W9-BSB-125

THE NATION'S BEST SCHOOLS

HOW TO ORDER THIS BOOK

BY PHONE: 800-233-9936 or 717-291-5609, 8AM–5PM Eastern Time

BY FAX: 717-295-4538

BY MAIL: Order Department
Technomic Publishing Company, Inc.
851 New Holland Avenue, Box 3535
Lancaster, PA 17604, U.S.A.

BY CREDIT CARD: American Express, VISA, MasterCard

PERMISSION TO PHOTOCOPY-POLICY STATEMENT

Authorization to photocopy items for internal or personal use, or the internal or personal use of specific clients, is granted by Technomic Publishing Co., Inc. provided that the base fee of US $3.00 per copy, plus US $ .25 per page is paid directly to Copyright Clearance Center, 222 Rosewood Drive, Danvers, MA 01923, USA. For those organizations that have been granted a photocopy license by CCC, a separate system of payment has been arranged. The fee code for users of the Transactional Reporting Service is 1-56676/95 $5.00 + $ .25.

THE NATION'S BEST SCHOOLS

BLUEPRINTS FOR EXCELLENCE

Volume 2
Middle and Secondary Schools

Evelyn Hunt Ogden, Ed.D.
Vito Germinario, Ed.D.

LANCASTER · BASEL

RENFRO LIBRARY
MARS HILL COLLEGE
MARS HILL, N.C. 28754

The Nation's Best Schools—Volume 2
a **TECHNOMIC**® publication

Published in the Western Hemisphere by
Technomic Publishing Company, Inc.
851 New Holland Avenue, Box 3535
Lancaster, Pennsylvania 17604 U.S.A.

Distributed in the Rest of the World by
Technomic Publishing AG
Missionsstrasse 44
CH-4055 Basel, Switzerland

Copyright © 1995 by Technomic Publishing Company, Inc.
All rights reserved

No part of this publication may be reproduced, stored in a retrieval system, or transmitted, in any form or by any means, electronic, mechanical, photocopying, recording, or otherwise, without the prior written permission of the publisher.

Printed in the United States of America
10 9 8 7 6 5 4 3 2 1

Main entry under title:
The Nation's Best Schools: Blueprints for Excellence—
Volume 2/Middle and Secondary Schools

A Technomic Publishing Company book
Bibliography: p.
Includes index p. 417

Library of Congress Catalog Card No. 94-60605
ISBN No. 1-56676-278-2

R
371.2
O34n
v.2

NOV 15 2011

To Muska Mosston . . .
he saw what others could not see
he heard what others could not hear
he did what others could not do . . .
he made a difference, and his monumental work lives on in education.

Evelyn Hunt Ogden

To Cheryl Haines for her unconditional support, encouragement, and love.

Vito Germinario

THERE is good news in education in the United States. In every state in every type of community, there are schools that meet the highest standards of excellence – Blue Ribbon Schools – world-class schools: schools where children learn and where education prepares students for active participation in the national and the world community of today and the 21st century of tomorrow. Within these schools are effective programs, processes, curricula, and instruction. *The Nation's Best Schools: Blueprints for Excellence, Volume 2, Middle and Secondary Schools* and *Volume 1, Elementary and Middle Schools* focus on what is good about education in the United States. It looks at what makes great schools great. It provides school staff, central administrators, boards of education, and parents with standards and a process for assessing their own schools. It provides blueprints for transforming poor schools to good schools and good schools to great schools. To paraphrase President Clinton's inaugural address, there is nothing wrong with American education that cannot be cured with what is right with American education. In recognizing the Blue Ribbon Schools in 1993, the President stated,

> The winners of the Blue Ribbon Awards . . . represent what is best in American education. If we could multiply the . . . schools . . . we could really revolutionize education in America. These are schools producing world-class results by any rigorous measure.
>
> [We have] to recognize the plain fact that notwithstanding the funding problems, notwithstanding the inequalities, notwithstanding all the problems of American education, you can find virtually every problem in our country solved . . . in an astonishingly effective fashion if you look at these schools. . . . The challenge for us . . . is to figure out how to replicate them.

Blue Ribbon Schools, the Best Schools, can play an important role in bringing about the needed educational reform required to prepare children for the 21st century. While representing only 2.5% of the total number of the 110,000 public and private elementary and secondary schools in the nation, these 2809 world-class schools – located in every state; in suburban, urban, and rural communities; serving children from the highest to lowest socioeconomic areas – serve as a powerful repudiation of the often heard cry from less effective schools that "We can't do that here because . . . !" Another important role of the Best Schools is to serve as demonstration sites, operational blueprints, for other schools striving to improve education. Educators want to "see it in action" as they contemplate new ways to meet needs. Theoretical research on learning has little widespread effect until examples of applications appear in "real" schools and classrooms. The movement from research-supported and -validated practice to mainstream school practice has, unfortunately, often taken as much as twenty years.

Transforming a less than effective school to a world-class school involves long-term planned change involving the whole of the organization, as well as change and development in a multiplicity of specific practices and programs. There is no magic bullet. Blue Ribbon Schools serve as models of the whole – models of how to conduct the business of learning – as well as models for the plethora of significant parts that are essential for school effectiveness. What they also model is that even the Best Schools must have the habits of mind to continually review progress against outcomes and to be continuously open to change. The Best Schools constantly reach out for models (in nearby schools, across the state, across the nation, in other countries), network with other schools, seek examples of how others have solved problems (i.e., the National Diffusion Network programs), and adopt or adapt practices from other schools that connect with their total vision for school development. The geographical proximity of at least one Blue Ribbon School, with similar demographics, to virtually all other schools in the nation provides the potential for a powerful network of demonstration and training sites. This book seeks to hasten the process of school development by showing the connections among educational goals, objectives, and standards; current research and theory; and the practices, processes, and programs already in place in the Best Schools.

The book is based on the following premises:

- We learn more from focusing on success than on failure.
- The wealth of great schools in the United States; in each and every state; in rich and poor districts; in cities, suburbs, and rural areas is evidence that we in the education profession know enough about what it takes to create effective schools in all types of communities and for all children.
- Principals, teachers, central office staff, boards of education, and parents are interested in and can use what the Best Schools do to make their own schools more effective.
- Frequently, the most credible source of standards, practices, processes, and programs for school improvement are those found in another school.
- Practices, programs, and outcomes within the Best Schools are highly congruent with research on learning, the National Goals Education, and National Standards.

The Nation's Best Schools: Blueprints for Excellence consists of two volumes. Volume 1 focuses on elementary education and Volume 2 on secondary education. Middle school practices appear in both volumes. The books are designed as guides for promoting school effectiveness; providing practical frameworks for evaluating practices, programs, processes, and student outcomes in schools; and serving as guidelines for school improvement, as well as serving as desk references of effective practice, related research, and standards.

The purpose of the school is to maximize learning for all students. The most obvious way schools do this is through direct instruction in the curriculum areas; however, the organizational climate and the systems that support the learner play powerful roles in determining learning outcomes for students. "Part One: Environments, Structures, and Supports That Promote Student Learning" addresses the roles of school vitality, school leadership, teaching environment, and student environment in maximizing school success for all students.

Students spend approximately 7700 hours in direct instruction in their passage from sixth through twelfth grade. How this time is spent in the study of the language arts, mathematics, social studies, science, the arts, information processing, and other subjects determines what they know and what they can do at any given point in their elementary school experience. The instructional program is addressed in "Part Two: 7700 Instructional Hours – The Middle School and High School Curriculum."

The 110,000 schools in this country are parts of some 16,000 school districts or umbrella organizations. The role of the district in school development and learner outcomes is addressed in "Part Three: The Role of the District in Effective School Development."

How Blue Ribbon Schools of Excellence are identified, how schools can use the Blue

Ribbon Standards as a basis for self-evaluation, and how schools can become Blue Ribbon Schools are the questions answered in "Part Four: The National Recognition Process."

Within the chapters, information concerning what children should learn, how they should be taught, and how learning should be assessed was based on the National Goals, National Standards Projects, educational research and theory, and national and international assessments. Each chapter contains a section describing how the Best Schools have translated theory into practice. Descriptions of practices, processes, and programs in the Best Schools were based on Blue Ribbon School applications; on-site school validation reports; interviews with principals and staff from recognized schools; and materials provided by the schools, districts, states, and the U.S. Department of Education. While descriptions of practices in all recognized schools were available, it was obvious that not all schools could be included among the illustrations of specific practices. The 260 middle and secondary schools recognized in 1993 represent a cross section of public and private education across the United States. These schools are located in large central cities (20%), mid-size cities (29%), suburbs (34%), small towns (12%), and rural areas (4%). The smallest of the schools was a private school with forty-eight students and the largest a public school with 3051 students, with an average of 1042 pupils. Eighty-two percent of these recognized schools were public, and 18% were private; they include schools from forty-three states, the District of Columbia, Puerto Rico, and two Department of Defense Dependent Schools in Germany.

Illustrations of practices were drawn mainly from this group of 260 middle and secondary schools; however, some illustrations are drawn from previously recognized schools. In most cases, the schools were randomly selected from the applications. The decision about which school was picked to feature for a particular program was based upon the degree of detail provided in the application and a desire to use schools representing different community types and examples from as many states as possible. Schools featured in one section could just as easily have been used to illustrate a different practice in another chapter. In other words, while not a scientific sample of Blue Ribbon Schools, the full range and scope of the successful schools are included. In some cases where the same approach, practice, or program was found to be widely used, the names of several schools using that approach, practice, or program are included in parentheses in the chapter. Again, these specific lists in no way indicate that these are the only schools using the program or practice; to the contrary, they are indicators of widely used specific programs and practices in Blue Ribbon Schools. Nationally validated programs disseminated through the National Diffusion Network of the U.S. Department of Education and identified by Blue Ribbon Schools are marked as (NDN) in the text.

The Appendices of the book are designed to be a resource. They include a list of the names and addresses of all (2809) Blue Ribbon Schools across the country, a list of state liaisons for Blue Ribbon Schools, a description of National Diffusion Network programs and a few other used programs widely used in Blue Ribbon Schools, a list of the state facilitators in the National Diffusion Network, parent involvement resources, and the National Goals of Education.

THE two books in this series, *The Nation's Best Schools: Blueprints for Excellence, Volume 1, Elementary and Middle Schools* and *Volume 2, Middle and Secondary Schools,* were born out of the knowledge and frustration that, each year, over 200 world-class schools are identified in which students are highly successful and whose programs and practices reflect the best of what is known about effective educational practices, and yet there has been only the most limited dissemination of what these schools do and little acknowledgement that these schools represent the national standard for education. This is particularly frustrating in light of the constant stream of reports and press coverage that often leads the public and educators alike to the belief that nothing works in education. Granted, only 2.5% of the nation's schools have been identified as meeting the criteria of a national Blue Ribbon School of Excellence; however, there are undoubtedly many other schools that will be identified in the future. This book is an attempt to open the door to the nation's Best Schools.

It would not have been possible to write this book without the cooperation and assistance of the recognized schools. The illustrations of programs and practices were drawn directly from their own reports and from the reports of the on-site evaluators. We are sure that, in many cases, a school would have selected a different program as most representative of its programs or practices than the one we used as an example. However, time, resources, and book space required that the authors limit illustrations. We would like to thank the principals who provided us with additional information about their schools and who took time to discuss their practices with us. The book contains illustrations from over 100 different schools, mostly from those recognized in 1993; we wish we could have used an example from each recognized school. To those not used for illustration, we apologize; it was the luck of the draw, not the quality of your schools, which accounts for your not being specifically referenced.

The authors wish to acknowledge the contributions of the staff of the Blue Ribbon School Program, U.S. Department of Education: J. Stephen O'Brien, Kathryn E. Crossely, Patricia A. Hobbs, and Jean D. Narayanan, former Director of the Recognition Division. This dedicated and highly knowledgeable group provides the vision and the backbone of the Blue Ribbon School Program, and, without their encouragement, assistance, and cooperation, these books could not have been written.

The authors also wish to thank Dr. Robert Hendricks, Superintendent of Flowing Wells Schools, and Dr. Robert Reeves, Superintendent of Poway Unified School District, for their insights on the role of the district in school development, as well as Linda Jones of the National Diffusion Network, U.S. Department of Education.

Finally, the authors are indebted to Diana Robinson for hundreds of hours of editing and rewriting; Karen Phillips for her friendship and typing of the manuscript; Timothy Wade for assistance in the analysis of the Blue Ribbon Schools; Cheryl Haines for her assistance in research and editing, and Amy Fisher for photography.

PART ONE

ENVIRONMENTS, STRUCTURES, AND SUPPORTS THAT PROMOTE STUDENT LEARNING

CHAPTER 1

The Essence of Schools: Organizational Vitality

THEY fly a flag proclaiming excellence, the President of the United States calls them the "world-class schools of now and the 21st century . . . the models of what schools should be," states honor them, communities applaud them, parents cherish them, children learn in them; they are the nation's Best Schools, the Blue Ribbon Schools of Excellence. What makes the Best Schools stand head and shoulders above, unfortunately, the majority of schools? It is necessary to look at the myriad specific practices, programs, and outcomes that are the parts of the place we call school. However, the Best Schools are far more than the sum of their individual parts; they are schools bound together by intricate webs of connected and integrated practices, programs, curricula, and support systems. In order to understand the "essence" of these schools, to understand why they are so successful, it is necessary to understand: a) what drives them—to know how they see the world, what they believe, what they value; b) how what they believe and value affects daily, as well as long-range, decisions concerning leadership, teaching, curriculum, student support, and, most importantly, student outcomes. Chapter 1 looks at the following questions:

- How do beliefs about learning, teaching, students, parents, and community determine values and, therefore, roles, practices, procedures, rewards, and outcomes that define the "essence" of all schools?
- What are the characteristics of effective schools—Blue Ribbon Schools, the Best Schools?
- How does the vitality of the school as an organization serve to determine actions and outcomes in the Best Schools?
- What is the process for school improvement in the Best Schools?
- How do the Best Schools respond to research findings, local, state, and national assessments; standards and goals?
- What are the problems the Best Schools have encountered and overcome?
- What do the Best Schools identify as future challenges and improvement agendas?

CONVENTIONAL, CONGENIAL, AND EFFECTIVE SCHOOLS

Formal studies of effective and ineffective schools and the observations of those who have worked with "failing," "ho-hum," "emerging," and "knock-your-socks-off" schools generally identify three types of schools. The set of characteristics of each type of school supersedes the importance of any individual practice or program in determining the outcomes of instruction. The dominant value and belief systems of a school determine the observable characteristics and the essence of the school as an organization, a place. These underlying values and beliefs define "what we do in this school," "how we make decisions," "how we respond to parents and the community," "what the real operating objectives are that we act upon in this school," "what we perceive as our accountability for what students learn," "what we consider important for students to learn," "how we interact with our colleagues," "what we believe about what students can learn," "why the staff works here," and "what we perceive as valued by the board of education, the central office, parents, and community." No school or district is purely one type; however, how the school leadership and staff, how district leadership and staff, and how boards of education act on the answers to these questions creates the culture, the climate, the character, and, ultimately, the degree of effectiveness of the school and school district in terms of student learning.

THE "CONVENTIONAL" OR "COLLECTED" SCHOOL

In the "conventional" or "collected" school, classrooms function largely as autonomous units: the school is a loose "collection" of these separate classrooms. These are schools that have no common goals, no collective sense of what they are trying to accomplish as a whole, as a school. Each classroom is like a mini-school. Teachers work in isolation within their own rooms. Although people usually work very hard, they view their work as what they do in their own classroom or maybe at their own grade level. What happens in the individual classroom depends on the beliefs, values, knowledge, and experiences of the individual teacher. Most of the staff believe that everyone else in the school shares the same beliefs about teaching and learning that they do; however, this is rarely the case.

The principal views his/her role primarily as that of a manager, that is, someone who makes sure that the school runs well – teachers have the materials they want, discipline is maintained, parent complaints are handled, and the PTA receives assistance for projects they undertake. Rules and sets of operational procedures often give the impression of strong building-level leadership and control; however, what are controlled are the operational aspects of the school. The principal's beliefs, often shared by district administration, form the basis of how he/she interprets his/her role, what he/she values, and the basic climate and culture of the school. Among these underlying beliefs are the following:

(1) Instructional leadership
- Good teachers make good schools; teaching is an "art"; either you have good teachers or you don't; what goes on in the classroom is the prerogative of the teacher; the principal can do little to affect what goes on in the classroom, other than hire "good" new teachers when there is an opening, prevent "bad" teachers from getting tenure, and encourage older "bad" teachers to retire.
- Teachers are the ones who know instruction and the needs of the students in their class; a good principal is one who lets teachers alone, insures that the teachers have the materials they want for instruction, supports his/her teachers with parents and the district administration, and insures that the school is orderly, clean, and safe.

(2) Management
- Ensuring a safe and orderly school environment is the most important function of the principal; in order to operate efficiently, the school needs sets of common procedures and practices such as disciplinary policies and processes, schedules, textbooks for each grade and course level, a standard report card, parent conference procedures, and the means for reporting standardized test scores to parents as required by law or district policy.

(3) Instructional accountability
- The effectiveness of the school in terms of learning is the responsibility of the

individual teacher; however, effectiveness is limited by the motivation, ability, and the ''problems'' children bring to school.

- Ultimately, the degree of effectiveness of the school and the individual classroom is largely a matter of ''perception''; if the parents, central office staff, and the board of education are satisfied with the teachers, the classes, and the school, then it is a good school; median standardized test scores, at or above the national norm, serve as confirmation of effectiveness and support current practice; poor test scores are rationalized largely as a reflection of the quality of the students.

(4) Educational research

- There is little useful knowledge outside of the school or district that is available to educators; research has little potential for impacting on classroom practice, since most schools are pretty much the same; schools touted as exemplary must have more resources and are ''lucky'' to have better kids and maybe better teachers; national and state reports recommending the need for change and new approaches to education are developed by people who don't know what the world of the school is ''really'' like.

(5) School improvement and planning

- The schools can always be improved by increased fiscal resources to enhance the building, hire more staff, and/or buy more materials.
- ''You shouldn't try and fix it if it can't be proven that its broken''; mandates for change in program, practice, or curriculum originate from outside of the school—such as parents' complaints about the way something is being done or the lack of computers in classrooms; changes in procedures emanating from the central office; or new state testing mandates; all of these can be expected to have little positive effect; however, they hold the potential of ''rocking the boat''—a good year is one in which there have been few calls for change.

These underlying beliefs create the climate of the school and directly affect decisions concerning what will be valued and reinforced, how people will interact with each other and for what reasons, what the faculty talks about, how outsiders are viewed, and the school's relationship with the district. It follows from the beliefs associated with the conventional school that ''leadership'' will be defined in terms of efficient operational management and public relations. Stability, lack of conflict, and minimal intervention in terms of the instructional process will be valued. Broad-based instructional planning, for example, would conflict with the value placed on individual teacher autonomy and stability and, therefore, is not characteristic of these schools. Even where the district has ''installed'' site-based management in these conventional schools, planning is usually confined to such areas as development of a new disciplinary policy, bus loading and unloading procedures, or student scheduling. Planning for change in instructional practice is considered inconsistent with the ''belief'' that this area is the prerogative of the individual teacher. Since the concept of development of staff is inconsistent with beliefs concerning the importance or, in fact, the ability of teachers to make major changes in practice, little value is placed on staff development and teacher evaluation in the conventional school. Inservice opportunities are usually limited to specific days in the district calendar and provide a smorgasbord of activities designed to allow for maximum options for individual teachers to make decisions about what to attend. Staff meetings are kept to a minimum and focus mainly on procedures and events involving the entire school, i.e., schedules for ''back to school'' night. Teacher evaluation is considered a bureaucratic requirement; at best, the formal evaluation process provides the opportunity to support, in writing, what teachers are doing and a means for weeding out weak nontenured teachers; at worst, the formal evaluation process is viewed by the principal and teachers as an unwelcome and unnecessary interference in the individual classroom and a waste of valuable time.

In conventional school districts, positive assessment of the school by district administration is often in terms of what is *not* happening; i.e., there were no major problems at the school, no major parent complaints, no grievances filed by staff, and no violence or major vandalism. The perception that the school's effectiveness is judged largely and informally by parent, public, central office, and board of education opinion discourages the indepth analysis of data that might identify and expose problem areas. Standardized norm-referenced tests may be criticized by staff for not measuring what is important in what they teach; however, when the median score is above the 50th percentile, these tests are used to reassure parents and the community that the school is doing well. Lower standardized test scores, however, are explained in terms of the "problems" students bring to school. This is reflective of a pervasive belief that the school can only have a limited impact on what students "bring" to school and a tacit acceptance that some will succeed, most will do okay, and, invariably, some will fail.

Unfortunately, most of the schools in America are "conventional" schools (Glickman, 1993). They predominate in suburban, urban, and rural settings, in rich and poor districts, and in high and low socioeconomic communities.

THE CONGENIAL SCHOOL

The congenial school gives the impression of being a cohesive unit with common goals. There are a lot of meetings and a lot of communication. The employees have a strong sense of being a school; it is a nice place to work. However, close inspection of the operational goals and priorities reveals that the focus is on the adults: improving the climate for adults, improving communication among teachers, and relieving teacher stress (Glickman, 1993). The belief is that the school should also be a nice place for students—friendly, supportive, concerned with self-esteem—and that there should be a friendly relationship between staff and parents. In other words, the "happy" school is the "good" school; however, when you get past the focus on affect, particularly for the adults, there is little difference between the congenial school and the conventional school in terms of beliefs about how children should learn, how instruction should be delivered, and how learning should be assessed. Means frequently are confused with ends. According to Glickman (1993), most of what is seen around the country as site-based management takes place in congenial schools and has more to do with adult wants than student needs.

As in the conventional school, the principal's role is defined mostly in operational and management terms. His/her role is to provide support for individual teachers in terms of classroom material, discipline, and support with parents; however, greater emphasis is placed on pleasing and being liked by parents and teachers. The value placed on public relations leads to actions that minimize the potential for conflict, to an even greater extent than in the conventional school. Value is placed on getting along by going along with the school as a clean, safe, and fun place to be. Change is viewed as having the potential of "rocking the boat." Since common goals concerning the instructional outcomes of education are missing, classroom practices reflect beliefs concerning the autonomy of teachers within the classroom; the idea that learning is limited, based on what the child brings to school; lack of relevance of knowledge and practice outside the school; and satisfaction with the status quo. The emphasis on effect frequently leads to lower standards for at least some children, justified by the belief that, if children are challenged, they may experience failure and low self-esteem. A reward for staff for working in the congenial school comes from the "family-type" atmosphere throughout the school. However, the rewards for students in terms of learning may be no greater than in the conventional school.

THE EFFECTIVE STUDENT OUTCOME-BASED, PROFESSIONAL, OR COLLEGIAL SCHOOL – THE BLUE RIBBON SCHOOL

The third type of school, frequently referred to in the literature as the "effective," "professional," "collegial," or "student outcome-based" school, operates from a very different belief system concerning the nature and purposes of the school. Satisfaction is derived from professional work accomplished together and from the achievement of children. These schools are bound by a strong sense of common mission and student learning outcome goals. Characteristic of the leadership and staff is that they are never satisfied, that it can always be better. They believe the following:

(1) Instructional leadership
- The purpose of the school is student learning; all children can learn to a very high set of standards.
- The most important roles of the principal are to make explicit the belief and value systems of the school, exhibit behaviors that reflect the beliefs of the school, lead the continuing effort at improvement, foster staff development, find "time" for planning and analysis, and communicate the mission and outcomes to parents, the community, and the central office.
- The principal is the instructional leader of the school instructional team, emphasizing that we know more together about effective practice than any one person alone.

(2) Management
- Ensuring a safe and orderly school environment is an important function of the principal; in order to operate efficiently, the school needs sets of common procedures and practices such as disciplinary policies and procedures, schedules, written curriculum and textbooks for each grade level, standard report card and parent conference procedures, and means for reporting assessment results to parents

(3) Instructional accountability
- The staff of the school is accountable for the learning of students – if we only work hard enough and are smart enough and creative enough, then every last child will achieve mastery in every content area.
- Standards for student achievement proposed by professional associations, national committees, and states are valuable for determining what children should learn.

(4) Research on instruction and learning
- As a profession, educators know a great deal about how students learn and how they should be taught; their findings are applicable to what happens in this school.
- Teachers and principals continue to learn, to get better at what they do.
- Colleagues have valuable lessons to share; working together will improve education for children.

(5) School improvement and planning
- ''Education is never totally fixed, and we shouldn't wait until it breaks to work at improving it''; data concerning the outcomes and processes of education should continually be probed to identify areas of need; it is okay to share flaws with staff, parents, and the community, since they can be trusted to know that the school is working on continuous improvement.
- The change process takes time: time to study data, time to ask fundamental questions, time to research solutions, time to make connections among programs and practices, time to plan, time to train staff, time to implement, and time to reassess; participating in these activities is a vital part of being in the education profession.
- The staff needs to share a common vocabulary and set of common definitions so that they can communicate effectively among themselves, with students, and with parents.
- Change brings an expected degree of anxiety and stress; however, change is essential; not everyone will be totally happy with everyone else's position on every issue; not everyone will agree on certain means or even the value of certain ends, but that is the price we are willing to pay on the road to creating a more effective school.
- Carefully thought-out risk taking is encouraged – it is okay to ''play'' with new ideas.
- Outside agencies, universities, businesses, parents, and other schools can help in the quest.
- The highest form of satisfaction, as a professional, comes from the intrinsic knowledge that you have made a difference – been part of something beyond personal goals.

These underlying beliefs create the climate of the student outcome-based or professional school and determine what is valued, what is reinforced, what is done, and what the outcomes are. It follows, then, that, in these schools, ''leadership'' is defined largely in terms of instruction. Therefore, the principal needs to know a lot about how children learn; about instructional practice and curriculum; and how he/she can assess outcome data, monitor instruction, study the research, and network with instructional leaders outside of the school. Teachers believe in the benefits of the collegial process of instructional improvement; it follows, then, that they must be actively involved in ongoing learning and staff development, as well as being participants in planning. As a result, staff development is a high priority in effective schools. Since staff act on the belief that every student will learn, data concerning the outcomes of learning are disaggragated and studied. Since standards for learning are valued, the staff is concerned with setting standards and, therefore, is willing to look outside for proposed standards for instruction and learning.

EFFECTIVE SCHOOLS

For more than twenty years researchers have produced studies that identify the factors associated with effective and less effective schools (Edmonds, 1978; Brookover and Lezotte, 1977; Rutter, 1985). The factors associated with effective schools are clearly those characteristic of ''Blue Ribbon professional/collegial/student outcome-based'' schools. These schools have the intrinsic ability and habits of mind to continually renew themselves. They have the organizational vitality to self-assess, to set and revise student-centered objectives, to plan, to act in unity, and to reassess. It is interesting that studies show that effective schools have the greatest "dissatisfaction" with their own teaching and learning [Brookover, reported by Glickman (1993)]. They believe that "seeking improvement . . . enlivens the organization for adults and students alike and [that] improvement is possible regardless of the current state of the organization" (Joyce et al., 1993).

On the other hand, research on less effective schools shows that they have the greatest satisfaction with their teaching and learning [Brookover, reported by Glickman (1993)]. Because less effective schools do not share common goals within the schools, they leave teachers alone to plan what they teach, with little guidance from colleagues or articulation of program from year to year [Oates, reported by Glickman (1993)]. These practices are consistent with the beliefs held in both the "conventional/collected" and "congenial" school. Such "self-satisfied" schools lack intrinsic organizational vitality; they respond only to external forces, such as central office and state mandates or parental dissatisfaction. They make changes only when the "cost" in terms of disruption and conflict is perceived as less than the "cost" of maintaining the status quo. However, changes in response to these externally identified crises or intrusions are apt to be quickly planned or inadequately implemented, and frequently represent more form than substance.

Can conventional and congenial schools become effective schools? The literature is full of case studies of successful turn-around schools, including many schools designated as Blue Ribbon Schools. Within every school, there are individual teachers who hold the beliefs and values associated with effective schools, and their classrooms are successful places where students learn a great deal. However, leadership is needed to unite not only these effective teachers but also their less effective colleagues, behind a mission that supersedes individual interests. Leadership that values self-criticism, models continuous learning, rewards professional risk taking, initiates and supports broad-based child-centered planning and development, and accepts accountability is essential for effective school development.

Leadership is the most important role of the principal. In case after case, it has been demonstrated that it was the principal who has made the most significant difference in the transformation of a school from a loose collection of individual classrooms to an effective connected school with a shared mission and successful student outcomes. This is not to say, however, that others both inside and outside the school do not participate in very significant ways in the transformation of the school; nevertheless, at the school level, the principal is the individual who, on a day-to-day basis, can establish the school climate, set the level of professional standards and expectations for the school, and largely define what roles others will play in the operation and development of the school. Effective principals have a vision of what they want the school to become; a long view of the process of becoming; extensive knowledge of educational practice and program, which allows them to see the connections among decisions, practices, programs, and outcomes; a drive to know more; and a belief that the school can do better. These professional characteristics need to be combined with a leadership style, personality, and "people skills" that can motivate others and engage them in the mission of the school and the management skills necessary to successfully maintain the operational aspects of the school.

Unfortunately, in most schools, principals have been hired and, once hired, reinforced based on their ability to "run a tight unrocking ship," and their "people skills" are directed at being "liked" by parents and staff. However, without the instructional leadership piece, the status quo will be valued and maintained. Changes that do take place in response to pressure will usually be inadequately understood and disconnected enhancements that mainly provide the illusion of effective practice, i.e., "We 'did' cooperative learning last year; this year we are 'doing' higher order thinking skills; next year we are 'doing' manipulatives."

BLUE RIBBON SCHOOLS, THE BEST SCHOOLS–ORGANIZATIONAL VITALITY

On-site visitors to schools nominated for Blue Ribbon Schools recognition and others who evaluate effective and less effective schools frequently say they can "smell an effective school within five minutes of entering the building." What they mean by this is that, through experience with observing in many different schools, they have learned to pick up a host of clues in what they see, hear, and sense, which seem to signal that this is an "effective school," "a developing school," or a "less effective school." This sense of the school comes from such things as what people are talking about; observed interactions between students, staff and students, principal and staff, and parents and staff; and what is displayed in the school, in the classroom, and in the principal's office. Taken together, these clues reflect the vitality of the school. In some cases, the more systematic review of the school's programs, practices, and processes of the school, which follows the first impression, results in a change in that initial impression. This can be particularly true in schools that have recently developed the organizational vitality characteristic of the most effective schools but have not had the time to align and connect all programs and practices in a manner that maximizes effective learning for all students. Getting even most of it "right" takes time–usually three to five years to move a less effective school to Blue Ribbon standards under the best of leadership. Getting it right is also affected by the context of the school. The presence of large numbers of at-risk students and negative factors outside of the school undoubtedly make the job more difficult and complex than in other contexts, where most students come to school prepared for learning and where parents themselves have had successful associations with education. However, all schools have to face challenges that make the job of school improvement difficult. Among the Blue Ribbon Schools are many schools that have met the most challenging of environmental problems successfully under the most difficult circumstances.

The Best Schools exhibit the beliefs, drives, actions, and outcomes described by researchers as effective, professional, collegial, or student outcome-based schools. They are in a continuous state of growth, trying to make it better. A significant reward for staff working in the Best Schools is participating with colleagues in probing data, researching alternatives, working for something beyond personal goals, and knowing that they are making a difference.

While the teacher is the person who establishes the climate for the classroom, it is the principal who is the force that sets the tone and provides the drive and the one who clarifies the belief system of the school, who models the values, and who reinforces the staff who seek to improve instruction. Best School principals really believe that "we can get it right in this school, for every kid." Like the principal of a "congenial" school, he/she places importance on creating a positive teaching environment, positive interactions among staff, and a happy place for kids. But this principal also believes that the satisfaction staff derive from their professional success and that which the students derive from learning will be valued most. Without effective or outcome-oriented leadership, it is virtually impossible for a school to become a Blue Ribbon School of Excellence. Some great things can happen within individual classrooms or even at a grade level, but the glue is missing for the total school. The role of the principal is well documented in creating the vitality of the Best Schools, as well as in all the research on effective schools. It is interesting that 12% of the principals of elementary schools recognized as Blue Ribbon Schools in 1991–1992 had been principals of other schools that had previously been recognized.

The organizational vitality of the Best Schools is reflected in every program, practice, and instructional outcome; illustrations abound throughout the chapters of this book devoted to the specific programs and practices of effective schools. However, how these schools have defined obstacles in the past, how the schools reach out to continue to learn, and how and what they view as future challenges provide a context for understanding the myriad specific approaches used in the Best Schools.

THE BEST SCHOOLS – THE SCHOOL IMPROVEMENT PROCESS

Central to the success of the Best Schools is a well established process for ongoing school improvement focused on the outcomes of the 7700 hours of instruction in which children will be involved in their journey from sixth grade through graduation. The process includes both formal and informal means for involving the entire staff and, frequently, parents in a continuous cycle of collecting data on the effectiveness of current practice, identifying unmet needs of students, studying research and effective practices generated outside of the school, establishing improvement objectives and priorities, deciding how instructional time will be used, planning specific programs, developing curriculum, training staff, implementing planned change, developing and identifying assessment strategies, and assessing the impact of the changes on students. In many cases, the process itself has emerged within the school; in other cases, the process is part of a district-developed planning model, state-disseminated or -mandated process, or a process shared by schools in a school improvement network such as the Network of Essential Schools, Missouri's Network of Accelerated Schools, or the Effective Schools Network.

School Improvement Process Illustrations

GOVERNOR THOMAS JOHNSON HIGH SCHOOL, FREDERICK MD

Governor Thomas Johnson High School is now a comprehensive senior high school for a stable population of approximately 1300 students in grades 9–12. While the numbers seem to paint a picture of an average American high school, "T. J." is recognized by students, staff members, and the public at large as a school of considerable diversity, even stark contrasts. A large portion of the students come from homes with considerable financial and cultural resources, yet we also draw students from the city's two largest low-income housing projects. The school includes the system's largest emotionally disturbed and multi-handicapped population and houses the magnet school for students gifted in the performing arts.

The statements, "All students can learn," and "We have high expectations for students," do not, in the school's opinion, go far enough and are not specific enough to present students, parents, and staff members with a target they can find inspiring. As a result, the overriding goal for the past three years has been "to become the type of school where all students are honor roll students." With this extremely challenging (some might say unrealistic or impossible) goal, obstacles are identified and then attacked with practical and realistic approaches.

One small example of a schoolwide practice based on this approach might help make Governor Thomas Johnson's routine method of operation more understandable. For the past two years, teachers have been asked to complete a grading grid each marking period that helps them analyze why students in their classes earn less than a "B." Generalizations for entire classes or groups are not accepted. Each student is coded with a variety of "causes." This information is then compiled and analyzed in order to achieve a schoolwide picture of why students are not achieving the lofty standard. Specific programs have been designed to address these impediments to high achievement. For example, to convince students the school staff is serious about the goal, they instituted academic detention as teachers saw fit for failure to complete homework, to study for tests, to complete reading assignments, and so on. In some cases, teachers went so far as to offer detention (often referred more positively as after-school tutoring lessons) to students who failed to earn 80% or better on tests or assignments. At first, students and even some parents were shocked by the idea that students could be "forced" to achieve such a high level. Now, the idea that all students are expected to earn A's and B's is firmly in place and widely accepted. The fact that honor roll membership has increased 48% in a short time indicates that these approaches are moving the school community along the right path.

The school goal and specific practices and policies that have emerged from the analysis of data are communicated frequently with all members of the school community. Each year begins with a staff review of important yearly targets and explanations about the special programs and practices that are designed to help us reach those targets. The principal, assistant principals, director of attendance, and guidance counselors routinely make presentations to students in small group settings in the first week or two of school to inform them about objectives and to elicit their feedback. The ninth grade orientation program is the first opportunity to inform parents about the overriding goal and the year's specific objectives and to encourage their participation and support. This past August, a four-page School Profile Summary containing important data analysis and identifying significant trends was mailed to all parents. An offer was also made to share the entire 100-page Profile with them. Monthly parent newsletters, periodic inservice sessions, weekly faculty bulletins, and daily public announcements are used to review progress toward the objectives. In a recent faculty bulletin, for example, the first month's summary data on grades, attendance, and discipline were reviewed for all staff members.

The efforts to promote a positive school climate are based on the simple notion that, when people dedicated to education (staff members, parents, and students) are provided with sufficient information to help them analyze their performance, they will respond by, first, identifying concerns and then, invariably and aggressively, beginning to attack those concerns. Once this process is set in motion, it is imperative, for its ongoing success, that a few key ingredients are always present.

First, information must be thorough and understandable. It was with this goal in mind that Governor Thomas Johnson has dedicated so many hours to the compiling of the vast amount of data that now fill the School Profile.

Second, the analysis of the data and use of the information must be thoroughly honest—perhaps the most important factor of all. Many districts and schools now claim to be "data-driven" and "outcomes-based," but too often, the review of information is nothing more than a search for good news, for items that are more appropriate for promotional press releases than for intelligent and sophisticated determination about what is going well and what is not. With this in mind, most of the energy is spent identifying problems, rather than gloating about success.

Third is the need for action. In most cases, when people identify a problem, they offer suggestions, but should the suggestions become trapped in an endless loop of debate, the participants soon grow weary of accomplishing nothing. Governor Thomas Johnson has taken the position that it is better to experiment with solutions and carefully examine the results of the experiments, tossing out approaches that do not work, than to move so cautiously that little, if anything, new is ever tried. It is this spirit that has led to a wealth of programs being implemented in a short time.

Believing that all students can learn and having high expectations for all students are goals that are included in the mission statements of almost all secondary schools. Having the willingness to search for imperfections, to hold them up where everyone can see them, to experiment with new ideas, and, hardest of all, to admit when these experiments fail are tasks much harder than developing an acceptable mission statement. At the school, they believe that they do these things consistently and well. In 1988, when school goals had for years been quite similar to what they are today, only 52% of the staff agreed that the "school displays a climate of expectation that students can reach extended levels of achievement." After two years of using the practice described above, the mission itself has changed only by becoming more specific and challenging, but 80% of the staff now believes the school community can display such a climate.

Michael N. Riley, *Principal, Grades 9–12, 1262 Students*

SCHAUMBURG HIGH SCHOOL, SCHAUMBURG, IL

Schaumburg High School is located twenty-six miles northwest of Chicago in a residential neighborhood. The village has experienced dramatic growth in the last twenty years, both in terms of population and geographic expansion due to annexation of unincorporated areas. The current population of 68,586 is expected to increase 35% to 45% by the year 2010. The community served by the school is relatively young, well educated, mostly white, and middle income. Ten percent of the households are headed by a single parent. Seventy-eight percent of the school's 1992 graduates continued their formal education. Thirty-two percent of these students matriculated at the local community college. The school's faculty is an experienced group of professionals, constantly searching for new ways to help students become more successful.

Outcome statements have been determined for each course in the curriculum. Students completing courses take common, comprehensive criterion-referenced examinations that test for mastery of outcomes. Results are examined course by course and outcome by outcome. Teachers compare their students' scores with district average scores and scores from previous years. As some of the tests are nationally normed, national comparisons are also available. Comparative weaknesses are identified, and teachers meet to review the nature of instructional strategies applied to these outcomes. Strategies are amended to address the weakness aggressively and decisively. For example, it was in order to better meet the needs of the 32% of the students who attend the community college and others who seek an alternative to the traditional four-year college path that Schaumburg High School became a pilot campus for a new level of educational programming called Tech Prep in 1990. Targeting the "under-represented majority," or so-called average students, Tech Prep links high school technical and academic courses with paid corporate internships and two years of community college training. With the help of local business and industry partners, Tech Prep has expanded its focus from one to thirteen career areas. In September, the U.S. Department of Labor affirmed the program's success in pioneering new approaches to prepare youth for the workplace. It bestowed upon it the 1992 Labor Investing For Tomorrow (LIFT) Award.

The principal provides a positive, nurturing environment for students and staff so all can discover the skills and talents to become the best they can be. His vision of an interdisciplinary curriculum focusing on problem solving and critical thinking has resulted in linkages between departments and brought new relevance to concepts previously taught in isolation. A major eight-year remodeling effort has equipped the school with exemplary classrooms and laboratories. Forty percent of the school budget has been allocated to purchase technical support that makes it easier for teachers to do their jobs and enables them to spend more time working directly with students. Advisory groups of parents, teachers, and students meet regularly with the administration to provide input and pave the way for constructive, positive change. Input from these groups is used to evaluate and monitor the day-to-day activities of the school and the educational needs of students.

Department chairs and the principal comprise the school improvement team that meets weekly and holds annual strategic planning sessions. State and local assessment scores are reviewed in light of local and district expectations. Departmental improvement plans that contain specific activities designed to strengthen curriculum and instruction are submitted as part of an all-school improvement plan. School climate issues are addressed through established communication forums such as the P.A.C., the Faculty Council, and the P.A.B. Teacher-driven staff development plans focus on refining instructional strategies to enhance overall teacher effectiveness. The North Central Association self-study completed last spring was deliberately structured so that teachers, rather than administrators, chaired the process. This philosophy of empowerment has fostered the faculty's ownership and commitment to implementation of action plans for improvement.

Jack Gaza, *Principal, Grades 9–12, 2224 Students*

THE BEST SCHOOLS – THE USE OF EDUCATIONAL RESEARCH FINDINGS, NATIONAL ASSESSMENTS, AND THE NATIONAL GOALS

The Best Schools are constantly asking questions about what their students should be learning, how they can best teach and support student learning, and how well their students are doing. Characteristically, they look outward, as well as at their own resources, practices, and assessment approaches in answering these questions. The Best Schools have formal and informal knowledge concerning the broad goals of education, standards for student achievement, and curriculum-related research generated at the nation level or by professional associations, universities, state agencies, and other districts and schools. They share information within the school, visit other sites to observe programs based on research, participate in intensive staff development, and adopt/adapt practices shown to be effective elsewhere. They do not want to reinvent the wheel. Frequently, the staffs of the Best Schools are also actively involved in large-scale improvement efforts beyond their school, serving on state and national advisory and development committees, piloting programs and assessment procedures, training staff from other schools and districts, hosting observers from other districts, and developing programs that will be used by other schools. In many cases, the school has been designated as a "demonstration site" for effective practices by the district, state, or networks.

Illustrations of the Use of Research, Assessment, and Goals

CULVER CITY HIGH SCHOOL, CULVER CITY, CA

Culver City High School serves approximately 1390 students in grades 9 – 12. While there has been a decline in enrollment over the past three years, the relative percentage of all ethnic groups has increased. Approximately 41% are Caucasian, 14% African-American, 14% Asian, and 30% Latino. Nineteen percent of the students are limited English proficient, representing thirty-four languages. Approximately 19% receive free or reduced-price lunch. The socioeconomic level of the community is reflected in a working population that consists of 64% white collar and 36% blue collar employees.

The principal's leadership and vision have established shared leadership and collaboration among administrators, faculty, parents, and students. The vision and mission of Culver City High School pivots on the determination to provide the student population with a stimulating, lifelong learning environment that fosters maximum individual development to become responsible, productive members of society. This goal is accomplished through a foundation of basic skills; a broad-based curriculum; accountability for results; utilization of community resources; input regarding decisions from students, staff, parents, and community members; support systems for all students and staff; safe, secure facilities; valid learning programs; and sound fiscal policies.

The administrative team promotes an open and challenging climate that allows the experienced staff to stimulate and motivate student learning. The on-campus community developed the philosophy statement, "Together We Do Better," which has become the guide for decision making, evaluating accomplishments, and creating a more cohesive school climate.

School improvement is an ongoing process at Culver City High School. "The National Goals," the State of California's Subject Matter Frameworks (K – 12), the "Quality Criteria for

High Schools," and "The Model Curriculum Standard" (9–12) are used by committees of teachers, parents, and students to find ways to improve.

During the 1991–1992 school year, teachers, parents, students, classified staff, and community members spent six months producing a 606-page self-study covering nineteen areas. The document was used by the six-member combined WASC/School Improvement Review and Accreditation Committee prior to and during a four-day visit. A six-year accreditation was awarded to the school, along with commendations and recommendations for improvements that are addressed in an action plan booklet written by the committee.

Other areas of the improvement process include various committees on campus that constantly evaluate school policies and procedures. Furthermore, as a part of the district's general strategic planning process, there is a task force on restructuring that has already begun implementing restructuring efforts at the high school site through a collaborative model for consensus building, including students, staff, and parents. The initiative for improvement comes from within our high school community. Its leadership is school-based with mostly staff, students, and administrators.

In response to all research that shows the importance of writing, a writing across the curriculum program has been established. The English Department has implemented "The Writing Project," funded by school improvement to implement and practice new motivation for student writings.

The school is working toward implementing a Scope, Sequence, and Coordination (SSC) program for science. It is an international program of integrated science modeled after the European science curricula. The program is an integrated science program with an emphasis on themes that Culver City has begun to use with the at-risk students in the Team Integrated Program (TIP) program.

Culver City Unified School District is at the forefront in bilingual education, with a K–12 Spanish Immersion Program; this year is the first of a Japanese Immersion Program. At the high school, there is a two-way immersion program with course offerings for native Spanish speakers combined with the English-speaking immersion students. In addition, there are three levels of English as a Second Language (ESL) and sheltered classes across the curriculum. Partly in response to the Department of Education's Language Report, the school is looking at expanding the current program offerings.

Culver City is developing a graduation requirement of community service. It is designed to build responsible citizens, inspire further learning, and show students the importance of their rights and responsibilities in a free society.

Laura Plasse, *Principal, Grades 9–12, 1368 Students*

LINA MILLIKEN MIDDLE SCHOOL, LEWISVILLE, TX

The Lewisville Independent School District, situated in the Dallas/Ft. Worth area, is one of the fastest growing districts in Texas. Milliken is currently one of six middle schools in the district. In the face of unprecedented growth, they have maintained a high level of professional collegiality and student success. Opened in 1976, Milliken student capacity was designed for 750, but it has served as many as 1200 students in phenomenal growth periods. Persistent growth, coupled with frequent rezoning for new schools, has resulted in high student mobility rates (34%) and staff expansion (eighteen new teachers) in 1991–92. Typical of school district patterns, they serve a predominantly middle-income population (6% socioeconomically disadvantaged) and a low ethnic mix (8% minority). The constant growth and turnover has challenged the cohesive, positive learning environment, reinforcing the value of a team-based approach to education.

Milliken administrators and faculty remain abreast of educational research and stay in the forefront in implementing goals for middle school restructuring. Due to the successful efforts towards becoming a "New Generation of American Schools," Milliken has been named a 1992 Texas Mentor Middle School. The North Central Texas Middle School Association highlighted target areas for programmatic restructuring, and Milliken was one of a few mentor schools that met or exceeded expectations in at least fifteen of nineteen areas: advisor/advisee programs, interdisciplinary teams, flexible scheduling, student recognition programs, intramural programs, peer tutoring/counseling (New Focus), parent involvement/parent volunteers, community service/student volunteer programs, student leadership opportunities training (POPS and New Focus), at-risk/dropout prevention programs, site-based decision-making teams, content mastery programs (total inclusion/co-teaching), multicultural sensitivity activities/programs (A World of Difference), and Channel One programming.

Milliken is currently researching multi-media centers, modification of science curriculum to include Science I/Science II, and a homework hotline. In line with National Goals, the school strives to provide improvements in curriculum and instruction to better prepare students as responsible, skillful citizens in a modern economy. They address equity through heterogeneous grouping, inclusion, and providing "gifted" curriculum to all students. Cooperative learning teaches students to work with others for a common goal. Academic teaming and flexible schedules encourage interdisciplinary planning of units that promote understanding of relationships between subjects. Technological awareness is promoted through computer literacy classes, computer writing lab, and technology applications in all classrooms. Strategic Thinking Skills teaches students to adapt to their individual learning styles and instills organizational skills. Writing across the curriculum promotes literacy by demonstrating the necessity for writing in all areas of life. Quest, New Focus, and integrated drug awareness curricula develop responsible decision making and promote a "no use" message.

Barbara Stagner, *Principal, Grades 6–9, 861 Students*

C. E. WILLIAMS MIDDLE SCHOOL, CHARLESTON, SC

C. E. Williams Middle School, a suburban school, is a part of Constituent District 10, one of eight constituent districts that comprise the Charleston County School District. The school has an economically diverse student body, ranging from upper middle- to very low-income families. Over the last ten years, 32% of the students have been eligible for free or reduced lunches. The school draws its population from the West Ashley area of Charleston County. There are five elementary schools that feed into out school. The ethnic distribution is about 48% Caucasian, 51% African-American, and 1% Hispanic and Asian.

C. E. Williams Middle School has addressed the findings of The Carnegie Council on Adolescent Behavior report and the National Goals through the following: 1) dividing grades into smaller communities by instituting team teaching; 2) standardizing and strengthening a core of common knowledge in the five instructional areas given in the National Goals; 3) organizing classes to ensure success for all students by incorporating heterogeneous grouping; 4) implementing the school-based management concept through committees and staff development cluster groups; 5) upgrading teacher certification beyond the bachelor's degree level and educating staff concerning new successful instructional techniques such as cooperative learning, team teaching, hands-on curriculum, and writing across the curriculum; and 6) involving parents and the community in the school's activities through the volunteer program, an active PTSA, and the School Improvement Council.

James E. Mobley, *Principal, Grades 6–8, 848 Students*

THE BEST SCHOOLS–OVERCOMING PROBLEMS AND IMPEDIMENTS

It is easy to believe when you look at the current programs, practices, processes, and outstanding student outcomes that the Best Schools have not had to deal with the myriad problems facing less effective schools. This is not the case. In some schools, there has been a long history of pursuing excellence, while in others something happened, frequently a new or revitalized principal, to change the path of a less than effective school. However, Best Schools exist in all types of communities and collectively serve the full range of children in the United States. They have faced not only instructional problems, but also changing school populations, increasing numbers of children at risk, facilities problems, staffing problems, community problems, and funding problems. None of these problems ever really go away; however, the Best Schools recognize problems as challenges, not excuses for inaction.

Illustrations of Challenges and Factors Identified by the Best Schools That Contributed to Their Success

METRO HIGH SCHOOL, CEDAR RAPIDS, IA

A combination of many factors makes Metro a dynamic and unique high school in Iowa. The purpose of the school is to provide educational opportunities to the high-risk students, the dropouts, and students with special needs. Everything they do is designed to meet the needs of those students. Academic expectations are high. The dropout rate is less than 3%. The average daily attendance rate is above 90%.

The majority of students who enroll at Metro do so at the recommendation of a counselor or administrator from their previous school. Approximately 78% come from the district's middle schools or other high schools. Around 20% enroll at Metro after being discharged from one of the state's residential treatment programs or at the request of the juvenile justice system. A few students enroll with no outside referral, having been out of school for an extended period of time.

Most of the students at Metro come from dysfunctional families and reflect lifestyles of poverty. Approximately 38% of the female population are either pregnant or parenting. Nearly 25% of the students live on their own or in residential programs. An estimated 60% of the students are adjudicated juveniles or children in need of assistance (CINA).

The school believes the following conditions and changes have contributed most to the success of Metro:

- Outstanding leadership and staff are committed to educational excellence and serving the needs of the challenged students. In the past five years, they have added four Metro graduates to the staff and increased the people of color on the staff. The staff comes from diverse backgrounds of religion, age, and outside interests. All of the staff share the desire to help students succeed.
- The district has continually supported Metro. The support ranges from spending more than a million dollars to rid the facility of asbestos in 1989 to increasing the computer density tenfold. Central administrators are supportive and respect the need for an alternative school.
- There has been consistent success at increasing the academic expectations while maintaining a caring, supportive environment.
- Services were increased to the district's special education population by adding specific services for learning disabled students.
- The school has developed the schoolwide portfolio process and the schoolwide demonstration of mastery in all content areas.
- There exists a commitment to gather, maintain, and interpret student data and to make appropriate changes as a result of that data.

Mary Wilcynski, *Principal, Grades 9–12, 661 Students*

MILWAUKEE LUTHERAN HIGH SCHOOL, MILWAUKEE, WI

The school is located in a residential area that grew up around it in the last three decades. With a twenty-acre campus, Milwaukee Lutheran has ample space for several athletic fields, a track, and an innovative confidence course modeled after Outward Bound. The student population is drawn from families of unskilled blue collar workers, skilled technicians, and professionals. Though it began as a school for the Lutheran churches in the area, students from other churches and denominations (along with some students who list no religious affiliation) currently attend the school. Approximately 11% of the students are considered minorities. The school also enrolls students from other countries to increase international exposure beyond even that provided through an Active American Field Service Program. More than 80% of the graduates of Milwaukee Lutheran go on to college or other postsecondary schools.

Since 1988, there has been a complete administrative change, beginning with the superintendent and including the principal and some assistant principals. The teamwork and collaborative efforts of the new administrative team have set the tone for implementing a new vision for the school. Corresponding to this change, there has been a new emphasis on educational restructuring. Successful grant applications to foundations resulted in more than $150,000 in resources for staff development, an amount unmatched in prior years. There has been strong encouragement and support for well-planned educational change directed toward preparing students for the 21st century. Impediments have been, primarily, limitations in funding. Grants have guaranteed progress, and a new funding campaign with a significant goal for academic program enrichment will continue to assure success in the future.

Paul M. Bahr, *Principal, Grades 9–12, 781 Students*

THE BEST SCHOOLS–MAJOR EDUCATIONAL CHALLENGES FOR THE NEXT FIVE YEARS

The Best Schools take the long view of school improvement. It is not unusual in reading about the development of a specific program or practice to discover that the school has been actively involved in transforming the program or practice continuously for five, ten, or even 20 years. Therefore, it is not surprising that the Best Schools are actively working on agendas with five or more year time lines. A survey of the 1993–94 Blue Ribbon Middle School and Secondary School principals, conducted by the U.S. Office of Education, identified the areas they plan to devote greatest attention to in the future (see Table 1).

A review of the concerns for the future of many of the Best Schools reveals that issues

TABLE 1. School improvement topics to receive the greatest attention (by percent of schools).

Rank Order	Among Top Five Priorities	Topics
1	50.6	Technology (computers, satellite hookups, VCRs, laser discs, CD-ROM)
2	46.5	Student performance assessment (testing, portfolios, exhibits, mastery)
3	44.0	Critical/higher order thinking skills
4	36.2	Multicultural education/education for pluralistic society
5	35.8	Teacher efficacy/professionalization/new roles and responsibilities
6	30.9	Strengthening curriculum content
7	30.9	At-risk students/dropout prevention
8	27.2	Community-school/business-school partnerships
9	23.5	Other school improvement and/or restructuring efforts
10	23.5	Schedule revamping, including major changes in class periods, school day, length of school year

related to feared or real decreased funding, growing student bodies, and increasing populations of at-risk students are among the challenges to be faced in the next five years. Two examples from Best Schools illustrate more specifically what schools view as challenges for the future.

Illustrations of Future Agendas

JOHN WALLACE MIDDLE SCHOOL, NEWINGTON, CT

This small school serves a middle-class Hartford suburban community of approximately 30,000 people. Among the parents, 30% work in blue collar jobs, 64% in white collar, and 5% are self-employed. A large number of apartments and condominiums are in the area of town served by this school. Annually, about 10% of the student population moves out of the district, with a similar percentage entering. Over the last five years, the composition of the student body has changed. There is a higher percentage of minority students than in the town population as a whole; there are more children from single-parent families and more living with guardians or foster parents.

Implementing our vision in spite of societal problems that affect our students, providing services to a changing clientele, restricting resources for schools, educating students for their roles in a diverse society with increasing population, and shrinking traditional resources are known challenges. Economic hard times are a reality. There are increasing percentages of poor and minority students, and these increases will continue. They face a continuing challenge to improve programs and services without increased public funding. More students will need social services in order to become ready to learn. Monitoring students and assessing educational effectiveness will continue. Maintaining communication and expanded coordination with social service providers are priorities. The NEAS&C self-study highlighted goals in the areas of curriculum, personnel, facilities, and equipment. This report, the district's strategic plan, student demographics, and fiscal reality provide direction for their efforts. The school remains committed to providing a nurturing environment with high academic and behavioral expectations for students.

Anne R. Giddings, *Principal, Grades 6–8, 456 Students*

CAPITAL HIGH SCHOOL, CHARLESTON, WV

Located in the rolling hills of Meadowbrook near WV 114 on the site of a former golf course, Capital High represents the Kanawha County Board of Education's commitment to offer secondary students a variety of learning pathways. The school board that designed this school was bold and innovative in their effort to provide the best preparation for 1400 students, representing a broad cross section of cultural and socioeconomic backgrounds. The 25% low socioeconomic population, 26% minority population, the 18% special education population, and all other learners are challenged by high expectations for achievement while being provided a nurturing environment with numerous support systems.

The goal is to provide an equitable and stimulating educational opportunity for all students by removing the "ceilings" placed on students when they find themselves in a "tracked" environment. Owing to the changing concept of the family unit, the task of socializing children often falls on the school. In fact, in many cases, the school must assume the role of the family. Forming tightly knit, smaller groups within the school (through the SAP and other counseling oriented groups), where more individual needs can be met, seems a positive tack to pursue. Though in the infant stages, the continuation and expansion of many of Capital's innovative programs will be a great help in meeting the educational challenges in the next five years. Plans are under consideration to increase the number of children able to be accommodated by the day-care program, which emphasizes parental training and responsibility. Better quality education increases a child's chances of success and increases his/her options in the work force. Integrated studies will help students better understand the relationships between facts and ideas and the reality of everyday life. It is essential that the community service aspect of the curriculum be expanded, a course that is presently being pursued. Also, plans are under consideration to change the school calendar year to provide better use of the building plan, while allowing staff more preparation and planning time. Eliminating the long summer vacation would also eliminate having to reteach much material after a three-month lapse. As the demands of the technological society become greater, more cost-effective and time-effective education will be demanded. A priority consideration in experiencing success in dealing with these problems is an innovative, concerned leadership, aware of the latest research and willing to implement promising programs. With leadership, accompanied by teacher mentoring programs as initiated this year, Capital can continue to be a leader in achieving better ways to help children compete in changing global economy.

John K. Clendenen, *Principal, Grades 10–12, 1387 Students*

SUMMARY

The underlying beliefs and values about education, students, staff, ''possibilities,'' and goals determine the organizational vitality of schools and, ultimately, the learning outcomes for students. The characteristics associated with the less effective conventional and congenial types of schools and the instructionally effective Blue Ribbon Schools of Excellence—the Best Schools—are identified. Illustrations from the Best Schools show how they maintain a continuous state of school improvement, use research, overcome challenges, and plan for the future.

REFERENCES

Brookover, W. B. (1977). ''Elementary School Social Climate and Student Achievement,'' *American Educational Research Journal*, 15(2):301–318.

Brookover, W. B. and L. W. Lezotte. (1977). ''Changes in School Characteristics Coincident with Change in Student Achievement,'' Lansing, MI: College of Urban Development of Michigan State University and the Michigan State Department of Education.

Edmonds, R. R. (1978). ''A Discussion of the Literature and Issues Related to Effective Schooling,'' paper prepared for the *National Conference on Urban Education*, St. Louis, MO: CEMREL.

Fullan, M. G. (1982). *The Meaning of Educational Change*. Toronto, Canada: Ontario Institute for Studies in Education.

Glickman, C. (1993). ''Promoting Good Schools: The Core of Professional Work,'' assembly presentation, ASCD Convention.

Joyce, Bruce, et al. (1993). *The Self-Renewing School*. Alexandria, VA: Association for Supervision and Curriculum Development.

Lezotte, Lawrence W. and Barbara C. Jacoby. (1992). *Sustainable School Reform: The District Context for School Improvement*. Okemos, MI: Effective Schools.

Rutter, M. (1985). *Changing Youth in a Changing Society*. Cambridge, MA: Harvard University Press.

U.S. Department of Education. (1993). ''A Profile of Principals: Facts, Opinions, Ideas, and Stories from Recognized Secondary Schools of 1992–93,'' Blue Ribbon Schools Program, Washington, D.C.

CHAPTER 2

Planning and Leadership

THROUGHOUT the past two decades, much has been written about what constitutes "effective schools." In particular, high school programs have become a central focus of school reform initiatives. The demand for such reform throughout the country has generated much debate concerning the fundamental aspects of the goals of education, the content of curriculum, school governance structures, and the changing roles of students, parents, teachers, and administrators in today's high schools.

The nation continues to demand accountability from its schools and value for the increasing financial support they are asked to provide. Yet, despite over a decade of rhetoric, most of the nation's high schools have yet to install comprehensive reform plans. In a comprehensive survey of over 3000 schools, fewer than half were using techniques such as cooperative learning and standard-based mathematics education, and barely a quarter were experimenting with outcome-based education or school-to-work transition programs (Cawelti, 1994).

Cawelti and Roberts (1993), after analyzing the results of over 10,000 surveys sent to high school principals throughout the country, concluded that "there's a lot of activity going on, but there have been very few high schools that have been able to put it all together."

Despite the reluctance of some schools to initiate school improvement programs, there is significant evidence to support that schools throughout the country are succeeding (Carson, Hullskamp and Woodall, 1993). In particular, there are schools that have established the mechanisms that promote the framework for planning for success and have the inspired leadership to transform action plans into meaningful student-centered outcomes.

This chapter will examine the critical nature of establishing and prioritizing goals as a focus for sustained school improvement. Additionally, it will explore leadership patterns and practices in successful schools. Finally, this chapter will provide examples, from the nation's best high schools, that illustrate the characteristics of effective planning and transformational leadership.

Specifically, this chapter will address the following questions:

- What are the essential characteristics of productive educational planning?
- How do Best Schools organize and prioritize goals?
- What goals have Best Schools established for their schools and students?
- What are the most important characteristics of school leaders?
- How do principals in Best Schools high schools inspire staff, parents, and students to accomplish school goals?

CHARACTERISTICS OF EFFECTIVE PLANNING

Successful schools have long known the benefits of systematic planning. These schools look upon planning as an organic, ongoing process not initiated by crisis or the need to institutionalize innovations. Instead, successful schools have developed a culture that initiates the planning process by recognizing and accepting what is good about their schools, but they are secure enough to create a level of dissatisfaction that essentially says, "We can always do better."

Although a variety of strategies can provide a framework for effective planning in a general way, decisions that evolve from the process should be 1) based on research, 2) made by consensus, and 3) intended to be in the best interest of students and education.

Sashkin and Egermier (1992) have identified the four broad strategies that are most often utilized in the planning for change in schools:

(1) *Fix the parts by transferring innovations:* Get new information into practice by developing and transferring specific curricular or instructional programs.
(2) *Fix the people by training and developing professionals:* This includes the comprehensive remodeling of pre-service and inservice training of administrators and teachers.
(3) *Fix the school by developing the organization's capacities to solve problems:* Help people in the school to solve their own problems more successfully. This strategy has grown out of the organization development (OD) movement that has schools collect data to identify and solve problems and to evaluate critical outcomes. Frequently, consultants are brought into the school to guide this strategy.
(4) *Fix the system by comprehensive restructuring:* Often called systemic change, school districts adopt a multi-level approach involving the school/district major stakeholders reaching out to examine and change the fundamental culture of the school community.

Following an examination of the writings and activities of proponents of school improvement, Joyce (1991) has identified five major emphases associated with initiatives for school change:

(1) *Collegiality:* developing cohesive and professional relations within school faculties and connecting them more closely to their surrounding neighborhoods
(2) *Research:* helping school faculties study research findings about effective school practices or instructional alternatives
(3) *Site-specific information:* helping faculties collect and analyze data about their schools and their students' progress
(4) *Curriculum initiatives:* introducing changes within subject areas or, as in the case of the computer, across curriculum areas
(5) *Instructional initiatives:* organizing teachers to study teaching skills and strategies

The Best Schools across the country have utilized individual and a combination of these strategies. Yet common themes can be associated with the Best Schools. The goal in planning for success is to create a professional culture in which instructional and curricular decisions are based on informed research; support inquiry, consultation, and cooperative collaboration; and establish a primary concern for the successful achievement of all students.

Whether urban, suburban, or rural, these schools utilize a systematic planning process to initiate and sustain school improvement. Through the development of a common understanding of shared beliefs, the school community is empowered to establish a clear vision for their school. This vision becomes the centerpiece by which the quest for school success is based.

Vision provides a clear statement of what the school should look like and deliver, as well as describes the environment in which it will operate. It includes the identification of an "ideal world" or construction of the "best or preferred future" before injecting reality data (Kaufman and Herman, 1991).

Glickman (1992) speaks to a "super vision" for school success. He states that for a school to be educationally successful, it must be a community of professionals working together toward a vision of teaching and learning that transcends individual classrooms, grade levels, and departments. The entire school community must develop a covenant to guide future decisions about goals and operation of the school.

The vision of the Best Schools is most often expressed in a mission statement as a broad general description of purpose. It can be motivational, inspirational, and/or directional (Kaufman and Herman, 1991). In developing a mission statement, no single format works equally well for all schools. But whatever process is used, it must be agreed upon by, and actually involve representatives from, all aspects of the school community. Although it can and should be stated in many different ways, it should emphasize that all students in a school are capable of achieving mastery in all areas of the curriculum and that the teachers and administrators accept responsibility for making this a reality (Lezotte and Jacoby, 1992).

Rogers (1990) attempts to simplify the definition of a mission statement by describing it as "a statement of an organization's vision of itself that serves to guide program planning, development, and evaluation."

Mission statements are not ends to themselves. Instead, they are clear statements that conceptualize and communicate the vision. The realization of the vision depends upon the successful implementation of workable action plans. Herman (1990) recommends a five-step process to facilitate this activity, which includes the following:

(1) Identify all tasks that must be accomplished.
(2) Place a sequential number beside each task that has been identified.
(3) Identify the person or persons who are responsible for completing the task.
(4) Identify the resources necessary to accomplish the objective.
(5) State the measurement that will be used to determine whether or not the objective has been achieved.

A common planning strategy in Best Schools is to promote more decentralized vehicles for the meaningful involvement of the major stakeholders within the school community. Under the general rubric of school-based management, school councils, school-based improvement committees, etc., have become increasingly popular mechanisms to engender support and expertise for school improvement initiatives. There are many definitions of this phenomenon that vary with implementation and practice, for example, "a means of empowering the stakeholders of the school to make important decisions" (Herman, 1990); "schools given the freedom and flexibility required to respond creatively to its educational objectives, and above all, to meet the needs of students" (Hanson, 1990); and "a process of decentralization in which the school becomes the primary unit of management and educational improvement" (Educational Research Service, 1991).

Through a collaborative process, school councils are developed to assume an increased governance role in establishing school goals, priorities, and practices. Principals, teachers, parents, and students accept increased ownership in their schools as they realize that their collected views are not only respected but acted upon.

According to the American Association of School Administrators (AASA), the National Association of Elementary School Principals (NAESP), the National Association of Secondary Principals (NASSP), and other sources, school-based management

- allows competent individuals in the schools to make decisions that will improve learning
- gives the entire school community a voice in key decisions

- focuses accountability for decisions, leading to greater creativity in the design of programs and redirection of resources to support the goals developed in each school
- leads to realistic budgeting as parents and teachers become more aware of the school's financial status, spending limitations, and the cost of its programs
- improves morale of teachers and nurtures new leadership at all levels of the school organization

Results from a recent research study involving twenty-six North Carolina principals, conducted by Peel and Walker (1994), identified the characteristics found to be common among principals who have successfully instituted site-based management in their schools:

- a strong commitment to shared decision making
- a willingness to take risks
- a willingness to communicate
- an awareness of potential problems associated with shared ownership

Many school districts across the country have successfully developed school-based planning councils as a means of transferring significant decision-making authority from state and district offices to individual schools. Many of America's Best High Schools have embraced the concept and have successfully integrated school-based planning councils as a vehicle for school improvement.

THE BEST SCHOOLS–PLANNING AND ORGANIZING FOR SUCCESS

The Best Schools throughout the country have developed clear mission statements that help operationalize the school's collective vision. Additionally, they have developed precise statements of goals and priorities, which establish the parameters for school practices.

Schools have used a variety of vehicles to establish goals and priorities. Many utilize broad-based staff, community, and, at times, business partnerships in the formative stages of planning to guide school improvement. Examples of strategies used in our Best Schools are illustrated next.

Planning Illustrations

CLOVIS HIGH SCHOOL, CLOVIS, CA

The Clovis High School campus, on eighty acres, opened in 1969. It is located in a residential area just two miles east of the city of Clovis, which has a population of about 55,000.

Clovis Unified School District is approximately 200 square miles in size, located within Fresno County in Central California. Based upon 1990 figures, Fresno County's population has grown 30% since 1980. The percentage of children living in poverty has increased by 55% in the last ten years. The median family income is $26,377, and the percentage of families of four below the poverty level of $12,674 annually is 21.4%. The unemployment rate for the county in August 1992 was 12.8%.

Even though Clovis Unified receives less money per student than the state average, it is one of the fastest growing districts in the state. Demographic data show that half of the school families have lived in the district less than five years. Clovis High's ethnic composition in 1991–92 was 72.9% Caucasian, 16.1% Hispanic, 2.0% African-American, 7.6% Asian or Pacific Islander, and 1.4% American Indian.

School goals and priorities are defined and established in a collaborative manner. School-site personnel recommend goals and priorities directly to the principal through various formal and informal groups. The governing board establishes district goals and priorities, and each school site blends these with their own goals and priorities. This process has been considered in developing Clovis High's current strategic plan, which lists the following objectives and priorities for Clovis High's students:

- Clovis High's students will meet or exceed all academic standards measured by national, state, or district standards.
- Clovis High's students will meet or exceed physical fitness standards measured by national, state, or district standards.
- All Clovis High students will participate in at least one co-curricular or community service activity prior to graduation.
- Clovis High will meet or exceed state and national graduation rates.
- Fifty percent of Clovis High graduates of the Class of 1993 will complete UC/CSU entrance requirements.
- Twenty percent of the Class of 1996 and 40% of the Class of 2000 will complete at least one honors-level course successfully.
- Clovis High will receive a 90% "A" or "B" response on the school climate assessment portion of the SART Survey.
- Clovis High will increase the percentage of under-represented minorities in co-curricular activities and school committees. The enrollment of under-represented minority students in honors-level classes will be equal to or greater than their school enrollment percentages.
- Clovis High will show improved ethnic relations, as measured by the frequency of racial/ethnic incident reporting.
- Clovis High will be below national and state averages in the areas of vandalism and student violence.
- All Clovis High students will participate in a yearly counseling session regarding their progress toward graduation and career goals.

Steven R. Weil, *Principal, Grades 9–12, 3043 Students*

PELHAM MEMORIAL HIGH SCHOOL, PELHAM, NY

Pelham is a suburban middle/upper middle-class community, which is bordered by three cities. The town of 13,000 people is divided into two villages with their own separate governments.

The residents are, for the most part, college-educated professional or business people who earn their livelihoods in one of the nearby urban centers. It is a town that develops great loyalty among its residents, and many of its students are the children and grandchildren of graduates of the high school.

This small New York town has a diverse student population consisting of approximately 86% Caucasian, 7% African-American, 3.5% Hispanic, 4% Asian-American, and 0.5% Native Indian.

Each year, the school conducts a comprehensive assessment of the entire school program with parents, teachers, and students. Each group begins this assessment process with a written survey, which asks for evaluative comments in all major curriculum areas, special areas, communications, physical plant and environment, and safety. The group then develops a list of concerns in order of priority, and from these lists are developed the goals and priorities for the following year. For this year, Pelham has four major goals: 1) to redefine and improve the K–12 math curriculum and math instruction through analysis and application of standards identified by the National Council of Teachers of Mathematics; 2) to identify through curriculum mapping the content and sequence of all curriculum areas in order to align the curriculum in such a way as to reinforce and complement instruction throughout the grades and to provide opportunities for interdisciplinary instruction; 3) to develop strategies for ensuring that all teachers, students, and parents accept each other as individuals sharing similarities and enriched by differences; 4) to initiate specific activities related to a general awareness of the Compact for Learning.

These goals are reviewed continuously and interim reports are presented at significant benchmarks throughout the year to all constituencies.

Dr. John M. Conroy, *Principal, Grades 9–12, 472 Students*

SPOTSWOOD HIGH SCHOOL, SPOTSWOOD, NJ

Spotswood is a community of 8000 residents located in southern Middlesex County, New Jersey. Although it is composed of various ethnic backgrounds, the vast majority of the population is Caucasian and falls in the middle or lower middle socioeconomic range. The student body, however, is heterogeneous and diverse in its interests, capabilities, and needs. There are two industries and a number of independently owned stores in the community. These few ratables, combined with property taxes, provide a limited financial base for the school system.

Spotswood High School was founded in 1976. It provides an educational program in grades 9–12 for approximately 550 students from Spotswood and the neighboring sending districts of Milltown and Helmetta, New Jersey.

The primary goal of Spotswood High School is to nurture students' intellectual, social, emotional, and physical growth by providing a variety of curricular and co-curricular programs in a supportive environment. The school strives to create a school community that builds students' self-esteem and gives them the confidence necessary for mutual respect, open-mindedness, and academic achievement. In order to accomplish this goal in the context of a rapidly changing world, the principal and staff have four related priorities:

- to create a curriculum that reflects the profound interrelatedness of knowledge and learning through the development of interdisciplinary programs, close articulation with other schools in the district, and communication with the local community, our neighboring educational institutions, and with business and industry
- to encourage the use of reading, writing, problem solving, and critical thinking as the principal means of learning across the curriculum
- to integrate modern technology within the instructional program so that students understand both its potential and its limitations and are comfortable using technological tools
- to encourage the ongoing reeducation of the faculty in order to ensure that current theory and practice inform instruction at all times

The goals and priorities of the school are developed by a committee comprised of teachers and support staff, as well as representatives of the community, the board of education, and the student body. A statement of philosophy and goals is included in the faculty handbook, the student/parent handbook, and the curriculum guide. It is also read formally at meetings of the board of education, the student council, and the faculty. Finally, goals are articulated for students in semi-annual grade level assemblies. The philosophy and goals are reviewed every three years in order to ensure that they reflect current vision and purpose.

Peter F. Karycki, *Principal, Grades 9–12, 542 Students*

VIVIAN FIELD JUNIOR HIGH SCHOOL, FARMERS BRANCH, TX

Vivian Field Junior High School is located on the north edge of Dallas in the city of Farmers Branch. The thirty-two-year-old building is surrounded by a neighborhood where the majority of the economically disadvantaged students (39%) live. Students who live on the east and west attendance zones come from country club areas. The ethnic composition has become almost equal, 51% Anglo, 49% minority, mainly Hispanic, with other races including Black, Asian, and Indian. This diverse community constantly presents challenges to overcome obstacles to learning.

Vivian Field embraced the opportunity to restructure education through its selection as a Partnership Initiative Campus by the Texas Education Agency. They started the effort by developing a school mission, philosophy, goals, and priorities through a site-based management process. The entire staff developed the mission statement and motto:

- *Mission:* The mission of Vivian Field Junior High is to guide students to become problem solvers through the development of higher order thinking skills so that they may have continuing academic and social success as contributing members of a culturally diverse society.
- *Motto:* Their motto is "Partners in Problem Solving."

Based upon the mission and motto, the entire staff identified issues and prioritized them. Cross-department committees were formed to outline the issues and problem solve on solutions. The Campus Improvement Council (CIC), made up of teachers, staff, parents, and business representatives, then adopted the following goals to restructure and establish a "New Generation of American School":

- *Evaluation through a collegial coaching assessment system:* Develop an assessment system based upon teachers coaching one another's professional performance to increase student learning.
- *Educational quality:* Create an educational accountability system for students, teachers, and parents through quality concepts.
- *Interdisciplinary curriculum:* Develop an effective way to reinforce common objectives through an interdisciplinary approach.
- *Education supporting parents:* Reduce the achievement gap of at-risk and language minority students by providing parents with on-site social services.
- *Academic indicators performance objectives:* Establish academic performance indicators that will reflect improved student learning.

The mission and motto are framed and posted in the main entrance. A campus improvement plan containing the mission, motto, philosophy, goals, and objectives is printed and distributed to the CIC, staff, and board of education. The principal presents the goals formally and informally through PTA meetings, newsletters, and key communicators. The goals are evaluated and revised each spring in planning for the upcoming year.

Conan A. Reinken, *Principal, Grades 6–8, 687 Students*

DIMENSIONS OF LEADERSHIP

The literature of educational improvement is filled with calls for better and stronger leadership, yet a categorical model of effective school leadership still remains elusive. In fact, in recent years, the role of school leaders has become somewhat diffused. In the midst of restructuring initiatives, school-based management teams, peer coaching, and teacher empowerment movements, some question the true role (or significance) of today's principal. Despite its critics, the role of school administration, particularly the building principal, continues to be at the core of successful schools. According to Eaker, Ranells, and DuFour (1991), "The leadership skills of the principal are critical to a school improvement initiative."

The role of the principal in today's successful schools has transcended the traditional notion of functional management, power, behavioral style, and instructional leadership. The Best Schools have principals who consider their most important task as establishing a school culture. Whether through collaboration, consensus building, personal influence, or modeling, the principal is able to promote a school's vision for success by promoting a culture where staff, students, and community members have school goals that become more important than their own self-interests. In this new role as cultural leader, the principal seeks to define, strengthen, and articulate enduring values and beliefs that give the school its unique identity.

Sergiovanni (1984) describes educational leadership within a framework of five forces defined as the means available to reverse or bring about changes needed to improve schooling. These five forces include technical, human, educational, symbolic, and cultural dimensions. Sergiovanni argues that the first two forces, technical and human, receive far more attention in the literature and in administrative training programs. Far more important, Sergiovanni believes, are the last two forces, symbolic and cultural, which are closely linked to the leader's vision for his/her school.

Manarsee (1986) provides a distinction between the leader and the traditional role played by managers. He further emphasizes the central role the vision plays in separating the two functions:

> Leadership . . . involves determining the direction (vision) of an organization and then leading the organization in that direction (strategy). It is the existence of vision, out of which evolves strategy, that differentiates leadership from management, though some of the actual activities of the individual encompass both management and leadership. (p. 150)

Manarsee (1986) goes on to identify four components of vision that educational leaders can use in their efforts to bring about school success:

- *Organizational vision,* based on a systems perspective, assumes that the parts of the whole are dependent on each other and that their behavior can best be understood in terms of their relationships to their context and their connections. Organizational vision enables leaders to put systems in place that create a capacity for high performance and, at the same time, frees them personally to concentrate on activities with the highest payoff in relationship to their vision.
- *Future vision* is a comprehensive picture of how an organization will look at some point in the future, including how it will be positioned in its environment and how it will function internally. Future vision incorporates the systems perspective of organizational vision, available information about expected developments, and the personal values and beliefs of the leader. Synthesizing an appropriate direction for an organization requires intuitive as well as rational processes, plus the exercise of moral imagination in the selection of alternative conceptions of goodness. Leaders rely heavily on symbols, metaphors, models, and interpersonal competence in conveying their vision to their organization.
- *Personal vision* requires both self-awareness and the ability to identify, mobilize, and coordinate complementary skills and resources. Through personal vision, leaders select situations that allow them to position themselves toward their strengths. Leaders see themselves as learners and create organizations that value innovative learning. Such learning encourages change, renewal, restructuring, and problem reformulation, all of which, in turn, enable people to see change as opportunity, rather than threat.
- *Strategic vision* connects the reality of the present to the possibilities of the future in a personal way that is unique to the organization and its leader. Strategic vision gives members of the organization confidence that there is a rationale behind individual actions or decisions. It guides behavior toward consistency and organizational integrity. Strategic vision requires skill in managing the change process and facility in the use of symbols and metaphors to link the present to the future vision. It is strategic vision, molded from the intersection of organizational, future, and personal vision, that gives life, energy, meaning, and a sense of purpose to an organization.

The achievement of vision depends heavily upon the transformation of the culture to facilitate systemic school improvement. The vision of the principal in shaping and reinforcing school culture has become a central theme for administrators in successful schools.

Deal and Peterson (1990) offer a list of guidelines to aid educational leaders in their efforts to shape positive school cultures:

- Read the existing culture. Understand the inner workings of the school's history, values, and norms and reflect on their match with your own hopes and fears for the school.
- Identify the norms, values, and beliefs you want to reinforce, as well as those you want to change. Develop a deep sense of new elements that are needed.
- If change needs to be dramatic, make an explicit commitment that is known to others.
- Work with all the school's stakeholders to clarify the mission and purposes of the school.
- Reinforce the core values and norms of the school by consistently modeling; coaching; attending to detail; observing ceremonies, rituals, and traditions; and telling stories that identify heroes and heroines that all support the school's mission.
- Confront resistance; don't avoid or withdraw from it. Use conflicts to explain and signal the mission and values of the school.
- Highlight the priority of additional values and beliefs you seek to encourage that are not now prominent in the existing culture but that support a vision of the school's mission. Encourage deep structures that support those values and recognize those whose actions illustrate them.
- Recruit teachers and staff who share your view of the mission of the school and whose values and beliefs are consistent with those you are trying to establish.
- Encourage the potent school ceremonies and traditions that celebrate the purposes and goals of the school. Recognize and celebrate successes (both small and large) as often as possible, and involve all members of the school and community in doing so.
- Keep track of what's going on. Regularly reevaluate the extent to which students, teachers, parents, and the community share a vision of the school's mission and degree to which cultural patterns are mutually reinforcing and supportive of the school's mission.

This change in the leadership role of the principal has prompted a major shift among those who study leadership and among those who practice it. Despite different styles, principals in successful schools have a transformational effect on the people who work in the shadow of their leadership. As Roberts (1985) explains,

> The collective action that transforms leadership generally empowers those who participate in the process. There is hope, there is optimism, there is energy. In essence, transforming leadership is a leadership that facilitates the redefinition of a people's mission and vision, a renewal of their commitment, and the restructuring of their systems for goal accomplishment. (p. 1024)

Leithwood (1992) describes transformational leadership as a form of consensual or facilitative power that is manifested through other people instead of over other people. The "old" way of leadership is hierarchical and authoritarian; the "new" way seeks to gain overall participation of others.

Walker (1993) defines three dimensions of the research that illustrates transformational leadership encompassing the following elements:

(1) *A collaborative, shared decision-making approach:* Such leaders believe that organizational goals can be better accomplished by shared commitment and collaboration.

(2) *An emphasis on teacher professionalism and teacher empowerment:* Such leaders believe all teachers are capable of leadership and encourage them to be self-directed.
(3) *An understanding of change, including how to encourage change in others:* Such leaders are agents of change and are committed to educating students for the 21st century.

John Gardner (1990) concludes that the primary skill for contemporary leaders is to "understand the kind of world it is and have some acquaintance with the systems other than their own with which they must work." To function in such a world, leaders need critical skills:

(1) *Agreement building:* Leaders must have skills in conflict resolution, mediation, compromise, and coalition building. Essential to these activities are the capacity to build trust, judgment, and political skills.
(2) *Networking:* In a swiftly changing environment, traditional linkages among institutions may no longer serve or may have been disrupted. Leaders must create or recreate the linkages needed to get things done.
(3) *Exercising nonjurisdictional power:* In an earlier time, corporate or government leaders could exercise almost absolute power over internal decisions. The new leaders must deal on many fronts with groups or constituencies over which they have no control (for educators, that might be taxpayers with no children in the schools). Their power comes from the ability to build consensus and teamwork, and to translate others' ideas into action. They must be sensitive to the media and to public opinion. New leaders use "the power that accrues to those who really understand how the system works and perhaps above all, the power available to anyone skilled in the art of leadership."

Sagar (1992) reports that an increasing trend in schools where teachers and students report a culture conducive to school success is that a transformational leader is the principal. He goes on to suggest that these principals consistently utilize identifiable strategies:

- a clear and unified focus that empowers professionals to act as both individuals and members of the school
- a common cultural perspective that enables teachers to view other schools through a similar lens
- a constant push for improvement emphasizing the importance of the simultaneous application of pressure and support during educational change

Through the development of schools as more open systems, leaders no longer decide what to do and set standards in isolation from other major stakeholders. For many successful schools, the principal's role has been redefined by assuming more of a facilitative role. In fact, the ability of principals to make this transition from one leadership perspective to another, to perceive power as something that is multiplied rather than reduced when it is shared, seems to be one of the key issues of school improvement (Goldman, Dunlap, and Donley, 1991).

Despite the emphasis on leadership as a transforming phenomenon, successful principals have a keen sense of the importance of the stresses placed on school stakeholders during the change process. As cultural anthropologist Jennifer James (1990) concludes, "Change that is too fast tears some of the fabric of the school culture." To be successful, change agents should never abruptly strip people of their illusions of yesterday but, instead, permit one step backward before moving two steps forward, keeping those things that they believe are most important for future improvement.

Sergiovanni (1992) concludes that the only thing that makes a leader special is that he or she is a better follower: better at articulating the purposes of the community, more passionate about goals, and more willing to take time to pursue them.

THE BEST SCHOOLS–LEADERSHIP PRACTICES

The examination of our Best High Schools uncovers literally hundreds of special leaders, principals who were able to transform the culture of schools, create a shared vision, and empower the school community to act on behalf of its children. Yet there does not appear to be any one specific profile of an effective high school principal. A study conducted for the Blue Ribbon Schools Ceremony by Research and Evaluation Associates, Inc. (U.S. Dept. of Education, 1993) generated the following profile that applied to the majority of the 1992–93 Blue Ribbon secondary school principals:

- are male (65% males, 35% females)
- are forty-five through forty-nine years of age
- supervise a staff of more than ninety people
- administer a grades 9–12 public school with nearly 1100 students
- have been a principal for slightly more than ten years and have spent nearly half of that time at the award school
- entered the profession because of an educator's influence during earlier years
- consider time management the most difficult aspect of being an effective principal
- see instructional leadership and advocacy as the two areas in which they need to improve their skills
- think educators should use less jargon
- perceive their efforts to empower, relate to, or listen to people as key success factors
- see student success as a result of a continuing parent-teacher collaboration

The role of the principal is of special significance in successful schools. Consistently, these dedicated professionals have been respected, admired, and in many cases, loved by students, parents, and staff. Time and space prohibit an all-inclusive description of the nation's outstanding principals, yet some more closely approximate the characteristics described in this chapter.

Illustrations of Outstanding Principals (Leadership)

BOB JONES HIGH SCHOOL, MADISON, AL

Located in Madison, Alabama, Bob Jones High School serves a community rich in cultural and technical resources. Madison is one of the fastest growing, most affluent communities in the state. The population has doubled from 7500 to 15,000 over the past ten years.

Bob Jones serves a broad spectrum of students. On one hand, parents in the city limits are well educated, possessing masters and Ph.D. degrees, and often earning $60,000–$100,000 per household with both parents working. Engineers, physicists, and computer scientists work at high-tech facilities at Research Park, NASA, and the Marshall Space Flight Center. Encompassing international students and young people from all fifty states, the student body has diverse curricular and social needs. Many advanced courses have been added to the course catalog, and course requisites have been strengthened as the community has evolved from a small, rural agricultural town to a high-tech, predominantly college-oriented suburb.

On the other hand, Bob Jones also serves students from very low-income homes with approximately 100 students qualifying for free lunch or fee waivers. Many students live in apartments with only one parent and do not enjoy the same cultural advantages that affluence affords. In meeting needs of students who do not seek a professional career, Bob Jones has strengthened its "technical prep" curriculum to motivate students to prepare for a two-year associate or technical degree.

Instructional leadership is pervasive within the school. The greatest impact comes from the principal, who sets the standard for excellence. He outlines his expectations in the annual teacher handbook. The assistant principal of instruction spends 100% of her time on the academic program. She reviews lesson plans, supervises instruction, and coordinates extensive staff development. Target areas have been critical thinking skills, questioning techniques, motivation, self-esteem, discovery learning, cooperative learning, interpreting test scores, improving SAT and ACT problem-solving skills, and stress management. Additionally, the administration trains the staff in effective schools research, how students learn, writing effective lesson plans, questioning techniques, engaged learning, and using higher cognitive skills.

Beyond verbal commitment to instructional priority, the normal routine reflects the goals of instruction: protected instructional time, well-organized lesson planning and accountability, and high grading standards and expectations. Teaching of each period and preparing detailed lesson plans are congruent with course objectives.

Empowerment to master teachers and department chairpersons has been one of the secrets of success in instructional leadership. Utilizing a common planning period, department chairpersons meet regularly to coordinate academic competitions and to articulate strengths and weaknesses they perceive. They share the responsibility for training new teachers, for registration, for creating the master teaching schedule, and for the community accountability update.

Billy Broadway, *Principal, Grades 9–12, 883 Students*

PONTOTOC JUNIOR HIGH SCHOOL, PONTOTOC, MS

Pontotoc Junior High School is a sixth through eighth grade school in the small rural town of Pontotoc, Mississippi. Pontotoc is located in the northeastern part of the state, which is legally classified as Appalachia. The school is one of four schools in the Pontotoc City School District. In the poorest state in the nation, the district is in the bottom 5% of the state in per pupil expenditure, as reported by the Mississippi State Department of Education. The students are not from affluent families—almost half receive free or reduced lunches.

The majority of the citizens are life-time residents of the area. The student population is made up of 68% Caucasian and 32% African-American.

The primary function of the principal in the school is to provide instructional leadership. Prerequisite to this is for the principal to be trained in curriculum and leadership. In particular, it is the responsibility of the principal in the school to provide instruction for teachers in methodology, planning, evaluation, reporting, remediation, refinement, and management. The district teacher evaluation plan has provided all teachers with a common educational language and a common teaching framework that places the principal in a position where he must be knowledgeable about what is good teaching, and he must establish credibility. Specifically, the principal helps identify school priorities through data disaggregation, use of educational experts, employment of current research, establishing study committees, and sharing of ideas. It is the responsibility of the principal to constantly monitor and evaluate instructional practices at Pontotoc Junior High School, and this is accomplished by:

- performing components of the comprehensive teacher evaluation
- conducting monthly focused faculty meetings
- monitoring grade distributions each six weeks
- interpreting test data
- monitoring progress in teaching essential skills as identified by the school's instructional management plan

The counselor is in a staff position that serves as a resource person for the principal and the teachers. Administration and interpretation of tests, counseling students into appropriate programs, providing personal data for teachers, scheduling, and serving as a liaison between students, teachers, and administrators are all functions of the counselor in assisting in instructional improvement.

Conwell Duke, *Principal, Grades 6–8, 442 Students*

ALEXANDER HAMILTON HIGH SCHOOL, ELMSFORD, NY

Hamilton School, the smallest public high school in its county, serves a population that is racially and culturally diverse. Fifty percent of the students are African-Americans, 30% are Caucasian, and 20% are Hispanic and Asian. Currently, the school district takes responsibility for twenty-eight group home students. Consequently, students experience a high degree of mobility. For example, in any given year, as many as fifty of the students may transfer in and out of the school.

The school district is located in the fourth poorest community in an otherwise affluent county. The most recent demographic study indicated that 50% of students' parents had not received a high school diploma. In contrast, approximately 85% of our students go on to a postsecondary institution, while maintaining a low dropout rate of less than 2%.

The school and community attribute much of the success to administrative stability and leadership. As in all areas of the school, the principal is the key to the instructional program. A major strength of the principal is knowing how to motivate staff members to work to their potential. His enthusiasm is infectious, and, in that way, he "lights fires" for others to share in his vision.

- *Department meetings:* Due to fiscal cutbacks the procedures have somewhat changed in recent years. The school no longer has department heads. Now, the principal has taken on the responsibilities that once belonged to chairpersons. The principal is the instructional leader and works collaboratively with staff members to discuss issues and share ideas.
- *Principal's cabinet:* The principal chairs a decision-making cabinet comprised of a cross representation of teachers. All instructional plans are shared at these meetings.
- *Informal network:* Because of the size of the school and the principal's open-door policy, programs, policies, and procedures are discussed on a daily basis. The staff does not wait for faculty meetings to discuss "burning issues."
- *Faculty meetings:* Faculty meetings are held monthly in order to coalesce and synthesize the discussions that arise from other formal meetings, the principal's cabinet, and informal meetings. In this way, the entire staff is well informed on all vital school issues.

In addition, the principal circulates in the building more than a few times a day, frequently visiting classes. And, yet, his most notable achievement in the instructional process is his use of staff talent and expertise. The principal is especially effective when it comes to organizing diverse staff members into decision-making productive teams.

Leonard Mecca, *Principal, Grades 7–12, 245 Students*

KASTNER INTERMEDIATE SCHOOL, FRESNO, CA

Kastner School began operation in 1979. Since that time, the student population has become quite diverse. Located in suburban Fresno, ten elementary schools, covering a very large geographic area, "feed into" Kastner.

The majority of students are transported to school each day by bus. Many students come from single-parent households and many live in lower socioeconomic conditions. The number of languages spoken at Kastner has grown to fifteen. In 1991–92, students from fourteen countries were enrolled. Kastner has been successful in assimilating the many diverse nationalities and wide span of socioeconomic backgrounds into a happy and productive school culture.

The principal believes all students can be successful learners; all teachers can be effective and inspirational leaders to children; and all parents should be shareholders in their children's education. The principal helps create the vision and inspiration to accomplish school goals through collaborative decision making and goal sharing. A parent stated, "Mrs. Snauffer is talented and accessible and has good rapport with students and parents." Pride in being part of the Kastner family is reflected in a collective pride inspired by the principal and staff. The positive and optimistic feeling that exists on campus is felt by every visitor. Every year, a new theme highlights the school's efforts. The recently selected motto, "In a League of Our Own," was presented in the opening week assembly and reflects the pride in accomplishments and the spirit of the "Kastner team" that exists among students, staff, parents, and community. This theme communicates the commitment to excellence and to achieving school goals.

The principal conveys her vision and high expectations to students, staff, and parents by directing all policies, programs, and resources toward the achievement of school goals and priorities. Shared decision making and collaboration are encouraged among staff and parents. The Kastner Academic Council, the Principal's Advisory Council, the School Site Council, the Kastner SART Committee, the Kastner Parent Club, the Multicultural Advisory Committee, department chairpersons, Student Council, House of Representatives and business and community partners all play a role in creating programs and resources that develop from the school goals and priorities. The principal helps develop support and financial resources necessary to achieve goals.

The principal provides vision and direction for curriculum and instruction. Curriculum areas are assigned to the learning directors according to individual strengths and expertise. The learning director works with the resource teacher and other teachers to develop and monitor instructional programs. Mentor teachers organize inservices, conferences, and seminars and provide instruction to new teachers through such programs as "Dear Beginning Teacher." The library media teacher uses resource-based instructional units in a team-teaching approach. Teacher coaches are assigned to help new teachers with instructional management strategies. Peer coaching is used throughout the school to enrich instructional delivery systems.

Lynda Austin-Snauffer, *Principal, Grades 7–8, 1751 Students*

SUMMARY

The Best Schools consistently demonstrate the ability to plan and organize for success. Although the strategies to produce the plans vary based on the size, traditions, and needs of the school, many common elements exist. America's finest schools have a clear sense of purpose. Great care is given to develop a mission statement that often serves as the focus for school practices and improvements. The mission is always translated into clear goals that are aimed at the development of a school climate that expects each student to be successful. The Best Schools have principals who transcend the managerial tenets of their role—principals who understand that their primary role is to create and maintain a school culture that is student-centered and goal-oriented. Teachers who work in these schools receive satisfaction from the professional work that they accomplish together for the benefit of children. Principals in the Best Schools not only value the students, parents, and teachers, but systematically involve them in a variety of meaningful educational decisions. Teachers are not treated as hierarchical subordinates but are given the responsibility to make decisions that affect life in the school. Finally, the principals in America's Best Schools instill a belief within the school community that school improvement is an ongoing process of getting better, no matter how good they may perceive themselves to be now!

REFERENCES

Carson, C. C., R. N. Hullskamp, and T. D. Woodall. (1993). "Perspectives on Education in America: An Annotated Briefing," *The Journal of Educational Research* (May/June):20–25.

Cawelti, Gordon. (1994). *High School Restructuring: A National Study; ERS Report.* Arlington, VA: Educational Research Service.

Cawelti, Gordon and Art Roberts. (1993). *Redesigning General Education in American High Schools.* Alexandria, VA: Association for Supervision and Curriculum Development.

Deal, Terrence E. and Kent D. Peterson. (1990). "The Principals's Role in Shaping School Culture," Washington, D.C.: U.S. Department of Education, Office of Educational Research and Improvement.

Eaker, Robert, Mary Ann Ranells, and Richard DuFour. (1991). *Utilizing the Effective School Research: Practical Strategies for School Improvement.* Murfreesboro, TN: Middle Tennessee Chapter of Phi Delta Kappa.

Educational Research Service. (1991). *Site-Based Management.* ERS Information Aid, Arlington, VA: ERS.

Gardner, John. (1990). *On Leadership.* New York, NY: The Free Press.

Glickman, Carl D. (1992). "The Essence of School Renewal: The Prose Has Begun," *Educational Leadership,* 501:24–27.

Goldman, Paul, Diane Dunlap, and David Donley. (1991). "Administrative Facilitation and Site-Based School Reform Projects," paper presented at the *Annual Conference of the American Educational Research Association*, Chicago, April 4, 1991.

Herman, Jerry J. (1990). "Action Plans to Make Your Vision a Reality," *NASSP Bulletin*, 74(523):14–17.

James, Jennifer. (1990). "How to Cope with Cultural Chaos" (interview with Jack Blendiner and Linda T. Jones), *The School Administrator*, 3(47):27–29.

Joyce, Bruce R. (1991). "The Doors to School Improvement," *Educational Leadership*, 48(8):59–62.

Kaufman, Roger and Jerry Herman. (1991). *Strategic Planning in Education: Rethinking, Restructuring, Revitalizing.* Lancaster, PA: Technomic Publishing Company, Inc.

Leithwood, Kenneth. (1992). "The Move toward Transformational Leadership," *Educational Leadership*, 49(5):34–35.

Lezotte, Lawrence W. and Barbara C. Jacoby. (1992). *The District Content for School Improvement.* Okemos, MI: Effective Schools Products, Ltd.

Manarsee, A. Lorri. (1986). "Vision and Leadership: Paying Attention to Intention," *Peabody Journal of Education*, 63(1):150–173.

Roberts, N. (1985). "Transforming Leaders: A Process of Collective Action," *Human Relations*, 38(11):1023–1046.

Rogers, Joseph F. (1990). "Developing a Vision Statement–Some Considerations for Principals," *NASSP Bulletin*, 74(523):6–12.

Sagar, Richard D. (1992). "Three Principals Who Make a Difference," *Educational Leadership*, 49(5):13–18.

Sashkin, M. and J. Egermier. (1992). "School Change Models and Processes: A Review of Research and Practice," working draft prepared for the United States Department of Education's AMERICA 2000 initiative and for a research symposium presented at the 1992 *Annual Meeting of the American Educational Research Association*, Washington, D.C.

Sergiovanni, Thomas J. (1984). "Leadership and Excellence in Schooling," *Educational Leadership*, 41(5):4–13.

Sergiovanni, Thomas J. (1992). "On Rethinking Leadership: A Conversation with Tom Sergiovanni (interview with Ron Brandt)," *Educational Leadership*, 49(5):46–49.

U.S. Department of Education, Blue Ribbon Schools Program for Improvement of Practice/OERI. (1993). *The Blue Ribbon Schools Program: A Profile of Principals.* Washington, D.C.

Walker, Bradford L. (1993). "What It Takes to Be An Empowering Principal," *Principal* (March):41–42.

CHAPTER 3

Teaching Environment

AMERICA'S Best Schools have effective principals. These principals have the ability to develop and sustain an organizational climate that focuses their staff toward the achievement of school goals. Through the creation of a shared vision comes a foundation for the traditions, norms, values, and beliefs that form the framework for the school's culture.

The perception of this culture, held by staff, students, and parents, constitutes the climate of the school (Keefe and Kelley, 1990). These prevailing conditions, which establish the parameters for daily practices and routines, have proven to have significant impact on school success. The maintenance of a positive climate provides the framework to move the school's mission and objectives from the awareness and planning stages to the implementation and maintenance stages.

The literature reveals a variety of factors that characterize a positive climate. These, in general, include an emphasis on academics, an ambience of caring, a motivating curriculum, professional collegiality, and a sense of closeness to parents and community. Often, high faculty morale, job satisfaction, and increased productivity can also be associated with a positive teaching environment.

Although there are no categorical models that ensure a productive teaching environment, current educational literature contains substantial support for the systematic study and recognition of this phenomenon as a cornerstone for school improvement.

This chapter will examine the significance of a professional teaching environment as a focus for achievement of student-based goals. Additionally, special emphasis will be given to common strategies that have promoted productive teaching environments in successful schools. Finally, programs and initiatives from America's Best Schools will be provided to illustrate the unique application of research and strategies into enriching teaching environments.

Specifically, this chapter will address the following questions:

- What are the essential characteristics of a productive teaching environment?
- What strategies are utilized to maximize teacher expertise in school decision making?
- What provisions are made in Best Schools to enable staff to engage in collegial planning and implementation of educational programs?
- What do Best Schools do to support and strengthen the skills of beginning teachers and teachers new to the school?
- What procedures for supervision and evaluation of teachers exist in Best Schools?
- How do Best Schools support and encourage the recognition of teachers?
- What strategies are utilized in Best Schools to enhance teachers' effectiveness with students and to improve job satisfaction?
- What are the characteristics of staff development programs in Best Schools?

PRODUCTIVE TEACHING

Teachers' performance in schools is, in part, determined by the atmosphere or climate in which they work. It can be looked upon as a broad concept referring to teachers' perceptions of the work environment. There are a number of common terms used to refer to the general surrounding of an individual at work—ecology, milieu, setting, time, field, atmosphere, or climate. They all are used to refer to the internal quality of the workplace as experienced by its members (Hoy and Forsyth, 1986).

In a very real sense, the conceptual environment in which teachers work can distinguish successful from unsuccessful schools because of the impact and direct influence environment has on teachers' perceptions and behaviors. Similarly, a school's environment can have a significant effect on the learning and development of students and, in some cases, student academic achievement.

No single factor accounts for building a successful teacher environment, yet much research has been aimed at isolating those characteristics that facilitate student learning and school improvement. Research by Lezotte (1991) has shown seven operational characteristics, which seem to be present in the environments of successful schools:

(1) *Safe and orderly environment,* including an environment that is conducive to good discipline where rules and procedures are well defined and where students actually help one another
(2) *Climate of high expectation for success* where a commitment to well-defined goals directs the school's resources and where beliefs and behaviors are aimed at successful achievement for all students
(3) *Instructional leadership* characterized by behavior directed toward instructional goals, motivation of instructional improvement, and provisions for opportunities for staff growth and disbursement of leadership throughout the staff
(4) *Clear focus and mission* directing and unifying staff toward the primary goal of learning for all students
(5) *Appropriate opportunity for student learning and time on task* through the design and delivery of an aligned curriculum and instructional strategies that emphasize student-engaged learning time
(6) *Frequent monitoring of student progress* where a variety of evaluation methods are used, which provide students with feedback on learning and teachers feedback for modifying instruction
(7) *Home-school monitoring of student progress* where the mission and instructional focus of the school is communicated to parents and the community and where their support is elicited and their involvement encouraged

These underlying characteristics of effective schools have long been valued as a conceptual framework for school success. Increasingly, as indicated in the previous chapter, successful schools have instituted collaborative problem solving as a basic ingredient for school improvement. Teachers' and administrators' working together to make decisions and solve problems has proven to foster school excellence, as well as develop a sense of collegiality among staff.

School climate or environment has been characterized by a number of metaphors. The concept of school health (Hoy, Tarter, and Kottkamp, 1991) addresses the nature of student-teacher, teacher-teacher, and teacher-administrator interactions. A healthy school has been described as one in which harmony pervades relationships among students, teachers, and administrators as the school directs its energies toward its mission (Hoy, Tarter, and Bliss, 1990). Many organizational characteristics that are associated with effective schools and student achievement are closely aligned with the indicators of the health of a school.

Hoy and Woolfolk (1993) identify six dimensions of organizational health, which have been used to describe the health of a school.

- *Institutional integrity* is a school's ability to cope with its environment in a way that maintains the educational integrity of its programs. Teachers are protected from unreasonable community and parental demands.
- *Principal influence* is the principal's ability to influence the actions of superiors. Being able to persuade superiors to get additional consideration, and to be unimpeded by the administrative hierarchy are necessary skills to be effective as a principal.
- *Consideration* is principal behavior that is friendly, supportive, open, and collegial; it represents a genuine concern of a principal for the welfare of teachers.
- *Resource support* refers to a school where adequate classroom supplies and instructional materials are available and extra resources are readily supplied if requested.
- *Morale* is a collective sense of friendliness, openness, enthusiasm, and trust among faculty members. Teachers like each other, like their jobs, and help each other, and they are proud of their school and feel a sense of accomplishment in their jobs.
- *Academic emphasis* is the extent to which a school is driven by a quest for academic excellence. High, but achievable, academic goals are set for students; the learning environment is orderly and serious; teachers believe in their students' ability to achieve; and students work hard and respect those who do well academically.

Increasingly, school reformers (Glickman, 1989, for instance) argue convincingly that positive change in schools depends on allowing teachers to work toward their own solution to problems. Power sharing is built into this concept. For teachers, this signifies a greater degree of participation in collaborative decision-making opportunities. Through these opportunities, teachers develop a sense of ownership and control over the classroom and (in some cases) school life.

THE BEST SCHOOLS – TEACHER INVOLVEMENT

This common theme of teacher participation and empowerment is central in current research on successful schools. Although the vehicles for involvement may vary from school to school, the results are most often related to positive student outcomes and productive teaching environments. Best Schools actively create opportunities for the involvement of teachers in most every aspect of school decision making. They have capitalized on the skills and experiences of those who are closest and know most about the teaching-learning process. Although all successful schools have developed strategies for teacher involvement, examples of strategies that have proven beneficial in America's Best Schools are illustrated below.

Teacher Involvement Illustrations

HARTLAND HIGH SCHOOL, HARTLAND, MI

Hartland High School serves grades 9 – 12 of the student population from the town of Hartland in Livingston County, Michigan. The population includes rural, small town, and somewhat suburban-like students, who range from lower to upper socioeconomic status. In general, the community adheres to traditional American family values, with parents who have some type of formal education. Much of the adult population works outside of the community, since expressway routes easily reach Detroit, Ann Arbor, Lansing, and Flint.

The district covers ninety square miles with a relatively homogeneous population with few ethnic minorities or persons living below the poverty line. Ninety-two percent of the citizens own their own homes, and the community has traditionally strongly supported millage elections and bond issues.

Hartland is a growing district that has evolved from rural to suburban. Teacher expertise and experience are welcomed with many opportunities existing for decision making. The principal and assistant principals maintain an open door policy, as well as remaining visible and available for input. Changes in the curriculum guide are sought from students and staff. These proposals go from the department to staff, to curriculum council, and to the board of education. Evidence of teacher involvement includes a new dramatics class, OBE team-taught Algebra I, pre-calculus (analysis), jazz band, AP physics, information systems technology, debate, forensics, and the academic teams' letter. Teachers had a large voice, along with students, parents, support staff, and community members, with the adoption of the school's mission and beliefs statement.

Teachers have a major input regarding staffing considerations. Staffing needs are also dictated by student requests. Teachers meet in departments, making recommendations for scheduling. The principal determines staffing, however, trying to schedule to teacher strengths and interests. All staffing is decided on what would be best for students; most teachers receive the schedule that they desire.

Teacher involvement is evident in the development of student outcomes for math and science. Coordinated common course outlines are developed departmentally with staff making content and sequence decisions, with input from the principal and assistant superintendent for curriculum and instruction. The staff/principal "sounding board" meets the first Tuesday of the month. Staff decide on the restructuring of the class schedule, meeting times, and duty stations. Teachers also help recommend appropriate student academic placement for scheduling (especially math/English/science). Curricular needs drove the expansion of the educational bond issue of 1990. Teachers were integral decision makers in terms of space, equipment, and design of the new facility. The child development wing, new computer labs, fine arts wing, and media center all had the teachers' stamp of approval. The school improvement team was totally site-based selected, and the chairperson is a teacher. Consensus is the form of decision making used in this area.

James Basel, *Principal, Grades 9–12, 949 Students*

MOUNTAIN BROOK HIGH SCHOOL, BIRMINGHAM, AL

The city of Mountain Brook is a suburb of Birmingham, Alabama, with a population of 19,800. The school district has a long history of success, with many families moving to Mountain Brook to be part of the school's tradition of excellence. Because of this reputation, there is a large degree of community support for the school. Additionally, both staff and community share high expectations for its students and a genuine commitment for each student to achieve.

The primary vehicle used in recent years has been the implementation of the shared decision-making process, which we call the leadership team. Initially, the principal asked eight faculty members representing all departments in the school to assist him in improving the school. The input of everyone was solicited, and the faculty aimed at deriving decisions through consensus. The eight faculty members, along with the administration, worked extremely hard to insure that the process was successful. After getting input from the faculty about the most pressing problems facing the school, the leadership team decided on nine areas: class time/student attendance, curriculum, scheduling, teacher morale, student-teacher relations, administration-staff relations, athletics/extracurricular, communication, and facilities.

Because so many topics were undertaken, during the second year of the leadership team's existence, the focus was narrowed to some degree, and many of the ideas proposed the previous year were investigated further. For example, growing out of the initial student-teacher relations committee was an idea that too much weighting of grades existed in advanced and AP programs. A faculty committee evaluated many grading and weighting systems and proposed modifications of the existing system. This modification was agreed upon by the faculty at large and has been implemented during the present school year.

As shared decision making continues to evolve, other modifications have been introduced. Recently, the principal asked departments to elect representatives to the leadership team in place of those who had served on the initial team at his request. Also, two parent representatives have been added to the group. Since this process has been viewed as successful at the high school (as well as at the junior high in the district), the four district elementary schools have also adopted a similar model for implementation. Due to his experience with shared decision making, the principal has been given opportunities to speak to administrators in nearby districts who are also considering the process.

Aside from the organizational structure, which is based on teacher input, teachers are encouraged to bring their ideas to their departments, to their committees, and, of course, to their classrooms. Curriculum improvement is a constant process in the school, one in which each teacher has a vested interest. The entire staff share the responsibility and the opportunity to create the best school they can.

Dr. Tim Norris, *Principal, Grades 10–12, 670 Students*

KENMORE EAST SENIOR HIGH SCHOOL, TONAWANDA, NY

Kenmore East High School is one of two comprehensive high schools in Tonawanda. Tonawanda is characterized as a lower middle- to middle-class community of approximately 90,000 residents in close proximity to Buffalo, New York. Its student population is diverse, with students represented from most all racial and ethnic backgrounds.

The school planning team is the primary long-range planning agency for the school. Teachers have representation on the team. The CORE team, a group of teachers, counselors, and administrators, is involved in day-to-day problem-solving operations of the school. They meet daily to plan activities and weekly with administrators to discuss students who are at risk for dropping out of school. Instructional staff also have a wide range of alternatives and individual choices in becoming involved in the planning of programs and the operations of our school. Under the district's active encouragement of cooperative decision making and employee-management contracts, the staff is involved in curriculum committees, scheduling of the school day, teacher evaluation, hiring of new personnel, evaluation of the discipline and attendance procedures, and various ad hoc committees. Teachers in the school have been and are actively involved in:

- Revision of discipline and attendance procedures – A group of twenty-eight staff, parents, administrators, and students met for a week-long workshop to discuss the need to revise the discipline system and to address students at risk for dropping out of school. The new system created a supervisory role for teachers called "deans." They serve as an adjunct to the administrators, meeting students and assigning disciplinary actions at the entry level, thus freeing the administrators to deal with more difficult cases.
- Site-based hiring – Recent district practices have allowed representative building committees to interview and hire the principal, assistant principal, teachers, and noninstructional staff.
- Textbook selection – It is a longstanding practice that individual departments review, evaluate, and select the texts that are used in their courses. While approval of the principal and the school board is necessary for purchase, all texts recommended for adoption have been approved.
- Scheduling of classes – For many years departments have openly determined the assignment of teachers to the classes that student registration requires. The cooperative nature of this process insures that teachers have balanced schedules and can volunteer to accept new assignments.
- Curriculum revision – Each fall, revisions are made to the curriculum handbook, which outlines the courses to be offered the following year. These revisions are done by each department and provide continuous updating and renewal of curriculum.

- Role of department chairs – Each month, the heads of the various departments meet with the principal to discuss problems and issues that face the school. These meetings promote the free exchange of ideas, which, in turn, are discussed during frequent meetings of each department.
- Staff development – A committee consisting of fifteen teachers, noninstructional staff, and administrators plans and implements all staff development initiatives for the school.
- Ad hoc committees – Teachers are members of various ad hoc committees dealing with school policies regarding attendance, discipline, and other school issues.

Barbara Field, *Principal, Grades 9–12, 1038 Students*

Teaching in Isolation

More than most any profession, teaching is practiced in isolation. All too often, teacher opportunities for the development of professional dialogue and collaboration are limited to hurried episodes over plastic lunch trays or periodic moments while supervising students in the hallways or cafeteria. Most teachers are hungry for stimulating professional dialogue and experiences, yet, in many schools, little time is devoted to the provision of time or incentive for the sharing of similar dialogue or meaningful educational experiences.

Best Schools have recognized the value of enabling staff to engage in collegial planning for the implementation of educational programs in their schools. Empowering teachers through release time, shared planning periods, interdisciplinary teaching experiences, etc., has led to a collective autonomy where professionals collaboratively plan for student success. Several specific examples of strategies for collegial planning in Best Schools are provided next.

Collegial Planning Illustrations

NORTH FARMINGTON HIGH SCHOOL, FARMINGTON, MI

North Farmington High School is located in a suburban area populated by 75,000–80,000 people. The Farmington school system maintains three high schools, four middle schools, and thirteen elementary schools, with an overall student population of 11,093.

The socioeconomic makeup of the community varies from families who are in need to families who are affluent; however, the majority of the population is comprised of upper middle-class, college-educated people. Over sixty ethnic and racial groups are represented in the school community.

During the 1991–92 school year, faculty members invested hundreds of hours after school and during vacation time examining a variety of options for school improvement. The steering committee convened and began a dialogue about ways that they wanted to change. During the course of meeting, it was realized that meaningful change could not occur without total staff involvement. Plans to accommodate learning for the whole staff were developed. A variety of plans were discussed, and consensus on a direction was reached. As a result of school board support, a weekly two-hour block was developed. From 7:30 A.M. to 9:30 A.M. each Wednesday, the faculty and support staff meet to research and discuss pertinent issues in education. The Wednesday morning planning block is a reflection of current educational research advocating time for teachers to collaboratively research, plan, and implement change.

From this ongoing process, new links between departments such as art and journalism are being created. The staff is willing to invest multiple hours to projects they realize will be implemented, based on the knowledge and evidence that what's good for our kids is worth doing.

Deborah T. Clarke, *Principal, Grades 9–12, 1072 Students*

LOS ALAMITOS SCHOOL, LOS ALAMITOS, CA

Located about twenty miles south of Los Angeles, Los Alamitos High School is one of eight schools in the Los Alamitos Unified School District, along with five elementary schools, a middle school, a continuation high school, the Orange County High School of the Arts, and a preschool, for a total population of 7179.

Los Alamitos High School is the pride of its suburban, primarily middle-class community. The stability of the school population is attributed to the fact that most families locate in the area so that their children can attend its schools. The sociocultural population of Hispanic, African-American, Asian, Indo-European, and Pacific Islander backgrounds comprise 23% of the student body. Military families from the Naval Weapons Station and the Armed Forces Reserves Center, and the 265 students who come to Orange County High School of the Arts distinguish and expand the school culture.

Teachers are considered the most valuable component of school success at Los Alamitos; therefore, their involvement and commitment to educational program planning and implementation is always engendered. The curriculum within the high school is articulated through many formal and informal channels and instructional delivery systems that are developed. Subject matter teams have been established to review content, materials, methodologies, and testing. Intra- and interdepartmental collaboration has resulted in four teachers team teaching. Many teachers join forces to present topics to multiple classes. Groups of teachers have become experts in brain-based learning, cooperative and collaborative grouping, discussions, lecturing, plus debates, simulations, and other interactive teaching strategies. On-site staff development, release time, and summer work groups provide opportunities for these experts to work with other staff members to improve instruction. Last year, 289 release days and 1601 summer work group hours were used for teachers to collaboratively develop lessons. Peer coaching and mentor teachers provide feedback on lessons, and evaluation of student assessment records provides direction for future improvements. Departments and subject matter teams meet frequently with special education teachers to present, assess, and revise instructional strategies as well as to share successes.

Carol A. Hart, *Principal, Grades 9–12, 2320 Students*

SEWANHAKA HIGH SCHOOL, FLORAL PARK, NY

Sewanhaka High School is a comprehensive school that serves the students of four communities: Elmont, Franklin Square, Floral Park, and New Hyde Park. These communities are suburbs of New York City and are comprised of over 70,000 people. The communities themselves are a reflection of America inasmuch as they represent a cross section of economic, ethnic, and religious backgrounds. The racial/ethnic composition of the student population is 69% Caucasian, 16% African-American, 10% Hispanic, and 5% Asian-American.

Collegial planning is valued at the school and takes a variety of forms:

- Teachers meet and write curricula over the summer.
- A daily common free period is scheduled in most departments to allow for collegial planning.
- Library professionals meet with teachers in each discipline to plan and evaluate reading and research projects.
- New textbooks are selected by teacher committees.
- Vocational and technical teachers regularly meet in eight craft committees to review curriculum and equipment needs.
- Department chairpersons meet with district coordinators once a month to plan programs, curriculum, and future needs.
- Faculty meetings are literally run by the faculty.
- Interdepartmental collaboration is also encouraged: mentor teachers from the English, science, and mathematics departments use a team approach; study skills facilitators in

mathematics and English coordinate staff training; art, occupational education, music, and English department members work together in dramatic and musical productions. English and social studies departments meet to integrate curriculum; foreign language and home and careers departments present an international desserts evening.

David A. Kreutz, *Principal, Grades 7–12, 1234 Students*

PROCEDURES FOR SUPERVISING AND EVALUATING TEACHERS

In recent years, the movement toward accountability in education has touched virtually every aspect of educational delivery systems. In this regard, monitoring an evaluation of teacher competence has become an increasing point of focus. Many believe that the key to educational improvement lies in upgrading the quality of teachers. Prompted by both an empirical and commonsense perspective, teacher evaluation and professional development have become an important element of school improvement efforts; however, developing effective systems for assessing teacher competence has proven extremely difficult.

For decades, researchers and practitioners have searched for ways to accurately assess teacher performance. The search for a categorical system that meets the needs of both the teacher and the evaluator will forever be elusive. The issues embodied in evaluation are much too complicated to be reduced to checklists or annual narrative statements. Instead, evaluation systems that work have become part of the culture of the school, a culture that values constructive feedback as a vehicle to provide quality education for its students.

Best Schools see the value of evaluation as a tool for self and school renewal. Additionally, evaluation is looked upon as a collegial activity by which both the teacher and the principal develop a greater understanding of their roles and performance as it relates to the mission of the school. In Best Schools, evaluation is an ongoing process – something that is systematized and purposeful, something that does not happen just once or twice a year, but, in a very real sense, takes place each day. Best Schools also realize that the goals of evaluation systems must differentiate for teachers with different levels of expertise, experience, and needs. Finally, evaluation is perceived as not being within the sole domain of the principal, and that much can be gained through peer observation and coaching.

Yet to provide a conceptual framework to discuss teacher evaluation, a brief description of traditional methods of teacher evaluation would seem appropriate. In a basic way, teacher evaluation in America has two separate functions. The first centers on the improvement of teachers' skills so that they can perform their roles more effectively. This type of evaluation is frequently described as formative teacher evaluation, for its mission is to help modify (form) the teacher's classroom behaviors.

The second function of teacher evaluation centers around decisions such as whether to dismiss a teacher, whether to grant tenure to a teacher, whether to place a teacher on probation, or whether a teacher should advance on a career ladder. This type of evaluation is typically called summative teacher evaluation because it deals more with final, summary decisions about teachers. Summative evaluation is not improvement oriented; instead, it is aimed at making judgments about how teacher performance relates to a district's standards for continued employment.

In a more general sense, most writers (Denham, 1987; Harris, 1986; McGreal, 1983) seem to agree that the major purposes of an evaluation are:

(1) Provide a process that allows and encourages supervisors and teachers to work together to improve and enhance classroom instructional practices.
(2) Provide a process for bringing structured assistance to marginal teachers.

(3) Provide a basis for making more rational decisions about the retention, transfer, or dismissal of staff members.
(4) Provide a basis for making more informed judgments about different performance levels for use in compensation programs such as merit pay plans or career ladder programs.
(5) Provide information for determining the extent of implementation of knowledge and skills gained during staff development activities and for use in judging the degree of maintenance of the acquired knowledge and skills.

The supervision and evaluation of teachers has had a significant role in a teacher's perception of his/her teaching environment. Bureaucratic systems have long been associated with close organizational environments that tend to inhibit teacher creativity and growth and actually negatively impact on teacher performance. Conversely, laissez-faire or permissive systems tend to communicate misleading information and promote continuation of poor teaching behaviors. Ogden and Germinario (1994) have identified systems that tend to be based on the following concepts:

(1) The supervision/evaluation takes place within a professional context of collegiality and collaboration.
(2) A clear understanding exists between the supervisor and teacher as to the common language describing good teaching.
(3) Data collection methods that are utilized in the classroom are clearly understood by both the teacher and the evaluator.
(4) Data collected through classroom observation are valid (in terms of measuring what they are intended to measure) and reliable (in terms of their intended consistency from one application to another).
(5) Conferences are held by the teacher and evaluator to share data collection and exchange perceptions of lesson outcomes.
(6) Consideration is given to differentiated systems of evaluation for beginning, advanced, and expert teachers.

Manatt (1982) offers a similar framework that identifies strategies that are closely linked to the teacher performance cycle:

(1) Establish the "rules of the game."
(2) Orient teachers.
(3) Analyze lesson plans.
(4) Conduct a preobservation conference.
(5) Conduct classroom observation.
(6) Conduct a postobservation conference.
(7) Synthesize data.
(8) Write an evaluation report.
(9) Set job improvement targets (repeat sequence).

An analysis of America's Best Schools indicates the incorporation of many of the concepts listed above into an ongoing evaluation system. Specifically, many use a version of a clinical supervision model (Cogan, 1973). Although many variations of the model are used, the supervisory cycle in a clinical relationship revolves around eight phases.

(1) Establish the supervisory relationship: Build a relationship of trust and support and induct the teacher into the role of co-supervisor.
(2) Plan lessons and units with the teacher: Determine objectives, concepts, teaching-learning techniques, materials, and assessment methods.
(3) Plan the observation strategy: Teacher and supervisor discuss the data to be gathered and the methods for gathering the data.
(4) Observe in-class instruction.
(5) Analyze the observational data to determine patterns of behavior and critical incidents of teaching and learning.
(6) Plan the conference strategy: Set tentative conference objectives and processes.
(7) Confer to analyze data.
(8) Resume the planning: Complete the cycle by determining future directions for growth and planning the next unit or lesson.

Recently, researchers have maintained that there is no one best approach to the evaluation of classroom teachers but, rather, that the process should be tailored to the background, needs, and the developmental readiness of the individual teacher (Marczely, 1992). The basic premise for teacher improvement is based on the belief that everyone has the potential to improve and that the challenge for the supervisor is to treat teachers as individual adult learners to enable them to use their potential.

Glickman (1990) identifies two propositions for supervision that emerge from adult and generic teacher development:

- Proposition 1: Supervision, to be effective, must be a function that responds to the developmental stages of teachers. Teachers are not all alike in their thinking or their motivation for teaching; thus, they should not be treated as a homogeneous group.
- Proposition 2: Supervision, to be effective, must be a function that responds to adult life transitions of teachers. Initial enthusiasm should be encouraged by gradually increasing responsibilities through midcareer. Late in their careers, teachers should be given reduced responsibilities so they may pursue their remaining educational goals.

One emerging method of teacher evaluation that recognizes the complexities of teaching and teacher developmental readiness is portfolio assessment. A portfolio is an accumulation of personal data about an individual teacher. The folder can include a record of achievement; samples of work; observations made by a supervisor, a colleague, or oneself; parent and/or student comments or evaluations. Portfolios can help strengthen a faculty member's overall organization, demonstrate progress and innovative work, and provide information that helps improve performance and quality of the overall program (Perkins and Gelfer, 1993).

Typically, a combination of methods, including those that have been presented above, compensates for the shortcomings of using one method alone. It also offers the advantage of reflecting on the richness and complexity of teaching.

THE BEST SCHOOLS—SUPERVISING AND EVALUATING TEACHERS

Best Schools throughout the country utilize a variety of practices and procedures to evaluate teachers. Although stylistically different, each approaches teacher evaluation as an organic learning experience, an experience that closely aligns with the positive outcomes addressed in the research and reviewed in the previous discussion. Several of the evaluation systems utilized in Best Schools are illustrated next.

Supervision and Evaluation Illustrations

HARRITON HIGH SCHOOL, ROSEMONT, PA

Harriton High School serves the communities of Gladwyne, Villanova, Penn Valley, Belmont Hills, Haverford, and sections of Bryn Mawr and Ardmore in the Lower Merion Township. Harriton is one of two high schools in the Lower Merion School District. The district also includes five elementary and two middle schools, serving a total of 5444 students. Approximately 40% of the school-aged children in the district attend private schools.

In the early 1970s, the school district served 12,000 students in ten elementary, three junior high, and two high schools. In 1979, Harriton enrolled 1135 students; in 1984, 867 students; and currently, 517 students. Harriton is also becoming more multicultural, with the percentage of African-American students increasing from 4% in 1984 to 8.5% in 1992, and the percentage of Asian students increasing from 1% in 1984 to 3.3% in 1992.

The formal procedures for supervising and evaluating teachers have been revised by a committee of district teachers and administrators. This committee has deliberated and negotiated for three years and has created procedures that were implemented on a trial basis beginning in the 1993–94 school year.

The new procedures are designed to address research results that formal teacher evaluations historically have not improved instruction. The new procedure separates the processes of evaluation and supervision and encourages teachers to become involved in new areas, techniques, and practices. The plan encourages professional growth by promoting an atmosphere of mutual trust and by encouraging staff creativity and exploration.

The plan divides the professional staff into three tracks: Track One for satisfactory tenured professionals, Track Two for satisfactory nontenured professionals or long-term substitutes, and Track Three for provisional or unsatisfactory professionals. Track Two requires indepth formal evaluations to be completed two times each year for nontenured professionals and once per year for long term substitutes (those who have worked for at least ninety school days). Track Three professionals follow a three-level procedure which guarantees due process and provides opportunities for improvement.

Norton Seaman, *Principal, Grades 9–12, 518 Students*

WALTER M. WILLIAMS HIGH SCHOOL, BURLINGTON, NC

Located on Burlington's major thoroughfare, Williams High School has been the cornerstone of a developing neighborhood since 1951. The Williams community is largely middle class. The school population is 78% Caucasian and 22% minority. The minority population has become culturally diverse in the past few years, with a particular rise in the Asian population. More than 80% of the graduates go on to higher education each year.

As a participant in a state pilot program for the career ladder plan, Williams has made a differentiated pay program part of the school improvement plan. This program has spurred the staff to refine the formal evaluation program. District policies specify the number of formal observations that each teacher will face and the personnel who will perform the observations. Each observation lasts a full class period. The number of observations range from eight (half announced, half unannounced) for an initially certified teacher to four observations for a candidate for Career Status I to three observations for a teacher at Career Status II. These formal observations are conducted by outside observer-evaluators, the principal or his designees (assistant principal), and mentors (for initially certified teachers only). Each department chairperson also observes the teachers within her or his department. All observers have had extensive formal training in techniques of evaluation and conferencing and in the use of the primary data-gathering device, the FODA (Formative Observation Data Analysis), and its supplement. The observers make summary comments in eight major areas:

- instructional time

- student behavior
- instructional presentation
- instructional monitoring
- instructional feedback
- facilitation of instruction
- interaction within the educational environment
- performance of noninstructional duties

Pre- and post-observation conferences give teachers and observers an opportunity to review the FODA and discuss the teacher's strengths and needs. The intent of the observation process is to help teachers succeed with their students, and the conferences are considered to be helpful rather than punitive.

After completing the required observations, observers reach consensus on a summative evaluation using the teacher performance appraisal instrument to indicate the level of performance (superior, well above standard, above standard, standard, below standard, or unsatisfactory). The evaluators review the FODA as well as the teacher's professional development plan and professional activities profile, which are submitted annually. The principal or his designee holds a summative conference with each teacher before the end of the school year. If a teacher requests or if serious problems exist, the principal or his designees can agree to additional formal and informal observations and conferences. Teachers with serious problems receive suggestions for improvement, such as observing other teachers in their classrooms or talking with master teachers. Sometimes the teachers are required to collaborate with other professionals on a formal improvement plan.

The evaluation process serves two primary functions. First, the information strengthens the total instructional program by helping teachers do a better job in the classroom and take on greater responsibilities. Second, those teachers who choose to participate in the career development program (originally called career ladder plan) earn more money if they qualify for a higher status on the two differentiated pay levels.

James D. Daye, *Principal, Grades 9–12, 984 Students*

ARAPAHOE HIGH SCHOOL, LITTLETON, CO

Arapahoe is one of three high schools in the Littleton Public School District. Predominantly a middle-, upper middle-class community, this suburban school serves a diverse student population consisting of 92% Caucasian, 3% Hispanic, 3% Asian-American, 1% African-American and 1% American Indian.

The school has a 95% graduation rate, with 88% of its graduates going on to post-high school education. The school endorses a philosophy that "not for school, but for life we learn." This attitude fosters high expectations for students and teachers.

The teacher evaluation process for the Littleton public schools is built around two major concepts. The responsibilities and performance standards listed in the position description for each certificated position ensure that all teachers in the same position are evaluated on the basis of the same set of expectations. Position descriptions are supplemented by performance criteria and observable behaviors for each standard. Secondly, the format is organized to communicate clearly a teacher's performance status, to provide evaluative feedback, and to support growth and improvement as appropriate to the individual.

The evaluation process for probationary teachers provides for formal observation and feedback early in the school year, which results in the implementation of a professional growth plan to improve performance and/or enhance effectiveness. Formal and informal observations, conferences, continuous feedback, and progress toward professional growth objectives culminate in a summative evaluation.

The evaluation process for tenured teachers has three levels, which provides the impetus for professional excellence, clearly communicates performance status, and ensures due process for teachers. Level One (teachers whose performance meets or exceeds district performance standards) includes an annual review of a professional growth plan, observation of performance, conferences, ongoing feedback, and summative evaluations every one, two, or three years. Level Two provides assistance to teachers whose performance does not meet the criteria for one or more standards. A specific plan of remediation is completed by the evaluator, members of an assistance team and the teacher. At Level Three, the district notifies the teacher of intent to begin formal dismissal proceedings, or the district provides professional career counseling to assist the individual in making the transition to another job.

Each Arapahoe administrator is involved in the evaluation of teachers. Conferences are held within seven days of each formal observation and immediately after each informal observation if the administrator observes behaviors that need improvement. Teachers have access to the notes from observations and provide input for the summative evaluation through the use of portfolios. Teacher-developed professional growth plans are generated from information contained on the summative evaluation. The evaluation process helps to develop a working partnership between administrator and teacher in order to create and ensure quality performance.

All new teachers are supported by the mentor teacher program. They have an on-site mentor who meets with them "on-call," as well as in regularly scheduled meetings. Each first- or second-year teacher is assigned an additional mentor with expertise in his or her subject area; if not on-site, they are easily reached by phone. After initial orientation with administration, department and school leaders, and mentor(s), ongoing support varies according to need and desire. Ten days per year are routinely provided for visitations, observations, inservice training, and direct aid. Each year, the district mentor program provides several training days, with follow-up for all first- and second-year teachers, typically on subjects such as classroom management, cooperative learning strategies, etc. The school improvement program supplements this training, covers all conference fees/expenses, and provides release time with department leaders for curriculum integration and direct aid. All of this occurs in addition to normally planned staff development within each department, the school, and the district.

Ronald H. Booth, *Principal, Grades 9–12, 1870 Students*

THE SUPPORT OF BEGINNING TEACHERS AND TEACHERS NEW TO THE BUILDING

Few things in education are more difficult than one's first year as a teacher. The research on new teacher attrition is dramatic:

- Almost 15% of new teachers leave teaching after one year.
- Between 40% and 50% of new teachers leave after fewer than seven years.
- As a group, the most academically talented teachers are the least likely to stay in the profession.
- Young teachers, when compared to more experienced teachers, report more emotional exhaustion and a greater degree of depersonalization (Tonnesen and Patterson, 1992).

Although the reasons for these phenomena vary, there is significant support that the difficulties are environmental in nature. Gordon (1991) has identified six such environmental factors: 1) difficult work assignments, 2) unclear expectations, 3) inadequate resources, 4) isolation, 5) role conflict, and 6) reality shock.

What happens during the first few months after a teacher is hired establishes that teacher's future attitude about him/herself and about the profession. A school's failure to adequately induct, orient, and support these teachers leads to an excessive "dropout rate."

Best Schools recognize the need to provide activities aimed at successfully integrating teachers into the school and the profession. They realize the critical nature of the first few days of school and the need to provide ongoing support for novice teachers. While the term *induction* is not new, the particular meaning that it has now taken on is somewhat different from meanings it has formerly been given. Whereas induction often referred to the informal, often reactionary, and ritualistic socialization of new teachers, its use now refers to more sophisticated and systematic efforts to initiate, shape, and sustain the first week experiences of prospective career teachers (DeBolt, 1992).

Induction programs have become increasingly more popular throughout the last decade. Realizing the greater challenge facing today's novice teachers, school districts have initiated programs to help new teachers meet the demands of current day teaching. These challenges, associated with the diverse nature of children in classrooms, the extensive curricular expectations to teach more, the greater variety of instructional tools from which to choose, and increasing accountability from school officials and parents, all lead to the complexities associated in teaching in today's schools.

Once in the classroom, novice teachers experience a sense of panic, feeling that their teacher education programs left them ill-prepared to deal with actual classroom life. Almost invariably, new teachers engage in stressful trial-and-error periods during which they figure out what works, with survival as their primary goals. No longer having the safety nets associated with student teaching, the teachers are awakened to the stark reality that the accountability for planning, organization of instruction, and assessment of students is now their sole responsibility.

Induction programs are aimed at minimizing the stresses associated with beginning teaching by providing programs that seek to add to the experiences of becoming a teacher. Huling-Asten et al. (1989) list five common goals of programs designed to assist beginning teachers:

(1) To improve teaching performance
(2) To increase the retention of promising beginning teachers
(3) To promote the personal and professional well-being of beginning teachers
(4) To satisfy mandated requirements related to induction
(5) To transmit the culture of the school (and the teaching profession) to beginning teachers

Sandra Odell (Huling-Asten et al., 1989) has condensed a somewhat different set of goals that represent a more comprehensive view of the purpose of induction programs:

(1) Provide continuing assistance to reduce the problems known to be common to beginning teachers.
(2) Support development of the knowledge and the skills needed by beginning teachers to be successful in their initial teaching positions.
(3) Integrate beginning teachers into the social system of the school district and the community.
(4) Provide an opportunity for beginning teachers to analyze and reflect on their teaching with coaching from veteran support teachers.
(5) Initiate and build a foundation with new teachers for the continued study of teaching.
(6) Increase the positive attitudes of beginning teachers about teaching.
(7) Increase the retention of good beginning teachers in the profession.

In pursuit of goals such as these, induction programs have been developed into programs involving new teachers in a wide variety of activities. While programs may vary from providing intensive and continuing support to less structured or more informal "buddy" systems, Best Schools tend to formalize the induction process, providing specific vehicles for the orientation, support, and improvement of beginning teachers.

Strategies to assist in this process include the use of support groups. The use of such groups is not for personal "therapy" but, rather, as an opportunity for relaxed reflection concerning the professional demands that novice teachers experience (Thies-Sprinthall and Gerler, 1990). These groups provide support and challenge (Hall and Loucks, 1978) described as personal adaptation to teaching, which provides the following stages for personalizing staff development:

- Awareness—"I'm not concerned about new ideas or methods."
- Informational—"Maybe I need to find out more about the requirements."
- Personal—"How will this affect me?"
- Management—"How can I organize my methods to control the class?"
- Consequence—"How does my teaching affect the pupils?"
- Collaboration—"Now I'm ready to share my ideas with other teachers."
- Refocusing—"I'm developing new methods that are working even better."

One promising program, increasingly used by successful schools, is mentoring. While traditionally an informal relationship between new and veteran teachers, mentoring has emerged as a central theme of many induction programs. Mentoring, as the term suggests, provides for an experienced teacher to assist the new teacher as he/she faces the challenges of teaching. Anderson and Shannon (1988) offered a definition of mentoring that includes the following attributes:

- the process of nurturing
- the act of serving as a role model
- provision for the five fundamental functions of the mentor—teaching, sponsoring, encouraging, counseling, and befriending
- a focus on professional and/or personal development
- an ongoing caring relationship

Typically, mentors who are usually excellent teachers, good role models, and positive people are matched with new teachers within their discipline or grade level. Program design includes a design that 1) promotes interaction, including class visitation, between new and veteran teachers; 2) shares research and experiences on effective teaching strategies; and 3) disseminates information on school policies, procedures, and routines. Often, specific times are provided within the workday to facilitate these activities. In a few schools (and mandated in a few states), a stipend is paid to the mentor for this assignment.

Galvey-Hjornevik (1985) found consistent evidence to support the importance of mentorship programs. The contention is made that the assignment of an appropriate support teacher is likely to be the most powerful and cost-effective intervention in an induction program. In fact, most of the beginning teachers in the study reported that having a mentor was the single most helpful aspect of induction activities because it provided a resource to turn to on a daily basis if and when problems arose.

As one would guess, induction-mentor programs also have benefits for experienced teachers who have an active role in program development and implementation. A review of the specific benefits includes:

- a mechanism to revitalize teachers who experience midcareer doldrums
- a vehicle to provide developmentally appropriate professional growth opportunities for experienced teachers

- a way to demonstrate appreciation and recognition of exceptional teachers
- an approach to develop and retain a high-quality teaching staff (Killon, 1990)

Tonnesen and Patterson (1992) provide a comprehensive summary of examples of concepts and activities that principals in schools with effective induction programs have employed:

- Treat new teachers like guests in your home; courtesy, acceptance, and support are crucial.
- Introduce them to everyone on the school staff. Set up meetings for beginning teachers and others – teachers, librarians, psychologists, nurses, and assistant principals – to exchange ideas.
- Hold individual and group orientation sessions.
- Meet regularly with new teachers. Discuss experiences and techniques that might help them.
- Visit new teachers' classrooms frequently.
- Assign strong, experienced teachers as mentors, and arrange for new teachers to meet their mentors before the school year begins.
- Offer praise and encouragement, but nip small problems in the bud before they become big problems.

To a varying degree, the issues facing novice teachers are also areas of concern for experienced teachers who may be new to a particular school/district. Although the experienced teacher comes to the school with a frame of reference that more readily provides the ability to predict classroom events and implement successful teaching and intervention strategies, issues related to integration into the school culture, social support, and a sense of the development of belonging are critical for his/her success. Thus, successful induction programs need to be not only planned around the goals and priorities of the school, but must be differentiated to meet the unique needs of teachers at different teaching and life stages.

THE BEST SCHOOLS – SUPPORT OF BEGINNING AND NEW TEACHERS

Best Schools have implemented a wide variety of strategies to meet the needs of their beginning teachers and those experienced teachers new to their districts. The following illustrations provide strategies used in selected Best Schools.

Illustrations of Supporting Beginning and New Teachers

PRINCETON HIGH SCHOOL, CINCINNATI, OH

Princeton High School serves students from the communities of Evendale, Glendale, Lincoln Heights, Sharonville, Springdale, and Woodlawn, as well as some township areas north of Cincinnati, Ohio. One high school, one junior high school, and nine elementary schools comprised of 6800 students make up the Princeton City School District. The high school has an enrollment of approximately 1800 students, of whom 40% are minority. The total residential population residing in the district is approximately 50,000. The school district is socioeconomically diverse with 26% of the students receiving free and reduced-price lunches. The mobility rate is approximately 21% among families, from the very poorest to the wealthiest in the state.

The district's director of personnel arranges for numerous recruiting activities at various universities during the spring of each school year. The district is sensitive to hiring teachers and other staff who are representative of the student population. An interview instrument used by all recruiters ensures consistency and fairness in the hiring process.

Beginning teachers and those new to the high school participate in a mentoring program designed to improve the effectiveness and performance of the first-year teacher through guidance and counseling by experienced teacher mentors. Mentors attend a three-day peer-coaching program designed to improve instruction by training them to use a nonjudgmental, nonevaluative process. Mentors observe the new teacher's classroom performance throughout the school year, lending support when needed.

Ongoing inservice sessions are presented by administrators to address issues of school policies and procedures. Opportunities for questions or concerns are provided during and at the end of each session.

Richard A. Dell, *Principal, Grades 9–12, 1854 Students*

RONCALLI HIGH SCHOOL, INDIANAPOLIS, IN

Roncalli High School is a Catholic high school sponsored by fourteen parishes that compose the South Deanery of the Archdiocese of Indianapolis. These fourteen parishes all contribute financially to support Roncalli, and the student population is drawn from the parishes.

The high school serves families from a wide variety of socioeconomic conditions, from very poor inner-city students to very affluent suburban students. Demographic studies of the south side of Indianapolis would indicate that the population is predominantly Caucasian.

Another unusual facet of the student population is that families tend to be much less transient than the typical urban family. It serves a large number of students whose parents and their parents before them attended Rancalli.

The school has initiated a systematic approach to the induction of new teachers. The basic premise for activities is that there are two types of new teachers, those with experience and those without. Those without any prior teaching experience participate in the beginning teacher internship program (BTIP). All teachers new to Roncalli start the year off with a separate day of inservice, which allows for a thorough presentation of school policies as well as a chance to hear from key administrators and staff. New teachers are also involved in six meetings throughout the course of the year. These meetings are timed to deal with key events in the school year such as Back-to-School Night, Open House, the end of grading periods, etc. The year is concluded with celebration!

The BTIP at Roncalli has been proclaimed exemplary by the Indiana Department of Education. In addition to the above meetings, beginning teachers are paired with a veteran teacher who serves as their mentor for the entire year. The school provides for release time for the mentor teacher to spend two full days with the beginning teacher. This allows for quality interaction between the two colleagues regarding instructional issues, as well as aiding in the introduction of the new teacher to the culture of the school. Teacher and mentor confer formally on a monthly basis to set goals, to review progress towards those goals, and to address problems, concerns, and questions.

Joseph D. Hollawell, *Principal, Grades 9–12, 724 Students*

LA PAZ INTERMEDIATE SCHOOL, MISSION VIEJO, CA

At the present time, La Paz is one of four intermediate schools in the district. Located in the community of Mission Viejo, La Paz houses approximately 1300 seventh and eighth grade students and seventy-six staff members. In 1990 and again in 1992, La Paz was recognized as a California Distinguished School, with CAP scores ranging about the 95th percentile level in statewide ranking. The current student population is 83% Caucasian, with the remaining 17% being primarily Asian-American and Hispanic. The students come from single-family homes; parents are well-educated and interested in their children's education. Most are middle-class; 4% are from low-income families, qualifying for free lunch, and need special financial consideration for school expenses.

All new teachers are supported by the mentor teacher program. They have an on-site mentor who meets with them "on call," as well as in regularly scheduled meetings. Each first- or second-year teacher is assigned an additional mentor with expertise in his or her subject area; if not on-site, they are easily reached by phone. After initial orientation with administration, department and school leaders, and mentor(s), ongoing support varies according to need and desire, from meeting every day to once a month. Ten days per year are routinely provided for visitations, observations, inservice training, and direct aid. Each year, the district mentor program provides several training days, with follow-up for all first- and second-year teachers, typically on subjects such as classroom management, cooperative learning strategies, etc. The school improvement program supplements this training, covers all conference fees/expenses, and provides release time with department leaders for curriculum integration and direct aid. All of this occurs in addition to normally planned staff development within each department, the school, and the district.

Dr. Ruth Lander, *Principal, Grades 7–8, 1305 Students*

STAFF RECOGNITION

Maintaining an effective school system requires the retention of the outstanding teachers that make up the lifeblood of every school. Approximately 40–50% of all teachers leave the profession within seven years. Increasing numbers of teachers state that, if they had it to do over again, they probably would not choose to teach in public schools. In a very real sense, teachers' satisfaction with the workplace depends on the environment in which they work and the success of their experiences in the classrooms. To this end, successful schools have actively engaged and empowered teachers to seek self-fulfillment and satisfaction. Strategies such as improving the management of existing resources, involving teachers in school-based decision making, minimizing bureaucracy, empowering teachers through greater knowledge about teaching and learning, and breaking down teacher isolation through team teaching and planning, are all efforts to professionalize teaching so that our best teachers remain in the profession.

Successful schools find ways to recognize the efforts of their outstanding staff members. Through intrinsic and external reward opportunities and incentives, schools have provided teachers with a sense of accomplishment, power, prestige, and, in some cases, money, so that children can continue to benefit from a master teacher's expertise. In a general sense, the purpose of recognition incentive programs is to establish an environment in which special achievements and contributions of faculty and staff are recognized and applauded on a regular, systematic basis. In so doing, the faculty and staff will be encouraged to develop and sustain the efforts to teach children.

Many surveys have been taken, with the results usually the same – school personnel desire positive recognition for their efforts. Some suggestions for recognition that are repeatedly heard include (a) plaques of commendation, (b) recognition in staff notes or district newsletters, (c) written praise with evaluation, (d) written notes of appreciation by the superintendent or principal, (e) verbal compliments, (f) parent-teacher organization awards, and (g) teacher of the month or teacher appreciation days (Karpinski, 1985).

THE BEST SCHOOLS – STAFF RECOGNITION

Best Schools actively seek ways to identify and recognize the accomplishments of their high-performing staff members. Through personalized efforts, officials in Best Schools have developed unique ways to applaud the achievements and dedication of those who serve children. Several Best Schools' programs and activities are illustrated next.

Staff Recognition Illustrations

CENTERVILLE HIGH SCHOOL, CENTERVILLE, OH

Centerville High School enrolls 2204 students in grades 9–12. It is the only high school in Centerville/Washington Township, Ohio, a midsize city of about 51,000. The student body is predominantly Caucasian (93%) and middle-class.

Qualities that characterize CHS include pride, respect, spirit, and overall excellence. All of the above are found in Centerville's large and excellent staff. Recognition of teachers occurs at the building, district, community, county, state, and national level. Within the building, teachers receive notes of appreciation, spirit pins and pens, and appreciation breakfasts and luncheons from the unit and coordinating principals. Also at the building level, a teacher of the week and unit teacher of the year are chosen.

The ELK Pride Recognition Program is a new program that creates the opportunity for faculty and staff members to recognize each other by writing notes of appreciation on tickets that will go into a drawing for prizes. The coordinating principal implemented the Quality Award in 1991. Designed to be given to four staff members whose contributions have benefitted the entire school community and whose performance has been above and beyond the norm, these recipients are selected from peer nominations by a district-level committee. The Centerville Board of Education hosts a cookout for all district staff at the beginning of the school year and formally recognizes teachers at each board meeting.

In 1991, CHS teachers received the Centerville/Washington Township Education Foundation Teacher of the Year Award and the Montgomery County Excellence in Education Award. In 1989 and 1990, CHS teachers received the American Chemical Society Chemistry Teacher of the Year Award, Marketing Education Teacher of the Year, and Business Week Award for Innovative Teaching in the U.S.A. CHS teachers have also been chosen to participate in programs funded by the National Endowment for the Humanities and the Arts. Nominations for local, state, and national awards are made annually.

David W. McDaniel, *Principal, Grades 9–12, 2204 Students*

VAN BUREN MIDDLE SCHOOL, ALBUQUERQUE, NM

Van Buren Middle School, one of twenty-four middle schools in Albuquerque Public Schools, is located in an area of unusual demographic variety and mobility, ranging from upper middle to low income, with the latter dominating. It rests in the middle of Bernalillo County. The Trumbull Park area, which surrounds the school, is one of the poorest neighborhoods in the city, but Van Buren's attendance area also includes military dependent youth from Kirtland Air Force Base, as well as students from Four Hills, one of the city's more prominent, upper-class suburbs.

Of the 902 students in the school, more than half, approximately 58%, are from ethnic minority groups–41% Hispanic, 9.7% Native American, 7.3% African-American, and 4.2% Pacific-Asian. Almost 33% of the families in the attendance area report an annual income of less than $10,000, but a substantial minority, over 7%, have incomes in excess of $50,000. Almost 30% of the students at Van Buren come from single-parent homes. The 1991–92 mobility rate for the school was 53.9%. The free lunch program serves 52.4% of the students in the school.

Teachers are formally supported and recognized for excellence in a variety of ways. One teacher a week is the recipient of the Falcon Award, a gold-plated pin, signifying exceptional contributions to students. This award is announced on the TV monitor during the Van Buren news so that the entire school is aware of the honor. At the end of the year, two staff members are formally recognized as the staff members of the year in an all-school assembly. These awards are given to two people who most exemplify the commitment, innovation, and interpersonal relationship skills that are needed for 21st century educators. Finally, all staff members who have dedicated their lives to education for twenty years are honored at a ceremony in the evening at a hotel. Informal support and recognition occurs daily and by all staff members. Grants are often written to support pilot or creative projects of the excellent teachers.

Gary Hocevar, *Principal, Grades 6–8, 902 Students*

RED BANK HIGH SCHOOL, CHATTANOOGA, TN

Located at the base of Signal Mountain, Red Bank is an incorporated city surrounded by metropolitan Chattanooga, Tennessee. Red Bank High School's zoned areas include the city of Red Bank, Signal Mountain, Lookout Mountain, and county areas to the north of the Chattanooga city limits.

The Red Bank area, a middle-class community, is relatively stable. The city of Red Bank has no new housing developments, while the Signal Mountain area is experiencing a high rate of growth. The areas to the north of Red Bank have moderate growth and development. The school's student population is composed of 94% Caucasian, 5% African-American, and 1% Hispanic and Asian-American.

Red Bank High School administration and faculty developed the Teacher of Outstanding Performance (TOP) Award to be presented annually to the faculty member who demonstrates outstanding performance in the classroom, concern for students, dependability, and participation in extracurricular activities; the recipient is presented a commemorative ring. Teachers have received grants from sponsors such as the Board of Regents Tennessee Collaborative, Chattanooga Venture, and Junior League of Chattanooga. Faculty members nominate peers for awards that provide recognition beyond the school. The Hamilton County Teacher of the Year title has been given to two Red Bank teachers in the last five years. The Hamilton County Education Association's Distinguished Classroom Teacher Award has gone to three members of the faculty, and three others were finalists. In addition, teachers have been awarded the Freedoms Foundation Valley Forge Teacher's Medal, Governor's School Distinguished Teacher honor, and Kappa Delta Pi's Charles Hyder Award. The upper 20% scholastically of the senior class choose their most influential teachers to be recognized at the annual Superintendent's Honors Banquet. Red Bank High is a school where faculty members recognize the contributions of their colleagues with small notes of appreciation and major awards of honor.

Donald R. Bishop, *Principal, Grades 9–12, 1519 Students*

OPPORTUNITIES TO ENHANCE TEACHERS' ROLES AND TO IMPROVE JOB SATISFACTION

Maintaining teacher job satisfaction in an attempt to motivate and keep the most capable teachers is critical to the success of school improvement. Reforms related to school restructuring, site-based management, empowering teachers, and implementing career ladders attempt to enrich the professional lives of teachers. Yet research conducted over the last decade yields no simple solution to increasing job satisfaction among educators (Hartzell and Wenger, 1989). Job satisfaction for teachers tends to be multidimensional rather than unidimensional in nature and, more often than not, is not consistently related to predictable demographic variables.

Although job dissatisfaction for teachers is commonly related to 1) negative student attitudes and discipline problems, 2) disappointment and stress, 3) low salaries, 4) poor working conditions, and 5) lack of professional recognition, little support is given to a categorical list of predictions. Instead, job dissatisfaction variables tend to revolve around a teacher's sense of powerlessness to appreciably affect the lives of students and satisfy the need to achieve, advance, and become self-actualized (Ellis, 1988).

Research conducted over the last decade yields no simple solution to increasing job satisfaction among educators, yet factions such as management style of principal, demographics, financial support, and class size find some support in the literature. Additionally, a school culture that stresses accomplishment and recognition is likely to elicit job satisfaction and commitment, whereas a culture emphasizing personal relationships and informal influence are of lesser importance. In most cases, clearly defined and reinforced lines of power have a negative influence on job satisfaction. Finally, teacher job satisfaction and commitment are most often associated with the behaviors of the school principal.

The research (Hartzell and Wenger, 1989) suggests that principals who develop and maintain satisfied teachers are those who:

- structure work opportunities that can fulfill higher order needs for recognition and self-actualization in teachers
- create a school climate for participatory management and teacher involvement in decision making
- nurture teacher autonomy, empowerment, and professional involvement
- cultivate, maintain, and use consideration behaviors, demonstrating concern for their employees, as well as for the task to be completed

THE BEST SCHOOLS–ENHANCING TEACHERS' ROLES

Emphasizing the importance of the teacher in school reform and improvement is by no means a new idea, yet effective schools have systematically supported school improvement efforts by allowing teachers a greater degree of challenge and a greater outlet for the need to achieve, to advance, and to have a significant role in affecting school life.

The schools illustrated below provide examples of how Best Schools actively provide opportunities to enhance the role of teachers.

Illustrations of Teachers' Roles

BRIGHTWOOD ELEMENTARY SCHOOL, MONTEREY PARK, CA

Brightwood is a K–8 school built by Los Angeles Unified School District in 1960. The school is located just east of the Los Angeles civic center in a hilly residential area in Monterey Park, California. East Los Angeles College and California State University at Los Angeles are neighbors to the south and north, respectively. Cultural centers, such as the Los Angeles County Museums, the Music Center, and playhouses, are minutes from the school.

The attendance area is a diverse community consisting of primarily single-family, three- and four-bedroom homes and modest, low-income housing situated in the cities of Monterey Park. The school serves residents who represent a cross section of the socioeconomic strata. Currently, 18.7% of our students are on free or reduced-lunch programs. The student population is multicultural, with over fifteen languages represented within the student body. Specifically, the student population consists of 69% Asian-American, 22% Hispanic, 9% Caucasian, and less than 1% African-American.

The principal works diligently to recognize and capitalize on individual teacher strengths/expertise. A high level of mutual respect and admiration exists among the staff members at Brightwood. They are the source of inspiration and encouragement for one another's creative experimentation with new strategies. Examples include innovative cross grade level cotraining projects: "Reading Buddies" and "Revision Buddies." Release time is provided for interested teachers to do peer observation/coaching and cross grade level demonstration lessons. Staff members with innovative ideas are connected with appropriate resources for access to funding and materials. Brightwood operates in a participatory management mode where input from staff is sought and valued. All site staff development activities and inservice opportunities are planned and organized to achieve school goals and priorities. More than 60% of the teaching staff in grades 5–8th are recognized district leaders in staff development. Three are mentor teachers. They have conducted workshops not only for their school, but also for teachers in other schools and districts. They have written curriculum that has been disseminated throughout the district.

Teachers are active planners, organizers and primary decision makers for quality programs/events:

- The Science Fair, culmination of month-long projects, demonstrates science knowledge. The high-caliber projects attract community attention and recognition.
- Red Ribbon Week, the antisubstance abuse campaign, promotes drug-free young people. Community dignitaries are involved in the closing pep rally.
- Athletic Field Day, a day-long athletic event, reinforces physical fitness and good sportsmanship.
- At the Community Read-In, community members from all walks of life are invited to participate in an afternoon of reading and sharing with the students, giving the community leaders direct involvement with school children.
- At the Vital Volunteer Tea, community volunteers are honored and recognized at this special annual event for their contribution to the school.
- In LITE (Leaders In Technology Education), teacher representatives plan program improvement activities and purchase materials for technology education.

Grace Love, *Principal, Grades 5–8, 366 Students*

SEWICKLEY ACADEMY, SEWICKLEY, PA

Sewickley Academy is a coeducational independent day school for grades pre-K–12, with an enrollment of 667 students. The school is separated into three divisions: the Lower School (pre-K –6), the Middle School (grades 7 and 8), and the Senior School (grades 9–12). Dating its origins to 1838 and in its present location since 1925, the Academy was historically a country day school that sent many of its graduates on to leading boarding schools in New England. In 1963, a secondary component was added with grades 10–12.

The current enrollment of 667 includes 331 boys and 336 girls. While 40% of students come from the local Quaker Valley School District, the rest commute from forty-nine different school districts, including districts in Ohio and West Virginia. Consistent with the board of trustees' commitment to economic and cultural diversity, approximately 23% of students receive financial aid. In the Senior School, 38% of students receive aid. Over 22% of the student body are non-Caucasian, and four students are foreign nationals studying at the Academy for one year.

Faculty members interact with their students outside the classroom in a variety of ways–as coaches, mentors, and sponsors of extracurricular activities. Math and science teachers meet students informally on Wednesday evenings to provide extra help. About fifty students typically show up to take advantage of this support. The English department runs a program of peer tutoring called Pendragon, whereby the best student writers help other students by providing a critical audience. Teachers have encouraged and assisted in the formation of new clubs such as the African-American awareness group, an Indian culture group, students against drunk driving, environmental awareness, and others that help meet the needs of our increasingly diverse student body. When the faculty approved the community service program, there were suddenly even more ways for faculty and students to work together. For example, five teachers teamed up with three minority students to design and conduct a one-week enrichment program for some disadvantaged local public school students. Finally, the school has made strides to address the growing need nationwide for school personnel to provide emotional, as well as academic, support to students. A number of teachers have been trained at highly respected counseling institutes to be effective advisors to their students. Each Senior School teacher is assigned a small advisee group, which meets once a week to offer support and enhance communication. Individual meetings between a student and advisor are conducted as needed. Teachers are extremely active and involved in all facets of students' lives, and they are very excited about what they are doing. Finding the time to implement all the ideas teachers generate seems to be the school's biggest obstacle.

L. Hamilton Clark, *Principal, Grades 5–12, 667 Students*

ELIZABETHTOWN HIGH SCHOOL, ELIZABETHTOWN, KY

Elizabethtown High is located in a progressive community in central Kentucky with a population of approximately 20,000. It is the only high school in an independent district, serving just over 2000 students.

The school has a diverse socioeconomic makeup. Approximately 30% of the families in the school community are below poverty level. A self-study in 1990 indicated 32% of the families have been changed by divorce, separation, death, or desertion of a parent. Although the largest representative work group is composed of the professionals (27%), there are many occupations represented in the community. The school serves students from diverse racial and ethnic origins; specifically, 86% of the students are Caucasian, 10% African-American, 4% Asian-American, and 1% Hispanic and American Indian.

The school prides itself on providing opportunities for teachers to enrich their satisfaction and commitment toward their profession:

- A peer coaching program for teachers was begun several years ago, which has spread to all teachers in the building. Approximately one-third of the staff has participated, and the number of participants expands each year.
- Teachers tutor in an extended day service program.
- Teachers are receiving ongoing training in research-based, effective teaching strategies. Over the past three years, teachers have received training in learning styles, motivation, classroom management, active participation, and levels of cognition, which are examples of the nineteen modules of this program.
- Teachers have held community forums on new programs at the school to orient parents and community to its offerings and to the state-initiated developments and AIDS education plan.
- Teachers of English received a state writing grant in 1989, which encouraged them to be innovative in the teaching process and in developing effective writing instruction.
- A local staff development grant provides monies, in addition to state professional development monies, for teachers to attend workshops or make visitations.

Phillip E. Owen, *Principal, Grades 9–12, 704 Students*

STAFF DEVELOPMENT IN THE BEST SCHOOLS

The vast majority of a total school budget is used to pay employee salaries. The framework for school success comes from the thoughts and actions of the professionals in the school. Thus, a logical place to improve the quality of education in a school is to systematically develop a continuous education program for educators.

It is well documented that staff development and successful innovation or improvement are undeniably related. Yet, despite the widespread interest and school district emphasis on staff development, much remains to be learned about the effectiveness of the process. All too often, schools embark upon one initiative after another hoping to affect individual and school development. Similarly, prominent experts move around the country in a series of isolated presentations whose impact on teacher or organizational behavior is, all too often, short-lived.

Best Schools address staff development with the same vision and commitment afforded all other aspects of school life. Staff development activities are not confined to one or two inservice days when faculty listen to a motivational speaker, attend a show-and-tell workshop, and chat with coworkers over coffee and Danish. Instead, staff development promotes true self and school improvement through thoughtful planning, long-term commitment to specific goals, and the appropriate nurturing from school administrators.

Staff development can be defined as those processes that improve job-related knowledge, skills, and/or attitudes of school employees. Typically, the staff development system is designed to generate three kinds of effort (Joyce and Showers, 1989): an *individual* component to enrich an individual's content knowledge or clinical competence as an instructor, principal, etc.; a *collective* component requiring the cooperative enterprise of the entire school staff; and a *systemic* component embodying a districtwide initiative requiring a coordinated effort among all branches of the school district organization.

The phrase *staff development* is often used interchangeably with the term *inservice*, yet there is an important distinction that is significant when directed at school improvement. Staff development is the total of learning experiences available to a professional that may be directly or indirectly related to his/her job responsibilities. Inservice involves a specific learning experience, sanctioned and supported by the school and/or school district that is often directly related to a predetermined goal of the organization (Orlich, 1989). Thus, inservice experiences are a subset of staff development.

Although a wide variety of topics may be addressed, Sparks and Loucks-Horsley (1989) have identified five major models currently utilized by staff developers:

(1) *Individually guided staff development* is where the teacher determines his or her own goals and selects activities that will result in the achievement of those goals. The model holds that individuals will be most motivated when they make their own personal assessment of their needs.

(2) *Observation/assessment* is most commonly implemented with a supervisor directly observing the teaching act using a predetermined criteria. A basic assumption underlying this approach is that reflection by an individual on his or her own practice can be enhanced by another's observations. Peer coaching where fellow teachers visit one another's classroom, gather objective data about student performance or teacher behavior, and give feedback in a follow-up conference is an increasingly common form of observation/assessment.

(3) *Involvement in a development/improvement process* is a combination of learnings that result from the involvement of teachers in the development of curriculum or engagement in systematic school improvement processes that have as their goal the improvement of classroom instruction and/or curriculum. Often, as with Best Schools, teachers serve on school improvement committees where they may be required to conduct research on priority goals for the school, learn group and interpersonal skills, or develop new content knowledge. In each instance, teachers' learning is driven by the demands of problem solving. Teacher involvement and ownership in organic school improvement initiatives provide a strong motivational foundation for this approach.

(4) *Inquiry strategies* result in an individual or a group of teachers utilizing their basic research techniques to formulate research questions and appropriate studies to improve instruction in their classrooms. Inquiry reflects a basic belief in teachers' abilities to

formulate valid questions about their own practices and pursue objective answers to those questions.

(5) *Training or workshop-type sessions* are given, in which the presenter is the expert who establishes the content and flow of activities inherent to this strategy in the hope that teachers' decision-making and thinking skills can be enriched through awareness, knowledge, and skill development. The basic assumption that guides this strategy is that teachers can change their behaviors and learn to replicate behaviors in their classroom that were not previously in their repertoire.

Considerable research exists on successful staff development initiatives that have had a positive impact on school culture, increased professional skills, and student achievement. Glickman (1990) provides a summary list of the common characteristics that are embodied in these projects:

(1) Training was concrete, continual, and tied to the world of the teachers.
(2) Local resource personnel provided direct follow-up assistance to teachers after the learning experience.
(3) Peer observation and peer discussion provided teachers with reinforcement and encouragement.
(4) The school leader participated in the activity.
(5) Regular project meetings were held with teachers for problem solving, adapting techniques and skills of the innovations that were not working as expected.
(6) Release time was used for teachers, instead of monetary payment for after-school work.
(7) Activities were planned with teachers prior to and during the project.

Elements of a successful staff development program do not evolve without the establishment of an organizational context in which teachers can individually and collectively grow. Thus, the notion of school climate and culture must be purposely nurtured for staff development initiatives to be successful. Interestingly, more may be gained from the transformation of school culture and/or the centrality of the focus of staff development activities than by the improvement of individual teaching skills. To that end, the topic chosen for staff development purposes may be of secondary importance. Instead, the real benefit of staff development may come from the activities that help focus a school's mission, promote professional dialogue, and center the school community on educational improvement.

Loucks-Horsley et al. (1987) attempt to describe that context as one where staff members have a common, a coherent set of goals and objectives that they have formulated, reflecting high expectations for themselves and their students. Additionally, administrators exercise strong leadership by promoting a spirit of collegiality, minimizing status differences between themselves and their staff members. Finally, teachers and administrators place a high priority on staff development and continuous improvement.

THE BEST SCHOOLS – STAFF DEVELOPMENT

Although the topics and delivery strategies may vary, there are several common traits that guide effective staff development activities in Best Schools:

- Activities support individual self-improvement efforts within a context of school goal setting.

- Activities are closely linked to the mission statement and priority objectives of the school.
- Activities emphasize professional and personal growth, rather than remediation of specific subskills.
- Activities incorporate sound principles derived from research on adult learning.
- Activities include a comprehensive planning process with extensive district, building, and/or individual contributions.
- Activities establish expectations and climate for successful integration of acquired skills and knowledge into daily practice.
- Activities include an evaluation system with appropriate feedback vehicles to assess the outcomes.

Staff development is an integral fact of successful schools across the country. Although different in their goals and delivery strategies, they are all systematized as part of a total personal/school improvement priority. Best Schools invest in staff development with the clear expectation that a high yield of return will be realized.

The following illustrations describe examples of specific strategies utilized in Best Schools.

Staff Development Illustrations

NEW CENTURY HIGH SCHOOL, LACEY, WA

New Century High School is a ''school of choice'' within the Lacey Public School System. Students from three school districts elect to attend this innovative, academic high school which operates during an evening time frame, utilizing the resources and facilities of a large day high school. New Century was selected in 1991 by the state of Washington Governor's Task Force as a School for the 21st Century.

New Century High School was created to offer possible solutions to modern day challenges. As its name implies, its mission is to explore new, future-oriented paradigms in education. These paradigms take into account today's changing demographics and the need for a learning environment focused on the technologically and the sociologically complex world of tomorrow.

New Century is a small, friendly school where teachers and students enjoy each other's company. Students discover how learning outside of the classroom applies to the curriculum. Community learning experiences are valuable additions to college or employment skills. Quality course offerings meet college entrance requirements. Students have opportunities to develop leadership skills and be involved in extracurricular activities.

New Century utilizes site-based leadership and shared decision making through consensus. Thus, staff development opportunities are aligned with the goals established by the site-based leadership team. Ten days are allotted to each teacher per year for curriculum development, collegial work, and inservice to meet the goals that have been established.

The school conducts three-hour monthly staff meetings where teachers provide inservice for their peers. As the site-based leadership team develops the budget for the year, they allocate resources for staff development for particular areas that are identified as needing staff inservice. Two examples are the Learning Community Project where the students relate classroom learning to the work world and an interdisciplinary curriculum presently being implemented.

Each teacher at New Century High School is encouraged to belong to their subject area professional association and attends one or more conferences in their subject matter area yearly. Additionally, the entire staff has been trained in the implementation of ''writing across the curriculum'' and interdisciplinary curriculum design. All staff attended a week-long inservice on developing school/business partnerships and integration of curriculum. Science and math teachers attend the national conferences for their subject areas annually.

An important component of the New Century High School model is the design and implementation of curriculum and instruction methods that move students from passive to active learning. The freshman interdisciplinary curriculum utilizes two-hour block classes that are taught by a four-person interdisciplinary team. During the school year, this team of teachers is provided a monthly five-hour block of release time to work together to design and implement interdisciplinary curriculum. The result of data collection indicates that student learning has increased as a result of our 21st century project.

Gail Covington McBride, *Principal, Grades 5–12, 195 Students*

JONAS CLARKE MIDDLE SCHOOL, LEXINGTON, MA

Clarke is one of two middle schools in the Lexington School District. The school serves an ethnically diverse population, which is reflected in its various linguistic and cultural groups. Lexington is a community located near colleges and universities, including MIT, Harvard, Lesley, and Tufts as well as Hanscom Air Force Base; the population includes students from such countries as Japan, China, Korea, Israel, Greece, India, and Italy. Several families remain for one or two years on tours of duty or special university-connected research projects. It is considered an upwardly mobile community that values education and has recently voted additional money for the schools.

Lexington's "Five-Year Strategic Management Plan" clearly articulates the goals of the system and extracts those that are important for the teachers and staff at Clarke. Within a framework of half a year, Clarke members selected those goals and objectives that were important to the teachers and staff at Clarke. Within a framework of half a year, Clarke members selected those goals and objectives that were important to the community and developed action plans. These were reviewed and updated and were incorporated into "Clarke's Guiding Principles of Education." The site council has developed intense planning stages as reflected in systematized training sessions. From the information and ideas generated at these training sessions, each council developed its own principles of education.

A centralized professional development committee has developed goals for the system, including alternative assessments; grant writing; cultural diversity; interdisciplinary, interdepartmental program integration; instructional technology; and special education inclusion.

A professional development booklet lists the variety of course and workshop offerings that address these and site council goals and priorities. A program in English focuses on reading in the content area and the development of the writing process within the writing lab and in the class. The essentials of Herber and Collins, as well as the work of others, influence each teacher's approach to writing. In mathematics, the school's nationally recognized math department teachers integrate reading strategies into math consistent with the University of Chicago textbooks. The science department incorporated a solar energy grant into the curriculum. Other science teachers are perfecting advance computer technology, including laser, video, and satellite connections in their classes.

A member of the social studies department has been instrumental in developing an immigration unit incorporating summer training and materials from a local industrial park.

Faculty members have the opportunity to apply for grants from the Lexington Education Foundation, which is a local funding source whose goals include funding proposals that "foster and promote sound, innovative approaches to enhance educational excellence in the Lexington public schools." Programs funded focus on "creative program development including, where appropriate, innovative materials, staff development and instructional resources related to the program."

Pamela B. Houlares, *Principal, Grades 6–8, 623 Students*

SUMMIT MIDDLE SCHOOL, EDMOND, OK

Located in a suburb near the state's capital city, this middle school is four years old and serves a predominately white collar population. Despite the fact that the community is located in an urban area, it is distinctly "small-town," with traditional expectations of civic involvement and academic excellence.

Planned as an exemplary middle school at its inception, it continues to maintain its reputation. At a recent National Middle School Association Conference, the school was featured and recognized as one of the nation's top middle schools, with new and innovative programs that meet the unique needs of middle school students.

The site-based staff development committee submits a needs assessment survey to the staff for its evaluation and comments. National, state, district, and school-site goals provide the basis for this survey.

An organized staff development committee consists of eleven teachers, three administrators, and two parents. The committee members serve two-year terms and are responsible for seeing that the action goals of the district's four-year staff development plan are met. The attainment of these goals is, in turn, audited by the state department of education. The district committee meets monthly to assess workshop needs (determined by teacher polls) and to organize them to promote the professional growth in priority areas. Staff development occurs on-site, within the district, and out of the district. The strongest staff development focus at our school is participation in outcome-based education and programs related to cultural diversity. The district offers five professional inservice days. Educators and other professionals present relevant workshops on teaching methods within the disciplines, uses of state-of-the-art technology, and issues concerning educational philosophies.

Roberta Gaston, *Principal, Grades 6–8, 907 Students*

SUMMARY

Best Schools value and systematically develop teaching environments that promote goal achievement and student learning. They facilitate a climate where professional involvement and growth are both encouraged and rewarded. Best Schools actively seek ways to involve their faculties. Whether through informal processes or formalized school-based management teams, the schools capitalize on the expertise, dedication, and commitment of the entire school staff.

Induction, staff development, evaluation, collaboration, and teacher recognition are all part of an organized process to promote the mission of the school and to foster an environment that promotes success.

REFERENCES

Anderson, E. M. and H. C. Shannon. (1988). "Toward a Conceptualization of Mentoring," *Journal of Teacher Education*, 39(1):38–42.

Cogan, M. L. (1973). *Clinical Supervision*. Boston, MA: Houghton Mifflin.

DeBolt, Gary P. (1992). *Teacher Induction and Monitoring*. Albany, NY: State University of New York Press.

Denham, C. (1987). "Perspective on the Major Purposes and Basic Procedures for Teacher Evaluation," *Journal of Personnel Evaluation in Education*, 1:2932.

Ellis, Nancy H. (1988). "Job Redesign: Can It Influence Teacher Motivation?" Paper presented at the *Annual Meeting of New England Educational Research Organization*, Rockport, ME, April 1988.

Galvey-Hjornevik, C. (1985). "Teacher Mentors: A Review of the Literature," Austin, TX: The University of Texas at Austin, The Research and Development Center for Teacher Education, ERIC No. ED 263 105.

Glickman, Carl D. (1989). "Has Sam and Samantha's Time Come at Last," *Educational Leadership*, 46(8):4–9.

Glickman, Carl D. (1990). *Supervision of Instruction: A Developmental Approach.* Second Edition. Needham Heights, MA: Allyn & Bacon.

Gordon, Stephen P. (1991). *How to Help Beginning Teachers Succeed.* Alexandria, VA: Association for Supervision and Curriculum Development.

Hall, G. and S. Loucks. (1978). "Teacher Concern as Basis for Facilitating and Personalizing Staff Development," *Teacher College Record*, 80(1):36–53.

Harris, B. (1986). *Developmental Teacher Evaluation.* Boston: Allyn & Bacon.

Hartzell, Gary and Marc Wenger. (1989). "Manage to Keep Teachers Happy," *The School Administrator*, 46(10): 22–24.

Hoy, W. K. and Patrick B. Forsyth. (1986). *Effective Supervision: Theory into Practice.* New York, N.Y.: Random House.

Hoy, W. K. and A. E. Woolfolk. (1993). "Teachers' Sense of Efficacy and the Organizational Health of Schools," *The Elementary School Journal*, 93(4):355–372.

Hoy, W. K., C. J. Tarter, and J. Bliss. (1990). "Organizational Climate, School Health, and Student Achievement: A Comparative Analysis," *Educational Administrative Quarterly*, 26:260–279.

Hoy, W. K., C. J. Tarter, and R. Kottkamp. (1991). *Open Schools/Healthy Schools.* Beverly Hills, CA: Sage.

Huling-Asten, L., S. J. Odell, P. Ishler, L. S. Kay, and R. A. Edelfet. (1989). *Assisting the Beginning Teacher.* Reston, VA: Association of Teacher Educators.

Joyce, Bruce and Beverly Showers. (1989). *Student Achievement through Staff Development.* White Plains, NY: Longman, Inc.

Karpinski, Joseph R. (1985). "Recognizing the Achievements of Your Staff–Ideas on How to Thank, Praise and Reward Employees for Their Accomplishments," *Journal of Educational Public Relations*, 8(1):22–26.

Keefe, James W. and Edgar A. Kelley. (1990). "Comprehensive Assessment and School Improvement," NASSP Bulletin, 74(530):54–63.

Killon, Joellen P. (1990). "The Benefits of an Induction Program for Experienced Teachers," *Journal of Staff Development*, 11(4):32–36.

Lezotte, Lawrence W. (1991). *Correlates of Effective Schools: The First and Second Generation.* Okimos, MI: Effective Schools Products Ltd.

Loucks-Horsley, S., C. Harding, M. Arbuckle, L. Murray, C. Dubea, and M. Williams. (1987). *Continuing to Learn: A Guidebook for Teacher Development.* Andover, MA: Regional Laboratory for Educational Improvement of the Northeast and Islands, and the National Staff Development Council.

Manatt, Richard P. (1982). *Teacher Performance Evaluation: Practical Application of Research.* School improvement model project. Ames, IA: College of Education, Iowa State University.

Marczely, Bernadette. (1992). "Teacher Evaluation: Research versus Practice," *Journal of Evaluation in Education*, (5):279–290.

McGreal, T. (1983). *Successful Teacher Evaluation* Alexandria, VA: Association for Supervision and Curriculum Development.

Ogden, Evelyn H. and Vito Germinario. (1994). *The Nation's Best Schools: Blueprints for Excellence, Volume 1–Elementary and Middle Schools.* Lancaster, PA: Technomic Publishing Company, Inc.

Orlich, D. C. (1989). *Staff Development: Enhancing Human Potential.* Boston, MA: Allyn & Bacon.

Perkins, Peggy G. and Jeffrey I. Gelfer. (1993). "Portfolio Assessment for Teachers," *The Clearing House*, 66(4):235–237.

Sparks, Dennis and Susan Loucks-Horsley. (1989). "Five Models of Staff Development for Teachers," *Journal of Staff Development*, 10(4):40–57.

Thies-Sprinthall, Lois M. and Edwin R. Gerler, Jr. (1990). "Support Groups for Novice Teachers," *Journal of Staff Development*, 11(4):18–22.

Tonnesen, Sandra and Susan Patterson. (1992). "Fighting First-Year Jitters," *The Executive Educator*, 14(1): 29–30.

CHAPTER 4

Student Environment

MUCH has been written concerning the significance of the relationship between the school environment and the academic and emotional well-being of students. Yet, while many of America's best secondary schools are places where the vast majority of students learn and prosper in a setting characterized by high expectations, a success orientation, and nurturing support systems, many high schools are places where large numbers of students are disenfranchised, where large numbers drop out and where their greatest concerns revolve around safety and security issues.

The criticisms aimed at many of our high schools have been well documented. Cawelti (1994) has provided a summary of several well-known findings:

- low student achievement, both on tests of basic skills and on tests of general knowledge in core subjects
- the need to move beyond only teaching basic skills and factual information to developing higher order intellectual skills such as critical thinking or problem solving and to provide classroom learning experiences that help students derive their own meaning from learning
- curriculum fragmentation, which prevents students from seeing the connections between school subjects and real life
- the impersonality of large high schools, in which many students feel little or no sense of belonging to the institution
- the failure to offer learning experiences that provide students with the skills needed for transition to meaningful jobs in the work world after graduation
- the predominance of students as passive learners and the failure to actively engage them in the learning process
- failure to provide the challenging curriculum needed by language-minority students and a culturally diverse student population

To address these complex issues, Best Schools have shifted the paradigm away from traditionally accepted modes of operation. They have challenged existing school organizational structures; the way time is used for instruction; the way personnel are utilized; and the way staff, students, and parents are used to broaden participation in school decision making.

Best Schools actively seek ways to enrich the school environment for students. The students' perceptions of the school environment tend to have a direct impact on the functioning of students within the school. Moreover, evidence exists that the learning environment is a critical element that can be either conducive or detrimental to student success. In a real way, "unfriendly schools" tend to promote student disengagement by establishing real or perceived obstacles for student success. These obstacles lead to student feelings of isolation, alienation, and, ultimately, feelings of failure. "Friendly" schools provide students with a climate that values involvement in school decisions, systematically develops students' interest in learning, and creates opportunities for students to build sustained relationships with teachers and other adults.

There is a strong relationship between school environments and students' feelings and behavior in them (Strother, 1983). An effective educational program for students does not require a change in the entire educational system; it does, however, take the vision of a committed professional staff to examine the environment that has been created for its students. It takes the dedicated leadership of the principal and school staff to analyze current school practices in terms of their impact on student learning and well-being. Finally, it takes courage and sustained effort on the part of the entire school community to modify existing school norms and teaching strategies to help ensure success for all children.

This chapter will examine the characteristics of a productive student environment in America's Best Schools. Additionally, examples of the best practices will be highlighted for use as a practical guide toward the development of a student climate that fosters learning and well-being.

Specifically, this chapter will address the following questions:

- What are the elements and practices associated with a productive environment?
- What classroom practices tend to enhance student learning and well-being?
- What policies and practices are used in Best Schools to facilitate transition of students into school?
- What programs, procedures, and strategies are utilized in Best Schools to develop students' interest in learning and to motivate them to study?
- What opportunities do Best Schools create to build sustained relationships with teachers and other adults?
- What programs and practices are initiated in Best Schools to identify and assist at-risk students?
- What extracurricular activities are available for students in Best Schools?
- What discipline strategies and policies exist in Best Schools?
- How do Best Schools prevent the sale, possession, and use of drugs, alcohol, and tobacco?
- What opportunities exist in Best Schools for students to influence classroom and school policy?
- How do Best Schools foster the development of sound character, democratic values, ethical judgment, and good student behavior?
- How do Best Schools prepare students to live effectively in a culturally diverse society?
- How do Best Schools prepare students to live effectively in a society that is globally competitive?
- How do Best Schools prepare students not continuing into postsecondary education for the demands of the workplace?

A PRODUCTIVE STUDENT ENVIRONMENT

The influence of school environment and culture as a vehicle for motivating students toward success can be found in most of the literature associated with high school restructuring. Traditionally, teachers have shouldered most of the burden for student motivation and success; however, because the research continues to demonstrate the powerful effect of school culture and climate on students' attitudes toward education, the entire school community must now share that responsibility (Renchler, 1992).

Recently, Maehr (1991) has studied the relationship between student motivation and success and the culture of schools. He draws many parallels between the school environment and the classroom environment, stressing the leadership roles of both the principal and teachers in establishing a school's "psychological" environment. The dimensions Maehr includes in his model of psychological environment of the school include,

- *accomplishment*—emphasis on excellence and pursuit of academic challenges
- *power*—emphasis on interpersonal competition, social comparison, achievement
- *recognition*—emphasis on social recognition for achievement and the importance of school for attaining future goals and rewards
- *affiliation*—perceived sense of community, good interpersonal relations among teachers and students
- *strength/saliency*—the perception that the school knows what it is about and that students know what is expected

In addition to the direct effect of the learning climate on individual children, there are significant effects of such instruction on the total school society of children, teachers, administrators, and parents. Teachers in orderly task-oriented schools experience less stress, students are not intimidated by the actions of other students, and principals have time to focus on instruction rather than discipline.

Additionally, the literature on effective schools consistently stresses the need for high expectations in schools. Teachers and principals in successful schools believe students (all students) can learn. In some ways, it is a paradoxical situation. Does the staff believe the students can learn, and, therefore, they do learn? Or do the students learn, and, therefore, the staff believes they can learn? It is probably more of the former. Staff's positive beliefs come first. However, success takes more than a belief that students can learn. It takes a commitment that all students "will" learn. Expectations always exist in schools whether they are implied or formally stated. In order to have a maximum impact on learning, expectations need to be agreed upon by staff, stated in understandable terms, and used as the basis for learning and for interactions of the society within the school.

To provide a positive student environment, many of America's Best High Schools have restructured the high school organization to make the school a more humane and welcoming environment. School-within-a-School, Teacher-Advisee Systems, and Team Teaching have been utilized to reduce students' feelings of alienation and disconnectedness, by giving them more personal contacts with caring adults (Cawelti, 1994).

- The school-within a school concept organizes students into smaller functional units to encourage student feelings of involvement and belonging. The idea, commonly referred to as a house plan, establishes three or four smaller schools within a larger institution, with predominantly its own faculty and student activities.
- Teacher-advisee programs are typically administered by assigning a group of students to a single teacher who provides a "home-base" for academic, vocational, or personal counseling. Typically meeting ten to twenty minutes per day, such one-on-one contact with a caring adult can increase a student's sense of belonging and self-esteem.
- In teaching teams where a specific group of teachers is responsible for the curriculum, teaching and evaluation of a predetermined group of students may enrich the student environment. Again, the emphasis is on identifying a given number of students responsible to a given set of teachers, thus making it more likely that both teachers and students are more intimately linked within the school experience.

Increasingly, students have been given a more active role in school governance. While schools vary greatly in the degree to which they include parents in formal school governance structures, students often play an integral part in the formation of their school's improvement efforts.

CREATING A CLASSROOM ENVIRONMENT FOR LEARNING

It is relatively easy to identify classrooms where a positive feeling and tone exist. These feelings are typically associated with a warm, supportive environment where students are more likely to raise their hands, take an active part in the learning process, and feel more confident about the responses they anticipate receiving from the teacher when they make mistakes or need assistance in learning activities.

Recent studies have begun to identify specific climate factors that are linked in both correlation and experimental studies to increases in student learning and feelings of self-worth. Teachers must systematically analyze their behaviors as they relate to the concepts discussed below to help ensure that their behaviors and routines actively promote success for all students.

Students are likely to work better and achieve at higher levels in an atmosphere that assures that they can and will succeed in the tasks established by the teacher. This success orientation is especially important for the at-risk student since there is a clear relationship between achievement gains of average and below average students and the number of successful responses they give in a classroom. Thus, teachers must plan strategies and events that are designed to provide opportunities for students to get the "right answers" and thus earn the praise and reinforcement associated with high achievement. In a practical sense, teachers should look for opportunities to provide a successful experience each day for students. Although difficult, the success a student receives in the classroom may be the only positive reinforcement he/she receives during a typical day.

Significant evidence exists to support the contention that typical elementary classrooms do not provide equal opportunity for student involvement and success (Good, 1982). Most teachers tend to call on those students who can be consistently depended upon to provide a correct answer. This is primarily done so that 1) a student not expected to know the answer does not get embarrassed, 2) the students in the class hear a correct and thoughtful reply, and 3) a certain degree of teacher reward occurs, which is associated with high-quality student performances (Kerman and Martin, 1980). This phenomenon produces an interesting paradox. Students will soon realize that they are less likely to be called on. Consequently, because they are not actually engaged in classroom interaction, they become less able. Knowing that they probably will not be called upon, many students are likely to seek attention and success through dysfunctional means or unresponsively drift through school.

If this pattern is permitted to exist, students become increasingly less likely to gain the benefits of praise and recognition associated with success and higher levels of achievement. Interestingly, many students may become so disengaged from active learning that they actually forget how to participate. A technique to help these students is to use paired or small group learning opportunities so that the reluctant learner can begin to model successful response strategies.

As the teacher systematically increases the learner's response opportunities, it is very important for the teacher to analyze the amount and quality of feedback those students receive. Frequently, the majority of feedback consists of short praise, routine comment, or corrections. The ongoing stream of one-liners such as "good," "okay," "no," "wrong," etc., adds little to a student's feeling of well-being in the classroom. Feedback has proved to be a powerful tool in motivating students and ensuring the correctness of original learning (Hunter, 1986). Praise can and should be used to extend pupil-teacher contact and to encourage and reinforce desired behaviors, yet there is significant evidence to support the idea that less able students actually receive less praise than higher achieving students (Good and Brophy, 1984). This was true even when less able students provided correct answers.

Hunter (1986) has provided a vehicle to help ensure that students receive appropriate and intended feedback to their responses. She suggests that each student comment/response should be "dignified" so that the student feels he/she has made an important contribution to the class. Secondly, the teachers should "probe" for the correct answer so that the students in the class will receive appropriate information. Finally, regardless of correctness of student response, he/she should be held "accountable" for providing information relative to the topic at a future time during the lesson.

Thus, an incorrect student response should be followed by a clarifying statement emphasizing the correct and/or thoughtful parts of a student's comments. Then, through a series of direct questions, the teacher should help "draw out" the correct response. Finally, regardless of the success achieved by the student, he/she is given credit for his/her contributions and told that he/she will again be asked to share his/her thoughts at a later time in the lesson.

Teachers must actively seek opportunities to provide personal contact and regard for their students. Thus, teachers should plan personal encounters with children. Comments related to positive feelings about a child's school work, athletic or aesthetic skills, class playground or cafeteria behavior, personal grooming, dress, etc., may provide the sense of security and worth needed to integrate the child into the mainstream of school life.

Effectively teaching and supporting efforts of students is a difficult task. Yet, it becomes critical that all educators continue to review the large body of knowledge embodied in effective schools and teacher effectiveness research to guide school and classroom practices. Moreover, they must go about this task with a high degree of commitment and enthusiasm. This enthusiasm in the classroom can manifest itself through the high energy level an individual teacher can generate, as well as by the personal, genuine encouragement a teacher shares with a child. Thus, concepts related to a teacher's inherent personality and/or "style" may have little to do with a child's perception of which teachers genuinely care about their profession, school, or, most importantly, their students. Instead, it is more important that each teacher behaves in a manner that clearly sends a message of enthusiasm and support.

Recently, specific teaching strategies have emerged as being closely linked to the improvement of class climate and student learning. One promising technique is cooperative learning. Organized to promote active student involvement, student responsibility, and interpersonal skills, students have shown that, used correctly, it can increase achievement for some students (Johnson et al., 1984).

The remainder of this chapter will examine specific school and classroom practices that enrich the learning environment for students. A wide range of topics linked to student success and well-being will be reviewed, with illustrations from selected Best Schools as a vehicle to provide an application of theory into practice.

ENSURING THE SUCCESSFUL TRANSITION OF STUDENTS INTO SCHOOLS

Entrance into high school is both an exhilarating and apprehensive time for most students. The sense of "coming of age" is often overshadowed by real and imagined fears of what high school will be like while the academic challenges and uncertainties create a certain degree of stress. The unknowns related to social acceptance, acceptable patterns of behavior, understanding routines and expectations, and the complex "newness" of the situation can sometimes prove debilitating for the unprepared freshman.

To some degree, the parents of incoming students are confronted with many of the same fears and apprehensions. Often, parents feel detached from the mainstream of school life they may have become familiar with in the more nurturing elementary school.

Successful schools recognize the importance of transitional activities for incoming students. The first several weeks of high school are critical to the establishment of a sense of expectation and belonging for the impressionable freshman.

THE BEST SCHOOLS–ENSURING SUCCESSFUL TRANSITION OF STUDENTS

Although a wide variety of strategies have proven successful, Best Schools typically provide a formal freshman (and new entrance) orientation program. These may include, but are not limited to, visits by guidance counselors, tours of the building, and initiations to social and athletic events. Many schools have effectively used students in the orientation process by providing "buddy systems," peer leadership, and/or peer listener programs.

Of great importance is the need for elementary/middle school teachers to review standard data and individual profiles of students with their colleagues at the high school. These meetings help ensure appropriate academic placement, identify potential problem areas, and provide the framework for immediate intervention for high-risk students, beginning the first day of their high school experience.

The appropriate "education" of parents is an integral part of the transitional activities. Carefully planned activities can facilitate the parents' role in their children's entrance into high school, provide a framework to help ensure success, and identify school personnel and programs that could be accessed when needed. During orientation and parenting sessions, parents are made aware of learning nuances and developmental expectations for the adolescent child. Handbooks containing the standard operating procedures of the school and strategies that parents can use to enrich the home learning environment are typically provided. Finally, schools often provide a list of referral agencies where parents can go to deal with a wide variety of issues and which may assist the family with circumstances that may limit a child's potential for success.

Best Schools, throughout the country, have accepted the challenges associated with providing a framework for success for entering students. The schools illustrated below provide comprehensive mechanisms that help children and their parents make that potentially difficult transition into high school life.

Transition Illustrations

WESTHILL HIGH SCHOOL, SYRACUSE, NY

The Westhill School District is located in the western suburbs of Syracuse, New York. The school community is best described socioeconomically as middle-class and as being primarily residential, with two different neighborhood types. One is distinctly traditional, with older homes, in a quiet, tree-lined setting. The second is quite new, more typically suburban in nature, and characterized by abundant new home construction. Currently, the school district is experiencing rapid growth as a result of the new home construction. Because of this phenomenon, transition of new freshmen and transfer students is given high priority, with several key activities held each year. In the spring semester of the eighth grade, the principal and/or assistant principal visit the middle school to explain course requirements and general high school expectations. Prior to the opening of school, a Student-Parent Orientation Night is held at the high school. Following a general informational session, parents meet with the principal, assistant principal, and director of guidance while the students meet with their counselors and upperclassmen. These small group sessions promote a free exchange of information about school life and help the students begin to feel that they are a part of the high school community. The evening concludes with a building tour and refreshments.

On the first day of school, upperclassmen are stationed on each floor to assist students in locating rooms, reading schedules, opening lockers, and, in general, making them feel welcome to the school. In addition, all transfer students are seen by their respective counselor within the first two weeks of school to assess initial adjustment, answer questions, and provide support.

Richard J. Cavallaro, *Principal, Grades 9–12, 496 Students*

RUTGERS PREPARATORY SCHOOL, SOMERSET, NJ

Rutgers Preparatory School is a private school that draws from a diverse student population throughout central New Jersey. It actively seeks students from different backgrounds ethnically, economically, and, to some extent, academically.

To facilitate successful integration of freshman students, the school conducts several interesting orientation activities. Admissions' Open Houses and having a student visit the school before registering help ensure a good match between the student's educational needs and the school's offerings. All new students attend an orientation before school begins in September, while the school staff runs a new-parent orientation. Freshmen participate in a peer leadership program and a three-day camping trip, especially developed to facilitate adjustment. Advisors are alert to the adjustment of new students, and the director of guidance meets individually with each new student within the first month of school. The first faculty meeting is devoted to a review of new students, and teachers write comments on each new student early in October. The school makes every effort to ensure that new students, especially those entering after the freshman year, are integrated into meaningful activity and into school life.

Dr. Steven Loy, *Principal, Grades 5–12, 326 Students*

COVINGTON MIDDLE SCHOOL, BLOOMFIELD HILLS, MI

Covington is one of four middle schools located in suburban Bloomfield Hills, Michigan. The vast majority of Bloomfield Hill's residents hold college degrees. Parents hold high expectations for their children and their school. Similarly, parents are supportive of their school and are actively involved in school activities, including the school's improvement committee.

The student population is predominantly Caucasian, with 4% of the students representing various minority groups.

The school has a comprehensive orientation for incoming sixth graders, to which all students new to the school are invited. In addition, new students are given individual assistance by the counselors, as needed.

The counselor who will have the sixth grade visits fifth grade classrooms two times in the spring, once bringing students who will conduct small discussion groups with the fifth graders. Fifth graders come to visit late in the spring, are given lunch in the cafeteria, and tours guided by the students. Parents receive an orientation in an evening meeting where they learn about the organization, policies, and home study requirements. In late August, parents and students are invited to another orientation meeting where they are given all the information needed for the first day. Following the meeting, they open lockers, follow their class schedule, and meet with the counselor or sixth grade team leader if needed. Assignment books and binders—complete with folders, paper, and materials, and Parents' Guide to Study Skills are sold at this time.

On the first half day of school, advisor/advisee groups meet first and new students are given further orientation. Their schedule is explained, and a short tour is taken to be sure students know the important places: lavatories, cafeteria, and bus pickups. On the first full day of school, classes are brought to the cafeteria for a welcoming breakfast. At that time, the lunch procedures are reviewed.

The advisor/advisee program continues to acquaint students with what they need to know, reviews the student handbook, and offers an opportunity for questions. Counselors organize a meeting for all students new to the area schools, and these students get the first counseling appointments of the year.

In October, parents are invited to join their daughters and sons for a breakfast. When the students return to class, a meeting for the parents informs them of the sixth grade program, expectations, counseling services, and current school news. Later in the year, the PTA offers a parent night at each grade level for more information and to address concerns of parents.

William E. Blackwell, *Principal, Grades 6–8, 468 Students*

STUDENTS' MOTIVATION TO LEARN

The goal of helping students acquire self-motivation that leads to an ongoing desire to learn should be at the core of any school improvement initiative, yet there is a longstanding list of conditions of school life that often limit student effort and academic achievement. Hunter and Tomlinson (1992) have identified four such conditions:

(1) Students have few incentives to study. Most schools reward high achievement alone, apparently assuming that the lure of grades and test scores will inspire effort in all. Hence, low ability students and those who are disadvantaged, who must work the hardest, have the least incentive to do so.

(2) Many school policies discourage student effort. For example, to increase graduation rates, some schools have offered to create far less rigorous alternatives to core subjects and award diplomas to students who merely stay in a course and accumulate credits. While increasing graduation rates, these schools have also allowed students to evade difficult tasks and have reduced the need for effort.

(3) Peer pressure may discourage effort and achievement. Peer pressure has a significant influence on the behavior of students. Unfortunately, some school cultures actively reject academic aspirations. High grades can be a source of peer ridicule with the consequence of strong social sanctions.

(4) Good intentions can backfire. In attempts to protect pupils' self-esteem, teachers may excuse disadvantaged students from the effort that learning requires. This practice obscures the connection between effort and accomplishment and shields children from the consequences.

Motivation can be characterized as a student's personal investment to compete and learn from a given task. Student motivation to learn can be conceptualized as either a general trait or as a situation-specific state (Brophy, 1987). The trait of motivation to learn is an enduring disposition to strive for content knowledge and skill mastery in learning situations. The state of motivation to learn exists when student engagement in a particular activity is guided by the intention of acquiring the knowledge or mastering the skill that the activity is designed to teach (Brophy, 1987).

Waxman and Walberg (1991) have identified five kinds of motivational knowledge. In performing tasks, all five kinds are involved in shaping a student's temperament, attitude toward the task, and persistence to accomplish the task.

(1) An *attribution* is an inference made that identifies a reason for why an event has the outcome that it does. Major dimensions of attribution theory include concerns of control, which attempts to explain the cause of an event's outcome as either internal (e.g., one's inherent ability) or external (teacher's help and support); stability addresses the consistency by which the cause of an outcome can be determined (e.g., ability is considered stable because it does not vary if the same task is reattempted, whereas luck and effort are considered unstable because they fluctuate over time); controllability deals with whether the cause is governed by oneself or is beyond one's influence (e.g., studying versus being ill).

(2) *Efficacy* is a belief about one's competency and ability to achieve. Typically, when approaching a task, students develop an expectation about being able to perform the task.

(3) *Incentive* provides the value that a goal has if it can be achieved. It is personally what the student wants from his/her effort but does not yet have.

(4) All tasks have *outcomes,* which define the results of individual effort. Clear, unambiguous goals help students determine what a finished task should look like.

(5) *Utility* establishes alternatives, causes of action, and parameters for judging the value of each relative to the others. Thus, a student can choose or not choose to participate in a learning activity once having assessed the value of each course of action.

Raffini (1988) proposes a fourfold approach that would remove motivational barriers and help students redirect their behaviors away from failure-avoiding activities toward academic applications. He describes how these four strategies can aid in promoting the rediscovery of an interest in learning:

(1) Individual goal-setting structures allow students to define their own criteria for success.

(2) Outcome-based instruction and evaluation make it possible for slower students to experience success without having to compete with faster students.

(3) Attribution retraining can help apathetic students view failure as a lack of effort rather than a lack of ability.

(4) Cooperative learning activities help students realize that personal effort can contribute to group, as well as individual, goals.

Understanding the various factors that shape an individual student's proclivity to be motivated or unmotivated in a particular situation has value. Yet, given the complexity of the issues related to motivation, it is highly unlikely that any single programmatic approach can serve as a panacea for motivating students. Brophy (1987) believes that no motivational strategies can succeed with students unless certain preconditions are in effect. These include the establishment of a supportive learning environment where learning activities are organized and classroom practices are well managed. This also includes appropriate management of students, parent support of their learning efforts, and providing an atmosphere where students feel comfortable taking intellectual risks.

Maehr (1991) describes the magnitude of motivation being influenced by the psychological environment of a school that gives meaning to the overall education experience. In an analysis of more than 16,000 students in 800 schools in Illinois, he found that school goals and culture that stressed motivation and achievement did have an impact and that the school leaders had a significant influence on the creation of that environment.

What is suggested is that motivation should not be seen as something existing solely within the student but, rather, as a complex outcome of meaningful participation in classroom and school activities. To this end, teachers must provide an appropriate level of challenge, ensuring that students can achieve high levels of success when they apply reasonable effort. Clearly, teachers must provide meaningful learning activities that are considered worth learning, either in their own right or as steps toward a higher objective. Finally, motivational strategies must be moderated for optimal effectiveness. Motivational attempts can be overdone, and any particular strategy can lose its effectiveness if it is used too often or too routinely.

Successful schools recognize the need to understand the importance of motivating students as an essential element in developing student interest in learning and study. Although many specific strategies, initiatives, and programs are utilized to meet the unique needs of individual students, classrooms, and schools, many common elements exist that may serve as a foundation for establishing a framework for student motivation and success (Ogden and Germinario, 1994):

- relevant, interesting curriculum and learning activities
- the maintenance of higher expectations clearly communicated through a positive sentiment that students can and will learn
- the utilization of well-conceived opportunities for both intrinsic and extrinsic motivations
- the effective use of rewards and positive reinforcement
- the development of a supportive environment that invites student success
- the spirit of mastery that embraces the need for students to feel competent and in control of their learning outcomes
- the teaching of cooperation that does not allow students to criticize themselves or allow others to criticize them
- the recognition that students need a sense of belonging, actively integrating them into the mainstream of school life
- the acceptance of the interdependence among students, parents, teachers, and principals in shaping a positive school climate directed toward student success

THE BEST SCHOOLS – MOTIVATING STUDENTS TO LEARN

Best Schools demonstrate the capacity to understand the nature and importance of motivating students and have translated that knowledge into unique, meaningful school programs and learning opportunities. The illustrations provided below attempt to describe how several highly successful schools actually plan and employ instructional strategies that develop students' interest in learning and motivate them to study.

Motivating Students Illustrations

BELFRY HIGH SCHOOL, BELFRY, KY

Belfry High School is located in the Appalachian Mountains within the easternmost section of Kentucky. Belfry serves an economically diverse community. Students' parents range from the highly educated to those who dropped out of primary school. Children live in traditional, one-parent, and no-parent households. They come from the employed, unemployed, and welfare, social security, and aid to dependent children recipients. The staff at Belfry have initiated both a curricular and procedural approach to help motivate students.

All freshmen are enrolled in a learning skills class. They work half-time developing computer skills and half-time in study skills, problem solving, and self-esteem classes. The class sizes are smaller so each student can receive individualized instruction. Each student has success, and this breeds future success. All students receive incentives for successful work completed, such as the red card and white card. The red card is awarded to those students with all A's and no days absent; the white card is awarded to those with no grade below a B and one day or less absent. A major motivating technique presently used is to include technology in the classroom, with the media center providing an expansion of the classroom. Program initiatives promote instructional strategies that allow for continuous learning and performance testing. The student can build from where she/he is, so she/he is never a failure.

Educational assemblies and guest speakers provide additional attempts to emphasize the importance of studying and achieving.

Frank T. Welch, *Principal, Grades 9–12 , 911 Students*

THE ACADEMY OF THE HOLY NAMES, ALBANY, NY

The Academy of the Holy Names is a private Catholic college preparatory school for young women located on sixty-four acres of former farmland on the outskirts of the city of Albany, New York. The 204 students in the school come from thirty-nine different schools or school districts in the capital area. Approximately 78% come from parochial and private schools, and 22% come from public schools in the area.

The school has developed various programs and procedures designed to fulfill the school's mission of preparing students for college and eventual careers. Flexible modular scheduling allows the students to take a maximum number of courses, both required and elective. A wide variety of electives offered by every department affords "something for everyone." Small classes give students an opportunity for individualized attention. Teachers, most willing to give extra help when needed, often are able to do so during a "free" (unstructured) period. The math lab, writing center, and tutoring club are all willing to offer their services both during and after the school day. There is a seriousness about learning at AHN. It is expected that everyone will try his/her best. In accord with this, teachers provide students with unit plans, which explain goals, objectives, course content, assignments, and methods of assessment. By means of the unit plans, students are able to organize their time, much as they will be expected to do in college. If a student does not fare well at evaluation time, "frees" are rescinded, and the student is assigned to the study room until such time as there is an improvement in grades. If the seriousness of the situation warrants, a group conference that includes parents, student, principal, advisor, and all subject teachers is called. Common problems are discussed, and a plan of action is devised. Senior privileges are revoked if the student is not performing well and are not reinstated until there is an improvement. For the student with special talent or interest, a variety of advanced or accelerated courses is offered. The number of students on the honor roll and in the National Honor Society attest to the fact that the students at AHN are serious about learning.

Mary Anne Vigliante, *Principal, Grades 9–12, 204 Students*

NORTHSIDE SENIOR HIGH SCHOOL, FORT SMITH, AR

Northside High School is an inner-city school, sixty-four years old, with many ethnic and socioeconomic differences represented. The student body has over 1300 members with 21% African-American, 15% Asian, 2% Hispanic, 1% American Indian, and 61% Caucasian. The large majority of students fall in the middle to low socioeconomic level, with about 21% below the poverty level. The school has capitalized on its collaboration with local businesses to promote student motivation and achievement potential.

The individual student at Northside is uppermost in the concerns of the school. Faculty and staff work to give all students the extra incentive to make the effort necessary for learning. Northside is very fortunate to have an active Partners in Education program. The volunteers from these businesses help reinforce the importance of education to an employer. Shadowing jobs requiring math, science, business, communication, and computer skills help students see the practicality of these courses. One partner provides speakers to classes on a variety of jobs. The most popular are those who speak about their personal education journey and the importance of education in the workplace. Many teachers use speakers from the community to emphasize the content of a course. Speakers provided by Partners in Education businesses encourage students to become proficient in skills used by that particular business. Planters Peanuts provides a group of employees who work with at-risk students to encourage them to stay in school. Four mornings a week, Planters' people staff a room from 7:15 A.M. to 8:00 A.M. as a study hall for students needing remedial or homework help. The students receive rich experiences through field trips and career day in the community.

Products from a business are provided to be used as incentives by teachers. A bag of peanuts for the highest score or the most improved score might seem insignificant for high school students, but the individual attention it brings causes students to raise their effort level and, thus, their grade level.

One business partner instituted an incentive program called GPA/GPA. "Grizzly/Planters" awards recognize every student whose grade point average has improved over the previous quarter. A certificate of merit and a tee shirt with the logo "Earn More/Learn More" is presented by a representative of the business and of the school. Presentations are made before the student's homeroom class. Second time winners are awarded a different colored tee shirt. The school has even had calls from the community asking to buy one of the tee shirts. This program was designed to recognize the students who improve their grade point and who are not recognized as top students.

Bill Barduck, *Principal, Grades 10–12, 1306 Students*

STUDENTS BUILD SUSTAINED RELATIONSHIPS WITH COUNSELORS, TEACHERS, AND OTHER ADULTS

Secondary schools are most often characterized by formal structures that stress specialization of teaching in large school settings that facilitate the offering of a wide variety of courses. In many cases, the outcomes associated with this traditional structure have served to depersonalize a student's learning experience. Successful schools conscientiously attempt to view schools as small societies where adult roles are diffused, division of staff responsibilities are minimized, and relationships are increasingly personal and, at times, social rather than only task-related.

Much support is given to the importance of social bonds that connect the student to the school. These bonds become an essential element in promoting a sense of belonging for the student. A primary indicator of a student's sense of belonging in a school is the quality of interactions and relationships he/she has with the adults in that school. It is those adults who help model the world for the child. It is those adults upon whom the child relies for security, support, and recognition. Through the development of trust between students and those adults around them, fear and apprehension are managed. Thus, students are far more likely to take intellectual risks in classrooms to feel free to engage in activities throughout the school and to seek adult assistance when confronted with a school or life problem.

Wehlage et al. (1989) have identified common elements that are impediments to a student's "membership" in secondary schools: adjustment, difficulty, incongruence, and isolation.

- *Adjustment* to school is a major contribution to membership. The transition from elementary to high school, introduction to new peer groups, experiencing of new social norms, confronting new teachers, and teaching methods are all significant adjustment issues.

- *Difficulty* of academic content is a primary cause of academic failure. Yet, academic success is essential if students are to become socially bonded to school.
- *Incongruence* describes the personal and social match between the student and the school. This match is based on the students' understandings of their own values, experiences, and projected future; elements of this perception include social class orientation and racial and ethnic values.
- *Isolation* refers to academic and social experiences. School membership requires that students have frequent and high-quality interactions with adults.

Most frequently, secondary schools view guidance counselors as the primary support service to students. Unfortunately, these counselors are confronted with large student-counselor ratios that prohibit meaningful outgoing, sustained relationships. Increasingly, schools have utilized *advisement* programs as an element to personalize a student's education. While guidance is viewed in terms of broad activities aimed at helping students understand themselves and their schools, advisement functions as a "helping link" between professional guidance functions and the day-to-day school life of a student (Keefe, 1986).

Teachers almost always assume the role of advisor in these relationships. Jenkins (1992) identifies the primary responsibilities of teachers as advisors:

- monitoring the academic progress of each student advisee to provide reinforcement, support, intervention, and help at appropriate times
- providing each student with an adult advocate who knows him or her personally and who will help him or her examine options and make responsible choices
- helping plan programs of study that are based on the needs, interests, backgrounds, and aspirations of each student
- establishing a system of in-school communication wherein all professionals concerned with a student have systematic and consistent information to help the student succeed academically
- suggesting study techniques for each student for improving classwork and homework

These general goals can be translated into several specific objectives that can give direction for establishing, evaluating, and refining an advisement program.

- Salient information is collected about each student from a variety of sources and used to develop individual educational plans.
- All students are helped to develop career goals consistent with their talents and interests and based on a clear knowledge of economic and societal trends.
- All students are helped to plan a program of studies in accordance with their goals, aspirations, strengths, and weaknesses.
- The progress of students in academic areas that they take for credit is monitored on a regular basis by an adult who knows them well and who can help them make necessary adjustments.
- A communication network is established among the teachers to share information that will help provide effective learning environments for the student.
- The parents of each student are contacted on a regular basis by someone who knows their child's schoolwork well enough to provide information about the student's progress.

- A system is established for continually evaluating the success of each student and used to make changes as appropriate.
- All students have someone in the school with whom they can talk and who can arrange help for them from more qualified persons when needed.
- Potential student problems are handled in practical ways and before the fact, rather than in the aftermath of incidents.
- Accurate and comprehensive information on all students is reported to colleges and universities, armed services, and other appropriate agencies.

Because teacher-advisories have been implemented longer at the grade 7–9 level in middle schools or junior high schools, there is more documentation of their implementation and its effects at that level than at the secondary level. A current review of educational practices for early adolescents (Braddock and McPartland, 1993) reviews studies that find that schools with strong adult advisory programs are more able to help students solve personal problems and connect to a caring environment at school. Students at schools with such programs report more frequent positive contact with teachers and more positive perceptions of teachers' interest and support.

To be successful, students need to view their school as a special place where teachers are caring, the principal is approachable, others are friends, and learning takes place. In an environment that conveys a sense of community, a feeling of family, there are many opportunities for children to meet and learn from adults.

THE BEST SCHOOLS – BUILDING SUSTAINED RELATIONSHIPS

Best Schools throughout the country maximize the opportunities to personalize the school experience for their students by providing a wide variety of planned strategies to enrich the relationships between students and school staff. Several illustrations are provided next.

Illustrations of Building Sustained Relationships

KENT-MERIDIAN HIGH SCHOOL, KENT, WA

Kent-Meridian High School is located midway between Seattle and Tacoma, Washington. It is the oldest of four high schools in the Kent School District, which serves 23,000 students, K–12.

The student population is quite diverse, represented by 79% Caucasian, 9.5% Asian-American, 6% African-American, 4% Hispanic, and 1.5% American Indian/Native Alaskan. The school operates large English as a Second Language, Special Education, and Vocational Transfer programs.

School personnel believe that, in a traditional program, it is very difficult for most students to build sustainable relationships with their teachers or even their counselor. For that matter, there is little encouragement even for teachers to form such relationships with each other.

Kent-Meridian High School has adopted the school within the school format because they no longer believe that the traditional high school curriculum is relevant to the majority of students' lives. The educational strategies that worked in the past are no longer viable. Collaboration with business leaders has further convinced them that many of the students, even those who achieve well in the classroom, are, in many cases, unable to cope with the simplest of problems or to cooperate with others in the workplace. It was decided, therefore, to align the curriculum to career paths and aim directly at developing those skills and attitudes that will help students be proficient problem solvers and responsible citizens.

Lawrence H. Nicholson, *Principal, Grades 10–12, 1379 Students*

GREENVILLE JUNIOR/SENIOR HIGH SCHOOL, GREENVILLE, CA

Greenville Junior/Senior High School is located in a rural northeastern California town of 1500 people. Over the past decades, Greenville has had a downward spiral of economic activity. Because of the low housing cost resulting from the depressed economy, Greenville has been described as a "poverty magnet."

Despite this phenomenon, Greenville has dedicated itself to restructuring education to meet the needs of its diverse student population. Specifically, the student population is represented by 83% Caucasian, 9% American Indian/Native Alaskan, 7% Hispanic, and 1% Asian-American.

The school has taken several innovative steps to promote the relationship between its staff and students. The counselor meets with every ninth through eleventh grade student once each year and with seniors more frequently. Choosing a college, arranging special tests, reviewing results, and providing guest speakers are also included in the responsibility of the counselor, along with keeping track of scholarships, grants, and monetary awards to seniors. An additional counselor, who is supported by special grant funds, provides personal counseling for "at-risk" students one day a week. Plumas County Department of Drug and Alcohol also provides group counseling sessions for students referred by themselves and staff. A career technician meets with each student once a year in an advisory capacity, helps students investigate career opportunities, and acts as a referral agent for district work-ability programs, job referrals from the community, work permits and work experience assignments.

Each week, as part of the regular school day, all students are assigned to the "Teachers As Counselors Too (TACT). During this advisory period, each teacher is assigned fifteen to twenty students. Each student remains with the same teacher for three years, either grades 7–9 or 10–12. Staff members choose which age group they want to work with and are committed to the needs of students that age. The purpose of TACT classes is to provide group support, to give individual academic advising information, and to offer the opportunity for students to form a closer relationship with one staff member. All TACT curriculum is developed within the staff so that the curriculum is staff-originated, staff-trained, and implemented schoolwide.

Additionally, seniors, as part of their senior project, are encouraged to work with a mentor, an expert in their field of study. Some staff members serve as mentors, but many are community members who are otherwise not associated with the school. This helps our students form a personal relationship with an adult inside or outside of the school.

Gary F. Hartman, *Principal, Grades 7–12, 248 Students*

ANNA MIDDLE SCHOOL, ANNA, TX

Anna Middle School (hereafter referred to as AMS) is one of three campuses that comprise the Anna Independent School District, located approximately fifty miles northeast of Dallas. The school has a 48.8% mobility rate. Families move in, move out, and often move back into the district, thus requiring a challenging and flexible program to meet individual academic and social needs of mobile students. The school is considered a "wealth below average" rural school district with 10% Hispanic minority students. Thirty-four percent of AMS students currently receive free or reduced lunches, and it is estimated that perhaps 15% of the remaining student population qualified for this service, but their parents did not choose to apply for it. Within the past five years, the free/reduced lunch population has tripled. In the 1990–91 school year, 66% of the AMS student body was classified as "at risk." As a result of teamwork and a number of positive factors, the at-risk population has been reduced significantly.

With a strong mission that focuses on *all* students achieving success, the AMS faculty has made a wide variety of program opportunities available to meet the needs of a mobile and low-income population. Programs are designed to get students actively involved in the life of the school and provide optimum agents for building faculty/student, counselor/student, and parent/community/student relationships. All AMS students take part in one or more of the following activities. Prime Time is a mentoring program where a teacher is assigned fifteen to twenty-five students to meet with daily. The first fifteen to twenty minutes of each day is spent in this group. Teachers build relationships with this group and discuss values and judgments, as well as provide helpful information and instruction to enrich the curriculum. People Energizing People (PEP) provides individual adult-student counseling and "friend-making time," which has proven to be beneficial, especially for the troubled student or one who is new to the district. Athletics and cheerleading competitions are excellent means of building relationships among instructors and students. Through the team concept, positive attitude, and discipline, students learn to build positive rapport. Since the adult coaches are also teachers of academic subjects, this positive relationship is regarded as important to building student self-esteem and encouraging student success in all areas. The peer assistance leaders group becomes naturally close to their sponsor, who builds a trusting relationship through active participation in such activities as a PAL trip to Austin to attend the state PAL Conference, and the day-to-day leadership provided as students learn to care about one another. Through the student council, student governors are able to work closely with their sponsor and the principal to refine the structure of the school's programs to support student mastery and success. Beta club members build a lasting relationship with their sponsor as they work toward community improvement. The BEST club (boosters of education and sportsmanship team) sponsor works closely with a small group of students to help them define and report the strengths and successes of all AMS students.

Christy Benedict, *Principal, Grades 6–8, 166 Students*

PROGRAMS AND STRATEGIES TO IDENTIFY AND ASSIST POTENTIAL DROPOUT AND OTHER AT-RISK STUDENTS

In previous decades, school dropouts were, more often than not, able to find gainful employment and provide for themselves and their families. Today's young dropout faces quite a different world. Today's employment market clearly provides a distinct advantage to those who are highly educated or those who have the knowledge and skills to adapt to a technological workplace.

In 1992, approximately 380,000 youngsters in grades 10–12 decided to drop out of school (National Center for Educational Statistics, 1994). The social and economic impact of these decisions are extraordinary. For example, it is estimated that one-half of the heads of households on welfare failed to finish high school; of the more than 1.1 million persons incarcerated in 1990, 82% were high school dropouts; over a lifetime, today's dropout can expect to earn approximately $200,000 less than a high school graduate (National Education Goals Panel, 1993).

In addition to the economic consequences, dropouts often lose their only real opportunity to interact with adults who may influence more purposeful lives and careers. School is clearly the best place, for most every adolescent, to learn basic academic skills, decision making, and interpersonal skills. When students drop out of school, they place themselves and society at significant risk.

In response to the significance of the dropout issue, our government continues to support the goal that by the year 2000, the high school graduation rate will increase to at least 90%. To achieve such an ambitious goal, schools must actively prepare for their at-risk populations. Best Schools across the country have embraced this challenge and have developed comprehensive mechanisms to identify the at-risk and potential dropout population and have developed school, classroom, and community-based responses.

The At-Risk Student

All youngsters are, at times, at risk of failure, yet most can effectively utilize the standard resources and support systems established at home or school to deal with the trials and tribulations of growing up. As a result of their positive developmental experiences, they emerge as young adults satisfied with who they are and pleased with the approval and pride from their families and friends. Similarly, children who achieve in school experience success and, typically, develop positive attitudes toward school and themselves.

Unfortunately, there is a portion of every school population that consistently shows a lack of necessary intellectual, emotional, and/or social skills to take full advantage of the educational opportunities available to them. Often, these students become disenchanted and, ultimately, passively or openly reject school. It is these students who are at high risk of failure.

There is no prototype at-risk student. Students who do not succeed in our schools come from all social, ethnic, and racial groups, yet various demographic characteristics tend to place certain students at a potentially higher risk for school failure.

Certain key demographic factors have been found to be more closely related to at-risk status. Pallas, Natriello, and McDill (1989) characterize the educationally disadvantaged child as one who has been exposed to certain background factors or experiences in formal schooling, family, or community. Although not a categorical model to predict at-risk status, these authors have determined that particular combinations of risk factors have been shown to be particularly detrimental to success. Examples of these are single-parent homes with low incomes and parents with limited English proficiency, who have no high school diploma. Similarly, a study conducted by the National Center for Education Statistics (U.S. Department of Education, 1986) identifies indicators of at-risk status. These include (among others) living in a single-parent family, low parental income and/or education, limited English proficiency, having a brother or sister who dropped out of high school, and being at home alone without an adult for a period greater than three hours on weekdays.

Although helpful in a general sense, demographic characteristics, in and of themselves, cannot consistently identify those students who will fail. An examination of characteristics and school behaviors of at-risk students can further help identify which students are at greatest risk for failure. Research has shown that the characteristics listed below are closely associated with school failure:

- attendance problems
- previous school retention
- prior school suspensions
- working two or more years below grade level
- lack of participation in extracurricular activities
- special program placement

From both an empirical and commonsense perspective, these behaviors can accurately identify those students who, for whatever reason, will not meet with success. Yet these characteristics tend to manifest themselves long after a student has begun to develop attitude and behavioral patterns that lead to school failure. Instead, it may be more beneficial to examine general descriptors of a student's profile to establish parameters for determining the nature of risk. A review of the research can help synthesize this profile by analyzing four basic conditions: self-concept, alienation, lack of school success, and student learning style.

Alienation

For at-risk students, lack of success in school both contributes to and results from an increased sense of alienation from school as an institution. Newman (1981) associates alienation in schools with disruptive student behaviors and poor achievement. He suggests that student disengagement generally goes unrecognized as the source of many school problems. He insists that reducing student alienation is key to engaging students in the positive benefits in their schooling.

Thus, schools need to identify and revise school and classroom practices that send negative messages about school membership and belonging. Common practices associated with class grouping patterns, discipline and attendance policies, school regulations, school curriculum, school rules, and special class placement may be rooted in good intentions, yet they may, in fact, lead to increased feelings of isolation and lack of belonging.

Level of School Success

Early success in school is a critical prerequisite to success in later schooling and, ultimately, in life.

Student Self-Concept

Student self-concept has been found to be related to students' grades, test scores, and other significant educational outcomes. Teachers instinctively know that, when students feel good about themselves, they tend to do better in school. It becomes critical that school personnel actively seek ways of promoting self-esteem in the classroom and of promoting a school climate that conscientiously attempts to foster students' feelings of pride in themselves and their schools. Broderick (1993) found that school transition (both to middle school and to high school) was a critical juncture in the academic careers of high school dropouts. At these times, school performance and engagement dropped dramatically. It was in the transition to high school, particularly, that many dropouts fell into serious academic difficulty.

The experience of being retained in a grade emerged as another important facet of the school careers of dropouts. Students who were retained were more than three times more likely to drop out of school than students who were never retained. According to Broderick (1993), approximately one-third of the higher dropout rate among retained youths could be explained by differences in the pre and postretention grades and attendance of retained and promoted youths. Even after controlling for grades and attendance through the ninth grade, however, students who repeated grades were substantially more likely to drop out than those who had never repeated a grade. This was true regardless of whether the students had been retained early or late in elementary school or middle school. School failure leads to messages of rejection and poor sense of self. Without basic academic and social skills, children face failure every day and may quickly reach the conclusion that they are incapable and that schools do not care about their learning.

Success, however, can come from a variety of aspects of school life. Achievement, not only in academics, but in areas related to athletics or aesthetics can lead to increased feelings of self with a greater sense of belonging to the mainstream of the school. It becomes imperative that schools continue to examine how they incorporate a success orientation in daily practices. Clearly, teachers have the greatest impact on the sense of success a student may encounter, yet the principal, coach, play director, custodian, and bus driver provide significant contributions to the at-risk student's feeling of belonging and worth.

Learning Style

Every student has a preferred learning style. While most students can learn through a variety of sensory stimuli and within different learning environments, enough research is available to support the notion that teaching to various learning styles can improve student learning (Dunn and Dunn, 1978).

There is some evidence to suggest that at-risk students may have measurably different learning styles. In fact, at-risk students may have predominant learning modalities that differ significantly from traditional teaching styles. In a recent study, at-risk learners were identified as having poor to fair auditory and visual learning capabilities. Moreover, a very large percentage of these students demonstrated high preference for tactile and kinesthetic learning experiences. It becomes important then, that we begin to train teachers to utilize a more multisensory approach with identified at-risk students. It seems logical that providing variability in instructional delivery systems will ultimately help all learners.

Program Rationale

Schools have an expressed obligation to educate all students. This responsibility is most typically met through direct instruction in the traditional curriculum areas; however, schools must now embrace the responsibility of successfully educating those students who, for whatever reason, come to school unable to maximize their learning potential and are at risk to drop out. No longer can schools afford to disregard the role that society has placed upon them.

There are a variety of factors that compel our schools to engage in early prevention and intervention initiatives to help ensure the success of students. The first is that many societal problems are, at least in part, the result of a poor education. Early success in school correlates with high school graduation. More than 80% of prison inmates are high school dropouts (U.S. Department of Education, 1990). The best way to reduce crime is to increase education, because the chances are greater that a high school dropout will go to prison than they are that a smoker will contract cancer (Hodghenson, 1990).

The second concern is the question of equity in access to educational opportunity. State and federal laws have been enacted to help educate learning disabled children, non-English-speaking children, gifted children, etc.; so it can be argued that the disaffected students, the majority of whom have normal intelligence, require specialized learning experiences and support systems to truly maximize their learning potential.

A third reason is linked to changing societal expectations for our schools. The world has become increasingly complex for the young adult. Confronted with increased pressure from familial, environmental, and social stresses, today's youngsters may have greater difficulty determining their places in the world. Increasingly, parents will look to the school for help. Schools have now been asked to assume a more direct role in teaching essential life skills that were traditionally within the domain of family and church.

Finally, schools have the awesome responsibility of preparing students for the roles they will be asked to play in our ever complex society. It is through our efforts that a significant foundation can be established to ensure success for a generation of young Americans.

THE BEST SCHOOLS–COMPONENTS OF A COMPREHENSIVE PROGRAM FOR AT-RISK STUDENTS

Because the factors that place a student at risk are numerous and complex, successful programming for potential dropouts must address multiple needs and be carefully tailored to meet the individuals they serve. Nonetheless, general parameters of effective programs emerge that can be identified.

Successful programs are comprehensive and intensive. They start with a viable mechanism to identify at-risk students and provide the systematic application of instructional strategies and school programs that 1) help students succeed in school, 2) help students overcome feelings of isolation and alienation, and 3) optimally, create an environment that formulates self-motivation and student interest in continued learning.

Germinario, Cervalli, and Ogden (1992) provide the framework for successful programs:

- Develop a curriculum basis for school improvement initiatives. Teachers are trained best to teach. Programs that are rooted in counseling or the dynamics of the family are best suited for psychologists and social workers. Schools must capitalize on the staff's ability to improve student learning and self-esteem as the most primary of all at-risk prevention vehicles. Providing a success orientation for students will significantly increase the chances of life-long success.
- Stress intimacy and individual attention. Virtually all successful programs provide for strong personal attention to each student. They strive to create a feeling of nurturing and belonging that is often absent from the home and school experience of at-risk students.
- Deal with the child as part of the family and the family as part of the neighborhood. Research clearly shows that student attitudes and performance are better when parents are supportive and involved in the school environment (National School Boards Association, 1988). Special care should be given to accommodate access to the school for the parents of at-risk students. Parenting classes, home visits, and a recognition of parental responsibilities in educating their children are examples of bringing parents into the mainstream of school life.
- Utilize a team approach to programming for the at-risk student. The responsibility cannot fall on the counselor, child psychologist, nurse, or special education teacher. The entire school community must learn to embrace its responsibility to assist in the education of at-risk students.
- Possess caring, dedicated staff members who have the time and the skills to build relationships of trust and respect with at-risk children and their families. Thus, the school must make a commitment to training the staff as to the nature of risk and in strategies that facilitate the learning of the at-risk student.
- Monitor the program. Very few programs fail because of lack of initial enthusiasm or the utility of purpose. Instead, many programs fail because they are either not implemented as designed, or they are not periodically assessed for their impact on the intended outcome.
- Obtain administrative and school board support. Through the development of policies or commitment to provide needed resources, effective leadership programs aimed at providing success for at-risk students (like all other programs) will prove beneficial.
- Evaluate the program. Once implemented, monitoring must be initiated to ensure that activities are being conducted according to plan. Evaluation mechanisms must be put into place to determine if expectations/objectives are being met.
- Many of America's Best Schools have developed systematic programs that effectively identify and provide interventions to assist potential dropouts and other at-risk students. Although different in their approaches, the schools illustrated below provide a sample of how successful programs operate.

At-Risk Program Illustrations

OLIVE PEIRCE MIDDLE SCHOOL, RAMONA, CA

Olive Peirce Middle School is located twenty-seven miles northeast of San Diego, nestled in the foothills of the Vallecito and Santa Maria Mountains, surrounded by the Cleveland National

Forest. The school's proximity to Mexico's border results in a large immigrant population within the community; third world ideology affects the social and cultural aspects of the school. The school has an exceedingly diverse student population yet has maintained an exceptional success tradition. The school has identified the at-risk student as one whose social achievement, progress toward promotion, and preparation for full participation in our society are in serious jeopardy. At-risk students are identified through referrals of concerned staff, parents, or other students to the student assistance team (SAT). The team is composed of two counselors, the assistant principal, health clerk, a Ramona Project crisis counselor, and eight teachers. The team meets weekly to assess the needs of individual students and make recommendations for parent contact, student contact, program modification, tutoring, counseling, or the Positive Educational Experience – Ramona support program (PEER – a self-contained, minimum day alternative middle school experience designed to meet the needs of students who have been identified as needing a highly structured, individualized academic setting).

SAT enables staff to understand the problems of students at risk, through workshops, training programs, and group facilitator training. Programs currently in place include peer helpers and tutors, PALs (Peer Assisted Listeners), "Each One Reach One," enrichment classes, lunch-time activities, advisory, PEER, student court, student support groups such as "Children and Divorce," buddy system, referral to outside agencies such as the Ramona Project, parenting classes, and study hall. For students requiring services beyond those appropriate for the school setting, we have established relationships with our community resources such as the Ramona Project. This connection with the service providers provides communication links for the total support of at-risk students.

Stephen B. Levy, *Principal, Grades 7–8, 967 Students*

CRAIGMONT JUNIOR/SENIOR HIGH SCHOOL, MEMPHIS, TN

Craigmont High School is located in the city of Memphis, Tennessee. The school is in an area of Memphis known as "Raleigh," a lower middle- to upper middle-class neighborhood with a mixed racial composition. The ethnic composition of the school is as follows: 59% Caucasian; 36% African-American; 5% Asian, Hispanic, and East Indian.

The school has successfully met the divergent needs of its students through a wide variety of curricular and support programs. Potential dropouts, underachievers, or other at-risk students are identified by teachers, counselors, and parents. Determinations are made based on age ("overage" for present grade), lack of regular attendance, inattentiveness in class, failing grades, and/or inappropriate/disruptive behavior.

Through multidisciplinary team meetings and support team meetings, students who fall in the above category are identified, counseled, and assisted by a team of specialists within the school. The following strategies and/or programs are effective to counsel and assist this particular group of students:

- involving parents in the learning process and making them aware of potential problems such as academic, behavioral, attendance, and emotional problems that are characterized with dropouts, underachieving, and/or at-risk students
- study skills session (class) to assist the student
- individual and/or small group instruction
- recommendations to move older students to a higher grade or to enroll in Middle College High School
- counseling the potential dropout at least once weekly
- providing vocational training at appropriate schools
- Lesson Line, a cooperative effort of First Tennessee Bank and Craigmont, as a means of assisting all students and their parents in keeping up with assignments
- night school programs for students who are planning to or already have dropped out but still desire to receive a diploma
- referring identified students to the Memphis City Schools Mental Health Center for further diagnostic testing

- an IEP (individual education program) for each student who qualifies as a resource student
- the VIP (vocational interest program) and the VAP (vocational assessment program) (VIP identifies children's interests and helps them pursue their interests and achieve their goals through school and community work-related programs. VAP assesses the child with special needs, such as the special education child.)

Dr. Ada Jane Walters, *Principal, Grades 7–12, 1881 Students*

MYERS MIDDLE SCHOOL, SAVANNAH, GA

Myers Middle School is located on the east side of Savannah, Georgia. The school services an extremely diverse student population. Specifically, the student population consists of 50% African-American, 48% Caucasian, and 2% Asian-American/Hispanic/American Indian. The school philosophy recognizes the uniqueness of this diversity and provides a wholesome environment to meet the needs of all students.

The school provides remedial and support services for over 200 students. Specifically, students requiring remediation are served by the academic support program (ASP), the comprehensive competencies program (CCP), Saturday school tutorial, and exploratory offerings.

The ASP serves the remedial needs of students who are two or more years behind their appropriate grade level. Tutoring offers remediation on an individual basis from a facilitator. "ASP students" sent by individual teachers receive help with specific assignments during their regular class period. Then the student returns to class to turn in the assignment.

After-school tutorial provides students with individual attention or computer-directed instruction in specific areas. Teachers, as well as parents, refer students in need of assistance. Individual classroom teachers monitor progress closely and acknowledge the student's increased understanding due to the personal help he/she receives on specific assignments.

The CCP is an individualized, self-paced, computer-assisted program serving middle school students who have repeated two or more grades and are at high risk of dropping out. The program offers a highly structured, intensive program, including language arts, mathematics, and reading in a hierarchial framework.

In addition, the "New Beginnings Program" is designed to meet the educational and behavioral needs of the students involved, in a self-contained setting. The program features individualized, prescriptive instruction with focus on skill mastery. Students are also involved in weekly counseling sessions and various other activities appropriate to the students' needs. Those selected for this program have demonstrated counterproductive academic and social behavior at school.

At-risk students are identified from computer lists sent to each site from the central office and from teachers' records within the school for inclusion in these programs. Teachers, counselors, and the facilitator monitor these students and make referrals based on the program criteria. The programs use various methods to encourage student progress and to reward achievement. Students receive incentive awards for academic, behavior, and attendance improvement. Students take field trips to expose them to offerings in the community. Speakers come to the school for demonstrations in their areas of expertise. Periodic outings such as picnics and luncheons foster social skill development. Parent volunteers assist in tutoring and chaperoning events.

Cheryl Reynolds, *Principal, Grades 6–8, 1332 Students*

EXTRACURRICULAR SCHOOL ACTIVITIES

Research studies have consistently indicated that participation in school activities benefits both the students and the school (Christiansen, 1984). Increasingly, student extracurricular activities play an important role in secondary school programs.

It is commonly agreed that extracurricular activities provide a mechanism for the "carryover" skills of life. While participating in student activities, students learn critical lessons in leadership, fellowship, character, communications, teamwork, decision making, self-worth, and individual potential (Biernot and Klesse, 1989).

Following an extensive review of the research on extracurricular activities, Holland and Andre (1987) concluded:

- Participation in extracurricular activities enhances self-esteem. (The state of California is so interested in this aspect of human growth that it has a legislative initiative regarding ways to foster self-esteem in schools and elsewhere.)
- Some extracurricular activities, such as competitive sports, are more successful than other efforts in promoting better race relations among students.
- Extracurricular activities promote positive behavior and establish lifelong habits of civic participation.
- Those who participate in a variety of extracurricular activities tend to have higher grade point averages and higher scores on college entrance examinations (though Holland and Andre skip over the question of which came first).
- Extracurricular participation is related to higher career aspirations and attainment, particularly for boys from lower socioeconomic backgrounds.
- Participation rates are higher in small schools than in large schools. (However, another research project found that the pressure on students to participate is higher in small schools and that there aren't usually enough students to carry out all the activities.)
- Best Schools plan for the success of extracurricular activities as carefully as they plan for daily academic lessons. Regardless of the availability of resources, successful schools recognize the importance of extending learning opportunities. Often, teachers and administrators volunteer their time and energy to help foster a sense of community for their students. The ultimate benefactors of these efforts are the students who learn and mature physically, emotionally, and intellectually under the watchful eye of a caring professional.

THE BEST SCHOOLS–EXTRACURRICULAR ACTIVITIES

Best Schools capitalize on every opportunity to extend student learning and well-being. To this end, many fine extracurricular programs have spawned exciting learning situations for their students. While all Best Schools have recognized the importance of extracurricular programs, several specific strategies are illustrated next.

Extracurricular Activities Illustrations

ELIZABETHTOWN HIGH SCHOOL, KY

Student participation in the life of EHS is encouraged with a monthly in-school activity period, which gives each student the opportunity to belong to at least one club. The offering of intramural athletics encourages students to participate in athletics even though they may not wish to participate in interscholastic sports. In the 1990 self-study, 100% of the student body was involved in at least one club or school activity. Forty-three percent regularly participate in interscholastic sports, and 40% participate in intramural programs.

The school offers the following clubs and activities for students: student council, future business leaders of America, Spanish club, French club, art club, math/computer club, tropical fish club, American field service club, future homemakers of America, Kentucky technology students association, fellowship of Christian athletes, chess club, beta club, students against drunk driving, academic team, mock trial team, *Panther Prowler* (student newspaper), *Etonian* (student yearbook), speech and drama, debate, environmental club, media, concert choir, and band; interscholastic sports—football, soccer, baseball, softball, and boys and girls swimming, cross country, golf, tennis, and track; intramural sports—flag football, volleyball, basketball, and ping-pong; pep club; and cheerleaders.

Special events such as the Belle of Louisville Dance, Sports Recognition Nights, Honors Night, Grad Night, Senior Spaghetti Supper, and Homecoming and Christmas Dances are offered throughout the year. In addition, the student council has been sponsoring mixers after some ball games.

CHERRY CREEK HIGH SCHOOL, ENGLEWOOD, CO

Cherry Creek High School is located in southeast metropolitan Denver. The school has a long tradition of excellence with 85–90% of its graduates attending college; 95% of those attend four-year institutions.

The students at CCHS come primarily from middle- to upper middle-class, professional families in suburban neighborhoods, and a small group comes from a working class, urban attendance area—both share in a strong commitment to the school's direction and achievement. Minority students comprise 7.4% of the student population. Thirteen different cultures and languages are represented in the student population.

CCHS provides a highly diverse program of extracurricular activities, including twenty-three athletic sports, thirteen for girls and eleven for boys; football is coeducational. The staff believes in full student involvement in the athletic program. Consequently, many sports have "no cut" policies, including cross country, football, girls' gymnastics, boys' and girls' tennis, boys' and girls' swimming, boys' and girls' golf, boys' and girls' basketball, baseball, field hockey, boys' and girls' lacrosse, boys' and girls' soccer, and volleyball which have varsity, junior varsity, sophomore, and one or two freshman teams. During the 1991–92 school year, 1670 students participated in athletics, with some athletes playing more than one sport. Overall, 51.5% of the student body participated in athletics during the 1991–92 school year.

Intramural sports are offered throughout the year at CCHS. The 1991–92 participation figures were ninety girls and 375 boys, for a total of 465 participants in six sports.

CCHS also offers a comprehensive activities program of sixty-four different interest clubs, service organizations, and performing groups. A complete list of activities and organizations is available to all students each summer, as well as to incoming freshmen and new students, and is sent to all parents of students new to CCHS. Each club and organization publishes meeting and sign-up information in the student newspaper, student announcements, and on posters in the halls. A review of the 1991–92 activities program reveals that the total enrollment in the activities program exceeded the total enrollment of CCHS, indicating that many students are involved in multiple activities. Nearly 75% of CCHS students are involved in at least one interest club, service organization, or performing group. The activities program is constantly expanding, adding six new clubs in the past year.

Dr. Mary C. Gill, *Principal, Grades 9–12, 2934 Students*

KESLING MIDDLE SCHOOL, LA PORTE, IN

Kesling Middle School is one of two middle schools serving sixth, seventh, and eighth grade students in the LaPorte Community School Corporation located in northwestern Indiana. There are 35,000 residents within the corporation boundaries, with over 22,000 residents in the city of LaPorte. The boundaries enclose 170 square miles, making it one of the largest in the area. Principal industries are farming and manufacturing.

Kesling's student population of approximately 750 comes from all levels of the socioeconomic scale. Three-fourths of these students are bus students. Free and reduced lunch students average 24% of the student population. About 10% of the student population changes during the average school year.

The school community values the positive impact of a comprehensive program of extramural activities. Twelve academic competition teams involve over 100 students. An additional 180 students participated in the National Geography Bee, Handwriting Contest, Spelling Bees, and the Indiana Math League during the 1991–92 school year. During this same period, club participation included seventy-eight students in the chess club, twenty-three students in the math club, and fifty-one students in the art club. Athletic participation included sixty-three girls in volleyball; sixty-eight boys in football; fifteen students in co-educational cross country; twenty students in wrestling; forty-eight boys and sixty-seven girls in basketball; thirty-two boys and twenty-two girls in co-educational soccer; and eighteen boys and fifty-six girls in track. Kesling has started a strong intramural program in the 1992–93 school year with flag football, basketball, and volleyball. Although participation in extracurricular activity is widespread among the student population, the hope is to get students who are not involved in other extracurricular programs positively involved in intramurals.

Student participation and the importance of participation are emphasized in orientations and in newsletters. A year-ending awards program for each grade level recognizes those students involved in extracurriculars. Participation is encouraged by a no-cut rule in all sixth grade athletics; a no-cut policy in all seventh and eighth grade athletics, with the exception of basketball and volleyball (because of gymnasium limitations); open club participation; and open academic team participation.

James A. Rubush, *Principal, Grades 6–8 , 753 Students*

STUDENT DISCIPLINE POLICIES AND PROCEDURES

Establishing and maintaining an orderly school and classroom is a primary determinant of teaching success, yet more and more of our youth go to school afraid; they are forced to deal with frequent disruptions, the threat of bodily harm, and pressure to use illegal substances. In a recent student survey conducted by the National Education Goals Panel (1993), direct measures of school discipline characteristics were reported. These included the following:

- In 1992, the majority of students in grades 8 and 10 reported that student disruptions were fairly common occurrences in their classes. About half of the students estimated that disruptions occurred only occasionally (five times a week or less), but 11–15% of the students reported that teachers interrupted class twenty times a week or more to deal with student misbehavior. About one in twenty eighth and tenth graders reported that other students interfered with their own learning at least twenty times a week.
- Skipping school and classes is a fairly common practice among eighth, tenth, and twelfth graders, according to student reports. Between 1990 and 1992, the percentage of twelfth graders who skipped class increased. Increases were most prevalent among black students.
- Substantial numbers of eighth, tenth, and twelfth graders continue to be victims of violent acts, theft, and vandalism at school, according to student reports. Over one-third of all students report that other students at their school belong to fighting gangs.
- In 1992, 9% of eighth graders, 10% of tenth graders, and 6% of twelfth graders reported that they had brought a weapon to school at least once during the previous month. The percentages of students, by grade, who habitually carried a weapon (ten or more days in the previous month) were 2%, 4%, and 3%, respectively.

- Sizable proportions of students and their parents report that they take one or more precautions to ensure students' personal safety at school or on the way to or from school. Staying in a group and staying away from certain places in school were the precautions most frequently cited by students; talking to students about ways to avoid trouble and setting limits on the amount of money taken to school were the precautions most frequently cited by parents.
- In 1992, one in ten eighth graders, nearly one in five tenth graders, and nearly one in four twelfth graders reported that they had been approached at school by someone trying to sell or give them drugs during the previous year.

Classroom and school discipline has continued to be a concern for children, educators, and the public for many years. For children, concerns range from loss of opportunity for learning to simply physical danger. For teachers, discipline problems are a serious threat to their ability to do their jobs and, in some cases, provide a fear. For the public at large, as evidenced in most public opinion polls (e.g., Gallup, 1992), discipline in schools continues to be viewed as the most significant problem confronting schools today.

Promoting effective discipline in the school requires a comprehensive program supported by everyone in the entire school community. As with all other aspects in successful schools, discipline programs are based on sound research and development. They are characterized by high expectations for teachers to systematically apply agreed-upon strategies and consistently administer the discipline code. Moreover, successful schools take the initiative to appropriately sensitize and train staff as to the nature of effective discipline in the classroom and throughout the school.

School discipline has two main goals: 1) to ensure safety of students and staff and 2) to create an environment conducive for learning. Serious student misconduct involving violent or criminal behavior defeats these goals and often makes headlines in the process. However, the most common discipline problems involve noncriminal student behavior (Moles, 1989).

Effective school discipline strategies should teach responsible behavior and self-discipline, as well as discourage misconduct. Blendinger (1993) describes a "Win-Win Discipline" system that embodies the following characteristics: 1) developing a discipline plan, 2) establishing classroom rules, 3) determining consequences for violating rules, 4) recognizing and celebrating good behavior, and 5) involving parents in their children's behavior.

Curwin and Mendler (1988) speak to three integrated dimensions of discipline that should be established as the cornerstone of the school's discipline program:

(1) *The prevention dimension:* what the teacher can do to actively prevent problems. To a large degree, these strategies are aimed at attacking problems long before they arise, through intensive organization and planning. In the classroom, they include (but are not limited to) the establishing and reinforcement of clear expectations for appropriate behavior; the maintenance of a positive classroom climate; provision for interesting, relevant, instructional activities; the development and communication of classroom routines; the monitoring of students within small groups and during other nondirected times; and involvement of parents in the development and implementation of classroom procedures.

From a schoolwide perspective, the selection of a schoolwide program is often difficult, yet consistent, uniform, total school discipline programs can have a positive effect on student behavior and performance. Often, successful schools have embraced a system to help systematize expectations for student behavior. A popular example is the use of assertive discipline (Canter and Canter, 1976), which emphasizes systematic reinforcement of clearly communicated classroom requirements. Assertive discipline requires teachers to take the following steps (MacNaughton and Johns, 1991):

– Make clear that they will not tolerate anyone preventing them from teaching, stopping learning, or doing anything else that is not in the best interest of the class, the individual, or the teacher.

- Instruct students clearly and in specific terms about what behaviors are desired and what behaviors are not tolerated.
- Plan positive and negative consequences for predetermined acceptable or unacceptable behavior.
- Plan positive reinforcement for compliance. Reinforcements include verbal acknowledgement, notes, free time for talking, and, of course, tokens that can be exchanged for appropriate rewards.
- Plan a sequence of steps to punish noncompliance. These range from writing a youngster's name on the board to sending the student to the principal's office.

(2) *The action dimension:* what actions the teacher can take when, in spite of all the steps taken to prevent discipline problems, they still occur. There are many approaches that can be utilized to stop minor discipline problems before they escalate into situations that increase loss of instructional time and precipitate the need for direct (often negative) teacher intervention. Cummings (1983) provides an approach for dealing with minor classroom disturbances that fills the gap between simply ignoring the student's inappropriate behavior and forceful, negative intervention. This approach organizes teacher response on a continuum using behaviors that take relatively little time and create little interruption to the learning environment (i.e., eye contact, physical closeness, etc.). The goals of this continuum of choices are:

- to maintain a positive feeling tone in the classroom
- to maximize time on task
- to present the teacher as a positive role model
- to avoid students generalized negative feelings toward teacher, school, and district

Palandy (1993) has identified intervention strategies that he believes should be in every teacher's repertoire:

- Nonverbal techniques, particularly at the beginning stages of misbehavior, can be an effective way of letting students know that one (or all) of them had better settle down. Eye contact, body posture, facial expressions, etc., are typical examples of effective nonverbal strategies.
- Exercise proximity control by walking up to and simply standing beside (and possibly putting your hand on a shoulder) the misbehaving student.
- Remove the source of a disturbance by either taking away the items (such as rubber bands, food, etc.) that may be involved in the misbehavior or permit the misbehavior to "run its course" by permitting a brief period of indulgence.
- Point out the consequences of misbehavior. Clearly, this is most effective when the "right" consequence can be matched with the student(s).
- Behavior modification techniques using a systematized reinforcement (as described earlier) can be an effective intervention strategy.
- Isolation of misbehaving students by asking them to leave the room or to go to the "time-out corner" can be effective in providing an angry student a chance to "cool off."

Punishment can be a necessary and, at times, effective intervention strategy. But when punishment is considered, certain principles must be kept in mind:

- Punishment should be used sparingly; the more often it is used, the less effective it becomes.
- Punishment should never constitute retaliation.

– Subject matter should never be used as punishment.
– ''Mass punishment'' is almost always ineffective.
– Corporal punishment should *never* be used.

The principal has a most significant role in ensuring a safe, orderly and productive learning environment. His/her primary role is to mobilize the students, parents, and teachers toward the establishment of high expectations, appropriate reinforcements, and, of course, a discipline code that clearly communicates consequences of student misbehavior. In addition, the principal must insist that students learn to understand that they must assume responsibility for their actions and, hopefully, learn the importance of the relationship between appropriate behavior and success in school.

The principal, parents or guardians, and teachers must collaboratively demonstrate to the students that adults at home and at school share the same expectations. The simple belief that deference, civility, courtesy, accountability, and respect are mutual behaviors to be reinforced in the home and school is the common ground on which conflicts are resolved and the teacher-learning process is elevated. The principal's responsibility includes working with misbehaving students and their parents to teach both, if necessary, that authority, civility, courtesy, and accountability are critical to everyone's interests (Hartzell and Petrie, 1992).

(3) *The resolution dimension:* what the teacher can do to resolve problems with chronic rule breaker(s) and the extreme, ''out-of-control'' student. Reaching these students requires a great deal of effort, with no real guarantee that there will be a truly effective resolution. General strategies can be characterized as in-house interventions and outside referral.

In-house strategies, like those described in the previous sections related to at-risk students, can, if systematically applied, have significant impact on modifying the behavior of chronic disciplinary problems. Common strategies include individual counseling, mentorships, and customized classroom strategies, such as modified assignments, peer tutors, or cooperative learning.

Unfortunately, in-house strategies are not always adequate to meet the complex school and often family needs of the student. Thus, referral to the district child study (special education) team and, at times, referral to outside social service agencies may be required. It is important, if a referral strategy is pursued, that the parent is involved in all stages of the resolution process. This is increasingly important because, many times, a child's behavioral problems in school are (at least in part) a function of family dynamics.

THE BEST SCHOOLS–DISCIPLINE POLICIES

Our nation has reinforced the need for schools to systematically address discipline in our schools. To this end, Goal 6 of our National Goals for Education states, ''By the year 2000, every school in America will be free of drugs and violence and will offer a disciplined environment conducive to learning.'' To attain this goal, Best Schools have planned, organized, and implemented effective discipline standards and procedures. They have committed to effective pupil management as a cornerstone to student learning and school effectiveness. In addition, they have taken the time to provide the necessary training to the staff to optimize staff involvement, develop common goals, and establish uniform behavioral expectations for all students. Examples from Best School's disciplinary strategies and programs that reflect the concepts and practices reviewed above are illustrated next.

Discipline Illustrations

CENTURY HIGH SCHOOL, BISMARCK, ND

Century High School is one of three high schools in Bismarck Public School District. Bismarck is the largest school district in North Dakota, with over 11,000 students, K–12.

The student population at Century High School reflects the Bismarck community as a whole–largely middle-class with no large concentration of ethnic groups. Overall, Century High School boasts a stable student population: last year, 91% of the members of the graduating class had begun their high school educations at Century at least three years earlier; furthermore, the attendance rate for the past three years has exceeded 97%.

In general, the discipline policy of the Bismarck School District "recognizes that effective discipline is intended to foster student growth while assuring each student an acceptable environment in which to learn." To that end, Century High School promotes a positive, preventative, and consistent approach to student discipline.

The school produces a student handbook, in which all rules affecting student discipline and attendance are outlined for students. The assistant principal visits all English classes and distributes the handbook to the students. At that time, he explains rules and consequences and answers student questions. Consequences for rule violations usually involve in-school detention–usually held on Monday nights from 3:30 to 6:30 P.M.–or out-of-school suspension. Usually ten to fifteen students are assigned to in-school detention each week; rarely is more than one student suspended out-of-school each week. Expulsion, as an extreme consequence, is never used. All students, regardless of the offense, are granted due process rights. Parents are informed at each step and, depending on the offense, are involved in conferences with either the assistant principal or the guidance counselors.

Students whose conduct proves to be incorrigible are referred to the student assistance team. The student assistance team is then able to establish linkages and make referrals to appropriate school or community agencies for assistance.

Jeffrey Geiger, *Principal, Grades 10–12, 819 Students*

ROCKFORD MIDDLE SCHOOL, ROCKFORD, MI

The Rockford School District is the fastest growing school district in the state of Michigan's fast-growing Kent County. The district covers 100 square miles and is located in the northeast corner of the county, ten miles north of Grand Rapids. Considered a suburban district, it truly is a rural district, with 75% of the students being bused.

The discipline of Rockford Middle School is designed to motivate students to make better choices and decisions. If it becomes apparent that one mode of discipline is not effective, others will be tried. The first step, involving minor behavioral problems, is teacher contact with the parent(s). Major discipline problems are dealt with immediately and contact with parents made after the fact (i.e., smoking, fighting, disrespectful conduct, etc.). The discipline philosophy is based on three general goals: 1) to provide an effective learning environment for all students at Rockford Middle School; 2) to provide students with a safe learning environment; and 3) to have students show respect for school property, student property, and all people at Rockford Middle School. Discipline procedures used range from parent contact and student/teacher discussions to noon-hour detention, detention assignments, Saturday detentions, and in-school and/or out-of-school suspension.

The school believes that it is important that parents, staff, and students work together to maintain a positive, educational atmosphere. The goal is that each student learn to be responsible for his or her own actions. Every student and staff member has a right to personal safety and freedom to learn; consistency for both administration and staff is held as a high priority.

There are five basic disciplinary actions available to teachers and administrators, which are listed next.

- *Demerit system:* Behavioral demerits are given to any student who violates school rules. A student who receives three demerits (and every third demerit thereafter) is issued a before- or after-school detention. Demerit examples are chewing gum; eating candy, cough drops, etc.; locker misconduct; classroom misconduct; cafeteria misconduct; inappropriate hallway behavior; tardiness (second and thereafter); failure to return signed progress report, inappropriate language; disrespect to school personnel, and harassing/mistreating another person.
- *Behavioral detentions:* Behavioral detentions are given to any student who fails to comply with school rules. A student is expected to act in a respectful manner. Students who receive three detentions (including any demerit detentions) in a nine-week period receive a one-day in-school suspension. These detentions are accumulative for a nine-week period. Appropriate counseling may take place following the first behavior detentions. Detention examples are profanity, major classroom disruption, or any behavioral act considered inappropriate by our school community.
- *Academic detentions:* Academic detentions are given at the discretion of the classroom teacher. These detentions are served with the issuing teacher. Academic detentions are not counted as behavior detentions.
- *Saturday detentions:* Saturday detentions are alternatives to suspension and are assigned by the principal or assistant principal only. When a student is assigned a Saturday detention, he/she reports to the assigned detention at 9:00 A.M. and is required to study until 12:00 noon. Saturday detentions are assigned to students for improper behavior that warrants firm disciplinary action.
- *In-school suspension:* Upon the third behavioral detention (and every third detention thereafter) a student receives a full-day in-school suspension. Detentions are accumulative for a nine-week period; parents are notified prior to the day students are serving this suspension.

James Jay Husford, *Principal, Grades 7–8, 896 Students*

BENJAMIN E. BANNEKER HIGH SCHOOL, COLLEGE PARK, GA

Banneker High School was created in 1988 as a result of a merger of two existing schools. The student population is predominately African-American (99%), and the students come from homes that range from high to low socioeconomic levels. The school is committed to maintaining a safe and orderly environment conducive to learning and student well-being.

The discipline policy at Banneker High School is consistent with the discipline policy established by the Fulton County Board of Education, which categorizes behavior infractions as minor, major, or critical. At the beginning of the school year, each student is given a discipline brochure published by the central office, as well as a Banneker handbook, which outlines behavioral expectations.

When discipline referrals are handled by any administrator, the "3F policy" is followed—firm, fair, and friendly. While staff may dislike a behavior, the worth of every student is never in question.

In August 1990, students made a commitment to improve their behavior and improve their school's discipline reputation. During the 1988–89 year, twenty-three students were referred to the discipline tribunal to respond to major infractions. In 1989–90, the number rose to twenty-five. After the commitment was made, only nine students were referred to the tribunal, and in 1991–92, the number dropped to three students, one of the lowest in the county. The number of students suspended has dropped from 361 in 1989–90 to 180 in 1991–92.

To address the issue of violence, the student government association developed a "Stop the Violence" campaign, held each January. During this week, students hear speakers, "rap" with other schools, write essays, and develop programs to address the serious problem of violence. Because of the success of the program, the "Stop the Violence" campaign has been expanded to all Fulton County high schools.

The improvement in school climate is a tribute to the maturity and commitment of students and to the many dedicated teachers who have worked to create a learning environment that discourages negative behavior.

Hansell Gunn, *Principal, Grades 9–12, 1202 Students*

THE PREVENTION OF DRUG AND ALCOHOL ABUSE

Drug and alcohol abuse in America's schools is an issue that has received much deserved national attention. Making every school in America free of drugs by the year 2000 is a major part of the sixth National Education Goal. While recent studies have shown a slight decline in drug abuse among high school students, more than one-third of all high school students have used some form of illicit drug (National Institute on Drug Abuse, 1991). More than one-fourth of all students report that beer or wine, liquor, and marijuana are easy to obtain at school or on school grounds. The vast majority of students report never being under the influence of alcohol or other drugs while at school; however, about one-third of all students report that they have witnessed other students high on drugs or drunk at school.

Although alcohol and other drugs are rarely used at school, overall use is much higher. In 1992, more than three-fourths of twelfth graders used alcohol during the previous year, and almost one-fourth used marijuana, according to student reports. However, overall student use has continued to decline since the early 1980s (National Education Goals Panel, 1993).

Schools have a legal, as well as a moral, responsibility to provide a safe school environment. Federal law requires schools to fight substance abuse on campus and the Drug Free Schools and Communities Act Amendment of 1989 requires educational institutions to adopt and implement programs and policies to prevent the unlawful possession, use, or distribution of illicit drugs and alcohol by students and employees.

To meet the legal, social, and educational responsibilities associated with substance abuse, successful schools across the country have implemented comprehensive prevention programs. In a meta-analysis of secondary school drug prevention programs, Tobler (1986) identified five basic modalities on which prevention programs were based:

(1) Programs that focus on knowledge and information
(2) Programs that focus on attitude change and the psychological side of drug abuse
(3) Programs that focus on both knowledge and attitude change
(4) Programs that focus on peer relationships
(5) Programs that focus on alternatives to drug use

While controlling student drug and alcohol use is difficult, schools can play a significant and positive role. Because the problem is complex, only a multifaceted program will be effective. Expectations for the program must recognize limitations, since no school program will prevent all substance abuse. The basic strategies available to the school include the following (Ogden and Germinario, 1988):

- effective teaching of decision-making skills, negative peer resistance skills, and facts concerning the dangers of drugs/alcohol
- setting tough policies, guidelines, and procedures that make it clear to students, staff, and parents that drug/alcohol use will not be tolerated
- training staff to recognize and act upon signs of drug/alcohol use
- providing opportunities for students to seek help for themselves or others

- establishing a proactive plan and procedures for identifying students with problems and assisting them to get help
- developing a plan for working with parents as a group and with parents of individual students
- establishing procedures and plans for working with community groups
- establishing a procedure for confrontation, complete with penalties, to get help for students who resist assistance or whose parents resist assistance
- enforcing the penalties for drug/alcohol use or sale established by the school board and law
- establishing procedures for working with the police
- building strong working relationships with outside agencies that provide therapy and support programs for addicted students
- providing group and individual support for school-related problems for students returning from treatment
- providing as much support as possible to all students so they will succeed academically and socially in the school environment

Horton (1992) identifies factors working against effective drug programs, which include myths about drugs (especially alcohol); mixed messages students receive from their parents, teachers, and other adults; negative adolescent peer pressure; seductive messages from the media; and erroneous, even dangerous, messages contained in some drug education materials. Further, he identifies several key components that, if attended in proper sequence, will help to minimize program impediments and help ensure program success. These components include 1) the organization of a unified community involvement; 2) a schoolwide articulation of program goals; 3) a strong focus on "gateway drugs" such as alcohol, tobacco, and marijuana; 4) systematic inservice training for teachers; 5) the mobilization of positive peer influence; 6) parent networking to support parents homebound efforts; and 7) ongoing evaluation mechanisms built into the program.

THE BEST SCHOOLS–DRUG AND ALCOHOL ABUSE PREVENTION

Essential to the development and implementation of a drug/alcohol prevention, intervention, and treatment program is the formulation and adoption by the board of education of a *policy* on drug and alcohol use. The policy protects the staff, by making it clear who is to do what, under what conditions. The policy makes it clear to students that drug and alcohol use will not be tolerated and what the consequences will be if they break the rules. The very existence of a clear policy is an initial step in assisting students to resist negative peer pressure. In schools in which it is recognized that penalties will be imposed for drug/alcohol use, it gives students another valid excuse for saying "no."

Policy needs to be built on federal and state law and precedent cases. In general, all boards of education have the responsibility for the health and safety of students. All states have laws concerning the use and distribution of controlled substances. Cases heard by the Supreme Court have also clarified the rights of schools, for example, to conduct searches when there are "reasonable grounds" for suspicion that a student has violated the law or school rules. The Comprehensive Crime Control Act of 1984 makes it a federal crime to sell drugs in or near a school. Before developing a policy and procedures, state laws should be reviewed. In many states, the department of education has gathered the pertinent laws together and made them available to school districts. Some states have mandated that districts adopt a policy concerning the use of controlled substances and have developed model policies. Whether a district starts from scratch or adapts/adopts a state sample policy, the district solicitor should review the policy before it is adopted by the board of education. The policy should make explicit (Ogden and Germinario, 1988):

- that drug/alcohol use will not be tolerated
- that it is the staff's responsibility to act on information concerning drug/alcohol use by students
- that the staff will be "held harmless" for reporting information concerning the use of or distribution of drugs/alcohol
- to whom and when information on drug/alcohol use or distribution is to be reported
- what procedures the school will follow to confirm the use or distribution of drugs
- if and how drug testing will be required and under what conditions
- drug/alcohol prevention curriculum requirements, grades K–12
- in cases of suspected distribution or sale, when and by whom the police will be informed
- that the use of drugs/alcohol by students constitutes a physical and mental risk to students and that information cannot be kept confidential and must be reported
- that not only do parents have the right to know that their child is suspected or known to be using a controlled substance, but they have the primary responsibility for treatment
- that lockers and personal possessions will be searched when there are "reasonable grounds" to suspect violations of school rules or laws
- what the school penalties will be for using, possessing, distributing, or selling drugs/alcohol
- what requirements the board will make concerning assessment and treatment as a condition of reentry into the school
- what assistance the school will make available to students concerned with drug/alcohol issues and for assistance during and after treatment
- what the roles of the student assistance team, counselors, administrators, and nurses will be in confirming suspected drug/alcohol use, abuse, distribution, or sale
- what medical procedures should be followed if a student appears to be physically at risk
- what the relationship is between the schools and public and private agencies, treatment centers, and hospitals

Finally, as with all other school programs, drug/alcohol prevention initiatives must be formulated with the staff and community. Additionally, systematic training for staff is critical in areas related to implementation of the drug prevention curriculum, identification of drug-related risk behavior, the standards and procedures set forth in board policy, and knowledge of appropriate referral services for those students (and/or families) that may be drug involved.

The illustrations of Best Schools' practices that successfully integrate school and community resources are provided next.

Drug and Alcohol Abuse Prevention Illustrations

MOHAVE MIDDLE SCHOOL, SCOTTSDALE, AZ

Mohave is one of five middle schools in the Scottsdale School District No. 48. Mohave initiated the innovative "house" concept in the fall of 1990. The "house" system creates small communities of learning. Teachers work with students in teams in these "schools-within-a-school" to promote cooperative learning, eliminate tracking, and establish flexibility in instruction. Mohave consists of thirteen buildings on a spacious campus, which is widely used by the community. The population of Mohave Middle School is 93% Caucasian and 7% African-American, Asian, Mexican-American, and Native American. The socioeconomic level ranges from lower- to upper-class. Daily student attendance was 93.6% during the 1991–92 school year, with 20% new enrollees and 15% withdrawals.

Mohave has programs for anti-drug use initiatives through a prevention team consisting of four staff members and a parent. This team works with the administration to establish an annual plan for prevention. The main focus is prevention activities, which are presented by teachers, parent volunteers, high school students, and other professional people within the community. Activities that enhance positive self-image and decision-making skills in students can often provide the turning point for students trying to find that place in which they feel they "fit in." These activities include the "after hours" program, peer mediation, leadership academy, student council, national junior honor society, and on-campus extracurricular activities. Over 65% of students are involved in these activities. Other examples of activities offered are Red Ribbon Week (drug awareness), alcohol presentation by a local hospital trauma unit, and a young lawyers' presentation, which addresses alcohol and substance abuse and how the law relates to teens.

The police liaison officer, funded by the city and school district, works very closely with the staff by making classroom presentations related to substance abuse and gang activity. Scottsdale Prevention Institute, a community-based organization, works with students referred for alcohol and other illegal substances by offering parent/adolescent counseling classes on Saturdays.

Dr. Carol Erickson, *Principal, Grades 7–8, 523 Students*

FORT CAMPBELL HIGH SCHOOL, FORT CAMPBELL, KY

Fort Campbell High School is a unique educational institution serving a transient military population. The mission of 101st Airborne (Air Assault) Division contributes to a highly mobile lifestyle and high student turnover. It is rare for a student to complete three or four years of high school at FCHS. The school experiences an approximate 35% turnover in student population each calendar year. Approximately 61% of the students qualify for the free or reduced lunch program. The parents of the students hold a military rank from the lower enlisted to the commanding general of Fort Campbell. However, the most distinctive feature of FCHS is that it is one of only two high schools entirely for United States Army dependent students in the continental United States. The community has a highly diverse ethnic composition, with English spoken as a second language in approximately 15% of the homes.

FCHS supports the national goal of maintaining a drug-free, safe, learning environment through current policies and procedures. All students are required to take health education and other courses that offer a comprehensive unit of study on substance abuse. Additionally, the unique position as a high school on a military installation where personnel are drug tested regularly impacts their drug-free emphasis. Military police and criminal investigation personnel monitor all school-sponsored events, and once students are admitted to an activity, they are not permitted to leave and reenter. Additionally, guidance counselors work closely with the post drug and alcohol unit counseling services.

Each spring, the school clinic sponsors a health fair during which health-care professionals from the civilian and military community provide information about substance abuse and sample health-care products and perform basic function testing (i.e., blood pressure and cholesterol).

To prevent traditional post-prom festivities, FCHS and parent volunteers sponsor Project Prom. Students participate in a closely supervised activity. Guest speakers, consultants for classes, and assemblies are conducted throughout the school year to emphasize the need for and benefits of a drug-free life.

Dr. J. Gary Stewart, *Principal, Grades 9–12, 643 Students*

ASSUMPTION HIGH SCHOOL, LOUISVILLE, KY

Assumption High School is a private, Catholic secondary school for girls in grades 9–12. It is sponsored by the Sisters of Mercy of the Americas. Assumption serves over 700 young women who come primarily from Louisville and Jefferson County. Students represent a wide range of socioeconomic levels, with 14% receiving financial aid.

In the community, Assumption has a reputation for being a school that stresses the individual needs of the student and that has high student expectations, a caring, professional faculty, effective administrative leadership, and strong parental support and involvement.

The school maintains a clear "no-use" message in its policies and prevention programs. Prevention programs include an "affective skills development" course, which is offered to freshmen to help in the development of personal power (ability to choose thoughts and actions to achieve results) and to make responsible life choices. Objectives of the course are to help students develop the ability to claim self-esteem, act responsibly, relate effectively, and solve problems and set goals. Additionally, the "talking with students about alcohol" curriculum is taught in all health education classes.

Sophomores, juniors, and seniors receive a five- to eight-day course supervised and evaluated by the community alcohol/drug abuse agency. Parents are invited to a four-session "talking with your children about alcohol" program and are encouraged to join a parent network that supports supervision and alcohol-free teen parties. Parent education is provided by community speakers and student assistance counselors.

A "no-use" message is promoted in the students high on life club, which promotes a healthy life without alcohol and other drug use. Peer leaders are selected from this group to facilitate small groups in the prevention-education program. These juniors and seniors make a "no-use" commitment.

The school participates in the Kentucky drug-free program, Champions, sending students to teen leadership conferences and having counselors present workshops in AWARE, a drug-free community program. The counselors are members of a coalition for community-parent education on drug and alcohol issues.

Karen Russ, *Principal, Grades 9–12, 766 Students*

INVOLVEMENT OF STUDENTS IN THE DEVELOPMENT OF SCHOOL POLICY

Educators' decisions affect the lives of students, and it is for this reason that input from students about their school life is important. A major concern of educators is that students will make irresponsible decisions, but experience shows that they will make excellent decisions when guided in the decision-making process by caring and open adults. To establish an environment that encourages students to value their school experience, schools must increasingly involve them in important decision-making efforts. There are many benefits to be derived from student involvement in decision making. For example, student involvement helps develop social skills, promotes an appreciation of democratic action, and promotes creativity and independent thought and action.

Decision making should be viewed as a deliberate process that can be taught as a basic classroom skill. Typically, six steps are embodied in systematic decision making: 1) identifying the problem or issue, 2) exploring the many alternatives available to resolve the problem/issue, 3) evaluating the plausibility of each solution, 4) making the decision/choice, 5) defending (justifying) the decision, and 6) acting and evaluating.

The school's primary function in teaching decision-making skills is to encourage and help the students to effectively use their abilities and insights in making their own decisions. This means that the school staff must approach the teaching of decision-making skills without any preconceptions or ready-made answers (Stewart, 1989). Thus, to successfully involve students in school decision making, teachers and administrators must:

- be willing to let the pupils share in making decisions and to have a "piece of the action"
- see themselves as members of the group, rather than the final authority on all topics
- free themselves of any feelings that the pupils will "run the class"
- be a helper and guide, rather than merely a transmitter of facts
- create a relaxed classroom atmosphere in which the pupils feel secure in being themselves
- be accepting of all the pupils' responses and recognize that each response has legitimacy and worth

THE BEST SCHOOLS–STUDENT INVOLVEMENT IN POLICY

Best Schools have created opportunities for students to actively influence school policy. Through the systematic learning of decision-making skills, students have been able to effectively access their school's improvement efforts. With these efforts, students have achieved greater ownership in goals of their schools, developed a greater sense of trust in the adults around them, and have obtained and practiced an extremely important life skill.

A wide range of strategies have been utilized by Best Schools to increase student decisional involvement. Following are several examples.

Student Policy Involvement Illustrations

ROCHESTER ADAMS HIGH SCHOOL, ROCHESTER HILLS, MN

Adams serves a thirty square mile suburban/rural area. Throughout the past two decades, the population within the school sending areas has increased over 50%. To accommodate the representative growth in student population, several facility expansion and enhancement projects have been undertaken. The expectation of the majority of our parents and students is that graduates will continue their education beyond high school (follow-up studies indicate that nearly all do).

Over 1700 students attend the school, which includes a racial/ethnic composition of 94% Caucasian, 2% African-American, 3% Asian-American, and 1% Hispanic.

Students are encouraged to be leaders through student council, club council, the Adams Coming Together (ACT), and representation on the school board. The school's philosophy encourages student involvement; this has been especially evident in the school improvement process. Student input was gathered, and the data provided direction for goal setting. Students were then asked to be a part of the committees that set school improvement goals. Students also serve on interview committees for all hirings.

Recently, Adams established a club council, made up of representatives from all clubs, class officers, and student council. Club council has tackled such issues as campus beautification, recycling, raising funds for the homeless, and it provides communication among the clubs themselves.

The ACT program seeks student input on a variety of issues. Typical issues to be discussed in homerooms are locker assignments, closed campus, and lunchroom procedures. This program provides a voice for all students.

The Student Court involves students in discipline problems. If a student involved in a discipline situation disagrees with the disposition of the administration, he/she may take the issue to a special session of student court, made up of students who take the role of judge, attorneys, and jurors. The court hears the case and then makes a decision to uphold the disposition of the administration or to reduce the consequence.

Caye Randolph, *Principal, Grades 9–12, 1739 Students*

BOZEMAN HIGH SCHOOL, BOZEMAN, MT

Bozeman High School is a four-year, comprehensive high school accredited by the Northwest Accrediting Association and the Montana Office of Public Instruction. The high school district covers approximately 1100 square miles in and surrounding the city of Bozeman, situated in the Gallatin Valley of southwestern Montana.

The school serves a predominately middle-class, white collar type community. The school has experienced a steady increase in student population, which has brought more diversity to the student population.

Students exercise great influence on school policies and practices in recent years. Recently, the district established a superintendent's student advisory committee, comprised of representatives from all groups and types of students in the population. A special effort is made to include non-mainstream students—those who typically remain uninvolved in school activities and student government and who, therefore, have little voice in decision making processes. This advisory committee meets with the district superintendent over lunch once a month; there is no structured agenda and students are promised anonymity and are encouraged to speak candidly on any issues which concern them. Changes which have come about through this process include revising the school attendance and grading policies, restructuring the counseling services, and easing the social pressures surrounding the prom and homecoming dance.

Officers of the student council meet with the high school principal every week. This forum permits students to have input on school policy matters on a regular basis. One recent incident that illustrates student influence concerned the selection of a speaker for this spring's graduation address. Student council officers indicated that they would prefer a speaker from outside of the school staff. This suggestion was accepted, and the school administration arranged for Montana's Senator Baucus to speak in the spring. However, student representatives expressed an interest in another speaker and took the initiative to invite NBC news anchor Tom Brokaw. The school administration yielded to the students' preference.

In addition to their input on high school matters, students also exert influence on the school board. Two students sit as nonvoting members of the board and are regularly involved by expressing student concerns and suggestions.

Lou Gappmayer, *Principal, Grades 9–12, 1375 Students*

BISHOP HENDRICKEN HIGH SCHOOL, WARWICK, RI

Bishop Hendricken High School is a Roman Catholic, college preparatory school for young men. It is conducted by the Congregation of Christian Brothers on behalf of the Diocese of Providence. The school is accredited by the New England Association of Schools and Colleges and the state of Rhode Island. Most of the students are from middle-class to upper-class suburban families. The community in which the school is located has similar demographics.

As part of the Bishop Hendricken High School community, students must be part of the collaborative effort to create the Christian environment that is essential to the school's uniqueness. Therefore, they have initiated the following programs:

- The principal meets every other week with the student council leaders to solicit input and to listen to concerns.
- The principal meets with all seniors in small groups to listen to concerns and to discuss his vision for the school. In addition, every senior participates in a "perceptionnaire," which asks for additional input and suggestions.
- Homeroom representatives receive input from their fellow students and share them with the administration during student council meetings.
- Juniors are encouraged to apply to participate in the peer ministry program. The candidates who are accepted as peer ministers work in a student retreat program and are in a good position to share student concerns with the chaplain.
- As part of the board of directors' strategic planning process, focus groups are formed

from all constituencies; among these groups are several student focus groups that have an opportunity to share in the planning for Hendricken's future.

Brother James A. Liquori, *Principal, Grades 9–12, 689 Students*

THE DEVELOPMENT OF SOUND CHARACTER

It is generally agreed that schools should be involved in teaching moral values and developing good character in students. In the not-too-distant past, many schools adopted a neutral position on the issues related to the teaching of values and character. Presently, increasing numbers of schools have aggressively accepted this challenge because of concerns about increasing moral problems in society, including issues related to youth violence, teen pregnancy, and drug abuse.

If morality and character can be effectively taught, Americans seem anxious for schools to get involved in the development of programs. At least thirty-one states have adopted guidelines offering encouragement and technical assistance aimed at developing courses aimed at teaching aspects of "accepted old-fashioned values," with the expectation of producing concerned citizens who will be proactive in the preservation of our democracy.

While moral education may be considered whatever schools do to influence how students think, feel, or act regarding issues of right and wrong (Association of Supervision and Curriculum Development, 1988), no universally agreed upon list of values or virtues to be taught to students exists. Yet it is not unusual for educators to present such lists as the cornerstone of program development. Although, on the surface, lists have public appeal containing such concepts as honesty, courtesy, and hard work, Lockwood (1991) has identified several problems with this approach. First, the relationship between values and behavior is exceedingly complex. Listing values often gives the misleading impression that the relationship is simple and direct. A second problem is that lists do not indicate when or to what degree one should implement the values or virtues. He describes, for example, obedience to legitimate authority as usually appearing on character education lists. Yet, at times, following this rule could be problematic. For example, "Imagine a twelve-year-old girl attending her father's fruit stand while he takes her ailing mother to the hospital. A uniformed police officer strolls by and says, 'Give me one of those apples.' The girl realizes her father can barely make ends meet. What should she do?" (Lockwood, 1991, p. 24).

While the goals of moral and character education in America's schools may be diverse, most curriculum writers would agree that a fundamental element of a program would include the development of students who understand what morality is, who are able to think in a moral way using good reasons, and who act accordingly. A second goal is to heighten students' moral awareness, enabling them to recognize moral issues and moral situations. A third goal is to develop improved moral reasoning skills (Yeazell and Cole, 1986).

To be successful, moral/character education programs must reflect the values and characteristics of its community. While programs differ, Heller (1989) identifies the examples of components of many programs:

- a policy statement outlining the program's educational philosophy and instructional goals, plus a code of ethics for students, teachers, and administrators; rules of student conduct, with consequences for violations; a code of sportsmanship; and a handbook of student rights
- an understanding that staff and school support personnel will be seen as role models for students
- a heavy involvement of parents

- extensive community involvement, perhaps including community service projects
- a study of the Constitution and crucial court decisions bearing on the rights and responsibilities of citizenship, featured in grade meetings, assemblies, and student council sessions
- activities to build class and school spirit, including volunteer service on school projects
- programs and activities aimed at developing self-esteem
- student activities in the school and in the community that promote wider friendships
- a study of religions and religious principles
- an emphasis on academic excellence
- family life and sex education
- a program of competitive events for individuals and groups that emphasizes cooperation, as well as competition, and involves awards and other recognition
- a human relations program that, among other things, explores equal opportunity and the elimination of discrimination and promotes student/staff rapport and mutual respect
- a drug education program
- an exploration of Constitutional, personal, and public values
- counseling, health services, and other forms of student assistance
- mentorships
- opportunities to practice real-life moral behavior
- appropriate moral education training for teachers
- periodic evaluation

THE BEST SCHOOLS – DEVELOPMENT OF SOUND CHARACTER

In today's moral environment, teaching our youth high moral standards can be both complex and controversial. Yet Best Schools across the country have successfully integrated strategies to promote sound character, democratic values, and ethical judgment in their academic and co-curricular programs. Several examples of such programs are illustrated next.

Development of Sound Character Illustrations

GRANGER HIGH SCHOOL, WEST VALLEY, UT

Granger High School opened in 1958 and is located in the Salt Lake Valley, an urban center of over one million people. In 1958, the area around Granger High School was predominantly rural/agricultural in nature, and almost 100% of the students were Caucasian. Since that time, the school and the surrounding area has undergone dramatic changes stemming from a transition from a rural neighborhood and homogeneous school to a highly mobile, multiethnic community and rapidly changing urban educational center.

The Granger High community consists of a highly mobile population, which contributes to a high transition rate of over 30%. Students from cultures such as Asian, Hispanic, Polynesian, and African-American add to the diversity and richness of the school. These diversities have been emphasized positively to add strength and character to the programs at Granger High and have helped create the congenial atmosphere found in the school.

There is a schoolwide citizenship program that requires students and staff to work together for students to earn citizenship credit required for graduation. If students have received unsatisfactory citizenship grades, they have the opportunity to have those grades changed to satisfactory by completing school or community service. This service has to be preapproved by an administrator. A community issues course also emphasizes community service. Many school organizations and branches of the school government carry out service projects throughout the school year. Granger students contribute heavily to the Utah Food Bank for the less fortunate and several groups are involved in "Sub-for-Santa" projects each year.

Danny L. Talbot, *Principal, Grades 10–12, 1630 Students*

HEWITT-TRUSSVILLE HIGH SCHOOL, TRUSSVILLE, AL

Trussville is a suburb of Birmingham, Alabama. Geographically, it is a large area where almost all of the students ride buses or drive cars to school. The students come from a wide spectrum of socioeconomic backgrounds. The socioeconomic status is predominantly middle-class. In the past decade, the community has experienced tremendous growth. A recent real estate survey revealed the Trussville area to be the fastest growing region in the Birmingham area. Numerous subdivisions have been built to serve the middle- and upper-income homeowners; therefore, the school population reflects both the original rural residents, as well as the newer members of the community. Both groups share a strong sense of community, and they value the small town atmosphere.

Good character and values are developed and nurtured at the school through the commitment of and example set by faculty. School assembly programs and motivational speakers often focus on this message. Each day, students and staff recite the Pledge of Allegiance, and the American flag is on display in every classroom. The Power of Positive Students is a program that has been initiated to promote good character and positive attributes in students. An encouraging thought is read daily over the intercom. Another recent campaign, "Courtesy Is Contagious – Let's Start an Epidemic," is designed to encourage respect for others.

Each teacher assigns a citizenship grade and makes comments on students' report cards concerning strengths and weaknesses. The principal makes additional positive comments on report cards, and students who consistently receive outstanding citizenship grades are honored on awards night. Two exemplary students per grade level are honored each month by the faculty.

Administrators and teachers encourage critical thinking and self-discipline by providing students opportunities to examine their choices. Hard work and good sportsmanship are emphasized in all extracurricular activities, particularly in the athletic program.

Several extracurricular clubs, such as service association, "Serteens," "Junior Civitans," and national honor society, specifically focus on serving the needs of the community. Schoolwide campaigns focus on helping others less fortunate; an annual student-faculty basketball game raises money for the needy at Thanksgiving; and drives are initiated in response to natural disasters, such as the recent Florida hurricane. Additionally, subject-area teachers organize out-of-class activities to help others, such as preparing and serving a meal in a homeless shelter, decorating pumpkins for a nursing home, or hosting a party for children whose families have suffered from domestic violence. In election years, students are encouraged to work in political campaigns of their choice. Through this civic awareness and responsibility, the school fosters the development of sound character and democratic values.

Dr. Connie K. Williams, *Principal, Grades 10–12, 1259 Students*

LAGUNA HILLS HIGH SCHOOL, LAGUNA HILLS, CA

The school is located in a relatively affluent suburban community with predominately single-family housing. Students come from diverse racial/ethnic backgrounds. Specifically, 69% of the student population is Caucasian, 17% Asian-American, 12% Hispanic, and 2% African-American. Additionally, students come from homes with a wide range of socioeconomic levels.

Good citizenship, respect for others, and responsibility for one's actions are underlying themes of life as a "Hawk." Laguna Hills employs a strong ethics policy, which reinforces ethical decisions and behavior and instills "Hawk Pride" in most all who step on campus. Excellence in student academic achievement, behavior, activities, and athletics is evident by the number of students recognized at Hawk Pride Awards and departmental awards programs. A special "I Can Make a Difference" (ICMD) conference has been developed and sponsored by PTSA, recognizing 120 students, recommended by teachers, who show potential for involvement and leadership but have not yet had an opportunity to demonstrate such talent and potential. Additional awards and programs, such as California Scholastic Federation, principal's honor roll, senior awards, and student leadership continue to prove beneficial and successful. In athletics, LHHS participates in a league sportsmanship program, whose purpose is to develop good qualities and habits of league athletes. This program requires athletes to create and document codes for each of their individual sports. The school's well-rounded, complete sports program offers students the opportunity to enjoy a constructive physical outlet for their aggression and energy. LHHS students learn and practice lifelong skills through their maintenance and operation of the student store, "The Hawk Stop." LHHS promotes positive interaction in a culturally diverse environment through many clubs and organizations. The culmination of these efforts resulted in an International Day, which taught the value of cultural uniqueness. International Day has been recently expanded to International Week. Key club promotes school and community service through its projects and policies. Each member is required to give at least five hours of service a month. In addition, over 2000 "man hours" were provided during the summer. Projects include a spring party for homeless children, a holiday toy drive that involves the entire student body, and a car wash with a portion of the profits going to provide Thanksgiving meals for needy families in the school, with the remaining funds donated to a home for abused children. Last year, the key club had over 5000 service hours and was chosen as one of the top key clubs in California, Nevada, and Hawaii.

Wayne Mickaelian, *Principal, Grades 9–12, 1597 Students*

PREPARATION FOR LIFE IN A CULTURALLY AND ETHNICALLY DIVERSE SOCIETY

The United States has always been a nation of many races, cultures, and national origins. Schools reflect this diversity containing a complex mix of races, languages, and religious affiliations. One of the most significant challenges to public education during the past two decades stems from the growth of various minority populations. Unfortunately, educational programs have often failed to adequately respond to this phenomenon. All too often, curricula and instructional strategies have continued to reflect the prevalent white Eurocentric emphasis they have maintained over the last century.

From an educational perspective, culture can influence the way in which a class is formatted, the way in which a needs assessment is conducted, and the judgments made about those who are economically, socially, and physically different from us (Briscoe, 1991). Successful schools have recognized this important dynamic of schooling and have responded with programs and instructional strategies directed at teaching students about cultural diversity. Education within a pluralistic society should affirm and help students understand their home and community cultures. Moreover, in a very real sense, all students need to be more culturally literate; to gain a broader view of the real world that includes people of many colors, traditions, and with two genders. This awareness does not only affect an appreciation of others, but helps students prepare for an economy that is now clearly globally competitive.

Successful schools have conscientiously infused a more multicultural perspective to educational programming. These programs not only address curricular content, but examine such issues as equity, poverty, racism, and the need for cross-cultural cooperation (Gollnich and Chinn, 1991).

Banks (1994) has identified five dimensions of multicultural education that can serve as the foundation of programs that respond to student diversity:

(1) *Content dimension* deals with the extent to which teachers illuminate key points of instruction with content reflecting diversity.

(2) *Knowledge construction dimension* deals with the extent to which teachers help students understand how perspectives of people within a discipline influence the conclusions reached within the discipline.

(3) *Prejudice reduction dimension* deals with efforts to help students develop positive attitudes about different groups.

(4) *Equitable pedagogy dimension* addresses ways to modify teaching to facilitate academic achievement among students from diverse groups.

(5) *Empowering school culture and social structure dimension* deals with the extent a school' s culture and organization ensure educational equity and cultural empowerment for students from diverse groups.

A school that is truly committed to teaching about diversity reinforces the curriculum with ongoing interdisciplinary opportunities for students to learn about culture, develop cultural sensitivity, examine their own biases (and the biases of others), and develop skills necessary to communicate effectively with all types of people and to survive in a multicultural world. Specific objectives common to multicultural programs include:

- knowing about and feeling proud of one' s own culture and ethnic identity
- knowing about and appreciating cultures different than one' s own
- recognizing contributions that all types of people—women and men, young and old, rich and poor, including those from minority and nontypical cultures—have made to the school, community, nation, and world
- developing skills for communicating effectively with people from different backgrounds
- recognizing and refusing to accept any behavior based on stereotypes, prejudice, or discrimination
- recognizing the economic interdependence among nations

An analysis of the current literature reveals several identifiable levels and approaches to the integration of diverse ethnic content into curriculum (Banks, 1987). These are:

- *The contributions approach*— is the addition of ethnic heroes into the curriculum.
- *The ethnic approach*—is the addition of a book, a unit or a course to the existing curriculum.
- *The transformation approach*—changes the basic assumptions of the curriculum and enables students to view concepts, issues, themes, and problems from several ethnic perspectives and points of view.
- *The decision-making and social action approach*—includes all of the elements of the transformation approach but adds components that require students to make decisions and to take actions related to the concept, issue, or problem studied in the unit.

The demographics of America are changing, and nowhere are the shifts better reflected than in the nation's public schools. From 1976 to 1986, white, non-Hispanic student enrollment declined by nearly 13%, while total minority enrollment increased by more than 16%. By 2020, demographers predict minorities will comprise nearly one-third of the United States population and nearly half of the school-age youth.

To an increasing degree, the task of erasing ethnic and racial stereotypes and prejudice has become the responsibility of America's public schools. Sociologists and policymakers see education as the key to overcoming bias and discrimination and fostering an appreciation for cultural and ethnic diversity. Developing K–12 multicultural programs that promote diverse ethnic and cultural perspectives has challenged educators. Multicultural content is still emerging and constantly changing.

To systematize a response to the need to address cultural diversity in schools, districts have adopted a number of policy statements. The example below provides excerpts from the policies developed by the New York City School District:

> RESOLVED, that the New York City Board of Education, by adoption of this resolution, hereby ratifies a policy of multicultural education and commits itself and its resources to providing an education to achieve the following goals:
>
> - To develop an appreciation and understanding of the heritage of students' and staffs' own ethnic, racial, cultural and linguistic groups.
> - To promote and foster inter-group understanding, awareness, and appreciation by students and staff of the diverse ethnic, racial, cultural and linguistic groups represented in the New York City Public Schools and the general population.
> - To enhance New York City youngsters' self-worth and self-respect.
> - To encourage a variety of teaching strategies to address differences in learning styles.
> - To identify the impact of racism and other barriers to acceptance of differences.
> - To develop opportunities for all students to become bilingual and proficient in at least two languages.
> - To develop a multicultural perspective (interpreting history and culture from a variety of perspectives).
> - To analyze human rights violations in our global society and the progress made in obtaining human rights.
> - To develop an appreciation of the cultural and historical contributions of a variety of racial and ethnic groups to the growth of the United States and world civilizations.
> - To develop the human relations skills needed in interpersonal and inter-group relations as well as conflict resolution, with a special emphasis on conflict arising from bias and discrimination based on race, color, religion, national origin, gender, age, sexual orientation, and/or handicapping condition. (National Center for Effective Schools Research and Development, 1992)

THE BEST SCHOOLS—PREPARATION FOR LIFE IN A CULTURALLY AND ETHNICALLY DIVERSE SOCIETY

Best Schools have committed to develop programs and provide activities that foster a curriculum that promotes understanding and appreciation for differences in culture and people. Several examples of such programs are illustrated below.

Illustrations of Preparation for Life in a Diverse Society

NEW HYDE PARK MEMORIAL JUNIOR-SENIOR HIGH SCHOOL, NEW HYDE PARK, NY

The school has a population of over 1200 students and is located in an area that benefits from both the cultural resources of New York City and the comforts of suburban living.

In the past decade, the school has seen a rise in minority populations from 11% to 22%. Since 1988, the school has embraced a nationally successful program of excellence known as the Academy of Finance. This innovative program involves an advisory board of prominent firms in the financial community, including banking, real estate, law, accounting, and investment brokerages. Admission to this program is selective. Students are chosen from among the five district high schools with special consideration given to minority candidates. The students, parents, administrators, and community mentors work together in a cooperative effort for the maximum benefit of the young adults in this program.

The school has systematically developed programs that provide students the opportunity to prepare for their economic future through diverse and challenging course offerings that will prepare them to live in a culturally and ethnically diverse democratic society. The social studies department offers a two-year required program in global studies, which promotes understanding and appreciation of different world cultures. A course offering in contemporary world problems introduces students to diplomacy, parliamentary procedure, and the geopolitical aspects of contemporary history. Out of this program, the model United Nations emerges to compete in statewide, national, and, ultimately worldwide academic competition. Through the study of American history, students learn about the contributions of African-Americans, Hispanics, the role of women, the influence of immigration, and the role of different minorities in the shaping of historical events. Courses in psychology and sociology provide a forum for insight, discussion, and analysis of diverse peoples and cultures.

In order to fully implement the global aspect of learning, the foreign language department offers many opportunities for students to explore world differences. During "foreign language week," all students participate in thematic units celebrating cultural and ethnic diversities. Similarities and differences among cultures are organized around instructional activities focusing on customs, music, art, poetry, and original skits. The ESL program has included students from Korea, Pakistan, India, Italy, Colombia, Poland, Japan, Norway, Hungary, Mexico, China, and Arab nations. These students provide a valuable contribution to the study of different cultures. The Asian student population has risen to 12.5% of the total school population. To promote Asian culture, the school has formed an Asian culture club.

The foreign language department also provides the Italian club, Spanish club, and European literary circle. Students of the Italian club visit Little Italy and Ellis Island to better understand their heritage. The Spanish club visits the Spanish "Barrio," the Spanish museum, and the Cloisters. The European literary circle meets to discuss great European works of literature and contemporary films. The female writers' course shows a point of view of minorities, and Bible as literature classes sensitize students to other people's values and religious ideals.

The school was awarded a district mini-grant for studying multicultural literature in order to eliminate stereotypes and highlight the increasing cultural diversity within the school. The school staff believes that they are meeting their objectives by emphasizing the interdependence of the world's peoples in all content areas and extracurricular activities.

Gerald E. Connors, *Principal, Grades 7–12, 1210 Students*

HATT OAK GROVE SCHOOL, HATTIESBURG, MS

Oak Grove Attendance Center, with approximately 2900 students, is made up of three schools within a school spanning grades K – 12. The middle/high school side of the campus houses 1725 students and is in a continuous state of construction. This year's enrollment reflects a 10% increase, with the majority in grades 5 – 8. Eight classrooms are under construction, the cafeteria is being enlarged, and every available space is being utilized until all construction is complete. This condition is not new and will continue to reoccur as this bedroom community is one of the fastest growing areas in the state.

The school serves a predominately Caucasian student population, 94%; the remaining 6% are African-American and Hispanic.

The school has implemented a team concept, which promotes cooperative learning in groups. It has enhanced not only student self-concept, but it has taught the students the ability to get along with others for the productivity of team and/or group progress. Examples from the curriculum include the teaching of the following: living skills, media awareness emphasizing the role mass media may play in the decision-making process and the choosing of positive role models, and a unit course on manners in which students are actually placed in social situations in the community. Also within the curriculum are a speaker's forum that includes people from all walks of life; Channel One, which acquaints students with people from other backgrounds and cultures; and field trips to cultural events in other states and, at times, other countries. Examples of student activities include the following: multicultural club, peer helpers, and fine arts programs.

Staff development programs relating to gangs, teenage depression and suicide, and AIDS awareness enable the staff to more effectively prepare students for a diverse society. It is also a school practice to incorporate foreign exchange students, therefore promoting classroom discussions of cultural mixtures.

Carolyn Lott Adams, *Principal, Grades 5–12, 1723 Students*

EAST HIGH SCHOOL, WEST CHESTER, PA

East High School is located on the outskirts of West Chester, the county seat of Chester County. It is a semi-residential community located west of Philadelphia and north of Wilmington, Delaware.

The students of East High School come from various socioeconomic backgrounds. Ethnically, East High School has reflected a stable student population over the last five years; 87% of the student body is Caucasian, 7% is African-American, and 6% is of Hispanic and Asian origin.

Students have consistently experienced success, with approximately 80% of the student population matriculating into two- or four-year colleges.

East High School emphasized improving the appreciation and understanding of cultural diversity within the school and the broader community. During the 1988–89 school year, the East committee for cultural awareness (ECCA) was formed consisting of teachers, caseworkers and administrators to analyze existing procedures, to brainstorm ideas, and to discuss possible strategies that would heighten the appreciation of cultural diversity of students, faculty, and parents at East High School. In order to achieve this goal, the school presented a series of lessons, lectures, and discussions by selected speakers. In April 1990, this committee was expanded to include parents. Students became actively involved in 1992. During the second semester of the 1989–90 school year, five programs were presented to the students and faculty. Professor C. James Trotman (West Chester University) spoke on Martin Luther King, Jr.'s, *Writings from a Birmingham Jail* (1963); Professor John Linder (Delaware County Community College) gave two seminars on student stress and human relations; Ms. Elleanor Jean Hendley (NBC reporter and hostess of the television program "City Lights") spoke on the relevance of effective communication and related life experiences; Philadelphia councilwoman Augusta A. Clarke, Esq., discussed how individuals can make a difference in society; and Dr. Judith Thomas (Lincoln University) explained why African-American students should strive to be better than average. ECCA presented an inservice day program for the staff. This "Multicultural Experience and Food Fest" highlighted five cultures: Asian, Hispanic, Indian, Jewish, and African-American. The program included an informative presentation on each culture followed by a luncheon featuring multicultural foods. ECCA featured Asian and Hispanic cultures with guest speakers and a luncheon of appropriate ethnic foods. The curriculum addresses cultural, ethnic, and economic diversity in various units and courses: sociology, law and rights of minorities and women, criminology, black history, ethnic dancing, minorities and women in literature, family living, and teenage survival. Student activities include the Hispanic support group, the black student union, Scottish cultural programs, and student trips to France, Spain, and Italy. Exchange students come to East regularly from a variety of foreign countries and make presentations about their cultures to various classes. School announcements include short biographical sketches of people from various cultures, such as Martin Luther King, Jr. The school acknowledges, on the public address system, religious observances of the various cultural groups. The cultural awareness committee has printed a calendar that highlights dates celebrated by various cultures. This calendar is distributed and posted throughout the school.

Dr. David E. Cox, *Principal, Grades 9–12, 1515 Students*

SCHOOL-TO-WORK TRANSITION

Unlike most other industrialized nations, the United States has no systematic procedure to help secondary students' transition from school to employment. Kazis (1993) reports a developing consensus in the literature and among practitioners on the basic building blocks of an effective career preparation system that should guide federal policy: 1) encourage continued experimentation with and learning from diverse school-to-work programs; 2) support development of the basic elements of a national skills training system; 3) focus federal resources on employer participation and teacher development; and 4) use its authority and resources to promote a new vision of government's role.

The fifth National Education Goal states, "By the Year 2000, every adult American will be literate and will possess the knowledge and skills necessary to compete in a global economy and exercise the rights and responsibilities of citizenship." A major objective associated with this goal is to strengthen the connection between education and work. This renewed emphasis on school-to-work transition has been prompted by such factors as changing demographics, the need for a more productive and competitive work force, and a concern about the economic well-being of many youth.

Kazis (1993) provides examples of program models that illustrate "best practice" in the integration of school and work. Some of these programs—such as apprenticeships, school-based enterprises, and service learning—get young people out of the classroom and into the labor market. Others bring work and career issues into the classroom. Examples of the latter are:

- *Career exploration*—Some school districts are experimenting with ways to build career education into school life early. For instance, a year-long, ninth-grade course in Cambridge, Massachusetts, called CityWorks, gives vocational education students a chance to "build" their city and to explore the kinds of jobs that are done by people who work there.
- *Tech prep*—This approach integrates high school and community college programs in specific occupational areas. The goal is to smooth the transition from high school vocational programs into more advanced postsecondary programs in the same field by coordinating course requirements, reducing duplication and, in some cases, granting advanced standing for courses already taken in high school.
- *High school career academics*—The academy model uses a "school-within-a-school" approach, builds curriculum and activities around a single industry cluster, and integrates academic and vocational learning through coordination among teachers who work closely together. The target population is "at-risk" young people in danger of dropping out of school.

A lack of formalized transition systems exacerbates the problem that many non-college-bound youth encounter as they try to obtain career sustaining employment. Yet carefully planned, integrated programs significantly increase the likelihood that graduates are able to find meaningful jobs without going through a transition period of unemployment or becoming dependent on public resources.

Smith and Rajewski (1992) have identified six key concepts needed for successful school to-work transition programs: 1) coordinated, nonfragmented provision of appropriate services, 2) strong education-business partnerships resulting in paid work experiences, 3) relevance in the learning process through linkage of instruction and work, 4) early and continuing career counseling and guidance, 5) program accountability to students and community, and 6) a wide range of career/employment options available upon completion of *transition* services.

THE BEST SCHOOLS–SCHOOL-TO-WORK TRANSITION

About 50% of the nation's young people enter some form of postsecondary education program the fall after they graduate. Of these, about half successfully graduate with a baccalaureate degree. For those who do not have marketable skills, the road to success is extremely difficult. If our nation is to improve its place in the world market, educators and representatives from industry must teach all perspective workers high-performance skills. Successful schools have viable programs that bridge the gap between the capabilities of high school graduates, especially those who are not college-bound, and the skills, knowledge, and work habits needed to be successful in the workplace. Illustrations of best practices in America's schools are provided next (see also pages 297–300).

Transition Illustrations

WEST BLOOMFIELD HIGH SCHOOL, WEST BLOOMFIELD, MI

The West Bloomfield School District is located in a multi-lakes area twenty miles northwest of Detroit. The community of 42,000 is predominantly upper middle-class with a significant segment of working class families.

The school district has a diverse population. A survey of languages in 1989–90 indicated that forty-two different languages were represented in the district in addition to English. The major languages represented were Chaldean, Arabic, Indian (Asian), Japanese, German, Hebrew, Chinese, Russian, Spanish, and Korean.

All tenth graders participate in career groups for six hours where career options are explored. Non-college-bound students have extensive options open to them. Eleventh and twelfth grade students have the opportunity to enroll for a half day at the Oakland Technical School, which offers eighteen programs in technical, vocational, trade, and service occupations. These same students are also invited to a spring non-college-bound fair where a personal "one-on-one" approach is used with potential employers (seventy-six students attended last spring). The marketing and DECA programs provide students an opportunity to be recognized and awarded for their job skills through participation in real-life situations and problem solving by meeting with business leaders, participating in national DECA contests, and working in the newly constructed school store. Co-op programs are available to marketing and business and services technology (BST) seniors in many areas of trade, industry, and human resources. Career day has many businesses geared for non-college-bound students as does the mock interview day. Classes such as Child Development III, welding, computer-aided drafting (CAD) and retail marketing provide real-life job experiences during the regular school day. The school also has specialized staff to counsel and help alternative and special education students achieve career aspirations.

Dr. Gary A. Faber, *Principal, Grades 9–12, 1485 Students*

HILLSDALE HIGH SCHOOL, SAN MATEO, CA

Opened in 1955, Hillsdale High School is a four-year comprehensive high school serving 1380 students largely from the middle-class, suburban communities of San Mateo and Foster City on the San Francisco Peninsula.

Guided by research describing effective schools, in 1983, Hillsdale inaugurated a "traditional school" program. The program features strong academic courses to prepare students for college work. A closed campus, regular homework, and a specific discipline and dress code ensure a campus environment that is productive, orderly, safe, and attractive.

All freshmen at Hillsdale take the guidance information systems (GIS) interest inventory, which provides information on aptitude, strengths, and work options. Students who set a course of immediate postgraduate entry into the workplace receive guidance assistance. During sophomore counseling sessions, the student develops an educational plan to meet his/her postgraduate goals. Additional information available through the GIS computer program helps students to preselect careers and pursue the development of necessary skills through four years of study. Counselors, parents, and the career/college placement advisor refine the initial interest and help direct the student's study. Many of the course applications also provide entry level skills for immediate employment, and the school's career center provides job placement information. The work experience/joint ventures program, involving two periods per day on a job site, permits students to receive school credit while meeting the minimum graduation requirements. The regional occupation program and adult school also provide study opportunities for students determined to move immediately into the workplace. Transition IEPs are available for special education students who will enter the world of work immediately after high school, and a district specialist is available to these students for one-on-one counseling.

Donald C. Leydig, *Principal, Grades 9–12, 1382 Students*

SOUTHEAST BULLOCH HIGH SCHOOL, BROOKLET, GA

Southeast Bulloch High School is a relatively small rural high school serving grades 8–12. Located one and a half miles south of Brooklet, Georgia, the site is centrally positioned among the attendance areas of three feeder schools. The students come from varied socioeconomic backgrounds. Approximately 40% of the student population receives free or reduced lunch. The composition of the student body is 77.3% Caucasian, 22% African-American, and .7% Hispanic. Student mobility has increased slightly in recent years; however, 80% of the student population remains stable.

Career interests are addressed with all eighth graders. The vocational program, introduced in an eighth-grade exploratory program, emphasizes involvement in job-related content and activities. A greenhouse provides additional opportunities for on-site study and application of job-related skills. The agricultural mechanics class has been expanded to include units on mechanics, welding, small engine repair, and concrete production.

Emphasis on application of content helps students transfer information to marketable job skills. The principal and counselor visit job sites to actively engage business and industry in planning appropriate job preparation programs. Direct lines of communication have been established with business, industry, the Chamber of Commerce, the local hospital and health department, service organizations, and civic groups.

Motivational speakers meet with students during career day activities held each year. All seniors spend a day at a community work site to gain first-hand information about a career interest. A special parent night held at Ogeechee Technical Institute (OTI) for parents of SEB seniors acquaints parents with programs that allow students to upgrade skills while maintaining full- or part-time employment. The campus is open to military recruiters. The counselor works with both formal and informal job networks to assist students in obtaining employment upon graduation.

Thomas F. Bigwood, *Principal, Grades 8–12, 673 Students*

SUMMARY

Best Schools throughout the country have made a strong commitment to the development and maintenance of an educational climate that promotes students' learning and well-being.

Through curricular and extracurricular initiatives, Best Schools take great care to ensure that their students successfully integrate into school; are challenged through relevant, interesting instructional activities; and have the appropriate support systems necessary to assist under-achieving and/or at-risk students. Within these efforts, several common themes become apparent: Best Schools value students and create opportunities for them to influence school goals and processes; they are committed to involving the parents and community as valuable resources; they provide a wide variety of extracurricular student activities; they expect students to demonstrate self-discipline; and they take the necessary steps to ensure safe drug-resistant environments. Finally, these schools have recognized the diverse nature of today's student body by actively promoted multicultural learning opportunities and transitional work programs so that students can effectively compete in today's global economy.

REFERENCES

Association of Supervision and Curriculum Development. (1988). "Moral Education in the Life of the School," *Educational Leadership*, 45(8).

Banks, James A. (1987). *Teaching Strategies for Ethnic Studies*. Fourth Edition. Boston, MA: Allyn & Bacon.

Banks, James A. (1994). "Transforming the Mainstream Curriculum," *Educational Leadership*, 51(8):4–8.

Biernat, Nancy A. and Edward J. Klesse. (1989). *The Third Curriculum: Student Activities*. Reston, VA: National Association of Secondary School Principals: Division of Student Activities.

Blendinger, Jack. (1993). *Win-Win Discipline*. Fastback 353, Bloomington, IN: Phi Delta Kappa Foundation.

Braddock, J. H. and J. M. McPartland. (1993). "Educational of Early Adolescents," in *Review of Education, Vol. 19*, L. Darling-Hammond, ed., Washington, D.C.

Briscoe, Diane Buck. (1991). "Designing for Diversity in School Success: Capitalizing on Culture," *Preventing School Failure*, (36):13–18.

Broderick, Melissa. (1993). *The Path to Dropping Out: Evidence for Intervention*. Westport, CT: Greenwood Publishing Group.

Brophy, Jere. (1987). "Synthesis of Research on Strategies for Motivating Students to Learn," *Educational Leadership*, 45(2):40–48.

Canter, L. and M. Canter. (1976). *Assertive Discipline*. Los Angeles, CA: Canter and Associates.

Cawelti, Gordon. (1994). *High School Restructuring: A National Study*. Arlington, VA: Educational Research Service Report, Educational Research Service.

Christensen, D. D. (1984). *Managing Student Activities*. Reston, VA: National Association of Secondary School Principals.

Cummings, Carol. (1983). *Managing to Teach*. Edmonds, WA: Teaching, Inc.

Curwin, Richard and Allen N. Mendler. (1988). *Discipline with Dignity*. Alexandria, VA: Association for Supervision and Curriculum Development.

Dunn, R. and K. Dunn. (1978). *Teaching Students through Their Individual Learning Styles: A Practical Approach*. Reston, VA: Reston Publishing Company.

Gallup, George E. (1992). "The 11th Annual Gallup Poll in Education," *Phi Delta Kappan*, 74:43–52.

Germinario, Vito, Janet Cervalli, and Evelyn H. Ogden. (1992). *All Children Successful: Real Answers for Helping At-Risk Elementary Students*. Lancaster, PA: Technomic Publishing Company, Inc.

Gollnich, D. and P. Chinn. (1991). *Multicultural Education in a Pluralistic Society*. Third Edition. New York, NY: MacMillan Publishing Company.

Good, T. L. (1982). "How Teachers' Expectations Affect Results," *American Education*, 18(10):25–32.

Good, T. L. and J. E. Brophy. (1984). *Looking into Classrooms*. Third Edition. New York, NY: Harper and Row.

Hartzell, Gary N. and Thomas A. Petrie. (1992). "The Principal and Discipline: Working with School Structures, Teachers and Students," *The Clearing House*, 65(6):376–380.

Heller, Jeanne. (1989). "Offering Moral Education," *Streamlined*, a publication of the National Association of Elementary School Principals (8):1.

Hodghenson, H., Director of the Center for Demographic Policy. (1990). Remarks from *American Association of School Administrators – Twelfth Annual Educational Policy Conference*. Washington, D.C.

Holland, Alyce and Thomas Andre. (1987). "Participation in Extra-Curricular Activities in Secondary Schools: What Is Known, What Need to Be Known," *Review of Education Research*, Winter: 437–466.

Horton, Lowell. (1992). *Developing Effective Drug Education Programs*. Phi Delta Kappan Educational Foundation Fastback, Bloomington, IN: Phi Delta Kappan.

Hunter, M. (1986). *Motivation Theory into Practice*. El Sequido, CA: TIP Publications.

Hunter, M. and Tommy Tomlinson. (1992). "Hard Working and High Expectations: Motivating Students to Learn," *Issues in Education*. Washington D.C.: Office of Educational Research and Improvement.

Imel, Susan. (1992). "School-to-Work Transition: Its Role in Achieving Universal Literacy," *ERIC Research in Action*, ERIC Clearinghouse on Adult Career and Vocational Education.

Jenkins, John M. (1992). *Advisement Programs: A New Look at an Old Practice*. Reston, VA: National Association of Secondary School Principals.

Johnson, D., R. Johnson, E. Holubec, and P. Roy. (1984). *Circles of Learning*. Alexandria, VA: ASCD.

Kazis, Richard. (1993). *Improving the Transition from School to Work in the United States*. Washington, D.C.: American Youth Policy Forum,

Keefe, James W. (1986). "Advisement Programs – Improving Teacher-Student Relationships, School Climate," *NASSP Bulletin*, 70:85–90.

Kerman, S. and M. Martin. (1980). *Teacher Expectations and Students' Achievement – TESA*. Bloomington, IN: Phi Delta Kappa.

Lockwood, Alan. (1991). "Character Education: The Ten Percent Solution," *Social Education* (55): 246–248.

MacNaughton, Robert H. and Frank A. Johns. (1991). "Developing a Successful Schoolwide Discipline Program," *NASSP Bulletin*, 75(536):47–57.

Maehr, Martin L. (1991). "Changing the Schools: A Word to School Leaders about Enhancing Student Investment in Learning," paper presented at the *American Education Research Association Conference*, Chicago, IL, April 1991.

Moles, Oliver C. (1989). *Strategies to Reduce Student Misbehavior*. Washington, D.C.: Office of Educational Research and Improvement, U.S. Department of Education.

The National Center for Effective Schools Research and Development. (1992). "Multiculturalism: Diversity or Divisiveness?" *Focus on Change. Vol. 7.*

National Center for Educational Statistics. (1994). *Dropout Rates in the United States, 1993*. Washington, D.C.: Education Department.

National Education Goals Panel. (1993). *The National Educational Goals Panel: Building a Nation of Learners: Volume One, 1993*. Washington, D.C.: U.S. Government Printing Office.

National Institute on Drug Abuse. (1991). *Drug Use among American High School Seniors, College Students, and Young Adults 1975–1990. Vol. II.* Washington, D.C.: United States Department of Health and Human Services, p. 3.

National School Boards Association. (1988). *First Teachers: Parental Involvement in Public Schools*. Alexandria, VA: National School Boards Association.

Newman, F. M. (1981). "Reducing Student Alienation in High Schools: Implications of Theory," *Harvard Educational Review*, 51(4):546–564.

Ogden, Evelyn H. and Vito Germinario. (1988). *The At-Risk Student: Answers for Educators*. Lancaster, PA: Technomic Publishing Company, Inc.

Ogden, Evelyn H. and Vito Germinario. (1993). *The Nation's Best Schools: Blueprints for Excellence, Vol. 1, Elementary and Middle Schools*. Lancaster, PA: Technomic Publishing Company, Inc.

Palandy, J. Michael. (1993). "Classroom Discipline: The Diagnostic Approach," *Streamliner Seminar*, National Association of Elementary School Principals, 11(6):1–4.

Pallas, A., G. Natriello, and E. McDill. (1989). "The Changing Nature of the Disadvantaged Generation: Current Dimensions and Future Trends," *Educational Research*, 18:16–22.

Raffini, James P. (1988). *Student Apathy: The Protection of Self-Worth: What Research Says to Teachers*. Washington, D.C.: National Education Association.

Renchler, Ron. (1992). *Student Motivation, School Culture, and Academic Achievement: What School Leaders Can Do*. Trends and Issues, Eugene OR: ERIC Clearinghouse on Educational Management.

Smith, Clifton L. and Jay W. Rajewski. (1992). *School-to-Work Transition: Alternatives for Educational Reform*. Arlington, VA: Educational Research Service.

Stewart, William J. (1989). "Improving the Teaching of Decision-Making Skills," *The Clearing House* (63):64-66.

Strother, D. B. (1983). "Practical Applications of Research: Mental Health Education," *Phi Delta Kappan*, 65(2):140–141.

Tobler, S. (1986). "Meta-Analysis of 143 Adolescent Drug Prevention Programs: Quantitative Outcome Results Compared to a Control or Comparison Group," *Journal of Drug Issues*, 16:537–568.

U.S. Department of Education. (1986). *What Works–Schools without Drugs*. Washington, D.C.: U.S. Department of Education.

U.S. Department of Education. (1990). *A Profile of the American Eighth Grader*. Washington, D.C.: Office of Educational Research and Improvement. National Longitudinal Study of 1988.

U.S. Government Printing Office. (1993). *The National Education GOALS REPORT: Building a Nation of Learners. Volume One: The National Report.* Washington, D.C.: U.S. Government Printing Office.

Waxman, Hersholt C. and Herbert Jed Walberg. (1991). *Effective Teaching: Current Research*. Berkeley, CA: McCutchan Publishing Company.

Wehlage, Gary G., Robert A. Rutter, Gregory A. Smith, and Nancy Lesko. (1989). *Schools as Communities of Support*. Philadelphia, PA: The Falmer Press.

Yeazell, Mary I. and Robyn R. Cole. (1986). "The Adolescent Novel and Moral Development: A Demurrer," *Journal of Reading*, 29:292–298.

CHAPTER 5

Parent and Community Support

IN many high schools, communication between the school and the home generally takes place only in times of emergency or when issues of immediate interest arise. All too often, parents know or hear little about their child's progress in school other than through periodic grade reports. Other communications from the school are usually negative and prompted by student academic or behavioral problems.

The forms of meaningful parental involvement vary, ranging from parents' encouragement of their children in the home to intense parent-school partnerships in which parents are involved in most every aspect of the educational process. In a recent study conducted by the Illinois State Board of Education (1993), summaries of selected studies were reviewed in three major categories: 1) parent-child relationships in the home, 2) parent training or involvement in performance contracts, and 3) parent-school-community partnerships. The research on parent behaviors and attitudes at home that promote children's learning indicates that parental encouragement of positive attitudes towards education and high expectations for student success have a profoundly positive effect on student achievement. The literature on parent training or involvement in performance contracts focuses on attempts by educators to provide parents with skills they can employ to foster their children's learning process. The studies on parent-school partnership models stress the involvement of parents in decision making and every other aspect of the educational process. The research cited in this review provides evidence that parent involvement is positively related to gains in achievement for students at all levels of income.

Despite these and similar results, existing forms of parental involvement often develop traditional and quite limited relationships between families and schools. Further, when significant distance exists among the values, structure, and language of school culture and the home culture of diverse class, racial, and ethnic constituencies, traditional forms of parent involvement often fail to reduce that distance (Fruchter, Galleta, and White, 1993).

Meaningful parent involvement is only achieved when the school creates an environment that makes parents feel welcome, reaches out in a wide variety of ways, connects parents to needed resources, and provides systematic opportunities for participation. Epstein (1988) suggests that a comprehensive program of parent involvement should include 1) techniques to help parents create home environments conducive to learning, 2) frequent and clear communications from teachers to parents about pupil progress, 3) the use of parents as resources in school (i.e., volunteers), 4) teacher assistance with educational activities in the home, and 5) involvement in school governance through such vehicles as the PTA and school planning committees.

Although approaches and strategies vary, in schools focused on excellence, the principal and staff realize that parents and the school are linked by the common goal of providing the best for the child. To facilitate this relationship, successful schools have developed partnerships with parents that ensure the following.

- Parents have a real voice in shaping the school's educational program.
- Parents are helped to increase their effectiveness in working with their children both in school and at home.
- Parents are given, through both formal and informal vehicles, specific information regarding their child's performance and progress in school.
- Parents' concerns regarding their role in parenting are facilitated through parent training opportunities.
- Parents are provided with the necessary resources and networks to ensure greater control over their own lives and their child's future.

When a trusting, nurturing climate has been developed by the school, which actually seeks and values parental involvement, everyone within the school community benefits. For children, substantial evidence exists to show that children whose parents are involved in their schooling demonstrate advanced academic achievement and cooperative development (Henderson, 1988). The parent-child relationship is improved, and parents become better teachers of their children at home and use more positive forms of reinforcement (Henderson, 1988).

Liontos (1992) summarizes the positive outcomes for children as a result of parent involvement in schooling:

- improved achievement
- improved student behavior
- greater student motivation
- more regular attendance
- lower student dropout rates
- a more positive attitude toward homework
- increased parent and community support

Research also indicates that parents benefit from involvement in their child's education. These parents tend to develop positive attitudes about themselves, increase self-confidence, and often enroll in programs to enhance their personal development (Becher, 1986). In a very real sense, parents not only become more effective as parents, but they become more effective as people. Their increased knowledge and participation fosters positive outcomes for the entire family.

Dauber and Epstein (1989) report that teachers have strong positive attitudes and perceive direct classroom benefits from parental involvement. In many respects, teachers discovered that their classroom lives go easier when they received help from parents. Additionally, involved parents tend to rate teachers' interpersonal skills higher, appreciate teachers' efforts more, and rate teachers' overall ability higher (Liontos, 1992).

This chapter will examine the characteristics of parental involvement in America's Best Schools. Additionally, examples of best practices will be highlighted for use as a practical guide for improving school-home relationships.

Specifically, this chapter will address the following questions:

- How do Best Schools encourage parental involvement in schools?
- How do Best Schools communicate student progress and overall school performance to parents and the broader community?
- What strategies do Best Schools use to encourage parents to provide supportive learning environments in the home?
- How do Best Schools support the needs of families?

- What types of opportunities do Best Schools provide for meaningful collaboration with other educational and community groups?

THE ENCOURAGEMENT OF PARENTAL INVOLVEMENT

As previously cited, the benefits of parental involvement in schools is profound! Families provide the first educational environment and strongly influence the child's intellectual growth, achievement, and attitude about schooling. Thus, schools must consistently develop structured opportunities to involve parents and (to a large degree) other community members in most all aspects of school life.

The strongest and most consistent predictors of parent involvement at school and at home are the specific school programs and teacher practices that encourage and guide parent involvement. These programs and practices take many forms, yet high schools have successfully used strategies from the list provided below:

- school support for families where human service agencies link up with schools to provide a variety of support services
- parents as learners, which includes parents' participation in workshops that train and educate in areas such as parenting skills and helping their children at home
- school-family communication about school programs and the child's progress
- family support of school and teachers that takes place at school and includes parents who assist teachers, administrators, or children in the classroom
- parents participating in decision making by membership on school councils or school-based management teams

Parent programs are more likely to be successful involving parents when they are designed with high expectations for parent involvement, when they provide a variety of ways for parents to be involved, when they accommodate the needs of particular families to be involved, and when they are comprehensive.

THE BEST SCHOOLS–ENCOURAGEMENT OF PARENTAL INVOLVEMENT

Best Schools recognize the powerful influence parents have in their children's success and the positive effect they can have on school effectiveness. Although research has not identified the "best" form of parental involvement, these schools have created the appropriate climate and meaningful ways to involve parents as partners in their schools. The following illustrations provide specific examples of Best School practices.

Parent Involvement Illustrations

QUAKER VALLEY HIGH SCHOOL, LEETSDALE, PA

Quaker Valley High School serves students from eleven municipalities within an area of twenty-five square miles. The socioeconomic status of the communities ranges from the very poor to the very affluent. Although about 90% of the student population is Caucasian, the 8% African-American population is well established both within the school and community at large. In recent years, immigrant families from Kuwait, China, Vietnam, Israel, Romania, Yugoslavia, and Hungary have contributed increased diversity to the student population.

The school values parental participation and encourages involvement in a variety of ways.

The clear choice of most parents is through the school's very active parent support/booster groups for parent network, band, chorus, football, girls' soccer, boys' soccer, girls' basketball, and boys' basketball. Parents are also the primary audience at athletic events, plays, and concerts.

Many school functions are designed to bring parents into the school: open house (153 families in attendance), sophomore orientation (50% of parents), newcomers welcome, college planning seminars (approximately fifty parents), meeting on topics of special interest, e.g., strategic planning, the law, and underage drinking. As part of a recent middle states self-study, questionnaires pertaining to the school and its programs were mailed to all families. More than 100 responses were received.

Parents are welcome at school programs and assemblies and may visit classes by arrangement through the principal. Parents do, upon occasion, act as resource persons or speakers for particular classes. Parents are important components of the strategic planning process. They serve on various task forces and committees, most recently on a task force to develop a joint grant proposal between Quaker Valley High School and Sewickley Valley Hospital to work with at-risk student subcommittees of the middle states evaluation self-study and on a committee to recommend procedures for the recognition of top senior students. The parent community has assisted in organizing a peer tutoring program, co-publishes the school newsletter, organizes the after-prom party, assists in making arrangements for a senior-alumni sharing experience, and sponsors teacher appreciation events.

Dr. Jeanne M. Johnson, *Principal, Grades 10–12, 401 Students*

LOS ANGELES CENTER FOR ENRICHED STUDIES, LOS ANGELES, CA

The L.A. Center for Enriched Studies, part of the Los Angeles Unified School District, came into existence in September 1977, as a new component of the voluntary integration program. It served grades 4–8 in the beginning but now goes through grade 12. The primary focus of the school is preparation for college.

Student enrollment comes from throughout the district by a computer selection process, with highest priority given to students who reside in racially isolated neighborhoods. All socioeconomic family levels are reflected in the student population which is approximately 30% Caucasian and 70% combined minorities. Approximately 90% of the students are bused into the school daily from all over the city.

At LACES, there is an open door policy for parents to meet with administrators or counselors, and appointments for teacher conferences or classroom visitations are readily available.

There are three structured vehicles for parent participation. The parent advisory council and executive board meet once a month to discuss general concerns and share information; the shared decision-making council (50% teachers; 50% parents, students, and clerical staff) meets monthly and formulates school policy. "Friends of LACES," the fund-raising arm of the parent advisory council, meets monthly.

There is a formal back-to-school night in the fall, open house in the spring, and an ongoing parenting class, which is required if the student is enrolled in the "guidance program."

Parents volunteer in classrooms, offices, and the college center. They chaperone dances and field trips, help coordinate student activities such as magazine drives and carnivals, donate materials and services for the classroom, conduct and train students for the "mock trial" competition, make costumes for performances, and give fund raisers through "Friends of LACES." Occasionally a particular parent will volunteer to teach a class in the after-school program. Parents also serve on community boards and committees to represent the school. There are numerous special parent meetings, such as senior parent night and ninth grade parent night. The school also has a number of college awareness programs and numerous performing arts programs. Approximately 90% of the parents visit the campus on several occasions throughout the school year.

Marion B. Collins, *Principal, Grades 4–12, 1460 Students*

EAGLEVILLE SCHOOL, EAGLEVILLE, TN

Eagleville School is unique, being the only K–12 school in the system. Located in the southwest corner of Rutherford County, Tennessee, Eagleville is a small town of approximately 800. Although the school is located inside the town limits, most students are drawn from homes as far away as fifteen miles. Students represent the social and economic diversity of the geographic area. Specifically, 94% of the student population is Caucasian, and 6% are African-American.

The Eagleville community is in a rural setting with a friendly hometown atmosphere; parent involvement and support of the school is an important asset to the school. Perhaps the most important way parents are involved at Eagleville School is the role they play in making decisions. One of these roles is fulfilled by serving on teams. All new teachers hired at Eagleville School are interviewed by an employment team. This team is made up of teachers and parents who help the principal make decisions concerning the hiring process. The school improvement team is also composed of parents and teachers working together to meet common goals. Parents are often called upon to serve on committees regarding decisions on fund raisers, school equipment, and special programs. At monthly PTO meetings, parents, teachers, students, and the administration come together to freely discuss plans and make decisions about present and future outcomes. Approximately 65% of parents are actively involved in this organization.

While being deeply involved in the education of children, the staff at Eagleville School feel a certain responsibility toward the education of the parents. Motlow State Community College Job Training Division opened a training site at Eagleville School. Continuing education classes are offered through Middle Tennessee State University, as well as through our local school system.

Eagleville School has an "open door policy," which is a standing invitation to all parents to visit at any time. Parents may feel free to visit their child's class or just come for lunch. Lunch time visits are strongly encouraged, and an invitation is sent out to parents providing a free lunch to parents on their child's birthday. This environment makes the atmosphere at school very inviting and comfortable for parents to be more at ease when visiting or doing volunteer work at the school.

Recognizing parents as a valuable resource, they are encouraged to volunteer their time to help either in the individual classrooms or in the school office. Some parents work with students who may need extra tutoring, some make bulletin boards, and some help count money after a fund raiser. Many parents take advantage of this opportunity to get to know teachers, as well as to take an active role in their child's school life. Many parents have been invited to speak to classes on a number of subjects. Recently, several fathers who served in Desert Storm told the students of their experiences. Other parents are involved in teaching a skill or craft to their child's class.

Dr. James Russ, *Principal, Grades 5–12, 444 Students*

THE REPORTING OF STUDENT PROGRESS AND PERFORMANCE

Parents have long sought accurate measures of their children's performance in school. Although at one time information relative to grades (e.g., A, B, C, etc.) was the only readily understandable vehicle for parents to assess their child's performance, most parents now expect information regarding a much broader spectrum of student performance and behavior. The essential ingredient of effective school/parent communication is embodied in the frequent, warm, respectful, and honest dialogue between the school and the home. With increased parental sophistication regarding the nature of student performance, as well as the heightened interest of community members in the results produced by their local schools, educators must develop meaningful ways to share these outcomes with their constituencies.

Communicating student progress is a critical component of the parental and community involvement process. Not only does it provide unique information about a child, it serves as a mechanism by which comparisons are made between schools and school districts. It is exceedingly important that outcome data is addressed in relation to local student/school/district performance, since, all too often, raw test data is used to make faulty judgments about a child or school.

THE BEST SCHOOLS–REPORTING STUDENT PROGRESS AND PERFORMANCE

Successful schools have developed a wide variety of strategies that provide parents and community members with meaningful information about their children and their schools. Warner (1991) describes several strategies that have been employed in the Indianapolis Public Schools:

- parent/teacher conferences
- Dial-a-Teacher program designed to give students and parents assistance and information about homework
- Homework Hotline–a live call-in television program produced by the school district to help parents help their children accurately complete assignments
- parent line/communicator or computerized telephone system that gives callers access to 140 prerecorded messages on a variety of school topics
- Parent Focus Series–a parent education and information program offering ninety parent-oriented workshops
- work-site seminars offered throughout the community for parents who cannot come to the school for seminars
- Teachers Involve Parents in Schoolwork (TIPS), developed by Joyce Epstein at Johns Hopkins University, which structures communication from home to school regarding homework and student progress

Additionally, strategies from successful schools are illustrated next.

Student Progress and Performance Illustrations

BEACHWOOD MIDDLE SCHOOL, BEACHWOOD, OH

Beachwood Middle School is a highly successful school, which was the first middle school built in Ohio. The school is guided by a list of learning outcomes that identifies its priorities and emphasis on student achievement. The acrostic SCORES represent Skills, Cooperation, Organization, Responsibility, Exploration, and Self-Concept.

The school has a strong commitment to communication of school news and accomplishments to parents and other citizens within the school community.

In addition to report cards every nine weeks, Beachwood Middle School parents receive a progress report at the five-week point. This informs parents of a student's academic standing at that time. This report strongly encourages teacher and parent comment.

A building policy expects each teacher to make at least two "positive" phone calls to parents each month. A large marquee in front of the high school announces the accomplishments of schools and students.

The various building and district committees are used equally for feedback and information sharing.

The Beachwood Middle School PTA executive board and the PTA co-presidents consult regularly with the principal to address parental concerns about educational programs and to share information. Each month, the *Principal's Bulletin* outlines the achievements of individuals, as well as the school. District publications such as *You and Your Schools* and *This Month in Beachwood Schools* inform community members of school activities and individual student and staff accomplishments. The district also produces an award-winning annual report.

Edward Bernetich, *Principal, Grades 7–8, 206 Students*

MARS HILL BIBLE SCHOOL, FLORENCE, AL

Mars Hill is a private Christian school located in northwest Alabama. The school has been continuously accredited by the Alabama State Department of Education since its founding in 1871. The school operates three preschool and elementary satellite campuses, as well as the main secondary campus located in Florence, a city of 36,426.

The school welcomes feedback from parents, grandparents, and other patrons. In September, each student is encouraged to invite his/her grandparents for a special program and classroom visit. Early in the school year, an open house is planned, whereby parents may visit classrooms and meet teachers. A variety of other activities bring the surrounding community to the campus. After the first grading period, one day is set aside for parent-teacher conferences. Other formal and informal conferences are held as parents and/or teachers deem necessary. Progress reports are sent home every third week and report cards every sixth week. The school publishes a number of documents that reflect achievement. Local media constantly report on school achievement, and the school advertisements chronicle results on television and radio and in local newspapers and periodicals. At the conclusion of the school year, all parents are mailed a questionnaire that allows them to evaluate the various aspects of the physical plant, faculty, and administration.

Dr. Kenny Barfield, *Principal, Grades 5–12, 381 Students*

BOOKER T. WASHINGTON JUNIOR HIGH SCHOOL, CONROE, TX

Booker T. Washington High School, one of four junior highs in the Conroe Independent School District, is located in a historical African-American section of Conroe, Texas. The school now serves students from as far as twenty miles, thus providing a unique cultural/ethnic mix of 78% Caucasian, 11% African-American, and 11% Hispanic. Using a systematic identification process, school officials estimate that 70% of the students are at risk for school failure, yet the entire school community supports the school motto, "All for Success and Success for All."

The school encourages parent conferences to notify parents of positive behaviors and progress, as well as to notify them of concerns and areas in need of growth. During the school year, approximately 400 parent conferences are held. This does not include telephone calls, progress reports, and other forms of parent-teacher communication.

Interdisciplinary teams (IDTs) have designated one meeting day per week for the purpose of school/home communication. Also the IDTs have designed their own progress reports, which include the students' three-week average, comments on conduct, and information concerning upcoming learning events.

The "Bulldog Calendar" is another avenue of communication. In addition, Bulldog "Happy Notes" are sent to parents and students in recognition of worthy contributions. These notes may be used by any staff member in highlighting students' efforts. This communicates to parents and students that school is a place for acceptance and reward.

Through an advisory program, students maintain a six-week assignment sheet, in which they must record an assignment or a comment concerning class activities. Parents are encouraged to check this assignment sheet regularly, and advisory teachers assist students in correctly using this study tool.

A new school newspaper, *The Washington Express*, brings together students with an interest in writing and allows them to explore the skills associated with newspaper publishing. In this newspaper, students include articles concerning student achievement, student and other awards, outlines of school goals, and editorials.

The school is represented by a faculty member whose assigned duty, one hour daily, is to communicate and coordinate newsworthy events on campus to local news media.

Rosalyn Bratcher, *Principal, Grades 7–8, 889 Students*

STRATEGIES TO ENCOURAGE PARENTS TO PROVIDE SUPPORTIVE LEARNING ENVIRONMENTS

According to a study released by the Center for School Change at the University of Minnesota (1994), only fifteen states require teachers to study ways to support parent participation in schooling and just seven require administrators to do so. Obviously, educators are often ill-prepared to assist parents in their efforts to promote positive home learning environments. Successful schools acknowledge the potential resource of the home as a viable mechanism to extend family influence on a child and, ultimately, enhance a student's attitude toward school and learning.

As the child's first teachers, parents have a significant role in influencing achievement and attitudes about school. When one considers that, from birth to age eighteen, a child spends approximately 12% of his/her life in school, the need to promote a productive learning environment in the home becomes very significant. Parents can create a curriculum at home that teaches children skills and the importance of school. Yet a study of American families (U.S. Department of Education, 1986) indicated that many parents are not actively involved in promoting school success for their children. For example, American women, on average, spend less than half an hour a day talking, explaining, or reading with their children. Fathers spend less than fifteen minutes.

THE BEST SCHOOLS–STRATEGIES TO ENCOURAGE PARENTS TO PROVIDE SUPPORTIVE LEARNING ENVIRONMENTS

Successful schools provide parents with the necessary skills and opportunities that foster the value of hard work, the importance of personal responsibility, and the importance of education as a significant contributor to greater success for their children. Several strategies parents can use at home that are directly linked to student success are discussed below (U.S. Department of Education, 1986).

- provide books, supplies, and a special place for studying
- observe routine for meals, bedtime, and homework
- monitor the amount of time spent watching TV and doing after-school jobs

Additionally, parents stay aware of their children's lives at school when they

- discuss school events
- help children talk about school problems and successes

Effective strategies that can be communicated to parents include the following [from Thomas (1992)]:

- sharing any concerns about the amount or type of homework assigned with the child's teacher or principal

- encouraging the child to take notes concerning homework assignments in case questions arise later at home
- providing a suitable study area and the necessary tools (for example, paper, pencils, and reference books) for the child to complete homework assignments
- limiting after-school activities to allow time for both homework and family activities
- monitoring television viewing and establish a specific homework time
- planning a homework schedule with the child—allowing for free time when assignments are completed
- praising the child's efforts, and if questions arise about the assignments, helping by asking him or her questions or working through an example rather than simply providing the answer

Successful schools promote parent education by offering courses on and (at times) off the school campus. They conduct home visits, distribute handbooks and other materials such as "Tips for Parents," and disseminate the names of organizations that may serve as resources to parents. Parent seminars, workshops, and support groups provide valuable opportunities for involvement with their children and their schools. As parents increase their understanding of child development, parenting skills, and the nature of teaching and learning, students reap the benefits in terms of motivation, achievement, and success. Jones (1991) provides a brief list and description of parent workshops or activities that schools may utilize to help parents create a productive learning environment in the home. Some are for parents only, others are for parents and children.

(1) *"Make It—Take It" workshops:* These are designed for parents to construct home learning materials. Parents may be asked to bring special materials, or the school can provide ready-to-assemble materials.

(2) *Family learning center:* The school is open two or more evenings per week with learning activities provided for all ages. When feasible, access to the computer lab and library is available to both adults and students.

(3) *Learning fairs:* Single-session workshops are held in the evening on a variety of topics, such as study skills, memory techniques, concentration, etc. Students, parents, and teachers are invited to attend.

(4) *Parent-support groups:* These are organized and run by parents with meetings held in homes or at school.

(5) *Family room:* This is a room at school containing educational books and games for loan to parents. Parents are welcome to drop in and participate in informal activities. Parents share with each other and learn ways of helping their children.

(6) *Child and adolescent development series:* These programs provide parents with a better understanding of their children's physical, social, and intellectual development.

(7) *Special topic workshops:* These focus on helping children learn and succeed in school. Popular topics include reading, math, study skills, self-esteem, motivation, alternatives to television, and creating a learning environment in the home.

Best Schools have capitalized on the potential for increased student success through parental involvement. Through the creation of a trusting parent-school climate, parent education programs and activities significantly extend the learning opportunities for children. Illustrations from selected Best Schools are provided next.

Illustrations of Parents Providing Supportive Learning Environments

HOLT HIGH SCHOOL, HOLT, MI

Holt is a suburban community located adjacent to a medium-sized urban center in central lower Michigan. The school serves a diverse student population in terms of its socioeconomic and racial, ethnic composition. The school has developed a variety of strategies to assist parents in their efforts to provide a supportive, home learning environment. These include

- Family/Community Involvement Coalition sessions are a series of four seminars on parenting skills.
- Parents serve on an athletic council to hear student appeals.
- Parents have instituted a phone network structure for alcohol and substance abuse problems.
- Each counselor is available one night a week for parents or students. The counseling center provides working parents the opportunity to speak to counselors regarding their children and/or to gather information about programs and colleges.
- The HIPS (Holt Instructional Processing Strategies) team has provided seven parenting seminars since January 1988. The goal is to keep parents aware of the same teaching skills the teachers are learning and practicing. Topics included "prior knowledge," metacognition," and "mapping."
- The school has sponsored parent awareness seminars on AIDS in the evening while their sons/daughters were attending concurrent seminars in school.
- A parent board evaluates and advises the consumer home economics program.

Thomas D. Davis, *Principal, Grades 9–12, 1000 Students*

SAFFORD ENGINEERING/TECHNOLOGY MAGNET MIDDLE SCHOOL, TUCSON, AZ

Safford Engineering/Technology Magnet Middle School is located in the Tucson Unified School District 1, in Tucson, Arizona. Founded and built in 1918, Safford's campus is located in the Armory Park Historic District of Tucson.

Safford has a middle school enrollment of 684 ethnically diverse students, with 58% minority students, 23% limited English proficient students, and 68% of the students receiving free or reduced lunch. The neighborhood students come from the surrounding barrios and projects, while magnet students are bused from all over the district, a radius of approximately twenty miles. In 1981, as a part of the Tucson Unified School District desegregation plan, Safford Middle School became a magnet junior high school specializing in computers, basic skills, and a bilingual curriculum. By 1987, Safford had met the changing needs of the community and district by evolving into a middle school focusing on engineering and technology.

Safford strives to have clear communication between home and school. Open houses, conferences, parent workshops and meetings, counselor presentations on parenting skills, and community workshops provide information for parents. The school has a clearly stated homework policy, a homework hotline, a student assignment calendar, a computer take-home program, and a parent newsletter that includes homework tips. The school also provides parents with literature regarding study skills and parenting tips in the "Take-One Handout Center." Flyers are posted on upcoming events and are sent home. Radio spots announce some activities and the phone master system automatically calls families and informs them of events. Community-based enrichment activities are offered after school and during the summer through the Recreation Investigation Program, the University of Arizona, and the Tucson Unified School District Programs.

Peggy Schroder, *Principal, Grades 6–8, 684 Students*

INDEPENDENCE MIDDLE SCHOOL, BETHEL PARK, PA

Independence Middle School is located in a suburban community located twelve miles from Pittsburgh. IMS was originally constructed as an open classroom school, which began operations in 1975–76, the bicentennial year. The name, Independence, was chosen by the students. In 1980, classroom partitions were installed. Following an extensive renovation project undertaken during 1991, IMS opened in the fall of that year as a beautiful, 21st century building, designed for a child-centered philosophy. It houses interdisciplinary team pods, technology throughout, and a new cafeteria/social center.

Staff members believe that effective education for students can best be achieved through cooperative efforts between teachers and parents. IMS emphasizes the importance of the home/school connection. As a means of achieving this connection, they publish homework guidelines, distribute parent/student handbooks and student assignment booklets, set up an information area in our school office, conduct a parent education series, schedule morning coffee hours and individual conferences, and publish an IMS parent information newsletter. An updated telephone system incorporates the use of voice mailboxes for district personnel. Parents can now easily leave messages for staff. In the homework guidelines booklet, parent responsibilities are defined for homework as follows: 1) share in responsibility for the student's completion of homework; 2) make every effort to create an environment conducive to successful completion of homework; 3) support the school and homework policy by reinforcing the value of homework; 4) be a guide or resource person but insist upon the homework being done by the student; 5) promote daily attendance, which is absolutely necessary to ensure consistent and thorough learning; and 6) communicate problems regarding homework to teachers and/or school administrators. Parents are also offered suggestions for developing study skills. The homework hotline has proven to be a very effective strategy. Each day, team homework assignments are placed on the homework hotline and may be accessed by either parents or students. A survey conducted revealed that 63% of the students regularly used the homework hotline.

The Summer Academy is held for students who desire to improve their skills in math or reading. Learning opportunities are offered outside the school through Community College of Allegheny County (CCAC). During the school year, "Kids College" offers many diverse educational opportunities, including computer training workshops. Summer school for students is also offered through CCAC. The Schoolhouse Arts Center, a community arts program offers students drawing and painting classes. The public library offers a summer reading contest. Cheerleading, basketball, baseball, soccer, and football are part of the athletic clinics offered outside the school. Students and parents are informed of learning opportunities outside the school by announcements 1) in classes, 2) in the daily bulletin, 3) in flyers to parents, 4) in the IMS newsletter, 5) in cable TV releases, 6) on the IMS activity hotline, and 7) in letters mailed to parents of individual students who may benefit from specific opportunities.

Dr. Robert S. David, *Principal, Grades 5–8, 1000 Students*

SUPPORTING THE NEEDS OF FAMILIES

It is clear that parental encouragement, activities and interest at home, and parental participation in schools and classrooms have significant positive influence on a variety of variables, including student achievement. Despite this evidence, parental involvement tends to decrease as students progress into high school. Most parents and teachers welcome the opportunity for increased involvement. A survey conducted by the Southwest Educational Development Laboratory (Sandfort, 1987) revealed that 1) parents and teachers agreed on the value of providing parents with ideas to help children at home and with homework, 2) parents wanted teachers to send more work home related to classroom activities, and 3) parents were interested in learning about their role as co-learner and tutor.

A critical question is, "How can schools increase parental involvement, and just as importantly, what types of social support systems are necessary to facilitate this involvement?" Price, Cioci, and Trautlen (1993) define social support as the provision of aid, affirmation, and affect. Supportive aid refers to practical services and material benefits. Affirmation refers to feedback that raises self-esteem and strengthens identity. Affect refers to the provision of affection, caring, and nurturance. The authors provide a graphic representation of how the support mechanisms for adolescents are interactively linked to family, school, and community organizations.

One way to gain information about the specific needs of parents as it relates to the education of their children is to conduct an in-school survey. Such surveys are relatively simple to construct and may provide the school with pertinent information regarding the needs of specific families (the National School Boards Association and the National School Public Relations Association are excellent sources for sample surveys).

Each survey should outline several vital areas of possible school assistance. For example:

- What specific aspects of classroom procedures are you most interested in (e.g., homework, building student self-esteem, testing, reading skills, etc.)?
- What special parenting sessions are you interested in (e.g., single parenting; child development; teaching your child about sex, drugs, or disease; etc.)?
- What is the best time to hold such meetings/workshops?
- Where would you like these meetings/workshops held?
- Do you need transportation for you (and/or your child) to attend a meeting/workshop?
- Would you like to speak directly to the teacher, principal, counselor, or substance abuse coordinator?

The surveys should be tailored to the unique needs of the school community. Often, the school can serve as a resource providing the names of community agencies and outreach programs that may help troubled or dysfunctional families. Other resources could include school/town library hours, car pooling opportunities, parent support groups, and state and national advocacy groups. Regardless of what format is utilized, it is important to first assess the needs of families, as they relate to their ability to help their children learn and grow and, secondly, to provide a variety of vehicles to disseminate appropriate information and provide appropriate support.

Davies (1991) cites the need for a new and broader definition of parent involvement. One that goes beyond the term *parent* and that more closely describes today's reality.

- *Family* is a more encompassing term that includes other significant adults who have some involvement in child care.
- Involvement should go beyond parent or family and include all agencies and institutions that serve children.
- Involvement should go beyond having family members come to school; services should be available at home or in the neighborhood setting.
- Involvement should not only include the readily available parent, but also those who are "hard to reach."
- Involvement should go beyond the agendas and priorities of teachers and school administrators to include priorities of the families.
- Involvement in urban schools should replace the old "deficit" views of pathologies, traumas, and troubles with a new mind set that emphasizes the inherent strengths of families.

THE BEST SCHOOLS—SUPPORTING THE NEEDS OF FAMILIES

The illustrations of Best Schools' practices, highlighted below, can serve as a guide to help promote active family involvement in schools. It is important, however, that individual school practices closely match the unique needs of individual families and communities.

Illustrations of Supporting the Needs of Families

EDWARDSBURG SENIOR HIGH SCHOOL, EDWARDSBURG, MI

Edwardsburg is the only high school within Edwardsburg School District. The district covers sixty-three miles and is located in the southwestern corner of Michigan's Lower Peninsula. Over 50% of the students have attended district schools since kindergarten. Approximately half of the students' parents graduated from the school district and maintain close ties within the community.

The school supports the needs of families through many of the services organized and/or promoted by the counseling office. The county drug and alcohol agency is invited to send representatives to the school to instruct students and provide small group interaction throughout the school year for those with substance abuse problems or where there is usage in the family.

The county mental health agency provides emergency help if a crisis arises in the school. This agency is recommended to parents as a place of counseling help. The community has a local chapter of Tough Love, which meets weekly. The counselors use this group as an excellent referral source for parents who are in need of support and direction with difficult teens. If a student is institutionalized for a period of time, there is cooperation between the school and the hospitals in the area. Homework is provided for the students, and a meeting is set up with student, parents, and teachers when a student returns to school.

Recently, due to the auto-related death of three students who attended or were attending the school, the president of the Michigan Funeral Directors Association was invited to spend an evening with students who were "hurting." Small group sessions were held by a counselor as a follow-up to his talk.

Peer tutoring is a relatively new program instituted for the students who are having difficulty in the classroom. If a student would prefer tutoring by an adult, a local church provides free tutoring every Monday evening. Progress reports are also sent to parents in the mid-term of each marking period to keep parents abreast of student progress. If a student is identified by a teacher as having learning problems in a specific area, a school psychologist is provided.

For the nontraditional student or the reluctant learner, an alternative education program is in place. If a student is eighteen years of age or older, he/she may attend adult education programs during the day or in the evenings at a different site from the high school.

For the special needs population, annual individualized educational plan meetings are held with school staff and parents. Weekly/monthly services are provided for the physically or otherwise impaired, visually impaired, and hearing impaired. A vocational counselor spends quality time with special education students, making sure their program includes a block of vocational studies. Transportation is provided for students to attend the area career center, math/science consortium center, and the county vocational programs.

To aid parents in keeping up with their child's homework, a homework hotline is available through the school. Every teacher puts his/her weekly homework assignments on the hotline.

For college and career information for parents, informative letters are mailed home, and invitations are extended to attend the local college/career night fair and the local career center. Many national and local scholarship opportunities are announced, and a financial aid meeting is held at the school for parents and seniors every year.

Sherman L. Ostrander, *Principal, Grades 9–12, 514 Students*

SWAINSBORO HIGH SCHOOL, SWAINSBORO, GA

Swainsboro is a small town located in Emanuel County, Georgia. According to the recent census, 20,546 people live in the county, with a per capita income of $10,203 and an unemployment rate of 9.9%. The economy is based primarily on agriculture, forest products, and manufacturing. At the present time, the economy is not strong. Unemployment is high, and, within the past few years, several industries have closed their doors along with some wholesale-retail businesses. Over one-third of the population receives some form of public assistance. Of the households receiving aid for dependent children, less than 1% have both parents in the home. The county has approximately as many divorces as marriages. Emanuel County has one of the highest number per capita of teenage pregnancies in the state. Thirty seven percent of the citizens twenty-five and older have less than a high school education.

Swainsboro's student population consists of 52.5% Caucasian, 46.5% Hispanic, and 1% African-American.

Swainsboro is a very successful school whose staff has dedicated itself to provide support for the diverse needs of the families they serve.

Swainsboro has been selected as one of fourteen communities that serve as a model, state "family connection" site. This charges the community to work together to establish collaborative approaches to address the needs of at-risk students.

The effort that developed from this initiative links the school, the Department of Human Services (health, police, child abuse, mental health) and the Department of Medical Assistance. The school district has a student service center in all the feeder schools and at SHS. This center ensures professional service to families and their children in need of medical assistance, family therapy, parenting skills, transportation services, and child abuse support. The school and community are committed to the philosophy of Family Connection.

The commitment to the collaborative support provided by the school is exemplified in its motto, "We have no families to waste in Emanuel County."

Desse E. Davis, *Principal, Grades 9–12, 934 Students*

QUEEN OF PEACE HIGH SCHOOL, NORTH ARLINGTON, NJ

Queen of Peace High School is a coeducational, Roman Catholic parish high school located in North Arlington, NJ, offering a college preparatory curriculum to an average of 1000 students. Although the town is in suburban Bergen County, over 60% of the students reside in communities in the more urban Hudson and Essex counties.

Many students are first generation Americans; over 45% live in households where English is not the primary language. Coming from economic circumstances as diverse as their cultures, the students' backgrounds range from the affluence afforded by parents who are in the professions through the more modest lifestyles of white and blue collar workers. This variety, which results from the plurality of the feeder communities, not only brings a richness to the fabric of school life, but also raises ever-new challenges.

Specifically, the school serves a diverse student population consisting of 58% Caucasian, 37% Hispanic, and 5% Asian-American, African-American, and other minority groups.

The school recognizes students' families as part of an extended family, sponsoring social activities, meetings, and programs that foster family unity and addresses their concerns. They maintain open lines of communication to provide needed support quickly and efficiently.

Annual social events offer opportunities for family members to share time in a positive atmosphere. Workshops on teen suicide, substance abuse, AIDS, college planning and financing are open to students, parents, and the community. These forums encourage open communication within families on difficult or sensitive topics.

Regular communication between the school and home enables school officials to respond to the needs of individual students and families. Personal requests for prayers often indicate home problems, cuing the staff to maintain contact and provide support. The entire school community has supplied emotional, spiritual, and, at times, even financial assistance to families struck by tragedy.

The guidance department provides counseling and referrals to proper agencies in cases of serious family problems. The school monitors progress, offers assistance, and follows up as needed.

For families with financial difficulties, the principal willingly makes special arrangements for school fees, and assistance is available to qualified families. The school works with families to solve students' daily commutation problems.

Local parishes and feeder schools form a significant part of students' extended families; the school maintains contact with them through visits by faculty and students, notification of their graduates' achievements, and invitations to school activities.

Brother Stephen Olert, *Principal, Grades 9–12, 966 Students*

COLLABORATION WITH EDUCATIONAL INSTITUTIONS AND COMMUNITY GROUPS

The potential of a parent involvement program will be enhanced if it is treated as an integrated strategy with three distinct features: a means of attracting family members to the school; a means of reaching families at home; and a clearly supported, controlled way of engaging teachers in creating new kinds of connections with parents and other community resources (Davies, 1991). It is often that link to other educational institutions and community services that can truly fulfill the school's outreach strategy. The school may be limited in its potential to meet the divergent educational needs of its communities. Similarly, it is likely that it cannot meet most complex family-oriented social, financial, or mental health needs. To this end, successful schools have increasingly developed access to support networks for their children and their families.

THE BEST SCHOOLS–COLLABORATION WITH EDUCATIONAL INSTITUTIONS AND COMMUNITY GROUPS

Successful schools understand the benefits of working relationships with colleges and universities. Those schools fortunate enough to have such institutions in reasonable proximity have a ready source for active research, consultation, staff development, and educational opportunities for students.

Additionally, the financial impact of quality schooling continues to establish barriers to school improvement. To meet the ever-increasing demands of educating today's youth, many schools have formed active partnerships with local and regional businesses and corporations. These partnerships often provide reciprocal benefits. In return for financial or capital resource donations by corporations, schools may provide basic skills instruction for low-achieving corporate members and computer training or have its band or chorus perform at special activities. In any event, many schools have found a valuable resource through these partnerships.

Several illustrations of how Best Schools have utilized educational and community resources are provided next.

Collaboration Illustrations

SPRING HIGH SCHOOL, SPRING, TX

Spring High School is located twenty-three miles northwest of downtown Houston, Texas. In 1969, the school opened with 650 students; recent enrollment is approximately 2350. The school serves a suburban population whose socioeconomic conditions are very diverse. The student body is also quite diverse—represented by 78% Caucasian, 11% Hispanic, 9% African-American, and 2% Asian-American. Additionally, student mobility rates approach 26%.

To meet the ever-challenging demands of educating its students, Spring High School has developed and maintained cooperative working arrangements with many educational organizations and community resources. These include the following:

- There is involvement with several area universities such as Texas A&M, the University of Houston, and Sam Houston State University through their student teacher programs.
- North Harris County Community College fulfills many of the educational needs of both parents and students.
- Several students maintain concurrent enrollment with SHS and NHCC for college credit.
- For "College Night," the school invites all area and state colleges and universities to share information with parents and students on entrance requirements; over 100 universities throughout the United States send representatives.
- Members of the Armed Forces set up a table during lunch periods to answer questions of potential enlistees from the student body.
- The advisory committee on education involves parents and the business community in current school issues.
- The chamber of commerce meets with school personnel to discuss pertinent school/business issues.
- The PRIDE program receives financial support from First Interstate Bank and other area businesses.
- Pepsi Corporation provides a positive, uplifting message for students to be the best they can be through its "Be Excellent" program.
- County Health Services provides a mammogram van at the school once a year for staff members at a reduced rate and provides speakers on topics such as AIDS and teen pregnancy.
- MADD/SADD promote a drug/alcohol-free society through visual aids for classrooms. They also provide a Crash Car on campus for students to see reaction time under the influence of alcohol illustrated.
- Student council participates in the state student government summer camp at Southern Methodist University.
- Local businesses give coupons for free games/food for A's on report cards.
- Sam Houston State University and Lamar University sponsor counseling workshops.
- Local dentists and doctors provide reduced and/or free services for students in need.
- Daughters of the American Revolution give a scholarship to one student each year.
- Northwest Assistance Ministries sponsors a needy family in the area during the Thanksgiving and Christmas holiday seasons.

Gloria Marshall, *Principal, Grades 9–12, 2298 Students*

GONZAGA PREPARATORY SCHOOL, SPOKANE, WA

Gonzaga Preparatory School is located in the North Foothills section of Spokane, Washington, approximately two miles from the center of the city.

The school's 853 students come from the inland Northwest section of Washington and Idaho, which includes the cities of Spokane and Coeur d'Alene, the Spokane Valley, and other areas within a fifty-mile radius.

The student population is racially mixed, with approximately 10% of the students identified as Asian-American, African-American, Hispanic, Indian American, or Eastern Indian. Sixty-eight percent of the students are Roman Catholic. The student population is particularly stable, with a mobility rate of 0.5% over the past five years.

The school has a longstanding tradition of academic and athletic excellence, which has successful integrated resources from its surrounding communities to enrich student learning opportunities.

This begins with the school's longstanding relationship with Gonzaga University, through which several students attend college classes. The liberal arts curriculum enhances the preparation of students who are more vocationally inclined. For these students, there is an arrangement with the local school district, through which they are permitted to go to the "skills center." Still other students take courses such as drivers' education or participate on sport teams at public institutions.

Gonzaga Prep collaborates with other community agencies. There are two very active service clubs for juniors and seniors. One of the main goals of these organizations is to help meet the needs of the community at large. Events include organizing a picnic for the Big Brother/Sister agency, running dances for the mentally handicapped, sponsoring a casino night for the elderly, and helping an inner-city school with some special needs. Moreover, Gonzaga Preparatory School, through Project Lead, collaborates with the Spokane Junior League in setting up a leadership skills program. There is also cooperation with the Spokane Police Department in a drug and alcohol awareness program called "Project Dare."

A most interesting collaboration is developed through a required senior class called community services. Students work approximately four hours a week serving the community in a direct way. Naturally, a great deal of communication and joint effort is required to insure the smooth running of this class. The more than twenty-five agencies that the school works with include four area hospitals, four inner-city schools, several youth assistance agencies, elderly services, and three agencies that work with the mentally disabled. Students take the class for either nine or eighteen weeks.

John Traynor, *Principal, Grades 9–12, 853 Students*

McKINLEY MIDDLE SCHOOL, ALBUQUERQUE, NM

McKinley is one of twenty-four middle schools in the Albuquerque Public School District. Families from the school's attendance area are from very low to lower middle-income ranges. The student population consists of 49% Caucasian, 43% Hispanic, 4% African-American, 3% Native American and 1% Asian-American. Thirty-six percent of these students qualify for free or reduced lunch.

The school has maintained a tradition of success and has worked collaboratively with local schools and agencies to foster school improvement. Many staff members enroll in course work at the University of New Mexico, leading to advanced degrees in special education, educational administration, and curriculum and instruction. Some teachers have made presentations to university classes on particular teaching strategies, classroom management, individual reinforcement procedures, grouping practices, and new materials. Additionally, the school often has student teachers and administrative interns placed in the school through preservice preparatory institutions.

Local businesses show tremendous support for the school community. They donate time and materials to school programs. For example, Price Club employees serve as after-school intramurals coaches, and a local restaurant provides experiences for students in all facets of business. The school also collaborates with community organizations, sharing playing fields with the local little league group and the district athletic programs and by using the gymnasium facility of the neighboring Boys' Club. A member of the local sheriff's department lives on campus in a mobile home. He provides added security and a link between students and the law enforcement community.

As another example of community collaboration, students at the school regularly provide service to "Joy Junction," the only family homeless shelter in the city. They raise money, collect items, and prepare and serve meals. Youth Development Incorporated, cheerleaders of the University of New Mexico, the University of New Mexico's basketball team, and neighborhood high school students provide additional activities for McKinley students.

Dennie Lee Paschich, *Principal, Grades 6–8, 979 Students*

SUMMARY

The accumulated evidence overwhelmingly supports the importance of parent involvement in children's education. Some parents have the skills and the motivation to foster both cooperative opportunities and achievement motivation. More importantly, parents who do not have these skills can readily acquire them if the school makes a concerted effort to reach out and facilitate the training of parents. This can be most successful if the school 1) takes a proactive, positive role in creating a trusting, responsive climate; 2) seeks parent input in determining the needs appropriate to the involvement initiatives; 3) is willing to be flexible in meeting those needs by taking the program to homes, neighborhoods, and workplaces; 4) provides resources beyond the school to assist parents with complex family issues; and 5) inherently respects the values and cultures of the family.

The research shows that, when teachers and administrators are strongly committed to engaging parents in their children's education, the outcomes for the child, family, teacher, and school are almost exclusively positive.

REFERENCES

Becher, Rhoda. (1986). "Parents and Schools," *ERIC Digest*, ERIC Clearinghouse on Elementary and Early Childhood Education. Urbana, IL.

Dauber, Susan L. and Joyce L. Epstein. (1989). "Parent Attitudes and Practices of Parent Involvement in Inner-City Elementary and Middle Schools," John Hopkins Center for Research in Elementary and Middle Schools, Report No. 33, Baltimore, MD.

Davies, Don. (1991). "Schools Reaching Out: Family, School, and Community Partnerships for Student Success," *Phi Delta Kappan* (January):376–382.

Epstein, Joyce. (1988). "How Do We Improve Programs for Parent Involvement?" *Educational Horizons* (66):58–59.

Fruchter, Norm, Anne Galleta, and Lynee J. White. (1993). "New Direction in Parent Involvement," *Equity and Choice*, 9(3):33–43.

Henderson, A. (1988). "Parents Are a School's Best Friend," *Phi Delta Kappan* (October):148–153.

Illinois State Board of Education. (1993). *The Relationship between Parent Involvement and Student Achievement: A Review of the Literature*. Springfield, IL: Department of Planning, Research and Evaluation.

Jones, Linda T. (1991). *Strategies for Involving Parents in Their Children's Education*. Fastback No. 315, Bloomington, IN: Phi Delta Kappan Educational Foundation.

Liontos, Lynn Balster. (1992). *At-Risk Families and Schools Becoming Partners*. Eugene, OR: ERIC Clearinghouse on Educational Management.

Price, Richard H., Wendy Pennen Cioci, and Barbara Trautlen. (1993). "Webs of Influence: School and Community Programs That Enhance Adolescent Health and Education," *Teachers College Record*, 94(3):487–521.

Sandfort, James A. (1987). "Putting Parents in Their Place in Schools," *NASSP Bulletin*, 71:99–103.

Thomas, Anne Hill. (1992). "HOMEWORK: How Effective? How Much to Assign? The Need for Clear Policies," *Oregon School Study Council*, 36(1):20.

University of Minnesota, Hubert H. Humphrey Institute of Public Affairs. (1994). "Training for Parent Partnership: Much More Should Be Done," Minneapolis, MN: University of Minnesota.

U.S. Department of Education. (1986). *What Works—Research about Teaching and Learning*. Washington, D.C.: U.S. Department of Education.

Warner, Izona. (1991). "Parents in Touch: District Leadership for Parent Involvement," *Phi Delta Kappan* (January):372–375.

PART TWO

7700 INSTRUCTIONAL HOURS—THE MIDDLE SCHOOL AND HIGH SCHOOL CURRICULUM

CHAPTER 6

The Language Arts

LANGUAGE arts instruction occupies as much as 30% of a middle school and 15% of a high school student's instructional day, 1650 hours of a student's journey from sixth through twelfth grade. This chapter looks at the following questions concerning how this time is best spent in preparing students for their lives now and for life in the 21st century:

- What does theory say about what students should learn and how they should be taught in language arts classrooms?
- How have the Best Schools successfully translated theory into practice in language arts?
- How do the Best Schools assess what students know and what they can do?
- How have effective programs been developed and implemented; what were the resources needed for development and support?
- What do case studies of Best Schools show about highly successful language arts instruction in four very different community contexts?
- Finally, what are some of the practices, programs and resources used by the Best Schools, which are widely available to other program developers?

WHAT STUDENTS SHOULD LEARN

According to the National Goals of Education, by the year 2000,

> American students will leave grades 4, 8, and 12 having demonstrated competency in challenging subject matter including English . . . and every school in America will ensure that all students learn to use their minds well, so they may be prepared for responsible citizenship, further learning, and productive employment in our modern economy.
>
> Every adult American will be literate and will possess the knowledge and skills necessary to compete in a global economy and exercise the rights and responsibilities of citizenship.

The goal of language instruction has always been to develop literate citizens; however, what constitutes the literacy needs of every adult in the 1990s or the year 2000 is far different than it was 100 or fifty years ago.

Over the past ten years, educational organizations such as the International Reading Association (IRA), the National Council of Teachers of English (NCTE), and the Modern Language Association have developed expectations for what students should know and be able to do. Currently, the bipartisan National Standards Task Force on Standards and Testing is working to develop national standards for English for grades K–12. The format will include vignettes from elementary, middle, and high schools, illustrating the standards in the three strands of the language arts/English program: reading, writing, and oral language. In addition to national efforts to define what children should know, numerous states and thousands of teachers and experts in the field of communication and learning have worked to develop outcome objectives or proficiencies to serve as a basis for language arts instruction in states, schools, and classrooms. The results of these efforts have been definitions of literacy, which require very high levels of comprehension, fluency, transference, interpretation, analysis, and appreciation in reading, writing, and speaking.

HOW STUDENTS LEARN–HOW STUDENTS ARE TAUGHT

For many years, educators worked within a paradigm that held that children learn primarily "part-to-whole." This view of how children acquire knowledge had profound effects on the decisions made in schools concerning curriculum, lesson objectives, instructional methods, materials selected for classroom use, organization of students for instruction, use of time, and assessment practices. The dominant belief that children learn "part-to-whole" led to a curriculum based on the sequential acquisition of discrete skills and instruction organized to maximize the effectiveness of learning the parts. Grammar, handwriting, reading, literature, and spelling were treated as separate entities with separate time slots, separate basal texts, and separate activities. In turn, each content area was divided into finite subskills, taught in a given sequence. Three learning assumptions supported this instructional model. The first was that learning is linear; that is, it is necessary to master skills in an identified sequence. Each individual skill, therefore, must be learned before the subsequent skill. As a result, remedial programs focused on reteaching specific skills identified as deficient through testing. A second assumption of this model was that the student who mastered each discrete skill would automatically, or with little direct instruction, be able to put the skills together, emerging as a critical reader, a fluent writer. A third assumption consistent with this model was that grouping students homogeneously would reduce variability within the class in terms of skills and allow teachers to focus attention on the "correct level" of skills and adjust the "pace" of instruction for each group.

The emphasis on the acquisition of discrete skills, close monitoring of these skills, and remediation of skills was credited with increasing standardized test scores in the late 1970s and early 1980s, especially in disadvantaged educational settings. The commercial standardized tests and state-developed minimal proficiency tests of the era paralleled the prevalent view of learning, instructional objectives, and the content of textbooks; in other words, the tests assessed the acquisition of discrete skills.

A different type of test, the National Assessment of Educational Progress (NAEP) confirmed that there were slight gains in lower level skills and concepts between 1971 and 1988 (NAEP 1990). However, the NAEP also assessed higher level applications and concepts, such as the synthesizing of information from specialized reading materials and the understanding of material read. For these higher order skills, the NAEP found that there were almost no gains during the same period. The 1992 NAEP assessment of reading and writing found that only 37% of high school seniors reached the "proficient level" in reading, and, while high school seniors had some understanding of informative and narrative writing tasks they continued to have difficulty with persuasive writing [National Center for Educational Statistics (NCES), 1993, 1994]. The apparent differences in evaluation results between commercial standardized tests and the NAEP, and their concomitant impact on a district's educational program rest with the decisions about what is important for students to learn, as well as what and how they learn. The NAEP is much more aligned with emerging national and state standards.

Over the past twenty years, research on how students learn has challenged the assumptions upon which the discrete/linear skill model was based. Numerous studies have shown that the acquisition of isolated skills is not positively related to fluency in reading, writing, or speaking (Goodman, 1964). For example, learning grammar out of the context of writing does not improve writing ability (Mellon, 1969; Sherwin, 1969; Hillocks, 1986). The 1992 NAEP study found that students of teachers who placed heavy emphasis on literature-based reading instruction and less emphasis on phonics instruction had higher levels of proficiency than those of teachers who reported low literature and high phonics approaches to instruction (NCES, 1993). In the area of writing, top-performing schools were more likely to report that teachers stressed quality and creativity of ideas and placed less emphasis on mechanics (NCES, 1994). Studies of ability grouping of students have shown that, rather than helping lower ability students to overcome deficits, homogeneous grouping increases the learning gap and undermines self-esteem (Oakes, 1985; Slaven, 1987).

During the late 1970s and 1980s, research on learning and brain development began to lead to a revised view of what is important for students to learn, how children learn, and how instruction should be organized to maximize learning.

> Optimizing the use of the human brain means using the brain's infinite capacity to make connections and understanding what conditions maximize this process. (Caine and Caine, 1991, p. 9)

As part of the reassessment of how students learn, research distinguished between *surface knowledge,* i.e., the memorization of facts, procedures, and applications, and *meaningful knowledge,* i.e., connected learning, which makes sense to the learner. This expanded view of what children should learn and the research on how children learn meaningful knowledge led to the development of a whole or integrated approach to teaching language. Five assumptions underlie the integrated language arts (ILA) model. The first is that teaching must provide a student with experiences that enable him/her to construct meaning by making connections among content and skills, i.e., to perceive patterns and to make connections with previous learning. For example, vocabulary and grammar are best learned when they are integrated into a total reading/writing experience.

A second assumption is that learning is natural and motivational; thus, the classroom should be organized around natural approaches to learning and the student's own life experiences. For example, children have learned to speak and have developed an average vocabulary of 10,000 words by the time they enter school (ASCD, 1992). They accomplish this without memorizing rules of grammar, lists of spelling words, or rules of phonics. The model holds that to learn how to read, write, and speak, students should actively engage in reading, writing, speaking, and listening activities, much more so than the discrete/linear model suggested. Reading should be literature-based and whole books, rather than fragments or condensed versions. Writing should be taught as a process and for multiple purposes and audiences.

A third assumption is that, rather than fragmenting content, blocks of time should be set aside for the integration of the strands of language arts, with instructional emphasis on making connections among writing, reading, speaking, and listening. Individual skills continue to be taught; however, they should be taught in meaningful contexts that emphasize higher order thinking skills.

A fourth assumption is that students learn best when they are not placed in ability groups. Lower and average ability students benefit most from whole-class, interest groups, and flexible and changing skill support groups; however, high-ability students are not negatively impacted (Slaven, 1987). In fact, the integrated curriculum brings to all students an instructional approach that has traditionally been advocated and reserved for gifted students. The flexibility of the integrated language program provides challenges and opportunities for all students.

The fifth assumption is that assessment is best embedded in the instructional process; in other words, it is part of the instructional process, rather than an add-on to instruction. Assessment should provide evidence not only of what a student knows, but also of what a student can do. As much as possible, it should be performance-based.

THE BEST SCHOOLS – THEORY INTO PRACTICE IN LANGUAGE ARTS

The Best Schools, whether suburban, inner-city urban, or rural, teach their students in integrated language arts (ILA) programs, which focus on making meaning and connections among the strands of the language arts. The schools also integrate language arts with other curricular areas, through writing across the curriculum and literature related to history, science, and the arts. They are committed to achieving verifiable outcomes for all students in reading, writing, and speaking. Their curricula are based on the theory and research on learning, which support integrated teaching and learning of reading, writing, and speaking. They are using and developing various forms of more authentic assessment, which are aligned with their curriculum and local, state, and/or national standards. In practice, the integrated language arts programs in the Best Schools have many characteristics in common; however, integrated language arts or whole-language is only an approach to curriculum, teaching, and assessment. It does not come packaged as a series of textbooks; therefore, the ILA program must be developed to fit within the context of each school.

Illustrations in Language Arts: The Contexts (Case Studies)

J. A. ROGERS ACADEMY OF LIBERAL ARTS AND SCIENCE, KANSAS CITY, MO

In the 1986 desegregation court order for the Kansas City Missouri School District, the J. A. Rogers Academy of Liberal Arts and Science was designated as a magnet school designed to implement instructional content in a form appropriate to address the distinctive characteristics of the middle school, preadolescent child. The court order indicated that the school "shall take advantage of the students' natural inclination to experience and apply first hand the content of what is to be learned and taught through the curriculum . . . and shall be an exemplary interdisciplinary middle school program which uses the Arts and Sciences theme as its primary means of instruction."

The student population at Rogers is representative of that found in many large, urban school districts. Students are impacted by many facets of the inner-city environment, including drugs, gang violence, and lack of perceived opportunity. An eighth grader was killed last year over the issue of a Starter® jacket. Forty-six percent of the students qualify for free or reduced-price lunch. Students are drawn from the entire Kansas City, Missouri, school district, and nonminority students are recruited from surrounding suburbs. While the district maintains a minority enrollment of 74%, Rogers has been successful in attracting nonminority students to closely approximate the court target of 60% minority and 40% nonminority.

Linda K. Kondris, *Principal, Grades 6–8, 351 Students*

FOX CHAPEL AREA HIGH SCHOOL, PITTSBURGH, PA

Fox Chapel Area District is a region of physical and economic contrasts. Lying ten miles northwest of downtown Pittsburgh, which encompasses 33.96 square miles, the high school is set on a forty-acre site in a residential suburban area. The district serves six communities, of which the boroughs of Sharpsburg, Blawnox, and Aspinwall are urban centers along the

Allegheny River; Fox Chapel Borough and O'Hara Township are prosperous middle- to upper middle-class suburban areas, while parts of Indiana Township are agricultural or coal mining regions. The *Wall Street Journal* named this school as one of the country's hundred best in 1989. Three of the district's six schools have been named Blue Ribbon Schools of Excellence.

Charles J. Territo, *Principal, Grades 9–12, 1219 Students*

FLOWING WELLS HIGH SCHOOL, TUCSON, AZ

Flowing Wells High School serves a community of approximately 40,000 and is located in the northwest section of Tucson, Arizona. The campus encompasses seventeen acres and is surrounded by both commercial and residential areas, including mobile homes and apartment complexes. The community is characterized as having the highest population receiving assistance from the Department of Economic Security in the entire Tucson metropolitan area.

The school received recognition as a National Blue Ribbon School in 1987 and 1992 and the National Drug Free School Recognition Award in 1988. There are 1800 students enrolled in grades 9–12, with 35% of the students district-wide participating in the free or reduced lunch programs. All eight schools in the Flowing Wells School District have been recognized as Blue Ribbon Schools of Excellence.

Nicholas I. Clement, *Principal, Grades 9–12, 1800 Students*

BRONXVILLE PUBLIC SCHOOL, BRONXVILLE, NY

The high school is located in an upper income community with residents who work primarily in New York City. The village is one square mile, and the school district boundaries are contiguous with the village boundaries (the only district in New York State with coinciding district and village boundaries). The entire school district, K–12, is located in one building.

The population of the high school is college-directed. In any given graduating class, a few students may opt not to attend college directly, but the program of studies is college preparatory. The school is a member of the Coalition of Essential Schools.

John Kehoe, *Principal, (Alan J. Guma, Principal at time of recognition), Grades 9–12, 330 Students*

THE BEST SCHOOLS–CLASS ORGANIZATION AND INSTRUCTIONAL TIME

ILA in most of the Best Middle Schools is block scheduled for approximately 400 minutes per week. Class sections are heterogeneously assigned. Within the class, students are not divided into ability-based groups; instead, teachers work with the class as a whole for many activities and form temporary groups based on interest in a particular book or the need to introduce or reinforce a particular set of skills. Frequently students also work in cooperative groups, pairs, or independently. Class projects may involve cross-age groups. High school English classes integrate literature, writing, and speaking. Longer block scheduled periods in many schools allow for greater amounts of instructional time during some days of the week. The correlation of literature with other subjects, cross-subject team teaching, and writing across the curriculum increases instructional time for reading, writing, and speaking. In the Best Schools, low-level classes have been phased out, with all students now taking standard core English classes. Students wishing to take very challenging courses may elect honors or advanced placement courses. Special education students are mainstreamed to the greatest degree possible.

Class Organization Illustrations

J. A. ROGERS ACADEMY, MO

The J. A. Rogers' program is designed to meet the individual needs of each student and, as such, is basic to the process of running the total school program. All classes at Rogers are heterogeneously grouped, with the exception of the severe learning disabilities (SLD) classroom. The SLD students meet with their teacher during the core periods and are intermixed with other students for foreign language, the fine arts, physical education, and exploratory classes. Every student at Rogers meets with his/her advisor and parents three times a year to establish goals for academics, social interaction, and health and wellness. The plan is reviewed twice more during the year and is tailored to meet individual needs.

Students experiencing academic difficulty are identified early through the team families, and a plan of assistance is developed in consultation with the parent and child. One method of identifying special academic needs is through the use of a computer program that pinpoints the student's level of achievement in reading and mathematics. Each student in the school completes this review at the beginning of each school year. Computer-assisted instruction can be prescribed to meet the needs for both enrichment or remediation. In addition, four transition teachers work closely with teachers to support students in mathematics and humanities. The transition teachers work with students within the regular classroom setting so that students requiring special assistance do not leave their normal environment and become out of step with the progression of the regular classroom.

Every student participates daily in a special projects class. The school's ten resource scholars meet formally as a group at least once a week and informally daily. At the end of each quarter, the progress of each student is specifically evaluated to determine his or her placement for the next quarter. The Rogers system is flexible enough that it is possible for a student to participate in two special projects classes during the same quarter. For example, during one quarter, a student chose history as her special project. She began work on a history essay using primary documents from the Western Historical Manuscript collection at the University of Missouri at Kansas City. In her science class, she became interested in a microbiology project. A conference was held between the student and the science and history resource scholars. As a result the student spent the next quarter with the science resource scholar but continued to travel to UMKC weekly to work on the history project.

FOX CHAPEL AREA HIGH SCHOOL, PA

The staff of Fox Chapel Area High School recognizes that students have a variety of educational needs. Within the curriculum, there are standard, accelerated, and advanced placement groupings. Supplementing these courses are English with reading, integrated instruction, and resource room instruction. Twenty-six percent of the students elect to take more than the four years of required English.

Students receive support services in a variety of ways. Based on individual needs, students may be included in a combination of regular education classes and special education classes. Students may also be placed in classes that are co-taught by an educational support teacher and a regular education teacher. The special education teacher is also responsible for adapting the curriculum, establishing goals, and providing materials so that educationally handicapped students can be successful in regular education programs. Because of these efforts, Fox Chapel Area High School has been recognized nationally for its accomplishments in the process of inclusion.

Eventually, the district's strategic plan calls for writing of an individual education plan (IEP) for every student. This has been implemented for all educational support and gifted students. There is a strong emphasis on inclusion, allowing students to participate in the programs that they, their parents, and staff feel are important to their academic success.

FLOWING WELLS HIGH SCHOOL, AZ

Students at Flowing Wells High School are required to take four years of English; however, nearly 30% elect to take a fifth English course. Through collegial support networks, major efforts have been undertaken to break the isolation that teachers experience. Currently, there are four cross-curricular projects that require extensive collaboration between faculty members from different disciplines. These programs include American studies—two teachers are integrating junior English content with American history; honors block—three teachers are integrating honors English, biology, and global studies; re-entry and STRIVE—four teachers are teaming in a program designed to provide successful experiences to high-risk students and students who have dropped out; and freshman/sophomore block—two teachers integrating math, science, social studies, and English in a school-within-a-school. Teachers in these programs have been provided release time and summer curriculum time for planning. Teachers in the freshman/sophomore block have also been provided two hours of common planning time for ongoing collaboration.

For the honors/advanced placement students, the school offers five courses in honors English and advanced placement English. The honors program promotes and expects students to demonstrate higher level thinking skills. The current enrollment in honors classes reflects the student body's diversity: freshman English—eighty-nine, sophomore English—forty-three, junior English—twenty-five, and advanced placement English—eighteen. Students also have the opportunity to pursue college classes not offered in our curriculum at local universities. The district pays tuition for these courses.

Flowing Wells offers three levels of diplomas, each of which requires a more rigorous program than the minimum required by the state:

(1) Advanced Studies Platinum Diploma—four years of English, history, mathematics; three years of science; two years foreign language, health; twenty-three elective credits; a 3.0 GPA and in the top quarter of the class
(2) Advanced Studies Gold Diploma—four years of English; three and one-half history; two each mathematics and science; one year foreign language, health; twenty-three elective credits and in the top quarter of the class
(3) Blue Diploma—four years of English; two years each of mathematics, science, history, health, and electives

Students are not tracked by diploma goal, nor are they asked to indicate which diploma they wish to receive. The awarding of a particular diploma is based on the student's record at the completion of the senior year.

For the students at the remedial level, the school offers skills labs in math and English. These programs are designed to provide students with intensive instruction in essential math and language arts skills. Currently, 12% of the student population is enrolled in one or more skill lab classes.

Recent examples of responses to current research, assessments, and national goals include the discontinuation of tracking and ability grouping of students, except in the advanced placement classes; de-emphasis on teacher lecturing in lieu of student participation; and a restructured day concept with the departure from the traditional six fifty-five-minute periods. Two days per week, the school operates on a block schedule consisting of three 110-minute classes each day.

BRONXVILLE HIGH SCHOOL, NY

Students at Bronxville Public School are organized into homeroom and seminar groups that remain together for four years. Common planning time is provided in the master schedule for the academic departments, the two interdisciplinary teams (ninth and tenth grade, social studies, English, and art), the seminar teachers, and grade-level teams. Thus, the work of a collegial faculty is enhanced.

THE BEST SCHOOLS – CURRICULUM

The goal of instruction is for students to become fluent and self-motivated writers, readers, and speakers. In most of the Best Middle Schools, the curriculum is organized around themes (i.e., "people around the world," "discovery") determined by individual teachers and/or school or district committees. Frequently, the chosen themes correlate with the social studies and/or science curriculum at the given grade level. It is not unusual in the Best Schools for language arts and social studies to be planned as an integrated program. Every opportunity is taken to make explicit connections among content areas. Research projects are a central part of the program.

The high school curriculum is literature- and writing-based, with attention given to oral presentation. Writing fluently for various purposes is emphasized, with grammar and mechanics supporting the writing process. Themes are frequently used to make connections with other areas of the curriculum; in many cases, integrated courses that include English and social studies and, in some cases, the arts, have been developed with research playing a major role in the curriculum. Technology and media center staff and resources are closely tied to the English program.

Literature

A comprehensive literature program is an important component of ILA. Through assigned and self-selected books, students become familiar with literary genres, authors, style, and cultural traditions. The Best Schools use a host of strategies to motivate students to read. At the middle school level, time is often set aside every day for silent reading. In some cases, the entire school, including the teachers and principal, read at the same time. Two examples of this approach are the "Excited about Reading" schoolwide silent reading program developed in Brookmeade, Tennessee, and the "Drop Everything And Read" (DEAR) used in such schools as Irwin, New Jersey, and Wantagh, New York. It is common for an individual student to be reading three different books at the same time – a core book, a group interest book, and an individual selection. Teachers model reading by actually reading with and then sharing their reading experiences with the class. Also, contests and reading logs are used to motivate and monitor children's reading. Some of the contests are local in nature; others such as Book-It (Baker's Chapel, SC; Brookmead, TN; John Grasse, PA), sponsored by Pizza Hut, are national. The "Children's Choice Program" is a national program that involves children in critiquing new books (Wantagh, NY). Book lists encourage children to read during the summer recess.

It is not just the quantity of books children read that is central to an ILA approach, but students engage in reflection on what they have read – in conferences with the teacher, with other students, and through their writing. The focus is on comprehension, meaning, and making connections. Students engage in prereading activities, active reading, review activities, and a wide spectrum of response strategies. They read for various purposes. Often, literature connects across the curriculum with math, science, social studies, health, and the arts. Meaning, connections, and transference are emphasized throughout the day. The Junior Great Book (NDN) program and Philosophy for Children (NDN) program are used in a number of schools (A. J. Rogers Academy, MO; Guilliver Academy, FL; Pearl, NY; Wantagh, NY).

A wide variety of fiction and nonfiction material is central to a literature-based approach. There is an emphasis on multicultural literature, which allows students to make connections with their own cultural background and that of other cultures and history; as a result, high school programs go beyond the teaching of American and English literature to include the study of a wide range of world literature.

Writing

Writing in an ILA program is taught as a process and includes prewriting, drafting, revising, editing, and publishing. This approach to the teaching of writing gained wide acceptance through the Bay Area Writing Project and the New Jersey Writing Project (NDN) almost twenty years ago. In 1984, the National Council of Teachers of English (NCTE) identified centers of excellence (ten of which were in Blue Ribbon Schools), which provided models of outstanding language arts programs for schools across the nation (Tchudi, 1991). The centers provided additional impetus and support for the process writing approach.

Writing is frequently linked to what the students are reading. Students learn to write in order to inform, persuade, narrate, describe, entertain, or communicate via E-mail; they learn to consider the audience in their writing. They work in large, small, or cooperative groups or alone to review, to critique, and to edit work in progress prior to "publication." Students write every day; they keep individual journals, share their writing with others, conference with the teacher, and reflect on their own writing. Brainstorming, drafting, critiquing, redrafting, and editing all lead to the "publishing" of the final work. The published work is what is formally assessed by the teacher and/or the student. Young authors' conferences are often held to share the students' published works. Programs such as the AT&T Learning Network allow students, via telecommunication, to engage in problem solving, research, and writing in cooperation with students across the country, as well as in other countries.

The Best Schools use many strategies to develop and recognize the published products of students. Most of the Best Schools use word processing and publishing programs to enable students to prepare work for "publication." Computers used for publishing include single stand-alone computers, mini-labs of four to eight computers in classrooms, separate computer labs, and/or a cluster of computers in the library. In schools serving disadvantaged populations, computers may be available for students to take home (Mirabeau Lamar, TX; Loma Heights, NM). The use of computers as tools also supports the development of technological literacy.

Speaking and Listening

Speaking and listening are two important strands of the ILA program because each helps students to develop self-confidence, to expand their understanding by questioning and responding, to problem solve, to clarify their ideas, and to develop social skills necessary for successful participation in the school and work community. Informal activities for speaking and listening include small- and large-group sharing, task-related talk, impromptu talks, dialogues, improvised dramatics, and debates. Formal activities for speaking and listening include opportunities for formal presentations, panel discussions, note taking, and demonstrations.

Support Skills and Strategies

Support skills and strategies underlie the ILA program. Specific skills may be taught prior to, during, or after a more holistic activity. Strategies, processes for doing something, are generally taught prior to an activity and reinforced subsequent to an activity. Thus, a reading skill might be to identify fact and fantasy in a story, whereas a reading strategy might be to create a story-map of that story to determine if the fact and fantasy remain consistent. A literature skill might be to discuss a character in a story. A literature strategy might focus on comparison and contrast of two characters via a chart or graphic organizer. Writing skills might include editing one's own or another's paper for standard English spelling; a writing strategy might be to use webbing as a prewriting activity in order to discover and narrow down a topic.

Curriculum Illustrations

J. A. ROGERS ACADEMY, MO

The curriculum at Rogers is challenging and rigorous. All students complete three years of humanities (language arts/social studies integration); three years of mathematics, including pre-algebra in seventh grade and algebra in eighth grade; three years of science (an integrated math/science class in the sixth grade); three years of foreign language (a four-language exploratory course in sixth grade, including Latin, Chinese, Yoruba, and Spanish or French, and a single language taken daily in seventh and eighth grades); fine arts taken for three years every day for one semester per year; and family living arts taken every other day for a semester each year. Every student has a daily special projects class within his/her area of interest and a daily tutorial class to promote enrichment opportunities.

A comprehensive program of language arts is required of all students during each of their three years at Rogers Academy. Each grade must take a course in humanities that incorporates language, literature, social studies, and the arts. These courses are designed with whole-language approaches in order to emphasize reading, writing, listening, and thinking with each assignment.

Sixth grade students concentrate on the district language arts course, along with specific work in the development of writing skills; a unit in public speaking is included. Sixth graders are also required to write essays and theme papers. Seventh graders study oratory as the second phase of the speaking component; eighth graders continue the speaking component with the study of debate. All eighth graders are required to write an advanced research paper (junior thesis). Reading comprehension is stressed in all courses with the use of the Junior Great Books program (NDN). Literature and writing are infused into all courses at Rogers.

All grades use the AT&T Learning Network, an effective instructional program that provides creative ways of integrating communication technology in the classrooms. Using telecommunications, students enhance their communication skills by writing via E-mail for distant audiences, reading and evaluating the work of others—writing across the curriculum, across the country, and beyond and cooperative work strategies with teams of peers in other states and countries.

The writing-to-learn strategy is used across the curriculum and helps students solve problems, engage in discussions, use multi-media techniques, and engage in the processes of project production that provides a variety of opportunities for students to participate in authentic reading and writing tasks. Writing is assisted by student use of the computer writing lab with the Writer's Network software program. All teaching staff have been trained in this program in order to support writing in all content areas. Writer's Network gives students writing power through prewriting activities, organizing strategies, word processing, tools for proofing, and collaborative learning through peer review. Students are involved in authentic writing across the curriculum and increased metacognition through portfolio development.

The Philosophy for Children program (NDN) is a component of the sixth grade humanities course and assists critical thinking skills.

The Learning Resource Center (LRC) contains a large book collection meeting Missouri AAA requirements, which is augmented by an extensive periodical microfiche file, a variety of audiovisual materials, and computer technology. A structured sequence of instruction in retrieval techniques is begun in the sixth grade in the humanities classes. The LRC has six computers equipped with CD-ROM drives. References such as general and science encyclopedias and periodical abstracts are available on CD and expedite student searches. Three microfiche readers are available as well as a microfiche printer. The LRC is wired to receive cable programming, including ShareNet and Express Exchange. The librarian works closely with teachers to plan student use of the LRC resources in support of curriculum goals.

FOX CHAPEL AREA HIGH SCHOOL, PA

The English department at Fox Chapel offers fifteen courses that include electives in acting, public speaking, and composition. The communication skills of reading, writing, speaking, and listening are emphasized in all courses. Independent study is a unique feature in grades 9 and 10, which requires organizational competence, critical thinking, and analytical writing. Students earn accelerated status by successfully completing the independent study criteria while maintaining a B average in the course work.

Research has shown that students learn best when concepts are taught thematically, rather than in isolation. The English 9 curriculum exemplifies improvement in content and delivery due to its heterogeneous and thematic approach. Its title, "Story Makers and Story Tellers," includes the student as the maker and the teller. In these roles, the foundation is laid for English 10's emphasis on world literature, English 11's emphasis on American literature, and English 12's emphasis on British literature. Once the student sees the potential of storytelling/writing, she/he gains greater insight into the work of professional writers. Beginning with the learner as a teller/writer lends credence and balance to their English education.

The Academic Seminar is a unique course that was created through a cooperative effort of faculty and administration and is required for graduation. This course was developed to teach study skills while focusing on the ever-increasing demands on students brought about by new technology and through a continuing demand from the community that the school act as an instrument of social responsibility. The course is designed to prepare the student for a successful academic experience, as well as to address postgraduate concerns.

Chapter 1 services are provided through the REACH English program. Students who test two grades below reading level on the Test of Achievement and Proficiency are assigned to a class that is co-taught by an English and a reading teacher. They follow the regular curriculum for their grade, with special assistance and adaptation for their reading deficiency. The goal of the program is to allow students to return to the regular English program as soon as possible. Each academic department has a resource room where students may receive special tutoring by a member of the department.

Students utilize the composing process of predrafting, drafting, revising, editing, and publishing in their writing. This process writing allows students to focus on developing stages of a piece, rather than the graded final product. Clear communication to the reader supersedes the paper's evaluation.

A writing center is available and accessible to all students and is located near the English classrooms. Peer tutors are trained to help writers with any phase of their papers; teacher tutors are also present to assist "clients" with their writing concerns, ranging from getting started to writing the paper to polishing it for publication. The center is staffed every period of the day by a member of the English department or a peer tutor and is available to students who need remedial writing work in any subject.

Students are motivated to improve their writing because they do not write in isolation. Writing workshops are a part of the English curriculum; teachers keep journals and write with their students; "Writers of the Week" share original pieces that are "published" on the classroom walls.

"In-house" workshops on writing across the curriculum have sensitized the staff to the need for more writing in other disciplines. With our commitment to cooperative learning, a natural outgrowth has occurred: students write in other subject areas besides English, both formally and informally. For example, assignments have included artist of the week paragraphs (art), biography poems of famous scientists (chemistry), letters to the president from signers of the Declaration (history), and a tour guide's "diction" of a foreign city's points of interest (foreign languages). The school newspaper, *Foxtails,* and yearbook, *Renard,* are other avenues in which student writing can be published. *Tapestry Magazine,* published annually, includes minority students' prose and poetry for students in the Fox Chapel Area School District, as well as other nearby school districts.

Technology is in the forefront at Fox Chapel with a television studio that produces daily morning announcements, a television in every classroom, a satellite dish, and a planetarium. The writing center has a complete computer lab. A "Mac on the Desktop Program" has begun the process of providing each teacher with a MacIntosh computer. The district has also provided opportunities for teachers to purchase computers at reduced prices, allowing them to make payment through an interest-free payroll reduction program.

Students in need of gifted support can receive enrichment, acceleration, or both. Students can become involved in a variety of individual and small-group activities such as seminars, apprenticeships, mentorships, competitions, field trips, and independent study projects through the QUEST program for gifted students. These activities are related to each student's needs and abilities and encourage individual problem solving and inquiry. Students in the QUEST program may also participate in alternative programs such as early graduation, early college admission, college admission, college/university concurrent enrollment, and independent study. A resource teacher meets with each student to help plan the special activities for the year. During the 1991–92 school year, 238 students were involved in the QUEST program, and 3.5 teacher positions were assigned to the program.

The responsibility training program at Fox Chapel High School places a special emphasis on teaching students to produce quality work and to use their time in a productive and efficient manner. The program allows students to develop good work habits that will ease their transition to the world of work and business.

FLOWING WELLS HIGH SCHOOL, AZ

Students in grades 9–11 in Flowing Wells High School are scheduled for a grade-specific English course. During the senior year, the school offers ten different interest-based English courses. This diverse selection allows students to pursue their study of English through relevant topics of interest. Students can also take courses for college and high school credit at the local university at night or after school. Approximately thirty students each year take advantage of this option. In cases where the school does not offer the class because of low enrollment, i.e., the fourth year of some foreign languages, the district pays for the tuition.

Writing is stressed in all areas of the English curriculum and across all curriculum areas. Within the writing program, emphasis is placed on grammar, usage, and mechanics. In 1990, a pilot writing competency exam was administered by the department to all seniors. This exam measured each student's ability to write effectively upon completion of the English four-year scope and sequence. A total of 269 seniors were tested, of which 90% met or exceeded the criteria based on assessments from a team of graders who focused on usage, spelling, fluency, and organization. Parents received letters following the test with feedback regarding each child's individual performance grade. While students performed well on this assessment, it was decided that even higher standards should be set for writing across the curriculum. The English department established the framework and a scoring grid for term papers. Now students are required to develop a term paper as part of a course each year in order to receive credit for that course. In grades 9–12, the selected course was one required for all students: biology in grade 9, driver education in grade 10, history in grade 11, and English in grade 12. All papers must be typed; most students use word processing. Additionally, there are nine writing assessments required of each student by the state.

The English department integrates content with other disciplines. One example is the program of two teachers, one from English, one from social studies, who share fifty students and focus on the connectiveness between the two content areas. A two-week simulation is initiated where students assume the role of pioneers. The students read Westerns, develop diaries, and write research papers and make oral presentations based on the experience. In another example, the

English department, in cooperation with the social studies and science departments, has developed a comprehensive interdisciplinary ecology unit.

The English department publishes a yearly literary magazine including student poems and short stories. Students are also encouraged to enter a wide variety of essay contests. In 1990, a Flowing Wells student was runner-up in the Optimist State Essay contest. Students have composed original children's stories that are taken to the elementary schools and read to the students. The school newspaper has been the recipient of numerous awards, including the prestigious George Gallup Award (1986 Quill and Scroll) and the University of Columbia Medalist Award for Excellence in Journalism (1986).

The library has evolved into a research center that is designed to provide students with the latest technology in a warm, comfortable, and technologically sound environment. The school librarian is a technical expert trained in library science and state-of-the-art research technology. He utilizes those skills to train students to use research as a tool and for personal enhancement. Networked mini-labs of six to seven IBM computers available in each English classroom facilitate the revision, editing, and final preparation of papers and other writing assignments. The mini-labs and library resources are available before and after school and during lunch as well as during class time.

BRONXVILLE PUBLIC SCHOOL, NY

The English department at Bronxville Public School offers a wide range of courses adapted for students with varied educational needs. Interdisciplinary sections (9 – 10) present students with at least three different academic subjects simultaneously. Units are planned by the social studies, English, and art teachers. For example, the interdisciplinary course in the ninth grade interrelates history of Western civilizations with literature and the arts. Students study the history of Greece while reading the *Odyssey* and studying the architecture and the arts of ancient Greece. English 11 and 12 offer a survey of American literature and an intensive examination of archetypes of tragedy, satire, and irony, respectively. Advanced placement (12) presents high-powered and challenging analyses of literary genres.

Of particular significance are writing labs that are coordinated with the student's English class. Each English teacher is scheduled for four English classes, plus one lab. The existence of the labs emphasizes the importance of writing as a process and allows for immediate teacher-student and student-student response to a written work, thus encouraging intensive editing. Each student develops a writing portfolio as part of the writing and development process.

Higher order and critical thinking skills are addressed, in part, by the construct of "essential questions" for the year, which students can answer through both literature and history and to which they return throughout the year. As the course progresses, students probe more complex issues, such as "How does American literature evolve as a revolutionary type of writing?" Comparisons of novels, e.g., *The Scarlet Letter* and *The Catcher in the Rye,* allow students to undertake the critical task of exploring such evolution.

Curriculum areas are integrated in a very deliberate manner. For example, students may parallel their study of the explorations of Louis and Clark with the frontier writing style of Washington Irving, so that the students realize that, as the country expanded geographically, it also expanded creatively. Art is another viable part of the interdisciplinary curriculum. The student realizes the connections between social movements, literary shifts, and artistic trends in the development of American society.

THE BEST SCHOOLS – ASSESSING WHAT STUDENTS KNOW AND CAN DO

Consistent with the emergence of new and higher standards for literacy, states have been actively involved in developing assessment processes that provide for higher order and more authentic measurement of reading and writing achievement. These assessments may be used for identifying students requiring additional instruction and/or as a requirement to be met in order to graduate. Many states now include writing samples that are holistically scored based on rubrics that are shared with schools and that can be used by teachers in the classroom to enhance instruction. State reading tests are beginning to include long passages or complete stories or narratives and require higher level narrative responses, rather than multiple choice answer selection. Different forms of reading are assessed. State tests in New Jersey, for example, assess the student's ability to "read the lines," "read between the lines," and "read beyond the lines." Vermont is supplementing more traditional forms of assessment with portfolios of actual classwork, which are scored according to established standards. A number of the Best Schools cite new state testing programs as much more in line with the goals of their ILA programs than traditional standardized tests. Some of the Best Schools are working with state and private agencies to develop valid alternative forms of assessment.

The Best Schools give high priority to assessment and are evolving new assessment approaches that provide better information about student learning. Most of the schools continue to give nationally normed standardized tests at least at some grade levels. The more recent editions of the popular standardized tests have attempted to place more emphasis on higher order assessment; however, the schools still consider these tests to be of limited validity in terms of current literacy standards and the ILA curriculum. They give the commercial standardized tests because of state regulations and federal and state program requirements to assure schools boards and parents that students are acquiring reading and writing skills and because there are few alternatives available to assess the higher standards for learning at the school or district level. Most students in the Best High Schools also take either the Scholastic Assessment Tests (SATs) or the American College Testing (ACT) for college admission.

Assessment within the classroom and school is undergoing the greatest change. The bell curve view of assessment designed to rank students and sort them into "excellent," "above average," "average," "below average," and "failed" groups has been rejected. Students are judged to be proficient, not proficient yet, or demonstrating competency far above the proficient level. The goal is to determine what the student knows and can do in terms of criterion standards; it is expected that all students will meet the standards. For example, only the final product of writing is assessed after revision and editing, frequently using teacher-, school-, district-, or even state-developed rubrics. In addition, students learn to assess their own writing and reading as a significant component of the instructional process. Reading ability is evaluated through oral reading, writing, and individual teacher/student reading conferences. Writing portfolios of students' work are assessed over time to show individual growth and level of achievement, as well as overall class and school achievement. Acquisition of traditional skills is also monitored through criterion-referenced tests, checklists, and reading and writing assignments. A most important feature of assessment in conjunction with ILA is the continuous use of data to plan instruction for the class, groups, and individual students.

Assessment Illustrations

J. A. ROGERS ACADEMY, MO

The writing-to-learn strategy is employed at Rogers to improve students' ability to solve problems, to engage in classroom discussions as a focus for judging work, to incorporate reflection and rehearsal as forms of assessment, and to engage in a network of practices in the process of producing a project that turns assessment into an episode of learning. Students in all grades make journal entries and write daily. Electronic portfolios are used to evaluate projects, as well as to teach thinking skills. Involvement in the active process of portfolio development is a strong motivational factor for enhancing writing skills. Students participate in telecommunication projects in humanities courses that give meaningful opportunities for writing in realistic situations in which students have ownership. Parents play a key role in student writing proficiency as they periodically review their student's writing and offer comments as part of the student growth plan. Workshops are conducted to guide parents in this important process.

The writing lab uses Writer's Network software and affords students the opportunity to practice the "writing process" on a computer in a variety of strategies, all of which become components of a student's portfolio. Teacher utilities contain a full set of grading tools with holistic scales. Writer's Network gives students writing power through prewriting activities, organizing strategies, experience with word processing, and individual tools for proofing. The system promotes collaborative learning through peer review.

FOX CHAPEL AREA HIGH SCHOOL, PA

Mastery learning at Fox Chapel is a teaching technique that provides students with the opportunity to take an initial exam, receive correctives or enrichment, and then take a second version of the test if their first score is below a set mastery level. This program is mandated in every class throughout the district.

Writing is assessed using a variety of rubrics: holistic scoring, letter grades, or outcomes-based education's "not yet" labeling. Student writing folders are kept in the English classrooms, and quality pieces are chosen by the student to be graded at the end of the nine-week marking period. Journal writing, essay writing, term papers, and independent study projects are just a few of the specific kinds of writing being done by students.

FLOWING WELLS HIGH SCHOOL, AZ

Each department at Flowing Wells has developed an assessment program unique to its subject area and needs. The data are collected and analyzed for department-driven changes. State-developed exit examinations required for graduation are analyzed in terms of need for program development.

A unique feature of the assessment program is the requirement of four term papers that grew out of concern for student writing. Each year, students must produce a term paper in order to receive credit for the course. The English department developed the format and the rubric for scoring; however, only in the senior year is the paper part of an English course. In ninth grade, the term paper course is biology, in tenth driver education, and in eleventh history. Course teachers assess the papers. In addition, the state of Arizona requires nine assessments of writing. In grades 9–11, these are graded in-house using the state grid. In the senior year, the writing is assessed off-site by the state. The district-required term papers and state writing assessments are included in a portfolio that travels with students from grades 9–12.

Computerized progress reports are mailed every three weeks. The reports provide comments, indicating both positive and negative performance and discipline and attendance updates. Ongoing parent dialogue is presented through telephone and personal conferences. In certain circumstances, home visits are initiated. Teachers are requested to call parents of students in their classrooms each year and provide information regarding school procedures and events.

THE BEST SCHOOLS–PLANNING AND PROGRAM DEVELOPMENT

The Best Schools began the implementation of their ILA programs from three to twenty years ago and have agendas for further development of the program, extending over the next three to five years. In many cases, the writing process component of ILA has been used in the Best Schools for ten to twenty years. It is important to note that implementing an ILA program is very different than the process used to adopt a new basal reading, literature, or English textbook series. Integration of language arts requires administrative, teacher, and parent understanding, and commitment to new and higher standards and to the theory of learning that supports integrated instruction. Therefore, extensive and ongoing staff development and parent orientation is required. While ILA programs have many features in common, implementation at the local level among schools and even classrooms can vary substantially; in most schools, the move from a skill-sequenced basal dominated approach to a significant ILA program has taken from three to seven years.

Districts and schools vary in how ILA has been implemented. In some schools, ILA was started at the lower grades and was moved up through the grades at a rate of one or two a year. In many schools, individual or small groups of teachers who had an early interest in ILA were encouraged and supported in making the transition to the approach, with other teachers joining in subsequent years as they "saw the results" and had opportunities for training.

Planning and Program Development Illustrations

J. A. ROGERS ACADEMY, MO

The underlying philosophy that guides learning at Rogers Academy is the belief that all children can learn and that all teachers and administrators can help them be successful. Goals in support of this philosophy and the school's mission were first developed by the planning task force during the year prior to the opening of the school. A school improvement plan is developed annually through the collaborative efforts of the staff, parents, and students and addresses the progress of the school. Adequate time is scheduled to permit the school's improvement committee members to develop the plan in a manner that promotes understanding, clarity, and commitment. The school improvement plan addresses all aspects of the school – instructional programs, curriculum, facilities, co-curriculum activities, and school climate.

Progress and programs to ensure the achievement of the Rogers' mission are shared with the total school community through a program of broad communication. The principal sends a monthly newsletter, the *Rogers' Scholar*, to parents and patrons, which highlights the accomplishments of students and staff, reports student progress, and addresses means by which parents may cooperate in the educational process. The student council meets regularly with the faculty advisory committee to address areas that impact on the school climate and the school's goals and mission. The school's conflict mediation program also supports the school's mission and goals through constant focus on lifelong guidelines and lifeskills.

Teachers have three periods during the day for preparation of instructional materials and for professional development. One of those periods is a daily grade level "family" planning meeting that allows coordination of themes, strategies, and resources. Instructional programs are developed and adapted during these times. The services of resource scholars are sought, and new technology is learned. Teams work together during portions of most development days. The fine arts, practical arts, and foreign language teams also have a planning period common to all and meet regularly to address common needs and develop appropriate curricula.

The integrated thematic instructional model places the responsibility for planning and implementing instructional programs largely upon the shoulders of the teams of teachers. Each team, working within the framework of the magnet theme of the liberal arts and sciences, incorporates goals of multicultural appreciation and lifeskills throughout the school. However, the grade level families of teachers design their own programs with various degrees of student input. Integrated thematic instruction encourages teamwork and professional growth.

A room adjacent to the resource center has been designated as the teacher research student development center and supports staff collaboration and development of the educational programs. This area contains a seminar room with blackboard, bulletin board, VCR and monitor.

professional library, and a project work area. Teachers use this area to publish, develop demonstration lessons, and aid in the professional growth of colleagues. The school supports a group membership in the Association of Supervision and Curriculum Development (ASCD), which provides all teaching staff members and administrators a monthly copy of *Educational Leadership*. This professional journal is used to promote collegial discussion of current educational issues and research.

FOX CHAPEL AREA HIGH SCHOOL, PA

Fox Chapel High School recognizes the need for planning through a goal-setting process on all levels of operation; the school district has completed the development of a strategic plan. The planning process was guided by a steering committee made up of district administrators, teachers, parents, students, business leaders, and representatives from the local higher education community. Subcommittees drafted a five-year, eight-goal plan to guide every school in the district. The goal areas are ethical behavior, involvement, communication, learning/instruction, resource management/development, balance/wellness, leadership, and inclusion/appreciation of diversity. All employees and residents have received a booklet entitled "Success for All Students" in which these goals have been described in detail. As the school board has unanimously accepted the National Goals for Education, individual schools within the district have been directed to plan programs accordingly.

Department chairpersons set goals with subject area teachers dealing with curriculum content, staff assignments, student achievement, and budget. The three building administrators develop annual goals related to the building goals. Goal achievement is evaluated by their immediate superiors; degree of achievement has been established as a factor in the merit pay system developed for all district administrators. The high school also employs graduate students from Carnegie Mellon School of Urban and Public Affairs to evaluate the effectiveness of curricular changes in the English department.

The staff and curriculum development committee plans and monitors the creation and implementation of programs throughout the district. Within individual high school departments, frequent formal and informal meetings of those teachers who teach the same courses allow for a coordinated approach to instruction. When possible, these teachers are scheduled with common planning time.

FLOWING WELLS HIGH SCHOOL, AZ

In Flowing Wells High School, there is an improvement process based on effective school characteristics described in the literature. Each year, a school improvement unit comprised of students, teachers, staff, and parents gathers both quantitative and qualitative data reflecting outcomes within each of the characteristics. Annually, the team broadens the scope of the collection efforts. The results of the data collection and other outcomes, including test scores, attendance rates, North Central Association evaluations, and discipline rates, are utilized by the school improvement unit to develop a comprehensive, effective school plan based on the school's vision statement.

The objectives of the principal and educational staff include making a positive difference in the academic achievement and personal/social growth of students, recognizing each person's worth and attempting to satisfy individual needs and interests, and preparing students for life after high school. The essential belief maxims are that students *can* learn; teachers *can* teach effectively; the school *must* have high standards and expectations; students need rewards, praise, and success; students must be involved and engaged a high percentage of time in active instructional experiences; and students must believe that they *can* learn and be successful in school.

Each year, representatives from all of the various school and community groups are involved in the goal-setting process. Each of the six to eight teams, comprised of at least one teacher, student, parent, and community member, collect and evaluate school outcome data. These teams meet monthly to share and discuss their findings.

At a summer day-long workshop, the vision statement and school improvement plan is formulated. Small groups develop goal statements in the eight categories of effective schools, utilizing both the vision statements and the outcome data provided by the school improvement unit.

Once the goals are developed, a school improvement document is published and mailed to all faculty for review. Further attempts to communicate these goals include their publication in the parent newsletter and the first edition of the school newspaper. The goals are also reviewed during the first parent advisory meeting.

Bimonthly feedback forms solicit information from staff regarding personal achievements, educational concerns, student successes, and facilities issues. Curriculum scope and sequence development is an empowerment of the staff in a continuous and ongoing revision and refinement process. Planning time is provided throughout the year and during the summer. Department members also have the responsibility for selection of textbooks and supplemental materials and for the review and initial adoption of new courses that are submitted by faculty members. Increased accountability has been a primary focus of the principal and staff. Opportunities have been provided for teachers to break the barrier of isolation and to share with one another, to observe other methods, and to grow professionally. Curriculum and test scores are continually evaluated and the program revised in light of educational research.

People share a common vision for excellence and the need for accountability and innovation. A comprehensive schoolwide effort has taken place that has brought the school to a point where teaching and learning could occur in a positive, dynamic, student-oriented environment. The rising of the "Phoenix phenomenon" set the stage for what has occurred since the 1987 National Recognition Award. The quality of this most recent experience is in the persistence of the school to continue to develop and refine programs that are driven by a vision of outcome-oriented accountability and a positive school climate. This renewed vision strives to provide a quality educational program to all students by identifying programs that address the special needs of each child and the unique needs of an increasingly diverse population.

BRONXVILLE PUBLIC SCHOOL, NY

In Bronxville Public School, a broadly-based, long-range planning committee meets to establish school goals. Membership in the coalition of essential schools has committed the school to work toward establishing a curriculum that will teach students to think creatively, solve problems, and share in community responsibility.

Among its specific responses to recent educational research and nationally promulgated improvement recommendations, the school has undertaken the following initiatives:

- development of a writing instruction program that includes a realistic teacher/pupil ratio and creation of writing laboratories for teachers to work with students
- establishment of shared decision-making techniques to enhance student outcomes
- commitment to extensive training, including peer coaching, in cooperative learning techniques
- training in specific student learning and thinking strategies that have been developed and researched nationally
- teaching second languages for oral proficiency through training and coaching in techniques to develop communicative methods
- responding to the need for technology by providing computer hardware, software, and training

THE BEST SCHOOLS–STAFF DEVELOPMENT

Staff development is an essential factor in ILA program implementation; teachers need to understand the theory and research undergirding ILA. In addition, there are many specific strategies that require comprehensive training of teachers and principals, such as training in reading strategies, the writing process, and assessment approaches. ILA cannot be adopted like a new textbook with just a publisher's representative providing an orientation to the new textbook and teacher's edition. This is one of the major reasons why ILA has been implemented over a course of years. Training usually requires release time to observe other schools or classrooms where ILA is in use, as well as involvement in specific workshops in ILA theory and research, reading strategies, use of literature, writing process strategies, and assessment approaches such as holistic scoring.

The training required for implementing ILA is provided by district supervisory staff, state and regional agencies, National Diffusion Network programs, educational consultants, and/or highly skilled principals and teachers within the school or district. Early program adopters are frequently used as turnkey trainers for colleagues. Principals provide some of the direct training for their staff and provide an essential support role for the program in the school and classrooms. Training takes place after school, on release time, during the summer recess, and regularly at faculty meetings. Books and articles concerning ILA strategies are circulated to staff to support the program. In a number of cases, schools have linked themselves into networks or joined regional or national networks, which include schools that have already implemented ILA. Schools using an ILA approach serve as models for staff from other schools who are considering changing to ILA or who are in the initial stages of the change process. "Seeing" ILA in practice seems to be an essential first step in making a commitment to the approach.

In addition, curriculum development is a key factor in implementing ILA. Developing the grade level or course proficiencies and curriculum structure should be considered a part of the staff development process. In many schools, teachers form whole-language or ILA support groups, which meet to exchange information and reflect on classroom instruction. To facilitate this, many schools schedule common planning time for grade level or course-common teachers.

Staff Development Illustrations

J. A. ROGERS ACADEMY, MO

Staff development planning at Rogers is done jointly by the principal and the staff development committee. Both follow the overall guide set by the school improvement plan, as well as their knowledge of current research and the particular needs of the J. A. Rogers learning community. The staff development committee is elected by the faculty and regularly holds meetings open to all. Many faculty members have opportunities to attend outside conferences and workshops that are congruent with the school goals and priorities. For example, a team of faculty members attended the Active Learning in the Middle School Workshop at Harvard.

Each new and beginning teacher receives five days of orientation and inservice to acquire the vision of education of the district, as well as its unique history. During these days, procedures and policies are explained, classroom management techniques are reviewed, and the distinct multicultural mission of the schools is described. Beginning teachers are assigned a mentor teacher who helps guide them during their first year in the district. The mentor assists in putting together the beginning teacher's professional development plan. These plans are a means of identifying strengths and areas needing refinement, as well as a plan for growth.

FOX CHAPEL AREA HIGH SCHOOL, PA

The goal at Fox Chapel of developing a community of cooperative learners has been supported by extensive training for teachers in the philosophy and technique of cooperative learning.

Approximately 80% of the staff has completed the basic course in cooperative learning. Fifty percent of the staff has completed the advanced course, and five individuals on the staff have been trained as faculty coaches. In addition, all department heads and building administrators have completed the course, "Learning the Cooperative School."

The high school principal and district administration have pursued and received competitive grants for staff development in the areas of cooperative learning, secondary student support and social/emotional support, and integration of program. Instructional improvement is implemented through the actions of department chairpersons, peer coaches, and peer observers.

In line with the main vision of "Success for All Students," the major inservice programs of cooperative learning, mastery learning, and responsibility training have been the focus during recent school years. These programs have involved three- to five-day training programs either in the high school or in a nearby community hall. Substitute teachers have relieved the faculty of teaching responsibilities during these days. Reinforcement seminars and other training programs have taken place on inservice days or during after-school meetings. Peer coaching planning and training sessions have been held during the summer months, while peer coaching workshops are held during the school year.

A group of teachers serve as peer coaches, helping colleagues to implement five innovative instructional strategies: mastery learning, cooperative learning, responsibility training, technology-assisted instruction, and individualizing instruction. Each teacher chooses one of these areas for personal staff development and sets a goal for the year. At the end of the year, the teachers evaluate their success in meeting their goals and report this assessment to the principal.

English teachers have gained professional growth by participating in or presenting the following activities:

- Writing across the Curriculum Workshop
- Computer Integration in the Classroom Workshop
- Use of Electronic Mail in the School Workshop
- Cooperative Learning Workshop
- National Council of Teachers of English Conference
- Motivating Low-Ability Students Workshop

FLOWING WELLS HIGH SCHOOL, AZ

The American Association of School Administrators' (AASA) award-winning Flowing Wells District staff development program is the cornerstone of success in teacher renewal and growth. The program has been in place for seven years and currently offers workshops in several areas: essential elements of instruction, advanced essential elements, cooperative learning, advanced cooperative learning, clinical supervision, creative thinking, classroom management, concept attainment, task analysis, and tactics for thinking.

The faculty is committed to ongoing staff development as evidenced by the following statistics based on one academic school year: twelve teachers attended twenty-four hours of classroom management training; eleven teachers attended thirty-two hours of cooperative learning training; thirteen teachers participated in twenty-four hours of training in advanced cooperative learning techniques; seventeen faculty members attended eight hours of training in developing concept attainment lessons. In addition to district staff development opportunities, the faculty is also involved in ongoing training in their specific disciplines.

The district staff development program has incorporated the most recent research in providing more appropriate education through specific areas of development. The career ladder plan provides teachers with opportunities to observe and meet in study teams to develop action plans focused upon student learning and to peer coach one another. The principal sets aside time in faculty meetings to discuss instructional delivery issues and to share research-based updates from contemporary educational journals. Curriculum adoptions focus upon the most recent data regarding learning in the specific cognitive area being analyzed.

All new teachers are required to attend forty hours of staff training with a focus on effective classroom instructional strategies. New teachers are required to report one week in advance of the continuing teachers. During this week, they participate in an extensive staff development program. The new teachers are assigned buddy/mentor teachers who help orient them to their new work environment and answer questions regarding a wide variety of work-related issues. Throughout the school year, new teachers/mentors support groups meet informally during lunch. These sessions prepare new teachers for upcoming events and school logistical issues. The staff development specialist and the principal provide follow-up observations and coaching for all new teachers.

Over 75% of the faculty participate in the district career ladder (merit pay) incentive program. These teachers engage in numerous additional instructional improvement activities which include

- action plans that outline measurable student growth
- summative evaluations by trained external evaluators
- study teams to focus on new teaching strategies and techniques

Departing from the traditional faculty meeting format, the principal utilizes faculty meetings as an opportunity to model effective teaching. A lesson is fully prepared and implemented one hour per month. Concepts taught include effective homework design, inductive lesson design, creative brainstorming, and tactics for thinking. The principal visits classrooms and frequently teaches lesson units to model specific strategies.

THE BEST SCHOOLS–FUNDING DEVELOPMENT

Language arts instruction, whether the discrete/linear model with separate time scheduled for reading, English, and spelling or an ILA instructional approach, can occupy as much as 30% of the middle school day and 15% of the high school day. Since the purpose of schools is learning, it can be argued that all school-related costs should be calculated in terms of actual instructional time. With a national average per pupil cost of $5243, language arts instruction averages $1573 per student per year for middle school students and $786 per student per year at the high school level (National Center for Educational Statistics, 1992). In other words, language instruction is expensive regardless of the approach used.

Staff development, curriculum development, books, and assessment are the major expenditures in initiating and maintaining an ILA program. Class sets of core books have usually been purchased at a rate of three to four titles a year for each grade level or course. Interest books (six to twelve copies per title) have been added for each grade level or course over a period of years. Funds previously allocated for the purchase of workbooks, anthologies, and basal textbooks have been redirected to the purchase of these books. Because paperback books have a shorter life span than hardcover texts, they need to be replaced more often than hardback books; however, traditional textbooks used to support skills or as sources of literature are being replaced less frequently by schools. The print and technology resources of school libraries have been greatly expanded and have become the hub of the school.

It must be stressed that effective staff development requires, first and foremost, time. The Best Schools invest heavily in staff development. The two to four inservice days built into most school calendars provides some time for staff development; however, release time to observe and to receive training is also needed. Courses are offered after school either on a voluntary basis, with stipend, or for continuing education credits. Summer workshops for staff development and curriculum development are planned and implemented. In some states, requirements for continuing education of staff facilitate involvement in professional development. Costs for inservice training usually include the costs for substitutes for release time, travel to training sessions and to model ILA programs, summer and/or after-school workshop pay for teachers, inservice credits affecting movement on salary guides, workshop registration fees, professional literature, and training consultant fees.

Technology represents a major investment in the Best Schools. Library/media centers have been equipped with computers, CD-ROM, laser disc players, and modem access to resources through Internet, Dow Line, or Dialog. Most schools, in addition to general computer labs and designated writing labs, are focusing on equipping English/ILA classrooms with mini-labs of four to six computers. Multi-media computer stations allow for the development of sophisticated student projects, as well as for assisting teachers to develop engaging classroom lessons.

A Cost Illustration

FLOWING WELLS HIGH SCHOOL, AZ

The expenditures at Flowing Wells for the English program for the most part are what would be considered standard in most schools: teacher salaries, textbooks, and trade books. In addition, the district has made a commitment to technology. The school goal is to have mini-labs of six to seven computers in every classroom networked to extensive technology resources in the library. The district budgets $50,000 for technology for the high school each year. Another annual expenditure reflects the district's commitment to continuing staff and program development. The annual school budget for staff development is from $50,000 to $60,000. The funds are used to provide two to three consecutive days of release time courses (substitute pay), after-school courses for teachers ($12.50 per hour), and pay for consultants and in-house trainers. Approximately 90% of the staff takes courses each year. University courses taken by students, which are not offered by the school and therefore paid for by the school, are budgeted for $2000 to $3000 per year.

SUMMARY

The Best Schools have adopted standards for literacy that include not only what students know, but what they can do. They use integrated language arts (ILA) programs, which are reflective of current theory and research. Language-rich environments are created in integrated language arts programs. Instruction emphasizes the connections among reading, writing, and speaking. Development of a love of reading and writing is considered essential to successful learning. English/language arts courses are often integrated with other subjects, most frequently social studies and the arts. Writing across the curriculum is standard practice in the Best Schools. Literature study is frequently correlated with other curriculum areas and not only reflects multicultural school populations, but also recognizes the importance of a worldwide focus. Students are grouped heterogeneously; regrouping occurs within the class based on either interest or the need to introduce or reinforce skills. At the high school level, challenging honors level and advanced placement courses can be elected by students. Students who, in the past, were placed in low-level English courses are now taking standard-level courses with high expectations, new instructional approaches, and support. New forms of more authentic assessment have been introduced. The Best Schools, urban, suburban, and rural, have developed their ILA programs over a period of years and are involved in a process of continuous program development. Extensive and ongoing staff development is characteristic of the Best Schools. Essential to their success is an unwavering belief that all students in the school will read, write, and speak fluently.

REFERENCES

Anderson, R., et al. (1985). *Becoming a Nation of Readers: The Report of the Commission in Reading*. The National Institute of Education.

ASCD. (1992). *Making Meaning: Integrated Language Arts*. Alexandria, VA: ASCD.

Brophy, J. and T. Good. (1985). "Teacher Behaviors and Student Achievement," in *Handbook of Research on Teaching*. Third Edition, Wittrock, ed, New York, NY: McMillan Publishing Co.

Caine, R. and G. Caine. (1991). "Understanding a Brain Approach to Learning and Teaching," *Educational Leadership* (October).

The College Board. (1985). *Academic Preparation in English: Teaching for Transition from High School to College*. Educational Equality Project. New York, NY: College Entrance Examination Board.

Council for Basic Education. (1991). "Standards: A Vision for Learning," *Perspective*, 4(1).

Fisher, C. W., et al. (1978). "Teaching Behaviors, Academic Learning Time and Student Achievement," *Final Report of the Beginning Teacher Evaluation Study*. San Francisco, CA: Far West Laboratory.

Goodman, K. S. (1964). "A Linguistic Study of Cues and Miscues in Reading," *Elementary English*. Urbana, IL: National Council of Teachers of English.

Hillocks, George. (1986). *Research on Written Composition*. Urbana, IL: ERIC Clearinghouse on Reading and Communication Skills.

McDougal, Littel and Company. (1993). *Daily Oral Language*. Evanston, IL: McDougal, Littel and Company.

Mellon, John. (1969). *Transformational Sentence-Combining*. Research Report # 10, Urbana, IL: National Council of Teachers of English.

National Assessment of Educational Progress (NAEP). 1990. *America's Challenge: Accelerating Academic Achievement*. Princeton, NJ: Educational Testing Service.

National Center for Educational Statistics. (1992). *Digest of Educational Statistics for 1992*. Washington, D.C.: U.S. Department of Education.

National Center for Educational Statistics. (1993). *NAEP 1992 Reading Report Card for the Nation and the States*. Washington D.C.: U.S. Department of Education.

National Center for Educational Statistics. (1994). *NAEP 1992 Writing Report Card*. Washington D.C.: U.S. Department of Education.

National Center for Educational Statistics. (1995). *Windows into the Classroom: NAEP's 1992 Writing Portfolio Study*. Washington D.C.: U.S. Department of Education.

Oakes, J. (1985). *Keeping Track: How Schools Structure Inequality*. New Haven, CT: Yale University Press.

Ogden, Evelyn. (1992). "Profile of High Challenge Students." East Brunswick. Unpublished paper.

Sherwin, Stephen. (1969). *Four Problems in Teaching English: A Critique of Research*. New York, NY: International Textbook Co.

Slaven, R. E. (1987). "Ability Grouping and Student Achievement in Elementary Schools: A Best Evidence Synthesis," *Review of Educational Research*, 57:293–336.

Tchudi, Stephen. (1991). *Planning and Assessing the Curriculum in English Language Arts*. Alexandria, VA: Association for Supervision and Curriculum Development.

U.S. Department of Education. (1994). *High Standards for All: Putting Excellence in Education*. Washington, D.C.: U.S. Department of Education.

Vermont Portfolio Institute. (1994). *The Portfolio Source Book*. Shoreham, VT: Vermont Portfolio Institute.

(1993). *Educational Programs That Work: The Catalogue of the National Diffusion Network (NDN)*. 19th Edition. Longmont, CO: Sopis West Inc.

CHAPTER 7

Mathematics

MATHEMATICS instruction accounts for approximately 15% of a students's instructional day, or between 700 to 1000 hours of instruction from sixth through twelfth grade. This chapter looks at the following questions concerning the development of world-class competency in mathematics for students who will spend their adult years in the 21st century:

- What does theory and research say about what people should learn and how they should be taught?
- How do the Best Schools successfully translate theory into practice in teaching mathematics?
- How do the Best Schools assess what students know and what they can do?
- What do case studies of Best Schools reveal about how highly successful mathematics instruction is carried out in four different community contexts?
- Finally, what are some of the specific practices, programs, and resources used by the Best Schools that are widely available to other program developers?

WHAT STUDENTS SHOULD LEARN

According to the National Goals of Education,

> By the year 2000, American students will leave grades four, eight and twelve having demonstrated competency in challenging subject mater including . . . mathematics . . . ; and every school in America will ensure that all students learn to use their minds well, so they may be prepared for responsible citizenship, further learning, and productive employment in our Nation's modern economy.
>
> By the year 2000, U.S. students will be first in the world in . . . mathematics achievement.

Schools have always had as a goal the development of mathematical literacy. While literacy has not in the past been specifically defined in practice, it has generally meant the development of basic competence in mathematical operations such as adding, subtracting, multiplying, and dividing, with some attention to the use of mathematics in solving relatively simple problems for all students. In addition, for college bound students, mathematical literacy has traditionally included some level of competence in algebra and geometry, with the study of calculus limited to a highly motivated few. The National Goals set forth much higher expectations for defining mathematical literacy for children of the year 2000. Key words and phrases within the goals include: ''demonstrated competency,'' ''challenging subject matter,'' ''*all* students,'' ''prepared for responsible citizenship,'' ''prepared for further learning,'' and ''prepared for productive employment in our modern economy.'' These statements imply the setting of standards for *all* students far beyond the traditional standards for mathematical learning implicit in the instruction aims of mathematics in the past.

In 1986, the National Council of Teachers of Mathematics (NCTM) established the Commission on Standards for School Mathematics as a means for improving the quality of school mathematics. The resulting standards published in 1989 represent a broadly held professional consensus about the fundamental content of school mathematics, outcomes of instruction, and student and program evaluation. The NCTM standards provide the operational framework for the National Goals. Inherent in the standards is "a consensus that all students need to learn more, and often different, mathematics and that instruction in mathematics must be significantly revised" (NCTM, 1991, p. 1). The NCTM standards have been endorsed by virtually all of the mathematical and scientific organizations nationwide and serve as the voluntary National Education Standards in the area of mathematics. The National standards provide a focus for state and local efforts. Furthermore, many states have developed or are beginning to develop their own content standards or proficiencies to meet their own needs for curriculum blueprints, teacher preparation, professional development, and certification.

The need for new goals and standards is embedded in the changes in the society in which we live. The industrial society has been replaced with the information society. The availability of calculators, computers, and other technology has dramatically changed the nature of the physical, life, and social sciences and business, industry, and government. Electronic communication has supplemented and, in some cases, supplanted the voice and printed page. Information is shared instantly from desk to desk and across the world. "Information is the new capital and the new material, and communication is the new means of production" (NCTM, 1991, p. 3). New societal goals have replaced goals based on development of most citizens to become workers in fields and factories, with advanced education for the few who would be the managers, the professionals, and the leaders. Today, mathematically literate workers must understand the complexities and technologies of communication, assimilate new information, generate questions and propose solutions, work in cooperative teams, adjust rapidly to changes in roles and functions within jobs, and then totally change jobs four or five times during their careers. Mathematical knowledge has become a significant filter for employment and full participation in society; therefore, all students must have the opportunity to become mathematically literate, and educational equity is an economic necessity. Finally, mathematics itself is rapidly growing and being applied to continually expanding and diverse fields. The concept of the person as a lifelong mathematics learner has become a necessary reality.

In line with the need to develop students who can function effectively in mathematics, the NCTM standards include what should be taught and what students should be able to do as a result of instruction for students K–4, 5–8, and 9–12. There are thirteen standards for grades 5–8 and fourteen standards for grades 9–12. These are further delineated by descriptions of what students should be able to do as the result of instruction. The length of the NCTM standards precludes a listing of all of them in this chapter; however, following is an example of a 5–8 and a 9–12 standard (NCTM, pp. 94 and 157):

GRADES 5–8

Standard 7: Computation and Estimation

In grades 5–8, the mathematics curriculum should develop the concepts underlying computation and estimation in various contexts so that students can–

- compute with whole numbers, fractions, decimals, integers, and rational numbers;
- develop, analyze, and explain procedures for computation and techniques for estimation;

- develop, analyze, and explain methods for solving proportions;
- select and use an appropriate method for computing from among mental arithmetic, paper-and-pencil, calculator, and computer methods;
- use computation, estimation, and proportions to solve problems;
- use estimation to check the reasonableness of results.

GRADES 9–12

Standard 7: Geometry From a Synthetic Perspective

In grades 9–12, the mathematics curriculum should include the continued study of the geometry of two and three dimensions so that all students can–

- interpret and draw three-dimensional objects;
- represent problem situations with geometric models and apply properties of figures;
- classify figures in terms of congruence and similarity and apply these relationships;
- deduce properties of, and relationships between, figures from given assumptions;

and so that, in addition, college-intended students can–develop an understanding of an axiomatic system through investigating and comparing various geometries.

HOW STUDENTS LEARN–HOW STUDENTS ARE TAUGHT

What students are taught and how they are taught has changed little in mathematics in the past 100 years in most of the nation's schools. The mission has been to develop minimal competency in calculation and knowledge of facts and formulas for the majority of students and advanced mathematics for the few. For those who do not reach minimal proficiency levels, remedial instruction focuses on the reteaching of missing skills. For those students expected to go beyond minimal or practical everyday mathematics, each successive course is designed to prepare the student for the next higher level course.

The students in our schools today live and will work in a very different world than the students of 1900. The world of now and the future relies on computers, calculators, and a disposition for continuous learning. New mathematical concepts and applications are emerging, mathematics is recognized as a means of communication, and the workplace requires complex and creative problem solving. As a result, the mission of schools preparing students for the 21st century is for all students to develop broad-based mathematical power and mathematical confidence. The need for change in preparation of students in mathematics is confirmed by the results of the National Test of Educational Progress. Based upon 1992 data, the National Goals Panel found that only 25% of eighth-grade and 16% of twelfth-grade students met the performance standard of "mastery over challenging subject matter" (National Education Goals Panel, 1993). Only 7% of the seventeen-year-olds in 1992 achieved the top level, multistep problem solving and algebra, on the NAEP, results that have not changed since 1978 (NAEP, 1994). In the International Assessment of Mathematical Study, American students were outperformed by students from Korea, Switzerland, and Taiwan in all areas tested in 1991 and by students from France and Hungary in four out of the five areas tested (LaPointe et al., 1992).

The curriculum implemented and instructional approaches used in most of the schools of today are totally inadequate to prepare students to meet the national goals, the NCTM standards, and needs of the workplace and society of the 21st century. Thomas Romberg, who chaired the panel that developed the NCTM standards, notes that we are still teaching "shopkeeper arithmetic" and that many of our textbooks do not look much different than a 15th century accounting text. No other country teaches eight years of arithmetic, followed by a year of algebra, followed by a year of geometry. Other countries organize mathematics instruction differently (Lockwood, 1991). In terms of instruction, students reported that listening to the teacher explain mathematics and test taking were the activities they most often experienced in their mathematics classrooms (NAEP, 1994).

The National Council of Teachers of Mathematics (NCTM) and the Mathematical Sciences Education Board (MSEB) are providing leadership in the restructuring of the mathematics curriculum and instructional approaches. In *Everybody Counts: A Report to the Nation on the Future of Mathematics Education* (Mathematical Research Council, 1989) the MSEB put forth some tenets for mathematics education:

(1) Mathematics is for everyone.
(2) Mathematics is the science of patterns, a broad field with myriad applications rather than routines of arithmetic with limited "right answers."
(3) Teaching means engaging students in solving real problems and inventing mathematics for themselves rather than lecturing and testing for low-level skills.

The NCTM has, in the development of curriculum standards, shifted the focus of mathematics from simply knowing and being a competent calculator to mathematics as doing. Five general goals guide the development of the standards for curriculum for all students:

(1) That they learn to value mathematics
(2) That they become confident in their ability to do mathematics
(3) That they become mathematical problem solvers
(4) That they learn to communicate mathematically
(5) That they learn to reason mathematically

Not only must the content of the curriculum change, but the quantity of mathematics instruction for all students must be increased. While almost all middle school students are scheduled for mathematics, this is not the case for high school students, where only two or three years of mathematics instruction may be required for graduation. In 1990, only 35% of the graduates had completed Algebra I, Algebra II, and geometry, and only 7% had completed calculus. Students do not view mathematics as a dynamic subject, open to discovery and innovation; instead, they view mathematics as mostly memorization and rule-bound, and less than half the students expect to work in an area requiring mathematics (NAEP, 1990). Students' attitudes toward mathematics become increasingly less positive from fourth through twelveth grades, with only 53% of boys and 49% of girls reporting a positive attitude toward mathematics by twelveth grade (National Education Goals Panel, 1993). On the positive side, only 24% of the thirteen-year-olds and 28% of the seventeen-year-olds agreed with the statement, "I am taking mathematics only because I have to" (NAEP, 1994).

In the NCTM Curriculum Standards, mathematics is viewed as much more than a collection of skills and concepts. Instruction includes methods for investigating and reasoning, communicating about math, exploring properties, solving real problems, and exploring important mathematical ideas. Problem solving is central in the mathematics classroom; exploration, conjecture, and experimentation are the standard approaches to problem solving. Technology broadens areas in which mathematics is applied and has changed the discipline itself by changing the nature of problems and the methods for solving them. "It is now possible to execute almost all of the mathematical techniques taught from kindergarten through the first two years of college on hand-held calculators'' (Steen, 1992, p. 4.18). In 1992, 56% of eighth-grade students reported using calculators in their classes at least once a week. However, only 20% of eighth graders reported having computers in their classroom, compared to 44% of fourth graders (National Education Goals Panel, 1993). Because technology is changing mathematics and its uses, NCTM (1989, p. 8) believes that:

- Appropriate calculators should be available to all students at all times.
- A computer should be available in every classroom for demonstration purposes.
- Every student should have access to a computer for individual and group work.
- Students should learn to use the computer as a tool for processing information and performing calculations to investigate and solve problems.

The availability of calculators does not eliminate the need for students to gain some proficiency with paper-and-pencil calculations. However, students should be aware of and choose the appropriate procedure in a given context. Research has shown that the use of calculators and computers does not diminish the students' abilities to do mental or paper-and-pencil calculations; however, the use of technology allows for greater indepth exploration of important mathematical concepts and applications. Seventh- and eleventh-grade students who used calculators scored higher than their non-calculator-using peers on the NAEP (1987).

The curriculum standards also recognize changes in the understanding of how children learn. Students do not passively absorb information in retrievable fragments as a result of repeated practice. People approach new tasks with some prior knowledge, assimilate new information, and construct their own meaning; therefore, instruction needs to involve reflection (Resnick, 1987). There is also recognition that there isn't a fixed linear order to the teaching and learning of mathematics. In the past, great emphasis has been placed on ensuring that each identified skill in the curriculum was mastered before progressing to skills identified as of a higher order. This led to many students being stuck in drill and practice modes while higher achieving students were involved in problem solving or more advanced skills. The assumption of the fixed linearity of mathematics also provided the focus for remediation and served as the basis for tracking students in mathematics. As a result of this approach, the gap between lower achieving students and higher achieving students grew rather than narrowed over time. The new mathematical curriculum paradigm does not accept that there is a fixed order to learning.

The curriculum standards also provide for significant shifts in the content of mathematics for grades 5–8 and 9–12. In order to ensure indepth understanding rather than surface coverage of topics, new curriculum is being developed using the concept of ''less is more.'' Experimentation, application, integration with other subjects, cooperative learning, and written and oral mathematics communication, while more likely to result in the desired understanding of mathematics, requires more class time than lecture and recitation instructional methods. The use of calculators and computers reduces the time needed for routine operations and makes possible complex problem solving; however, curriculum developers must determine the most significant topics and concepts and edit out less important topics if adequate time is to be made available to teach for understanding. Changes in content and emphasis are summarized as follows:

Major Shifts in Instruction

From

- classrooms as simply a collection of individuals
- the teacher as the sole authority for right answers

- merely memorizing procedures
- emphasis on mechanistic answer finding
- treating mathematics as a body of isolated concepts and procedures

Toward

- classrooms as mathematical communities
- logic and mathematical evidence as verification
- mathematical reasoning
- conjecturing, inventing, and problem solving
- connecting mathematics, its ideas, and its applications

Topics to Receive Decreased Attention

Algebra

- word problems by type, such as coin, digit, and work
- the simplification of radical expressions
- the use of factoring to solve equations and to simplify rational expressions
- operations with rational expressions
- paper-and-pencil graphing of equations by point plotting
- logarithm calculations using tables and interpolation
- the solution of systems of equations using determinants
- conic sections

Topics to Receive Increased Attention

Algebra

- the use of real-world problems to motivate and apply theory
- the use of computer utilities to develop conceptual understanding
- computer-based methods such as successive approximations and graphing utilities for solving equations and inequalities
- the structure of number systems
- matrices and their applications

Topics to Receive Decreased Attention

Geometry

- Euclidean geometry as a complete axiomatic system
- proofs of incidence and betweenness theorems
- geometry from a synthetic viewpoint
- two-column proofs
- inscribed and circumscribed polygons
- theorems for circles involving segment ratios
- analytic geometry as a separate course

Topics to Receive Increased Attention

Geometry

- integration across topics at all grade levels
- coordinate and transformation approaches

- the development of short sequences of theorems
- deductive arguments expressed orally and in sentence or paragraph form
- computer-based explorations of two-dimensional and three-dimensional figures
- three-dimensional geometry
- real-world applications and modeling

Topics to Receive Decreased Attention

Trigonometry

- the verification of complex identities, half-angle identities
- numerical applications of sum, difference, double-angle
- calculations using tables and interpolation
- paper-and-pencil solutions of trigonometric equations

Topics to Receive Increased Attention

Trigonometry

- the use of appropriate science calculators
- realistic applications and modeling
- connections among the right triangle ratios, trigonometric functions, and circular functions
- the use of graphing utilities for solving equations and inequalities

Topics to Receive Decreased Attention

Functions

- paper-and-pencil evaluation
- the graphing of functions by hand using tables of values
- formulas given as models of real-world problems
- the expression of function equations in standardized form in order to graph them
- treatment as a separate course

Topics to Receive Increased Attention

Functions

- integration across topics at all grade levels
- the connections among a problem situation, its model as a function in symbolic form, and the graph of that function
- function equations expressed in standardized form as checks on the reasonableness of graphs produced by graphing utilities
- functions that are constructed as models of real-world problems

Other Topics to Receive Increased Attention

- statistics
- probability
- discrete mathematics

Communicating about mathematics is another important tenet of the curriculum standards. Students should learn to communicate mathematically in problem-solving situations where they have the opportunity to read, write, and discuss ideas that use the language of mathematics. Furthermore, students should reason mathematically by making conjectures, gathering evidence, and building arguments to support notions. Good reasoning should be valued more than the ability to find the right answer. In the workplace, most complex problems demand the talents of teams of people. Learning in the classroom should frequently take place in working groups where students can argue strategy, learn from each other, and communicate approach and solutions in writing.

The NCTM standards were adopted in 1989 after several years of development and review. It will take a number of years before the practices in most of the classrooms nationwide are congruent with the standards. Programs and textbooks appearing since 1991 have begun to reflect aspects of the standards, and those published beginning in 1994 are much more closely aligned with the curriculum standards. Two older programs, while predating the standards, are closely aligned with the NCTM standards; these are the University of Chicago School Mathematics Program (UCSMP) K−12 and the Comprehensive School Mathematics Program (CSMP) K−6 (NDN).

Change in curriculum is only one piece in the formula for ensuring that all students meet high standards in mathematics. How the curriculum is taught and the ability of teachers to actively engage students in learning are of vital importance. Wayne Welch in 1978 characterized the math classes he observed as classes with repetitive routines, which included 1) answers given for homework, with the hardest problems worked on the board; 2) a brief explanation of new material and the assignment of problems for the next day; and 3) time to begin work on problems while the teacher moved around the room to answer questions. Unfortunately, there is little evidence that instruction in most of today's classroom has changed since Welch made his observations (NCTM, 1989; Mathematical Research Council, 1989; Weiss, 1989). It is abundantly clear, however, that attitudes toward instruction, decisions about instruction, and instructional methodology must change if all students are to become motivated to, engaged in, and successful in achieving the new curriculum goals.

The NCTM *Professional Standards for Teaching of Mathematics,* published in 1991, address the delivery of mathematics instruction. These professional standards, including standards for teaching, evaluation of teaching, professional development of teachers, and support and development of teachers and teaching, hold equal or even more potential than the curriculum standards in bringing about the transformation of mathematics instruction and outcomes. The professional standards clearly call for major changes in the teaching of mathematics and how teaching should be supported and evaluated. In *Everybody Counts* (Mathematical Research Council, 1989, pp. 58−59), a new view of learning is summarized:

> Effective teachers are those who can stimulate students to learn mathematics. Educational research offers compelling evidence that students learn mathematics well only when they construct their own mathematical understanding. To understand what they learn, they must enact for themselves verbs that permeate the mathematics curriculum: "examine," "represent," "transform," "solve," "prove," "communicate." This happens most readily when students work in groups, engage in discussion, make presentations, and in other ways take charge of their own learning.

The NCTM *Professional Standards for Teaching Mathematics* can serve as criteria for individual professionals, departments, and school leadership for the evaluation of teaching and programs, as well as a guide for instructional and program improvement.

HOW LEARNING SHOULD BE ASSESSED

Most of the standardized norm-referenced commercial tests available to schools today measure only very limited aspects of the National Goals for mathematics and the more specific national standards. The NCTM *Curriculum and Evaluation Standards for School Mathematics* (1989) presents fourteen evaluation standards for general assessment, student assessment, and program evaluation. The evaluation standards are a critical component of reform. Changes in assessment also strongly communicate what is important for students to know. Evaluation must change not only in what is measured, but also how it is measured and evaluated. The advocated change in evaluation practices can best be summarized in terms of which aspects receive increased and decreased attention (see Table 2).

The National Assessment of Educational Progress (NAEP) has, in the past, attempted to measure higher level skills and has adopted the NCTM standards as the framework for future math assessments. Some states, most notably Vermont, have introduced new forms of criterion-based assessments, which attempt to provide for more direct measurement not only of what students know, but of what they can do. Open-ended questions require students to consider alterative approaches to complex problems, describe the process they used, justify their approach, and provide one or more answers. In some ways, it is at the assessment stage that the magnitude of the needed change in the curriculum and instruction in mathematics is most clearly focused. Now and for the future, it has become clear that the ever-expanding users of complex mathematics will not work in situations that require them to select solution a, b, c, or d answers. They will be presented with problems in the real world where the problem itself will frequently have to be identified, alternative approaches considered, and solutions justified.

The *Vermont Mathematics Portfolio Project* (Vermont Department of Education, 1991) provides insight into the type of assessment emerging in conjunction with the new standards in mathematics. In the Vermont fourth and eighth grades, model assessment is embedded in the instructional process. Throughout the year, students keep portfolios of their problem-solving work in mathematics. In the spring, students, in collaboration with their teachers select five to seven pieces of their best work in mathematics. Students also include mathematics-related writing, such as essays and journals. Portfolios are assessed based on certain criteria, by teachers within the district. A sample of portfolios from each school are then assessed at the state level by a second assessor; an additional sample is then independently

TABLE 2. **Recommendations for Evaluation.**

Increased Attention	Decreased Attention
• Assessing what students know and how they think about mathematics • Having assessment be an integral part of teaching • Focusing on a broad range of mathematical tasks and taking a holistic view of mathematics • Developing problem situations that require the application of a number of mathematical ideas • Using multiple assessment techniques, including written, oral, and demonstration formats • Using calculators, computers, and manipulatives in assessment • Evaluating the program by systemically collecting information on outcomes, curriculum, and instruction • Using standardized achievement tests as only one of many indicators of program outcomes	• Assessing what students do not know • Having assessment be simply counting correct answers on tests for the sole purpose of assigning grades • Focusing on a large number of specific and isolated skills organized by a content-behavior matrix • Using exercises or word problems requiring only one or two skills • Using only written tests • Excluding calculators, computers, and manipulatives from the assessment process • Evaluating the program only on the basis of test scores • Using standardized achievement tests as the only indicator of program outcomes

Source: NCTM, *Curriculum and Evaluation Standards for School Mathematics*, 1989, p. 191.

assessed at the state level to check for reliability in application of the criterion standards. The student's work is assessed based on the following criteria:

(1) Problem solving
  - the student's understanding of the task
  - how the student approached the task: the approach(es), procedure(s), and/or strategies adopted to attack the task
  - why the student made the choices along the way: the reflections, justification, analysis, rationale, and verification that influenced decisions
  - what findings, conclusions, observations, connections, and generalizations the student reached

(2) Communication criteria
  - language of mathematics
  - mathematical representations
  - clarity of presentation

Vermont uses the mathematics portfolios also to assess the mathematics instructional opportunities provided in the schools. Samples of portfolios from each school are assessed in terms of their reflection of instructional opportunities considered critical elements of effective mathematics programs, variety of content, and student disposition/empowerment in mathematics (Vermont Department of Education, 1991):

(1) *Instructional opportunities criteria:* portfolios reflect evidence of
  - group work
  - interdisciplinary work
  - construction of mathematical understanding through manipulation of concrete objects
  - the real-world nature of the problems and generalizability of skills to other contexts
  - assignments and products showing the use of calculators and computers

(2) *Content criteria:* portfolios reflect (for grade 8)
  - number relationships/number theory
  - operations/estimation
  - patterns/functions
  - algebra
  - geometry/spatial sense
  - measurement
  - statistics/probability
  - logic

(3) *Disposition/empowerment criteria:* narratives accompanying problem-solving entries reflect some evidence of
  - curiosity
  - flexibility
  - perseverance
  - risk taking
  - reflection

Vermont has organized schools into networks. Extensive teacher training in the development of mathematics programs and assessment is provided within each network.

Assessment in mathematics should become an integral part of learning. Assessment should be multidimensional and include not only assessment of what students know, but also what they can do. Furthermore, assessment should not be dominated by standardized multiple choice tests; more valid assessment practices are emerging. The framework for the NAEP for 1994 follows the NCTM standards closely. The *Report on Educational Research* (1992) paraphrases the NAEP proficient standards for assessment:

> *Eighth Grade:* Proficient students should apply concepts and procedures consistently to complex problems. They should make conjectures and defend their ideas. They should be able to relate connections among fractions, percentages and decimals, as well as topics such as algebra and functions.
>
> They should be familiar with quantity and spatial relationships in problem-solving and reasoning, and be able to convey underlying reasoning skills beyond arithmetic.
>
> Students should make inferences from data and graphs; understand how to gather and organize data; calculate; and evaluate and communicate results in statistics and probability. They should also be able to apply the properties of informal geometry.
>
> *Twelfth Grade:* By their senior year, students should consistently integrate concepts and procedures, showing an understanding of algebraic, geometric, spatial and statistical reasoning. They should perform algebraic operations involving polynomials, justify relationships and judge and defend answers.
>
> In addition, they should be able to analyze and interpret data in tabular and graphic form. They should make conjectures, defend their ideas and give supporting examples. (p. 3)

The National Council of Teachers of Mathematics is developing instruments to assess the national standards in conjunction with the National Council on Educational Standards and Testing. The tests will be made available to states and local districts for use on a voluntary basis. The national assessment will be made available to districts and schools on a voluntary basis.

In summary, as part of the reassessment of how children learn, research distinguishes between surface knowledge, i.e., the memorization of facts, procedures, and applications and meaningful knowledge, i.e., connected learning that makes sense to the learner. This expanded view of how children learn, what they should learn, and how learning should be assessed is reflected in the new standards for mathematics instruction. Six assumptions underlie the standards-based model. The first is that teaching must provide a student with experiences that enable him/her to develop connections among content and skills, i.e., to perceive patterns and to make connections cumulatively and over time.

A second assumption is that learning is natural and motivational; classrooms should be organized around real-life problems that build on previous experience and knowledge.

A third assumption is that children should be engaged in doing real math; children should learn to choose and apply appropriate procedures from among mental-math, pencil-and-paper, calculator, and computer in solving problems, and they should be proficient in using each approach.

A fourth assumption is that children should write and speak about mathematics; they should learn to prepare data visually through graphs and models, and they should appreciate mathematics as a language.

A fifth assumption is that the availability of technology allows for the expansion and revision of mathematical content for all children; indepth knowledge of topics, patterns, and relationships should take precedence over surface knowledge and rote memorization of discrete facts and procedures; curriculum development should be guided by the concept that "less is more."

A sixth assumption is that assessment is best embedded in the instructional process; in other words, it is part of the instructional process, rather than an add-on to instruction. Assessment should provide evidence not only of what a student knows but also of what a student can do. As much as possible, it should be performance-based. Assessment should not be dominated by multiple choice items, which simply ask the student to select from a fixed list of solutions.

THE BEST SCHOOLS – MATHEMATICS: THEORY INTO PRACTICE

The Best Schools have implemented mathematics programs aligned with the NCTM standards for instruction. It would probably be difficult to find a school in which mathematics is taught where the staff does not verbalize support for the NCTM standards; however, at this point in time, most school mathematics programs show little real change in practice. All too often, one hears teachers and administrators make the statement, "We are using the NCTM standards; we use manipulatives and calculators in math class." The new goals, content, instructional approaches, and assessment standards and professional standards represent a whole new paradigm for mathematics instruction. In the new paradigm, the use of technologies as an instructional tool plays a part; however, to equate their use with implementation of a program aligned with the standards is to miss the point of the new paradigm. A mathematics program that is consistent with the new goals, content, and assessment does not come packaged in a textbook. Newer texts are more closely aligned with the objectives; however, programs that prepare students to meet the standards require major changes not only in content, but in how students are taught and how they are assessed.

The Best Schools have adopted the new paradigm for mathematics instruction. Based on the theory and research on learning, which supports the NCTM standards, they have made major changes in how mathematics is taught in curriculum and in assessment. They have accomplished their mission with diverse social, economic, and physical contexts.

Illustrations in Mathematics: The Contexts (Case Studies)

JOHN BROWNE HIGH SCHOOL, FLUSHING, NY

"One World . . . Many Cultures" is the school's motto and also a reflection of the school itself. Students in this central New York City school come from sixty-one different countries; they speak forty-nine different languages, and 70% speak a language other than English at home. The population is 15% Caucasian, 42% Hispanic, 20% African-American, and 23% Asian. Forty percent of the students qualify for free or reduced-price lunch. The school offers a rich and diversified curriculum of more than 250 courses. Eighty-two percent of the graduating class attends college, half the students are enrolled in advanced placement and college-level courses, and the Regents competency rate for the past four years has been 98%. Success is met with in equal measure by all ethnic groups represented in the student population.

Patricia Kobetts, *Principal, Grades 9–12, 2908 Students*

RALSTON HIGH SCHOOL, RALSTON, NE

Ralston is a suburban high school in the metropolitan Omaha area, drawing students from the city of Omaha, city of Ralston, and Douglas County. The K – 12 district has six elementary schools, one middle school, and one high school. The socioeconomic status of Ralston patrons runs the gamut from fairly rich to fairly poor, with the majority in the middle. In 1990, Ralston

High School was chosen by ASCD to be one of twenty-four schools in the High School Futures Consortium (Princeton High School in Ohio, another Blue Ribbon School, is also a consortium member) to work for the development of the American High School. The average tenth-grade student scores at the 92nd NP in mathematics and the 95th NP in mathematics application on standardized tests.

Martha Bruckner, *Principal, Grades 9–12, 941 Students*

LA CANADA HIGH SCHOOL, LA CANADA, CA

La Canada High School serves mostly middle-class residents with occupations of a professional, scientific, or business nature. The Jet Propulsion Laboratory, Descanso Gardens, and Mt. Wilson Observatory are all within its boundaries. Many individuals have become directly involved in school/community partnerships, such as the Institutes for the 21st century. The 7–8 PTA and the 9–12 PTSA contribute over 10,000 annual hours of volunteer work. Twelfth-grade students scored at the 98th percentile, and eighth-grade students scored at the 99th percentile in math in the California Assessment Program. The mean quantitative score on the SAT in 1992 was 577, an increase of fifteen points from the previous year.

James E. Stratton, *Principal, Grades 7–12, 1669 Students*

PROCTOR JUNIOR-SENIOR HIGH SCHOOL, PROCTOR, VT

Proctor is a central Vermont town of 2000 people. The first graduating class in 1891 had only nine students; now, the current senior class has only twenty-four students. The seventh/eighth grades are organized as a middle school, with students heterogeneously grouped and a curriculum of core subjects. The senior high school students choose from a technical or college prep program or a mixture of both. The economy of the town was built on quarrying and finishing of marble. Now the town is primarily blue collar, with a scattering of management and professional as a bedroom community for Rutland. The school competes for tuition students from communities without high schools. In addition to recognition as a Blue Ribbon School, the school was selected as a partner in the New American Schools Corporation, National Alliance for Restructuring.

Marilyn Grunewald, *Principal, Grades 7–12, 164 Students*

THE BEST SCHOOLS—CLASS ORGANIZATION AND INSTRUCTIONAL TIME

The Best Schools have structured their mathematics program to reflect high achievement expectations for a core curriculum for all students. They usually require a minimum of three years of math in grades 9–12; however, their goal is for all students to successfully complete four years of study. Expectations concerning what all students study differ from many traditional course sequences. Gone are the high school math courses that are mere repetitions of low-level arithmetic skills. In some cases, the course titles are reminiscent of past practice, such as applied mathematics; however, the content and instructional approaches of these courses have changed drastically. For example, Applied Mathematics, developed by the Center for Occupational Research and Development, is an integrated two- to three- year course with forty modules that incorporate Algebra I, geometry, and some material usually covered in Algebra II and trigonometry, which is designed to prepare students for postsecondary education and careers (Methacton High School, PA; Apopka High School, FL; Proctor High School, VT). Algebra, geometry, and trigonometry are among the topics for all students, grades 9–12. This does not mean that all students study these topics at the same level of coverage or in the same amount of time. For example, Algebra I may be taught over a two-year period for some students or taught as part of an integrated course sequence, while other students study algebra at much higher levels of abstraction.

A typical course sequence in the Best Schools might include

(1) Integrated math (two- to three-year sequence integrating algebra, geometry and trig with real-life applications)
(2) Algebra I, parts A and B (two-year sequence), Algebra I, Algebra II, Algebra III—(standard and honors levels)
(3) Geometry (standard and honors levels)
(4) Trigonometry
(5) Pre-calculus, calculus, calculus honors, AP calculus
(6) Discrete math, statistics

Middle schools are cognizant of the need for a common curriculum core. There is an accepted assumption that all children will learn mathematics and a recognition of the negative effects of tracking on student learning. The curriculum and instructional approaches used in the Best Schools facilitate heterogeneous grouping of children in mathematics. Some of the schools use no grouping at all, with even Chapter 1 remedial and special education mainstreamed with in-class support. Other schools maintain some achievement-based grouping at some grade levels, for example, scheduling students who have demonstrated the ability to handle abstract concepts for algebra in seventh or eighth grade.

Instructional approaches that emphasize problem solving, writing about mathematics, experimentation, use of technology, and cooperative learning are accepted methodologies in the Best Schools. These approaches take more instructional time than a lecture—question and answer—approach. Careful restructuring of the curriculum to focus on the most important topics and material facilitates the use of more effective methods of instruction. Another approach to gaining instructional time for indepth study is to extend course content over more than one year, as in Algebra I, parts A and B. At the middle school level, mathematics is usually scheduled for at least one hour per day, and team scheduling may also extend opportunities for mathematics instruction. Another approach gaining in popularity at the middle and secondary levels is "double-block" scheduling. In this approach, each course is taught every other day for eighty to ninety minutes, or blocks of time are scheduled at specific times throughout the marking period. These longer blocks of time facilitate explorations, simulations, and experimentation. Some schools use a combination of traditional and double-block scheduling.

Class Organization Illustrations

JOHN BROWNE HIGH SCHOOL, NY

Students at John Brown High School are programmed heterogeneously within houses that are designed to serve as schools-within-the-school. The policy of the school is to enroll all students in appropriate and challenging academic mathematics courses, and it is the practice of the guidance department to enroll every student in the next mathematics course for the following year. Students are given the opportunity semi-annually to move to honors level courses, to enroll in special electives such as computer mathematics and computer programming. Courses beyond those required by New York State and the three years of mathematics required by the school, such as pre-calculus and advanced placement calculus, are open to any student who has passed the prerequisite course.

RALSTON HIGH SCHOOL, NE

Students at Ralston High School are encouraged to take as much mathematics as possible, and 70% take more than the required two years. In addition to algebra and geometry, the department offers Algebra II/trig (standard and honors levels), elementary analysis (pre-calculus), calculus, and math topics. At the ninth-grade level, a few students take fundamentals of algebra and geometry, which is a pre-algebra type course.

At the ninth-grade level in 1994–95, students were grouped into two interdisciplinary teams with five or six teachers. Each team consists of a mathematics, science, social studies, English, and physical education teacher. Students who elect to take keyboarding are placed in a team with a sixth teacher who teaches keyboarding. The team approach allows for interdisciplinary planning of program, flexible scheduling, and the support of a common group of students.

Every student has a "learning plan." Collection of information begins in grade 8. The plan is revised each year based on the input of both teachers and students; students are released early on two days to allow teacher advisors to review and revise plans. Each student is part of a multi-grade advisement group which meets daily for thirteen minutes. Almost all teachers serve as advisors.

LA CANADA HIGH SCHOOL, CA

Grades 7 and 8 at La Canada High School are organized into small schools, with approximately 140 students each, and are taught by a team of teachers. The program allows teachers to focus attention on individual student learning needs and to provide rich opportunities for interdisciplinary learning. At the 9–12 level, a core curriculum prepares students to enter a two-year or a four-year college upon graduation. In addition to the core curriculum, the school offers honors and AP courses and an ESL program; however, the school makes a concerted effort to enrich the curriculum for the "average" student by focusing on more engaging and facilitative instructional methodologies and performance assessment. Students are free to move into any program within the school and are actively encouraged by counselors to expand expectations and to sample vocational courses via the California Regional Occupations Program.

THE BEST SCHOOLS–CURRICULUM

The Best Schools have restructured their curriculum to align it with the NCTM curriculum standards. The focus is on indepth study, rather than topic coverage of the program. In order to gain time to cover topics in depth, decisions have been made to eliminate sections and/or whole chapters of textbooks. Many of the Best Schools estimate that 50% or less of math instruction is based on a textbook. They also gain time for significant study of content by using tools such as calculators and computers to do calculations that are time-consuming and have little learning value when done with pencil and paper.

Instruction in math classrooms in the Best Schools is based on helping students make connections–connections to previously learned material, connections to real-life situations, connections to other subject areas. Students are actively engaged in learning by collecting and analyzing data and participating in simulations. There are problems, units, and projects that integrate math with other subjects. For example, the AIMS integrated math and science program is used in many of the schools. Students learn which approaches to solving mathematics problems are most appropriate and efficient. Mathematics is taught as a means of communication; therefore, students reflect, keep math journals, write about, and discuss mathematics. Selecting the best approach for a problem and explaining and justifying the process used is central to instruction. Cooperative learning groups are used regularly to simulate real-life math applications, foster math communication, and increase problem-solving ability. Manipulatives, calculators, and computers are used extensively. Research has demonstrated that fears are unfounded that the use of calculators and computers decrease in learning of basic mathematics skills. For example, seventh and eleventh graders who used calculators in class outscored peers who did not use calculators on the NAEP (1988). Computer software enables students to create and use data bases and graph and analyze data to solve complex problems. Software such as ClarisWorks, Geometry Sketchpad, MacNumberics, and Geometry Supposer are used extensively. There has been a major decrease on lecture, rote memorization of facts and procedures, and paper-and-pencil practice of routine tasks.

The focus in the Best Schools is on maximizing achievement for all students and maintaining a "can-do/want-to-do" attitude toward learning mathematics. Teachers use highly engaging and learner-centered instructional approaches in the classroom as one means to accomplish this goal. In order to reinforce the connection between the classroom and the real world, speakers from local industry or such groups as the Junior Engineering Technology Society (JETS) visit the schools, and field trips are also common (Pine Tree Middle School and Pine Tree High School, TX). Also crucial are testing and grading approaches that are embedded in the instructional process and that focus on demonstration of mastery.

The Best Schools also provide opportunity for students to get individual assistance outside of the class period. In addition to before- and after-school help provided by classroom teachers, many schools provide math resource centers staffed by a math teacher for all or part of the day. Frequently, peer tutors are available in these centers during or after school. The goal is simple—make everyone successful in mathematics.

Curriculum Illustrations

JOHN BROWNE HIGH SCHOOL, NY

The curriculum in mathematics at John Browne consists of the New York State Integrated Mathematics Courses I, II, and III, precalculus mathematics, advanced placement calculus, a three-year sequence in computer science, math team class, and mathematics research class. On the freshman level, courses in fundamentals of mathematics and pre-sequential mathematics are offered to students whose scores on standardized tests indicate they are not ready for Regents level algebra. Selected students are offered Regents algebra seven times a week to give additional opportunities for tutoring, individualized, and small-group work. Students who do not pass the state-mandated Regents Competency Test at the end of the freshmen year are offered remediation using computer-assisted instruction. The goal of the department is to provide every student with a full and sound preparation in mathematics for college or career, to provide electives and honors classes, to encourage special interest in and talent for mathematics, and to provide the support necessary for *all* students to meet success in a challenging program.

The instructional formats used in teaching mathematics are large-group developmental instruction, small-group work, individualized instruction, and computer laboratory work. Classroom instruction emphasizes the connections between classroom mathematics and careers, daily life problems, and problems in business and science. The instructional resources available to teachers include a wide variety of the most up-to-date textbooks; texts in several languages; teacher resource kits; class sets of manipulatives such as algebra tiles, dice, game chips, cards, and geometric models; computer labs; software; videotapes; calculators; and overhead projectors. Computers are used in three ways: 1) for computer-assisted instruction, 2) as an "electronic blackboard," and 3) for solving mathematical problems (using software written in BASIC by students in the school).

RALSTON HIGH SCHOOL, NE

The focus of the mathematics program at Ralston High School is to make mathematics meaningful to all students. The school offers a variety of courses, and it is stressed that every student can successfully take four years of mathematics. For example, in Algebra I, all students must meet established course outcomes. Teaching methods include cooperative learning, team teaching, lecture, laboratory experiences, and the use of technology. Emphasis in the curriculum is on application of mathematics to real life. In addition, field trips and guest speakers are used to reinforce the connection of mathematics to the "real world."

One of the strongest aspects of the mathematics program is the use of technology. There are six computer labs (240 computers) in the school, and the math department makes heavy use of the MAC labs. Each classroom is equipped with a computer for teacher demonstration purposes. Clusters of four to six computers can be brought into the classrooms for special projects. Extensive use is made of software programs such as Geometric Sketchpad, MacNumerics, and ClarisWorks Spreadsheet. Classroom sets of TI-81 graphics calculators are available and used for instruction.

LA CANADA HIGH SCHOOL, CA

Probably the most unique course in the math/science department at La Canada is the transformation math/science course for ninth and tenth graders. The teachers of this course received a grant from GTE for the development of the course. In keeping with the California State Framework and the National Council of Teachers of Mathematics Standards, algebra, geometry, and pre-calculus are integrated. The class is taught back-to-back with the integrated biology and chemistry course. Both courses are organized around the unifying idea of transformations. Students experience a hands-on, discovery approach to learning, with frequent science and computer labs. The content of the course focuses upon the technology and problem-solving needs of students of the 21st century, and careful evaluation of topics has led to elimination of some of the traditional topics (such as an emphasis on factoring) to allow more time for computer and science labs. For example, in the first quarter, students are introduced to reflections, translations, rotations, and matrices–not the usual content for students who would traditionally be in geometry class doing two-column proofs.

In addition to the transformation course sequence, the school offers a more traditional course sequence, which includes algebra starting in grade 8, followed by geometry, Algebra II, pre-calculus, and calculus AB and BC.

Graphing calculators are available for all classes and are used almost daily. In addition, a classroom computer is used frequently for demonstration purposes and three computer labs are also available. Special projects in Algebra II and pre-calculus help students to understand the interrelationship between mathematics and other curricular areas. As an example, in Algebra II, students worked in groups on a topology project and submitted their final report on video. Some courses, such as pre-calculus, have been coordinated with science courses, and Algebra I students work with the social science department to do a unit on polling.

In pre-calculus classes, the students are assigned monthly projects that relate mathematics to topics such as engineering and architecture. In Algebra II, the students complete units emphasizing mathematics in music and in bicycles, while geometry students do projects on architecture and art. Math students are often taken outside of class to experiment, measure, and observe. Students are involved in group problem-solving activities and in using manipulatives to explore new topics.

A unique program called the Institute for the 21st Century involves groups of ten to twelve students with an outside mentor to create and carry out a project, which is showcased at evening sessions. Many of these mentorships involve the use of math in real-life situations. There are approximately fifteen institutes per semester; however, the goal is for all students to participate in at least one institute during their high school years. Career exploration is also incorporated within the math and science courses, and students are assigned outside projects that relate their studies to the world of work, e.g., design of a house.

PROCTOR JUNIOR-SENIOR HIGH SCHOOL, VT

All grade 7/8 students at Proctor take mathematics, and three years of mathematics is required at the high school level, with many students taking a fourth year. A diversified curriculum is offered based on NCTM and state and district standards. Cooperative grouping, interdisciplinary units, and teacher- and student-directed learning are the formats used to introduce the curriculum. Calculators and computers are used in courses. Specific courses include

- Algebra I, II, and III are offered in grades 9–12. Eighth graders take pre-algebra or may elect to take Algebra I. Pre-algebra is also offered to students who need reinforcement in ninth grade and to all eighth graders. The courses approach math in an interdisciplinary way, stressing math's applications to physics, chemistry, biology, business, social studies, and English. The Saxon series is used as the basis for instruction.
- Geometry is offered following Algebra II. The school is piloting the state's portfolio system for problem solving and applying math to real life. The Geometry Supposer and spreadsheet software are used, along with the Saxon-developed textbook.
- Calculus, discrete math, and statistics are taught via satellite using programs from the Virginia Department of Education. Students communicate with the teacher via phone. The satellite connection has allowed the school to initiate advanced math courses for its small student population. Currently, nine students are taking calculus, five discrete math, and eight statistics.
- Applied math (NDN) is a two year-sequence offered primarily to eleventh- and twelveth-grade students. It uses a unique approach to relating math to the real world. The program allows room for much discussion about problems that students will encounter upon graduation.
- Grade 7/8 math focuses on problem solving as an integral part of the curriculum. Interdisciplinary units are also used in the courses. Approximately 20% of the class time is devoted to lab work based on the Vermont portfolio development and to piloting the math teaching and assessment materials of the National Standards Project. Saxon textbooks are used in the courses.

THE BEST SCHOOLS–ASSESSING WHAT STUDENTS KNOW AND CAN DO

The Best Schools are not waiting for finalization of new national or state assessment to expand their assessment approaches beyond the traditional multiple choice or work-the-problem, provide-the-correct-number tests. The schools are developing their own more authentic assessments, which focus on demonstration of understanding mathematical concepts; examples of such approaches include lab reports, portfolios of best works, multiple step problems, visual representations, open-ended questions, applications, and cooperative group projects. While the assessment strategies have become much more comprehensive, the approach to grading has also changed. The object is for all students to master the content, and multiple opportunities are frequently given for students to demonstrate their achievement. There are criteria or standards set for the course, and the assumption is that all students can and will meet the standards. Grading is in terms of fixed criteria standards, rather than how one student does in comparison to another. The goal is to have a strongly skewed curve, not a normal curve, of grades. For example, the standards for Algebra I are set in terms of what students should know and be able to do, apply to all students taking Algebra I, and are shared with the students. Each student is judged or graded against this standard, rather than how other students are doing in the individual class section.

Assessment Illustrations

RALSON HIGH SCHOOL, NE

There is a commitment at Ralston that every student will successfully meet mastery requirements in Algebra I and geometry. The courses are designed to focus on important concepts and understandings, which are assessed through three department-developed mastery tests per marking period for each course. A variety of instructional methods and technologies are used to maximize student success in the classroom. A modified school calendar allows for three intersessions at the end of each quarter. The semester ends before the winter vacation, which lasts for two and a half weeks, one week of which is considered the intersession. During these intersessions, students can attend intensive two full days of Algebra I or geometry classes to gain understanding of concepts not understood during the marking period and can retake the competency tests for the marking period. Regardless of in-class work, projects or homework, each student must pass each competency test at the 80% level. When students are assigned to a remedial class due to a previous failure, they must complete homework or remain after school. Students who do not complete the work after school are referred to the principal. Three referrals and the student is dropped from the course.

Nebraska requires the administration of standardized tests at the tenth-grade level. These tests are given during the intersession. Approximately 97% of the students come to school to take the tests during this period; the remaining students take the tests in scheduled blocks after school. Scheduling testing in this manner eliminates the need to take time from instruction for standardized assessment.

PROCTOR JUNIOR-SENIOR HIGH SCHOOL, VT

Proctor is a member of the Vermont pilot school program on portfolio assessment in math and English. Problem solving is an integral part of the curriculum. The state system of portfolio assessment is used in grades 7/8. The mathematic portfolio contains five to seven pieces of each student's best pieces in four categories. An example of a portfolio might include

(1) The solution to a math puzzle with an explanation concerning the strategy
(2) A problem requiring the use of technology to develop a table and a paragraph explaining the approach
(3) A graph that shows the data from a survey investigation conducted in the school
(4) A real-world experience with math, such as a series of estimations of the number of seeds in a pumpkin, with written observations concerning estimation

Based on developed rubrics, the portfolios are holistically scored from 1–4 by the school staff. In addition, the Vermont State Department evaluates a sample of the school's eighth-grade portfolios and provides district and state results of the assessment. Portfolios for grade 7 are evaluated by the teachers within the school.

As part of the school's participation in the National Alliance (New American Schools), it is piloting assessment of the National Mathematics and English Standards. This assessment approach also includes a teaching component. Over a series of days, students are pretaught a topic in order to bring them to the same level of knowledge. A problem is then presented in a forty-five-minute assessment period. Using a rubric, a score of 0–4 is given.

The National Assessment of Standards approach is similar to the Vermont Portfolio approach in terms of its use as a teaching tool, as well as for assessment of achievement. One way in which they differ is that the National Standards approach uses a specific topic and problem while the Vermont system of assessment uses an open-ended approach to selection of items for the individual portfolio.

LA CANADA HIGH SCHOOL, CA

In La Canada, open-ended questions and investigations are used in many courses, with some students submitting mathematics portfolios as a record of their growth in mathematical thinking. Every course requires some writing, from explanations of procedures to investigation write-ups patterned after science lab reports. All students are involved in problem-solving activities, frequently in collaborative groups. Expectations are high, and students are called upon to analyze and synthesize in many different situations such as group work, tests, projects, reports, and daily work. In addition to school developed assessment, students take the UCLA Diagnostic Tests at the end of each course to ensure that they have met the criteria to allow for success in the next level of the program.

THE BEST SCHOOLS–PROGRAM DEVELOPMENT AND SUPPORT IN MATHEMATICS

Many of the Best Schools began to transform mathematics education a number of years ago, prior to the release of the NCTM standards. Emerging state standards for assessment, more consistent with NCTM standards, also served to stimulate reform. Also, many of the Best Schools serve as pilot sites for state, professional network, and/or national initiatives. What all the Best Schools have in common is a recognition that *all* students need to learn meaningful mathematics and that both the curriculum and mode of instruction have to be aligned to the principles of how people learn, such as the following:

- Learning is natural and motivational.
- People learn by making connections to previously acquired knowledge.
- Learning involves making connections with real-life situations.
- Rather than fragmented skill-sequenced curriculum, students learn better when instruction emphasizes connections among content areas and topics.
- Learning of surface knowledge, i.e., memorization of facts, formulas, and procedures, does not automatically result in the learning of meaningful knowledge or understanding.
- Assessment should be embedded in instruction and assess what students can do, as well as what they know.

The transformation of mathematics instruction in the Best Schools was a planned change. Those that began the process in the late 1980s had to rely almost totally on materials they developed and on supplemental programs developed by others. Starting in 1991, new textbooks began to reflect the NCTM standards. "Drill and skill" computer programs were replaced by problem-centered software, such as the Geometry Supposer and easy-to-use integrated packages, which include data base, spread sheet, and word processing. Scientific and graphing calculators became less expensive and more user friendly. However, a program that meets the NCTM standards is far more than textbooks, software packages, supplemental materials, calculators, and computers. The program requires major changes in curriculum and modes of instruction. The Best Schools are committed to ongoing curriculum development; each year, the program is reviewed and the curriculum refined based on student outcomes and available resources. Each school continues to design connections to other subject areas and to incorporate real-life problems relevant to their own context.

Program Development Illustrations

PROCTOR JUNIOR-SENIOR HIGH SCHOOL, VT

Proctor is a very small school with fewer than thirty students at each grade level. Some teachers teach as many as seven different courses each day. It has always been a source of pride for the community it serves. The principal upholds high expectations for the faculty, and the faculty have high expectations for students. Faculty members are expected to review curriculum on an ongoing basis and to keep abreast with current trends in their fields. Teachers are encouraged to attend workshops and visit model programs and become involved in professional activities. The principal serves as an instructional model by participating with teachers in staff development, i.e., training in the Vermont portfolio assessment and serving as the resource and on satellite courses. The school has actively sought participation in state and national programs. The program is always in development, always moving forward, and always improving.

In 1993, the school became one of fifteen Vermont schools to join the National Alliance, a multistate multidistrict project of the New American Schools Coalition. This project provides some direct resources ($28,000) for local training and curriculum development and technology and access to a national network of schools working toward continuous improvement and toward becoming directly involved in the piloting of assessment for the National Standards Projects. Each school in the Alliance is working on five design tasks: 1) establishment of standards; 2) learning environments (science, math, English, history, and transition to work); 3) high-performance management (strategic planning, change strategies, site-based management); 4) community services and support; and 5) public engagement. Many of these areas were well developed already at Proctor; however, the development of community support and services has been an initiative that has been very successful. The Alliance connection supports and enhances strategies for development already valued by the school, such as networking with other schools, staff development and piloting innovations.

RALSTON HIGH SCHOOL, NE

In 1990, Ralston High School was chosen by ASCD to be part of the Futures Consortium of twenty-four schools to seek ways to improve the American High School. Six goals were established to serve as the basis of a five-year plan. The goals were generated by a nineteen-member planning team consisting of administrators, teachers, and parent representatives. A steering committee, which includes the principal, the superintendent, an assistant principal, a board member, and four teachers, works together to plan strategies to keep the school working toward its goals. Within the overall five-year plan, groups have developed twenty-three related action improvement plans. Department chairpersons are credited with the initial push for change and for involvement with ASCD. Department chairpersons meet weekly to decide issues related to curriculum, assessment, and scheduling. Department members are heavily involved in discussion and implementation of curriculum changes within their departments. Curriculum study groups such as the interdisciplinary team also play a significant role in ongoing program development. The principal and assistant principals provide energetic leadership that encourages staff to increase their knowledge of education, to plan, and to take the risks necessary to develop a high school of the future.

LA CANADA HIGH SCHOOL, CA

The staff, students, and parents of La Canada High School came together in a series of special workshops to define the major goals for the school, which are to 1) provide for continuous personal growth, 2) prepare students for productive work and home lives, 3) prepare students for participation in a culturally diverse society, and 4) prepare students for participation in a democracy as effective and informed citizens. Each department reviews these goals annually as they set specific objectives for curriculum revision, staff development, and instructional reform. Every change that occurs in the classroom (e.g., increased use of technology or implementation of performance assessment) is linked back to the purposes of schooling and to the vision, and these connections are emphasized by the administration and faculty leadership. Members of the school site council have incorporated the goals and vision into the annual school site plan. Students are informed of the school goals through class meetings, articles in the paper, individual meetings with the principal, and classroom presentations.

Expectations and standards are clearly established by the principal, who believes in a participatory style of decision making. When the principal chairs a decision-making group, the role he models for those present, particularly those who will lead other meetings, is Socratic, asking questions that cause participants to define, augment, and clarify proposals. He encourages debate, plays devil's advocate, challenges members to prioritize their concerns, and, ultimately, to build consensus for what becomes the collective will of the school. Elected staff leadership, whether they are department chairpersons (elected biannually), 7/8 team leaders, or faculty association leaders, act as liaisons between the committees on which they serve and the faculty at large. Key components of this collaborative model are the instructional planning team, instructional council, and the school site council.

A common planning period for department chairs facilitates interdisciplinary efforts and coordination. Curriculum is developed in the summer and frequently involves more than fifty staff members.

JOHN BROWNE HIGH SCHOOL, NY

The principal and the staff at John Browne High School believe that all students can learn and that nothing is as important to the individual and to society than a sound education. Their goal is to have young people know and understand themselves, to respect one another, to love the world of books and ideas, to seek enlightenment from the arts, and to become contributing citizens who value truth, justice, fair play, integrity, and freedom and who accept responsibility for their own actions. School goals and priorities were developed by the entire staff as part of a comprehensive improvement planning process. Outside college and business groups work in conjunction with staff planning teams in making suggestions for change and in providing expertise and support in a variety of areas such as grant writing. The improvement of instruction is ongoing and lies at the heart of all development efforts.

Planned improvement is not new to John Browne. When the principal arrived ten years ago, there were many identifiable needs, but there was also a cadre of teachers ready for change. She brought these people together and energized them. The principal serves as a model in the instructional leadership process. In addition to the principal, there is an assistant principal for curriculum, a vice-principal for supervision, and ten department heads, one for every subject, who also hold the title of assistant principal. Supervising assistant principals are primarily responsible for the day-to-day operations of their departments. They assess and improve instruction from the planning stages with staff to the recording of final grades. They work with teachers to implement new curriculum, monitor standards, and assist teachers to establish effective classroom instruction. The principal meets regularly with a committee of teachers representing each subject area, along with the union leader regarding school programs, designs, concerns, and restructuring.

THE BEST SCHOOLS–MATERIALS

A wide variety of programs, materials, and equipment are used in the teaching of mathematics in the Best Schools. The Applied Math (TechPrep NDN) program, developed by the Center for Occupational Research and Development, is a widely used program (Methacton High School, PA; Apopka High School, FL; Proctor High School, VT). The two- to three-year program integrates higher levels of math, such as algebra, geometry, and trigonometry, with real-world applications. Representatives are available in every state to assist schools in implementing this program. The AIMS program, which integrates mathematics and science, is also used by a number of schools. STAMM (Systematic Teaching and Measurement Mathematics) (NDN) is a program that focuses on the application of mathematics skills to daily life experiences and links problem solving and critical thinking skills to other school subjects.

Classroom sets of scientific and graphing calculators are available in the Best Schools. In addition, many school libraries have calculators that can be checked out. Most of the schools have a computer in each mathematics classroom for demonstration purposes, four to six computers for student use in the room or which can be moved into the classroom, and computer labs available for math instruction. Extensive use is made of utility software such as ClarisWorks or Microsoft Works, which combine spreadsheet, graphing, word processing, and data base capabilities. Software developed specifically for enhanced mathematics instruction is also widely used, such as the Geometry Supposer and PreSupposer (Sunburst/Wings for Learning Inc.). Some middle schools, such as Pine Tree Middle School, Texas, use Josten's Learning Lab. Manipulatives are used extensively at the middle school level, and their use continues into the high school programs.

Materials Illustration

RALSTON HIGH SCHOOL, NE

Textbooks at Ralston are selected based on NCTM standards and emphasis on mathematical applications. More than 240 computers are available in various labs, in small clusters, and stand-alones for student use. All the computers are Mactintoshes, except for one business-oriented lab, which has IBM computers. Every classroom is equipped with a computer and large-screen monitor for teacher demonstration. Extensive use is made of software programs such as Geometric Sketchpad, MacNumerics, and ClarisWorks Spreadsheet. In addition, classroom sets of TI-81 graphics calculators are available.

THE BEST SCHOOLS – STAFF DEVELOPMENT

The National Council of Teachers of Mathematics, in their *Professional Standards for Teaching Mathematics,* elegantly states the critical need for continuous professional development to meet the curriculum and evaluation standards for students. Professional teachers and administrators are committed to increasing their own knowledge on an individual, as well as a collective, basis. Teachers and administrators need to understand the theory and research undergirding curriculum, instruction, and assessment. In addition, there are many specific strategies that require comprehensive training of teachers and principals. For example, teachers need to learn how to select the appropriate tools of learning and also how to use such tools as computers, calculators, and manipulatives to support a problem-solving mode of instruction. Even with new textbooks more fully aligned with the NCTM standards, the new curriculum and approaches to teaching mathematics cannot be implemented with a short inservice conducted by a textbook representative. The Best Schools have been willing to make an extensive commitment over time to staff development, and there is an active commitment from the staff to continuous learning and improvement.

Training in the Best Schools has been provided by district supervisors, teachers, principals, state department staff, university staff, and network and coalition partners who are dedicated to the new paradigm of instruction. Schools have provided release time for teachers, used scheduled inservice (usually from five to ten days per year), built on continuing education requirements and programs, and used voluntary professional development time. What the Best Schools have in common is the recognition of the need for comprehensive, focused, and ongoing staff development.

Staff Development Illustrations

RALSTON HIGH SCHOOL, NE

Staff development in Ralston High School is ongoing. Teachers are involved in planning and staff development for three to four days before the start of school, one day between each marking period, and three to four additional days scheduled throughout the year. In addition, groups of teachers work on curriculum during intersessions and during the summer recess. Experts in the field of mathematics are brought to the school, and in-school "experts" provide training for colleagues. Two of the staff have won Cooper Awards for innovative practices in mathematics, and another has had articles published concerning the teaching of mathematics. Another teacher was named a finalist for Outstanding Mathematics Teacher for Nebraska; the same teacher was selected to participate in a two-week NASA space camp for math educators.

Many staff development activities have related to goals developed through work with the ASCD Futures Consortium, such as individual learning plans, assessment, interdisciplinary and multicultural curriculum, changes in the school day and year, and technology. For example in 1991–92, all staff members were included in five days of inservice related to the use of technology in a school and classroom; as the year progressed, sessions were planned to move from general knowledge to specific curriculum related information as planned by individual departments. Math, English, social studies, science, industrial technology, and practical and fine arts departments met with "Apple Fellows" who were experts in the utilization of technology in their specific curricular areas.

LA CANADA HIGH SCHOOL, CA

Each year in La Canada, over one-third of the school improvement budget of approximately $100,000 (the district applies for these state funds, and they are prorated to the schools) is devoted to staff development. The funds, support such items as release time for the planning team (they teach four rather than five periods), half-time science lab aides, the math resource center aide, workshops, and conferences. District mentor grants are given to staff who volunteer to develop a new approach to instruction. The teacher receives $4000 for out-of-school time and a $1600 budget for materials, travel, etc. An example of a mentor grant program is one to increase the use of technology in math. The staff development program reflects the long- and short-term goals developed for the district by the administrative team and the district curriculum council. Goals for 1992–93 included implementation of district curriculum documents, implementation of authentic assessment, collaborative learning, technology in the classroom, and creation of increased interdisciplinary connections. Five full-day inservices are held throughout the year, and all staff participate. In addition, teachers are encouraged to attend workshops and conferences that pertain to the goals set for the year, or to increase curriculum expertise. The principal places great emphasis on increasing the staff's knowledge of curriculum and instruction. For example, he takes teachers on study retreats. A recent retreat with eighteen teachers and administrators focused on brain research and its implications for current instruction.

Teacher evaluation is seen as a critical tool in the enhancement of student learning. The responsibility for improved student learning is the shared responsibility of the teacher and site administrators. The evaluation process recognizes excellence in teaching while encouraging all to grow and improve. Permanent teachers are evaluated every two years using a standard or self-directed model. Self-directed teachers are encouraged to create broad goals in the areas of curriculum, technology, and instructional strategies. Standard evaluation teachers generate specific classroom goals and also tailor classroom teaching to a list of performance exemplars. Teachers who encounter difficulty complete a certificated assistance plan along with the supervising administrator and receive help remediating problems. These teachers are observed twice every year.

The principal and other administrators place great emphasis on instruction. Being in classrooms and discussing instruction with teachers are top priorities. The principal attends individual department meetings to participate in curriculum discussions and teaches sample lessons from each of the departments' curriculum guides. For example, in one two-week period, he taught honors English, geometry, and French classes.

THE BEST SCHOOLS–FUNDING DEVELOPMENT

Mathematics instruction occupies approximately 15–20% of the instructional day. Based on the national average cost per pupil of $5342, mathematics instruction costs on the average $800 to $1070 per pupil per year (National Center for Educational Statistics, 1992). In other words, no matter what the outcomes of instruction, mathematics instruction is expensive.

Salaries, benefits, and operational expenses account for the great majority of instructional costs. Staff development, curriculum development, textbooks, supplementary materials, computers, calculators, manipulatives, and software are minor costs in terms of overall school budgets, but highly significant costs in terms of outcomes on initiating and maintaining effective mathematics programs. An extensive array of manipulatives are needed for each classroom. Class sets, library sets, and individually assigned calculators need to be available to insure that all students have access to calculators. Sufficient computers need to be available to make them a viable instructional tool. The Best Schools have computers available for teacher demonstration, for classroom use, and for use in laboratories. Technology has been purchased by the Best Schools through reallocation of district funds and grants. The PTAs and PTOs have been major fund raisers to support the acquisition of technology for the schools. Business partnerships have also been effective sources of technology and expertise. Few schools have been able to purchase all of the support materials and technology at one time; rather, they have developed plans to ensure that they will have the needed resources and technology in a fixed period of years. They also recognize that technology will change over the years and will have to be supplemented, enhanced, or replaced.

In general, there has been little or no increase in staffing resulting from the transformation of mathematics programs. In schools where there are mathematics or exploration labs, the classroom teacher accompanies the class to the lab and conducts the lab experience. In some cases, a trained instructional aide has been added to assist in the lab experience. Other schools have made use of volunteers. In schools with many computers, technical services are provided. Frequently, a staff member is provided a stipend and/or released from other duties to coordinate the use of technology and maintain the networks and software.

Effective staff and curriculum development requires time. The Best Schools invest heavily in development. Most of the Best Schools incorporate at least five inservice days into the school calendar for staff development; however, release time to observe and to receive training is also needed. Courses are also offered after school on either a voluntary basis or for continuing education credits. Summer workshops for staff development and curriculum writing are planned and implemented. A number of states have requirements for continuing education, which facilitate professional development. Because of the need to work with technology, most schools encourage faculty to take computers home during holidays. In many schools, the goal is that eventually all teachers will have a computer on their desks; in some schools, this is a reality. Costs for inservice training usually involve the costs for substitutes for release time, travel to training sessions and to observe model programs, summer workshop pay for teachers, inservice credits that may affect movement on salary guides, workshop registration fees, professional literature, and training consultants' fees. In addition to district funds, many schools use their Education for Economic Security Dwight D. Eisenhower Mathematics and Science Education Act funds for inservice. Many of the Best Schools have found business partners who provide technical assistance and, in some cases, financial resources. University partners are also sources of technical assistance and training. Most of the schools are involved with networks of other schools working toward similar goals. These network connections may not provide direct financial resources, but they provide free or low-cost expertise and support. The Best Schools, because of their commitment to staff and program development, have managed to find the resources for development, regardless of their economic status.

Funding Illustration

RALSTON HIGH SCHOOL, NE

Expenditures at Ralston High School, compared to other schools in Nebraska, are high, $5340 per student in 1993–94 (close to the average expenditure nationwide). The school has a budget of $390,000 for textbooks, library books and resources, equipment, and instructional supplies. Most of the 240 computers were purchased at one time under a three-year lease-purchase agreement. The standard teaching schedule is six periods per day. Two full-time paraprofessionals provide technical support and assistance in the computer labs. Twelve days for inservice, curriculum development, and planning are built into the staff calendar. In addition, teachers who provide instruction during intersessions are paid $20 per hour. Teachers involved in intersession or summer inservice of curriculum development are paid $13 per hour.

Ninth- and tenth-grade teams have a release day once a quarter to allow for lengthy planning for the upcoming marking period. In cases where groups of teachers do not wish to take time from instruction, the superintendent has given special permission for these teachers to work on their own time for pay equal to that which would have been paid to substitutes.

SUMMARY

The Best Schools have adopted the NCTM *Curriculum and Evaluation Standards,* which focus on not only what students know, but what they can do, and the NCTM *Professional Standards for Teaching Mathematics*. They have developed mathematics programs that are reflective of current theory and research. They are committed to the belief that all students can learn and develop an appreciation for a high level of mathematics achievement. Instruction is centered on problem solving and making connections with real-life situations. A rich environment of materials, computers, calculators, and manipulatives support higher level programs for all students. New forms of more authentic assessment are being introduced. Gone are tracked/basal/worksheet/select-the-right-answer math classes. The Best Schools, urban, suburban, and rural, have developed their mathematics programs over a period of years and have plans to continue program development. In addition, there has been and will continue to be extensive staff and program development in the Best Schools. The Best Schools reach out to the community, business, state departments, parents, and networks of schools for aid in developing programs.

REFERENCES

AIMS Education Foundation. (1989). "Project AIMS Update," Fresno, CA: AIMS Education Foundation.

Association for Supervision and Curriculum Development (ASCD). (1989). *ASCD Curriculum Handbook: A Resource for Curriculum Administrators*. Alexandria, VA: ASCD.

Association for Supervision and Curriculum Development. (1989). *Toward the Thinking Curriculum: Current Cognitive Research,* L. B. Resnick and L. E. Klopher, eds., Alexandria, VA: ASCD.

Bennett, William J. (1986). *First Lessons: A Report on Elementary Education in America.* Washington, D.C.: U.S. Government Printing Office.

Bennett, William J. (1988). *James Madison Elementary School*. Washington, D.C.: U.S. Government Printing Office.

California State Department of Education. (1987). *Mathematics Model Curriculum Guide*. Sacramento, CA: CA State Department of Education.

Center for Occupational Research and Development. (1992). *Applied Mathematics.* Waco, TX: Center for Occupational Research and Development.

Educational Testing Service, Center for the Assessment of Educational Progress. (1991). *The 1991 IAEP Assessment: Objectives for Mathematics, Science, and Geography*. Princeton, NJ: Educational Testing Service.

Flanders, J. R. (1987). "How Much of the Content in Mathematics Textbooks Is New?" *Arithmetic Teacher,* 35:18–23.

LaPointe, Archie E., et al. (1992). *Learning Mathematics*. Princeton, NJ: Educational Testing Service, Center for the Assessment of Educational Progress.

Lockwood, Anne T. (1991). "Mathematics for the Information Age," *Focus in Change*, The National Center for Effective Research and Development (Winter):5.

Mathematical Research Council. (1989). *Everybody Counts: A Report to the Nation on the Future of Mathematics Education*. Washington D.C.: National Academy Press.

McKnight, C. C., et al. (1987). *The Underachieving Curriculum: Assessing U.S. School Mathematics from an International Perspective*. Champaign, IL: Stipes Publishing Co.

National Assessment of Educational Progress (NAEP). (1987). *Learning by Doing: A Manual for Teaching and Assessing Higher-Order Thinking in Science and Mathematics*. Princeton, NJ: Educational Testing Service.

National Assessment of Educational Progress (NAEP). (1988). *The Mathematics Report Card: Are We Measuring Up?* Princeton, NJ: Educational Testing Service.

National Assessment of Educational Progress (NAEP). (1990). *America's Challenge: Accelerating Academic Achievement*. Princeton, NJ: Educational Testing Service.

National Assessment of Educational Progress. (1994). *NAEP 1992 Trends in Academic Progress*. Washington, D.C.: Educational Testing Service with the National Center for Educational Statistics. U.S. Department of Education.

National Center for Educational Statistics. (1992). The Condition of Education 1992. Washington, D.C.: U.S. Department of Education, Office of Educational Research, U.S. Government Printing Office.

National Council of Teachers of Mathematics (NCTM). (1989). *Curriculum and Evaluation Standards for School Mathematics*. Reston, VA: NCTM.

National Council of Teachers of Mathematics. (1991). *Professional Standards for Teaching Mathematics*. Reston, VA.: NCTM.

National Council of Teachers of Mathematics. (1992). *The Road to Reform in Mathematics Education: How Far Have We Traveled*. Reston, VA: NCTM.

National Education Goals Panel. (1993). *The National Educational Goals Report: Building a Nation of Learners: Volume One 1993*. Washington, D.C.: U.S. Government Printing Office.

National Research Council. (1989). *Everybody Counts: A Report on the Future of Mathematics Education*. Washington, D.C.: National Academy Press.

Oakes, J., et al. (1990). "Multiplying Inequalities: The Effects of Race, Social Class, and Tracking on Opportunities to Learn Mathematics and Science," Report No. R-3928-NSF, Rand Co., Santa Monica, CA.

Phi Delta Kappa, Center on Evaluation, Development, Research. (1987). *Exemplary Practice Series: Mathematics*. Bloomington, IN: Phi Delta Kappa.

Report on Education Research. (1992). "NAEP Board Approves New Math Standards," Alexandria, VA: Capitol Publications.

Resnick, L. B.(1987). *Education and Learning to Think*. Committee on Mathematics, Science and Social Sciences and Education, National Research Council, Washington D.C.: National Academy Press.

Steen, Lynn A. (1992). "Mathematics," in *Curriculum Handbook*. Alexandria, VA: Association for Supervision and Curriculum Development.

Stevenson, H. W., et al. (1990). *Making the Grade in Mathematics*. Reston, VA: National Council of Teachers of Mathematics.

Sunburst/Wings for Learning, Inc. (1992). *The Geometric Supposer Series*. Pleasantville, NY: Sunburst/Wings for Learning, Inc.

U. S. Department of Education. (1991). *America 2000: An Educational Strategy*. Washington, D.C.: U.S. Department of Education.

Vermont Department of Education. (1991). *Vermont Mathematics Portfolio Project: Teacher's Guide*. Vermont Department of Education, VT.

Weiss, Iris. (1989). *Science and Mathematics Education Briefing Book*. Chapel Hill, NC: Horizon Research.

Welch, Wayne. (1978). "Science Education in Urbanville: A Case Study," in *Case Studies in Science Education*, R. Stake and J. Easley, eds., Urbana, IL: University of Illinois.

Willoughly, Stephen S. (1990). *Mathematics Education for a Changing World*. Alexandria, VA: Association for Supervision and Curriculum Development.

CHAPTER 8

Social Studies

SOCIAL studies is a term used to collectively describe a number of related disciplines, including history, civics, geography, sociology, psychology, economics, archaeology, anthropology, political science, and law. Some professionals maintain the importance of separating these disciplines for instructional study, arguing that, in combination, course content is watered down to the point where no individual discipline receives enough attention to have meaning. However, others argue that the separation of the disciplines is largely an artificial distinction made by scholars and that integration of the disciplines within courses leads to higher levels of understanding. They also make the cogent argument that instructional time within the school day and school year does not allow for separate courses in each discipline. This chapter looks at the following questions concerning the development of world-class competencies in social studies for children who will spend their adult years in the 21st century:

- What does theory and research say about what students should learn and how they should be taught?
- How do the Best Schools successfully translate theory into practice in teaching social studies?
- How do the Best Schools assess what students know and what they can do?
- What do case studies of Best Schools reveal about how highly successful social studies instruction is carried out in four very different community contexts?
- Finally, what are some of the specific practices, programs, and resources used by the Best Schools that are widely available to other program developers?

WHAT STUDENTS SHOULD LEARN

According to the National Goals of Education,

> By the year 2000, American students will leave grades four, eight and twelve having demonstrated competency in challenging subject matter including . . . civics and government, economics, . . . history, and geography; and every school in America will ensure that all students learn to use their minds well, so they may be prepared for responsible citizenship, further learning, and productive employment in our Nation's modern economy.
>
> By the year 2000, every adult American will be literate and will possess the knowledge and skills necessary to compete in a global economy and exercise the rights and responsibilities of citizenship.

One of National Goals for Education includes achievement in civics and government, economics, history, and geography as four of the nine subject areas in which students must demonstrate competency. The supporting objectives recognize the ever-increasing diversity of the nation (by the year 2000, one in three students will be a minority) and the need for students to have knowledge of our diverse cultural heritage and about the world community; the need for all students to increase achievement in subject areas and to demonstrate ability to "reason, solve problems, apply knowledge, and write and communicate effectively"; and the need for "all students to be involved in activities which promote and demonstrate good citizenship, community service and personal responsibility." Another of the goals focuses on the knowledge and skills necessary to compete in a global economy—an area that requires study of world history and cultures, economics, and world geography. A second part of this goal includes development of the knowledge and skills necessary to exercise the rights and responsibilities of citizenship, areas traditionally taught as part of United States history and civics.

The results of the National Assessment of Educational Progress (NAEP) indicate that the current social studies programs in most schools are not effectively preparing students to meet these goals and objectives. The NAEP reported concerns about the achievement of students in history, civics, and geography. Published in three separate reports, *The Civics Report Card* (Anderson et al., 1990), *The U.S. History Report Card* (Hammack et al., 1990), and *The Geography Learning of High School Seniors* (Allen et al., 1990), NAEP found that students in the United States have a high level of "knowledge of simple facts" but low achievement in "understanding basic terms and relationships" and almost no competence to "interpret information and ideas." NAEP (1990) concluded that

> . . . for any curriculum area, only about half of our high-school seniors may be graduating with the ability "to use their minds" to think through subject related information in any depth. Fewer than 10% appear to have both an understanding of the specialized material and ideas comprising that curriculum area and the ability to work with these to interpret, integrate, infer, draw generalizations, and articulate conclusions. (p. 29)

Instruction in social studies has traditionally been part of the middle school and high school curriculum. However, the amount of time and the quality of time spent on instruction in the social studies content areas has varied greatly from district to district and even classroom to classroom. Only 45% of 1990 high school graduates had completed courses in United States and world history, and only 21% had completed a course in geography.

No less than ten major reports can be credited with refocusing the nation and the schools on social studies. These include 1) the results of the NAEP; 2) the establishment of the National Goals for Education, explicitly including history and geography; 3) the issuance of a geography curriculum framework by the Joint Committee of the National Council for Geography Education/Association of American Geographers; 4) the issuance of nine recommendations concerning the teaching of history by the Bradley Commission on History in the Schools; 5) the report of the forty-five-member commission established by the American Historical Society, the Carnegie Foundation for the Advancement of Teaching, the National Council for Social Studies, and the Organization of American Historians; 6) the results of the four National Standards Projects in United States history, world history, civics and geography; and 7) the *Curriculum Standards for the Social Studies* developed by the National Council for the Social Studies (1994).

Guidelines for Geographic Education: Elementary and Secondary Schools (Natoli et al., 1984) was the first report to propose a change in the way social studies was taught in the schools. The report advocated for a significantly increased place in the curriculum for the teaching of geography. The authors of the report argued that geography needs to have a separate identity within the curriculum and that the subject matter should be organized around broad themes, rather than focus on the memorization of names of places—the traditional focus of geography within the social studies curriculum. The five themes around which the new curriculum would be organized were as follows.

- location (e.g., the absolute and relative position of people and physical objects)
- place (e.g., the distinguishing physical and human characteristics of locations)
- human-environmental interaction (e.g., human sustainability and environments, responses and adaptations to physical attributes in each place)
- movement (e.g., transportation of materials and communication by people between places)
- region (e.g., the study of political, governmental, linguistic, physical, and democratic areas unifying features)

Four years after the issuance of the guidelines for geography, the Bradley Commission (1988) issued a report, *Building a HIstory Curriculum: Guidelines for Teaching History in Schools*. This report focused on the teaching of history as the core of social studies instruction in schools and recommended how practices could be improved. The Commission argued that "history is the discipline that can best help [students] to understand and deal with change, and at the same time to identify the deep continuities that link the past and present."

"What should children know and be able to do in the field of social studies if they are to lead effective public and personal lives in the century ahead?" was also the subject of the National Commission on Social Studies in the Schools (NCSSS). The final report (NCSS, 1989) recommended that

- Social studies should be taught every year, grades K–12.
- Course work is to be based on a matrix of history and geography, but each course should be infused with information and methodologies from the other social sciences.
- The curriculum must provide a sound grounding in United States history and government but should devote equal time to other regions of the world so that students will understand the economic and cultural connections between nations.
- Course work should incorporate and act as a bridge between the humanities and sciences.
- Teaching materials and teaching strategies are to be chosen to help students become both independent and cooperative learners.
- Emphasis must be on a selective and coherent core knowledge that promotes depth of understanding, rather than on superficial coverage.
- Community service should be an element of the curriculum.

In 1991, Congress established the National Council on Educational Standards and Testing, a bipartisan panel that recommended the establishment of voluntary national standards and voluntary national assessment. The U.S. Department of Education made grants to major professional and scholarly organizations to develop standards in American and world history, civics, and geography. Each project involves many organizations, prominent scholars in various fields, school administrators, and teachers. Drafts of proposed standards were distributed widely for comment and then revised and refined. The resulting documents represent a broad consensus about what is important and relevant to teach, what students should know and be able to do by the end of certain grade levels, and how learning should be assessed. While separate standards were developed for each discipline, the standards do not constitute a curriculum to be followed by schools. The standards set forth knowledge, understanding, and abilities that students should demonstrate as a result of their K–12 education. The curriculum standards suggest what should be the focus of instruction across the grades, with implications for how content should be taught. However, the standards are voluntary, and it is up to the states, districts, and schools to develop the curriculum. In developing the working curriculum, schools must decide on the degree of integration or separation in the teaching of geography, history, and civics. Examples from the United States Civics and Government Standards and the Geography Standards illustrate not only the form of the standards, but also the perspective of each group concerning themes (Center for Civic Education, 1994, pp. 66–69, 131–132).

National Standards for Civics and Government

Grades 5–8: How does the American political system provide for choice and opportunity for participation?

Content Summary and Rationale

The American political system provides citizens with numerous opportunities for choice and participation. The formal institutions and processes of government such as political parties, campaign, and elections are important avenues for choice and citizen participation. Another equally important avenue is the many associations and groups that constitute civil society. All provide ways for citizens to monitor and influence the political process.

American constitutional democracy is dynamic and sometimes disorderly. Politics is not always smooth and predictable. Individually and in groups, citizens attempt to influence those in power. In turn, those in power attempt to influence citizens. In this process, the public opinion regarding these issues is formed.

If citizens do not understand the political process and how to deal with it effectively, they may feel overwhelmed and alienated. An understanding of the political process is a necessary prerequisite for effective and responsible participation in the making of public policy.

Content Standards

The public agenda: Students should be able to explain what is meant by the public agenda and how it is set.

To achieve this standard, students should be able to

- explain that the public agenda consists of those matters that occupy public attention at any particular time, e.g., crime, health, education, child care, environmental protection, drug abuse
- describe how the public agenda is shaped by political leaders, interest groups, the media, state, and federal courts, individual citizens
- explain how individuals can help to shape the public agendas, e.g., by joining interest groups or political parties, by making presentations at public meetings, by writing letters to government officials and to newspapers

What are the responsibilities of citizens?

Content Summary and Rationale

The purposes of American constitutional democracy are furthered by citizens who continuously reexamine the basic principals of the Constitution and monitor the performance of political leaders and government agencies to insure their fidelity to constitutional values and principles. In addition, they must examine their own behavior and fidelity to these values and principles.

Citizens also need to examine situations in which their responsibilities may require that their personal desires or interests be subordinated to the common good. To make these judgements requires an understanding of the differences between personal and civic responsibilities as well as the mutual reinforcement of these responsibilities.

Personal responsibilities: Students should be able to evaluate, take, and defend positions on issues regarding the personal responsibilities of citizens in American constitutional democracy.

To achieve this standards, students should be able to

- explain the distinction between personal and civic responsibilities, as well as the tensions that may arise between them
- evaluate the importance for the individual and society of
  - taking care of one's self
  - supporting one's family and caring for, nurturing, and educating one's children
  - accepting responsibility for the consequences of one's actions
  - adhering to moral principles
  - considering the rights and interests of others
  - behaving in a civil manner

Civic responsibilities: Students should be able to evaluate, take, and defend positions on issues regarding civic responsibilities of citizens in American constitutional democracy.

To achieve this standard, students should be able to

- evaluate the importance of each citizen reflecting on, criticizing, and reaffirming basic constitutional principles
- evaluate the importance for the individual and society of
  - obeying the law
  - being informed and attentive to public issues
  - monitoring the adherence of political leaders and governmental agencies to constitutional principles and taking appropriate action if adherence is lacking
  - assuming leadership when appropriate
  - paying taxes
  - registering to vote and voting knowledgeably on candidates and issues
  - serving as a juror
  - serving in the armed forces
  - performing public service
- evaluate whether and when their obligations as citizens require that their personal desires and interests be subordinated to the public good
- evaluate whether and when moral obligations or constitutional principles require one to refuse to assume certain civic responsibilities

Geography for Life: National Geography Standards 1994 (Geography Education Standards Project, 1994) defines a geographically informed person as one

(1) Who sees meaning in the arrangement of things in space
(2) Who sees relations between people, places, and environments
(3) Who uses geography skills
(4) Who applies spatial and ecological perspectives to life situations

Eighteen standards have been developed under six essential elements: the world in spatial terms, places and regions, physical systems, human systems, environment and society, and the uses of geography. For grades K–4, 5–8, and 9–12, each standard explains what the student should know and be able to do and is supported by examples of learning opportunities.

Sample Standard–Geography Standard 12 Grades 5–8

Human Systems the Processes, Patterns, and Functions of Human Settlement

By the end of eight grade, the student knows and understands:

(1) The spatial patterns of settlement in different regions of the world
(2) What human events led to the development of cities

(3) The causes and consequences of urbanization
(4) The internal spatial structure of urban settlements

Therefore, the student is able to:

(a) Identify and describe settlement patterns, as exemplified by being able to
List, define, and map major agricultural settlement types (e.g., plantation, subsistence farming, truck-farming communities) . . .
(b) Identify the factors involved in the development of cities, as exemplified by being able to
Describe the kinds of settlements that existed before cities emerged (e.g., stopping places on the routes of hunters and gatherers, isolated farmsteads, villages) . . .
(c) Analyze the ways in which both the landscape and society would change as a consequence of shifting from a dispersed to a concentrated settlement form, as exemplified by being able to
Describe and explain the structural landscape changes that would occur if a village were to grow into a city (e.g., larger marketplace, city walls, grain-storage areas) . . .
(d) Explain the causes and consequences of urbanization, as exemplified by being able to
Explain the links between industrial development and rural-urban migration (e.g., the movement of people into the mill towns of New England) . . .
(e) Identify and define the internal spatial structures of cities, as exemplified by being able to
Using the concentric zone model of a city, explain how nearby city reflects that model (e.g., central city has the highest buildings, general decrease in density away from center). . . .
(Geography Education Standards Project, 1994, pp. 167 – 168)

While the four National Standards Projects developed four separate sets of discipline-based standards, the National Council for the Social Studies (NCSS) developed a set of standards designed to be used either as an umbrella framework for the discipline-based standards or as a stand-alone set of standards to guide development of social studies programs, instruction, and assessment. The integrated discipline approach of the NCSS standards recognizes the trend toward more integration of subject matter across the curriculum and that

> Social studies is the integrated study of the social sciences and humanities to promote civic competence. Within the school program, social studies provides coordinated, systematic study drawing upon such disciplines as anthropology, archaeology, economics, geography, history, law, philosophy, political science, psychology, religion, and sociology, as well as appropriate content from the humanities, mathematics, and natural sciences. (NCSS, 1994)

Recognizing that within the school day and school year, it is impossible to teach everything, the NCSS standards establish the criteria for the scope of the curriculum and specific student performance, which is the measure of program quality. Standards provide the basis for making decisions about why, what, and how to teach, as well as suggesting the means for assessing outcomes. The NCSS standards, using multiple perspectives, categorize the standards as follows:

- culture
- time, continuity, and change
- people, places, and environments
- individual development and identity
- individuals, groups, and institutions
- production, distribution, and consumption
- power, authority, and governance
- production, distribution, and consumption
- science, technology, and society

- global connections
- civic ideals and practices

An example of the NCSS standards (1994) illustrates the integration of disciplines as a guide for curriculum development:

Power, Authority, and Governance

> Social studies programs should include experiences that provide for the study of how people create and change structures of power, authority, and governance, so that learners can:
>
> Middle Grades
>
> (a) Examine persisting issues involving the rights, role, and status of the individual in relation to the general welfare;
> (b) Describe the purpose of government and how its powers are acquired, used and justified;
> (c) Analyze and explain ideas and governmental mechanisms to meet needs and wants of citizens, regulate territory, manage conflict, and establish order and security;
> (d) Describe the ways nations and organizations respond to forces of unity and diversity affecting order and security;
> (e) Identify and describe the feature of the United States' political system, and identify representative leaders from various levels and branches of government;
> (f) Explain conditions, actions and motivations that contribute to conflict and cooperation within and among nations;
> (g) Describe and analyze the role of technology such as transportation systems, weapons systems, communication systems, and information systems in contributing to creating and resolving conflicts;
> (h) Explain and apply concepts, such as power, role, status, justice, and influence to the examination of persistent issues and social problems;
> (i) Give examples and explain how governments attempt to achieve their stated ideals at home and abroad.

The five sets of standards, four from the National Standards Projects and the one set from the National Council of Social Studies, have the potential for providing the framework for raising the quality of instruction within both the individual disciplines and social studies as a whole. The existence of five sets of standards may appear to establish competing demands for time, space, and resources within the school curriculum, and, in fact, difficult decisions have to be made at the state and/or school district level concerning course offerings, content, and articulation of programs K–12. However, all of the sets of standards have many characteristics in common and many areas of overlapping content. For example, they all

- focus on the desired outcomes of instruction—what the student should know and be able to do
- emphasize on important themes, rather than the memorization of facts, dates, and names
- recognize that students cannot learn it all and they need to make decisions about what are the most important aspects of the disciplines
- advocate teaching for indepth understanding, rather than surface coverage of topics
- include the teaching of more and different geography and history
- make connections with other strands of the curriculum, including writing, literature, the arts, science, technology, and mathematics

- include curriculum that addresses reoccurring important controversial issues
- promote active, inquiry-based approaches to instruction
- establish learning benchmarks at various grade levels
- establish standards for forms of assessment of learning that require students to apply knowledge, justify positions, compare and contrast, and connect new knowledge to previous learning

HOW STUDENTS LEARN–HOW STUDENTS ARE TAUGHT

A review of elementary textbooks for social studies over the past years confirms that a consistent scope and sequence, commonly referred to as the "expanding horizons curriculum," has endured for more than fifty years (Bennett, 1988). Starting in kindergarten, children learn about those things closest to them–home, school, and community. These subjects are then covered in more depth in first, second, and third grades. This is then followed in grade 4 by the study of their state and region; and in grades 5–8 with United States history, world history, geography, and a second year of United States history; and at the high school level, by one or two years of American history and electives such as world history and psychology. The scope and sequence have been criticized for their failure to include "real content," particularly history and geography, in the lower grades and their shallow coverage of topics in the upper grades.

Allocation of time to the social studies curriculum is an essential ingredient in effective instruction. Too often, social studies has been viewed as of minor importance at the middle school level, a subject to be taught from a textbook when the "important" language arts and mathematics instruction is done. Even in districts with well-articulated curricula, there have often been widespread variances between the printed curriculum and the taught curriculum. Assessment practices that emphasize achievement of reading, language, and mathematics skills on standardized tests have also contributed to the view of social studies as a less important subject. Even in districts where social studies is included in the annual testing, little importance has been attached to the results. In order to implement the new social studies effectively, increased time must be allocated to the subject. Some of the time can be found through integration of at least some of the social studies curriculum with instruction in language arts, mathematics, science, and the arts.

At the high school level, social studies requirements for graduation have frequently been limited to the study of one or two years of United States history. Often, the secondary school program has not been articulated with the middle school or elementary programs. As a result, United States history has been repeated with only marginal increases in the depth of study at multiple grade levels. World history, particularly non-Western European and modern, has frequently played little or no part in the required curriculum.

If students are to achieve world-class standards in social studies, instructional approaches must change, as well as curriculum content. Students need to become excited about social studies and see the relevance of study to their lives now and in the future. Too often, students consider social studies their least favorite and most uninteresting subject. All too often, particularly at the middle school level, teachers also have been less than excited about the subject matter in the social studies curriculum. This may be because of their own limited indepth knowledge and training in the disciplines and/or because of the competing priorities of other subject areas. In order for both students and teachers to become actively interested in social studies, instructional methods must change. Without sacrificing content, students can become actively engaged in social studies at all levels. Rote memorization of historical facts and place names and read-the-chapter/answer-the-questions-at-the-end-of-the chapter methods must be replaced with indepth study of concepts, discussion, written argument, and oral discourse. Multiple sources, original documents, and historical narratives need to be used to help students understand history, geography, and civics. Students need to write essays, use technology, research information, produce individual and group research papers, evaluate and critique sources, draw conclusions, debate, and construct logical arguments as a regular part of their social studies program at all grade levels. The instructional skills of effective social studies teachers are the same skills required to teach other subjects effectively.

In addition, because the social studies curriculum deals extensively with issues of diversity and because the goals of the program include development of understanding and appreciation of similarities and differences, tracking or grouping of students by ability flies in the face of basic aims of the program. From a learning point of view, tracking has also been shown to be ineffective; however, while tracking is an undesirable practice, flexible groupings and cooperative groups have immediate benefits in terms of learning content and for learning to function as part of a team. In addition, honors level and advanced placement courses can provide opportunities for interested students to explore subjects at very high levels.

HOW LEARNING SHOULD BE ASSESSED

While many schools do not use commercial standardized tests in the assessment of social studies, most book tests and teacher-developed tests have been of the short-answer or select-the-right-answer variety similar to common standardized testing formats. Assessment of students must be aligned with the goals, objectives, and standards of the program. Assessment in social studies should provide the opportunity for students to read and interpret maps, graphs, diagrams, pictures, and charts; to retrieve and analyze information from books, data bases, documents, newspapers, and periodicals; and to organize and express ideas orally and in writing. This type of assessment, individually and as part of a group, requires formats for assessment, which include essays, oral reports, and project products. These forms of assessment require time for student preparation and are best developed as part of the instructional process. Each of the sets of standards for social studies recognizes the importance of assessment and includes standards for evaluation of student learning.

In summary, as part of the reassessment of how children learn, a distinction must be made between surface knowledge—the memorization of facts, procedures, and application—and meaningful knowledge—connected learning that makes sense to the learner and prepares the student for further learning. The goals and standards for social studies are grounded in the following assumptions:

- History, geography, and civics are essential subjects that should be a required part of every student's educational program.
- There is a need for more significant study of content, particularly from the disciplines of history and geography; however, the instructional emphasis should be on indepth study, not coverage of surface facts and information.
- Learning is natural and motivational; instruction should be organized to make connections among strands of the social studies curriculum, events, and real-life experiences of students.
- Students should be actively engaged in learning, rather than in passively receiving teacher recitations or textbook readings.

- Students should write about, speak of, and discuss social studies; they should learn to critique sources and develop cogent arguments to support positions.
- The availability of technology allows for the expansion of resources available to students and teachers in accomplishing the aims of the social studies curriculum.
- Finally, assessment is best embedded in the instructional process, rather than considered a terminal activity. Assessment should provide evidence not only of what a student knows, but of what a student can do. As much as possible, it should be performance- and product-based.

THE BEST SCHOOLS–THEORY INTO PRACTICE IN SOCIAL STUDIES

In the Best Schools, social studies is an important subject that is seriously attended to. Programs reflect the National Goals, studies, reports, and standards that make recommendations concerning the social studies curriculum and methods of instruction. At the middle school level, social studies is frequently integrated with other subjects; however, individual integrity of the disciplines of history and geography are maintained. At the high school level, the Best Schools require the study of world history, as well as American history, for all students, with physical and cultural geography integrated into the history courses and the scope and sequence of subject matter constructed to build on middle school study. Large numbers of students take four or more years of social studies. Significant electives include indepth study of national and international governing structures, courses that emulate the work of political bodies. Frequently, these courses include competitive experiences such as mock trial, We the People . . . The Citizen and the Constitution competition, and Model UN.

How social studies is taught in the Best Schools is consistent with how students are taught effectively in other subject areas. Emphasis is on the development of higher order thinking skills and development of indepth knowledge and understanding, rather than rote memorization of names and dates and surface knowledge of historical events. The curriculum is enriched through literature, field experiences, technology, research studies, community service, and projects related to broad themes. The Best Schools have accomplished their mission with diverse social, economic, and physical resources.

Illustrations in Social Studies: The Contexts (Case Studies)

EAST BRUNSWICK HIGH SCHOOL, EAST BRUNSWICK, NJ

In 1950, dotted with apple and peach orchards, East Brunswick was a farming town with a population of about 5700 and four four-room elementary schools for students in grades K–8. Today, East Brunswick has a largely middle- to upper middle-class population of approximately 43,000 who are employed primarily in business and professional occupations. Townhouses, apartments, and condominiums sit beside small, medium, and large single-family homes. People with children generally move to East Brunswick because of the excellent reputation of the schools; therefore, they have high expectations and aspirations for the education their children will receive. Residents make a point of staying informed and becoming involved in school programs. More than 93% of the graduates enter two- or four-year colleges. Since the township has no "Main Street" and few recreational facilities, the schools also serve as community centers and are used constantly by the Township Recreation Department and various community organizations. Currently, the school population is growing and becoming increasingly ethnically diverse with Asian Indians and Chinese representing the largest minority groups.

Charles M. King, *Principal, Grades 10–12, 1626 Students*

LEMON G. HINE JUNIOR HIGH SCHOOL, WASHINGTON, D.C.

Lemon G. Hine Junior High School is located in the shadow of Capital Hill in an affluent neighborhood; however, it draws its 98% African-American student body from across Washington, with many students coming from drug-plagued neighborhoods and low-economic, matriarchal families. The school has gone from a dilapidated physical plant known as "Horrible Hine" to a well-equipped successful school now referred to by staff, students, and the community as "The Thrill on Capital Hill." A once hopeless, hostile school population has been transformed into a proud, cohesive family of students, parents, staff, and community. The school has embraced the theme, "All teachers will teach, all children will learn, and Hine will be successful."

Princess D. Whitfield, *Principal, Grades 7–9, 900 Students*

BLACK MOUNTAIN MIDDLE SCHOOL, SAN DIEGO, CA

Black Mountain Middle School is a school community of the Poway Unified School District, which has achieved excellence by focusing decision making around its goals, stated as seven core values. The student body earned a GPA of 3.0 or above in 1990, and there was a 99.7% promotion rate. The school received special recognition in history in 1991 as part of the Blue Ribbon Schools recognition process. Black Mountain Middle School is one of the nine schools in Poway Unified School District that have been recognized as a Blue Ribbon School.

Candice Toft, *Principal (former Principal of La Mesa Middle School, La Mesa, CA, Recognized Blue Ribbon School 1991) (M. Jo Bechtold, Principal at time of recognition), Grades 6–8, 1535 Students*

BROAD MEADOWS MIDDLE SCHOOL, QUINCY, MA

Broad Meadows Middle School was built in 1957 and is located on a peninsula in the historic city of Quincy, Massachusetts. The school services approximately 300 students from several diverse neighborhoods, including the only low-income housing project in the city, a middle-class residential area facing Quincy Bay, and a fishing and lobstering community of blue collar families, many of whom live in converted summer homes. The challenge is to blend an increasing diverse population into a cohesive student body, while being sensitive to individual needs. The student population also presents other challenges, in that 40% are eligible for Chapter 1 services, 25% are certified special needs students, and 50% receive free or reduced-price lunches. No school buses are provided; therefore, students must take public transportation at their own expense. Broad Meadows Middle School received special recognition in history as part of the Blue Ribbon School designation.

Anne Marie Zukeuskaf, *Principal (Thomas M. Hall, Principal at time of recognition), Grades 6–8, 337 Students*

THE BEST SCHOOLS–CLASS ORGANIZATION AND INSTRUCTIONAL TIME

The Best Schools teach social studies in heterogeneous classes; however, at the high school level, there are opportunities for students to take honors level and advanced placement courses. Students also have the option of taking, and most do take, electives such as the institute for political and legal education (IPLE) and psychology. Based on the purposes and structure of lessons, whole-class, small-group, and cooperative learning groups are used. The middle schools schedule between 150 minutes and 250 minutes per week for social studies classes; however, integration of social studies content into other areas of the curriculum provides for considerable extended study. Most of the schools use the literature strand of the language arts curriculum to have students read fiction and nonfiction related to history. The writing strand of language arts is also used for joint social studies/English research and writing experiences. Science is also often integrated with social studies. For example, at Labay Junior High School in Houston, Texas, interdisciplinary units include research in science and social studies, reading skills in all content areas, and novels and sort stories in history and science. Students in eighth grade read *Johnny Tremain* in language arts while studying the American Revolution in United States history and read Jack London stories while studying arctic ecosystems in science and the former USSR in world cultures.

Class Organization Illustrations

EAST BRUNSWICK HIGH SCHOOL, NJ

Every attempt is made at East Brunswick to provide students with programs that best suit their individual needs and allow them to develop to their full potential. Courses are offered on standard, honors, and advanced placement levels. Flexible grouping within classes is a common practice used to develop cooperative learning projects. Special education students are mainstreamed into standard and, in some cases, honors courses. Courses are designed to meet the needs of general and college-bound students, as well as those who are seeking vocational training.

Students are required to take 110 credits for graduation. The vast majority of students graduate with thirty credits above the school requirement; they are aware that a more challenging program better prepares them for the future. Three years of history are required; however, more than 80% of the students take additional social studies electives.

LEMON G. HINE JUNIOR HIGH SCHOOL, D.C.

In grades 7–9, students of Lemon G. Hine Junior High School are scheduled for three social studies courses. Seventh grade takes western hemisphere geography and eighth grade American history to 1877. Ninth grade students take one semester of D.C. history and one semester of world geography. In addition, about half of the ninth graders take the civics elective course. Another elective is crime team, which focuses on the judicial system and participates in mock trial competitions. Forty-five percent of the students are involved in community service, such as work with hospitals and senior citizen centers. All students must complete 100 hours of community service by the end of twelfth grade in order to graduate. Special education students are mainstreamed and function well with the support of cooperative learning, peer tutoring, and individualized instruction.

BLACK MOUNTAIN MIDDLE SCHOOL, CA

Students at Black Mountain Middle School are heterogeneously grouped for science, basic ed (language art and social studies), electives, and physical education. Students identified as gifted are clustered three to five per room in basic ed classes. Special education students are mainstreamed to the maximum extent. All students are required to complete math, science, language arts, social studies, PE, and two semesters of electives each year. Mastery is the goal and promotion is based on a combination of passing academic subjects and proficiency tests or passing support courses after school and in summer. All students are scheduled for 1639 instructional minutes per week. Students in danger of retention are identified in December and become involved in intensive interventions that include daily or weekly parent contact, behavioral contracts with rewards and consequences, and strong tutoring support.

Black Mountain incorporates language arts and social studies as part of a three-period "basic ed'' block. This extended time block (690 minutes per week) allows teachers to integrate language arts and social studies and to plan activities and lessons using a wide range of strategies.

BROAD MEADOWS MIDDLE SCHOOL, MA

All students at Broad Meadows Middle School are required to pass the core courses which include language arts, reading, math, science, and social studies. Additionally, students are required to take the following courses: physical education, art, music, home economics, technical education, and health.

THE BEST SCHOOLS–CURRICULUM

The Best Schools provide a content-rich program in social studies, which includes history, geography, and other areas of social science. Broad themes are used to organize the social studies program at each grade level. The scope of the curriculum has been purposely reduced to allow time for indepth study of areas that are central to the program. Repetition of content has been eliminated by planning the curriculum K–12; however, important themes may reoccur and be connected to previous study from grade to grade. Students are engaged in a wide variety of instructional strategies that make the subject interesting. They read fiction and nonfiction; conduct research studies; work with CD-ROM, laser, and remote data bases; discuss issues; work on projects in cooperative groups; visit museums and historical sites; and participate in multi-media lessons, community service, and competitions. For example, at Shulamith High School for Girls, in Brooklyn, New York, students in the economics course are involved in a month-long project called ''Market Basket.'' The students are required to select a supermarket and visit it four times, once a week, in order to collect prices on fifteen diverse consumer items. They then have to arrive at written conclusions using their knowledge of the rules of inflation and the consumer price index. As another example, in River Bend School, Chesterfield, Missouri, sixth-grade students participate in a unit on acid rain. Students study their community in depth, including population density, industry, and prevalent modes of transportation. Through Kidsnet (National Geographic Society) via telecommunications, they share data with schools across the nation and analyze the data to determine the relationship between human and environmental factors.

In the Best Schools, much of the literature used in the language arts program is correlated with the social studies curriculum. Students read both fiction and nonfiction related to periods of history, including biographies of historical figures. Writing assignments relate to both language arts and social studies curriculum.

Geography is usually integrated with the study of history. Within the context of the historical period, instruction includes the five themes of geography: location, place, relationships within place, movement, and region. Software such as Jenny's Journey, Where in the World Is Carmen Sandiego? and Oregon Trail are frequently used software programs for reinforcing geographical knowledge at the middle school level. Many different kinds of maps, globes, and multi-media sources are used to enhance understanding with students making maps and graphs and collecting data in the field. Classes are frequently organized into collaborative, mixed ability teams for activities and projects as the diverse cultural and ethnic nature of the class, school, region, and nation is used to study geographic areas.

Throughout the social studies curriculum, the emphasis is on the development of higher order critical thinking skills. Instruction is organized to make connections among the strands of the social studies curriculum, events, and real-life experiences of children. The focus is on indepth study of "real content" and understanding, not on surface coverage of facts and information. Although textbooks are used in most schools, they are only one source of information in the program.

Curriculum Illustrations

EAST BRUNSWICK HIGH SCHOOL, NJ

The social studies department at East Brunswick offers students a wide range of required and elective courses covering various aspects of history, government, law, economics, and psychology. Ninth-grade students take U.S. History 1 (junior high school); tenth-grade students take world history and Cultures; eleventh grade students take U.S. History 2 or AP American history. Electives are open to all students and include Institute for Political and Legal Education 1 and 2 (a nationally validated program, formally disseminated through the NDN), psychology, sociology, New Jersey studies, racial and cultural minorities, women in history, and the history of the Vietnam War. The following electives are open only to eleventh- and twelfth-grade students: economics, Psychology 2, The Law and You—Part 1 and 2, AP European history, and international studies. More than 80% of the students opt to take a fourth-year elective in social studies.

While understanding individual course content is important, the department has over-arching goals of development of critical thinking skills and creation of independent learners. Each curriculum is structured to achieve these goals and is supported by instruction that uses modern technologies, higher level questions in every lesson, student debates, cooperative projects, multi-media research requirements, and oral assessment. Teachers are actively involved in the development and use of test items that require students to analyze, synthesize, and evaluate. Students demonstrate critical thinking skills and independence as learners through preparation of performance assessment projects at the end of ninth, tenth, and eleventh grades.

There exists a formal bridge between social studies and the library media department, which supports the social studies curriculum and research projects through development of print collections correlated to the curriculum and technology sources such as DowLine, Info-Track, News Bank, laser discs, CD-ROMs and videos.

The focus of the curriculum is indepth study of periods and events, rather than the traditional surface coverage of topics, people, and dates. In order to accomplish this, repetition in program across the grades has been eliminated, with many traditional topics also eliminated or organized into thematic studies. For example, students in eighth grade study early American history, followed by U.S. History 1 in ninth grade, with the year 1865. U.S. History 2, which all students take in the eleventh grade, is a truly modern course, with indepth study of events occurring after the election of 1932. Many students also take AP American history as an elective. In tenth grade, world history and cultures focuses on non-Western, as well as Western European, history and cultures. Ancient world history is taught at the middle school level. AP European history is a popular elective course for eleventh- and twelfth-grade students.

It has been the goal of the department to enliven history by a thorough examination of controversial issues. For example, in the U.S. History 2 program, students participate in examinations of the Holocaust, the civil rights movement, and the Vietnam War. To assist in these examinations, additional supplements have been purchased, and the staff has been given inservice training. Major historical themes are stressed at all grade levels of the history program. In order for students to appreciate the importance of the past and the continuing consequences of human decisions, the program develops an understanding of major principles, concepts, and themes. These themes serve as threads that are articulated among the three levels of history.

All required social studies courses have a major infusion of geography. Atlases, historical map sets, and contemporary maps have been added to classroom collections. In addition, the five themes of geography have been incorporated into the required curriculum. Geographic analysis is a focal point of world history/world cultures. Students study the distinctive regions of the world to understand the cultural forces and technological improvements of our increasingly interdependent world. Social sciences are also infused into required courses and exist as areas of specialization in the elective program. Students annually compete in competitions such as the Lincoln-Douglas debates, mock trial, model Congress, model United Nations, and the We the People . . . The Citizen and the Constitution.

A year-long course, institute for political and legal education, taken annually by more than 120 students at East Brunswick High School, develops strong citizenship skills. Students are given "hands-on" leadership opportunities while developing knowledge of the political ideas and principles found in the Declaration of Independence, the Constitution of the United States, the Bill of Rights, and the United Nations' Declaration of Human Rights. Students simulate the use of procedures and techniques of government at the local, county, state, and federal levels; they acquire independently and cooperatively the process of writing political and legal materials and apply this research to verbal expression.

The institute for political and legal education at East Brunswick High School has evolved into a unique program from the original IPLE model that some New Jersey high schools adopted over twenty years ago. For the first twelve weeks of the course, teacher and students examine the historical and philosophical basis of the United States Constitution. One key strategy that is employed for this unit of work is an oral assessment activity. Simulating a congressional hearing, groups of students working collaboratively present prepared timed responses to higher cognitive-level questions. Students must also respond to extemporaneous questions that are posed by the teacher and guests who serve as judges. In addition, groups are engaged in debates about Constitutional issues facing today's society. Grades are derived from research products and group interaction during panel preparation and presentation.

After examining the Constitution, IPLE students apply research techniques and basic legal precepts to current issues in daily debate. The debate schedule is prepared for a sixteen-week period, with all members of the class assigned "pro" and "con" propositions on current topics. Besides thorough research of each topic, members of the class master Robert's Rules of Order, write sample legislation that proposes solutions to problems under scrutiny, write proposition papers, and chair the proceedings on a rotating schedule. The teacher acts as a facilitator—evaluating individual presentations and ruling on matters of parliamentary procedure questions that may arise. Foreign policy topics and the United Nations global agenda are the focus of similar research and debate late in the second semester.

LEMON G. HINE JUNIOR HIGH SCHOOL, D.C.

The social studies program at Lemon G. Hine is distinguished by the way the courses are organized and the teaching resources used. Characteristic of the program is the sequencing of knowledge, which exposes students to a continuum that starts with a hemispheric outlook, moves to a national historical view, narrows to a detailed study of local history, and expands to global geography. The process begins in seventh-grade geography, in which students are introduced to a sweeping view of the western hemisphere, inclusive of land and water forms, continents, countries, and cultures therein. In addition, the course equips students with map and global skills necessary to do more advanced work in the subject area. In eighth grade, students are exposed to the historical development of North America up to 1877, including the history of the Native Americans. In ninth grade, students examine local history and how it connects to both national and world history and world geography.

The very nature of the D.C. history course is distinctive in the way that the social, economic, and political situations are presented as microcosms of issues and debates that are national in scope. In addition, due to the historically unique African-American population in D.C., the opportunities arise to view historical events from the perspective of African-Americans.

An important thrust in the history courses is to teach basic understanding of major historical themes. Such themes are important because they teach students to analyze the past, interpret the present, and direct the future. To teach these themes, the department aims to lay a prerequisite foundation, stressing comprehension of historical chronology, basic facts and documents, significance of past events, and historical literature. The department stresses critical and analytical thinking skills and cause/effect relationships.

The social studies department collaborates with the science, math, English, and art departments; courses are broadly integrative. The geography units on physical features of the earth, the earth in space, and the environment reinforce similar seventh-grade science objectives. The literature of the eighth grade corresponds to the eras of American history studied. Earth Day activities/information involve the science and humanities departments. Finally, skits and plays produced by the social studies department are greatly enhanced through cooperation with the visual arts department.

The school takes full advantage of its location in Washington. The school is seven blocks from the United States Capitol building which is used, geographically, to demonstrate to seventh and ninth graders the point from which streets and avenue flow. The eighth graders see Article I of the Constitution come to life. Students then walk across the street to see Article III of the Constitution when they visit the Supreme Court. Guest speakers include congressmen, congressional aides, historians, and publishers, as well as local poets and storytellers. The school has a comprehensive and diverse tutorial system with tutors and mentors from many different agencies and organizations. Embassies, museums (particularly the Smithsonian), and libraries (both local and national) offer a wide variety of programs and learning opportunities. A specific example is the National Gallery's program. Their docents come to the classrooms, and then students complete assignments at the gallery.

An elective course, crime team, focuses on the judicial system. Students not only study the judicial system, but actually run a court within the school for minor offenses. All students in the school are eligible for jury duty and are selected randomly to serve on juries. Students from the class serve as lawyers, prosecutors, and court officials. The police department provides judges. Students may elect to have cases heard by the court. Students from the crime team class also successfully compete against public and private schools in mock trial.

The history program is further enhanced through students' participation in such activities as a national history fair. Geography students participate in a national geography week. A portable geography lab equipped with desk maps, globes, puzzles, games, and independent activities provides increased opportunities for hands-on activities in the classroom. Field trips are a regular part of the social studies program.

BLACK MOUNTAIN MIDDLE SCHOOL, CA

The basic ed three-period block provides time to plan and employ integrated lesson strategies. Teachers use lesson designs that foster interactive and cooperative learning, debates, simulations, role play, readers' theater, and primary documents to stimulate students. There is a special emphasis placed on geography's impact on historical events. Using a hands-on approach, each grade emphasizes the geographic area specific to the region, culture, and history being studied.

HISTORY

History and language arts are presented in a basic education time block. This unique arrangement enables integration of literature, language, and history. Rather than using a survey approach, teachers have selected important historical themes on which to focus in each of the three years of required study. The objective is to provide students with an indepth experiential understanding of these major themes.

In the sixth grade, all students study history and geography of ancient civilizations beginning with the early people of Africa and Asia. Students develop a model community where they explore real-life issues and implement an economy, political structure, and community services.

In grade 7, the sequential study of world history and geography continues from the decline of the Roman Empire through medieval and early modern times in Europe, Africa, and Asia. To stimulate student interest in medieval times, students even create and present a schoolwide Renaissance fair each Spring with drama, poetry, foods, entertainment, and jousts from the Middle Ages.

In grade 8, all students concentrate on United States history and geography from the framing of the Constitution through World War I. The focus is on the Constitution, citizenship, and the judicial system, concluding with classroom simulations of trials and a field trip to the San Diego County Courthouse. Past winners of grade-wide Constitution and civic competitions have traveled to Sacramento, toured the capital and historic sites, and met with state representatives to discuss community concerns.

The overall success of our history program is attributed to the staff's commitment and enthusiasm for imparting an understanding of history, with the impact of cultural change on today and tomorrow. Teachers use various instructional strategies to foster interactive and cooperative learning among students. Debates, simulations, role playing, readers' theater, social seminars, and the use of primary documents are implemented to engender student interest and enthusiasm. All classes are heterogeneously grouped to include students of all abilities and language backgrounds. The goal of the social science curriculum is to provide to all students close encounters with powerful ideas, great events, and major issues that are important to men and women of all cultures. This year, the faculty includes three district mentor teachers in the areas of writing, literature, and social science. Under the guidance of these mentors, collaborative teaching teams are working together to integrate literature and writing with the study of history. Historical novels, plays, and short stories such as *The Red Badge of Courage, Across Five Aprils, Escape from Warsaw,* and *The Book of Greek Myths* are used to blend literature with historical themes. Students are assigned to respond to these readings by the use of journals, personal essays, dialogues, diaries, and historical newspapers. Incorporating writing across the curriculum, students experience "a moment in time."

GEOGRAPHY

Geography is integrated throughout the curriculum and is presented in each of the three years of required social science study. The Black Mountain theme is, "Without geography, you are nowhere." World geography is presented at grades 6 and 7 and American geography at grade 8. Geography also impacts language arts. Understanding location and historical background enhances the novels read. Earth and physical science present geographic phenomena such as ocean currents, land forms, and mineral deposits and how to use them. Life science focuses on geography in terms of weather, illustrated by latitude and its contribution to natural habitat. In United States history, students see how humans have interacted with natural features to create social and economic change. Students see how such events as the westward movement of people and industrialization changed the shape of landscapes.

At grades 6, 7, and 8, students learn to locate places, sites, and regions. They relate patterns of transportation, communication, and migrations of people in a global context and relate these patterns to the spread of culture and civilization. The most unique geography program is geography joust. This special program is similar to a spelling bee with teams. It is a year-long intramural, competitive activity among seventh graders. This interscholastic competition motivates students to learn the location of over 1000 cities, countries, mountains, rivers, and other natural landmarks and landforms. The competition spurs great student enthusiasm, interest, and participation in the learning process. Exercises include map making, map reading, and globe skills.

Social, economic, and political geography are infused into the study of location and region. Students learn not only how to find a country or city on a map, but why those countries developed into the culture and civilizations that they are today.

EFFECTIVE USE OF RESOURCES

The learning resource center (LRC) is the hub of the school. A librarian and two assistants provide research help, a balanced collection of fiction and nonfiction, and a computer-assisted instruction area for social studies, language arts, math, and science. The district has made it a priority to expand history/geography through technology. Programs include Hypermedia (an interactive video that displays pictures, maps, and narration), GTV, Grolier's Electronic Encyclopedia, PC Globe, Carmen San Diego Programs, EcoSystem, Voyage of Mimi, and Oregon Trail. Video disc units, on carts with projectors, expand the magic of this new technology to classrooms.

CNN Newsroom and other special television programs are taped for teacher use. Reading and reference materials are prepared ahead for classes to use in the library for projects. Scholarly periodicals, such as *American Heritage* and *Civil War Times* are catalogued as resources for teachers. Students attend lectures with prominent visiting authors, readings by the librarian, cultural and theme exhibits, and demonstrations of new technology for student use. The librarian presents five reference skills lessons to 480 sixth graders. All basic education teachers take classes to the library and send individual students for research projects. The LRC is open before and after school and during lunch for student use. All books and equipment are processed with computerized check-out systems, which allows the staff time to work with students—the highest priority.

BROAD MEADOWS MIDDLE SCHOOL, MA

Many innovative teaching approaches and teacher-initiated activities distinguish the Broad Meadows history program from the average. Interdisciplinary learning units, team teaching, cross-grade programs, and collaboration with specialists in the allied and fine arts are commonplace. At all levels, there is a concerted effort to blend the literature curriculum with history objectives.

Each grade level has a specific course of study in history and geography. Additionally, there are schoolwide efforts in human rights and local history instruction. Through these programs, students gain a basic knowledge of historical chronology and major historical themes so that they can come to understand the significance of past events and the enduring consequences of human choice. By integrating language arts, literature, and science programs around historical themes, teachers have created unique opportunities for these objectives to be achieved.

GRADE 6

The curriculum focuses on a study of ancient civilizations and Greco-Roman culture using the framework of the "Seven Aspects of Culture." Study is enhanced in reading and language arts classes, where students read and interpret fables, myths, and legends. Creative writing experiences in these genres are also offered. Long and short research reports are written by students who incorporate art activities such as models, dioramas, and posters into an oral presentation of their topics. With the assistance of the art staff, colorful corridor displays related to historical themes are created by students. A variety of media is used to help students gain a deeper understanding of themes, including the rise of organized religions, the growth of cities and trade, the development of nations, and the growth of democracy.

GRADE 7

Using United States history and government as its unifying themes, students are offered a unique interdisciplinary program for middle school history instruction. Through a collaborative effort, all seventh-grade teachers have redesigned their subject curriculum to parallel, chronologically, the American history course of studies. Combining the efforts of all academic and specialist teachers, the seventh-grade team has developed a program called "Farm-to-Factory-to-Technology." Students at this level immerse themselves in the study of United States history through novel reading, journal writing, role playing, dramatics, scientific inquiry, music, art, dance, and culinary and industrial arts, as well as a variety of carefully planned field experiences. As a culminating experience, all seventh-grade students and teachers share in the production of a musical drama related to the course. This exciting approach to learning has resulted in increased student/parent enthusiasm, as well as significant improvement in reading achievement test scores and school attendance.

An additional ten-week local history course is a requirement for all grade 7 students. This course is an offshoot of the farm-to-factory-to-technology program. It is presented so that students can develop a better understanding of the local historical events, thereby enriching their regular United States history course while fostering a sense of pride in their community. One of the finest accomplishments of the local history course is the development of an award-winning student-produced video, "Quincy Pride: Quincy Shipbuilding," shown on CNN. This documentary was the culmination of a two-year oral history project. Men and women who had worked at the shipyard decades ago were interviewed by students, and the historical perspectives of the workers became the foundation of the video.

GRADE 8

While the primary focus of the grade 8 social studies program is world geography, the entire literature and writing program continues to reinforce human rights goals from an historical perspective. The ideas of scapegoats, prejudice, and poverty, the black experience, Japanese internment, the Holocaust, and the struggle for self-awareness are further explored through the reading of a variety of historical novels centered on these themes. Students react to these readings individually in personal response journals and share their views in lively peer discussion groups. In their world geography classes, students can draw inferences about the ways these concepts can influence the developing global community. The Scholastic Computer Network allows students to interact with students in other places. The World of Difference Curriculum focuses on human rights. By increasing student awareness regarding the nature and manifestations of prejudice in the world, students begin to understand the importance of past events and the effect of individual actions on development of social attitudes.

THE BEST SCHOOLS–ASSESSING WHAT STUDENTS KNOW AND CAN DO

The Best Schools use some form of criterion-referenced assessment rather than, or at least in addition to, commercial norm-referenced tests to assess social studies progress. Products such as graphs, maps, research reports, dramas, reenactment of events, debates, and oral reports, which are developed by individual students and/or groups, are some of the means used in assessment. These are criterion-based approaches to assessment, where the work that students produce is compared to achievement criteria rather than to the performance of other students. Culminating projects, including written, visual, and oral work, are frequently used for assessment. More traditional criterion-based tests are also used as checklists.

Assessment Illustration

EAST BRUNSWICK HIGH SCHOOL, NJ

Assessment within each course at East Brunswick focuses on higher level thinking skills. Department-developed mid-term and final exams in required courses include essay questions, while an oral assessment component involves the development of projects and oral presentation of findings. The project based on the curriculum, but selected by the student, is assessed by using instruments to evaluate the following components: 1) the research process, 2) the research product, 3) students' self-evaluation of cooperative group work, 4) the active participation of the student audience, and 5) the oral presentation. Multiple assessors (class teacher, a second teacher, and a building or central office administrator) rate the projects using the following rubric:

ASSESSING THE ORAL PRESENTATION

For each criterion listed, score the group on a scale of 1 to 5, with 5 being the best score for each item.

1–2 = Fair 3 = Average 4 = Above Average 5 = Excellent

Criterion	Group Score	Notes
Delivery and Understanding: • uses verbal strategies that engage the audience (such as metaphors, rhetorical questions, colorful examples, strong verbs) • speaks clearly and audibly • maintains eye contact		
Understanding, Reasoning, Application: • provides a clear introduction to the topic • gives relevant supporting data to convincingly answer the question • knowledge of facts		
Responsiveness: To what extent did students answer the questions asked by the assessors?		
Participation: To what extent did group members orally contribute to the group's presentation? • assisting other group members with questions • contributing further information		

Total possible score is 20 Group Total: ______________________

Group: ______________ Date: _________ Period: ______________________

Following the students' presentation, the assessors and students in the class ask questions of the panel members, and both the presenters and students in the class are rated on the quality of the questions and responses. The assessment approach grew out of the methods used in the national We the People . . . The Citizen and the Constitution. This project, repeated from grades 4–12, provides an ever-increasing opportunity for students to work cooperatively; to demonstrate higher level thinking, writing, and speaking skills; and to function independently as learners.

THE BEST SCHOOLS–PROGRAM AND SUPPORT IN SOCIAL STUDIES

The Implementation Process

The Best Schools share a consistent view of how students learn, which includes the need for active engagement of learners, the need to make connections between content of real-life and other content, the importance of indepth knowledge versus surface acquisition of facts and information, the need to develop higher level thinking skills, and high expectations for all students. The development of curriculum in social studies has taken place over time and is grounded in learning research and meaningful content from the disciplines. There is a recognition that effective curriculum development goes far beyond the periodic updating of textbooks. Program development is a continuous process of assessment, data analysis, revision, and refinement.

Program Development Illustrations

EAST BRUNSWICK HIGH SCHOOL, NJ

Development of the East Brunswick articulated K–12 social studies program is continuous. In the high school, the department develops specific objectives to accomplish its mission within the district and building framework. Individual teams of staff members participate in planning through the student assistance program, curriculum committees, and faculty, departmental, and districtwide meetings.

Teachers work with the district supervisor and department chairperson to design and implement all curricula. Together, they develop the proficiencies, scope and sequence, activities, and assessment processes for all courses. A kindergarten through twelfth grade scope and sequence, a three through twelve student research sequence, and a four through twelve oral assessment process are some of the means staff have developed to ensure vertical articulation of programs across the grades. The social studies department works closely with the library/media staff and the English department to develop research skills. The *East Brunswick Research and Style Manual*, developed on three levels of sophistication and used by all students in all schools is an example of collaborative efforts by these three departments. The State Core Proficiencies and the National Standards Projects in civics, history, and geography and the NCSS standards for social studies provide the base for setting course objectives and expectations. Textbooks are reviewed and piloted. Summer workshops and department meetings provide opportunities for curriculum and assessment development. The district curriculum committee reviews textbooks and courses before submission to the board of education for final adoption.

Building-level procedures augment the formal efforts of program review established and conducted by outside consultants on a five-year cyclical plan. Quarterly, grades in all courses listed by individual teachers are reviewed and analyzed. Insight into possible curriculum problems is provided by analysis of the number of D's and F's. The focus is clear: the curriculum must reflect the needs of the students and provide them with the best opportunities to excel.

BLACK MOUNTAIN MIDDLE SCHOOL, CA

Instructional leadership at Black Mountain is the principal's most vital function. Her highest priority is to implement the most valid strategies to expand student learning. Initiating, implementing, and evaluating curriculum and learning strategies is a joint effort. Staff and principal determine criteria, programs, and evaluation processes. The principal delegates action activities to assistant principals and lead teachers in each department. They follow through to reach criteria for that specific project. In February, progress is reported by team leaders to staff during a professional development day. The organization structure and the actual program evaluations are supervised closely by administrators and lead teachers.

Black Mountain Middle School has an effective school improvement process in operation. The school improvement plan is developed by using information provided by site staff, site administration, parents, students, and two external reviews by accrediting agencies. Specific parts of the school improvement process include

- *The California Quality Program Review*—Every three years, the staff conducts a self-study that searches for evidence to confirm that school improvement programs, goals, and objectives are being met and to make further recommendations for improvement. Then, a team of trained outside reviewers complete a separate study in three days. Upon conclusion of reviews, a new school improvement plan is developed, and plans are implemented to correct deficiencies.
- *The Western Association of School and Colleges (WASC)*—Accreditation takes place at regular intervals. The school is currently on the maximum accreditation period.
- *Long-Range Strategic Site Planning*—In 1990, the staff initiated a site-level strategic planning process that goes far beyond previous procedures, by allowing staff and community to plan and attain long-range goals for student learning.
- *Teacher Committees for Curriculum, Instruction, Technology, Advisement, and Wellness*—These meet monthly to identify needs relative to core values and to initiate activities and evaluate programs.
- *Leadership Team*—The school-site leadership council meets monthly to review reports from the decision-making site committees, to address site problems and implement improvements in instruction.
- *Annual and Special Issue Surveys*—Parent, teacher, and student survey results are used to identify specific areas for curricular change and policy revision.
- *National and State Standardized Tests*—Standardized test results are analyzed by site staff and site administration to identify curriculum areas that need strengthening.

BROAD MEADOWS MIDDLE SCHOOL, MA

The school system has a director of curriculum and various other coordinators who guide and support development in specific disciplines. The director and coordinators meet with the principal, as well as with individual teachers, to discuss and define the curriculum. The principal is then responsible for supervising the instruction of all teachers in the school.

Within the school, staff teams (grade 6, grade 7, grade 8, personnel, special education, and allied arts teams) have a chairperson who is responsible for the program agenda to be considered at the weekly team meeting. Each team has common planning time, which enables team members to meet for up to three hours each week, as necessary. The administration participates in all team meetings, primarily as a resource.

THE BEST SCHOOLS—STAFF DEVELOPMENT

Staff development is a major commitment in the Best Schools. It is recognized that teachers must continue to be learners if they are to work effectively with children. Staff development is related to the program objectives of the school, as well as the needs of individual staff; in addition, staff development is planned as part of every new or revised program. The aim is for indepth understanding of the concepts and themes underlying the curriculum, methods of instruction, and knowledge of content. These aims cannot be accomplished in single training sessions; they require time, practice, and follow-up. A good deal of staff development occurs as staff—teachers, principals, subject specialists, librarians—develop curriculum; current practices are assessed; research and theory are reviewed; resources are identified and decisions are made concerning scope and sequence, inclusion or exclusion of topics; unifying themes are developed; and assessment practices are designed.

Staff Development Illustrations

EAST BRUNSWICK HIGH SCHOOL, NJ

East Brunswick has identified five major goals for the staff development program: staff will receive timely and adequate information to carry out procedures and programs required by law, policy, or adoption; staff will increase their knowledge in the content areas; staff will prove their increased knowledge in the instructional process; staff will identify risks to student learning and participate in student assistance; and staff will show knowledge of interrelationships among programs, schools, procedures, and subject matter. To carry out these goals, the district has developed a plan with eight components: districtwide, full-day inservice programs; inservice programs mandated by law (i.e., Right-to-Know); faculty and department meetings; summer curriculum development workshops; "Curriculum Mondays"; out-of-district conferences; the observation/evaluation/IIP process; and graduate study.

The staff incorporates interdisciplinary projects into the curriculum and has developed the *East Brunswick Research and Style Manual,* a guide used by all teachers to teach research skills and to guide the research process. Teachers have been trained in new technologies, implementing the "stock market" game, critical thinking skills, and writing of instructional objectives. As a result, they have identified a further need to develop ways to incorporate critical thinking skills into everyday instruction and to carry out the curriculum through cooperative learning.

LEMON G. HINE JUNIOR HIGH SCHOOL, D.C.

Staff development programs at Lemon G. Hine Junior High School involve the entire administration and teaching staff in ten scheduled half-day sessions during the school year. In addition, teachers have a week or more of planning and inservice time before the start of school each year. Monthly faculty meetings are frequently used for staff development. Teachers, department chairpersons, regional resource teachers, and administrators serve as facilitators of well-planned pertinent staff development sessions. The sessions are designed to give every teacher an opportunity to discuss educational programs and share innovative strategies. The staff interaction extends to lunchtime mini-workshops that enhance professional growth. Teachers also take evening, weekend, and summer classes with coworkers. While many of these courses are given in conjunction with universities and carry graduate credit, staff can also apply these courses to the required six credit hours of inservice required over each five-year period. All departments share cooperative learning techniques with colleagues; the quest for professional growth lends itself to cohesive, collaborative instruction.

BLACK MOUNTAIN MIDDLE SCHOOL, CA

Staff development at Black Mountain is the primary vehicle for achieving the school goal of *all* students learning. The integration of literature and writing into the total curriculum, use of quality instructional techniques and long-range site planning are top priorities at Black Mountain Middle School. Ongoing staff development efforts focus on increasing all teachers' use of collaborative learning, development of a strong at-risk intervention system, and kinesthetic learning. Staff development opportunities are congruent with priorities, as illustrated below:

- One year, the school released three full-time teachers to work as resource teachers in writing and literature. These teachers provided in-class demonstration lessons on a daily basis to all sixth, seventh, and eighth grade basic education (language arts/social studies) teachers. Instruction focused on the eight writing domains; the writing process; integrating literature into the curriculum; "into, through, and beyond" strategies for teaching literature; and reading remediation for students identified as reading two or more years below grade level. The computer lab for writing was in use eight periods a day, five days a week. Writing achievement scores of eighth graders (based on the last three years' CAP scores) were in the 94th percentile (or above) in the state. In another example, over a two-year period, twenty sixth and seventh grade basic education teachers attended forty hours of workshops focusing on lesson design to enhance study skills.

BROAD MEADOWS MIDDLE SCHOOL, MA

Continuous staff development at Broad Meadows is a priority. Twice each month, students are released early from school so that teachers may meet to discuss team, building-level, or citywide concerns. In addition, summer workshops, conferences, and staff development programs are commonplace for the faculty.

A myriad of staff development opportunities abounds in the school. Some are designed by teachers, some have been made available by staff grant writers, and some are offered by the Quincy Public School system and outside agencies. In many workshops and courses, academic teachers, special teachers, and special needs teachers work collaboratively. Three specific examples include local history (Quincy Historical Society, Society for Preservation of New England Antiquities), farm-to-factory-to-technology (in-house development project), and women's studies (Annual Conferences—The Network/Massachusetts Department of Education).

THE BEST SCHOOLS—FUNDING DEVELOPMENT

Social studies instruction in all schools has associated costs. Based on just the national average cost per pupil, a program that occupies 10% of instructional time would cost $524 per student, and one that occupies 20% of instructional time would cost $1048 per student (National Center for Educational Statistics, 1992). In other words, no matter what approach to social studies is used, instruction is expensive.

In addition to staff salaries, expenses include staff development, curriculum development, maps, globes, fiction and nonfiction books, software, multi-media, news sources, field trips, computers, and general materials for projects. Basic books, resources, and supplies are purchased through district funds. Staff development is also an area in which districts and schools have made budget-related commitments. Field trips may be supported by the school or PTA, and/or may be financed by students. Technology and multi-media may be purchased with district funds, through grants, or through special fund-raising. In some cases where schools do not use textbooks, money normally spent on these resources has been allocated to other resources that support the social studies program.

Funding Illustrations

BLACK MOUNTAIN MIDDLE SCHOOL, CA

At Black Mountain, instructional leadership means that all efforts and resources focus on student learning. The greatest thing done for children is to provide excellent teachers in every classroom with the lowest possible class size and the strongest learning resources. In the past year, seven outstanding teachers were hired, and $35,000 was allocated for staff development activities to expand competencies of all teachers and support staff. Individuals and teams develop goals based on school objectives, and school improvement funds are distributed to projects that target areas of need and that maintain areas of strength. In one year, $30,000 was spent for materials and equipment for program improvement and $10,000 for the advisory student support program. Also, $94,000 in state school improvement program/lottery funds and funding from district lottery and corporate sources for a total of over $100,000 were targeted for staff development, classroom learning resources, and student self-esteem projects. To provide a stimulating environment, the school spent $40,000 to renovate and equip areas for learning, office operation, counseling, and volunteer activities. A new $100,000 exploring technology lab and four auxiliary workrooms were built. A vocational skills program (COMMERCE) was established, and students were trained to be vitally involved in school operations.

BROAD MEADOWS MIDDLE SCHOOL, MA

At Broad Meadows in Quincy, there is a strong commitment to program and staff development. Students are released at noon every other Tuesday to provide time for planning and development. Broad Meadows has received tremendous administrative and community support for their innovative history programs. In a time of increased budget constraints, the administration has provided funds to assist the research and development of programs. For example, funding was granted to the seventh-grade team to provide summer workshops for the development and refinement of the farm-to-factory-to-technology program. Buses for field experiences ("classrooms on wheels") have been provided free of cost to subsidize students and to allow for full participation. Substitutes have been hired so that teachers can avail themselves of special conferences and workshops relating to the goals. Recently, a city councilor donated $500 to the program from his personal funds. The language arts and social studies coordinator provided additional funds to purchase novels that correlate with the curriculum objectives. There has been funding for speakers from Amnesty International, Facing History and Ourselves, and the Cambridge Oral History Project. The World of Difference curriculum was purchased for each grade, and an inservice workshop was provided. Several awards and citations have been presented to Broad Meadows by the Quincy School Committee, the Quincy Council, and the Massachusetts Department of Education for outstanding efforts in human rights and local history education.

SUMMARY

The Best Schools take instruction in social studies seriously and have effective K–12 articulated programs, which include from 150 to 250 minutes of instruction in social studies, increasing the allocated time through integration of social studies with other subjects at the middle school level. At the high school level, they require more courses in social studies and have developed significant elective courses that attract major portions of the student body. The literature and writing strands of the language arts program are frequently correlated with social studies. Emphasis in the social studies program is on the development of indepth knowledge of content and higher order thinking skills, rather than on the acquisition of surface information. The social studies curriculum includes significant content in history and geography, as well as civics, current events, and other strands of the social sciences. Gone are tracked/basal/select-the-right-answer social studies classes. Students are actively engaged in activities that stimulate interest and promote deep understanding. The Best Schools, urban, suburban, and rural, have developed their programs over time with programs grounded in theories of learning, as well as content. The National Standards Projects in United States history, world history, civics, and geography, as well as the standards of the National Council for the Social Studies, provide the framework for curriculum development, assessment, and program evaluation. In addition, there has been and continues to be a commitment to program and staff development.

REFERENCES

Allen, R., et al. (1990). *The Geography Learning of High School Seniors*. Princeton, NJ: Educational Testing Service.

Anderson, L., et al. (1990). *The Civics Report Card.* Princeton, NJ: Educational Testing Service.

Bennett, William J. (1986). *First Lessons: A Report on Elementary Education in America*. Washington D.C.: U.S. Department of Education.

Bennett, William J. (1988). *James Madison Elementary School.* Washington D.C.: U.S. Department of Education.

Bradley Commission on History in the Schools. (1988). *Building a History Curriculum: Guidelines for Teaching History in the Schools*. Washington, D.C.: Educational Excellence Network.

Center for Civic Education. (1994). *National Standards for Civics and Government*. Calabasas, CA: Center for Civic Education.

Geography Education Standards Project. (1994). *Geography for Life: National Geography Standards 1994.* Washington, D.C.: National Geographic Research & Exploration.

Hammack, D. C., et al. (1990). *The U.S. History Report Card.* Princeton, NJ: Educational Testing Service.

History-Social Science Curriculum Framework and Criteria Committee. (1988). *History-Social Science Framework for California Public Schools Kindergarten through Grade Twelve*. Sacramento, CA: California State Department of Education.

National Assessment of Educational Progress. (1990). *Accelerating Academic Achievement.* Princeton, NJ: Educational Testing Service.

National Center for History in the Schools. (1994). *National Standards for United States History Exploring the American Experience—Grades 5–12.* Los Angeles, CA: National Center for History in the Schools, University of California.

National Center for History in the Schools. (1994). *National Standards for World History: Exploring Paths to the Present—Grades 5–12.* Los Angeles, CA: National Center for History in the Schools, University of California.

National Commission on Social Studies in the Schools. (1989). *Charting a Course: Social Studies for the 21st Century.* Washington D.C.: National Commission on Social Studies in the Schools.

National Council for Geography Education. (1993). *The National Geography Standards: Geography for Life*. Indiana, PA: National Council for Geography Education.

National Council for the Social Studies. (1994). *Curriculum Standards for the Social Studies.* Washington, D.C.: National Council for the Social Studies.

Natoli, S. and Joint Committee on Geography Education. (1984). *Guidelines for Geography Education: Elementary and Secondary Schools.* Washington D.C.: Association of American Geographers and the National Council for Geography Education.

Parker, Walter C. (1991). *Renewing the Social Studies Curriculum.* Alexandria, VA: Association for Supervision and Curriculum Development (ASCD).

Risinger, C. Frederick. (1992). *Current Directions in Social Studies.* Boston, MA: Houghton Mifflin.

U.S. Department of Education. (1991). *America 2000: An Educational Strategy.* Washington, D.C.: U.S. Department of Education.

CHAPTER 9

Science

SCIENCE instruction is a regular part of the instructional program for most sixth- through eighth-grade students, accounting for as much as 950 hours of study. However, science study requirements and course taking patterns vary tremendously at the high school level, with only 19% of students completing a course sequence, including biology, chemistry, and physics (National Goals Panel, 1993). This chapter looks at the following questions concerning the development of science literacy:

- What does theory and research say about what students should learn and how they should be taught?
- How do the Best Schools successfully translate theory into practice in teaching science?
- How do the Best Schools assess what students know and what they can do?
- What do case studies of Best Schools reveal about how very successful science instruction is implemented in three very different community contexts?
- Finally, what are some of the specific practices, programs, and resources used by the Best Schools that are widely available to other program developers?

WHAT STUDENTS SHOULD LEARN

According to the National Goals of Education,

> By the year 2000, American students will leave grades four, eight and twelve having demonstrated competency in challenging subject matter including . . . science . . . ; and every school in America will ensure that all students learn to use their minds well, so they may be prepared for responsible citizenship, further learning, and productive employment in our Nation's modern economy.
>
> By the year 2000, U.S. students will be first in the world in . . . science achievement.

Science has traditionally taken the back seat to other curriculum areas; in 1993, only 40% of the schools enrolling eighth graders and 35% of those enrolling twelfth graders identified science as a priority (National Goals Panel, 1993). Among the reasons for the second-rate status of science are low value placed on the development of science literacy for all students beginning at the elementary level; competing priorities for instructional time in a crowded academic day; the lack of training on the part of teachers, principals, board members, and parents in science; the perception that understanding science is for those who will become scientists and, to a limited extent, the college bound; prevalence of textbooks, materials, curriculum, and methods that focus on science as memorization of selected "facts," which turn students off to science [by twelfth grade, only 57% of girls and 74% of boys report positive attitudes toward science (National Goals Panel, 1993)]. The National Goals set forth much higher expectations for defining science literacy for all students and adults of the year

2000 and beyond. Key words and phrases within the goals include "demonstrated competency," "challenging subject matter," "all students," "prepared for responsible citizenship," "prepared for further learning," and "prepared for productive employment in our modern economy." These statements imply the need for setting standards for *all* students far beyond the implicit low standards for scientific learning that are traditionally part of the science program. Clearly, there is a need for change in time commitment, content, and methods of teaching science if the National Goals are to be achieved and if students are going to function effectively in the 21st century.

In 1990, the American Association for the Advancement of Science (AAAS) published *Science for All Americans* (Rutherford and Ahlgren 1990), which "consists of a set of recommendations on what understandings and ways of thinking are essential for all citizens in a world shaped by science and technology." The report and subsequent book was the result of a three-year collaboration involving several hundred scientists, mathematicians, engineers, physicians, philosophers, historians, and educators. The recommendations include mathematics and technology, as well as the natural and physical sciences, and are applicable to all students. Recommendations concerning content are based both on scientific and human significance: knowledge is doubling every five years; science has been fractionated into over 40,000—fields over any given two day period, there may be as many as 3000 discoveries in chemistry alone. The framers of *Science for All Americans* recognized that schools cannot teach it all, and, in fact, schools need to decrease content in order to teach it better. Curriculum developers need to focus more on what to eliminate, rather than what to add to the curriculum. The recommendations for content included in the publication were selected based on what was judged as worth knowing now and for decades to come. Concepts were chosen that could serve as a lasting foundation upon which further knowledge could be built. Choices for inclusion had to meet criteria having to do with human life and broad goals within a free society including utility, social responsibility, intrinsic value of knowledge, philosophical value, and childhood enrichment. *Science for All Americans* is not a curriculum, nor does it make recommendations for learning outcomes at particular grade levels; rather, it defines what students should retain after graduation from high school, the cumulative effects of a K–12 education.

What students should learn, as put forth in *Science for All Americans,* has been presented in sets of related topics, which, taken together, lay out a conceptual framework for understanding science and which can serve as a basis for further learning. The topics are not meant to be sequentially incorporated into a school curriculum nor dealt with as distinct topics. A major recommendation of the report is that the boundaries between the scientific disciplines be softened and that the connections between science and other disciplines be emphasized. The following list represents the recommended conceptual framework and the conceptual categories with which all students should be familiar, but not the specific content (Rutherford and Ahlgren, 1990, pp. xxiii–xxiv):

Science Framework and Conceptual Categories

(1) The Nature of Science—The Scientific World View, Scientific Inquiry, The Scientific Enterprise;
(2) The Nature of Mathematics—Some Features of Mathematics, Mathematical Processes;
(3) The Nature of Technology—Science and Technology, Principles of Technology, Technology and Society;
(4) The Physical Setting—The Universe, The Earth, Forces that Shape the Earth, The Structure of Matter, Transformations of Energy, The Motion of Things, The Forces of Nature;
(5) The Living Environment—Diversity of Life, Heredity, Cells, Interdependence of Life, Flow of Matter and Energy, Evolution of Life;

(6) The Human Organism—Human Identity, Life Cycle, Basic Functions, Learning, Physical Health, Mental Health;
(7) Human Society—Cultural Effects on Behavior, Group Organization and Behavior, Social Change, Social Trade-offs, Forms of Political and Economic Organizations, Social Conflict, Worldwide Social Systems;
(8) The Designed World—The Human Presence, Agriculture, Materials, Manufacturing, Energy Sources, Energy Use, Communication, Information Processing, Health Technology;
(9) The Mathematical World—Numbers, Symbolic Relationships, Shapes, Uncertainty, Summarizing Data, Sampling, Reasoning;
(10) Historical Perspectives—Displacing the Earth from the Center of the Universe, Uniting the Heavens and Earth, Uniting Matter and Energy, Time and Space, Extending Time, Setting the Earth's Surface in Motion, Understanding Fire, Splitting the Atom, Explaining the Diversity of Life, Discovering Germs, Harnessing Power;
(11) Common Themes—Systems, Models, Constancy, Patterns of Change, Evolution, Scale; and
(12) Habits of Mind—Values and Attitudes, Skills.

Science for All Americans was part of the larger and ongoing Project 2061. *Benchmarks for Science Literacy,* developed by Project 2061, details the progress all students should make by the end of grades 2, 5, 8, and 12 on the way to becoming scientifically literate (American Association for the Advancement of Science, 1993). The benchmarks are organized around the twelve conceptual categories delineated in *Science for All Americans* and were developed by six school district teams, assisted by university faculty and extensively reviewed by teachers, curriculum specialists, and content supervisors. The following examples from the "Nature of Science" category are illustrative of the benchmarks. (In these statements, *know* is shorthand for understanding ideas well enough to use them in a variety of meaningful contexts.)

By the end of the 8th grade, students will know that

- If more than one variable changes at the same time in an experiment, the outcome of the experiment may not be clearly attributable to any one of the variables. It may not always be possible to prevent outside variables from influencing the outcome of an investigation (or even to identify all the variables), but collaboration among investigators can often lead to research designs that are able to deal with such situations.

By the end of the 12th grade, students should know that

- Hypotheses are widely used in science for choosing what data to pay attention to and what additional data to seek, and for guiding the interpretation of the data (both new and previously available). (American Association for the Advancement of Science, 1993, pp. 12, 13)

The National Science Education Standards and Assessment Project, commissioned in 1991, has as its goal to develop national science education standards for grades K–12 and to build consensus among a range of constituencies nationwide to adopt those standards. The standards include not only content standards, but also program, teaching, assessment, and support and resource system standards. The standards offer a coherent vision of what it means for all students to become scientifically literate. The National Standards represent a consensus of what defines successful learning but does not define a national curriculum.

The standards focus on fundamental content that represents central scientific ideas and principles, has rich explanatory power, guides fruitful investigations, applies to situations and context common to everyday experiences, can be linked to meaningful learning experience, and is developmentally appropriate for students. These criteria are apparent in the following examples of "Science as Inquiry" draft standards.

(1) As a result of inquiry-oriented activities in grades 5–8, all students should develop these abilities.
   - Identify appropriate questions for a scientific investigation.
   - Design and conduct a scientific investigation.
   - Use appropriate tools and technologies to gather, analyze, and interpret data.
   - Construct explanations and models using evidence.
   - Think critically and logically about relationships between evidence and explanations.
   - Recognize and analyze alternative explanations and procedures.
   - Communicate scientific procedures and explanations.

(2) As a result of inquiry-oriented activities in grades 9–12, all students should develop these abilities.
   - Identify the questions and concepts that guide scientific investigations.
   - Design and conduct a full scientific investigation.
   - Use technologies to improve investigations and communications.
   - Construct and revise scientific explanations and models using logic and evidence.
   - Recognize and analyze alternative explanations and models.
   - Communicate and defend a scientific argument.
   - Analyze a historical or contemporary scientific inquiry.

HOW STUDENTS LEARN–HOW STUDENTS ARE TAUGHT

Traditionally, the teaching of science at the middle and high school levels has been based on the premise that science is solely knowing what science has already discovered, with a collection of identified facts for each grade level. Memorization has frequently been the major form of learning; little emphasis has been placed on science as doing. In the 1960s, there were several large-scale curriculum development efforts from which emerged science programs based on science as inquiry and science as doing, the most popular of which was BSCS (Biological Science Curriculum Study). During this period, the National Science Foundation and other groups sponsored institutes to provide training to teachers. Nevertheless, by the late 1970s, national-level funding for training in science education had largely dried up, and funds for program development were also in short supply. Most schools returned to a textbook-centered approach. In 1993, 54% of eighth-grade teachers reported that they relied primarily on textbooks to determine what they taught, and only 62% reported that their students did experiments (National Goals Panel, 1993). Teachers reported that they implemented science with whatever knowledge they brought with them to the job. However, some schools do make science a priority, actively engage students through hands-on activities and meaningful content, and provide continuing training and adequate resources for teachers.

The United States has paid a price for its lack of attention to meaningful science instruction. The National Assessment of Educational Progress (NAEP) found that, by 1992, science proficiency was higher at age nine than in 1970 and that scores for thirteen year olds were back to the 1970 level; however, the scores of seventeen year olds were still below the 1969 level. An international assessment of science, including the United States, France, Hungary, Korea, Switzerland, and Taiwan, found that American thirteen year olds were outperformed by students in Hungary, Korea, and Taiwan in three out of four areas tested. Only in assessment of knowledge of the nature of science did American students equal the performance of students from all other countries tested (National Goals Panel, 1993).

If students are to achieve the goals of scientific literacy, dramatic changes must be made in what students are taught and how they are taught in most of the nation's schools. It is necessary that what is known about how people learn be applied in the classroom. People construct their own meaning based on their previous knowledge and perceptions and on new information or experiences encountered. Concepts are best learned and need to be taught using multiple contexts, which build on previous knowledge and, at the same time, insure that previously held incorrect knowledge is replaced. If learning is to go beyond surface knowledge (i.e., the memorization of facts, procedures, and applications) to the development of meaningful knowledge (connected learning that makes sense to the learner), then students must be given time to explore concepts, apply ideas to novel situations, receive feedback, and reflect on what is learned.

The need for time has at least two immediate implications for the middle and secondary curriculum. First, more lab time needs to be devoted to the teaching of science. Second, more time must be devoted to teaching important concepts and less time to covering a vast array of facts and information. "Less is more" in the development of the elementary science curriculum. Those content areas that are included in the curriculum need to be covered and explored in the depth necessary to insure understanding. In AAAS's publication *Science for All Americans*, the following characteristics of effective science instruction are identified (Rutherford and Ahlgren, 1990, Chapter 13):

- Students should have experiences with the kinds of thought and action that are typical of science, mathematics, and technology.
- Students should be engaged with challenging subject matter and, at the same time, be provided with opportunities for success; understanding, rather than vocabulary, should be the main purpose of science teaching.
- Instruction should begin with questions and phenomena that are of interest to students; problems should be given that are appropriate to their developmental level and that require them to decide on the relevance of evidence and to offer their own interpretations.
- Students need to have opportunities to learn to use the tools of science, such as thermometers, hand lenses, cameras, microscopes, calculators, and computers and to use the tools in various contexts.
- They need opportunities for observing, collecting, sorting, cataloging, surveying, interviewing, note taking, and sketching.
- They need to have time and opportunity to question, puzzle, and discuss findings; to collect, sort, and analyze evidence; and to build arguments based on evidence; any topic that can be taught in a single lesson is probably not worth learning.
- They should have opportunities to study scientific ideas in a historical context in order to develop a sense of how science happens, by learning about the growth of scientific ideas.
- A high priority needs to be placed on effective oral and written communication; emphasis should be on clear expression of procedures, findings, and ideas.
- The collaborative nature of scientific and technological work should be strongly reinforced by frequent group activity in the classroom; group approaches should be the norm in the science classroom; competition among students for high grades can distort what should be the prime motivation for science: to find things out.
- The nature of inquiry is determined by what is being studied, and the method used determines what is learned; teaching scientific reasoning as a set of procedures separate from any particular substance is as futile as solely imparting accumulated

knowledge of science to students; "science teachers should help students to acquire both scientific knowledge of the world and habits of mind at the same time."

- Teachers should value and foster creativity, imagination, and invention as distinct from academic achievement.
- Teachers should make sure that students have some sense of success in learning science and mathematics, de-emphasizing getting all the right answers as being the main criteria of success; students should be aware that, particularly in science, knowledge is not absolute; teachers should make students aware of their progress and encourage further study.
- Teachers should encourage all students in science and provide the opportunities for both boys and girls to gain proficiency in the use of scientific tools; teachers should exploit the larger community and involve parents and other concerned adults in useful ways.

The National Standards also establish standards for review of science programs and science teaching, which focus on development of K−12 articulated programs based on achievement of content standards coordinated with the mathematics program, inquiry learning, discourse about scientific ideas, and development of scientific habits of mind and which incorporate a positive attitude toward science. The following draft of National Science Education Standards illustrate the focus for instruction:

(1) Teachers of science should guide and facilitate science learning. To do this, they
- Interact with students to focus and support their inquiries.
- Orchestrate among students the discourse about scientific idea.
- Recognize student diversity and ensure that all students participate fully in science learning.
- Challenge students to take responsibility for their own work and also to work collaboratively.
- Encourage and model the habits of mind, curiosity, excitement, and creativity of those involved in science.

(2) Teachers of science should design and manage a learning environment that provides students with the time, space, and resources needed for learning science. To do this, teachers should
- Structure the time available so that students are able to engage in extended investigations and indepth inquiry.
- Provide a setting for student work, which is flexible and supportive of science inquiry.
- Provide students with access to the tools and materials they need for hands-on investigation.
- Ensure a safe working environment.
- Make available print and media resources.
- Identify and use resources outside the school.
- Engage students in designing the learning environment

At the state level, the California State Department of Education (1990) has developed a set of expectations for science programs as a part of the *Science Framework for California Public Schools*. The science program expectations serve as a model and as a set of criteria for review of current curriculum and as a guide for curriculum development (California State Department of Education, 1990).

(1) The major themes underlying science, such as energy, evolution, patterns of change, scale and structure, stability, and systems and interactions, are developed and deepened through a thematic approach.

(2) The three basic scientific fields of study are addressed, ideally each year, and the connections among them are developed.

(3) The character of science is shown to be open to inquiry and controversy and free of dogmatism; the curriculum promotes student understanding of how we come to know what we know and how we test and revise our thinking.

(4) Science is presented in connection with its applications in technology and its implications for society.

(5) Science is presented in connection with the student's own experiences and interests, frequently using hands-on experiences that are integral to the instructional sequence.

(6) Students are given opportunities to construct the important ideas of science, which are then developed in depth, through inquiry and investigation.

(7) Instructional strategies and materials allow several levels and pathways of access so that all students can experience both challenge and success.

(8) Printed materials are written in an interesting and engaging narrative style; in particular, vocabulary is used to facilitate understanding rather than as an end in itself.

(9) Textbooks are not the sole source of the curriculum; everyday materials and laboratory equipment, videotapes and software, and other printed materials such as reference books provide a substantial part of the student experience.

(10) Assessment programs are aligned with the instructional program in both content and format; student performance and investigation play the same central role in assessment that they do in instruction. (pp. 8–9)

There are great similarities and reflected consensus among the work of Project 2061, the National Standards Committee, the California Science Framework and Criteria Committee, and other similar state initiatives. All of these projects have been influenced by national and international science achievement studies, the recommendations in *Science for All Americans*, and the National Goals for Education. In addition, many of the same individuals and professional associations are involved in more than one of these projects.

THE BEST SCHOOLS–THEORY INTO PRACTICE IN SCIENCE

The Best Schools have evolved their science programs over many years, and the programs continue to evolve. The goals and objectives of these programs are congruent with national science literacy projects. Instruction is organized into units of instruction that allow all students to explore topics in depth and to be involved in hands-on lab-centered activities that foster understanding of concepts. Programs have been developed to fit within the context and environment of each school; however, they are consistent with the new standards for science education.

Illustrations in Science: The Contexts (Case Studies)

E. O. GREEN SCHOOL, OXNARD, CA

E. O. Green School is one of eleven schools in the Hueneme Elementary School District, serving the residents of Port Hueneme and South Oxnard. Green is a sixth-, seventh-, and eighth-grade middle school. It is located in a lower middle-class, multi-ethnic residential neighborhood made up of apartment buildings and single-family homes, many of these currently housing multiple families. Parent occupations are primarily blue collar and related to regional military installations, agriculture, commercial labor, and service industries. The student population is made up of approximately 54% Latino, 36% Caucasian, 3% African-American, 5% Filipino, and 2% Native American/Asian/Pacific Islander. Fifty-five percent of the student body qualifies for free or reduced meals, 14% qualify for Aid to Families with Dependent Children, and 13% are limited or non-English proficient. Eighth-grade students score at the 96th and 89th percentiles in mathematics and science, respectively, on the California Assessment for districts with similar demographics. E. O. Green received special recognition in both mathematics and science as part of recognition as a Blue Ribbon School. No other schools in the district have been recognized to date.

Deloris Carn, *Principal,* Edward Jones, *Assistant Principal, Grades 6–8, 900 Students*

JACKSON HOLE HIGH SCHOOL, JACKSON, WY

Jackson Hole High School lies just inside the city limits of the town of Jackson, which is considered the gateway to both Grand Teton and Yellowstone National Parks. The population ranges from upper middle-class executives to seasonal workers in the tourist industry. The high cost of living in the valley creates a high degree of transiency in both the community and school populations. It is not uncommon for the high school to enroll or check out 20% of its population within a year. Jackson' s tourist-based economy has flourished in the last decade. There has been consistent growth in the hotel and restaurant sector and in other businesses that serve the tourist industry. However, during the same period, the state of Wyoming has undergone financial hardship due to the decline within the state of the energy and minerals industry. Because education is funded in Wyoming largely by royalties from energy and mineral extraction, education funding in Wyoming has reflected economic hardship. In 1992, 61% of the graduating class entered college. Jackson Hole was recognized initially as a Blue Ribbon School in 1986–87 and then again in 1992–93. In 1992–93, Jackson Hole received special recognition in science as part of its recognition as a Blue Ribbon School.

Albert M. Storrs, *Principal, Grades 9–12, 539 Students*

WESTMINSTER HIGH SCHOOL, WESTMINSTER, CA

Westminster High School is located in the city of Westminster in the Hunterton Beach Union High School District, Orange County, California. Westminster is an "edge city," with a rapidly changing demography, characteristic more of an urban than suburban environment. The school has a highly transient population of 2350 students from low to middle socioeconomic status, with one-third on Aid to Families with Dependent Children. In 1991–92, 770 new students enrolled beyond normal freshmen grade advancement, and 419 students transferred out of the school. The student population is approximately 27% Caucasian, 26% Hispanic, 35% Asian or Pacific Islander, 5% American Indian, and 7% other. Thirty-seven percent of the student body is limited English proficient. Daily announcements are made in three languages. Ninety-two percent of the graduating class enters two- or four-year colleges. Westminster received special recognition in science as part of its recognition as a Blue Ribbon School in 1992–93.

Bonnie J. Maspero, *Principal, Grades 9–12, 2443 Students*

THE BEST SCHOOLS–CLASS ORGANIZATION AND INSTRUCTIONAL TIME

Science is a priority for all students in the Best Schools. Science courses are problem- and activity-centered, with class time spent in lab explorations. Many of the schools use a block schedule all or part of the time. Under this approach, three or four classes meet for double periods on alternate days. This schedule not only facilitates the lab-centered approach to science, but favors indepth coverage and hands-on activities in other subjects. Time is also extended through science activities integrated with other subject areas and field experiences. Core science classes are heterogeneously grouped. The emphasis is on all students successfully completing a minimum of three years of study; however, most students elect to take four or more full-year courses. Special education students are mainstreamed to the degree possible within the classes; many of the schools use in-class support to ensure the success of special needs students within the regular program. Individual accommodations are made for students who need to learn at different paces or need to express what they have learned in different formats. Cooperative learning groups are used extensively in science to enhance instruction and to model how scientists work in the real world.

Class Organization Illustrations

E. O. GREEN SCHOOL, CA

The needs of sixth-grade students at E. O. Green School are met through a modified departmentalized program. Two days a week, the students have a period of science with the sixth-grade teacher, who specializes in science, and one period per week, they have science with their homeclass teacher. Seventh and eighth grades are departmentalized for core subjects, and students are scheduled for a period each day. At the seventh-grade level, math and science teachers have classes scheduled back-to-back, which allows them to plan double-period classes whenever necessary. At the eighth-grade level, students change from science classroom to the laboratory and back every two weeks.

Each subject area class is heterogeneously grouped with an emphasis on mainstreaming for special education students. The use of cross-curricular integration throughout the school allows for strengthening, blending, and focusing of efforts, preventing any student from "falling between the cracks." The school aggressively pursues its philosophy that "every student can and will learn."

JACKSON HOLE HIGH SCHOOL, WY

Students at Jackson Hole are required to take three years of science, including one year of life science and one year of physical science. Almost all students take from four to six semesters of the integrated science courses. Some students elect to take accelerated chemistry or chemistry, biology, and physics or life science and physical science, instead or in combination with integrated science. Most students take four years of science, and a substantial number "double up," taking five or six courses. Other courses offered at Jackson Hole include Biology II, food science, AP biology, AP chemistry, and AP physics. All courses are open to all students. One hundred percent of the students take integrated science and biology, 85% chemistry, 50% physics, and 60% an additional biology course. Special education students are mainstreamed into regular science courses. Special education teachers coteach in classes most often elected by special students. In 1992–93, fewer than thirty students out of the total school population were not enrolled in a science course.

The school strives to stimulate interest in the sciences and to provide an opportunity for all students to successfully meet high expectations. The diversity of courses allows students to select individualized courses of study that can meet broad-ranging needs from non-college-bound to college-bound future engineers and doctors.

All science courses are lab courses. Because labs can take more than the traditional fifty-minute period, once a month, the school blocks schedules, providing four double periods one day and three double periods the next day. These block-scheduled days are planned a year in advance to allow teachers to coordinate lengthy activities.

WESTMINSTER HIGH SCHOOL, CA

Students at Westminster High School are organized into heterogeneously grouped classes throughout the core curriculum. All students take the same placement tests (prior to entry into ninth grade) and are randomly placed in classes by a computer. In addition to the heterogeneously grouped classes, there are honors and advanced placement classes for GATE identified students. There are LEP and sheltered classes for students who do not read and write English well enough to succeed in the regular program. Special education students participate in the regular program. The special education staff offer alternative instructional strategies to teachers and provide assistance to classified students. Resource teachers team teach with regular education teachers in required graduation subject areas. Special day students are mainstreamed according to individual educational profiles.

A block schedule, with three 113-minute periods, lunch, and an optional half-hour tutorial, operates four days a week. The tutorial period (8:00 to 8:30 A.M.) provides time for students to obtain special assistance from teachers, make up work, and use the library or computer labs. On the fifth day of the week, there are six fifty-seven-minute periods, plus lunch. Under this schedule, each class meets 283 minutes per week. The change to this schedule increased greatly the use of interactive instructional strategies and increased depth, rather than breadth, in subject matter.

THE BEST SCHOOLS – CURRICULUM

The Best Schools have moved away from the focus on discreet study of science disciplines, as advocated by national studies and reports, such as *Science for All Americans*. Two- to three-year sequences of integrated science have replaced the traditional earth science, biology, chemistry, and physics sequence. These integrated science courses combine the study of each discipline into units that stress the relationship among the disciplines in the context of real-life applications. Even in cases where the traditional course titles have been maintained, curriculum has been modified to incorporate cross-discipline learning. The emerging sequence for all students is two to three years of integrated science, followed by or taken simultaneously with elective study of such courses as advanced biology, chemistry, physics, environmental science and/or advanced placement courses.

Curriculum in the Best Schools is thematically based. Curriculum units may be drawn from programs such as Activities that Integrate Math and Science (AIMS) or National Geographic's KidsNet and/or others developed by states and locally by staff. In many cases, units have been developed locally to take advantage of local environments and opportunities. The emphasis is on comprehensive understanding of concepts, rather than surface coverage of large quantities of information. In order to maximize understanding, many modes of instruction are used. Students read about science, hear about science, and, most importantly, are actively engaged in doing science. Students learn to use the tools of science – from simple measuring devices to microscopes and computers; they observe, collect, and record data; make hypotheses; analyze data; and communicate and support findings. Textbooks, if used at all, are used largely for reference. In order to "do science" and provide for hands-on activities, the schools rely heavily on science labs and make the most of the school and neighboring environments. In many cases, they have extended facilities, including natural areas outside of the building.

Technology is used extensively to support science programs in the Best Schools. Many of the schools have elaborate computer networks that allow students to access library resources, data bases, and software from virtually every location in the building. Computers with peripherals are used to collect and analyze data. Modems connect science labs to resources around the world, local universities, private research labs, and students in other schools. Lab reports often incorporate word processing, graphics, data bases, spreadsheet, and digitized photography. The capability of laser and CD-ROM technology to hold large amounts of still and moving images and the ability to easily access and organize material for instruction is well suited to science education.

Day field trips are a regular occurrence and overnight and even week long experiences are incorporated into the program. Local resource people from industry, colleges, and museums serve as speakers or provide leadership for special science-related activities.

Science activities are frequently integrated with other areas of the school curriculum. Math and science are integrated in the real world, and it is logical to integrate math and science in the curriculum. A number of the Best Schools use the integrated math/science investigations developed by the AIMS Education Foundation; however, the science program also incorporates the history of science and social and ethical issues. An emphasis on writing across the curriculum is another characteristic of the Best Schools. Students keep records of their investigations in science journals and logs and communicate findings through oral and written reports. If students are to learn the processes and attitudes of science, they need to be involved in activity-oriented investigations. This active learning increases understanding and retention. In addition, involvement in investigations stimulates curiosity and motivates students to explore and learn. Finally, schools develop their own investigations, frequently related to their own environment.

Curriculum Illustrations

E. O. GREEN SCHOOL, CA

Science has a high priority at E. O. Green School. Science literacy is developed through activity and investigation by allowing students to construct their own understanding of concepts after observing the world around them and developing hypotheses to explain their observations. To guide instruction, a curriculum framework aligned with the California science framework was developed within the district over a three-year period of time.

Students receive three years of science using a thematic approach. As the curriculum spirals through life, earth, and physical science, students see different aspects and interconnected perspectives of real-world phenomena. Math concepts are also interconnected with science, especially in the seventh-grade Science Union Math core. This ninety-minute per day program is designed to facilitate student hands-on connections between science and mathematics by aligning two closely related frameworks. Care is taken to cover the scientific content areas and themes and the mathematical strands and unifying ideas. Students have the advantage of relevant tasks, posed in a concrete manner, with a myriad of resources and technological tools for investigating and solving problems. The goal of the program is not to teach all the facts of science and math in a rote manner, but rather to provide rich experiences in doing science and math with the curiosity, tools, and mental set of scientists and mathematicians. Students are assessed formally throughout the project. There are a variety of audiences for their work and a range of feedback from peers, instructors, and self-evaluation.

The eighth-grade curriculum is also inquiry-based and focuses on the connections among subjects. Activities that Integrate Math and Science (AIMS) materials are used as part of the eighth-grade curriculum. Students rotate back and forth from the classroom to the laboratory every two weeks. Language arts is coordinated through the many writing activities required and shared with English teachers. Students are taught that any person can make a difference through scientific contribution.

Science is student-centered. Activities build on students' prior experiences. High-interest, performance-based investigations that are "hands-on" keep students motivated, thinking, and communicating. For example, "Gorgues" were strange little globs that began appearing all over the campus. As students noticed them, they were asked to describe and construct theories about them. "Are they alive? Do they eat? Do they reproduce?" Reactions were interesting; some stated, "Gorgues were viruses that had spread throughout the campus." Others said, "They were a new type of mushroom." This critical thinking activity permitted students to apply the scientific method and discover that, in science, there is no absolute on scientific inquiries. Students were challenged to combine their prior knowledge and experience of life forms to defend their opinions about "Gorgues."

Students are engaged in many multi-media activities and simulations. One such program is the NASA-Marsville Mission, which is part of the eighth-grade curriculum. This problem-solving activity, designed by NASA, asks students to design and build a community on Mars. Part of the activity involves the challenge of bringing down a payload from a spacecraft that was unable to land due to severe dust storms. NASA held a teleconference for classes to compare results with their team. Additionally, students demonstrate enthusiasm for science through the math/science club, science fairs, environmental projects, and Earth Week observances. Other examples of hands-on multidimensional programs include KidsNet in sixth grade and Voyage of the MIMI in seventh grade.

Each science classroom is equipped with computers, videocassette recorders, televisions, laser disc player, and overhead projectors. The smart classroom, in operation since 1987, is a prototype for computerized multi-media education in the United States. Concepts originally designed and tested at Green are being used throughout the world. The "wet laboratory" is coupled with the smart classroom to add the experiential dimension to computer-assisted instruction through hands-on laboratory investigations. Students find themselves in the wet lab during 50% of their science time. It is here that most life science takes place. Technology Lab 2000 also links science application to technology. At thematic stations, students gain an understanding of the physics of manufacturing, communication, construction, fabrication, and transportation activities.

JACKSON HOLE HIGH SCHOOL, WY

While the actual courses at Jackson Hole are diverse, several common threads run strongly throughout all of them. All science courses are lab courses; all courses utilize new technology to improve student success; all courses strive to remain relevant in the eyes of students through the use of real-world examples; and all courses engage students in higher level thinking. In various courses, students may discuss relevant current events, read current science articles and apply the information in small cooperative groups, or write abstracts on articles that they have read in current scientific journals. Students are encouraged to utilize prior understandings in their synthesis of current course work. During class discussions, it is a common occurrence for students to refer to prior experience, material learned in another science course, or a piece of information gleaned from outside reading or television when formulating a question or an answer.

The relatively small size of the science department facilitates regular communication and coordination of class progress, material covered, instructional techniques, integration of courses, and future plans. To achieve the goal of hands-on/minds-on science, the staff uses a variety of techniques, including traditional labs, cooperative group work, independent investigations, research, small-group and individual presentations to the class, field trips, and technology, including tutorial programs, computer-interfaced labs, computer-generated graphing and lab reports, CD-ROM, and interactive programs on laser discs.

The science department is committed to teaching science as a process and as a body of intimately related disciplines, rather than as discreet content areas consisting of their own elements of information. For example, the biology courses all include elements of chemistry and earth science. Another is the food science course, which integrates nutrition, biology, and chemistry. However, the two-semester integrated science course totally integrates the major discipline areas of biology, ecology, chemistry, earth science, and physics through lessons designed around the locally relevant themes of the Greater Yellowstone Ecosystem and Rivers. The staff wrote the hands-on thematic units with regional and local emphasis, and they supplement the curriculum with field trips and weekend enrichment activities (i.e., a snowmobile trip to Yellowstone National Park to study the ecosystem as it exists in winter). Cooperative learning strategies are used extensively to help all students, but specifically those who have traditionally not done well in science, to gain greater appreciation and understanding. Some of the assessment strategies are based upon the synthesis and application of concepts in a final product. For example, student teams build various sections of a three-dimensional relief map from their interpretations of a topographical contour map.

The Principles of Technology course uses the Center for Occupational Research Design (CORD) curriculum and materials. Students are involved in numerous projects such as building model cars using nontraditional energy sources, robots to lift and move objects, and telephones that connect theory and application.

Just as the department strives to ensure integration of the science disciplines in courses, they also work to involve the other academic disciplines. Every science course requires students to utilize and improve communication skills. Opportunities to improve communication skills include reading texts or journals and newspaper and magazine articles; using the written expression of ideas in lab reports, research papers, abstracts, journaling, and essays; and making individual and group presentations in class. Increasingly, students are required to synthesize written material in a small group, make a verbal presentation, and write a paper as a final product for a course. The science and math departments actively cooperate with one another to ensure that students are given the tools necessary to use math skills in the science courses.

Regardless of all other achievements, no science program can truly be deemed successful if it fails to involve the students' experiences, validate their personal interest, and draw upon their natural curiosity. The staff believe that only through touching students on a personal level can they get them to accept the challenge of personal achievement and instill in them the belief that they, as individuals, can have personal success and impact in the field of science. To achieve these goals, they draw upon a variety of local resources and work with students on a personal level. In addition to using all the previously discussed instructional techniques, the science department provides ample opportunity for individual remediation and enrichment. Every year, the department hosts a series of science speakers who discuss a variety of science and applied science topics. Last year, each of the fourteen lectures drew over 200 students in a cross-curriculum cooperative effort. Students routinely meet with teachers before and after school and at lunchtime to make up work, get extra help, or pursue topics of personal interest. Some science courses offer evening study sessions to help prepare students for upcoming tests or to provide extra time for class projects. All science teachers are involved with providing individualized enrichment activities outside of class time. Last year, these opportunities included an overnight snowmobile trip to Old Faithful in Yellowstone National Park, a tree planting and forest ecology trip that planted over 700 trees, a camping trip and opportunity to work with a wildlife biologist on a fisheries habitat improvement project and an owl nest survey in a proposed timber sale area, a trip by bus through Grand Teton and Yellowstone National Parks, an informal aeronautics club that has students actively applying scientific principles through making and flying model airplanes, and a recycling club that recycles aluminum and paper on a schoolwide basis.

WESTMINSTER HIGH SCHOOL, CA

The science department offers many successful and innovative courses that are modeled by other schools in the area. Students are required to take two and a half years of science, including the equivalent of one year each of life and physical science; however, most students exceed the requirement. Courses offered include

(1) Integrated science
(2) Physical science technology

(3) Introduction to college prep science
(4) Biology
(5) Chemistry
(6) Physics
(7) Anatomy and physiology
(8) AP biology
(9) AP physics
(10) AP chemistry
(11) Sheltered physical and life sciences for LEP/bilingual

The integrated science course is the most exemplary of the collaborative efforts of content improvement by the department. This is a vertical, rather than horizontal, approach to science. It is a six-semester program covering physics, chemistry, biology, and earth/space science. The subject matter is connected through the following themes: energy evolution, patterns of change, scale and structure, stability, and systems and interactions. Focus is on indepth coverage of a limited number of themes, not broad coverage of all science areas. Concepts are logically developed through scope and sequence using a storyline format. Course work is team planned, taught, and assessed. Primary documents are used in preference to a single textbook. Westminster is piloting several coordinated textbooks following a constructionist approach through Wiley and Sons Publishing in Canada. Teachers communicate regularly with the authors and publishers. Some materials from ChemCom and Conceptual Physics are used in the program. The greatest indicator of success is the 400% increase of middle ability students who now enroll in a full third year of science. Of the 300 integrated science students who took the course in 1991–92, only eight said they preferred lecture, note taking, and traditional multiple choice tests when compared with experiential and discovery learning. All students, except those identified as gifted and limited English proficient and some special education students, take at least four semesters of integrated science.

Over 40% of the course is hands-on, laboratory, and activity based. Students are given many open-ended problems to solve in cooperative teams, using their critical thinking skills, primary documents, and observations. Proper laboratory reports are required. Students are required to analyze, synthesize, and apply their learning through writing in journals. More and more assessment involves essay exams and practical application situations.

The school was one of the original 100 schools to receive a grant under the California State Department of Education for planning for integrated science. This course was evaluated by both the state and federal departments of education and has been approved for two years of laboratory science credit and one year of elective entrance credit for the University of California.

Anatomy and physiology is the most popular elective science course. The physical science technology course is team taught by a physical science and automotive teacher, stressing physical science concepts and their applications in technology. A new course, introduction to college prep science, combines life and physical science and replaces IPS physical science for gifted students. A Health Science Academy, for up to 100 at-risk students, operates as a school-within-a-school to prepare students for health occupations, with assistance from the local regional occupational program and business partners. All students in this program take six semesters of integrated science, plus a year of anatomy and physiology. The program is supported in part by an ongoing grant that was written by the principal.

Students in all science courses are engaged in finding answers to questions about the world around them and in making connections to their prior understandings through a combination of exploratory hands-on activities, inquiry-based laboratory activities, and constructionist teaching strategies.

The science program is language-based. Students read textbooks and primary documents for comprehension, evaluation, and application. They discuss and defend their positions in small and large groups. Students listen to teachers and fellow students for information and direction, and they write concept maps, journals, and laboratory analyses. Mathematics is used as appropriate in the collection and analysis of data and more extensively in formulas for chemistry and physics.

Teachers often bring into the classroom household items or everyday apparatus to demonstrate science concepts. Students are challenged to earn extra credit by searching for examples in their households to illustrate scientific phenomena. Food, clothing, and everyday articles are used to demonstrate scientific principles. Consumer choices are also analyzed as possible critical thinking exercises. Included in each course is a safety unit that must be passed before each student may participate with dangerous chemicals and equipment.

THE BEST SCHOOLS–ASSESSING WHAT STUDENTS KNOW AND CAN DO

As a means of assessing achievement in science, traditional standardized multiple choice science tests are rarely used in the Best Schools. These tests are considered invalid measures of the understandings, processes, and attitudes that are the heart of the science curriculum in these schools. In place of standardized tests the schools are developing more performance-based assessments using oral and written reports, open-ended and essay tests, projects, experiments, and observations of the processes used to determine progress of students. Individual writing and oral presentations of findings, teacher- or district-made tests, portfolios reflecting work over time, and products of cooperative groups are some of the means used. In some states, such as Texas, performance-based science testing has been introduced as part of statewide assessment.

Assessment Illustrations

E. O. GREEN SCHOOL, CA

Assessment at Green is embedded in all activities. Data, observations, conclusions, and reflections are included in laboratory notebooks. Portfolios provide dynamic evidence of student growth and are used in all core subjects. At the end of each marking period, students select three of their best works (research paper, cooperative project, exam, lab report, etc.) for their portfolio and write a reflection piece on their selections. Students meet with their teacher to discuss their growth and their selections. Portfolios are then used in meeting with parents and forwarded to the high school at the end of eighth grade. Performance-based assessment strategies that align with the California science framework and the California assessment program are being piloted. In 1992, 90% of the student body was achieving at or above a "C" average.

In addition to individual assessment, evaluations are conducted in each department to review goals and assess alignment with schoolwide curricular goals using the California program quality review state criteria guidelines for schoolwide and curricular areas. Annual recommendations from this assessment are monitored for progress and/or completion. Recommendations are made for curricular change, staff development, and/or innovations in program delivery. Examples of programs developed through this process are Science Union Math, interdisciplinary math/science, and distance telecommunications.

A school effectiveness survey administered annually permits parents, staff, and students to provide their perceptions on fourteen key indicators.

JACKSON HOLE HIGH SCHOOL, CA

No science program can be exemplary without a variety of methods to assess student progress and an introspective spirit toward self-evaluation and improvement. Jackson's science department's philosophy towards student assessment strives to check for the demonstration of true learning. Assessment strategies include course proficiency, aligned criterion-referenced tests, quizzes, written assignments, research papers, portfolios, individual and group projects, and presentations. Staff believe that an accurate assessment of student achievement is important; however, they also recognize that student achievement in the sciences is largely determined by the quality of the science program. For example, prior to the introduction of integrated science, there was a very high rate of ninth-grade failure in science; now the rate of failure is well below 10%, and students have an increased interest in science and have developed much higher levels of scientific understanding. The average score on the advanced placement science examinations in 1992 (on a five-point scale) was 3.76, compared to a national average of 2.95. On all nationally and state-normed tests, the students consistently average higher than state and national norms in the area of science.

The school uses both internal and external resources to provide regular evaluation of the science program. Within the department, an ongoing dialogue is carried on concerning effectiveness. The school improvement team meets a minimum of once a month to assess various aspects of the school program. Standardized assessment data is shared with the entire staff through the school improvement team. Criterion-referenced course assessments are shared within departments. Recently, the district completed a two-year formal evaluation of the science program districtwide. Based on the findings of the study, current research, shared experiences, and ideas, programs and practices are routinely adjusted, changed, or fine-tuned. For example, based on recent findings, general biology and physical science courses have been dropped, and integrated science, life science, AP biology, AP physics, and AP chemistry were added. In addition to local means of evaluation, the school also looks to statewide and national standards of achievement and evaluation.

WESTMINSTER HIGH SCHOOL, CA

Assessment at Westminster is embedded and performance-based. Teachers assemble portfolios that involve student projects, models, videotapes, audiotapes, and research papers. The goal throughout the department is for at least 40% of class time to be activity-based with hands-on learning. Students are required to analyze, synthesize, and apply their learning through writing journals, which are tools to assist students in achieving higher levels of thinking as they complete their laboratories and predictions and discuss content and observations. Students are also asked to reflect upon their experience through classroom questioning and discussion, making concept maps and metacognitive activities.

THE BEST SCHOOLS – PROGRAM AND DEVELOPMENT SUPPORT IN SCIENCE

Program development is a continuous process in the Best Schools. In the area of science, many of the programs have roots going back to hands-on approaches and environmental studies initiated in the 1960s. However, the programs in use in the schools today reflect a commitment to developing high levels of scientific understanding for all students, the growth in knowledge of how students learn, use of advanced technology, and greater focus on standards of student performance.

Integration of science content with, for example, writing across the curriculum has been facilitated by the change in the English programs that focus on reading, writing, and speaking for multiple purposes. Reading, writing, and speaking are recognized as essential parts of the science program. Also, the expanding view of mathematics as more than arithmetic has facilitated the integration of math and science. Recognition of the need for students to understand the role science has played in history and the impact of science on the modern world has led to greater integration of social studies and science. The congruence of views on how students best learn across all content areas; the work to establish meaningful standards for achievement at the national, state, and, in the Best Schools, at the local level; a well-entrenched ''habit'' in the Best Schools of continually assessing programs and developing curriculum; and interest in and, in many cases, participation in university, state, or nationally developed initiatives and networks aimed at improving instruction are among the reasons for development of their current science programs. The Best Schools also reach out to form partnerships with universities and businesses that have provided important support in the development and implementation of science programs.

Program Development Illustrations

E. O. GREEN SCHOOL, CA

The vision of an integrated curriculum at E. O. Green was developed five years ago when the principal joined the staff. The staff is committed to continuous learning and improvement. Curriculum emphasis was initially placed on research skills and writing in the language arts program. As teachers were trained, they then trained other teachers to incorporate writing across the curriculum. Three years ago, work was begun on the science curriculum framework; interdisciplinary themes were developed and continue to be developed. The existing technology was harnessed throughout the years and new technology and programs were introduced. Each year, the staff evaluates the program and sets new objectives; there is continuous staff and curriculum development. There is ongoing staff research and outreach to identify effective programs and instructional strategies. Vacancies on the staff have been filled with teachers who have content knowledge and strong commitment to and expertise in working with student-centered, integrated curriculum and technology.

JACKSON HOLE HIGH SCHOOL, WY

The science program at Jackson Hole has been developing for many years. The current program, with its focus on integration, traces its roots back seven years to the integration of computers into chemistry and physics. The increased interest on the part of students in science, as a result of the technology, such as staying late to get more accurate results in labs, led the staff to seek new approaches for other courses. The high failure rate of ninth grade students, the limited interest in science of middle ability students, and recognition of the need for all students to achieve high levels of mastery in science led the staff to totally rethink the science curriculum four years ago. The result was the development of the six-semester integrated science course, as well as greater integration of content within all other department courses. The use of technology has expanded over the years. Advances in technology, assessment and refinement of curriculum, availability of new materials and software, desire to motivate all students, and efforts to make assessment more authentic and mastery-centered ensure an unending emphasis on program development.

WESTMINSTER HIGH SCHOOL, CA

Program development at Westminster is a continuous activity based on student needs and program assessment. In 1989, Westminster teachers analyzed the number of failures in the entry-level science courses. They looked for a better and more meaningful way to bring science to all students, not just those in the honors level. Various research and inservice activities, including the 1989 paper ''Essential Changes in Secondary School Science'' by Bill Aldridge in the February/March issue of *Science Teacher; Science for All Americans* (Project 2061), published by the American Association for the Advancement of Science; and the work of Marge Gardner led to the department's decision to develop a three-year team-taught integrated science program, combing physical, life, and earth sciences by themes. With the new course, the failure rate is now well below 10%. In another case, concern over the number of students whom teachers saw each day, the inability to cover subjects in depth in a short period of time, and increasing use of hands-on activities across the curriculum led to review of the school schedule. The result was the block-schedule, which was implemented after extensive off-campus school visitations and a teacher and student voting process that determined the best use of instructional time and a reduction of the ratio of pupils to teachers on block-schedule days.

In 1994–95, Westminster High School will become a magnet math/science/technology school under the California schools of choice initiative. The goal is to maintain all current students and attract an additional 100–700 students. Among changes in the program will be the further integration of technology in science and mathematics and the implementation of integrated mathematics.

Illustrations of Links with Other Agencies and Schools

E. O. GREEN SCHOOL, CA

Three adjectives describe the collaboration between E. O. Green and other educational and community organizations: meaningful, effective, and diverse. Whether across the street or across the nation, "working effectively with others" empowers the school to increase student success. For example: curriculum alignment and articulation with feeder and high schools are ensured through monthly meetings; service clubs support activities; two E. O. Green teachers serve on the state of California Math and Science Framework Committees; and motivational programs are sponsored by the University of California at Santa Barbara Outreach, Oxnard College Min-Corps, Indian Education Consortium, and Work Opportunity.

JACKSON HOLE HIGH SCHOOL, WY

The district is one of fifteen in the state of Wyoming that has joined the Wyoming School-University Partnership. The partnership was selected by John Goodlad (National Center for Educational Renewal) as a site for inclusion in his work to model the best practices in teacher education and the renewal of public schools. Eleven staff members have been involved in the leadership team to 1) restructure teacher education training at the University of Wyoming; 2) restructure administrative leadership training at the University of Wyoming; and 3) infuse the newest technology into school settings, including interactive video.

The school is linked as a partner with Sweetwater School District in Green River in order to collaborate on the development of "teaching and learning centers" within the school districts. The purpose of the teaching and learning centers is to promote innovative educational opportunities within each district.

WESTMINSTER HIGH SCHOOL, CA

The school is affiliated with the California Science Project and articulates and demonstrates at feeder schools, the California Science Implementation network, and the Orange County Science Education network. Most teachers belong to state and national groups such as the National Science Teacher's Association regional planning committee; the Science Laboratory Specialist Committee Action Research for Scope, Sequence; and Coordination Instructional Television and the Scope, Sequence and Coordination Assessment Committee. Several teachers teach at the university level, provide inservice to professional groups, and demonstrate lessons at feeder schools.

THE BEST SCHOOLS–MATERIALS

The Best Schools have science laboratories within the school but also use areas outside the school for study. The Best Schools provide students with the "tools" of science, such as measuring devices, stereo microscopes, electronic meters, still and video cameras, calculators, and computers. Some schools maintain animals, garden plots, and natural areas for study. Many others take full advantage of the existing environment of the community and nearby areas.

Science in the Best Schools is primarily based on thematic units with many hands-on activities. Most of the schools use a variety of university, foundation, commercial, and locally developed units, which focus on development of indepth understanding of limited topics. They may include written material for each student, problems and investigations, field experiments and observations, visuals, computer software, and multi-media. Textbooks, if purchased at all, are usually used mainly for reference.

Material Illustrations

E. O. GREEN SCHOOL, CA

A great deal of technology is available at E. O. Green to support the curriculum. Four servers, networked through a Tokin Ring, connect all but a few computers in the school, allowing teachers and students to access a wide variety of software. All classrooms are equipped with TV, and, through cable and satellite dish, connect to outside programming and in-school television transmission. The interdisciplinary approach to curriculum allows for maximum use of technology. For example, the eleven language arts classrooms and the special education resource room each have eight computers that can be used for accessing data bases, word processing programs, and the total software inventory of the school.

Specifically in the area of science, the eighth-grade students use the Smart Classroom developed in conjunction with WYCAT in 1987. The room is equipped with thirty-two student computers. The teacher station is equipped with a lab table, computer, projection screen, cable TV, satellite dish connection, a bank of Smart laser disc players, and CD-ROM. From the teacher station, there is individual control of each student station. For example, one student could be watching a program from the satellite dish, another typing a report using Word Perfect, a third student taking a test, and the rest working with various Edunetics science programs from EduQuest. About 50% of student science time is spent in the "wet lab." This is a traditional science lab, except for the addition of two student-use computers, a teacher station equipped with computer and projection device, and cable TV.

Approximately 150 seventh- and eighth-grade students elect to take a half year physics-based course called Tech Lab 2000. This course is taught by the Technology 2000 lab teacher in a special lab developed by Creative Systems in San Diego. Technology Lab 2000 is equipped with multi-media learning stations, including twenty computers.

Seventh-grade science is taught in two science rooms. One room, in which the program centers around oceanography, is equipped with eight computers and a computerized teacher station. The other classroom, which has the interdisciplinary math/science program, has a teacher station equipped with a computer and projection device, which allows access to all school software. In addition, the NTN science computer in the room is connected to eight student key pads. This equipment allows for eight students to respond simultaneously to questions projected on the central screen and records their responses on pads connected to the computer.

The five sixth-grade classrooms use the Eduquest System 40, and there are four networked computers in each room. In addition to Eduquest, Children's Writing Workshop, and Microsoft Works software, students can access any other software in the school. The classrooms also have access to four CD-ROM data bases. Each teacher station is equipped with a computer, VCR, CD-ROM, and monitor/TV.

Students also have telecommunication access to the University of California data systems and to Internet to access programs such as KidsNet.

JACKSON HOLE HIGH SCHOOL, WY

Technology resources include twelve IBM compatible computers on carts and server drop cords in each science room; these allow teachers to convert regular science labs and classrooms for technology use. The triple room computer lab adjacent to the library includes twenty-three IBM compatible computers and twenty-nine Macintoshes. Twenty-two IBM compatible 486 computers, linked using Windows for Workgroups, equipped with sound cards and video digitizing boards, along with scanners and equipment for making CD-ROMs, are used primarily for students for developing multi-media science presentations. Integrated science classes are regularly involved in projects in this room. In addition, a MAC Centrex on a rolling cart can be brought into any science classroom to develop multi-media productions. In 1992–93, the school produced a multi-media program for the U.S. Forest Service. The library has CD-ROMs for periodical research and computer modem connection to the University of Wyoming library for additional research capability. Computers are frequently used to collect and analyze data.

Many of the courses at Jackson Hole are based almost entirely on teacher-developed units, with primary documents, textbooks, and software used as resources. For example, the physics course uses a lab manual written for the course by the teacher and refined over many years. Another example is the integrated science course, which utilizes theme units developed by the staff. Moreover, the principles of technology course uses the CORD (Center for Occupational Research Design) curriculum and materials.

All physics labs include some aspect of computer use–whether it is collecting data or analyzing data collected manually. These experiments have proven popular, and physics enrollment is now approaching 50% of graduates. Software used includes Chap II, Excel 5.0, and Labpartner. Integrated science students create multi-media presentations using Asymmetrix Compel and Toolbook. These include video, still images, and sound. The final program is then recorded onto a CD-ROM at the school and used for display in the local visitors' centers. Interactive programs utilizing laser discs are also created by some of the advanced classes. Currently, the advanced students are working on interactive tutorials for experimental techniques and a computer simulation of qualitative analysis labs in advanced chemistry. Software for data processing, graphing, and word processing is available in all labs and classrooms.

THE BEST SCHOOLS–STAFF DEVELOPMENT

Staff development is of major importance in the development and implementation of science programs. Effective science programs cannot be implemented by purchasing a textbook and holding a half-day orientation on the use of the teacher's edition. The types of hands-on programs that focus on indepth understanding of science concepts require extensive staff development if the staff is to implement these programs effectively. The Best Schools recognize this need. Professional contracts frequently provide for eight or more days of staff development each year; in addition, provisions are made for time and support for planning, assessment analysis, and curriculum development.

Staff development is accomplished through in-house programs and courses, as well as through state and regional training programs, summer institutes, and university courses. Partnerships can also be a source of staff development, for example, the California Science Project through ULCA-Urbine, the Indian Education Consortium, and the Wyoming School-University Partnership. Programs disseminated through the National Diffusion Network, such as FAST (Foundations Approach to Teaching Science), provide and require training of staff for schools adopting their programs. The AIMS Foundation also provides training for staff either at the school site or in regional training sessions. Curriculum development in itself is a powerful part of the staff development process.

Staff Development Illustrations

E. O. GREEN SCHOOL, CA

Good schools produce lifelong learners, and teachers should be models of that concept. When students see their teachers involved in class work and workshops, they understand their school experience is part of a larger life pattern and not just hours clocked at a desk.

Each year, following the identification of goals and priorities, staff development plans at E. O. Green are implemented. Many activities take place on-site as part of the school improvement program during eight student-free days each year set aside for staff development. Other staff development takes place through classes and workshops off campus.

The school district has provided technology, training, and support for science teachers. Teachers are encouraged to continue their professional development. They have participated in training in Tech Lab 2000 Systems, technology and interactive television, science framework, mastery teaching, teacher expectations and student achievement (TESA), and portfolio assessment. In addition, they have participated in the California Science Project Advisory Board, South Coast Science Project, California Science Teacher Association, Tri-County Math Project, Edunetics Interactive Technology Conference, and Great Expectations in Math and Science (GEMS).

Many programs and materials are used in conjunction with the school developed themes. Among these are KidsNet, AIMS (Activities that Integrate Math and Science), and NASA Marsville Mission. Classroom sets of textbooks are available; however, the program is not textbook-based.

JACKSON HOLE HIGH SCHOOL, WY

A strategic planning process at Jackson Hole resulted in definition of goals and priorities. A staff development needs assessment was developed and correlated to the goals and priorities. Staff development opportunities are based upon the needs identified from an annual survey and are provided during evenings, weekend seminars, and summer courses. Two days are provided within the school calendar for staff development. In addition, four "floating days" are included within the professional contract. Staff are committed to using these floating days for participation in evening, weekend, and/or summer staff development.

One school strategy for staff development is to encourage teacher-led pilot programs of new ideas, techniques, and programs. For example, two teachers are piloting an A, B, C, Incomplete grading system to encourage students toward greater mastery; another team is piloting an integrated studies class with an interdisciplinary goal. Each pilot teacher reports quarterly to the staff and provides inservice to those teachers interested in implementing their programs. In addition, the staff who have been trained in various instructional techniques (TESA, cooperative learning, assessment, applications of computers in science, etc.,) provide formal class opportunities for other staff to be trained.

Teachers are encouraged to attend conferences and seminars. Recent involvement has included state-level meetings on alternative assessment, a conference on the integration of the newest technology into curriculum, advanced placement class workshops, Wyoming Science Teachers' Association meetings, and school visitations. One of the science teachers was awarded the IBM Teacher of the Year in Wyoming for his innovative use of computers in the science lab and was also awarded a $20,000 grant in 1991–92 from the Fletcher Jones Foundation for the same reason (Jackson Hole High School was the only high school in the nation to be awarded a grant from this foundation).

WESTMINSTER HIGH SCHOOL, CA

Teachers in the science department are involved in professional activities and are models of lifelong learning. Three teachers are involved in state-level training in test construction, several attended Project Physical Science at Lawrence Hall of Science, and one is a project writer.

The district provides for eight staff development days within the school calendar. Summer, after school, and release time provide for additional staff development opportunities. Funding for some of these activities comes from the Eisenhower Grant. Many staff development activities are provided through the five district collaborative inservice programs (the high school district and four elementary feeder districts). Teachers involved in the California science project through UCLA-Urbine meet monthly with feeder, as well as other, schools in the network. Mathematics teachers, through project C Cubed, are developing integrated mathematics courses.

THE BEST SCHOOLS–FUNDING DEVELOPMENT

The major cost for all instruction, including science, is for staff. In comparison, costs for equipment, field trips, materials, supplies, and staff training are small; however, the Best Schools invest in the tools of science and in staff and curriculum development. Many of the tools of science used in science, such as hand lenses and calculators, are inexpensive, while computers, software, physics interfaces, CD-ROMs, and laser discs can be costly. The Best Schools, while varying greatly in terms of financial resources, have made a commitment to provide the modern tools of science for all students.

Effective staff and curriculum development requires time. The Best Schools invest heavily in development. Inservice training is provided through scheduled inservice days (frequently eight or more each year), summer and after-school workshops, college courses, and special training programs associated with adopted curriculum. Release time is provided to staff to observe instruction within the school and district and in other districts. A number of states have requirements for continuing education, thus facilitating professional development. Costs for inservice training usually involve the costs for substitutes for release time, travel to training sessions, summer workshop pay, inservice credits that may affect movement on salary guides, workshop fees, and, in some cases, consultants. Many schools use their funds from the Education for Economic Security Dwight D. Eisenhower Mathematics and Science Education Act for inservice. Schools that have hired a science specialist have added to the overall cost of the science program. While there are some costs associated with much of staff and curriculum development, the staffs of the Best Schools also characteristically involve themselves in a wide range of professional activities.

Field trips are another expense associated with the science program. In some cases, these may be trips to local areas for a few hours, to museums and science centers for the day, or overnight trips for indepth study. Some schools pay for these trips as part of the school budget, while some are supported by PTAs or PTOs, other fund raisers, or partnerships; in other cases, parents pay for the field experiences. Students whose parents cannot afford the expense are subsidized by district or donated funds. The Best Schools, because of their commitment to staff and program development, have managed to find the resources for development, regardless of their economic status.

Funding Illustrations

E. O. GREEN SCHOOL, CA

The Hueneme Elementary School District has a reputation as being frugal. However, eight years ago when state lottery money and federal 874 Military Installation funding became available, the district made a commitment not to use these funds for basic school ongoing expenses. The acquisition of technology became a district priority. As a result, E. O. Green has had a budget for technology of approximately $100,000 per year.

Staff development is supported through eight or more inservice days built into the school calendar and based on school objectives. In addition, the school allocates funds from its school improvement program budget for stipends for summer curriculum development and training. The SIP budget for the school is based on $28 per seventh- and eighth-grade student.

Other program support comes from the regular school budget, which is comparable to other school budgets in the area.

WESTMINSTER HIGH SCHOOL, CA

Eight days of staff development time are provided within the school calendar at Westminster.

Grants and district funds provide for substitutes for release time and for summer and after-school workshop stipends.

A planning grant under the Specialized Secondary Schools Program, for $32,000, was received for development of the new magnet program. A $100,000 science grant based on the plan provides support for implementation.

SUMMARY

Science programs in the Best Schools have many of the characteristics of instruction advocated for development of scientific literacy goals for the 21st century. Instruction is based on a constructionist's view of how students learn. Curriculum has been developed based on the recognition that "less is more," that it is more important for students to gain indepth understanding of concepts, the methods of science, and scientific "habits of mind" than to cover large quantities of surface information about science. Two- or three-year integrated science programs, heterogeneously grouped, are replacing introductory discreet discipline courses such as earth science, biology, chemistry, and physics for all students. New forms of performance-based assessment are being utilized. The Best Schools, urban, suburban, and rural, have developed their programs over time and have a commitment to continuous development. Extensive staff development is characteristic of the Best Schools. Underlying all their efforts and programs is the commitment that science is for all students and that all students can achieve high levels of scientific literacy.

REFERENCES

Ahlgren, Andrew and F. James Rutherford. (1993). "Where Is Project 2061 Today?" *Educational Leadership*, 50(8).

AIMS Education Foundation. (1989). "Project AIMS Update," Fresno, CA.

American Association for the Advancement of Science, Project 2061. (1993). *Benchmarks for Science Literacy.* New York, NY: Oxford University Press.

Association for Supervision and Curriculum Development. (1989). *Toward the Thinking Curriculum: Current Cognitive Research,* L. B. Resnick and L. E. Klopher, eds., Alexandria, VA: ASCD.

Association for Supervision and Curriculum Development. (1992). *ASCD Curriculum Handbook: A Resource for Curriculum Administrators.* Alexandria, VA: ASCD.

Bennett, William J. (1986). *First Lessons: A Report on Elementary Education in America.* Washington, D.C.: U.S. Government Printing Office.

Bennett, William J. (1988). *James Madison Elementary School.* Washington, D.C., U.S. Government Printing Office.

California State Department of Education. (1990). *Science Framework for California Public Schools Kindergarten through Grade Twelve.* Sacramento, CA. State Department of Education.

Educational Testing Service, Center for the Assessment of Educational Progress. (1991). *The 1991 IAEP Assessment: Objectives for Mathematics, Science, and Geography.* Princeton, NJ: Educational Testing Service.

Fort, Deborah. (1993). "Science Shy, Science Savvy, Science Smart," *Kappan*, 74(9).

Jones, Lee R., et al. (1992). *The 1990 Science Report Card: NAEP's Assessment of Fourth, Eighth, and Twelfth Graders.* Washington, D.C.: U.S. Department of Education, National Center for Educational Statistics.

LaPointe, Archie E. (1992). *Learning Science.* Princeton, NJ: Educational Testing Service, Center for the Assessment of Educational Progress.

Loucks-Horsley, Susan, et al. (1990). *Elementary School Science for the '90s.* Alexandria, VA: Association for Supervision and Curriculum Development.

National Assessment of Educational Progress (NAEP). (1987). *Learning by Doing: A Manual for Teaching and Assessing Higher-Order Thinking in Science and Mathematics.* Princeton, NJ: Educational Testing Service.

National Assessment of Educational Progress (NAEP). (1990). *America's Challenge: Accelerating Academic Achievement.* Princeton NJ: Educational Testing Service.

National Assessment of Educational Progress. (1994). *NAEP 1992 Trends in Academic Progress.* Washington, D.C.: Educational Testing Service with the National Center for Educational Statistics, U.S. Department of Education.

National Committee on Science Education Standards and Assessment. (1993). *National Science Educational Standards: July '93 Progress Report.* Washington, D.C.: National Research Council.

National Goals Panel. (1993). *The National Education Goals Report: Building a Nation of Learners, Volume One: The National Report 1993.* Washington, D.C.: U.S. Government Printing Office.

Oakes, J., et al. (1990). "Multiplying Inequalities: The Effects of Race, Social Class, and Tracking on Opportunities to Learn Mathematics and Science," Report No. R-3928-NSF, Rand Co., Santa Monica, CA.

Rutherford, F. James and Andrew Ahlgren. (1990). *Science for All Americans.* New York, NY: Oxford University Press.

U.S. Department of Education. (1991). *America 2000: An Educational Strategy.* Washington, D.C.: U.S. Department of Education.

CHAPTER 10

The Arts

IN 1988, the National Endowment for the Arts reported that schools were giving increasing attention to the arts as an essential and valued part of the academic curriculum, with as many teachers of the arts employed by districts as science teachers. In 1993, a survey of principals of the nationally recognized Blue Ribbon Schools listed visual and performing arts initiatives as among their curriculum priorities. This chapter looks at the following questions concerning the role of the arts in preparing children for the 21st century:

- What does theory say about what students should learn and how they should be taught the arts?
- How have the Best Schools successfully translated theory into practice in the arts?
- How do the Best Schools assess what students know and what they can do?
- How have effective programs been developed and implemented; what were the resources needed for development and support?

WHAT STUDENTS SHOULD LEARN

To some who remember their school art experiences as little more than perspective drawing and an annual choral concert, the arts seem like the last arena of the curriculum that would be able to define what students should know and be able to do in measurable terms; however, this is not the case. The arts are specifically included among the academic subjects in the National Goals as amended by Congress in 1994 as part of the Goals 2000: Educate America Act:

> By the year 2000, American students will leave grades four, eight and twelve having demonstrated competence in challenging subject matter including . . . arts. . . .

The Consortium of National Arts Education Association was charged with defining "what every young American should know and be able to do in the arts." They saw no contradiction between the arts as a creative individual process and the desirability of defining what should be the outcomes of arts education in grades K–12. The task force published the *National Standards for Arts Education* in the spring of 1994.

Art in the National Standards Project means creative works and the processes of production, as well as the whole body of artworks that make up intellectual and cultural heritage. The art disciplines include dance, music, theater, and the visual arts. Within each discipline, the standards are organized based on three learning tasks:

- creating and performing
- perceiving and analyzing
- understanding cultural and historical contexts

While the standards recognize the importance of maintaining the integrity of each discipline, the importance of making connections among the disciplines has also been recognized by the task force.

Essentially, the standards ask that students should know and be able to do the following by the time they have completed secondary school (Consortium of National Arts Education Association, 1994):

- They should be able to communicate in the four arts disciplines (dance, music, theater, and visual arts). This includes knowledge and skills in the use of the basic vocabulary, materials, tools, techniques, and the intellectual methods of each arts discipline.
- They should be able to communicate proficiently in at least one art form, including the ability to define and solve artistic problems with insight, reason, and technical proficiency.
- They should be able to develop and present basic analyses of works of art from structural, historical, and cultural perspectives, and from multiples of those perspectives. This includes the ability to understand and evaluate work in the various arts disciplines.
- They should have an informal acquaintance with exemplary works of art from a variety of world cultures and historical periods and a basic understanding of historical development in the arts disciplines, across the arts as a whole, and within cultures.
- They should be able to relate various types of arts knowledge and skills within and across the arts disciplines. This includes mixing and matching competencies and understandings in art making, history and culture, and analysis in any arts-related project.

Specific curriculum and achievement standards provide guidelines within each discipline for grades K–4, 5–8, and 9–12. At the secondary level, standards have been developed at the "proficient" and "advanced" achievement levels. The proficient level is intended for students who have completed courses in that discipline for one to two years beyond grade 8. The advanced is intended for students who have completed three to four years of study beyond the eighth grade. Following are examples from the *National Standards for Arts* Education (Consortium of National Arts Education Association, 1994):

Theatre Grades 5–8

Content Standard:

Researching by using cultural and historical information to support improvised and scripted scenes

Achievement Standard:

(a) apply research from print and nonprint sources to script writing, acting, design, and directing choices

Visual Arts Grades 5–8

Content Standard:

Choosing and evaluating a range of subject matter, symbols, and ideas

Achievement Standard:

(a) integrate visual, spatial, and temporal concepts with content to communicate intended meaning in their artwork
(b) use subjects, themes, and symbols that demonstrate knowledge of contexts, values, and aesthetics that communicate intended meaning in artworks

Music Grades 9–12

7. Content Standard:

Evaluating music and music performances

Achievement Standard, Proficient:

(a) evolve specific criteria for making informed, critical evaluations of the quality and effectiveness of performances, compositions, arrangements, and improvisation and apply the criteria in the personal participation in music
(b) evaluate a performance, composition, arrangement, or improvisation by comparing it to similar or exemplary models

Achievement Standard, Advanced:

(c) evaluate a given musical work in terms of its aesthetic qualities and explain the musical means it uses to evoke feeling and emotions

Dance Grades 9–12

3. Content Standard:

Understanding dance as a way to create and communicate meaning

Achievement Standard, Proficient:

(a) formulate and answer questions about how movement choices communicate abstract ideas in dance
(b) demonstrate understanding of how personal experience influences the interpretation of a dance
(c) create a dance that effectively communicates a contemporary social theme

Achievement Standard, Advanced:

(d) examine ways that a dance creates and conveys meaning by considering the dance from a variety of perspectives
(e) compare and contrast how meaning is communicated in two of their own choreographic works

The project recognizes that there are many paths to development of the envisioned competencies in each of the arts disciplines. The standards do not represent a national curriculum; rather, they provide the standards for curriculum development and establish the expected outcomes of arts instruction for all students.

HOW STUDENTS LEARN–HOW STUDENTS ARE TAUGHT

The shift in emphasis in the other academic disciplines away from rote memorization and discreet sequential learning of basic skills toward a curriculum focused on the development of thinking skills, connections, reflection, and the construction of knowledge has also impacted on instruction in the arts. First, the retreat in other areas from repetitive drill and practice of multitudes of "basic skills" has increased the time available to the arts in many schools. Second, the restructuring of other academic areas has facilitated integration of subject matter, especially of the arts. Third, the methodologies currently advocated, based on research on learning in other subject areas, are congruent with those of effective instruction in the arts.

In order to accomplish the objectives of arts education, it is essential that students be actively involved in a comprehensive, sequential, and articulated curriculum from year to year. Less comprehensive approaches may result in skill development in specific areas and even exceptional performances; however, without an encompassing articulated framework, these remain only pieces and parts, with little potential for all students to meet the objectives of arts education.

The National Endowment for the Arts (1988) in a report to the President and to Congress, described the characteristics of a desired school program for the arts:

- is comprehensive across all grades for all students and defines the curriculum content in the arts that all students, not just the gifted and talented or college-bound, should have, particularly in terms of the knowledge and skills, concepts and principles necessary to be knowledgeable and appreciative of the arts
- encompasses, over the course of thirteen years of schooling, all of the arts disciplines and assures students opportunities for the study of history and criticism of the arts in a sequential and structured curriculum, as well as the making, exhibiting, and performing of art
- interrelates components of various art forms where appropriate, while providing for interdisciplinary learning across non-arts subject areas where relevant
- utilizes, as part of an integrated system of art education, specially trained arts teachers, supported by general elementary and teacher specialists in other areas who are well grounded in the arts, along with artists and scholars in residency programs and field trips to museums and performances
- provides for ongoing professional growth in the arts and humanities for all staff, including general teachers, arts specialists, administrators, superintendents, and board members
- assesses and measures students' achievement and program effectiveness
- takes place in school facilities that are compatible with program goals
- is supported by instructional and reference materials and supplies that are both appropriate and adequate in numbers
- uses media and modern technology both as a curriculum content and a process to learn about the arts.

In the past, the arts education program in most schools was focused almost entirely on production designed to encourage creativity. While students still produce art in schools, the importance of skill development has been established, and there is recognition that participation is not the same as education. In addition to art production, students should develop the ability to analyze and critically view the arts. The history of the arts and the relationship of the arts to culture and history are important parts of the arts curriculum. Discipline-based arts education (DBAE) is the approach that has been broadly disseminated and supported by the Getty Center for Arts Education and has impacted on art education in many schools. DBAE advocates development of a program in the arts, which engages students every year in the study of four disciplines: art history, criticism, production, and aesthetics.

HOW LEARNING SHOULD BE ASSESSED

The arts have a long history of the use performance and product-based assessment techniques, such as portfolio assessment in the visual arts and auditions in dance, music, and theater. These techniques are representative of the types of authentic assessments that other academic disciplines are seeking to develop. While the arts are experienced with individual assessment techniques, there have been few attempts to assess the outcomes of art instruction for large groups of students exposed to specific types of instruction, to assess outcomes across programs, or to determine the national levels of achievement of students in the arts. In most cases, the assessment of student achievement in the arts and evaluation of arts programs have been left to local school initiative.

The National Assessment of Educational Progress, however, is developing a framework for national assessment of the arts by 1996, which will coincide with the voluntary national standards. The project is jointly funded by the Getty Center for Education in the Arts and the National Endowment for the Arts.

THE BEST SCHOOLS—THEORY INTO PRACTICE IN THE ARTS

In 1989–90 and 1990–91, the Blue Ribbon Schools Program designated the arts as an area of special emphasis. While the excellence of the total school is the basis for recognition, forty-two schools received special recognition for exemplary programs in the arts. The reviewers found that the schools shared the following characteristics:

- a philosophy that holds that arts education is a basic and necessary component of a balanced educational program for pre-kindergarten through grade 12 students
- a broad understanding of arts curricula and pedagogy that is matched with the highest quality instructors available—arts specialists, artists/teachers, and highly trained classroom teachers
- a balance of art forms, including music, dance, drama, poetry, creative writing, and visual and media arts (Music, visual arts, and drama were offered most frequently, and poetry, creative writing, dance, and media arts, less frequently.)
- a realization that the arts need time, space, and financial and administrative support (Time spent in direct arts instructions ranged from two to seven hours per week. The ratio of arts teachers to students ranged from 1–80 to 1–250.)
- an understanding of the instructional power that comes from using the arts as part of an integrated approach to teaching (Every school infused the arts into other parts of the curriculum.)
- a commitment to *all* students that ensures access to instruction in the basic art areas and also provides for differentiated levels of instruction based on student motivation and talent
- parent involvement as volunteers, program designers, and fund raisers
- a strong and vital connection to the local arts community and an awareness that successful arts programs lead to wider community support for education in general

The Best Schools have evolved their programs in the arts over many years and are continuing to give priority to these areas of the curriculum. Changes in other academic subjects have resulted in increased recognition of the arts as a valuable part of a more integrated school curriculum. Programs have been developed to fit within the context of each community.

Illustrations in the Arts: The Context (Case Studies)

PINEDALE MIDDLE SCHOOL, PINEDALE, WY

Pinedale Middle School is located in Pinedale, Wyoming, a small rural community of just over 1000 in population. Historically, cattle ranching has been the heart and soul of the local economy. Recent years have seen oil and gas as major contributors to the community. However, 21% of the students qualify for free or reduced-price lunch.

The school serves the least populated county in the least populated state in the country. It is recognized that most students will not remain in this isolated rural setting; therefore, emphasis is placed not only on the quality of the education students receive while they are there, but also in preparing them to leave.

Kyle B. Walker, *Principal, Grades 6–8, 136 Students*

NEW TRIER TOWNSHIP HIGH SCHOOL, WINNETKA, IL

A ninety-year-old educational landmark on Chicago's North Shore, the ivy-covered, red-brick complex occupies a twenty-five-acre campus on Winnetka Avenue, near the shore of Lake Michigan. The school serves residents of five communities. In these tree-shaded suburbs, just twenty-five miles north of Chicago's Loop, stability and "quality of life" are paramount. Often, several generations of a single family have attended the school. Most residents of the communities hold college degrees, and most value quality education. The tradition of parent-school reciprocal accessibility keeps school programs responsive to community and student needs. The atmosphere is warm, respectful, competitive, and highly demanding.

The typical student is actively engaged in a strong college preparatory program. The average combined SAT score is 1043. Over 300 courses are offered in the eighteen departments, ranging from advanced placement to tutorial programs for slower learners. Typically, more than 96% of the graduates continue their formal education in 300 colleges and universities across forty-two states and a number of foreign countries.

At the heart of the school experience is the advisor (guidance) system, in place since 1922, ensuring that every student in school, for all four years, has an adult advocate on the faculty. The advisor is a person who knows his/her students and their families. Each advisor group, consisting of twenty students, serves as a base of support, friendship, solidarity, and continuity.

Dianna M. Lindsay, *Principal, Grades 9–12, 2711 Students*

H. B. PLANT HIGH SCHOOL, TAMPA, FL

Diversity, stability, transition, tradition, and innovation are appropriate descriptions of H. B. Plant High School. Plant High School was opened in 1927 and has operated continuously in the same building since. The school is in an older neighborhood. Many of the students come from advantaged families that heavily value education. Many of the neighborhoods have been through a cycle of decline and development, leaving a patchwork of gentrification side-by-side with working-class homes and Section Eight publicly subsidized housing.

The student body is representative of the city's population. In addition to many advantaged households, 23% of the families live below the poverty level. The neighborhood is racially integrated at all socioeconomic levels, but the majority of minority students come from public housing projects that teem with the problems of poverty, including single-parent households, teenage pregnancy, and a flourishing trade in illicit drugs. A number of students are living independently and providing their own support. The neighborhood also includes the most significant concentration of Jewish families in the city.

James P. Hamilton, *Principal, Grades 9–12, 1050 Students*

EAST ANCHORAGE HIGH SCHOOL, ANCHORAGE, AK

East Anchorage High School opened in 1962 and is the second oldest senior high school in Anchorage. The school is regarded as an "inner-city" school in Anchorage. The school population reflects its varied socioeconomic, cultural, and ethnic community. There is a wide range of socioeconomic conditions, with many of the students coming from low socioeconomic homes. Slightly over 40% of the students are minority, including over 200 Alaskan Native and Eskimo students. The student body is a mixture of students from long-time community families and from highly mobile families. An average of about 300 students enroll and 400–500 students withdraw during each school year.

Rita J. Holthouse, *Principal, Grades 9–12, 1624 Students*

THE BEST SCHOOLS–CLASS ORGANIZATION AND INSTRUCTIONAL TIME

The National Endowment for the Arts recommends that, at the elementary and middle school levels, 15% of instructional time be devoted to the arts. Many of the Best Schools meet this criteria, and some exceed it. The arts in these schools are considered an integral part of the total educational process. Heterogeneous grouping has always been the rule in elementary art programs, as it has been accepted that instruction in the classroom can and should allow for differences in ability or talent. However, the arts have also recognized the need for individual and group study for those students who have special talent and/or interest in an art form. Especially in music, schools have provided for and encouraged choral and instrumental groups. The Best Schools also provide opportunities for all interested students to learn to play an instrument. Special opportunities are also provided in the Best Schools for students interested in art forms through electives and/or special projects and teaching artists.

Class Organization Illustrations

PINEDALE MIDDLE SCHOOL, WY

Pinedale Middle School employs specialists to teach the visual arts, drama, vocal music, and instrumental music. There is a written and sequential curriculum for the visual arts and the music programs. Vocal music and instrumental music meet for forty-one minutes every day for the entire year. Students may elect to take vocal or instrumental music. Sixth-grade students are required to take one or the other. One semester of visual arts is required of all middle school students each year. Classes are held daily for a forty-five-minute period. Drama is a quarterly elective for the seventh and eighth grades and part of the schedule for all sixth-grade students.

NEW TRIER TOWNSHIP HIGH SCHOOL, IL

The division of performing arts at New Trier is an interdepartmental organization of music, speech, drama, dance, and theater production. The unifying purpose of the division is to bring a rich, artistic program to students and the community based on a strong curricula foundation. The curriculum is sequential with approximately 2000 students involved. Seventeen fully accredited teachers are in the division. The majority of the faculty holds masters degrees. Two full-time technical directors/designers assist the division. Dance has a full-time accompanist. This year, the division will produce thirty dance concerts, music concerts, musical theater, and theater productions. Ninety-nine percent of the students involved in the productions will be enrolled in one or more curricula offerings. Classes in all departments meet for five forty-minute periods, with all arts courses treated equally and enthusiastically supported by the administrators, faculty, and support staff. Rehearsals for productions occur after school for two hours or more.

Physical facilities for all arts are superior. The well-equipped theaters include a 220-seat little theater, and a 1600-seat auditorium. An extensive scene shop, prop room, lighting room, two costume storage and construction rooms, a large make-up room, and four dressing rooms are available. The lighting board is an auto transformer; the little theater is a proscenium thrust with a computer light board. Other theater resources include an extensive library of plays, poetry and prose, video cameras, a fully equipped television studio with technical support, a radio classroom with broadcast facilities, and a fully equipped radio station. The dance facilities include a well-equipped dance studio, an office, and extensive storage space. The music wing is supplied with numerous practice spaces, a fully equipped recording studio, and large/small rooms for orchestras, bands, and choral programs.

H. B. PLANT HIGH SCHOOL, FL

Plant High School offers a unique and exemplary program in the visual and performing arts. Despite the relatively small size of the school and the large number of students taking intense academic loads, Plant has a complete performing arts program, with over 800 pupil periods scheduled in speech, drama, visual arts, dance, instrumental music, choral music, and humanities. Classes in the arts are organized and scheduled daily for fifty minutes. Students can and do schedule more than one class in the performing arts. Advanced placement credit is provided in art-drawing portfolio, art-general portfolio, and music theory. Six hours of college credits are available in dual-enrollment humanities courses.

The arts programs are a centerpiece of Plant High School. They provide hundreds of students an opportunity to develop an appreciation of the arts by participating in the wide variety of programs available. They enrich the lives of thousands of other students at Plant and the feeder schools and are a source of pride throughout the community.

EAST ANCHORAGE HIGH SCHOOL, AK

The fine arts program consists of 760 students enrolled in fine arts classes such as instrumental music (orchestras and bands), choral music, art, modern dance, and photography. The fine arts courses are taught by teachers who have received degrees in their areas and who, in some cases (band and art especially), are also performers. Wide use is made of community people and professional artists and dancers to enrich the lessons.

THE BEST SCHOOLS–THE ARTS CURRICULUM

The Best Schools have structured sequential curricula in the arts. Skill development, as well as creativity, is fostered across the grades in art production. Art history, criticism, and aesthetics education is embedded in the programs at each grade level. In addition to scheduled group art instruction, the arts are integrated into other areas of the school curriculum. Provision in the Best Schools is made for the development of individual talents and interests.

Curriculum Illustrations

PINEDALE MIDDLE SCHOOL, WY

The literary arts are important at Pinedale. The curriculum reflects the scope of writing, including poetry, stories, reports, letters, essays, etc. Pinedale publishes a school newspaper and utilizes the computer extensively in student writing. A portfolio containing samples of student writing is kept as a profile of each student's abilities and progress.

The school has a fully developed art room, complete with all necessary materials, allowing students to experience the different art forms such as pottery, enameling, drawing, painting, sculpture, origami, printmaking, and jewelry making. Not only do students receive instruction from the visual arts teachers, all classroom teachers schedule visual arts projects that integrate with other areas of their curriculum. The walls are alive with artwork produced in the classroom and art room.

Art history, criticism, and aesthetics are an integral part of the formal arts instruction. The history of composers from classical to contemporary is presented with the introduction of new selections. In drama, the study of the theatrical history from Shakespeare to Marcel Marceau and Emmett Kelly is incorporated. The art department hosts regular art shows, providing opportunities for students to analyze, interpret, and judge works of art from a number of artists using a wide variety of medias.

The drama and music students enjoy a new fine arts auditorium equipped with state-of-the-art sound and lighting systems, separate rooms for vocal and instrumental music, and individual practice and storage rooms. This facility itself demonstrates the commitment and value that the community places on the performing arts.

The music department schedules performances throughout the year to showcase students' abilities in music. Students go into the community to perform at senior citizen's centers or the retirement center or for special occasions. Many middle school-age students participate in the high school stage and marching bands. Concerts are scheduled throughout the year in conjunction with holidays, special occasions, inter-school festivals, and at the end of the year.

The middle school principal has an extensive background in music and drama and is very supportive of the arts in our school. In fact, he occasionally takes time out of his day to teach dancing to the entire middle school. He promoted the foundation of a "show choir." He allows students release time for music lessons and performances at community functions and encourages them to take advantage of every opportunity to use their talents.

NEW TRIER TOWNSHIP HIGH SCHOOL, IL

The performing arts division at New Trier strives to create in students an awareness and understanding of associate arts and to afford the community a broader and more complete program of performance. Thirty performances scheduled during the school year represent the process that is grounded in classroom instruction in dance, music, theater, and theater production. In each of the specific areas, the performances reflect the goals of instruction. In general, the goals can be seen in the variety of genre and style in the performances and in the increased complexity of material being performed. The theater curriculum is based on a written and sequential four-year program. Each year's sequence is defined by goals, objectives, and learning activities that develop an aesthetic awareness, an understanding of the basic relationships of the individual to the theater, and the relationship of theater to the world in which we live. Theater courses are offered in theater workshop, acting workshop, acting, advanced acting, performance studies, and stagecraft and lighting. The dance offerings include beginning dance, boys' dance, intermediate dance, advanced intermediate dance, advanced dance, and dance composition. The speech offerings include speech communication, radio workshop, radio practicum, television production, discussion and debate, debate, performance studies, and creative communications. Each course in the sequential curriculum is evaluated by the faculty every two years. In the past three years, this evaluation has resulted in adding a performance studies class, offering of playwriting on an independent study basis, adding theater history in the acting workshop curriculum, and adding a film unit in advanced acting. The dance faculty continually dialogues as they share course content ideas, observe classes and projects, and track students after they leave the program and continue to study in college. The ultimate evaluation of the arts program, however, is our high enrollment. In addition, our unique faculty merit evaluation plan encourages our faculty to be innovative, effective, and eager to assess their work.

The school takes advantage of the truly exceptional resources and opportunities Chicago has to offer to augment the curriculum. In addition to field trips, visiting artists, guest conductors, lecturers, and performers, the teachers are fully involved in the cultural scene in Chicago. The school's teachers are associated in leadership roles with the Northwestern University Schools of Education, Drama, Speech, Dance, and Art. A professional make-up artist and graduate students work with the division. Numerous professional troupes, dance companies, and actors appear in the classes and on the school's stages. Active participation in the Illinois Arts Council and the National Endowment for the Arts is encouraged by administrators. A special parents' association exists for the full support of the fine arts program.

THEATER

The complete performance repertoire is published annually in a professionally prepared calendar for subscribers and faculty. The theater performances include five plays, two musicals, an evening showcase of the advanced acting classes, and numerous directing projects. Theater productions consist of two Shakespeare productions that alternate between comedy, tragedy, contemporary, and classical literature and include a variety of themes. The autumn, winter, and spring theater productions are primarily geared toward sophomores, juniors, and seniors. The plays are selected as a challenge to the serious, committed, and experienced theater students. Auditions, however, are open to everyone. Two of the yearly productions, the freshman/sophomore play and the freshman/sophomore musical, are limited to freshmen and sophomores. The repertoire provides a variety of production styles, allowing the technical theater students to experience varying degrees of complexity.

Performance goals include:

- understanding the interrelationship of the actor, author, and audience in a theater performance
- valuing theater as a means of self-expression
- working with others in all areas of theatrical productions
- understanding technical theater
- exhibiting a functional understanding of the skills and techniques of reading, interpreting, and performing dramatic material

DANCE

Dance training for students is concerned with the art process and includes experience in technique, moving through space, improvisation, choreography, and performance. The desired outcome for our students, as a result of their hands-on experience with the creative process, is increased self-awareness, greater bodily articulation, the ability to communicate in a nonverbal manner, an understanding of the art process, and an appreciation for all performing arts. The primary concern has been the development of the creative, aesthetic self through a dance curriculum that is both comprehensive and sequential.

In addition to formal performances, a dance day is celebrated at our school. "Dance Day" involves students of all levels in an informal showing and sharing of choreography. The day provides an opportunity for many students who would otherwise not have the experience of performing on stage. The program occurs without special lighting or costumes. The day is a popular part of the program for both the performers, who number around 200, and the audience. Sometimes, there are 800 or 900 hundred students in the auditorium at any given period to see the work of their peers. "Dance Concert" is a major performance of the advanced and advanced/intermediate classes involving live music provided by the symphony orchestra, jazz ensemble, or wind ensemble. The concert is an outgrowth of the composition class, with all work presented choreographed and directed by students under the supervision of the dance faculty. Students choreograph, direct, design costumes and sets, and sometimes write their own music or sound scores. "Kinesis Dance Company" is a student company from the advanced dance class that collaborates to choreograph and present outreach programs in the community throughout the year. Students share directing and choreographing responsibilities, and rehearse a minimum of three afternoons a week.

Dance goals include

- understanding the body as an instrument of dance
- achieving enough technical skill to communicate ideas effectively through movement
- understanding the principles of art as they relate to compositional form
- making appropriate choices in the selection of music, lighting, and costumes for a compositional work
- evaluating the artistic merits of an aesthetic work

ART

The art department consists of seven full-time faculty members, of which six have masters degrees. All teachers are certified, practicing artists with exhibition experience. The faculty is active in regional, state, and national professional obligations. The art studios, classrooms, and student/community art gallery are attractive, well-lighted spaces with ample storage and display areas.

Philosophically, they believe that art knowledge is essential to a well-educated person's experiences. Art is offered to many students on a wide variety of levels. The introductory (prerequisite) courses are art and photography fundamentals. They also offer courses in drawing, painting, ceramics, sculpture, design, history of art, advanced photography, advanced studio art (AP Portfolio), and independent study. After the introductory art or photography fundamentals courses, students may take up to three years in sequence in a particular discipline, or elect to take advanced classes in several subjects, consecutively or concurrently. In the junior year, students may apply for the advanced studio art course (admission is based upon portfolio), which provides seniors in the department with a common setting for the preparation of a personal portfolio. The course is a keystone of the program, bringing together senior students from various disciplines, where they can learn and share together. For the majority of students, the portfolio is also submitted for the advanced placement studio art portfolio.

The advanced placement history of art class places great emphasis on history, criticism, and aesthetics with a modest amount of art production. The art fundamentals course has a much greater emphasis on the production of assignments and projects, which are then considered in light of the issues of history, criticism, and aesthetics. Through the selection of studio assignments, class discussions and critiques, reading assignments, field trips, and other activities, all of the disciplines become essential aspects of the art program.

To support the curriculum, an extensive school library collection exists. The collection includes art books, periodicals, on-line data bases and media resources, and slides. On campus, there is the Ann Brierly Memorial Gallery, managed by the art department, which is an excellent facility for showing the work of students and others in the community and for attracting outside exhibitions from the Illinois Arts Council, the Field Museum, and other cultural institutions.

H. B. PLANT HIGH SCHOOL, FL

All of the performing arts programs at Plant High School are based on written, sequential curricula. State and local curriculum frameworks and objectives and the curricula of the College Board's advanced placement courses determine the content of courses. The courses are taught by certified art educators. The music educators and the drama and speech educators are also appropriately trained and certified. Additionally, the art teachers are artists who have exhibited and sold their work. The music educators are performers in local vocal and instrumental groups. They also draw extensively upon the "Artists-in the Schools" program, which has provided artists to teach our students in visual arts, dance, and music.

ART

The visual arts include work in drawing, painting, sculpture, print-making, photography, computer graphics, and stained glass. Art productions use the widest variety of media, including graphite, watercolor, prisma pencil, pen and ink, stencil silk screen, photo silk screen, linoleum, batik, and collage. Sculpture is done in paper, clay, plaster, wire, aluminum, and wood. Photography includes composite imagery and manipulative techniques. Computer graphics utilize an IBM graphic computer, Hewlett-Packard ink jet printer, and Electronic Arts Deluxe Paint Enhanced Graphic Program.

Art history is integrated throughout the visual arts program. The textbook, *Discovering Art History;* "Art of the Western World" video series; "Art through the Ages" slide series; and the Reinhold Instructional Visual Posters are used. Visits to local museums include the Ringling

Museum, with an extensive collection of Titans, Reubens, and Baroque art; the Tampa Museum of Art; the St. Petersburg Museum of Art; and the Dali Museum.

Art criticism is ongoing. Students learn to evaluate their work and the work of others on a daily basis. They are required to critique their finished work, assessing creative merit based on the elements and principles of art. Students also evaluate works of known artists to judge their aesthetic worth and technical value.

The teaching of aesthetics is interwoven throughout the entire fine arts curriculum. The historical context of each medium is evaluated as to the aesthetic significance. Students are encouraged to judge the aesthetic value of their artwork based objectively on the compositional principles of design, rather than on subjective opinions. Students also critique works of both traditional and contemporary artists concerning their aesthetic qualities.

The community is a resource for the visual arts program. In addition to the museums cited earlier, teachers draw upon the University of South Florida, the Gasparilla Art Show, the Hyde Park Art Show, the Ybor Art Show, our speaker's bureau SERVE, Art in Public Places, and the University of Tampa. Contributions of materials have come from Palmer Paper, Fantastic Graphics, Schmidt Framers, Mona Lisa Art Supplies, and Computer Solutions.

Student work is extensively exhibited. Awards won include National Scholastic Art Exhibit—awarded Gold Key, and the drawing was exhibited in New York City; Best of Show—Hyde Park Art Show; Bar Association Law Day Creative Art Competition—six years; Empire State Bank Calendar Competition; Tampa Water Department Fire Hydrant Painting Contest—seven years; and the award-winning posters for Brotherhood and Sisterhood Week.

The art program is woven into the entire school. Student artists produce the covers for the student handbook and all of our program covers for our school ceremonies. Art students work with the drama department to produce the sets and backdrops for all of the theatrical productions.

The centerpiece for the art program has been an extensive arts-in-the-school program to produce works of art to adorn the school. A sixteen-month program raised $11,000 and produced four major and twenty smaller stained glass windows for our building. Fifty students worked with the practicing artists to produce these windows.

A second project spanned four months. A noted sculptor worked with 150 students to produce a life-size bronze statue of the school's namesake, H. B. Plant. The project was paid for with $9600 raised by the community art club, and the statue is displayed in the school lobby.

The latest project, spanning nineteen months and involving 250 students, utilized the services of Kirk Wang, a bronze medal winning artist from the People's Republic of China. The project produced eight statues of noted historical figures, including Ludwig van Beethoven, Susan B. Anthony, and Dr. Martin Luther King, Jr. These statues adorn the pilasters in the school auditorium. These projects, financed 100% from local sources, involved 450 students, 710 volunteer hours, spanned thirty-nine months, and received three and a quarter hours of television coverage and twenty-six newspaper articles.

The result has been numerous stunning works of art spread throughout the school. They have enhanced the building and the appreciation of art among all of the students and school patrons.

PERFORMING ARTS

The performing arts department includes an exemplary drama program. Students are instructed in five full classes of drama from introductory to advanced levels. The focus of the program is performance. Two major shows are produced each year. The fall show is a project of the third-year class and represents a straight theatrical production. Recent productions have included *Up the Down Staircase, All My Sons, Voices from the High School,* and *Flowers for Algernon.*

The spring production is a musical. Casting is drawn from schoolwide open auditions, and the competition is always intense. Recent productions include *The Wizard of Oz, The King and I, Grease,* and *The Sound of Music.* All of the productions are well attended, usually selling out each performance.

Additional productions are extensive. Classes produce forty- to fifty-minute excerpted productions. These productions are performed for students and other classes, giving wide visibility to the program throughout the school. The level of appreciation from the students in the audience is exceptional. Excerpted productions have included *Our Town, A Chorus Line, Barefoot in the Park,* and male and female versions of *The Odd Couple.*

The school is particularly proud of our children's theater productions. These programs are produced for the young children in the elementary feeder schools. They come to Plant for the productions, giving them both the experience of live theater and an early introduction to their high school. The students particularly enjoy these productions, which include *Cinderella, The Velveteen Rabbit, Alice in Wonderland,* and *Where the Sidewalk Ends.*

The thespian group participates in district and state competitions, with participation increasing every year. In 1989–90, twenty students competed at district and qualified for state competition. One of the students was cited as the top performer of the competition, as was the case in the previous year. Competition in the One-Act Competition has resulted in excellent and superior ratings.

Drama students at Plant have had the opportunity to work with several professional actors in the past five years. They have reviewed and critiqued these students at monologue workshops. The Tampa Arts Council has provided opportunities to work with professional set designers, costumers, and choreographers. Support has also been provided by the Plant Academic Foundation.

MUSIC

The music programs have also flourished and have experienced significant growth while the total school enrollment has declined. The repertoire includes works from the Renaissance, Baroque, Classical, and Romantic periods. Contemporary works include Neo-Classic, Neo-Romantic, Modern, and Avant-Garde pieces.

Instruction includes work in technique and music theory. In addition to performances for the school, the groups are in extensive demand throughout the community. They perform in concert at our elementary and junior high feeder schools. Two years ago, the choral music program performance, at the $100 per plate charity program to benefit H. B. Plant Museum, was sold out.

Both music groups compete at district and state festivals. They are judged for technical accuracy, tone, effort, intonation, interpretation, effect, and stage discipline and presence. Sight-reading criteria include technical accuracy, flexibility, interpretation, and musical effort.

EAST ANCHORAGE HIGH SCHOOL, AK

MUSIC

In the area of music, East High offers courses in music appreciation, symphonic band, concert band, stage band, keyboard, beginning/intermediate/advanced guitar, concert choir, swing choir, intermediate choir, concert orchestra, string techniques, chamber orchestra, music theory, and black music. Two of the music courses are cross-discipline (e.g., music theory is taught primarily on computers, and black music/black history is team-taught by the choral director and a social studies teacher). Students participate in four bands (symphonic, concert, stage, and pep), three choirs (swing, concert, and chamber), and two orchestras (concert and chamber). Eight evening concerts are scheduled for this year, in addition to eight music assemblies during the school day. Music students participate in five music festivals (All-State Honor Festival in Seattle, East Area Band Festival, and a school district music festival). Twenty-seven musicians from East High School qualified via audition tapes for the All-State Honor Music Festival, the most of any Alaskan School. Music groups frequently perform at all-school assemblies, graduation ceremonies, and during community tours prior to the winter holidays. The pep band plays at numerous athletic events and school assemblies throughout the school year. This fall, the symphonic band was contracted by the "Oprah Winfrey Show" to perform in a show segment that was filmed in Anchorage.

DANCE

East High is well known throughout the community and state for its unique modern dance program. The school offers five sections of modern dance courses open to all students, which is taught in a specially designed dance studio. One class features multicultural dances with a special unit on Eskimo dancing. During that unit, the students are taught several Eskimo dances by a local Eskimo elder who also teaches the students to make skin drums. East High has a performing group called Contempo that participates in numerous performances on auditions and is open to all students. Much emphasis is given to the students to choreograph their own or other students' dancing. Contempo produces a full-scale program each spring that is highly acclaimed throughout the community. In addition, the Contempo dancers perform in school plays, during schools and assemblies and music concerts, and for community groups and conventions. Each year, artists-in-residence work with the dance classes and with Contempo. Last year, dancers from India and Japan participated in the artists-in-residence program. This year, East High plans to host African and Hispanic dancers. For the past two years, Xsight, a professional dance troupe, has worked with the dance classes and Contempo, culminating in a joint dance performance. East High drama students also participated in the Contempo dance numbers for that performance.

DRAMA

Traditionally, the drama program has been based on three all-school plays. This year, only two plays will be produced, as the entire fine arts program will be involved with a large-scale musical, *Fiddler on the Roof.* Each year, the first school play is a children's play, such as *Alice in Wonderland* or *Charlotte's Web.* In addition to evening performances, the children's play is performed during the school day for elementary students who are bused to East High School and during a Saturday afternoon matinee for young children. The other two plays are geared more toward high school and adult audiences. This year, the winter play will be *The Outsiders;* in past years, plays such as *Picnic at Hanging Rock, Dandelion Wine, The Taming of the Shrew, Lady Windmere's Fan, J. B., 1984,* and *Screwtapes* have been performed. East High offers a course in stagecraft for students who wish to learn skills that will enable them to participate in backstage functions of play production. East High was recently recognized for having an active thespian troupe for twenty-five years. The school has its own small television studio, offering a course in mass media, during which the students write, direct, film, and edit video programs, both in the television studio and in the school and community. One of their videos was selected for nationwide broadcast last year.

ART

The art curriculum includes drawing and design, print-making, jewelry, pottery, fiber and fabric design (a combination vocational education and art course), painting, ceramics, and art studio. The art studio course is part of the EWE alternative program. It is taught from an Alaskan Native emphasis and draws upon the expertise of Eskimos from the community (e.g., beadwork and soapstone carving units). East High's art program is highly respected in the school district and includes many features. Drawing and design students create full-body paper costumes for Halloween and model their creations during a popular school assembly. This year, over 120 students participated in the Fourth Annual Art Department Halloween Fashion Show. Other features of the drawing and design course include the creation of a thirty-minute animated film and hot-air sculptures (the students work in groups to make ten-foot-diameter tissue paper hot air balloons). The basic curriculum in the painting course revolves around tempera, watercolor, oil, and acrylic. The students will be creating supergraphics—massive, permanent paintings (11′ × 19′) painted in various locations around the interior of the school. In pottery, students study raku firing, an Oriental firing technique in which pots are removed from the kiln when red hot and placed in combustible material to reduce extensive handbuilding techniques (such as pinch, coil, slab, vermiculite, nylon screening, styrofoam, and slip casting) and extensive pottery glazing techniques (such as slips, oxides, covercoats, luster, glaze pencils, and high and low temperature glazes). In print-making, students learn block-printing, etching, embossing, and silk-screening. They print posters and T-shirts for various school functions and organizations. The jewelry course includes work with copper enameling, fabrication, and lost wax casting. Sculpture course projects include life-size plaster people and giant (10′ × 60′) plastic sculptures, one of which was delivered to a school in the former Soviet Union as a gift. In fabric and fiber, students learn to do batik (wax resist fabric dyeing), Sumi Nagaski (water-base marbling done on fabric and paper), papermaking and bookbinding (occasionally made with handmade paper), and silk handpainting, during which the students use special techniques resembling watercolor style of painting. While these special projects may be unique to East High, the curriculum is also based on the school's scope and sequence (course descriptions, goals, and objectives).

One goal of the fine arts program is to integrate the various art forms—dance, drama, instrumental and vocal music, and art. A major instance of that integration was the musical, *Fiddler on the Roof.* The annual talent show showcases student talent from the music, drama, and dance programs. East High holds a talent and creative fair each spring during which creative work, including computer programs, science projects, poetry, photographs, art pieces, and many other types of items are displayed in the library with community people judging the entries by category. Classes visit the fair during the day and the public visits during a specified evening.

THE BEST SCHOOLS—ASSESSING WHAT STUDENTS KNOW AND CAN DO

Assessment of individual achievement in the arts takes place in the classroom based on the objectives of the curriculum. Children learn to critique each other's work and to understand the standards they and the teacher use in assessing works of art. Classroom assessment also includes knowledge and understanding of art history, criticism, and aesthetics. Some of the Best Schools use out-of-school individuals or committees to formally evaluate their arts programs every four to six years, in the same way that other academic areas of the curriculum are evaluated.

Assessment Illustration

NEW TRIER TOWNSHIP HIGH SCHOOL, IL

Evaluation occurs both formally and informally at New Trier. Our enrollment also supports our belief that what the program offers is important. Regular visits by representatives from art schools, colleges, and universities provide us with ongoing evaluations of our programs and the abilities of our students to meet their standards. The staff also meet with alumni, in schools and related professions, to learn of their evaluations of their education while at New Trier. Portfolio assessment is an important part of the assessment process.

THE BEST SCHOOLS—PROGRAM DEVELOPMENT AND SUPPORT IN THE ARTS

The Implementation Process

Seventeen of the Blue Ribbon Schools selected for their model arts programs participated in a symposium in Washington, D.C. Following is some of the advice these schools give for developing effective arts programs:

- Treat the arts as academics.
- Plan a curriculum thought out to integrate the arts with the other curricula.

- Encourage teachers to attend summer educational programs at museums and then bring back ideas to their classrooms.
- The location of the school and the unique community it serves largely determine the parameters of the community arts support that can be built, such as bridges to local museums and business partnerships. Locale can provide unique advantages.
- Involve senior citizen and other community members with or without children in the program.
- Engage in arts competitions. Recognition reinforces learning, encourages good teaching, and builds community support.
- The superintendent and school board are of vital importance in support for the arts; they need to be intimately involved in funding the arts. No one person can take total responsibility for building support for the arts; it must be shared responsibility.

THE BEST SCHOOLS–STAFF DEVELOPMENT

In the Best Schools, staff development in the arts involves more than opportunities for art specialists. The role of the classroom teacher is recognized, and much of the inservice activity involves these teachers. Resources of universities, art galleries, orchestras, opera companies, museums, and local working artists are frequently used for staff development. In some cases, the training is specific and in depth, such as working with a teaching artist in the classroom for several weeks or attending one- to three-week workshops at a center for the arts. Other training takes place in short-term inservice programs designed to enhance the links between the classes in the arts and other areas of the school curriculum. In addition, the Best Schools encourage their art specialists to continue their own work as artists and encourage all teachers to participate in the arts.

Staff Development Illustration

NEW TRIER TOWNSHIP HIGH SCHOOL, IL

A fifty-page document from New Trier delineates the paths that each department shall follow to achieve the five goals of the school. In the spring, each department meets to converse on each of the goals and develop department strategies to meet the goals. After the department meetings, department chairs meet in cluster conversation groups with the principal to review the discussion highlights. A consensus is achieved, and the department chairs formalize their staff development events. In addition to content specific efforts, the school's leadership facilitates further collaboration in special education, mathematics, English, social studies, the arts, physical education, and modern and classical languages. Collaborative efforts are encouraged in TESA and SPIRAL. Personal growth is gained from monthly Great Books style book discussions and first Thursday panels. Each semester, a professional institute is required, which is planned by faculty/administration to meet yearly goals. Monthly faculty meetings feature keynote speakers to address national educational trends. Each department has a substantial travel budget for professional conferences at the national level. Several teachers hold major offices in the organizations or have served as presenters.

THE BEST SCHOOLS–FUNDING DEVELOPMENT

The Best Schools provide support for the arts in terms of teaching specialists, materials, facilities, and staff development. Funds are budgeted for live performances at the school and for field trips to museums and performances. Frequently, the PTO or PTA, community groups, corporations, and production admissions provide additional funding for the arts. Artists and other volunteers are also recruited to work with staff and/or students.

Funding Illustrations

PINEDALE MIDDLE SCHOOL, WY

Community resources at Pinedale are utilized during National Arts Week, when the community members with expertise in the arts are asked to share their talents with the students in our schools through workshops and performances. The school district also has a strong partnership with the Pinedale Fine Arts Council. Jointly, they sponsor programs and residencies that span a total spectrum of fine arts. Last year, a community fund-raising effort resulted in the purchase of a $25,000 grand piano.

NEW TRIER TOWNSHIP HIGH SCHOOL, IL

The New Trier Board of Education and administration support the entire arts program through ample finances, written acknowledgements and confirmations, professional staffing, encouragement to attend professional conferences and meetings, constructing and maintaining separately designated areas for instruction and performance, allowing advanced classes to have a smaller enrollment than beginning and intermediate classes, and supporting the extensive extracurricular program by paying stipends to faculty involved in all after-school activities. The faculty supports programs through their attendance at productions and shows and with their encouragement of students who take our classes and perform in extracurricular activities. This support is shown by an art faculty of seven full-time teachers, a theater faculty of five full-time teachers, a dance faculty of three full-time teachers, two fully equipped theaters, a beautiful dance studio, a stipend budget for extracurricular theater activities in excess of $75,000, a curricular program that offers numerous sections of classes, an attractive art gallery, and special sound systems, lights, percussion instruments, etc.

H. B. PLANT HIGH SCHOOL, FL

Administrative support at Plant for all performing arts programs is intense. The staff is present at all performances. The principal sends written communications expressing appreciation and support to teachers and students. Financial resources are made a priority from the school budget, reflecting the support of other departments, and from the Academic Foundation. Flexibility in scheduling practices enhances the entry of students into the programs.

SUMMARY

The Best Schools consider the arts as important academic subjects. Structured sequential curricula include not only art production, but art history, criticism, and aesthetic education. Specialists in the arts provide instruction, and classroom teachers and, in many cases, teaching artists provide additional instructional support. Staff development provides opportunities for continuous development for the classroom teacher and administration, as well as the art specialists. Individual or small-group instrumental lessons are made available to interested students. Art productions enliven the total school program. A significant portion of the school budget contributes to supporting the arts programs; in addition, community groups are active supporters of the arts in the schools. Finally, the Best Schools reach out to local artists, centers for the arts, universities, and museums to enrich their programs.

REFERENCES

Consortium of National Arts Education Association. (1994). *National Standards for Arts Education: Dance, Music, Theatre, Visual Arts: What Every Young American Should Know and Be Able to Do in the Arts.* Reston, VA: Consortium of National Arts Education Association.

National Endowment for the Arts. (1988). "The Arts in America: A Report to the President and to the Congress," Washington, D.C.: National Endowment for the Arts.

Report on Educational Research. (1993). "Artists, Educators Craft Standards for Arts Education," *Report on Educational Research*, 25(6).

U.S. Department of Education, Office of Educational Research and Improvement. (1991). *Notes of the Blue Ribbon Schools Arts Symposium, September 25, 1991.* Washington, D.C.: U.S. Department of Education, Blue Ribbon Schools Program.

U.S. Department of Education, Office of Educational Research and Improvement. (1993). *A Profile of Principals: Facts, Opinions, Ideas and Stories from Principals of Recognized Elementary Schools of 1991–1992.* Washington, D.C.: U.S. Department of Education, Blue Ribbon Schools Program.

U.S. Department of Education, Office of Educational Research and Improvement. (1994). *Blue Ribbon Schools: Outstanding Practices in the Arts.* Washington, D.C.: U.S. Department of Education, Blue Ribbon School Program.

CHAPTER 11

Preparation for Life in the Information Age

WHAT STUDENTS SHOULD LEARN

ACCORDING to the National Goals of Education,

> . . . every school in America will ensure that all students learn to use their minds well, so they may be prepared for responsible citizenship, further learning, and productive employment in our Nation's modern economy.
>
> By the year 2000 every adult American will be literate and will possess the knowledge and skills necessary to compete in a global economy and exercise the rights and responsibilities of citizenship.

What does it mean to learn to use your mind well? How do you prepare students for further and continuous learning? What are the knowledge and skills necessary to compete in a global economy? One thing is clear: the answers to these questions cannot be found in one course or even a series of courses. The National Goals envision behaviors, skills, and knowledge that should be the outcomes of the total school experience; however, there are specific learning opportunities that schools need to provide within courses but that transcend individual courses that are essential for achievement of the goals and life in the information-based society of the future.

As we prepare to enter the 21st century, information is being generated at a dizzying rate in all fields. It is coming at the individual with lightening speed and, often, is contradictory. Information has become the new capital of the global economy. Those who know what questions to ask; where and how to get and exchange information; who can interpret, analyze, and synthesize data; and who are able to apply "information-based products" to problems are the new capitalists. Now students can not only study other cultures and places from textbooks, but they can actively participate with children across the street, across the country, or around the globe to exchange and create information and cooperatively solve problems and develop projects. Telecommunication provides students with direct opportunities to practice the skills needed for global understanding and future participation in a global economy. Students in geographically separate locations can simultaneously participate in the same course. The Community Learning and Information Network (CLIN) is creating a community-linked learning and information system designed to provide all Americans with equal access for America's "information super highways" of tomorrow. It is clear that the old school curriculum, with its emphasis on rote memorization of material and selection of *THE* right answer on paper-and-pencil tests, is inadequate to meet the needs of students in the 21st century. The new skills needed are reflected in new subject matter-related standards, in the research on how students learn complex skills, and in the work done by individual schools and universities.

The development of standards or statements concerning what students should be able to do to demonstrate information literacy is expected to come from the International Technology

Association (ITEA) working with the National Science Association (NSF). The Committee for Education and Human Resources is coordinating the efforts of sixteen agencies to develop a five-year planning framework to establish standards (Walter, 1994). In the meantime, information literacy standards might include the following sample:

STANDARDS: INFORMATION LITERACY

Students will be able to

- formulate questions and plan strategies for finding solutions
- find, collect, and analyze information from multiple sources to solve subject specific and transcurricular questions
- exchange, interpret, and develop information-based products cooperatively with other students within the school and through telecommunications with other students
- critique information in terms of validity and reliability of sources
- use research to propose solutions to everyday problems
- produce information-based products using multiple technologies

Students will demonstrate the skills to use tools necessary for information literacy by

- finding information using print sources, video, computer data bases, and telecommunication
- developing data bases and spreadsheets using technology
- developing one-, two, and three-dimensional and technology-generated visual representations of information
- using keyboarding, word processing, and desktop publishing skills to produce documents
- producing products incorporating multi-media

Students will demonstrate the attitudes and habits of mind for continuous learning and problem solving by

- using multiple information sources to solve problems on a regular basis
- demonstrating confidence in using the current tools of technology to gain and process information and confidence that they can and will learn to use emerging technologies to better solve problems
- demonstrate the ability to select the appropriate technology resources for specific tasks
- work cooperatively with other students to develop multidimensional solutions and projects

HOW STUDENTS LEARN–HOW THEY ARE TAUGHT

Schools have traditionally viewed the teacher and the textbook as the dispensers of knowledge; however, this paradigm cannot be used to prepare students to function effectively in the Information Age since there is simply too much information and the information itself is generated, revised, and discarded at too astonishing a rate. If children are going to learn processes and gain the flexibility of thinking required to meet ever-changing information and intellectual demands, then instructional methodology must also change.

A distinction needs to be made between how children are to be taught to operate the tools of information literacy and the methods used to assist students to internalize the processes necessary to function effectively by using, interpreting, analyzing, creating, and communicating information. Learning to use the tools is fairly straightforward. Keyboarding skills can be taught by a teacher, by the use of computer software, or by a combination of both. Simple word processing programs can be introduced as early as kindergarten, with more complex functions introduced over the years as student products gain sophistication. Skills for accessing information from books, CD-ROM, and laser disc sources can be taught as part of a library media curriculum or introduced at times when students need access to a source for a specific project. Skills for accessing and retrieving information through telecommunications can be taught in the library, using Internet and data bases such as Dow Jones Retrieval and Dialog, or in classrooms as students have the need to exchange information with students across the country and beyond, in KidsNet or AT&T Learning Circles.

Development of students' ability to effectively use sources to find, analyze, interpret, draw conclusions, and communicate information is much more complex from an instructional point of view than learning to operate the tools of information literacy. Just as learning to hold a pencil and to form letters is very different from learning to write effectively, there is also a big difference between learning to use the keyboard and being able to effectively gather, analyze, and communicate information. Learning research and learning theory indicate that, if students are going to make connections between what they learn in school and real-life situations, learn to apply basic skills to complex problems, and develop the very high-level thinking skills required for true information literacy, then the instruction must provide for the active learning and application of these skills.

Instruction across the curriculum has to be structured in such a way as to require students to pose questions, seek information, and evaluate alternative solutions. The new standards for individual subject areas are problem solving based. There is a growing congruency among individual content areas concerning the views of how students learn and how they should be taught. In addition to a focus on development of problem-solving skills, there is also an ever-increasing emphasis on integration of curriculum. Clearly, as students and adults encounter life in the information age, the perceived boundaries between fields continue to fade.

In order for students to have the opportunity to learn to use the tools of information literacy, schools must have available not only traditional print materials, but also computers, CD-ROM, modems for telecommunication, scientific and graphing calculators, videodisc players, satellite dishes, cable television, retrieval services, Internet access to remote data bases, software, laser discs, CDs, video- and audiotapes. They must also have these technologies available in sufficient quantity and quality to make their use by the student body feasible and realistic. The opportunity to use technology must be available to all students, and all students must be actively engaged in problem defining and solving. Some information resources such as VCRs or a telecommunication equipped computer for KidsNet can be shared by an entire class or, in some cases, among a group of classes. However, clusters of computers are needed to allow students to efficiently access the school's "card catalogue" and CD-ROM collections such as Infotrac and Newsbank and multi-media encyclopedias such as Grolier's Electronic Encyclopedia and PC Globe or MAC Globe. Some tools such as HyperCard for Macs or LinkWays for IBM or bar coded laser discs such as Living Textbook material from Optical Data are used primarily by the teacher to prepare lessons in order to more actively engage students in learning. Some activities are best carried out in cooperative groups and require only a computer for each group. However, other information-processing applications, such as word processing, require individual student access to computers for sustained periods of time. The computer has become the "pencil" of the information age, and scheduling the use of one or two of these modern "pencils" among an entire class is neither efficient nor effective for most purposes.

Equal educational opportunity is a major consideration in the use of technology. The school can be reasonably certain that all students have access to pencils and paper at school and at home, and research data shows that almost all households have some type of calculator. However, not all homes have computers, nor do all children in homes that do have computers have access to them. Furthermore, not all computers are equal in terms of facilitating learning. Some computers provide access to word processing and simple programs, while others equipped with CD-ROM and modems can provide students at home with access equal to or better than the resources of the school's library. While most households have some type of simple calculator, which can facilitate learning of mathematics in the lower grades, only some of the students will have access at home to the graphing calculators used in their high school classrooms. Educators must be careful not to widen the gap between the "knows" and the "non-knows" in teaching information processing. Providing ample opportunity within the school day is one way of ensuring equity; extending hours of access, i.e., keeping the library/computer centers open after regular hours, and loaning calculators and computer hardware and software for home use are some of the ways of ensuring equity.

A three-year study and development project by a team of researchers from Education Development Center (EDC) and Technical Education Research Centers (TERC) found that, if technology is to meet the diverse needs of students in the classroom, essential and interdependent elements must be in place at the curriculum, instructional, and organizational levels. The principal must assume overall leadership by communicating a vision of the value of technology in meeting the needs of students and the goals of the curriculum, fostering a spirit of inquiry among staff, providing motivation and resources, and allowing for individual differences in interest and expertise among staff in the use of technology. There is a need for a strong facilitator, an advocate who can work with teachers, providing training and guiding curriculum development. Finally, on the organizational level, there is need for a team consisting of administrators, facilitator, and teachers within each school building to guide curriculum development. Within this curriculum, interdisciplinary and thematically based programs assist students in inquiring, linking, and synthesizing ideas. Decisions concerning hardware acquisition, allocation, and scheduling should focus on curriculum goals and teacher expertise. When a mechanism to narrow software choices is matched to the curriculum, teachers are more apt to integrate technology into instruction.

At the instructional level, EDC advocates the use of an I-search or We-search process based on the work of Ken Macrorie (1988). By using a theme as a basis, students are engaged in a process of making meaning through posing an interesting question, gathering information, integrating information to build concepts and generate ideas, refining their thinking, and writing about how they have carried on their investigation and what they have learned. Instruction should also include the use of cooperative learning to enhance shared creativity and strengths and to build social skills and respect for each other. Finally, students should use, on a regular basis, a variety of technological applications to pose questions and solve problems, construct knowledge, and communicate ideas.

According to the National Goals,

> By the year 2000, the nation's teaching force will have access to programs for the continued improvement of their professional skills and the opportunity to acquire the knowledge and skills needed to instruct and prepare all American students for the next century.

Staff development is an essential component of any plan to use technology effectively. EDC/TERC found that "in-service workshops contribute to acquisition of knowledge, but are insufficient in helping teachers use this knowledge in their work with students. Teachers best learn to integrate technology successfully through ongoing school-based support and structures for collaboration and communication'' (in Zorfass et al., 1993, p. 11.54). In addition, if teachers are to use technology regularly, someone must be responsible for maintaining hardware and for solving technical problems.

HOW LEARNING SHOULD BE ASSESSED

Assessing students' skills in operating information-processing tools is, in many ways, an easier process than assessing basic skills in content-related areas. In some cases, the assessment is built into the learning process. For example, software that teaches students to type usually includes routines that also record the speed at which the student has learned to type. The proof of a student's ability to access a data base is that the connection is made and the data retrieved; in addition, the length of the connection and the specific data base assessed is frequently reported on a regular basis back to the school as part of the billing process. Word processing skills can be assessed by having students produce documents or edit text. Data searches can be monitored to determine how quickly and effectively a student can use descriptors to narrow and complete a search for specific information.

Assessing the students' abilities to effectively use the information tools to solve problems and communicate results is more challenging. A very limited amount of knowledge can be assessed through traditional paper-and-pencil tests. For example, this form of traditional assessment can be used to determine if students can identify the best sources for obtaining certain kinds of data in certain situations. However, complex problem solving takes not only access to data, but time. Students need to learn to define problems, explore data sources, deal with conflicting or incomplete information, draw and justify conclusions, and produce and communicate a product. The complex and most important forms of information processing need to be assessed based on the process and the product. Most often, projects developed over time and in various content areas are used to assess outcomes by using criteria such as

- problem definition
- appropriateness and variety of sources used
- accuracy of data reporting
- justification of conclusions reached
- effectiveness of mode of communication, i.e., graphs, charts, narratives

In summary, assessment of information literacy must distinguish between surface knowledge, i.e., learning to use tools, procedures, and rote applications, and meaningful knowledge, which is connected learning that requires active problem solving and communication. There are at least six assumptions that underlie emerging standards in information literacy:

- It is not possible to teach or for students to learn all the information needed for life in the 21st or even the 20th century.
- Knowing how to pose questions, access, process, and analyze information and having the ability to apply the results to real-life problems are essential skills transcending individual content areas or courses.
- Students must be actively engaged in real problem solving; they should learn to select and choose from among multiple resources and become proficient in using each approach.
- Learning to efficiently operate information tools is only a necessary step toward effectively learning to use these tools to solve meaningful problems.
- Information processing is needed by all students, and equal access needs to be ensured.

- Assessment is best embedded in the educational process as part of the instructional process, rather than an add-on to instruction. Assessment should provide evidence of what a student can do, as well as what a student knows; as much as possible, it should be performance-based.

THE BEST SCHOOLS–THEORY INTO PRACTICE IN INFORMATION PROCESSING

The Best Schools are keenly aware of the need for students to become information literate at a very high level. Information literacy goes far beyond the common objectives of development of computer literacy: to use a computer, including keyboarding and booting programs; to know the history of the computer; and to have a little knowledge of programming. The Best Schools assume that students have to learn to use technology, just as they have to learn to hold a pencil, print, and learn to write script, and they teach students these basic technology operation skills. However, the Best Schools also have as their prime instructional goals the ability of students to process, evaluate, use, and communicate information and solve problems. Since learning to use technology is the means to the ends and not the ends, information resources include not only computers, but also scientific and graphing calculators, televisions, CD-ROM, laser discs, telecommunication links, camcorders, fax machines, and a wide range of print material including books, charts, magazines, and prints.

The Best Schools recognize that access to information-processing resources is key to accomplishing instructional goals. All students have the opportunity for repeated and sustained access to technology. Their visions of what technology to use, the location of that technology, and the use of technology are very consistent. The library/media center is seen as the hub of information resources; however, multi-media teacher stations, classroom mini-labs, and class-size or larger computer labs provide access to technology matched to course needs and interdisciplinary projects. In many cases, all or most technology resources are networked to provide maximum access and flexibility throughout the school and/or district. Connections to Internet and other global communications can expand access to worldwide resources. In some cases students with access to modem-equipped computers at home can access the library/media center resources at any time from home. Recognizing the importance of home-school communications, schools have established E-mail systems (such as Parent Link or Home Work Hotline), which allow parents and students to dial in for daily classroom and school information and leave messages for teachers. Few of even the Best Schools have totally implemented their visions concerning use and availability of technology; however, they have made large strides in the use of technology and have specific plans to expand access. Components of their systems commonly include or are projected to include

- the library/media center as the central hub for technology access and distribution
- one or more labs for word processing, publishing, and exploration (including sets of portable computers, which can turn any classroom into a computer lab)
- five to seven computer mini-labs in most classrooms
- a multi-media teaching station in each classroom
- all computers networked to the server in library, to other schools, community resources, and local colleges and universities
- access from labs and classrooms to card catalogues (in school library, county, district, university libraries), video encyclopedias, telecommunication (other schools, national

data bases, worldwide data bases and exchanges, bulletin boards), videos, cable TV, and two-way interactive TV
- a computer loan system to ensure equal access
- multi-use software such as Microsoft Works or ClarisWorks, available to all students, as well as software, CD-ROMs, and laser discs for specific purposes
- ability to use different platforms in network mode (PC, Apple)
- ability to expand to homes access to school-based technology
- ability to take advantage of programs via satellite and cable
- access to worldwide resources through Internet
- installation of school/home E-mail communication systems

The new paradigms for instruction in language arts, science, mathematics, and social studies, grounded as they are in the development of complex problem-solving skills, make the development of information literacy essential in each of the several disciplines. Similarity in the goals for language arts, science, mathematics, and social studies also reinforces the interdisciplinary nature of learning and the use of interdisciplinary problems and projects in the learning process. In the Best Schools, technology is used to enhance learning in individual disciplines and in integrated units and projects.

THE BEST SCHOOLS – INFORMATION PROCESSING GOALS AND OBJECTIVES

Many of the Best Schools have developed specific goals and objectives for the development of technology skills and the use of technology as a research tool; other schools have developed objectives that are embedded in subject specific learning objectives. With the exception of keyboarding skills, skills related to learning how to use particular hardware or software are usually introduced in conjunction with the students' need to use the hardware or software. For example, if a project requires the use of a camcorder, then instruction in how to operate the camera is introduced in conjunction with the assignment. Word processing skills are introduced, as needed in the classroom, as students write using "user friendly" software such as the Children's Writing Center in the lower grades and more powerful word processing programs such as Microsoft Word or WordPerfect in the upper grades. Students learn to use Hypercard as part of the research process so that they can format research into multi-media systems for presentations that allow them to tie the computer, video camera, and video presentations into one report.

In addition to instruction provided on a "need to know" basis within the various curricular areas, courses or units specifically designed to teach all students to use the various technologies are required at some level in the school or district. The Best Schools also offer advanced elective courses and electives for students who entered the district after the grade level where required courses were taught.

Information Processing Goals and Objectives Illustrations

CROSSROADS SCHOOL AND SOUTH BRUNSWICK HIGH SCHOOL, SOUTH BRUNSWICK, NJ

COMMUNITY CONTEXT

South Brunswick is a growing community located midway between Philadelphia and New York City, half-way between Trenton and New Brunswick and half-way between Princeton and

Rutgers Universities. Symbolically, middle school students are at a crossroads between childhood and adolescence. The adult population includes large numbers of bankers, stock brokers, and financial advisors. It also houses professors from the nearby universities, scientists from businesses such as Squibb, and a number of computer application specialists who are in demand by local businesses. At the same time, the community includes the technicians who work for the scientists, the truck drivers who carry the cargo from the local businesses, the bureaucrats who work for the state of New Jersey, and the shopkeepers who own and manage small conveniences in town and in the local malls. Many of these people have been in the town for two or three generations; some have moved here recently from places as distant as Thailand or Pakistan. Some live in high-priced homes and others in trailer parks. Some speak English; others do not. More than forty world languages other than English are spoken by South Brunswick students. About 13% of the population is Asian-American; about 9% is African-American.

VISION

The South Brunswick School District incorporates technology into the existing curriculum as an instructional and communication tool to enhance and support basic skills, learning strategies, problem solving, and critical thinking skills. This integration of technology is accomplished through an ongoing program revision cycle, so that technological tools are incorporated into all curriculum areas.

OBJECTIVES

Students will be able to become proficient in finding, accessing, analyzing, and presenting information.

Teachers will be able to employ technological tools for expanding learning opportunities for all students.

Administrators and their secretaries will be able to use technology to access district information from centralized data bases. Administrators will foster the use of technology by the teachers in their buildings.

The district will provide support and staff development opportunities to assist each staff member in becoming fully competent with utilization for teaching and learning. Schools should be open after hours, on vacations, and during the summer to allow students and community members access to technological tools.

COMPUTER SCIENCE

The computer science curriculum at Crossroads plays an essential role in the schoolwide curriculum goals. It is a program that is both important and unique. The computer science program addresses the fact that the computer is a powerful tool and is essential in today's world of technology. The Crossroads School houses twenty-four Mac SE computers in one lab and the same number Mac LC computers in an adjoining lab. In addition to these student-use areas, the school also has a teacher tech area where there are several Mac SE computers, a portrait screen, LaserWriter printer, and Scanner.

Students in the seventh grade are provided with an introductory course, which enables them to understand the organization of the Macintosh computer and use it in ways to enhance and facilitate the learning process. Students are also introduced to a word processing/data base program and are taught the various functions of these applications; keyboarding skills are emphasized so as to raise the comfort and ability levels of students, thus reducing the stress of using the computer. These skills are used in the writing curriculum as students compose, edit, and revise their work before they develop a final product. In addition, other teachers use the lab on a regular basis for their classes: math spreadsheets for grades, science for projects, social science for simulations and reports, language arts for word processing. The computer lab at Crossroads also provides a variety of supplemental programs for students to learn and master all of the above areas.

TECHNOLOGY USE IN THE CURRICULUM

Skills learned in the computer labs and courses are used in other classes:

- The music department uses the computer as a full-time teaching aid. Through the use of electronic keyboards, headphones, computer, CD-ROM, and appropriate software, students are able to study music, to create their own music, and to find that part of themselves that is musical without fear of failure. Band scores are programmed into the computer so a clarinet class, for example, can hear all the other band parts while playing their own music. The pace of the music can be varied until mastery is gained.
- Students deficient in basic skills use technology to develop strategies for problem solving through a program called Higher Order Thinking Skills (H.O.T.S.) (NDN).
- Students across all grade levels are encouraged to use the computer for word processing.
- Students are encouraged to use the computer, videodisc, CD-ROM, and other technological tools to prepare and present their research findings for the sixth-grade assessment.
- Telecommunication is used at many levels to connect students to other schools or information sources around the country.
- Sixth-, seventh-, and eighth-grade students use LOGO to write procedures and super procedures to solve problems.
- Seventh- and eighth-grade students use Pagemaker to learn the principles of desktop publishing and good design.
- Seventh- and eighth-grade students use word processing to aid in the writing process and to format papers properly.
- High school students use computer-aided design to learn principles of drafting and architectural planning and execution.
- Students in grades 4–8 use a news service coming to the school via satellite from Penn State University called, "What's in the News?"
- Special education classes are linked to regular fifth-grade classes through a cross-curricular program, "The Voyage of Mimi."
- Parents are invited to join staff for an evening of hands-on time to learn about programs their children are using.
- Students from all grade levels share in preparing a daily broadcast of the news on their in-house TV station (WIFS) through use of the school's integrated information system.
- Physical education teachers use video cameras to tape their students in gymnastics. Students are then allowed to view the tape for critiquing.
- The school business department has students use the Macintosh computers for keyboarding and application skills and later moves them into the DOS platform for advanced courses.
- Independent study students at the high school work with all building resources to complete their projects.
- Graphic arts students use technology to take a product concept through all the stages of design to final production.
- In science labs at the high school, students use computers to take raw data from experiments and analyze results.
- Advanced placement students use a program called Interactive Physics which allows them to review first year physics in a third of the normal time.
- Libraries are central to the schools and serve as sources of print and nonprint material and play a key role in developing literacy. The media specialists teach students to use library resources for information retrieval and independent research through group and individual instruction. The libraries employ the following technologies to

motivate student learning: on-line computer search catalog, print bibliographies, tapes for teachers/students, laser discs, and available computers for word processing.

Dr. Frederick Nadler, *Crossroads Principal, Grades 7–8, 626 Students*
Richard Kay, *South Brunswick High School Principal, Grades 9–12, 1173 Students*

FOREST GLEN MIDDLE SCHOOL, CORAL SPRINGS, FL

COMMUNITY CONTEXT

Forest Glen was opened in 1987 as the third middle school in the flourishing city of Coral Springs, Florida. Coral Springs is a residential suburb of Fort Lauderdale, attracting young families, with a median age of thirty-five, seeking quality educational programs. The award-winning architectural design of the school facility has become a prototype for future middle schools in the district.

The composition and size of Forest Glen has evolved from 690 predominantly white upper middle-class students to the current enrollment of over 1750 students representing all segments of society. The school draws students from single-family homes, multifamily apartment complexes, and federally subsidized housing. Twenty-three percent of the students qualify for free/reduced price lunch. Adding to the multicultural base, Forest Glen is designated as the bilingual cluster for all middle schools in Coral Springs.

TECHNOLOGY COURSES

Business and computer education play an essential role in preparing the students for success in the 21st century. At Forest Glen, business and computer classes are available to both seventh and eighth graders. In business education class, students learn the competencies and responsibilities of occupations, including accounting, data processing, clerical, and secretarial. They interact with equipment to develop skills in keyboarding, calculation, and word processing. To consolidate all the above competencies into a meaningful unit of instruction during a nine-week course, the business education teacher developed an innovative program, CITY INTERNATIONAL MALL. Initially, the students receive instruction in economics; then the classroom is transformed into a shopping mall. Students become presidents of their own businesses, rent store space, and simulate many true life business activities. During the events, students learn to use computer applications, including word processing to write business letters/resumes, data bases to list employees/customers, and spreadsheets to calculate monthly budgets. Throughout the program, students are involved in selling merchandise and distributing and paying bills with their personally designed checks. The business education class is equipped with 28 Tandy 2500/SX25 computers and Microsoft Windows and Microsoft Works software.

The computer education program at Forest Glen is located in a laboratory classroom supplied with state-of-the-art equipment—thirty-two Macintosh LC computers with eight ImageWriter networked printers. Computer education classes are available for seventh and eighth graders. Students are introduced to computers using Symantec Greatworks software containing eight applications. True Basic software is used in the computer lab to provide instruction in programming. The Computer II course offers an extended program in which students complete several projects demonstrating their competency in word processing, spreadsheet, data base, and graphic applications. This program is the impetus for the computer academic competition club, which has received awards in the following categories: computer problem- solving contest, lo-resolution animated graphics computer fair, computer programming computer fair, logo design contest, and the computer-generated art contest.

The business and computer education programs provide the students with quality instruction using state-of-the-art equipment and software to enable students to creatively complete projects that will prepare them for success in the workplace of tomorrow.

David A. Goldstein, *Principal, Grades 6–8, 1762 Students*

LABAY JUNIOR HIGH, HOUSTON, TX

COMMUNITY CONTEXT

Labay Junior High is a part of the Cypress-Fairbanks Independent School District, located northwest of Houston, Texas. The district is one of the fastest growing districts in the United States, and the growth directly affects Labay. Labay serves junior high school sixth-, seventh-, and eighth-grade students. The students come from a diverse background, ranging from poverty to upper middle-class. The area has over twenty subdivisions and five apartment complexes that offer a diverse and culturally mixed student body. There is a definite shift to more Hispanic students in the past few years. The only common bond to be found unifying these areas is the school district. The community voted in 1993 to adopt a year round school calendar, rather than construct additional facilities; however, they approved a $14,000,000 bond issue to expand technology resources. Labay was recognized as a Blue Ribbon School in 1988–90 and 1991–92. Six of the district's forty-one schools have been recognized as Blue Ribbon Schools.

COMPUTER LITERACY

The required computer literacy curriculum at Labay is continually being updated to prepare students to be productive members of society in the 21st century. Students learn basic technology skills and apply problem-solving strategies and cooperative skills in real-life situations. Student evaluation includes authentic assessment, essays, and student self-evaluation. Skills learned in this class are applied in all subject areas. Six computer labs facilitate use of technology in all curriculum areas. Applications include: word processing in language arts, reading, social studies, and science; problem solving in math, science, social studies, reading, and industrial technology; new technological evaluation strategies in science, social studies, and industrial technology; and research skills in language arts, reading, social studies, science, industrial technology, and speech. The course helps students understand the relationship of knowledge from one subject area to another and the value of technology as a tool. The course also supports the school curricular objectives in writing, technology, and authentic assessment. Computer Literacy II, industrial technology, and keyboarding are also offered as electives.

The Labay Library is the heart of the school. It provides all students with the necessary skills to research independently. Innovative technology can be found in the library. Students are taught to master all information technologies so they will become self-reliant, lifelong learners. A computer card catalog enables students to conduct productive, thorough research quickly. There are several levels of search strategies available; every student and teacher is taught how to use Dialog, an on-line information retrieval system. The librarians model the use of all information retrieval systems such as Dialog, Newsbank, SIRS, vertical files, multi-media encyclopedia, and text on microfiche for CD-ROM.

Mr. Bob Warner, *Principal, Grades 6–8, 1346 Students*

WILLIAMSBURG HIGH SCHOOL, WILLIAMSBURG, KY

COMMUNITY CONTEXT

Williamsburg High School, a secondary school enrolling students in grades 7–12, has a rich tradition of excellence. Located in a small, rural community with a population of 5480, the school is known for its quality academic programs, competition in extracurricular activities, and overall community support. The school has been accredited continuously by the Southern Association of Colleges and Schools since 1927.

Williamsburg High School is confronted with challenging demographics in that the percentage of disadvantaged students enrolled has almost doubled in the past two years. A majority of these students live in public housing and are transient. The school's mobility rate has averaged 23% for the past three years.

TECHNOLOGY EDUCATION

A state-of-the-art technology education program was initiated with the 1992–93 school year, which exposes students to 21st century technology in a modern, fully equipped laboratory setting. Rotating through modules, students study robotics, engineering, aerospace, research and design, computer-aided design, computer applications, desktop publishing, computer graphics, alternate energy systems, applied physics (pneumatics), mechanisms, transportation systems, audio/video production, photography, laser/fiber optics, electronics, digital technology, production, and computer numerical control.

In conducting research through experimentation with technology, students are required to analyze, synthesize, and evaluate. As with other subjects "writing to learn" is emphasized and skills acquired in the class are used in completing interdisciplinary projects.

Jerry L. Hodges, *Principal, Grades 7–12, 422 Students*

THE BEST SCHOOLS–LIBRARY/MEDIA CENTERS

The library/media centers in the Best Schools play a central role in the development of information processing. The use of technology in no way reduces the importance of books and print materials; the Best Schools are proud of their book collections and the high level of circulation to all students. In most of the library/media centers, the catalogue and circulation systems are computerized. Technology has had a profound effect on the reference sections of the libraries–on-line data bases, laser discs, data retrieval services, video collections, and CD-ROM. For example, CD-ROM interactive video encyclopedias such as Grolier's and Compton's are being used extensively at the middle school level. These encyclopedias allow students to conduct searches for information, identify multiple sources, allow students to select references for indepth study, and, on most topics, provide video footage based on actual events. For example, if a student is interested in why President Truman gave the order to drop the atomic bomb, the student can find a listing of many sources, narrow the search using additional "search words," actually read material (on screen or printout), and watch and listen to President Truman explain to the nation the reasons for his decision. Unlike regular encyclopedias, the interactive video encyclopedias are updated regularly. Another resource widely available in library/media centers is NewsBank and InfoTrac. These resources bring to the libraries magazine and newspaper resources that are beyond the funds available for individual subscriptions, are easier for students to use, and reduce the need for storage and shelf space. Many other CD-ROM-based resources are also available. CD-ROM towers allow multiple student access to these resources at the same time within the library and, in some cases, from every classroom in the school. Laser discs provide access to huge video, graphic, and data bases in the arts, history, science, and literature.

Library/media centers in the Best Schools are also equipped for telecommunications. Via modem, the library/media center is linked to electronic networks outside of the school. Such a service is Dialog, which allows librarians, teachers, and students to conduct on-line searches for material. Dow Jones provides a reduced rate to schools so that students can access their data bases through DowLine. This latter source provides much more than stock information; however, it is often used in conjunction with the Stock Market Game. Prodigy is another source that provides a low-cost connection to multiple data bases and, like DowLine, is easy to use. Library/media centers are also frequently linked to other libraries in the district and/or to town or county-level libraries via modem and fax. These connections allow students to search further for resources and allow libraries to share resources. A number of the Best Schools have developed links with universities and businesses to access not only their data bases, but also their professional staff.

In order to access and process the various forms of information available in the library/media centers, the facilities are equipped with computers, CD-ROM, laser disc players, videocorders, camcorders, scanners, and printers. One goal of the Best Schools is to expand constantly the availability of resources, to have students access their resources, to make decisions concerning relevance of information for solving specific problems, to evaluate information in terms of credibility, to use information to solve problems, to justify their conclusions, and to communicate results. In order to accomplish this, the Best Schools have plans for or have already networked the library/media technology with computers in individual classrooms and computer labs. In order to ensure equal access for all students, libraries are also loaning hardware (computers and calculators) and software to students (Mirabeau Lamar, TX).

Computer laboratories are frequently adjacent to the library/media centers and allow for whole-class, small-group, and individual computer work. Classroom teachers bring students to the facility to work on projects. In some schools, a trained technology assistant is available in the lab, and, in a number of schools, volunteers are used to assist classroom teachers and students. Teachers also use the lab computers to prepare materials for lessons; in many of the schools, there are also computers in each classroom for teacher demonstrations and material development.

Library/Media Center Illustrations

FOREST GLEN MIDDLE SCHOOL, FL

The media center serves as a focal point for instruction at Forest Glen. Materials in a variety of formats are accessible to students and staff through the card catalog. Reading is promoted schoolwide through participation in the Sunshine State Young Readers' Award program and the Pizza Hut "Book-It" program. Students checking out the most books from the media center are recognized with a "Super Reader" award at the year-end awards assembly. The Media Center uses the Book Brain computer software program to help students generate a personal recreational reading list. All sixth graders receive a comprehensive orientation on the use of the media center by the media specialist through their English classes. Reference and retrieval skills are taught in collaboration with teachers for such projects as the invent America competition, science fair, and social studies fair. As part of their English instruction, eighth-grade students complete an extensive research project, which is team taught by the media specialist and the English teacher.

The state-of-the-art media center has a number of data bases available for student use, including Compton's Multi Media Encyclopedia, Information Finder, The Electronic Encyclopedia, and the TOM periodicals data base. The media center also has the Social Issues Research Series (SIRS) and subscribes to the Abridged Newsbank microfiche program. The media center circulates books using the Book Trak computer program. The Sunlink computerized union catalog links many high school and middle school library collections throughout Florida. A media advisory committee, composed of interested parents and teacher, meets monthly with the media specialist to assist in the formulation of policies and priorities. A dedicated cadre of parent and grandparent volunteers staff the checkout desk, shelve books, and process new materials to allow the media staff extra time to interact with students and teachers.

A schoolwide television network is maintained and educational television can be accessed in each classroom. CNN Newsroom is available for current event instruction. The Partner-in-Excellence, Cable TV of Coral Springs, provides a cable television connection as part of the "Cable in the Classroom" program.

WILLIAMSBURG HIGH SCHOOL, KY

The media/information center is housed in a new facility that is technologically active. Both the circulation and card catalog are fully automated, allowing students immediate access to the center's holdings. The librarian/information technology specialist operates the center on a flexible schedule and works cooperatively with the school's technology coordinator to ensure students quick access to information retrieval services. The center contains two computer labs, with a total of sixty networked computers. Grolier's Electronic Encyclopedia is available at each work station in the media center, as well as in the classrooms.

The media center also has a video digitizer that converts video images to the computer graphics employed in multi-media applications. Short-range plans call for the purchase of additional CD-ROM players, enabling students to use a variety of research reference works on CD-ROM discs. The center is in the process of converting periodical and additional reference materials to CD-ROM discs which contain extensive full-text magazine and newspaper articles and standard reference works such as almanacs, atlases, etc. The center provides all types of technology equipment for use in the classroom, including VCRs, audiotape players, and video production equipment. Computer labs are available for students both before and after school hours, and students frequently come in and run software of their own choosing. The center has an inkjet color printer and a full-page scanner, providing additional resources and motivation for students as they write research papers, incorporate graphics, and access information from both electronic and printed sources.

Extensive use of technology (e.g., Carmen Sandiego, PC USA, and PC Globe) is made in teaching geography. The media center provides students access to two- and three-dimensional maps and globes, atlases, etc. Every classroom has access to a networked electronic encyclopedia. Students studying global issues have participated in AT&T's "Learning Network" classroom. Mathematics teachers make extensive use of computer software, which includes packages that cover an entire year of geometry and two years of algebra. Graphing calculators are used in the classrooms and two, thirty-two-station multiuse computer labs are available to classes.

The center has a total of 4480 volumes in the high school section, along with an extensive collection of printed and automated reference materials, VCR tapes, filmstrips, slide sets, pictures, transparencies, charts, maps, globes, etc. This is updated often to promote reading.

RICHLAND NORTHEAST HIGH SCHOOL, COLUMBIA, SC

COMMUNITY CONTEXT

Richland Northeast High School is "inside the beltway" and has many of the elements of inner-city schools. There is a continuing struggle not to fall into the "urban blight" patterns that have engulfed other schools. The students come from a wide variety of socioeconomic backgrounds. The school serves those who live at Fort Jackson, the Army's largest basic training facility. Many students' families live in apartments. Eleven percent of the students qualify for free and reduced-price lunch. The students are exceptionally mobile; a study done in 1989 indicated that 26% of the school's students had been in four or more schools. Since that time, the school has added more Fort Jackson students. Recent statistics reveal that the turnover rate is approximately 20% per year. In 1985 and 1993, the school received the Secondary Schools Blue Ribbon School Award.

LIBRARY/MEDIA CENTER

Numerous and varied resources are available to students at the school to become information literate. The library provides access to paper and microfiche journals and newspapers. CD-ROM access to periodicals and newspapers as well as on-line access to Dialog, prepare the students to use new technology that they will find in public and university libraries. All students receive orientation to the services of the media center when school begins. Working within the scope and sequence for library skills and the curriculum of this school, a media specialist covers skills in general research based upon the needs of each grade level. For example, for ninth graders, skill instruction corresponds to geography, English, and biology class requirements. In the tenth grade, skills are further developed as students become more familiar with biographical and scientific resources as well as with the historical materials needed to complete assignments for courses on this level. Eleventh-grade media center instruction moves to English and American history as students prepare to write a literary paper, as well as to investigate issues and events in United States history. Following this sequencing, seniors report that they feel comfortable and competent using the school media resources.

Electronic searching and/or borrowing privileges are available to students who wish to search the local public library system and/or that of the University of South Carolina. The media center has borrowing privileges with the South Carolina State Library for materials to supplement the school's collection for specific classroom assignments; last year, students borrowed and returned over 800 books from the state library.

Telecommunications capabilities developed since 1987 give students access to information not available in any other way. Students participate in discussions with students from around the world through AT&T's Learning Circles. A continuing link with a school in Canberra, Australia, allows teachers and students to interact on topics of mutual interest in both curriculum and personal arenas. Additionally, a statewide network of educators provides resources such as "Spacelink" and weather data bases for general use.

Information retrieval of career and college data is an integral part of the services provided in the media center to seniors. Subscriptions to an on-line data base from the South Carolina Employment Security Commission (SCOIS), as well as a purchased data base for financial resources for higher education (CASHE), form the cornerstone of assistance in this area. Students request information, and a network of parent volunteers access these data bases for the materials requested. No fees are charged.

Each year, the media specialists set a goal for inclusion of recreational reading through the English classes. Teachers are encouraged to bring all levels of their ninth- and tenth-grade students for a book talk every nine weeks. Focus is on titles from the fiction and story collection, nonfiction, and biography, which appeal to teenagers. Recent circulation statistics indicate that students at this higher school are reading a number of recreational reading titles, which is equal to or greater than the national average. This reading is in addition to the required reading for classroom activities.

Overall, the media center operates in a cost-efficient manner. Through use of library borrowing privileges with local and state library sources, the actual collection is increased significantly. The use of on-line computer and electronic resources provides access to very costly data—otherwise not affordable in-house. Sponsorship of resources by clubs and organizations expands the effectiveness of and the commitment to the media center. Student access to other libraries makes retrieval of additional resources more efficient. Finally, parent participation in the delivery system builds valuable contacts that strengthen the effectiveness of the total program and the positive perception of the school in the community.

Ronald F. Hill, *Principal, Grades 9–12, 1631 Students*

ST. THOMAS MORE CATHOLIC HIGH SCHOOL, LAFAYETTE, LA

COMMUNITY CONTEXT

Located on a twenty-five-acre tract in Lafayette, a city of approximately 100,000, in southwestern Louisiana, St. Thomas More is a Catholic high school for students in grades 9–12. Students come from the unique Acadian-Cajun culture, which values family life, hard work, and *joie de vivre* (joy of life). Although the school is surrounded by farmland, commercial development is rapidly expanding into the immediate area. Lafayette is the professional center of the eight-parish (county) Acadiana region. The city is a leader in the medical field and in the oil and tourist industries. The 16,500-student University of Southwestern Louisiana is the community's largest employer. The school has an open admissions policy and serves students from Lafayette Parish and surrounding areas.

LIBRARY/MEDIA CENTER

The library was originally designed as a focal point of the school, following state and national guidelines for organization of space and function. What began as primarily an aging book collection housed in a new and dramatic space has evolved quickly into a library/media center that compares to the best in the country. The five-year goal focuses on making the student a confident seeker of information and imagination in all media. Student and teacher use of the library has grown exponentially in relation to both the growth of the collection and growth in understanding the central role of the library in lifelong learning. Librarians stay current with changes in school libraries by attending local, state, and national conferences and workshops and by taking courses.

Students take advantage of available information technology in the research process. Books are located using the card catalog automated on Macintosh computers. Research for current information in magazines is usually done by computer, rather than the Reader's Guide. Infotrac TOM, a CD-ROM index to magazine articles, is easy for students of all abilities to use. A CD-ROM product called Newsbank Plus, which indexes newspapers as well as magazines, allows for Boolean searches.

Both Infotrac TOM and Newsbank Plus are keyed to microfiche; the media center currently has 115 indexed magazine titles in print and/or microfiche. Newsbank includes a number of national and international newspapers on microfilm. A microfiche reader-printer makes it possible for students to copy articles. Students' rate of success in searches for current information is multiplied many times with the addition of this technology.

Other CD-ROM information products such as Grolier's Electronic Encyclopedia and PC Globe are also used for research. The addition of two Macintosh computers with CD drives and eight compact discs brings a new dimension to reference sources. Sound and motion illustrate the written word, making it possible to hear King's "I Have a Dream" speech, as well as read it and read about it. A videodisc player, purchased for use in the classroom, works much the same way.

Access to CD-ROM sources, as well as the library card catalogue, is available from any of the networked Macintosh computers in the library. Plans have been made to network to other Macintoshes in the school so that information from the card catalog and the CD-ROM will be accessible from the classroom. Eventually dial-in access for students, teachers, and parents will be provided.

All freshmen complete a four-day series of library exercises involving skills, use of the card catalog, periodical indexes, reference sources, and computer searches. Student enthusiasm for computers lends itself to quick mastery of computer skills and leads to cooperative learning situations. Expansion of research skills takes place when teachers and the librarians plan research assignments cooperatively. A recent example of such a project was the collaboration of the environmental science teacher and a librarian in planning a vertical file to be prepared by students.

Normally, the library is open before and after school, as well as during lunch; however, hours are often extended to late afternoon and evening when requested by students and teachers. Three Macintoshes and one Apple IIe equipped with simple word processing programs are accessible to students during library hours. The library does not close during the school year for preparation or inventory.

Reading promotion is another area in which teachers and librarians work cooperatively. The media specialists rely on various means—reading lists, enticing displays of books and magazines, articles for the parent newsletter, suggestions for classroom reading, and announcements on the PA system—to encourage reading. After observing that part of the reluctance to read is in not knowing how to select a book, one librarian developed a novel-selection exercise to develop the students' judgment in deciding whether or not to check out a book. Her idea was published in *Ideas Plus* (National Council of Teachers of English, 1991).

A major part of promoting reading is in having an alternative and current print collection that addresses the recreational and curricular needs of students. The per pupil expenditure for library/media of $35 per student from all sources allows for significant additions of new materials each year. Students and teachers may suggest new acquisitions. About half of the print budget is spent on magazines – one of the primary sources teens choose to read. All materials, including magazines and reference books, can be checked out.

Raymond Simon, *Principal, Grades 9–12, 724 Students*

THE BEST SCHOOLS – TECHNOLOGY AND INFORMATION IN THE CONTENT AREAS

The curriculum in the content areas in the Best Schools is experiential and problem solving-based. Technology is widely used to access information, to organize and analyze data, to chart and visually present information, and to produce documents. Laser discs are used by teachers to incorporate visual material into classrooms. For example, art and social studies teachers can access artwork from the National Gallery or the Louvre laser discs in their classrooms. Computer-assisted design programs such as MacDraw enhance art programs. Software programs such as ClarisWorks allow students to create data bases, import information, analyze data, and create graphs. Computer technology is used to support problem solving, rather than for "skill and drill." In some states, educational television is used to enhance specific areas of the curriculum; for example, current events information is downloaded to videotape and used in the classroom to connect studies to real-world events. In other schools, such as Proctor Junior-Senior High School in Vermont, students receive instruction in advanced mathematics courses via satellite from the Virginia Department of Education.

One of the most powerful uses of technology is the opportunity now available to link students across the district, the nation, and the world. KidsNet (National Geographic) is such a program used in many of the Best Schools. With this program, students are linked with students in other schools. Data is collected concerning real problems such as pollution. Local data and data from linked schools is analyzed, conclusions are drawn, and students then interact with scientists concerning their findings, and a report is developed. Another program, AT&T Learning Network, connects seven to nine distant classrooms via telecommunications into learning circles, which provide the opportunity for students to expand perspectives, generate new ideas and solutions, and cooperatively develop products through units such as "Society's Problems," "Global Issues," "Energy and the Environment," and "Mind Works." For example, during the Gulf War, students in East Brunswick communicated daily via modem with children in Saudi Arabia, sharing insights about the effect of the conflict on the lives of students. State-developed systems, such as Kentucky Educational Television – NET – is used by students at Williamsburg High School, Kentucky, to communicate with students via E-mail with students across the state and to exchange writings. Each of the previous chapters also include numerous examples of how technology has become the tool of instruction.

Integration of Technology Illustrations

COLUMBIA HIGH SCHOOL, MAPLEWOOD, NJ

COMMUNITY CONTEXT

The students served by Columbia High School (C.H.S.) are part of professionally based, relatively affluent communities (Maplewood Township and South Orange Village) that have become significantly more diverse during the last decade. While only 2% of the high school students are eligible for free and reduced lunch, South Orange and Maplewood have witnessed strong demographic changes with an influx of African-American, Asian, Hispanic, and Eastern European families, which has resulted in much cultural and bilingual diversity in the school. The high school's nonwhite student population in the fall of 1992 was 37% of the total student enrollment of 1438. Almost 77% of this minority group was African-American. Another indication of diversity is found in the number of students represented in the ESL program. The languages reflected include Spanish, Polish, Bulgarian, Portuguese, French Creole, Japanese, Thai, Turkish, Romanian, Chinese, and Greek. Of the 1992 Columbia High School graduates, 89% attended college.

MATHEMATICS

In 1988, C.H.S. entered a long-term collaborative relationship with four other New Jersey high schools initiated by the Center for Improved Engineering and Science Education (CIESE) at Stevens Institute of Technology. Ten C.H.S. mathematics teachers worked to create videotaped model lessons using computer technology for nationwide distribution. Implementation was furthered through a $120,000 equipment grant from IBM Corporation. Development and monitoring occurred at monthly meetings, two-week summer workshops, and annual conferences at Stevens. Six Columbia math teachers participated in a program sponsored by Satellite Education Resource Consortium (SERC) and CIESE. Model lessons were videotaped for nationwide distribution. Eight teachers made presentations in the area of application of computer technology at the National Council of Teachers of Mathematics Regional Conference in 1990. Many math teachers make presentations on a regular basis (i.e., NJEA). Several teachers completed a ten-credit summer program and/or thirty-credit program with Stevens Institute on computers and math in the curriculum.

Departmental innovations have included the infusion of data analysis and the integration of technology (computers and graphing calculators) into the curriculum. The partnership with Stevens Institute of Technology (CIESE Project), combined with the IBM grant, has solidified the staff's commitment to infusing the use of computer software into the teaching of mathematics. The staff has encouraged students for more than ten years to use calculators when taking in-class tests and to use computers and calculators for take-home assignments. The recent inclusion of open-ended type problems in all areas of the math curriculum clearly addresses critical thinking and communication skills.

The one course that best exemplifies the school's efforts at content improvement is geometry. Traditional synthetic Euclidean geometry does not reflect contemporary geometric thinking. Staff emphasize transformational geometry because the use of motion (translating, rotating, reflecting, and size transforming) seems more suitable for developing abstract ideas. These transformations are introduced through manipulatives (protractors, rulers, compasses, and MIRAs) and computer software, and they are consistently infused throughout the course. This integrated course combines algebraic methods, vector analysis, matrix operations, and coordinate representations to unify fundamental mathematical constructs.

The unified math curriculum (written by the school's staff) is structured into a four-year program of sequential units, rather than the traditional full-year courses. This allows any group or team (of students and teacher) to set its own pace and, with each team evaluating progress continually, finish the year at any point in the curriculum.

The computer lab is an integral part of instruction. Teachers may sign up for selected available periods. The two overhead imaging systems are regularly used, as well as graphing calculators. Additionally, students are encouraged to have their own calculators. The students have created their own computer games, simulations, and graphing projects (polar and trig graphs), including twin students who wrote their own computer program in three-dimensional modeling and fractal curves.

ENGLISH

The English curriculum of the high school has as its basis the K–12 integrated language arts curriculum. This curriculum is based on the most recent research in language learning, including the basic tenets of whole-language. The primary goals of the department are to develop lifelong readers and writers who have the ability to use language to create meaningful lives for themselves.

The writing process is integrated into a variety of departments, including mathematics (open-ended item assessment), social studies (research and critical papers), foreign language, science (labs and research papers), art, and business. The process of revising, using the computer, and using established standards for exemplars of good writing is part of the classroom activities throughout the school.

SCIENCE

The one course that exemplifies the school's best effort at "content improvement" is the tenth grade "pre-physics" course. Knowing that 75-80% of the students elect physics and chemistry as upperclassmen, the school wanted to increase the probability of their success in physics by giving them earlier and more practice in representing reality in abstract/mathematical terms. There is no textbook; content is limited to only four units of study—direct proportions, heat, machines, and electricity—so that the school can treat each in sufficient depth to reach its goals. A six-week unit on computer literacy is spread throughout the year. In effect, students begin this course by feeling a weight, then putting it on a spring, and seeing that stretch. They then take what they "know" and learn to represent it or graph it by using a computer graphing program, also learning to write a few sentences in BASIC to solve for each variable. As the course progresses, relationships between these variables become more abstract. Eventually, students are able to talk about the relationships between these variables and represent them in abstract/mathematical ways.

HISTORY

History and the skills associated with the gathering and interpreting of data are a major theme in the school's required program. Writing is a major skill developed in its world history and United States history courses. The writing skills range from concept mapping to organizing data to writing of essays, as well as developing research activities and writing papers. These writing and researching activities are coordinated with the library/media center, where social studies teachers are available to assist students.

TECHNOLOGY

The school's computer graphics program has played a critical role in integrating technology with several different curricula and has demonstrated the results of combining a high-quality and creative staff with high-quality technology. As a result of the talent, interest, and initiative of a dually certified industrial arts/art teacher, the school received a three-year grant to acquire a MAC/desktop publishing lab in the graphics room. Moreover, the school now offers two Commercial Art I and II/computer graphics courses that are team taught to integrate art and graphics, a production journalism course team taught with the journalism course to teach students the totality of publishing a newspaper (and the problem solving needed to go along with it), and a computer graphics course to students in the alternative school. The lab is also used in the alternative school. Beyond linking technology with varied curriculum, the lab is also used for special projects throughout the school—program, budgets, etc. The art, music, English, and industrial arts programs have intertwined. Further, the initiatives taken in this area have spilled over to the entire art and music programs, with tech labs in each room allowing students to practice the connections between technology and the skills being learned in their courses.

LIBRARY

The library program reaches all levels of students and is designed to be "needs-oriented" and "subject-related" as a fully infused component of Columbia High School's courses of study. The guiding philosophy maintains that the most effective learning and application occurs when library skills are taught using a variety of assignments within the course work of the following departments.

- In grade 9, English students are introduced to the high school library's various resources and services.
- In grade 10, science students are introduced to the importance of locating current information.
- In grade 11, social studies students are introduced to theory and organizational process skills essential for the preparation of a research paper.
- In grade 12, through business/guidance, non-college-bound seniors are introduced to the concept that libraries are designed for lifelong learning.

The intellectual life of a school depends upon reading. To this end, the library provides a pleasant, friendly, and supportive atmosphere, as well as flexible hours. The library works to promote pleasure reading through bestseller list displays, bibliographies, booktalks, rotated book displays, literary contests, and individual reader advisement.

The utilization of technology at the Columbia High School library fosters ways of expanding the resources available in our collections and bringing them efficiently to the hands of students through ASAP (Academic, School, and Public Library Consortium), which links Seton Hall University, Maplewood Memorial, South Orange Public, and the school libraries for patron borrowing and information sharing; Dialog (an online information retrieval system); HERMES (Hudson-Essex Regional Materials Exchange System); ILL (InterLibrary Loan) to locate periodicals, journals, and books from libraries throughout the state and across the nation; and Readers' Guide on CD, which allows students to retrieve periodical citations.

Dr. Judith Weiss, *Principal, Grades 5–12, 2881 Students*

E. C. GLASS HIGH SCHOOL, LYNCHBURG, VA

E. C. Glass High School's theme, "A Tradition of Excellence," dates back to its establishment as Lynchburg's first high school in 1874. The student body is markedly diverse. The socioeconomic composition of students comes from both affluent and depressed neighborhoods. The ethnic composition is 58% Caucasian, 40% African-American, 1.5% Asian/Pacific Islander, and 0.5% Hispanic. The student makeup continues to change, with a gradual increase in students with academic, social, and cultural differences. However, E. C. Glass has not had an exodus of students to private and suburban schools; in fact, the school continues to attract tuition students from the suburban schools. E. C. Glass High School was first recognized as a Blue Ribbon School in 1983 and again in 1993.

SCIENCE

The science curriculum consists of earth science, biology, chemistry, physics, and college biology. Also offered are courses in computer science and research and statistics. Significant improvements to science courses include the following: revising the curriculum and all lab manuals; team teaching in basic-level earth science and biology courses (in collaboration with special education teachers); placing new emphasis on problem solving as an integral part of science; increasing the number of computer applications in laboratory experiences; implementing CD-ROM living textbook materials in biology and earth science; total upgrading of all computer science hardware, including video microscopy in biology; and double blocking for an extended lab period in chemistry.

All computer science applications are directed toward usage in daily life. Two examples are word processing for preparing reports and data bases for cataloging information. Mathematical reasoning is enhanced in all science courses. Graphing, data analysis, conversions, quantitative chemical analysis, calculator skills, and scaling in map reading and modeling are some skills inherent in all content areas. In addition, the random number theory is part of the computer science curriculum. Glass students have access to instructional technology such as CD-ROM, video microscopy, content-specific software, two IBM computer labs, video and video-support equipment, and library research references.

GEOGRAPHY

A special course called world geography is offered, in addition to the incorporation of geography into the other courses. After attending the National Geographic Society Summer Institute for Teachers, members of the department implemented the five themes for teaching geography: location (absolute and relative), place (physical and human characteristics), human environment interactions (relationship with places), movement (mobility of people, goods, and ideas), and regions (how they form and change). These five themes are reinforced with computer activities. Students use Mac Globe on the Power Book 100 to identify countries and their geographical features and to reinforce the concept of location and relationships between locations. Students are required to write answers to critical thinking questions, collect data, and develop a base of questions and research answers on the computer. The course stresses global interdependence in the technological age.

TECHNOLOGY

Today's high-tech, multicultural society requires that the career-technical education department offer a variety of skill-oriented programs to enable students to become productive citizens. The department offers courses requiring the integration of all academic disciplines, especially math, science, and language. Courses are offered in the following disciplines: marketing, education for employment, business education, keyboarding, COE, accounting, materials and processes, manufacturing, graphics, basic technical drawing, engineering drawing, architectural drawing, ICT, home economics, machine trades, auto mechanics, power train technology, dental careers, Air Force ROTC, and photography.

The department has undergone a major revitalization in recent years. Programs have been added and targeted for support by industry. One of these partnerships resulted in the addition of the dental careers program financed by matching funds of $20,000 from the Lynchburg Dental Society and the federal government. The machine trades course is supported by the local machine trades partnership, which donated $8000 to renovate and update the lab. Wiley and Wilson, a local engineering firm, donated computers, printers, and software used in the mechanical drawing program. The addition of state-of-the-art computer technology in almost all areas, as well as the total renovation of the labs (supported by advisory groups), has enhanced the school's image with the public and improved the learning atmosphere.

ENGLISH

In all English classes, writing is an ongoing process. From basic skills required in the literacy passport class to the advanced techniques taught in college composition and AP English, good writing is emphasized. Every course outline identifies several key writing experiences required for each student. Many teachers further reinforce writing skills by means of journals, writing portfolios, writers' notebooks, and writing style books. In addition, twenty-seven laptop Macintosh computers circulate as a mobile lab to classrooms for use in writing instruction and social studies.

LIBRARY

The library/media center provides an attractive learning environment that encourages investigation, allows for independent thinking, and develops effective study habits. The library maintains an open schedule before and after school and during lunches so that the students and teachers have sufficient time to use the facilities. Creative bulletin boards encourage students to read for information and enjoyment.

The library has an up-to-date collection of current print materials, periodicals, microfiche, and vertical file information. Teacher/department input is solicited every year, with a percentage of the budget given to each department for new materials.

The library staff offers many services to the students, such as bibliographies, orientation lessons, library skills instruction, Readers' Guide lessons, a twenty-computer Apple IIGS lab, Dialog information retrieval, interlibrary loans, reserve collections, and individual instruction and assistance. All ninth-grade students receive instruction in library skills and use.

Technology plays an important part in the total learning process. The staff provides instruction in word processing using the computers in the library. Two satellites enable the library to provide instructional programming in all disciplines and to tape programs requested by teachers. The Whittle Network provides daily news. The in-house instructional television system allows the school to see live, student-produced and -directed television morning announcements. The latest technological additions are multi-media stations, which allow students to use CD-ROM, laser discs, and computers simultaneously for information retrieval, report development, and independent learning.

MATHEMATICS

The mathematics department provides appropriate learning activities in fifteen different courses. To emphasize practical applications of mathematics, the consumer math class studies personal banking skills and paying taxes. Geometry students apply their skills to the worlds of architecture, design, and construction. A partnership with Babcock and Wilcox enables advanced students to see how math is used in nuclear engineering.

The diverse curricula and variety of teaching styles accommodate different learning styles. Instructional formats include cooperative learning—pioneered at this school by the math department—team teaching, question-answer techniques, tutoring done by advanced students, and individual instruction. It is rare to find an empty math classroom before or after school. Calculator use is encouraged in all classes. Graphing calculators are provided for math analysis. Computers are used to illustrate concepts and generate tests. Television monitors, cassettes, and overhead projectors are also available. A library of the latest textbooks, instructional aids, and state and national information is kept in the department office. Videocassettes are collected for classroom use.

Howard Hurt, *Principal, Grades 9–12, 1310 Students*

LABAY JUNIOR HIGH SCHOOL, TX

MATHEMATICS

The math program at Labay strengthens knowledge of basic facts with problem solving as the base. Calculators and computers are used throughout the program. Key components include computer problem solving, cooperative learning, authentic assessment, manipulatives, essay writing, and problem-solving strategies. Math is integrated into science through the use of equations, graphs, and measurements. Math integrated with social studies units includes latitude and longitude and project business activities. The eighth-grade, on-level math class best exemplifies the content improvement with computer problem solving, calculator use, numerous manipulatives, group tasks, surveys, and authentic assessment.

SCIENCE

The science curriculum for all three grades is laboratory based for problem solving. Skills are emphasized, and students use cooperative learning, authentic assessment, essays, manipulatives, word processing, and computer problem solving. The course that best exemplifies the efforts at content improvement is sixth-grade science; in order to involve all students in active learning, an invention convention is held. Students also participate in discovery projects throughout the year. Laser disc use and word processing have been added to maximize problem solving.

HISTORY

The history program is characterized by the approach to chronological events through all social studies disciplines: geography, history, culture, economics, and government. Students use cooperative learning, essays, word processing, a history fair, and the research process to better understand events and their interrelatedness. The skills of mapping, graphs, and designing time lines assist students in analyzing and comparing and contrasting social studies concepts. The word processing computer labs are utilized in social studies (grades 6 and 8) to allow students to apply technology in their study of history.

GEOGRAPHY

Geography is incorporated into all three social studies courses. It is taught according to the fundamental themes of location, place, regions, movement, and relationships within places. Higher order thinking skills are addressed in essays, authentic assessments, cooperative learning, word processing, and United Nations Day. Interdisciplinary units in short stories are shared with language arts, endangered species and ecosystems with science, and Dialog and research with reading.

The course that best exemplifies content improvement is world cultures. Word processing and data base are technologies that have been recently added. Students work in pairs using a data base in the computer lab to call up a variety of statistics such as population, literacy rate, life expectancy, and temperature ranges of the fifty-two countries in Africa. With this information, the students write comparisons and contrasts of countries and draw conclusions about lifestyles in specific countries. The data base culminates in a relocation agency simulation in which students draw clients and must select a country in Africa for that client to live in based on the client's preferences and the country's statistics. Students write a letter to the fictional client stating why their selected country is appropriate. In addition, meaningful relationships have been explored through pen pals to the former Soviet Union, United Nations Day, efforts to save the African elephant, and schoolwide surveys.

THE BEST SCHOOLS–PROGRAM DEVELOPMENT AND SUPPORT FOR TECHNOLOGY

Technology and Research Implementation Process

Many of the Best Schools began to introduce technology more than a dozen years ago. In some cases, they began with a computer lab, and, in others, they began by placing a single computer in as many individual classrooms as possible. Much of the software initially available was either the "skill and drill" type or games. However, schools saw the potential of the technology, and these initial efforts have developed along with the technology and applications. Commodore and Apple 64 K computers were replaced with more powerful machines, and these, in turn, are being replaced by much more powerful multi-media computers; however, in most cases, these highly durable second generation machines purchased by districts are still being used for some purposes. Other technology, such as laser discs, CD-ROM, satellite dish, and VCRs, has been introduced as it has become available.

The Best Schools, like most schools, began instruction using computers by focusing on computer literacy. The aim was to teach students about computers–how to boot a program, how a program was written. Students enjoyed playing computer games, and teachers complained about the lack of relevance and about the quality of software. The Best Schools have not only upgraded software, but have developed plans and curriculum to utilize computers and other technologically powerful learning tools. They recognize that new technology will constantly appear in the marketplace. Some of the new technology will find immediate application in their schools; however, each new contender will be reviewed in terms of what it really adds to the instructional process. For example, more powerful and faster computers are appearing all the time; however, these machines are not necessary for word processing. The schools move the technology around, placing the available machines where they can be most appropriately used. New technology is then placed where it can be most effectively used. The Best Schools do not wait for the "ultimate" technology; they buy what is adequate for their curriculum and, as much as possible, what is compatible with what they already own. However, they recognize that, just as textbooks become outdated, even the most carefully purchased technology will become obsolete.

Most of the districts in which the Best Schools are located have developed long-range technology plans. These plans have been developed by board members, administrators, teachers, and community members. Standing committees annually monitor progress toward implementation of the plan and emergence of new technology and then revise the master plan.

Implementing a Technology Plan Illustration

COLUMBIA HIGH SCHOOL, NJ

The use of technology at Columbia High School dates back many years. One of the first efforts was a partnership with Stevens Institute of Technology to develop the use of technology to enhance learning in curriculum areas. At the time, most technology instruction was dedicated to teaching programming languages. As part of the pilot to use technology for instruction, IBM donated two computer labs to the school.

In 1991, a districtwide technology plan was developed with input from every grade level, content area, and school. Board of education members and community people were also part of the development process. This plan, which is updated and monitored each year by a standing technology committee, guides the funding priorities and acquisition of technology in the district. The district's director of technology and media centers, with a staff of four, is responsible for implementation of the plan.

LABAY JUNIOR HIGH SCHOOL, TX

The district that includes Labay Junior High School has a five-year technology plan developed by central office administration with input from staff and the community. A standing committee of twenty people oversee implementation of the administrative and instructional branches of the plan.

THE BEST SCHOOLS–STAFF DEVELOPMENT

Teachers and administrators in the schools today did not grow up with technology beyond television, nor, in general, did they learn to use technology as part of their degree training. The training of staff is an essential part of any effective technology program. Not only do staff members have to learn to operate technology, they also need to become comfortable in using it and must see the value of its use in the education process. A recent survey of schools shows that 90% planned to spend money on technology training in 1992–93. Nineteen percent of the schools surveyed planned more than ten hours of training per person (Quality Education Data, 1992). The Best Schools provide extensive and continuous staff development. In the early years of computer use in the schools, staff development was usually provided by the school computer "hackers." Unfortunately they frequently "turned off" their colleagues by attempting to teach programming to teachers. Today's technology is much more user friendly than earlier models, and hard drives and networks make access to programs much easier than in the past. Training has also changed; now, the focus is on teaching how technology and specific software can be used to enhance the curriculum and student learning. Every effort is made to make the use of technology simple and understandable, and staff receive training in specific applications, with computers being available for their use and practice. Many schools encourage teachers to take computers home for weekends and vacations. Because a goal of most of the Best Schools is for every teacher to have a computer, in some schools, there already is a computer on every teacher's desk. In addition, some schools have also initiated plans to assist teachers in buying computers for home use, through reduced price contracts and payroll deductions, or have, in some cases, provided all teachers who are trained in technology with a computer for home use.

Staff Development Illustrations

CROSSROADS SCHOOL AND SOUTH BRUNSWICK HIGH SCHOOL, NJ

During the summers, training in technology has been offered to district personnel. Classes are offered by district teachers in areas such as

- early childhood applications of technology highlighting specific programs that teachers found successful
- troubleshooting technology – allowing teachers hands-on practice
- introduction to the MAC – for folks who are new users
- previewing new software
- graphing on the computer

Demonstration lessons showing the integration of technology into the curriculum are regularly offered by the district technology coordinators. Information about out-of-district workshops relating to technology are offered to all teachers. Staff development courses are offered throughout the year on a building- or on a districtwide basis for continuing education credits (CEUs).

LABAY JUNIOR HIGH SCHOOL, TX

All of the inservice at Labay is focused to support the campus improvement plan (CIP) goals and objectives. In 1992 – 93, every staff member attended three hours of inservice in departmental activities that define the CIP, six hours in technology (teacher tools) training, three hours on authentic assessments, three hours on reading in the content area, and four hours on portfolios. Every teacher also receives training in writing in the content area, word processing with students, cooperative learning, and high expectations.

The district offers a wide variety of technology courses in its computer center. Teachers who complete twenty-one hours of training and pass exams are given a computer for their personal use. Approximately twenty-three Labay teachers have received computers, and the goal is that, by the end of 1994 – 95, each teacher in the school will have a personal computer. Many teachers who already own computers select a classroom computer (for every three classroom computers selected, a laser printer is provided). Within the school, the priority for instructional management is training all teachers to use Grade Book II, in order to streamline administrative tasks related to instruction.

Teachers also receive technology assistance from the computer liaison, who teaches computer literacy but also has responsibilities to assist teachers, and from the computer aide who maintains equipment but also works with teachers on applications.

E. C. GLASS HIGH SCHOOL, VA

The district provides three days of inservice prior to the opening of school and five half days of inservice time during the year. These days provide opportunities for technological training of staff. Department chairs also provide training in subject specific technology use within the department, during planning time and after school. Districtwide courses are also offered. The superintendent places a priority on development of technology skills for teachers.

THE BEST SCHOOLS–TECHNOLOGY HARDWARE

Hardware in most schools has been purchased over time; however, often, there has been a concentrated period of time based on a district plan during which major resources have been devoted to technology acquisition. The type of computers used depends largely on the availability and desirability of software at the time of purchase. For example, many in-class computers purchased five or more years ago are Apple IIes or Apple GSs. These machines were relatively inexpensive, and most of the classroom software was available for this platform. Many of these machines are being replaced by MAC LCs, a much more powerful and flexible computer. On the other hand, software for computerizing libraries was available first for IBM PCs or compatible machines (Columbia Library, Winnebago, or Follette Library systems), and many of the schools adopted PCs for library use. In some cases, computer labs were purchased for specific software applications that required specific hardware. Today, while much of the software is available for both MAC and PC formats, there is still specific and often excellent software being developed that requires either the Mac or IBM platform. Technology now allows the networking of these various types of computers throughout the school and the Power MAC allows for use of both MAC and PC software on the same computer. The aim of the Best Schools is to network all technology in the school.

The schools also have CD-ROM-equipped computers for interactive video, laser disc players, modem-equipped computers for telecommunication, VCRs and cable for accessing television, and, in many cases, satellite dishes to access instructional television.

Technology Hardware Illustrations

E. C. GLASS HIGH SCHOOL, VA

The high schools become part of the districtwide technology plan in 1994–95; however, technology development has been a school priority over the past six years. Hardware includes

- twenty-five MAC computers in the library, computerized card catalog, and circulation
- two MAC labs networked to the library (access to card catalogue, CD-ROM, and menu of programs)
- one IBM compatible lab not yet networked used for techprep (fifty to sixty students) technology education course
- twenty-seven portable MAC computers based in a classroom but available to be moved to other rooms or borrowed individually
- mini-lab of six to seven computers in science and math
- districtwide E-mail
- systemwide TV through local cable company providing programming and information to homes
- a priority to add more multi-media stations and laser technology during the next two years
- districtwide PC-based administration systems (SIMS-NCS)

LABAY JUNIOR HIGH SCHOOL, TX

Labay Junior High School introduced technology many years ago with Commodore computers. Now, the school has six computer labs equipped with IBM compatibles. Five of the labs have twenty-eight computers each and the science lab has nine or ten. In addition there are two computers in each reading classroom, two each in social studies, and three in industrial arts. Language arts classes make heavy use of the full labs, as does mathematics. The science department uses the mini-lab.

The library's card catalog and circulation are completely automated. Other resources include Dialog, Newsbank, SIRS, verticle files, multi-media encyclopedia, and text on microfiche for CD-ROM.

COLUMBIA HIGH SCHOOL, NJ

Columbia High School has acquired technology over time based in large part on the district technology plan. Currently, Columbia has

- two IBM labs and one MAC lab for general instruction use
- one MAC lab for graphics and art
- one MAC writing lab
- two IBM business labs
- one foreign language networked computer lab

All of the labs are heavily used. There are computers in the teacher department resource rooms. In addition, the library has computerized card catalog and circulation, OPAC stations, CD-ROM, and modem-equipped computer(s) to access Dialog and other libraries. The school's administrative functions are computerized using Columbia software.

CROSSROADS SCHOOL AND SOUTH BRUNSWICK HIGH SCHOOL, NJ

Macintosh computers are used throughout the school district by teachers and other school personnel. Laser disc players are used in elementary schools, the middle school, and the high school. CD-ROM players are available in media centers. New computers being purchased have CD-ROM drive built in. IBM computers are used for high-end business applications and beginning composition at the high school. Fax services are available to the administrative and student population at all levels. Telephone line access and telephones are available in most classrooms. On-line card catalogs are in libraries. Modems are available to all teachers in all buildings.

THE BEST SCHOOLS–FUNDING DEVELOPMENT

Technology is expensive. While prices have been reduced consistently over the years, technology, in the quantities needed for effective instruction, still requires a significant and ongoing commitment of funds. Except for new construction, where it is not uncommon to include the technology as part of the bonding cost or in the cases where districts have issued bonds solely for technology, most schools are faced with the acquisition of equipment over time. As new and more powerful equipment is purchased, older less powerful, but still usable, machines are moved to classrooms that can make use of older technology. Funding for technology has been provided in most schools by numerous sources, including the PTAs and PTOs, district funds, redemption of coupons, donations, grants, and partnerships with business and industry. Federal Chapter 2 grant monies have been widely used for purchase of technology hardware and software.

Funding Technology Illustrations

LABAY JUNIOR HIGH SCHOOL, TX

The district has had a major commitment to technology for many years, demonstrated by four to six cents of the tax rate allocated to technology each year. In 1993, the district passed a $14,000,000 bond issue to purchase technology over a five-year period. Each school is required to have certain technology, such as writing labs. In addition, each school develops a priority plan for technology.

A major portion of the bond money will be used to continue the personal teacher computer program. Teachers who take and pass twenty-one hours of training at the district computer center and pass mastery tests may select either a portable or classroom computer with printer for their personal and classroom use. Courses offered by the computer center are varied, and teachers can select courses based on their needs. It is the goal of Labay Junior High School that all teachers will have personal computers provided by the district by the close of the 1994–95 school year.

There is a computer liaison in each school, who teaches computer literacy and works with teachers. A trained computer aide maintains the technology equipment and assists classroom teachers. The aides are used to provide assistance to students in the labs; however, teachers have also developed the expertise necessary to work with their students in the labs.

CROSSROADS SCHOOL AND SOUTH BRUNSWICK HIGH SCHOOL, NJ

Local funding has been provided for ongoing technology use in all areas and for construction of a new elementary school that is state of the art.

Partnerships are ongoing cooperative ventures with local businesses and industry. For example, staff development on new software has been provided without fee from a vendor. Apple Partnership has provided some teachers with training in Apple's Early Language Connection, as well as hardware to be used directly with staff and students. Community education has helped to increase the number of computers in several schools by purchasing computers for the after-school program.

COLUMBIA HIGH SCHOOL, NJ

Except for the initial funding of two labs in 1988 by IBM as part of a project ($120,000), district funds have been used for the purchase of technology, based on the districtwide adopted plan. Approximately $400,000 has been allocated for the high school annually since 1991 for acquisition of new technology and replacement of old equipment. Limitations of available funding has slowed the process of networking computers schoolwide and increasing student access to technology as quickly as desired.

The district (nine schools) has a full-time director of technology and media services, who has a staff of four. Most of the staff have both classroom, as well as technology, backgrounds. Librarians in all schools lead teachers at the elementary level, and principals all play direct roles in the implementation of technology in instruction and for administrative purposes.

E. C. GLASS HIGH SCHOOL, VA

District funds have paid for computer labs and library systems. Funds are made available to the school, which sets priorities for spending. In addition, the school has run fund-raising events and activities with proceeds going for department technology. Occasionally, there have been technology donations. Partnerships have also provided specialized technology for specific areas such as dental careers and mechanical drawing.

SUMMARY

The Best Schools have goals, objectives, and curriculum for information literacy that go far beyond computer literacy. Technology is used within individual subjects to support instruction of higher level thinking skills and is also used to support integration of instruction. All students in the Best Schools use a wide range of technology and software. The library/media center is the hub for technology; however, technology is also available in individual classrooms, mini-labs, and in full-class size labs. In most cases, technology has been purchased over time and through multiple funding sources. However, frequently, there have been concerted efforts to make major purchases of technology through bond issues and budget set-asides. Staff development has been extensive and is a continuing part of an overall plan for achieving the goal of information literacy.

REFERENCES

AT&T Learning Network. P. O. Box 4012, Bridgewater, NJ 08807.

Community Learning and Information Network (CLIN). (1994). *The CLIN National Initiative: An Overview.* Washington, D.C.: CLIN.

Macrorie, K. (1988). *The I-Search Paper.* Portsmouth, NH: Boynton/Cook Publishers.

National Geographic Society. (1993). KidsNet. Washington, D.C.: National Geographic Educational Technology.

Peck, Kyle L. and Denise Dorricott. (1994). "Why Use Technology," *Educational Leadership,* 51:7.

Quality Education Data. (1992). *Ed Tech Trends, 1992–93.* Denver, CO.

Walter, Judith A. (1994). "Technology Education Summary," *ASCD Curriculum Handbook.* Alexandria, VA: ASCD.

Zorfass, J., et al. (1993). "A School-Based Approach to Technology Integration," *ASCD Gurriculum Handbook,* Alexandria, VA: ASCD.

CHAPTER 12

Other Areas of the Curriculum

IN addition to the dimensions of the middle and high school curriculum covered in the previous chapters, schools also provide physical and health education and other subjects that address goals and objectives that they consider important for students to learn. This chapter looks at the following questions concerning other areas of the curriculum:

- What are some of the additional subjects that round out the curriculum?
- What are some examples of how these are implemented in the Best Schools?

THE BEST SCHOOLS – FOREIGN LANGUAGE

According to the National Goals of Education,

> By the year 2000, America students will leave grades four, eight, and twelve having demonstrated competency in challenging subject matter including . . . English . . . foreign languages . . . ; and every school in America will ensure that all students learn to use their minds well, so they may be prepared for responsible citizenship, further learning, and productive employment in our Nation's modern economy.
>
> By the year 2000, every adult American will be literate and will possess the knowledge and skills necessary to compete in a global economy and exercise the rights and responsibilities of citizenship.

Two types of programs potentially address these objectives: first, the teaching of a non-English language to English-speaking children and, second, the teaching of English to children whose native language is other than English. The American Council on the Teaching of Foreign Languages (ACTFL), in conjunction with the American Association of French (AATF), the American Association of Teachers of German (AATG), and the American Association of Teachers of Spanish and Portuguese (AATSP), is developing the national standard for foreign language education.

Foreign language instruction, whether English or other than English, aims today to develop the ability of students to function in real-life situations in the target language. Instruction focuses on the development of student competencies in speaking, listening, reading, and writing, and the assessment of proficiency includes actual demonstration by students of their ability to speak, write, read, and comprehend the spoken language. Leadership in the area of assessment has been provided by the American Council on the Teaching of Foreign Languages (ACTFL), which has defined eleven performance levels, ranging from "no ability to speak the language" to that of "native speaker." Performance levels have also been developed in reading, listening, and writing.

To achieve communicative competence requires a continuous and sustained sequence of instruction. Research indicates that it takes a highly motivated adult with an aptitude for foreign language 720 hours of intense instruction (equivalent to five and a half years of one-period-per-day instruction) to achieve high levels of proficiency (Liskin-Gasparro, 1982). Spanish and French oral proficiency studies in East Brunswick Public Schools show that the average student reaches the "intermediate–mid" level on the ACTFL scale after four years in a foreign language program. The studies also show that students achieve an "intermediate" level of writing ability in four years, with students achieving "intermediate–high" and "advanced" levels at the end of the fifth year in advanced placement courses (Lester, 1992).

The focus of instruction needs to be on communicative tasks. Instruction in a second language attempts to mirror the natural ways children acquire their native tongue. Because a successful foreign language program teaches students to communicate in the language, rather than solely to demonstrate knowledge about it, emphasis is on use of language in real-life, culturally appropriate contexts. This is accomplished through listening, speaking, reading, and writing at predetermined levels of accuracy; however, in learning a second language, the child is usually at a disadvantage in that he/she is not a part of a nonschool group that regularly uses the language to communicate. The same factors that characterize good teaching in general are also those that characterize good foreign language teaching. East Brunswick Public Schools have identified the following features that should characterize a foreign language classroom:

TEACHER BEHAVIORS

- Teachers "demystify" the language by focusing on and teaching to meaningful and achievable goals.
- Teachers state objectives in terms of communicative functions/tasks.
- Teachers use the target language with ease.
- Teachers use the target language in instruction whenever appropriate.
- Teachers employ a variety of communicative/interactive activities to meet instructional goals in listening, speaking, reading, and writing, focusing on the learning styles of the students.
- Teachers use a variety of instructional strategies that are functional, meaningful, and contextualized; integrate the language skills; and provide opportunities for personalization.
- Teachers utilize questions in a manner that invites/facilitates normal conversation.
- Teachers provide opportunities, including use of audio, video, and computer technology, for language practice leading to creative language use.
- Teachers provide an instructional language-rich environment with many authentic foreign language books, magazines, newspapers, games, visuals, cultural displays, and other realia.
- Teachers demonstrate a sensitivity to individual students and, in turn, foster student sensitivity to others.
- Teachers demonstrate authentic cultural behaviors.
- Teachers present grammar as a "tool" for communication.
- Teachers use the textbook as a "springboard."
- Teachers accept oral and written errors as a natural part of the language learning process.
- Teachers use a flexible classroom organization, incorporating pairing, grouping, and moving about of students and teacher.
- Teachers use assessment that reflects instructional techniques and learning styles.

STUDENT BEHAVIORS

- Students engage in meaningful activities that have real-world functions and purposes.
- Students participate in activities that allow for the development of listening and speaking skills.
- Students talk and write about ideas they have read and heard.
- Students work in large and small groups, as well as one-on-one with the teacher.
- Students are involved in activities that reflect the beliefs and customs of other cultures.

Cognizant of the length of time required to achieve communicative proficiency in a second language, the Best Schools begin formal instruction in one or more languages at the elementary or middle school level. High school programs continue instruction in foreign language in programs designed to provide the time necessary to achieve proficiency. Most of the schools offer Spanish and French, with some offering German. Latin is offered in many schools; however, students are encouraged to take a modern language as well. Some schools are also offering other languages (Los Angeles Center for Enriched Studies, CA, Japanese; Barrington High School, IL, Russian).

Foreign Language Illustrations

HEBREW ACADEMY OF GREATER WASHINGTON, SILVER SPRINGS, MD

The Hebrew Academy of Greater Washington is a private school that combines instruction in Judaic studies with a general education curriculum for kindergarten through grade 12. Its student body reflects the variety of socioeconomic classes and countries of origin found in the Jewish homes of the surrounding neighborhood. Parents of students include government professionals; immigrants from Russia, Iran, and Israel (all of whom speak English as a second language); business owners and employees; professionals in private practices; tradespeople; and other workers. Currently, 31% of the student body receives tuition assistance. A similar percentage of students are children of highly educated, upper middle-income parents.

After completing the required four-year foreign language curriculum at the Academy, students will be able to understand, read, speak, and write Spanish in everyday situations. Classes are conducted almost entirely in Spanish, since the students' level of proficiency increases with the level of exposure to and interaction with the target language.

Time in class is spent practicing Spanish, not "learning" it; the students understand that rote memorization is to be done as homework. This approach guides students to high-order, critical-thinking skills. Instead of being given explicit grammar rules, students deduce and formulate many of the rules for themselves based on the class conversations and exchanges. A particularly successful technique has been the teaching of vocabulary, not by giving the English equivalent of a list of words, but by using elaboration of new words in already familiar Spanish and using Spanish synonyms or antonyms. This approach enables the students to construct vocabulary nets with words intimately linked, rather than vocabulary lists.

In every Spanish course, content is the study of language, not study of mere grammar and vocabulary. The students learn to summarize and analyze the main points of a text, deduce meaning from context, and express themselves – all skills that reinforce the content of other areas of the curriculum.

The middle and high school course of study in Judaic studies essentially requires all students to take one period per day of Hebrew language. An attempt is made not only to advance Hebrew language as an additional foreign language, but also to help students become truly proficient in it by means of immersion, by having all intensive-level Judaic studies courses being taught entirely in Hebrew. Proficiency in Hebrew, constituting a link with the Jews' historical means of expression down through the ages is not only considered an important educational and cultural value, but it also has important practical ramifications, in light of the greater number of Academy graduates who opt to spend at least one year of study following their completion of the twelfth grade in an Israeli educational institution.

Deena Levine, *Upper School Principal, Grades 5–12, 310 Students*

SOLON HIGH SCHOOL, SOLON, OH

Solon High School is a four-year comprehensive high school with an enrollment of 1030 students. Solon is a middle- to upper middle-class suburb of 19,000 people located twenty-two miles southeast of Cleveland. A contemporary community, it reflects the cultural and intellectual interests of its residents whose occupational status is predominantly business and professional. Approximately 90% of the graduates immediately pursue post-high school education.

The goal of the foreign language department is to develop in the students an international competence in foreign languages. More than 70% of the students are enrolled in foreign language courses. Emphasis is on communication and articulation in the foreign language as both the main objective and the enabling activity of classroom learning. Textbooks are carefully selected to enhance the development of communicative skills. They are designed to emphasize the receptive and productive skills of listening and speaking in the entry levels and reading and writing in the advanced levels.

Cultural study is integrated throughout the program in all languages. Beliefs, customs, social structures, behaviors, and gestures common during greeting, meeting, and departure taking are studied and practiced. In order to have an international competence in the foreign language, the students must be able to function appropriately in other cultures and be sensitive to cultural differences.

As a department, the ACTFL guidelines for proficiency are followed to set expectations of function and content abilities at the novice (years I and II), intermediate (years III and IV), and advanced (Level V advanced placement). The advanced placement courses are designed to parallel the skill development of a third-year college course in advanced composition and conversation. The courses focus on the mastery of the four skills, not on the content of specific texts. Thus, the teachers have the freedom to design these courses tailored to the needs and interests of their students.

Travel abroad programs have also been made available during the summer months for students who wish to experience language learning firsthand. As a result, they are able to bring alive what they have learned in the classroom. Trips to France and Spain are offered on alternating years. Usually twenty to thirty students travel each year with school staff.

The addition of advanced placement courses in French, German, and Spanish best exemplify the efforts at content improvement in the department. These courses extend the existing four-year program and provide students an opportunity to demonstrate fluency in the target language.

E. James Kotora, *Principal, Grades 9–12, 1039 Students*

NILES WEST HIGH SCHOOL, SKOKIE, IL

Niles West serves about 1700 students in the suburban villages of Skokie, Morton Grove, Lincolnwood, and Niles. According to realtors, the mainly middle-class community is drawn to the area because of quality schools and close proximity to Chicago, which provides easy access to business opportunities. The school shares its southern boundary with the Chicago Public Schools; the ninety-four-acre school property is surrounded on two sides by residential property and business and by industrial property on the other sides. The community uses the school frequently for adult education programs and other activities. The community's emphasis on education is highlighted by the fact that 93% of graduates continue their education after graduation.

The foreign language department offers four or five years of instruction in four languages (Spanish, French, German, and Hebrew) with a variety of difficulty levels available to students. The department embraces and uses the tenets of "proficiency instruction" from the guidelines set forth by the American Council of Teachers of Foreign Languages (ACTFL). Instructors use cooperative learning techniques consistently through the year to advance the concept of proficiency instruction. Students spend over half the period orally practicing the lessons presented in class, because communicative competence is a discernible goal of the department.

Writing skills are heavily emphasized through the frequent use of journals and development of journal articles into expository essays. In addition, teachers require students to write out their own definitions of new vocabulary words presented in class. French teachers have assigned their students pen pals to whom they write two to three times per year. Students in the fourth year and advanced placement classes (in French, German, and Spanish) routinely respond to higher level critical thinking questions in their target language. Questions are based on readings in the language.

At senior level, Spanish students may choose from advance placement, honors, or two regular-level classes, one of which is a highly specialized Spanish conversation course, which focuses intensely on language production and reception. Using a strict immersion-type approach, students speak only in Spanish for the duration of the class. Students demonstrate quantitative and qualitative improvement after completing this year-long course that caps the student's high school experience in Spanish. When enrollment permits, the course will also be offered in French and German. Enrollment in foreign language study over the last five years has approximated 60%, considerably higher than the national average.

Donald G. Ring, *Principal, Grades 9–12, 1701 Students*

MONTGOMERY HIGH SCHOOL, SKILLMAN, NJ

Montgomery Township is less than twenty minutes from the industrial/technical complex of the Route 1 corridor between Princeton and New Brunswick, the academic community surrounding Princeton University, and the New Jersey State capitol in Trenton. Montgomery, a rural-suburban community of approximately thirty-four square miles, is characterized by a growing population in an attractive rural setting. The community is comprised primarily of high middle-income households whose wage earners hold professional, managerial, and executive positions.

The Montgomery Township schools offer a strong six-year foreign language program beginning in seventh grade for study of French, German, and/or Spanish. If a student progresses beyond the courses mentioned, Montgomery has a relationship with Princeton University that permits students to take courses during the day at no cost. Eighty-six percent of the current student population, grades 7 – 12, is studying foreign language.

All levels of language instruction stress active student performance in that language. Students are encouraged to use the language for creative self-expression. Written assignments include student newspapers, scrapbooks, poetry books, journals, essays, and travel brochures. Computers are used extensively to enhance the writing process. Intensive speaking opportunities such as discussion, debate, videotaped skits, and mock elections allow students to become proficient in the spoken language. Grammar is taught in a communicative context with practical application of oral and written activities. Students are encouraged to use deductive and inductive reasoning, hypothesis, and analysis to gain a real understanding of grammatical structures.

Foreign language instruction is enhanced through an interdisciplinary approach. The music and foreign language departments coordinate holiday programs and a multicultural evening featuring song, food, and dance from many nations. French VI students and English IV students work together on a unit about the French Revolution. Exchange and travel programs with France, Germany, and Spain help to enlarge the student's global perspective.

Anne Marie Current, *Principal, Grades 9–12, 417 Students*

ENGLISH AS A SECOND LANGUAGE (ESL)

It is estimated that, by the year 2000, one in three people in the United States will be either African-American, Hispanic, or Asian-American (Malarz, 1993). The largest non-English-speaking minority group is Hispanic; however, many other native languages are spoken by students. More than 2.3 million limited english proficient (LEP) students attend schools in the United States. More than 40% of all LEP students are also immigrants, representing many cultures as well as languages (GAO, 1994). The purpose of English as a second language (ESL) programs is to facilitate the language and cultural transition to English. The focus of the curriculum is to enable students to learn English to the degree necessary to function in an English-speaking classroom. In the ESL classroom, English is spoken exclusively, and, in any given class, there may be children who speak several different native languages. In terms of classroom instruction in English, there is little observable difference in instructional approach between a classroom where children are learning English and the classroom where native English speakers are learning a second language using the authentic language approach.

Bilingual education differs from ESL in that, while the student is gaining competence, the student also receives academic instruction in some subjects in his/her native language. Bilingual instruction allows for more detailed and richer coverage of academic subjects until students become proficient in English. Schools with small numbers of LEP students and those students who speak many different languages may be unable to offer bilingual education and may be limited to ESL approaches. Training of all teachers in the school in English language acquisition, cultural diversity, and strategies for instructing LEP students in academic areas is an essential part of effective instruction.

The rate at which a child learns a second language varies; however, the motivation for learning and the amount of time spent using and hearing the second language affect the speed and quality of acquisition. Educators frequently remark on how quickly a non-English-speaking child learns English. Unable to communicate with peers or to participate in English-speaking classes, these children are usually highly motivated to learn English. In addition, the child is exposed to English outside of the ESL class for as much as five hours per day in school, and that time may be extended through play time and, in some cases, at home. In communities with high concentrations of a particular non-English-speaking population, children may take longer to become proficient in English, since there may be many people who communicate with the child in the native language and, therefore, less motivation to learn English and less exposure time to English.

The non-English-speaking population in the United States is not distributed evenly across school districts. Some districts have students who speak many different languages (i.e., East Brunswick, New Jersey, with fifty-five native languages), while other districts draw students from only one or two non-English language groups; still other districts have no non-English-speaking students. For many districts, non-English-speaking students represent only a small fraction of the population; however, in other districts, more than 80% of their student bodies may have native languages other than English. Children who maintain their native language and become fluent in English achieve the national objective of fluency in two languages.

THE BEST SCHOOLS–ENGLISH AS A SECOND LANGUAGE

The Best Schools provide ESL and/or bilingual education based on the needs of their population. In addition to formal class work, many schools also provide the support of peers who speak the language, parental contact in the native language, bilingual tutoring, advisory groups, and Saturday and summer programs. In addition, emphasis has been placed on the training of all teachers in the school in methods of regular classroom instruction, which assist students whose native language is not English. Some schools also take advantage of the presence of students who speak other languages to support their programs to teach foreign languages and culture.

English as a Second Language Illustrations

ALAMEDA HIGH SCHOOL, ALAMEDA, CA

Alameda High School, founded in 1874, is situated near the center of the city. Although a part of the East Bay metropolitan area, Alameda maintains a small-town atmosphere. The student mobility rate and dropout rate have always been low (under 2%). At the same time, the majority of the students and families are new Alamedans and/or new Americans. Currently, there are more than twelve ethnicities represented on campus, and 31% of the student body speaks a primary language other than English, with 8% of the students needing ESL instruction. The 1279 member school community crosses all socioeconomic categories. Some families live on the ''Gold Coast'' in huge Victorian mansions, while others live in one-bedroom apartments with twelve people sleeping in shifts. The juxtaposition of old and new, of rich and poor, of tradition and innovation gives solidity and vitality both to the school and community.

LEP (limited english proficient) students participate in classes designed to meet their needs. There are three levels of English language development (ELD) classes: beginning, intermediate, and advanced; there are sheltered classes in history and in English to allow these students to have access to content while they acquire English. Students are identified when they enroll in school through a series of oral and written tests. The program is completed when a level of competence is achieved that will enable the student to work independently. LEP students are closely monitored both while they are in the program and after they enter mainstream classes. The apprenticeship program recruits fully bilingual students who are assigned to beginning, intermediate, and mainstreamed classrooms. These students, who receive credit, are trained in sheltering, ELD, and translation techniques in order to aid LEP students in the classroom. After school, peer tutoring, study nights (also involving English-speaking students studying a foreign language), and the international club (open to all students) provide additional support. Students who consistently use after-school tutoring improved an average of fifteen points per subject on an eighty-five–point scale on an ESL teacher assessment tool, while those who did not use the tutoring registered no progress on the scale.

The school strongly encourages family involvement in the ELD program. Forms are translated and messages home are taped in a number of different languages to encourage families to become actively involved. Parents are invited to a September breakfast and tour of the school, and international parent-teacher-student breakfast and dinner buffets throughout the year nurture and develop the feeling of community for the families. The bilingual advisory committee, made up of parents, teachers, students, and staff, meets regularly throughout the year.

Betty J. Ruark, *Principal, Grades 9–12, 1279 Students*

ROSEMONT JUNIOR HIGH SCHOOL, LA CRESCENTA, CA

Nestled in the foothills of La Crescenta, Rosemont Junior High School is one of four middle schools in the Glendale Unified School District. Rosemont's student population represents a suburban, middle-class unincorporated community of nearly 22,000. In recent years, the community has become more cosmopolitan and ethnically diverse with a language minority population of over 30%, with 15% qualifying for LEP instruction.

The LEP program integrates instruction with the core curriculum through ESL reading and

English courses, sheltered courses in science, United States history, and world history and geography. Cultural literacy, along with American ethics, values, customs, and beliefs, is prevalent throughout the program. Students use listening, speaking, reading, writing, and critical thinking to understand and express ideas and for creative expression.

The ESL curriculum is aligned with the core curriculum in English, social science, and science, and it is supported by materials appropriate for LEP students. Intermediate and advanced ESL students read core literature available for native English speakers. A library of core curriculum literary works in Korean and Spanish is available to beginning ESL students, who also have access to the English core curriculum through nonprint media.

While they are developing English proficiency through ESL and sheltered classes, students are also learning English and content in the areas of math, physical education, skills for adolescence, art, chorus, orchestra, and home economics.

All students who speak more than one language are initially tested for proficiency in oral language, writing, and reading at the district's Welcome Center, and placement is made depending upon the results. Students are also tested at the school site three times a year with a standardized test per level in writing, reading, grammar, and oral proficiency. Rosemont's rate of reclassification of LEP students to fluent English proficiency (FEP) averages 15% yearly.

Lois W. Neil, *Principal, Grades 7–8, 994 Students*

NEPTUNE MIDDLE SCHOOL, KISSIMMEE, FL

Neptune Middle School serves the growing community of Osceola County. This county remains among the fastest growing in the nation. Once predominately agricultural, Osceola County is today dominated by tourism. The demographics of the school reflect the diversity of the larger community. Recent data indicate a community of 86% Caucasian, 6% African-American, and 8% Hispanic. The Hispanic population is the fastest growing. This trend is expected to continue as long as Caribbean and South American immigration continues. Osceola also draws Hispanic residents from the Northeast (mainly New York) and south Florida. Four percent of the students qualify for the ESL program.

The goal of the English for speakers of other language program (ESOL) is to develop the LEP students' proficiency in the English language. To qualify, students must score below specified scores on identified language tests. The teacher is bilingual in Spanish and English, and most of the students are Hispanic, although the school has also had Russian-, French-, German-, Chinese-, Portuguese-, and Vietnamese-speaking students. The teacher has the students for two periods a day for reading and language arts; they attend regular classes the remainder of the school day. However, sixth-grade students have a teacher for mathematics, social studies, and science who is bilingual. One hundred percent of the faculty have been trained in ESOL teaching strategies effective in communicating with LEP students.

The ESOL teacher uses listening/writing exercises to help students learn English. For example, she reads a short story every day to the students, who take notes of names and characters, settings, events, problems, and solutions. Students then write a summary of the story. Students also write in their journal every day. Students select books and then rewrite the story by changing events to make it their story. They then illustrate the stories and the teacher binds the books for them to share their stories with the class.

Rose J. Kish, *Principal, Grades 6–8, 1047 Students*

CHARLIE RICHARD LYLES MIDDLE SCHOOL, GARLAND, TX

Lyles Middle School, located across from a lake and surrounded by trees, was opened in 1987, with 750 students; it has now reached its maximum capacity of 1040. This phenomenal growth is due in part to Garland's "parental choice" plan. The student body is composed of 31% minority students and 60% Anglo students. Much of the student population comes from the apartment areas that surround the nearby interstate highway. Over 600 students, including sixty-two ESL students, are bused to the school.

ESL classes are a part of the instructional program at Lyles. Students are placed into ESL classes for one, two, or three periods, depending on their level, and are mainstreamed into mathematics, science, social studies, electives, and physical education classes. An ESL extended day program and a aummer/Saturday tutorial program are supported through a grant. The idea for a summer/Saturday program came as result of a preassessment test developed by the school and administered to sixth graders. Teachers decided a summer tutorial program was needed to review concepts and prepare students to take the seven-grade state test.

Marlene C. Carter, *Principal, Grades 6–8, 1037 Students*

TRANSITION TO WORK PROGRAMS

Fifty percent of American high school graduates do not go directly on to postsecondary education, and an additional 25% who go on to college do not complete the bachelor's degree. It is estimated that half of all high school graduates have not found a steady job by the age of thirty. Rather, they move from one low-paying job to another, with little hope of advancement or little opportunity for job training. About one-third of high school students are enrolled in a largely random sequence of general courses, which do not prepare them for work or college, yet, at the same time, from 60–80% of students hold part-time, in some cases, full-time, jobs while in school. However, these jobs are low level, with little potential for long-term careers and bear little relationship to school-based studies. It is said that the United States has the worst school-to-work transition record in the industrialized world (Olson, 1994).

The National Education Goals state that

> By the year 2000, American students will leave grades four, eight, and twelve having demonstrated competency in challenging subject matter . . . and every school in America will ensure that all students learn to use their minds well, so that they may be prepared for . . . productive employment in our Nation's modern economy.
>
> By the year 2000, every adult American will be literate and possess the knowledge and skills necessary to compete in a global economy. . . .

The school-to-work transition is a priority under the Goals 2000 initiative. The President, in signing the School-to-Work Opportunities act, called the measure a "whole new approach to work and learning." Programs funded under the act provide a combination of school- and work-based learning, skill certification, and, where appropriate, a postsecondary credential.

The new programs focus on high expectations for academic learning, which prepares students for postsecondary education, as well as entry into the work force. Academic courses have high standards and make connections to real-world problems and experiences. For example, Applied Mathematics, developed by the Center for Occupational Research and Development (CORD, 1994), is a two- to three-year math course with evidence that students who complete the course score as well as those who complete traditional Algebra I courses. Moreover, the highly motivational lab-oriented program uses career-oriented problems that make clear to students the answer to the question, "Why do we have to know this?" Other courses developed and supported through CORD include Applied Chemistry and Principles of Technology. Schools are also developing their own courses as they seek ways to develop connections for all students to make between classroom study and the real world.

Academic study is combined with study in one of several career clusters. The area of study is usually finalized by the eleventh grade. In many schools, programs are designed to coordinate with two years of postsecondary education, most often a community college. From the community college, students can enter the work force or, in many cases, continue into a baccalaureate program.

An important part of the school-to-work transition is the opportunity to experience careers directly through mentorship programs, internships, and/or work-study programs. In these, the emphasis is on making connections between the classroom experiences and the real world.

The aim of the new programs, such as TechPrep (NDN) (developed by CORD, a nonprofit public service organization working with state education agencies in forty states, which provides instructional materials and support for TechPrep programs throughout the country), is to ensure that no students will drift through high school in a general program of unrelated courses that prepares them for neither work nor college. In order to accomplish this goal, provision has to be made starting at least in the middle school to provide opportunities for career exploration in order to help students to identify their interests and aptitudes and to begin to think about education in relationship to careers. The emphasis in the first two years of high school should be on further exploration of careers, with specific information about occupations. Such orientation should not be limited to a specific course but should be infused into all academic areas. Finally, the stigma too often associated with old forms of "vocational" education, which leads many students to enroll in a "general" curriculum, needs to be eliminated in both the minds of students and parents.

THE BEST SCHOOLS–TRANSITION TO WORK PROGRAMS

Not all students in the Best Schools are college-bound. Represented within these schools are the full range of student goals and aspirations. One of the characteristics of Best Schools is their attention to meeting the needs of all students, including those who may or may not continue their education directly from high school. The emphasis is to replace the so-called "general curriculum" with a highly challenging academic program for all students, to provide career orientation and to make connections between academics and careers for all students, and to provide serious career study and hands-on work experience for those planning to enter the work force from high school or after two years of postsecondary education.

Illustration of Transition to Work Programs

BARRINGTON HIGH SCHOOL, BARRINGTON, IL

Barrington High School serves a geographically large and socioeconomically diverse community. The aspirations of many parents for their children and their expectations for the school serving them are reflected in ACT scores that are the highest in the northwest suburbs of Chicago; in the record number of national semifinalists; in the number of students taking AP exams and earning college credit; and in the nationally recognized academic and fine arts programs. However, in so diversified a student body, expectations cannot be defined solely for the college-bound students. Some students expect to be qualified to enter the workplace upon graduation from high school; therefore, the high school has made a whole-hearted commitment to the nationally recognized regional career cooperative, combining with two other districts and Harper College.

Barrington students may enroll in the following programs while in high school:

- cooperative careers program (with paid internship in a participating company) in either banking or insurance
- TechPrep programs (with a paid internship) in the following areas: law enforcement, manufacturing and fabrication, heating and cooling, marketing and management,

corporate careers, computer aided design, child development, hospitality management, food service, electronics, office careers, and fire science

The career cooperative programs are planned jointly by academic and vocational educators and business and industry representatives. They are based on defined academic competencies (e.g., writing and reading skills, scientific understanding, mathematical skills) acquired in high school course offerings and vocational/technical competencies acquired in high school courses, junior college courses, and/or work experiences. Employers among seventy-five regional businesses and industries have committed themselves to paid internships and hiring preferences for employment at the conclusion of the program. Students may terminate the program with high school graduation or continue at Harper Junior College to earn an associate degree in the particular skill or occupation.

Edward J. DeYoung, *Principal, Grades 9–12, 2014 Students*

SCHAUMBURG HIGH SCHOOL, SCHAUMBURG, IL

Schaumburg High School serves its community in a tradition of educational excellence with equity for all levels of students. A comprehensive high school, it finds creative ways to meet the needs of all its students. Seventy-eight percent of the school's 1992 graduates continued their formal education. Thirty-two percent of these students matriculated at the local community college.

It is to meet the needs of these students and others who seek an alternative to the traditional four-year college path that, in 1990, Schaumburg High School became a pilot campus for a new level of educational programming called TechPrep. Targeting the "under-represented majority," or so-called average students, TechPrep links high school technical and academic courses with paid corporate internships and two years of community college training. With the help of local business and industry partners, Tech Prep has expanded its focus from one to thirteen career areas. In September 1992, the U.S. Department of Labor affirmed the program's success in pioneering new approaches to prepare youth for the workplace. It bestowed upon it the 1992 Labor Investing For Tomorrow (LIFT) Award.

Jack Gaza, *Principal, Grades 9–12, 2224 Students*

LAKOTA HIGH SCHOOL, WEST CHESTER, OH

Located twenty-five miles north of Cincinnati, Lakota High School is a sprawling facility of 259,000 square feet designed to meet the various needs of a middle-/upper middle-class community. Over 1900 students in grades 10–12 represent diverse backgrounds and an enrollment that is increasing at a rate of approximately 100 students per year.

Approximately 75% of the Lakota graduates attend postsecondary education programs. The school provides those who do not choose to pursue that goal with a range of alternative programs. The occupational work experience program is a two-year program that is geared to eleventh- and twelfth-grade students who wish to earn both school and work-study credits. The Marketing I and II program does likewise. The Joint Vocational School (JVS) offers a variety of training programs for students.

The special education department at Lakota is an exemplary program, which addresses the academic and vocational goals of individual educational plan students. All special education students are eligible to be vocationally assessed at the vocational school. This is an intense two-day evaluation process, and the detailed results are shared with students, parents, work-study coordinator, job trainers, and related agencies. Students wishing to attend JVS during their high school career or as a thirteenth-year student also use this information to make program choices.

A unique feature and unusually effective program is the use of the supported-work model. Students identified as needing individual training at a job site are provided with a job trainer who evaluates the job skills, teaches those skills, and trains the students to master the skills in the work environment. This process varies in length, based on individual needs; the training may be reinstated at any time that the job requirements change or if the student needs reinforcement of the skill learned. Students also work and are trained in an enclave model. Groups of multiply handicapped students are transported to selected work sites to learn about the work environment as a team. They are accompanied by a teacher, two aides, a job trainer(s), and a language therapist. Students participating in these programs are compensated for their work and receive a grade. A Butler County Transition Coordinator uses this work experience and information to assist students and families in preparing for entry into the community workplace. Vocational education is integrated into the curricular areas of mathematics, social studies, English, and reading. In addition to mainstreaming handicapped students into academics, students may participate in the keymakers club, which integrates handicapped and nonhandicapped students for social and recreational activities.

Craig C. Ullery, *Principal, Grades 9–12, 1935 Students*

THE BEST SCHOOLS–OTHER SUBJECTS

Private schools among the recognized schools frequently have specialized programs that are central to their mission. For example, the Hebrew Academy devotes as much as 50% of the instructional day to religious instruction. Other schools affiliated with religious groups also incorporate religious curricula. Multicultural, global, and character education are also taught as a distinct part of the curriculum in some private, as well as public, schools.

Many of the Best Schools are also working toward development of a totally integrated curriculum; examples of this are found in previous chapters.

Other Curriculum Illustration

SEABURY HALL, MAKAWAO, HI

Seabury Hall is an independent, college preparatory school with a faculty of about forty-five skilled professionals, a middle school population (grades 6–8) of 118, and an upper school population (grades 9–12) of 206. It was founded in 1964 under the aegis of the Episcopal Church and continues to operate on the original site, in a rural, ranching area on the island of Maui. Although the school is no longer owned by the Episcopal Church, the school continues to develop programs and courses to foster sound personal values and high ethical standards.

The department of religion and philosophy offers challenging courses that explore issues of ethics and faith. Because these courses emphasize not only writing and critical thinking skills, but also the development of personal values and self-awareness, they feature them as uniquely suited to the school philosophy.

In "The Philosophy of Belief and Faith," for example, students are guided in close textual study of works by the Western world's greatest philosophers. The class traces the development of the medieval concept of the soul into more recent concepts such as ego, self, and (in the instructor's words) "nothing." Students evaluate these ideas primarily by comparing them with their own articulated beliefs and views.

In developing these unique programs, the philosophy teacher often confers with faculty of other departments. He works with the computer lab to focus attention on ethical issues raised by new technology. The teacher collaborates with English, history, and art teachers in a wide variety of ways.

Thomas P. Olverson, *Principal, Grades 6–12, 324 Students*

SUMMARY

In addition to language arts, mathematics, social studies, science, the arts, and information processing, the Best Schools make provision for the learning of a second language, whether that be English for non-English speakers or a second language for native English speakers. Transition to work programs are part of the curriculum, even in schools where the majority of students are college-bound. Most of the Best Schools are working toward a more integrated curriculum, making connections among subject areas and thereby reducing an overall curriculum often burdened with content, but with little time left for development of indepth understanding.

REFERENCES

ACTFL (American Council on the Teaching of Foreign Languages). "ACTFL Oral Proficiency Guidelines," Yonkers, NY: ACTFL.

CORD (Center for Occupational Research and Development). (1994). "A Report on the Attainment of Algebra I Skills by Completers of Applied Mathematics 1 and 2," Waco, TX: CORD.

GAO (United States General Accounting Office). (1994). *Limited English Proficiency: A Growing and Costly Educational Challenge Facing Many School Districts.* Washington, D.C.: GAO.

Lester, Kenneth. (1989). "Foreign Language Program Evaluation: East Brunswick Public Schools," East Brunswick, NJ.

Lester, Kenneth. (1992). "Foreign Language Program Evaluation: East Brunswick Public Schools," East Brunswick, NJ.

Liskin-Gasparro, Judith. (1982). *ETS Oral Proficiency Testing Manual.* Princeton, NJ: Educational Testing Service.

Malarz, Lynn. (1993). "Bilingual Education: Effective Programming for Language Minority Students," *ASCD Curriculum Handbook.* Alexandria, VA: ASCD.

Olson, Lynn. (1994). "Bridging the Gap: The Nation's Haphazard School-to-Work Link Is Getting an Overhaul," *Education Week* (January 26).

Rosiello, Linda. (1989). "Envisioning East Brunswick's Foreign Language Program," East Brunswick, NJ: East Brunswick Public Schools.

PART THREE

THE ROLE OF THE DISTRICT IN EFFECTIVE SCHOOL DEVELOPMENT

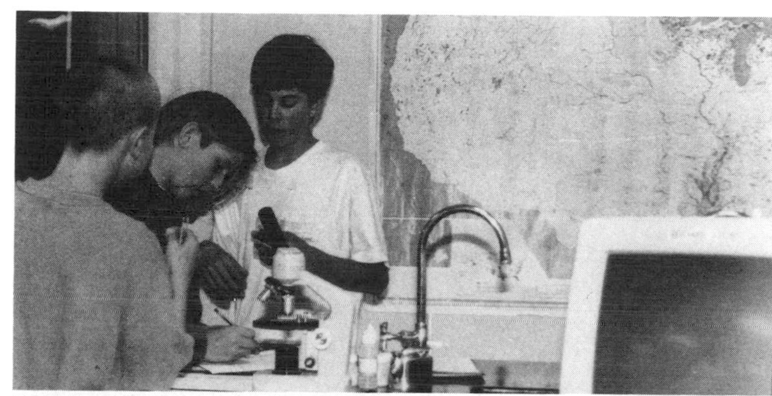

CHAPTER 13

The Effective School District

THE emphasis in the literature and in the media on the individual school as the focal point of educational reform has frequently distorted or overlooked the role of the district in school improvement. It is true that effective instruction occurs classroom by classroom, school by school; however, if successful schools are to become the rule rather than the exception, the role of the district in providing a unified mission, instructional leadership, and support must be recognized. There are over 110,000 schools in the country, but only 16,000 school districts. Standards for the 21st century will not be met merely by hoping that 110,000 effective principals will emerge spontaneously and, with only inconsequential central organizational support, "create" 110,000 successful schools. "The individual school may be the unit of change but frequently change is the result of system initiatives that live or die based on the strategies and supports offered by the larger organization" (Fullan, 1991, p. 73). "Researchers who have studied innovation in general [have] found that it is most likely to be successful when it combines elements of 'bottom up' planning and decision making with 'top-down' stimuli and support in setting directions and guiding the change process" (Levine and Lezotte, 1990, p. 44). This chapter looks at the following questions concerning the roles of school districts in providing effective education for students:

- What does theory and research say about effective school districts?
- What is the role of the district in effective school development?
- What do effective districts do to foster and support the Best Schools?

CHARACTERISTICS OF EFFECTIVE SCHOOL DISTRICTS

School districts operate in a manner consistent with their underlying belief systems. "Conventional" and "congenial" districts operate much like the less than fully effective conventional and congenial schools (see Chapter 1). The leadership of these districts focus on operational matter; they determine which schools are "good," based on efficiency of operations and the opinion of the community as expressed by significant individuals or groups concerned with each individual school. While there may be a multitude of "district"-defined practices, procedures, textbooks, curricula guides, and testing procedures, which may give the appearance of centralized control, in fact, principals are left to function pretty much as they see fit. Interaction among schools is minimal and usually limited to operational concerns. In the conventional or congenial types of districts, effective principals are viewed as "born" and "seasoned by experience," not made, and the definition of who is a successful principal may have little congruence with characteristics associated with high levels of student learning. Whom the central leadership and the board of education hires at the central office and principal levels and which administrative behaviors central leadership reinforces reflect their underlying beliefs about education and determine the culture, climate, and, ultimately, the effectiveness of the district.

Unfortunately, since conventional and congenial type schools predominate, it follows that there is also a preponderance of conventional or congenial districts in the nation. Conventional and congenial districts are the sum of their parts at any specific time in any specific place; there are no mechanisms, no mission, no vital forces, no perceived incentives within the district to transform it or improve it. Any force for change in these districts comes from outside. With little experience in planning, little knowledge of the change process, and little knowledge of effective practices, the response to outside forces that cannot be ignored is usually the "quick fix," the solution that will impact least on the staff and business as usual. Fortunately, there are districts that demonstrate through their actions, beliefs, mission, values, and goals congruence with those factors associated with effective schools research and student outcome-based schools. Lawrence Lezotte (1991) describes four kinds of schools that exist within districts:

(1) Effective and still improving
(2) Not yet effective but improving
(3) Effective but not improving
(4) Neither effective nor improving

Effective schools are those that have met standards of accomplishment. An improving school is one that is able to show continuing progress toward achievement of the standards. Effective and/or improving school districts are those striving to have only the first type of schools, which provide consistent support for both the first and second types of schools and which will not tolerate the third and fourth types of schools.

Just as the characteristics of effective schools are not very different than the characteristics associated with the effective classroom, the characteristics of the effective district are not very different than those of the effective school (Lezotte and Jacoby, 1992):

- strong instructional leadership
- a clear and focused mission
- a climate of high expectations for success of all children
- a safe, orderly environment
- the opportunity to learn and adequate time spent on academic tasks
- frequent monitoring of student progress
- positive home-school relations

The board of education is at the top of the pyramid in provision of district and school leadership. What the board believes and values provides the basis for its definition of its own roles and the powers it bestows on and the roles it defines for the superintendent. The superintendent, in turn, empowers and defines the roles of central and building-level administrators. It is the superintendent who "is the single most important individual for setting the expectations and tone of the pattern of change within the local district" (Fullan, 1991, p. 191).

The need for continuous improvement is necessary even in the most effective district. Improvement requires change. Recognition of the continuous need for change, refinement, and adjustment in the local educational system's practices, programs, and approaches to "doing business" may be the most fundamental of all differences between effective districts and those less effective districts that are organized to maintain the status quo and that initiate change only when external pressures demand.

The roles of the central office in the ongoing journey of school improvement have many dimensions. Clarifying the beliefs of the district and communicating, by word and action, what is valued are the most significant of these. This may be done through the development of a district mission statement, belief statements, and/or the development of explicit statements of expected student learning outcomes. However, much more is involved than the development and dissemination of written documents. The central office must "talk the talk and walk the walk." School staff have often learned "not to take change seriously unless central administration demonstrates through actions that they should" (Fullan, 1991, p. 74). This means that central administration's day-to-day interactions with individuals and with groups, both inside and outside of the schools, reflect the commitment to the mission and the values of the district. What the district leadership does is far more important than what it says is important. How resources are allocated, where and on which issues time is spent, which behaviors are supported and which criticized, which activities are monitored and evaluated, the type of individuals hired for positions, and the way staff is evaluated all speak powerfully to what is "actually" valued in the district. Effective districts reflect in their mission and act on their beliefs that "all students in a district are capable of achieving mastery in all areas of the curriculum and that the teachers and administrators accept responsibility for making this a reality" (Lezotte and Jacobs, 1992, p. 85).

A study by Pajak and Glickman of school districts that have demonstrated sustained improvement over time has identified variables that contributed to their success:

> . . . The superintendent and central office supervisors played critical roles in improving the quality of instruction. . . . Each of the superintendents communicated to the community and to the district's faculty that "children come first." These superintendents also sought financial support from the community for improving instruction in the district.
>
> A common language which centered on instruction and curriculum refinement was found in each district. . . . Talking about students, lessons, and curriculum was the norm, not an aberration.
>
> . . . Districts put into place an organizational structure in which supervisory support was established to encourage instructional dialogue. These districts established either supervisory positions at the central office level or an instructional lead teacher at each building whose primary responsibility was to engage teachers in talking about pedagogy, students' progress, and curriculum. These districts also committed time to allow teachers to meet for the purpose of analyzing information, planning strategies, and sharing ways of implementing new techniques.
>
> . . . Each superintendent established and articulated a clear purpose for the . . . [organization]. This message was clear to the administrators, teaching staff and community. . . . [Each district] also approached the task of improving student learning as a collective effort and recognized the talent and leadership that existed within the district—both in the administration and in the ranks. (from abstract of Pajak and Glickman in *Effective Schools Research Abstracts*, 4(2):62; reported in Lezotte and Jacoby, 1992, pp. 31–32)

Other studies speak to the important role of advocacy in successful districts.

> Initiation of school improvement efforts never occur without an advocate (or advocates). The efforts of the superintendent and other district administrators are usually the most critical in initiating and/or supporting school improvement. Even when the source of school improvement initiation is elsewhere in the system, perhaps at the building level, a powerful determining factor is how the superintendent and others in central office react. The superintendent and other district administrators are such powerful influences on change that they can advance or block progress in school improvement efforts. (Lezotte and Jacoby, 1992)
>
> . . . except in the case of isolated maverick schools that have become effective largely on their own, success . . . requires considerable direction and support of central leadership. (Levine and Lezotte, 1990, p. 40)

Creating a climate of high expectations for staff, as well as students, is an essential role of instructional leadership. While all central administrators contribute to the establishment and reinforcement of expectation, it is the superintendent who is the single most important individual in this regard. One of the ways a climate of high expectations is actualized is through the personnel hiring and evaluation system. Effective districts seek professionals who have the knowledge, attitude, and skills that will contribute to ongoing school improvement, whether that be in the classroom, at the building level, or in central office. Job descriptions should reflect what is important to the district. For administrators, particularly principals, leadership roles and expectations should be clearly stated and outcome-based. Teacher job descriptions should be performance-based, reflect research on effective teaching, and establish the expectation for continuing professional growth. The evaluation system at all levels in the organization should be centered on instructional outcomes. The evaluation system should serve as a basis for ongoing improvement and development and make provision for terminating those who cannot or will not contribute to the overall mission of the district.

Another important role of the central office, in particular the superintendent, is "in ensuring continuity of [effective] leadership at the building level" (Lezotte and Jacobs, 1992, p. 33). However, continuity is important at all levels of the administration. Change in leadership can lead to positive examples of turn-around schools and districts or can quite quickly turn a successful or improving school or district into a less and less effective school or district. Successful practices and programs carefully implemented can quickly be derailed with a change in expectations and priorities of new leadership.

"One of the key beliefs of [administrators of] effective schools is that the people in the schools are already doing the best they know how to do, given the conditions under which they find themselves" (Lezotte and Jacobs, 1992, p. 209). In some cases, change can be brought about by changing conditions, i.e., adding materials, changing equipment, building facilities; however, change most often must occur in what people know. This requires investment in staff development at all levels of the organization. The typical school district in the United States spends less than 2% of its resources on staff development. Effective school districts recognize the ongoing need for growth in the knowledge of their staff, and they allocate substantial resources to this area. Staff development means more than what happens on staff inservice day; it includes the district's observation and assessment process, curriculum and program development, individual guided staff development, training programs related to specific program changes, observations of practices outside of the district, peer observations, opportunities for staff to share ideas and expertise, opportunities to receive feedback on implementation of practices, and involvement in networks, professional associations and leadership projects.

Planning is a critical role of central administration in effective districts. It begins with a belief that there is a need for ongoing improvement and a belief that planning is essential in bringing about positive change. Lawrence Lezotte and Barbara Jacoby (1992) point out in *Sustainable School Reform*, ". . . that school improvement planning is a meaningful process—a journey—not an event." Every district administrator gives lip service to the importance of planning; however, most districts show few signs of systematic planning as a basis for either major or minor change. Most of what passes for planning is the quickly adopted solution implemented in response to "crisis" or the periodic establishment of committees to review new textbooks. Resource allocation is an essential aspect of planning. First, planning takes time—time to assess information concerning the needs; time to disaggregate and analyze data; time to study research and effective practices; time to collaborate; time to define clearly the expected outcomes of change; time to train staff for plan implementation; time to implement, monitor, refine, and revise practice. Effective districts value planning as the base for large-scale changes and for changes in the myriad practices and programs in the district. A major factor in the successful implementation of planned change is the commitment that central office staff makes to monitoring and nurturing the activities incorporated in the plan. Effective superintendents and supervisors are "cheerleaders" for planned change.

Another essential role of the district is to ensure that all students will achieve mastery in all curriculum areas. The district needs to have a process for defining "mastery," developing and implementing curriculum, and assessing what is learned. School administrators may do many things in a day, which are only indirectly involved in instruction; however, students and teachers spend 13,600 hours from kindergarten through grade 12 directly involved in the learning process. When the district says *all* students, it implies that the expected outcomes of instruction will apply equally to the outcomes of all the schools in the district. The role of the district in curriculum development is essential. The first step in the process is the identification of what is worth learning – the statements of proficiency expected of all students as outcomes of their instruction. Curriculum development then follows from the expected outcomes and should be based on the research on learning and effective programs and practice in each area. Finally, means must be identified and/or developed to determine if mastery has occurred. In effective districts, schools, and classrooms, the written, taught, and tested curriculum is aligned (English, 1988); the instruction reflects the relationship between intended outcomes, instructional processes, and instructional assessment. It seems as if this would be standard practice in all schools and districts; however, this is not the case:

> Lack of excellence in American schools is not caused by ineffective teaching, but mostly by misaligning what teachers teach, what they intend to teach, and what they assess as having been taught. (Alan Cohen, 1989, in Lezotte and Jacobs, 1992)

The district's role is to ensure that expectations for learning are set, that curriculum based on research is written, and that valid assessment procedures are established; further, it is the central administration's responsibility, along with that of building administrators, to ensure that curriculum and instructional alignment occurs at the classroom level.

An additional role of the central office is to communicate to the community, parents, and the board of education the mission, goals, programs, practices of the district, and the need for and direction of change. How well the district staff, primarily the superintendent, does this is often critical in maintaining school improvement efforts. It is essential that the stakeholder understand and support what is happening in the schools. Effective district superintendents are decisive in carrying out this role.

Finally, it is the role of the district administration to operate the district, ensure a safe environment, hire staff, manage buildings, build budgets, pay bills, respond to "crises," and meet the mandates of state and federal agencies. Both effective and less effective districts, however, usually do these things well.

THE ROLE OF THE DISTRICT IN SCHOOL DEVELOPMENT

The relationship between the district and the individual school is crucial. The district must provide support for the school as an entity with a mission and, at the same time, insure that the school is also a functioning part of the larger entity – the school district. Levine and Lezotte (1990) describe this as "a kind of directed autonomy" (p. 44).

The central office needs to take the initiative in the development of the district mission, in the establishment of the district and school planning process, in the determination of desired outcomes, and in the setting of guidelines for evaluation of outcomes. However, the central office must also encourage initiative at the school level, within the overall context of the district mission. One of the ways districts accomplish this balance is through the establishment of planning guidelines that require each school to develop improvement plans using district-established criteria. The central office staff plays a significant role in supporting the efforts of the school staff in implementing the plan and in ongoing monitoring of milestones and, ultimately, must hold the school accountable for outcomes.

Another important function of the central office is the coordination of plans and activities among the schools. This requires the development of a sense in each school that they are part of a greater district mission. The involvement of principals and teachers in districtwide planning is one means of accomplishing this. Principal/central office meetings, used to discuss school improvement and to provide the opportunity to share instructional initiatives and concerns, are another important strategy for supporting coordinated development among schools and the central office. Central office also needs to take an active role in monitoring programs districtwide, collecting, disaggregating, and analyzing data, and in communicating findings as a basis for further program development.

Selection of building leadership is a critical central office role. The criteria that district leadership and boards of education use in selecting principals reflect what they believe and value in their schools. Their ability to select the leaders who reflect and who can operationalize those values and beliefs and define which behaviors are encouraged, reinforced, or discouraged determines, to a great degree, the type of schools in the district. Regardless of the process used—a central office committee or a committee involving parents, teachers, and other administrators—a process needs to be established, which will insure the selection of building administrators with the characteristics of effective principals. In the case of a school with a long history of "status quo leadership," building staff may have no experience and no basis for identifying other forms of leadership. Fear of the unknown may steer teachers away from selection of a principal with a different yet effective leadership style. In such cases, involvement of building staff needs to be balanced with others' involvement to maximize the potential for selection of the most effective candidate.

In some districts, Best School principals were hired with full knowledge of the district leadership that they possessed the characteristics to develop Best Schools; in others, they have been hired because of their personality and/or management skills; however, they brought more than "expected" and, in some cases, more than desired to the job in terms of educational knowledge, commitment to change, willingness to take risks. There are also cases where district leadership has changed, and conventional and congenial principals have been swept up, revitalized, and transformed into instructionally successful principals. Unfortunately, there are also cases at the building and district level where changes in central leadership and/or boards of education have resulted in regression of successful schools into conventional molds.

THE BEST SCHOOLS—THE ROLE OF THE DISTRICT

Successful schools can be found in districts that have few characteristics of effective districts. In these cases, the relationship between the school staff and the district leadership can, at best, be described as indifferent and, at worst, antagonistic. The problem stems from their differing views, values, and beliefs concerning the form of the "elephants" we call districts and schools. A district in which the board of education and central administration hold values and beliefs congruent with the less effective "conventional or congenial school" will not understand the priorities and goals of a school staff that is acting on beliefs congruent with those of student outcome-based/professional/collegial schools. It takes particularly strong, passionate, self-initiating, and clever leadership within such schools to persist, survive, and succeed despite the mismatch of school and district culture. Frequently, in such districts, outside recognition of a school for excellence is valued only for its publicity value. In other districts, an individual successful school may never even be allowed to seek recognition, since such recognition might create community pressure on other district schools to change and improve. There may also be central office fear of negative community response should a district apply for recognition and fail to be recognized.

There is no formal Blue Ribbon School District recognition program and, therefore, no specific process in place for examining the districts of which the Best Schools are but a part. However, a review of the Blue Ribbon Schools list for 1991–92 reveals that more than 50% of them were from districts in which at least one other school has been recognized and some where many have been recognized. It can be inferred from the number of multiple school recognitions emanating from these districts that, at a minimum, the district and the schools share the beliefs and values characteristic of effective schools and that there is active support for excellence.

The Role of the District Illustrations

POWAY UNIFIED SCHOOL DISTRICT, POWAY, CA

Poway Unified consists of twenty-nine schools organized into three regions, each with a high school, one or more middle schools, and the feeder elementary schools. Located in the hills northeast of San Diego, Poway is considered a low-wealth district. Nine of the twenty-nine schools have been recognized as Blue Ribbon Schools of Excellence (see Black Mountain Middle School, Chapter 8 , and Chaparral Elementary in Volume 1, Chapter 7, for specific school examples) and as California Distinguished Schools. The district serves a diversified growing community. The superintendent has been in the district for more than twenty years. He is described by principals as a strong instructional leader with clear and high expectations for all students, all staff, and all schools.

In 1988, the district initiated a two-year strategic planning process, involving the union, principals, staff, and the community. From the process, a set of seven core values were developed, with "learning for all children" and "excellence in everything" serving as the bookends for the other values. These core values define the playing field for secretaries, principals, teachers, and the community. The core values include

(1) All students learning
(2) Competent and caring staff
(3) Respect for individual differences
(4) Staff participation in decision making
(5) Safe, orderly, and attractive environment
(6) Effective use of resources
(7) Excellence in all we do

The district is committed to being tops in everything, not just a few things, and *means* that all children will learn.

The organization of Poway Unified represents a balance between centralized and decentralized responsibilities. The organizational philosophy or model, initiated by the superintendent, is "site-based delegation to principals," with a strong partnership with the union. Administrators follow the tenant of the situational leadership model: "Do only for the followers what they can't do for themselves." Let people take the leadership as long as they stay within the playing field.

Decisions, concerning budget, staffing, use of time, and use of nonstaff resources are made at the level closest to the student—the school and classroom. However, there is a critical districtwide vision and unity of purpose based on the core values and district culture, which binds the district together and produces consistently excellent results for students. Curriculum staff work with grade-level teams and cross-grade-level teams to develop program articulation. Administrative autonomy at the regional and school level is monitored and encouraged based on experience. Principals work with the superintendent to develop the district budget.

The superintendent views as essential roles the establishment, communication, nurturing, and maintenance of the district culture of high expectations based on the core values. These values are not mere written statements to be reviewed annually, but the basis for passionate implementation. They define the playing field and set the parameters.

Monitoring the outcomes of the educational process is another major role of the central office staff. One way the district operationalizes the core values is through set annual districtwide objectives, developed by the superintendent with the board of education. For example, information and needs concerning the transition points in the district, elementary to middle school and middle school to high school, were widely discussed with staff. Data was gathered and disseminated and problems defined. A districtwide improvement objective was set. Then, as the superintendent describes it, "The power of the staff was unleashed to solve it." Another example of a districtwide goal stated that "by the end of 3rd grade every child will be reading on grade level if parents will enter into a pact with the district when their child is in kindergarten." Another significant role of the superintendent and other staff is the initiation of new staff into the culture and traditions of the district.

Investment in staff development is key to success. Administrators are trained in various instructional models, from which they choose and develop their own style. Dynamic research-based teacher training has been a high priority in the district for many years. Despite the absence of financial incentives, most teachers are active participants in staff development programs because such participation is expected of professionals. Teachers are also encouraged to give presentations within and outside the district, which reinforces the professionalism of the staff and creates enthusiasm for further learning. Teachers from each school attend monthly forums with the superintendent. Administrators frequently participate with teachers in training programs and are required to attend series of workshops on clinical supervision, leadership, and management. The results of research are highly valued and used to guide program development, solve problems, and provide the basis for staff training.

The characteristics of the superintendent in Poway parallel the characteristics of effective school principals, but with schools rather than classrooms—a unifying vision; high expectations; passionate belief that schools (like students) can learn and continually improve; knowledge of instruction and program; consistent monitoring of results; the ability to work with administrators, teachers, unions, and the community to make it happen; willingness to take risks; positive reinforcement of professionalism; willingness to delegate power; and effective communication of results.

Dr. Robert Reeves, *Superintendent, Grades K–12, 20,000 Students*

MOORESTOWN TOWNSHIP PUBLIC SCHOOLS, MOORESTOWN, NJ

The Moorestown Township public school system is a comprehensive K–12 district located in a suburban community in the southern portion of New Jersey, approximately twenty miles from Philadelphia. The school district has maintained a long history of excellence in education. During the past five years, all three of the district's elementary schools have received national Blue Ribbon School awards.

A foundation of the district's success is its commitment to a systematic planning process. The district has been guided by a strategic plan since its development in 1987. This plan is an organic document that serves as the basis for budgeting, curriculum development, staff development, and strategic school improvement initiatives. Specifically, through the collective governance of K–12 subject advisory committees, five-year operational objectives are developed from the more general strategic plan goals. These objectives are prioritized by the superintendent and his central administrative team. The annual school/district's objectives are presented to the school board for funding as "program initiatives." Each year, the district supports 1/2 to 1% of the annual operating budget for initiatives directly associated with the implementation of school improvement (strategic) projects. Using a variety of financing strategies, the district typically commits from $250,000 to $300,000 annually toward this effort.

The curriculum development process is guided by a systematic assessment of student performance and program needs. This is accomplished by curriculum audits. These audits, which have been conducted by district staff (internal) or by noted educators with specialized knowledge and skills in a content area (external), form the basis of establishing the direction for curricular change. Using current research to provide a benchmark for the "ideal curriculum" (e.g., NCTM Standards, Project 2061 – Science, etc.), these audits carefully assess the status and utility of current content and curricular standards and provide short- and long-term direction for program improvement.

The district places considerable emphasis on staff development, instructional support systems, and supervision to ensure quality and consistency in daily instruction. A district instructional model provides the foundation for essential teaching skills in the district. Originally developed in 1988, this instructional framework has been modified to reflect the latest research on how students learn best. Each staff member in the district has participated in at least ten hours of intensive inservice training by the superintendent on the nature of the model and how it can be integrated into the planning and delivery of daily lessons. Although not a categorical model for effective teaching, the model ensures a core set of teaching skills for all teachers, provides a common language by which school staff can focus professional dialogue, and is the basis for the evaluation of novice and advanced beginning teachers.

As teachers demonstrate proficiency in the delivery of daily instruction, they begin to integrate more complex instructional strategies into daily lessons. The district provides a wide variety of staff development opportunities for its proficient and expert teachers. Topics such as cooperative learning, teaching through student learning styles, whole-language, TESA, etc., are available to promote ongoing professional dialogue and skill development for experienced staff. Often, these teachers will utilize their skills and knowledge to conduct inservice training in their schools or by mentoring a novice or advanced beginning teacher.

Student academic achievement has been consistently well above state and national benchmarks. Student progress is monitored on an ongoing basis, with special attention given to students who fail to take advantage of the educational opportunities offered in his/her school. To this end, the district has implemented a student assistance program. This program, which has gained state and national recognition, utilizes a team [principal, teacher(s), school nurse, member of the child study team] approach to identify and program for the success of at-risk students. Through collaborate efforts with parents, a wide variety of intervention strategies are put in place to help the student(s) achieve and find success both in and out of school. Strategies that have proven to be particularly successful include the district's "grandparent unlimited program," which provides a support system for identified elementary at-risk students by matching them with a trained senior citizen, mentorships that provide social and academic support for middle school students by matching identified at-risk students with staff members, and the "teens need teens" program, which provides peer support and referral for high-risk high school students.

Recently, planning for school improvement has become increasingly decentralized. Through the formation of school-based planning committees, the school principal, staff, community members, and students (at middle school and high school) meet to discuss school needs and plan for school improvement. Specifically, each school has the responsibility of developing at least two multi-year challenge goals to maintain or improve a student-centered phenomenon in the school. To maintain a sense of parity among the schools, these goals may be unique to the school but must be developed and implemented within the framework of district curriculum and school board policy. Through these initiatives, a sense of collective autonomy has developed in the schools. It is hoped that participation by the major stakeholders within the schools will help focus the objectives of school improvement efforts and foster an increased sense of ownership within the school community.

Finally, the district school board has consistently placed its policy development and financial resources toward instructional and student learning outcomes. Moreover, through the leadership of the school board, administration, and staff, the citizens of Moorestown have acknowledged the success of the school district and have demonstrated their support by consistently passing school budgets and building referendums.

It is through this sense of commitment toward students, systematic planning, school climate, and instructional improvement that the Moorestown schools continue to promote educational excellence. Although successful, the staff of the district continues to recognize the need for ongoing school improvement. "We're good, but we can be better" is an attitude that is instilled within each member of the school community. This predisposition of high expectations for staff and students has been a cornerstone of this fine school district.

Vito Germinario, *Superintendent, Grades K–12, 2643 Students*

SUMMARY

While there is no Blue Ribbon Award for school districts, it is clear there are districts of excellence. Among the characteristics exhibited by these districts are many of the characteristics associated with the individual effective school. These districts are committed to and believe that each of their schools can meet the highest standards of excellence, and they provide the leadership, practices, processes, programs, and resources necessary to accomplish their mission. They provide effective balance between control and autonomy and between encouragement and accountability. In the Best Districts, the individual schools are active participants in the accomplishment of a shared district vision. The number of districts with multiple Blue Ribbon Schools is evidence of the powerful and specific roles the central district leadership and school boards play in the development of schools of excellence.

REFERENCES

Black, John A. and Fenwick W. English. (1986). *What They Don't Tell You in Schools of Education about School Administration.* Lancaster, PA: Technomic Publishing Co., Inc.

Caulfield, James M. (1989). *The Role of Leadership in the Administration of Public Schools.* Union, NJ: Nevfield Press.

David, Jane L. (1989). *Restructuring in Progress: Lessons from Pioneering Districts.* Washington, D.C.: Results in Education, Center for Policy Research, National Governors' Association.

English, Fenwick W. (1988). *Curriculum Auditing.* Lancaster, PA: Technomic Publishing Co., Inc.

Fullan, Michael G. (1991). *The New Meaning of Educational Change.* New York, NY: Teachers College Press.

Joyce, Bruce, et al. (1993). *The Self-Renewing School.* Alexandria, VA: ASCD.

Levine, Daniel U. and Lawrence W. Lezotte. (1990). *Unusually Effective Schools: A Review and Analysis of Research and Practice.* Madison, WI: The National Center for Effective Schools Research and Development.

Lezotte, Lawrence W. (1991). *Correlates of Effective Schools: The First and Second Generation.* Okemos, MI: Effective Schools Products, LDT.

Lezotte, Lawrence W. and Barbara C. Jacoby. (1992). *Sustainable School Reform: The District Context for School Improvement.* Okemos, MI: Effective Schools.

Pajak, Edward F. and Carl D. Glickman. (1989). "Dimensions of School District Improvement," *Educational Leadership,* 46(8):61–64.

Waterman, Robert H., Jr. (1987). *The Renewal Factor.* New York, NY: Bantam Books.

PART FOUR

THE NATIONAL RECOGNITION PROCESS

CHAPTER 14

On Becoming a Blue Ribbon School of Excellence

OF the nation's 110,000 public and private elementary, middle, and secondary schools, a total of 2809 have been awarded national recognition as Blue Ribbon Schools of Excellence since the program's inception in 1982. Schools from every state, very small to very large schools, rural to inner-city schools, schools serving very low to very high socioeconomic areas, have been among the approximately 2.5% of the schools nationwide that have met the standards of excellence necessary for national recognition. This chapter looks at the following questions concerning the development and recognition of schools of excellence:

- What are the purposes of the Blue Ribbon School Program?
- What is the process for application to become a Blue Ribbon School?
- What is the process for selection?
- What are the standards of excellence for schools?
- How can a school use the standards as part of the process for self-assessment and improvement?
- What is the value to the school, community, state, and nation of meeting the standards for recognition?

The purpose of the Blue Ribbon School Program, begun in 1983, is to identify and give recognition to public and private schools across the United States that are truly effective in meeting the goals of education for all students. These model schools collectively serve as evidence that schools can successfully provide education for children now and for the 21st century in many different community contexts and within the full range of socioeconomic and multicultural backgrounds that comprise American society. Foundations, magazines, professional organizations, researchers, states, and individual federal programs have long recognized the importance of identifying models in education. The Blue Ribbon Schools Program differs from other recognition programs in that 1) the achievements of the total educational program are used for identification, rather than a specific program or set of programs, i.e., Chapter 1, Drug Free, mathematics programs; 2) a broad range of criteria based on research on effective schools and school practices is used as the basis of the selection process, and the criteria cover all aspects of the educational process, rather than being limited to such items as test scores; 3) all schools both public and private are eligible for recognition; and 4) credibility of the recognition process is established through the multistage selection process starting at the local and state levels followed by a three-stage national review, which includes two reviews of written documents and an independent on-site validation process.

THE BLUE RIBBON APPLICATION PROCESS

Public and private middle and secondary schools with some combination of grades 5–12 may apply for recognition every other year. In alternating years, elementary and middle schools with some combination of grades K–8 may apply. A middle school may not apply as a secondary school if it applied the previous year under the elementary recognition program. Applications are distributed through each state's department of education.

The quality of each school is judged in the context of how successfully it meets its own goals and how well its programs are tailored to local needs. Nevertheless, for a school to be judged deserving of national recognition, it must show significant progress in meeting state and the national goals, must offer an instructional program that meets the highest standards, and must have attained a standard of overall excellence that is worthy of respect and emulation by schools elsewhere of similar size and characteristics. In seeking successful schools, the program also welcomes schools that have overcome serious obstacles or problems and are making significant improvements. Schools selected to receive the Blue Ribbon Schools Award are looked to for exemplary practices to support the achievement of the national goals.

The application has seven sections:

(1) Leadership
(2) Teaching environment
(3) Curriculum and instruction
(4) Student environment
(5) Parental and community support
(6) Indicators of success
(7) Organizational vitality

Each section is further divided into subsections that require specific information concerning each of the areas. In addition, there are two areas of special interest designated each year. These are areas in which the U.S. Department of Education is seeking outstanding model programs. These are optional areas and a school is not penalized for not applying for special recognition.

Applications are usually developed by committees; however, the actual writing is most often done by one or two people. Response space is limited in the narrative section to twenty-eight pages. Clarity of response is the most important writing criteria, since many topics must be covered in limited space. From their reading of the application, panels of reviewers must be able to visualize and understand the programs, practices, and outcomes of the school. The preceding chapters contain many examples of application responses from winning schools. Several people at the local level, including a good editor and one or two people not terribly familiar with the programs in the school, should read the application to be sure that it is clear and understandable.

In addition to describing each program and practice required in the application, schools that are applying for a second or third time (they must skip at least one round after each recognition) must highlight changes and improvements since they were previously honored.

The completed application must be certified as to its accuracy by the principal, the superintendent, and, in the case of public schools, the president of the board of education.

HOW SCHOOLS ARE SELECTED FOR RECOGNITION

Each state administers its own program for selecting public schools to be nominated to the national level. Panels of reviewers are used in most states; in a few cases, on-site visits are also part of the state selection process. Frequently, states provide their own form of recognition for schools selected at the state level. Schools selected within the state are nominated by the chief state school officer to the U.S. Department of Education. The number of schools a state can nominate in a given year is indexed to the state's population. The Council for American Private Education nominates private schools, and officials of the Bureau of Indian Affairs and the Department of Defense Dependent Schools also nominate schools.

At the national level, the applications are reviewed by a panel of some 100 outstanding public and private school educators, college and university staffs, school board members, medical professionals, business representatives, and the general public. Subpanels of three to four members review fifteen to twenty applications. Not only is training provided for all panel members, but each panel has as a facilitator a person who is knowledgeable of the broad range of educational research, programs, and practices associated with effective schools. Special attention is paid to assigning schools, particularly private and special type schools, to reviewers with relevant experience. Panel members do not review schools from their own states or schools with which they have had previous personal or professional involvement.

The standards for school identification are based on research concerning practices and processes associated with high academic achievement and demonstrated learning outcomes. Standards within curricular areas are reflective of the national goals, recognized curriculum, and program standards in each area and research on learning. Standards for leadership, student services, and parent and community involvement are consistent with research in those areas. Over the history of the program, the standards have been revised to reflect new research findings and evolving program standards; however, the basic framework for Blue Ribbon School standards has remained unchanged.

National review panels begin the selection process at Stage I, by rating each section of the application as individuals and then developing consensus ratings as a group, using the following scale and criteria.

U.S. Department of Education Blue Ribbon School Rating Scale

(1) *Very Strong (V):* This segment of the program is truly excellent, that is, within the top 5% of the nation. It describes something that "knocks your socks off" and could be used as a model for presentation to any school.

(2) *Strong (S):* Although a very good program and above the norm, this component does not have the quality of an exemplary program. This part of the school program would exceed that of 60% of the schools in the nation.

(3) *Adequate (A):* This segment meets the general standards of quality expected of schools and represents the norm for schools of this type.

(4) *Inadequate (I):* This segment has serious deficiencies and is clearly below the norm for this type of school.

(5) *No Evidence (NE):* There is insufficient evidence in the application to make any kind of judgment about this aspect of the program, or the section is not addressed.

U.S. DEPARTMENT OF EDUCATION
1994–1995 BLUE RIBBON SCHOOLS PROGRAM
FOR SECONDARY SCHOOLS
Review Panel Instrument

Stage I: Recommended for Site Visit? _____ Yes _____ No
Stage II: Recommended for Recognition? _____ Yes _____ No

Honors Candidate? _______ Parent Involvement
_______ Technology

School Name ____________________

Justification for Decision (include any extenuating circumstances):

____
____
____
____
____
____
____
____
____
____

For Research and referral purposes:

1. Based on your review of the entire nomination form, do you think that the abstract statement accurately reflects the school's nomination? (Circle one)
   a. Yes, to a great extent b. Somewhat c. Not as closely as it should
2. Did you find any particularly exceptional or unique program(s), strategy(ies), approach(es) at this school that might be of value to other schools? ____________Yes ____________ No. If yes, please complete the following:

Program Title or Focus	Nomination Page Number

LEADERSHIP

V S A I NE

○ ○ ○ ○ ○ A1. Goals and priorities appear appropriate for the school and are clearly articulated. Goals and priorities are developed with input from the school's major constituents; formally reviewed and revised regularly; and effectively communicated to staff, students, parents, and the wider community.

○ ○ ○ ○ ○ A2. The principal and staff have a clear vision for the school and its students. This vision is operationalized in terms of specific objectives and the policies, programs, and resources needed to accomplish the school's goals and priorities. School leadership has created a sense of shared purpose among faculty, students, parents, and community to accomplish the school's mission.

○ ○ ○ ○ ○ A3. The principal and staff have a common understanding concerning the importance and structure of instructional leadership within the school. There are written guidelines concerning who performs the various functions.

TEACHING ENVIRONMENT

V S A I NE

○ ○ ○ ○ ○ **B1.** Teachers are substantively involved in decisions about curriculum, instruction, discipline policy, teacher and program evaluation, and other activities. Teacher input is instrumental in the operation of the school.

○ ○ ○ ○ ○ **B2** Special provisions are made for the support and training of beginning teachers and those new to the school. Recruitment and selection procedures appear appropriate to the school.

○ ○ ○ ○ ○ **B3.** The recognition of excellent teachers is supported and encouraged both formally and informally at the school level and beyond.

○ ○ ○ ○ ○ **B4.** A variety of opportunities, including common planning time, are provided to expand or alter teachers' roles to enhance effectiveness with students, improve job satisfaction, and reduce teacher turnover.

○ ○ ○ ○ ○ **B5.** A significant number of staff members participate in staff development activities directly related to school priorities and in programs aimed at strengthening subject matter expertise in the five core subjects.

○ ○ ○ ○ ○ **B6** Teachers are formally and informally supervised and evaluated on a regular basis by designated individuals, provided with useful feedback, and monitored to ensure that evaluations effect improvement.

CURRICULUM AND INSTRUCTION

○ ○ ○ ○ ○ **C1.** Differing student needs and the school's mission are reflected in school and classroom organization. Instructional placement procedures are reasonable and fair. Students have flexibility of movement among instructional/academic groups as their skills and interests change.

○ ○ ○ ○ ○ **C2.** Graduation requirements are challenging and indicate that more is expected of students than minimum standards. A substantial percentage of students exceed the school's graduation requirements. (Middle schools describe requirements to be promoted from the school.)

○ ○ ○ ○ ○ **C3.** Ongoing curriculum development has resulted in a rigorous and rich curriculum offered for all students in

a. English
b. Mathematics
c. Science
d. History
e. Geography
f. The Arts
g. Foreign Language

V S A I NE

○ ○ ○ ○ ○ **C4.** The school has highlighted two well-conceived courses that clearly contribute to schoolwide curriculum goals.

○ ○ ○ ○ ○ **C5.** The school has implemented specific strategies for ensuring that students learn to write effectively and has an assessment process to measure progress.

○ ○ ○ ○ ○ **C6.** Special programs are provided by the school to adapt the academic program to meet the needs of specific groups of students. The identification and placement of students is equitable. Individual progress is closely monitored, and there is clear evidence that strategies/programs are effective. Suitable programs are provided for the following:

a. Special education students
b. Students requiring Chapter 1 services, limited English proficient students, returning students, and students in need of remediation

○ ○ ○ ○ ○ **C7.** A variety of advanced study or enrichment opportunities are provided for unusually talented or motivated students. If participating students do not represent student body diversity, a defensible explanation has been provided.

○ ○ ○ ○ ○ **C8.** The library/media center is an integral component of the school's overall instructional program and plays a key role in developing students' information literacy.

○ ○ ○ ○ ○ **C9.** Regular, systematic, building-level program evaluation efforts result in identifiable instructional improvement.

STUDENT ENVIRONMENT

○ ○ ○ ○ ○ **D1.** School policies and practices ensure that beginning students and transfer students can participate successfully in all aspects of school life and that students have a smooth transition out of the school.

○ ○ ○ ○ ○ **D2.** The school uses incentives, motivational programs, and/or special instructional strategies to help develop and sustain students' interest in learning.

○ ○ ○ ○ ○ **D3.** Opportunities to build sustained relationships with counselors, teachers, or other adults are varied and readily available. Programs are in place to provide counseling and advisement, and these approaches are systematically reviewed for effectiveness. A significant number of students representative of the student body take advantage of these opportunities.

○ ○ ○ ○ ○ **D4.** Effective procedures are employed for identifying, counseling, and assisting potential dropouts and other at-risk and underachieving students. A significant number of these identified students are served.

○ ○ ○ ○ ○ **D5.** A variety of extracurricular activities are available for students.

V S A I NE

Participation is encouraged, and a substantial number of students representative of the student body regularly take part.

○ ○ ○ ○ ○ **D6.** A sound, well-articulated discipline policy prevents violence and encourages students to behave in an orderly fashion without excessive constraints. The school has implemented safeguards against violence and has established violence control procedures.

○ ○ ○ ○ ○ **D7.** The use of drugs, including alcohol and tobacco, is prohibited at school and is discouraged away from school through a comprehensive "no use" drug prevention program and broad-based community efforts.

○ ○ ○ ○ ○ **D8.** Students play an active role in influencing classroom and school policy. Student input is valued, and student participation in problem solving is representative of the student body.

○ ○ ○ ○ ○ **D9.** School programs, practices, policies, and staff foster the development of sound character, democratic values, ethical judgment, good behavior, and the ability to work in a self-disciplined and purposeful manner.

○ ○ ○ ○ ○ **D10.** The school effectively employs curricular and other strategies to prepare students to live productively and harmoniously in a society that is culturally and economically diverse.

○ ○ ○ ○ ○ **D11.** The school effectively employs curricular and other strategies to prepare students to live productively and harmoniously in a society that is globally competitive.

○ ○ ○ ○ ○ **D12.** The school helps non-college-bound students make the transition from the school to workplace.

PARENT AND COMMUNITY SUPPORT

○ ○ ○ ○ ○ **E1.** The school provides evidence of various types of parent involvement. A substantial number of parents are involved, and they are representative of the student body.

○ ○ ○ ○ ○ **E2.** Student progress and overall school performance are regularly communicated to parents through formal and informal means, and a mechanism is in place to receive feedback from parents and the community.

○ ○ ○ ○ ○ **E3.** The school encourages and helps parents to provide a supportive learning environment in the home and informs them about other learning opportunities.

○ ○ ○ ○ ○ **E4.** The school makes a concerted effort to support the diverse needs of families.

○ ○ ○ ○ ○ **E5.** The school provides specific evidence of valuable collaboration with other educational institutions and community groups to support school activities and programs, promote learning outside the school, and provide integrated services to children and their families.

INDICATORS OF SUCCESS

V S A I NE

○ ○ ○ ○ ○ **F1.** Through the use of tests developed and normed at the national or state level:

a. The school reports student achievement results in a manner readily interpretable.

b. Student outcomes are more positive than those reported in schools with similar demographic characteristics.

c. Improvements in student outcomes have been realized over the past three years, or results are consistently outstanding.

○ ○ ○ ○ ○ **F2.** College-bound students perform well on college entrance examinations.

○ ○ ○ ○ ○ **F3.** Student and teacher attendance and the number of students involved in serious disciplinary incidents compare favorably to those of similar schools.

○ ○ ○ ○ ○ **F4.** Concerning the school's dropout rate:

a. The dropout rate compares favorably with that of other schools with similar demographic characteristics.

b. The school has succeeded in lowering its dropout rate or in sustaining an already low rate over the past five years.

○ ○ ○ ○ ○ **F5.** Postgraduate pursuits compare favorably with those of similar schools.

○ ○ ○ ○ ○ **F6.** The school, staff, and students have received a variety of noteworthy awards and recognition over the past five years that are indicative of school success.

ORGANIZATIONAL VITALITY

○ ○ ○ ○ ○ **G1.** The school's climate reflects its mission and provides an atmosphere that is orderly, purposeful, conducive to learning, respectful of diversity, and open to change.

○ ○ ○ ○ ○ **G2.** A school improvement planning process is in place, with evidence of leadership, support, and progress.

○ ○ ○ ○ ○ **G3.** School staff are cognizant of the findings and recommendations of major educational reform studies, national assessments, efforts to establish challenging national standards in the core content areas, and the National Goals, and they have implemented or are considering related changes.

○ ○ ○ ○ ○ **G4.** The school has effectively introduced changes and/or overcome problems and impediments to educational excellence over the last five years while sustaining those conditions that have contributed most to its success.

○ ○ ○ ○ ○ **G5.** Major educational challenges the school must face in the next five years are realistically understood and reflect a careful assessment of changing student needs.

SPECIAL EMPHASES: PARENT INVOLVEMENT AND TECHNOLOGY

V S A I NE

○ ○ ○ ○ ○ H1. The school provides many different opportunities for all parents to be involved in their children's education, including shared responsibilities in decisions about their children's education, health, and well-being.

○ ○ ○ ○ ○ H2. The school uses technology to support instruction through strategies such as the following:

a. Application of technology appropriate for specific objectives
b. Use of distant learning to expand educational opportunities
c. Use of technology to support education of students with disabilities
d. Professional development of staff concerning the appropriate use of hardware and software
e. The use of interactive technologies where possible

Special emphasis topics are reviewed by expert panels convened after the Blue Ribbon Schools have been identified.

There is no calculation of a total score, nor is there a set number of "very strong" or "strong" ratings required for recognition. Based on the total application, the panel either recommends that the school should continue to Stage II of the review process, the site visit, or be eliminated from further consideration. Panels are not limited in terms of the number of schools that can be recommended for visits. Experience over the years has shown that from 40% to 60% of the schools that reach the national level are recommended for site visits by the review panels. The panel's recommendation to site-visit means that 1) based on the review of the application the school is judged worthy of recognition, and the purpose of the site visit is to validate the practices, programs, and outcomes reported in the application; or 2) the school has many exemplary and strong programs, and practices; however, there are some concerns or needs for clarification, which the site visit may be able to clarify or answer during the visit, which would allow the panel to recommend recognition. In addition, each section of the application must be validated by the on-site reviewer.

Two-day site visits are conducted at each school recommended during Stage I of the process. Site visitors are educators with extensive public and/or private school experience. The role of the site visitor is to verify the accuracy of the information in the nomination form and provide answers to specific questions posed by the review panel. Site visitors receive special training and follow carefully prepared guidelines in conducting their school reviews. During the visit, they observe in many, if not all, classrooms; meet with parents, students, staff, and administrators; and review achievement data. They arrange part of their time schedule in advance to insure that they see all aspects of the program and talk with all constituencies; however, much of the time on-site is not structured. During this unstructured time, the visitor may have lunch with students, drop into classes, talk to parents who happen to be in the school, review student work in classrooms, and talk informally with staff. For two days, the site visitor is totally immersed in the school. Then, the site visitor reports his/her findings back to the review panel. For each section of the application, the reviewer states whether he/she found the school's description as "overstated," "understated," or "accurately stated"; narrative comments are made for each section. In addition, the site visitor reports his/her findings concerning specific concerns or questions raised by the review panel. The on-site reviewer does not decide if a school will be recognized.

The review panel meets for a second time, Stage II, to review the site reports. Based on the report, the review panel decides whether their original ratings of each area were "too low," "too high" or "accurate," and then, based on all the information available to them, they decide whether or not the school will be recommended to the Secretary of Education for recognition.

In addition to the individual panels, there is a group of five panel members who review the actions on all nominated schools within state or private school communities where no schools have been recommended for site visits to insure that at least one school from each state and private school community is visited. However, there is no requirement that a school from each state or private school community will be recognized. In addition, this special panel reviews applications referred by other panels because of unusual circumstances. This panel has the authority to reverse the original panel. However, once a decision is made, no appeals are permitted. All schools reviewed at the national level receive a copy of the panel rating and a narrative statement concerning the reasons for the decision.

Schools selected for recognition are notified by phone and by letter of their selection. The schools are invited to send their principal and two other representatives to Washington for an award ceremony at the White House and receptions at which the schools receive the "Blue Ribbon Flags of Excellence," which will fly over their schools and plaques for the schools. The principals also receive recognition from the National Association of Secondary Principals. Communities, districts, and schools celebrate the award in many different ways.

SELF-ASSESSMENT AND IMPROVEMENT: DECIDING WHEN AND IF A SCHOOL SHOULD APPLY FOR RECOGNITION

The Review Panel Instrument can be used as the basis for an assessment of all aspects of the school's programs, services, practices, and achievements. Frequently, an initial "quick and dirty" informal assessment is made by the principal and a few staff members. This usually identifies areas for further study and/or development. Initial assessment is then followed by a more comprehensive review by one or more committees of principal and teachers and, not infrequently, including parents, who take each Blue Ribbon Standard, seek specific standards, report and research concerning effective practice in each area, and then rate their school's own practices against these criteria. For example,

C2. Ongoing curriculum development has resulted in rigorous and rich curriculum offered for all students in: . . . b. mathematics . . .

This example requires schools to review their mathematics program in the light of research on the learning of mathematics, the NCTM Curriculum Standards for Mathematics, and the outcomes envisioned in the national goals and in developing standards, and ask the questions concerning their curriculum, instructional strategies, and outcomes for *all* students in the school.

The five ratings used by the national review panel can be used as a shorthand rating in each area. However, justification for the self-assessment rating should be documented so that it can be shared with the staff as a whole, serve as a basis for improvement, and/or be used in the application process.

Early in the self-assessment process, the committees may find that they have to rate parts of their programs or practices as "No Evidence." As staff focus in on specific programs and practices it often becomes necessary to better define what the actual practice is in the school and/or collect data concerning effectiveness. For example, the committee may be able easily to find a list of staff development activities in which teachers were involved or which were offered by the district; however, it may be necessary to collect additional information in order to determine the extent of involvement of all staff in development programs, the relationship of the involvement to school priorities and the need for subject matter expertise, and to determine how actual practice was affected in the classroom.

The self-assessment process itself has been characterized by many Blue Ribbon principals as one of the best forms of "staff development" undertaken by themselves and their faculties. In order to determine the status of practices and programs, much work must be done in terms of reviewing research concerning learning and program. Whether or not the match is close between the ideal and current practice, the staff learns much about what the ideal should be, reflects on current practice, and either validates their practices or is provided with the basis for planning improvement strategies. They also learn a great deal about the school as a whole and the full range of problems, strengths, and services within the school. In the words of five of the successful principals the impact of applying for national recognition was as follows (U.S. Department of Education, 1992):

> The Blue Ribbon Schools nomination process brought teachers, parents, and students together for a common cause. It provided a focus and single-mindedness to the entire school community.
>
> The process permitted faculty to focus on positive aspects of the school. In a school where everyone wants to do her or his best, the focus easily shifts to our flaws and results in disenchantment. But this process generated pride in the enterprise.
>
> A phenomenal team-building activity that magnified our knowledge of school programs, curriculum, and activities.
>
> There emerged a kind of pride that words are too anemic to describe. There now is an aura of academic supremacy that prevails among students, staff, and community. And we'll work hard to preserve that sense of achievement.
>
> We examined our school with a collective microscope. The process afforded us the opportunity to reflect critically on what we really are all about and to increase our understanding of where we are headed.

Based on the self-assessment, the school is in position to decide if they will seek formal recognition as a Blue Ribbon School. While the Blue Ribbon School standards encompass all aspects of the school program and practices, it is not necessary for a school to be rated "exemplary or very strong" on each standard. Successful applicants usually have a mix of "very strong" and "strong" ratings. Occasionally, a school with a rating of "adequate" in an area may be recognized if there are very high ratings in all other areas. It is not uncommon for schools to apply for recognition and, if rejected, then use the experience as a springboard for school improvement. Some schools have been rejected twice before recognition finally came. Discussions with principals in these schools indicate that, while they were disappointed in not being selected the first or even the second time, the process was a powerful agent for self-improvement and definitely worth the effort.

Time is also a factor in the development of Blue Ribbon Schools. In the preceding chapters, the time lines involved in evolving and implementing successful programs frequently extend over many years. A school that rates itself as "adequate" or "inadequate" in many areas will have to set priorities, establish program improvement objectives, plan staff development programs, and make a commitment to change and persist in development over a period of years. Those who have worked extensively with schools of excellence frequently conclude that it takes three to five years with the *right* leadership for an "adequate/inadequate" school to become a school of overall excellence. In addition, it takes leadership and commitment to excellence on the part of the district, or at least a willingness on the part of the district to let a school strive for excellence. This would seem to be a simple criteria; however, the leadership in far too many districts is afraid to take risks, to rock the boat, to assess and expose weaknesses, and to implement program changes that may be initially uncomfortable for teachers or some parents. Another concern of business-as-usual or "play-it-safe" districts is the fear that if one school is recognized, that the school will "stand out from the rest," creating unwelcome pressure for change at the district-level and at other schools in the district. There are, unfortunately, many stories of struggles on the part of principals and staffs to succeed with little encouragement outside the walls of the school. However, there are also many cases where district leadership has supported excellence at all levels over time; these are the districts with multiple Blue Ribbon Schools. If there were a district-level award, these would be the Blue Ribbon Districts of Excellence.

THE VALUE TO THE SCHOOL, COMMUNITY, STATE, AND NATION OF THE BLUE RIBBON SCHOOL PROGRAM

School and District

For the school, the Blue Ribbon School preapplication review process can be a powerful tool for self-improvement. Many schools have used the process to determine needs, to establish improvement objectives, and to make changes in practices and programs.

In addition to improving programs, the review and application process itself is often credited by Blue Ribbon Schools with increasing the unity of staff, parents, community, and students. The sharing of the "microscope" as the practices and programs are reviewed leads to many immediate, sometimes major, sometimes minor, improvements and enhances the understanding of the roles of all those involved in the success of the school. Some schools who have completed this stage of the process postpone formal application for recognition until the next round, while others go forward with application development. School districts also can find application of the criteria for recognition as a valuable form of assessment and use this as a basis for long- and short-term planning of school improvement.

Recognition as a Blue Ribbon School of Excellence is the public confirmation to all concerned that "this is a successful school." The announcing phone call sets off a professional "high" in the school, among parents, and in the community, which is unparalleled. Even schools who have been previously rejected one or even two times believe that it was worth all the effort and prior disappointments. There is no other award offered in education that matches the Blue Ribbon School of Excellence designation. Receiving the flag and plaque in Washington, the White House ceremony with the President of the United States, and the raising of the flag of excellence above the school are frequently described as the highlights in the professional careers of recipients. Educators, so often painted with the broad brush of criticism based on reports about "average" or poor practices and results, need the public confirmation that excellence can also be a characteristic of education.

Designation as a Blue Ribbon School does not mean that the self-improvement work of the school is complete. Just the opposite is true. Constant review, revision, and assessment are characteristic of the Best Schools, and the award just stimulates the schools to continue to reach for perfection. In fact, 116 schools have applied for and received recognition twice, and four schools three times, during the ten years of the program. In discussions with Best School principals, one of the messages that comes through most clearly is their commitment to future improvement. Discussions concerning what their schools are doing now, or what they have done, quickly turn to what the school is going to do this year and the following year or over the next five years to make the program even better for students. Also impressive is the knowledge of principals and the staff concerning newly developed materials, technology, research, assessments, large-scale state and national improvement projects, reports, and practices in other schools. For example, the day after Apple Computer introduced the Newton Computer, a principal in Texas brought the conversation around to speculating on all the ways this new technology could further enhance instruction in his school. He couldn't wait to talk to staff about the instructional potential.

Designation of a school as a Blue Ribbon School of Excellence has considerable impact on the district as a whole. Schools do not function in isolation within the district. Best Schools are willing to take risks to improve instruction; these schools are most often found in districts that also focus on continuous improvement of programs for children and that encourage innovation and risk taking. In many cases, programs in Best Schools have been initiated with the encouragement and support of the district. Priorities concerning leadership, planning, funding, staffing, curriculum, materials, and equipment at the school level reflect decisions and priorities at the central district level. Therefore, the district, as a whole, rightfully shares in the glory of even a single school's recognition. Where central district practices and programs parallel and support Blue Ribbon School standards, it is not unusual for multiple schools to be designated Blue Ribbon Schools over a period of years. Unfortunately, however, in other districts, the Blue Ribbon School reached its high level of excellence in spite of laissez-faire or indifferent district support.

Another positive effect of having Blue Ribbon Schools in the district is in the recruitment of new teachers, subject supervisors, and principals. Districts report frequently that outstanding professional candidates state that the fact that the district had one or more Blue Ribbon Schools was a major factor in their decision to apply. They see the award as an important indicator of a professional school and/or district committed to and willing to support excellence.

The success of one school in the district, many times, encourages other schools to work toward Blue Ribbon School recognition by stimulating interest in self-assessment and program development. However, the fact that another school has won the flag can also cause anxiety in some schools, based on fear that to apply and fail could be viewed negatively. Where district leadership supports risk taking, focuses on continuous improvement and growth as a district goal, and allows the school staff to decide when they are ready to apply for recognition, the effect of school fears can be minimized. Many districts in the country have multiple Blue Ribbon Schools, and a few, such as Flowing Wells, Arizona, have 100% of their schools recognized. In many districts with multiple winners, some of the winning schools were recognized the first time they applied, and others were not recognized until the second or third attempt.

Parents and Community

Parents have a gut-level feeling about the quality of the school their child attends; however, their perceptions are usually limited to such indicators as their child "likes" or does "not like" the school; the principal and teachers seem "caring" or seem "indifferent"; and/or the school's and their child's standardized test scores are "high" or "low." Assessment of the school's practices and programs in the light of Blue Ribbon School standards provides the confirmation that the opportunities enjoyed by their child are congruent with what is known about the most effective approaches and programs. This is important to parents. The enthusiasm of parents when a school receives Blue Ribbon status usually matches that of the staff and children. The community, as a whole, also gains confidence and pride, not only in the designated school, but frequently in the entire school district. Realtors report that, where parents have the financial flexibility to select the community they want to live in, the quality of the schools is a major factor in their determination of where to settle. Having one or more Blue Ribbon Schools in a district affects home purchasing decisions, property values, and, ultimately, support for the schools.

State and Nation

Many of the reports on education released over the past ten years could easily lead the public and even educators to believe that education in the country is a complete disaster. On national surveys, even parents who rate their own child's school at a fairly high level believe that education in other places is in bad shape. Educators are frequently little more positive than the public at large. At the local level, school and program failures are frequently blamed on parents and even the children themselves. At the state and national level, policymakers, researchers, and educational reporters seem to be determined to find flaws in and discard every program or practice that begins to receive positive reports. Groups that are advocating for a particular program or organizational pattern seem to feel compelled to minimize achievements of any other practice, program, or standard.

Blue Ribbon Schools represent only 2.5% of the nation's schools; however, they serve as ongoing testimony that education can successfully meet world-class standards. Undoubtedly, there are many many more schools across the country that meet standards of excellence, and, hopefully, they will be recognized in the future.

Educators do use models to improve programs and practices. This is particularly true of the Best Schools. Visits to other schools to observe particular programs are almost always mentioned as a starting point for evolving new programs or revising old ones. Release time for observing in other schools is part of the Best Schools' plans for staff development. Frequently, the principal and key teachers are the ones to go first to observe a promising practice in operation. Once a decision is made to adapt or adopt a practice or program, staff are frequently trained by staff from the school where the model is in place. The National Diffusion Network, which disseminates programs validated as effective, has long recognized the importance of model programs and the need for multiple sites where observations and training can take place. Blue Ribbon Schools are frequently the developers of new programs and practices and, in many cases, have served as demonstration sites for other schools.

The existence of over 2809 Blue Ribbon Schools of every socioeconomic type means that other schools can observe the programs and practices of schools with similar demographics to their own. The existence of Blue Ribbon Schools makes it impossible for educators and the public to sit back and say, "It can't be done with our population of students." Inner-city and schools serving low socioeconomic students are definitely not the only ones who can benefit from Blue Ribbon Schools because, many times, it is even more difficult to initiate program improvement in middle- and upper-class communities. The limited nature of most assessment, i.e., standardized math and reading scores which show high "achievement," makes the need for more comprehensive assessment and program development a risk that many educators are not inclined to take. In other words, "If the basic skills test scores are high and parents are relatively happy, why 'rock the boat'?" The dissemination of results, practices, and programs from federal and state levels can provide the education for parents, community members, administrators, and teachers, which can stimulate motivation to move beyond the "safe" to the "effective."

Blue Ribbon Schools are located in every state in the nation. States with aggressive school improvement efforts make maximum use of their knowledge about how schools change and of the existence of their Blue Ribbon Schools. Texas, South Carolina, and California, each state with many of the Best Schools, are examples of states that broadly disseminate the standards for Blue Ribbon Schools, encourage schools to use the standards for self-assessment, report on the practices and programs in Blue Ribbon Schools, and actively involve principals of Blue Ribbon Schools and higher education in training of school administrators and teachers statewide.

SUMMARY

Approximately 2.5% of the nation's 110,000 public and private schools have met the standards as Blue Ribbon Schools of Excellence since 1982. These recognized schools are in every state and serve the full range of student populations and community types, from inner-city to rural to suburban. Recognition is a powerful energizer for further improvement in recognized schools, as well as a stimulus for continued efforts by schools striving for excellence. The recognized schools serve as models for other schools seeking excellent programs and practices; they serve as testimony about what is right about education. The standards for recognition as a Blue Ribbon School can serve as a basis for self-assessment and school improvement. Based on their own assessment, a school can decide whether to apply for and participate in the Blue Ribbon process and seek to fly the flag of excellence over their own school.

REFERENCES

U.S. Department of Education. (1994a). Blue Ribbon Schools 1994-95 Secondary Program: Nomination Requirements and Application. Blue Ribbon Schools Program, Programs for Improvement of Practice, Office of Educational Research and Improvement, 555 New Jersey Avenue, Washington, D.C. 20208-5645, (202) 219-2149.

U.S. Department of Education. (1994b). *Review Panel Manual.* Washington, D.C.: Blue Ribbon Schools Program.

U.S. Department of Education, Office of Educational Research and Improvement of Practice. (1992). *A Profile of Principals: Facts, Opinions, Ideas and Stories from Principals of Recognized Elementary Schools of 1991–1992.* Washington, D.C.: Blue Ribbon Schools Program.

The Complete List of Elementary, Middle, and Secondary Schools Recognized 1982–1983 through 1993–1994

For further information, contact:
Blue Ribbon Schools Program
Programs for the Improvement of Practice
Office of Educational Research and Improvement
U.S. Department of Education
555 New Jersey Avenue, NW
Washington, D.C. 20208-5645
(202) 219-2149

SCHOOL	CITY	YEAR(S) RECOGNIZED
ALABAMA		
Academy for Academics and Arts	Huntsville	87–88
Bob Jones High School	Madison	92–93
Bush Middle School	Birmingham	83–84
C. F. Vigor High School	Prichard	83–84
Cahaba Heights Community School	Birmingham	85–86
Corpus Christi School	Mobile	89–90
East Highland Middle School	Sylacauga	84–85
Edgewood Elementary School	Homewood	91–92
Elvin Hill Elementary School	Columbiana	87–88
Enterprise High School	Enterprise	83–84
EPIC Elementary School	Birmingham	93–94
Eura Brown Elementary School	Gadsden	91–92
Grantswood Community School	Irondale	91–92
Hewitt-Trussville High School	Trussville	92–93
Homewood High School	Homewood	83–84
Homewood Middle School	Homewood	83–84
Indian Valley Elementary School	Sylacauga	89–90
Ira F. Simmons Junior High School	Birmingham	84–85
Julian Newman Elementary School	Athens	87–88
Leeds Elementary School	Leeds	93–94
Mars Hill Bible School	Florence	86–87, 92–93
Mars Hill Bible School (Elementary)	Florence	87–88
Maryvale Elementary School	Mobile	93–94
Mountain Brook High School	Mountain Brook	83–84, 92–93
Muscle Shoals High School	Muscle Shoals	90–91
Oak Mountain Elementary School	Birmingham	93–94

SCHOOL	CITY	YEAR(S) RECOGNIZED
ALABAMA (*continued*)		
Pinson Elementary School	Pinson	91–92
Riverchase Middle School	Birmingham	84–85
S. S. Murphy High School	Mobile	86–87
Saint Ignatius School	Mobile	87–88
St. Paul's Episcopal School	Mobile	88–89
Shades Cahaba Elementary School	Homewood	93–94
South Side Elementary School	Gadsen	89–90
Sylacauga High School	Sylacauga	84–85
Tarrant Elementary School	Tarrant	93–94
Valley Elementary School	Pelham	85–86
Vestavia Hills Elementary School	Vestavia Hills	85–86
Vestavia Hills High School	Vestavia Hills	90–91
W. P. Davidson High School	Mobile	90–91
Westlawn Elementary School	Decatur	89–90
ALASKA		
East Anchorage High School	Anchorage	90–91
Gruening Junior High School	Eagle River	84–85
Homer High School	Homer	88–89
Kenai Junior High School	Kenai	83–84
Mendenhall River Community School	Juneau	93–94
North Star Elementary School	Nikiski	93–94
Petersburg High School	Petersburg	86–87
Romig Junior High School	Anchorage	84–85
Rosamond Weller Elementary School	Fairbanks	87–88
Soldotna High School	Soldotna	82–83
Soldotna Junior High School	Soldotna	82–83
Tok School	Tok	85–86
Valdez High School	Valdez	82–83
West Anchorage High School	Anchorage	92–93
Yakutat Elementary School	Yakutat	87–88
ARIZONA		
Agua Fria Union High School	Avondale	82–83
Amphitheater High School	Tucson	83–84
Baboquivari Junior High School	Sells	86–87
Booker T. Washington School	Mesa	85–86
Centennial Elementary School	Tucson	93–94
Chandler High School	Chandler	82–83, 86–87
Cherokee Elementary School	Paradise Valley	87–88
Craycroft Elementary School	Tucson	91–92
Del Rio Elementary School	Chino Valley	93–94
Desert Cove Elementary School	Phoenix	87–88

SCHOOL	CITY	YEAR(S) RECOGNIZED
ARIZONA (*continued*)		
Desert Shadows Middle School	Scottsdale	86–87
Desert Sky Middle School	Glendale	90–91
Dobson High School	Mesa	86–87
Echo Mountain Elementary School	Phoenix	89–90
Flowing Wells High School	Tucson	86–87, 90–91
Flowing Wells Junior High School	Tucson	84–85
Frye Elementary School	Chandler	87–88
Green Fields Country Day School	Tucson	84–85
Greenway Middle School	Phoenix	86–87
Harvey L. Taylor Junior High School	Mesa	84–85
Indian Bend Elementary School	Phoenix	87–88
John J. Rhodes Junior High School	Mesa	82–83, 92–93
Kino Junior High School	Mesa	84–85
Laguna Elementary School	Tucson	85–86
Manzanita School	Tucson	93–94
Mesa High School	Mesa	83–84
Mohave Middle School	Scottsdale	92–93
Mountain View High School	Mesa	84–85
Page Elementary School	Page	85–86
Palomino Elementary School	Phoenix	89–90
Poston Junior High School	Mesa	83–84
Rancho Viejo School	Yuma	87–88
Richardson Elementary School	Tucson	87–88
Safford Engineering/Technology Magnet Middle School	Tucson	92–93
Saint Mary-Basha Catholic Elementary School	Chandler	93–94
Sandpiper Elementary School	Scottsdale	91–92
Santa Rita High School	Tucson	84–85
Sequoya Elementary School	Scottsdale	91–92
Shea Middle School	Phoenix	83–84
Show Low Primary School	Show Low	91–92
Shumway Elementary School	Chandler	93–94
Sirrine Elementary School	Chandler	89–90
Utterback Junior High School	Tucson	83–84
Veora E. Johnson Elementary School	Mesa	87–88
Walter Douglas Elementary School	Tucson	89–90
Weinberg Elementary School	Chandler	85–86
Westwood High School	Mesa	83–84
Willis Junior High School	Chandler	82–83
Xavier College Preparatory School	Phoenix	90–91
Yavapai Elementary School	Scottsdale	89–90
ARKANSAS		
Annie Camp Middle School	Jonesboro	82–83

SCHOOL	CITY	YEAR(S) RECOGNIZED
ARKANSAS (*continued*)		
Arkadelphia High School	Arkadelphia	90–91
Conway High School	Conway	84–85
Douglas MacArthur Middle School	Jonesboro	82–83
Jonesboro High School	Jonesboro	82–83
Louisa E. Perritt Primary School	Arkadelphia	87–88
Northside High School	Fort Smith	92–93
Parson Hills Elementary School	Springdale	93–94
Root Elementary School	Fayetteville	91–92
Southside High School	Fort Smith	82–83, 86–87
Thurman G. Smith Elementary School	Springdale	87–88
Westwood Elementary School	Springdale	89–90
White Hall High School	Pine Bluff	83–84
BUREAU OF INDIAN AFFAIRS		
Cherokee Central Schools	Cherokee, North Carolina	88–89
Cherokee Elementary School	Cherokee, North Carolina	87–88
Dzilth-na-o-dith-hle Community School	Bloomfield, New Mexico	86–87
St. Stephens Indian School	St. Stephens, North Carolina	93–94
Santa Clara Day School	Espanola, New Mexico	89–90
Santa Fe Indian School	Santa Fe, New Mexico	86–87
Sky City Community School	Acoma, New Mexico	90–91
CALIFORNIA		
Academy of Our Lady of Peace	San Diego	88–89, 92–93
Admiral Akers School	NAS Lemoore	86–87
Alameda High School	Alameda	92–93
Alamo Elementary School	Alamo	85–86, 91–92
Alvarado Middle School	Union City	83–84
Amy Blanc Elementary School	Fairfield	85–86
Anacapa Middle School	Ventura	90–91
Andersen Elementary School	Newport Beach	87–88
Anza Elementary School	Torrance	89–90
Argonaut Elementary School	Saratoga	93–94
Armijo High School	Fairfield	88–89
Arroyo Elementary School	Santa Ana	89–90
Artesia High School	Lakewood	83–84
Audubon Junior High School	Los Angeles	86–87
Balboa Boulevard Gifted/High Achievement Magnet School	Northridge	87–88
Bishop Amat Memorial High School	West Covina	83–84
Bishop O'Dowd High School	Oakland	90–91
Bishop's Peak Elementary School	San Luis Obispo	87–88
Black Mountain Middle School	San Diego	90–91

SCHOOL	CITY	YEAR(S) RECOGNIZED
CALIFORNIA (*continued*)		
Borel Middle School	San Mateo	83–84
Borrego Springs High School	Borrego Springs	84–85
Brea Olinda High School	Brea	92–93
Brightwood Elementary School (grades 5–8)	Monterey Park	92–93
Bryant Ranch School	Yorba Linda	93–94
Brywood Elementary School	Irvine	91–92
Bullis Purissima School	Los Altos Hills	91–92
Cajon Park School	Santee	92–93
Carmenita Junior High School	Cerritos	90–91
Caroline Davis Intermediate School	San Jose	92–93
Castro Valley High School	Castro Valley	84–85, 88–89
Cate School	Carpinteria	86–87
Cayucos School	Cayucos	86–87
Chadbourne Elementary School	Fremont	89–90
Chaparral Elementary School	Poway	91–92
Charles E. Teach Elementary School	San Luis Obispo	91–92
Charlotte Wood Middle School	Danville	92–93
Chico Senior High School	Chico	88–89
Chula Vista High School	Chula Vista	83–84
Claremont High School	Claremont	86–87
Clovis High School	Clovis	86–87, 92–93
Clovis West High School	Fresno	88–89
Collins School	Cupertino	87–88
Convent of the Sacred Heart High School	San Francisco	92–93
Corona del Mar High School	Newport Beach	84–85
Country Club Elementary School	San Ramon	93–94
Cuddeback Union Elementary School	Carlotta	93–94
Culver City High School	Culver City	92–93
D. Russell Parks Junior High School	Fullerton	86–87
Davidson Middle School	San Rafael	82–83
Del Cerro Elementary School	Mission Viejo	87–88
Del Dayo Elementary School	Carmichael	87–88
Del Mar Hills Elementary School	Del Mar	87–88
Diegueno Junior High School	Encinitas	92–93
Discovery Bay Elementary School	Byron	85–86
Dr. Jonas Salk School	Anaheim	89–90
Dry Creek Elementary School	Clovis	93–94
E. O. Green Junior High School	Oxnard	92–93
Earl Warren Junior High School	Solana Beach	90–91
Edison-Computech 7/8 School	Fresno	90–91
Eisenhower High School	Rialto	92–93
El Morro Elementary School	Laguna Beach	87–88
Eugene Padan Elementary School	Vacaville	87–88
Fairmont Private Junior High School	Anaheim	90–91
Fallbrook Street School	Fallbrook	87–88

SCHOOL	CITY	YEAR(S) RECOGNIZED
CALIFORNIA (*continued*)		
Fallbrook Union High School	Fallbrook	83–84
Ferndale Elementary School	Ferndale	86–87
Foothill Elementary School	Saratoga	91–92
Fort Washington Elementary School	Fresno	85–86, 91–92
Fred L. Newhart School	Mission Viejo	93–94
Fruitvale Junior High School	Bakersfield	90–91
Fullerton Union High School	Fullerton	88–89
Garden Gate Elementary School	Cupertino	85–86
Gardenhill Elementary School	La Mirada	93–94
George Leyva Junior High School	San Jose	82–83
George W. Kastner Intermediate School	Fresno	84–85
Glenn E. Murdock Elementary School	La Mesa	91–92
Gomes Elementary School	Fremont	87–88
Graystone Elementary School	San Jose	91–92
Greenville Fundamental Elementary School	Santa Ana	85–86
Greenville Junior/Senior High School	Greenville	92–93
Gretchen Whitney High School	Cerritos	86–87, 90–91
Grover Heights Elementary School	Grover Beach	93–94
Harbor View Elementary School	Corona del Mar	85–86
Harkham Hill Hebrew Academy	Beverly Hills	93–94
Harvard School	North Hollywood	88–89
Helen Estock Elementary School	Tustin	89–90
Hewes Middle School	Santa Ana	92–93
Highland High School	Bakersfield	88–89
Highlands Elementary School	Saugus	89–90
Hillsdale High School	San Mateo	92–93
Holy Names High School	Oakland	84–85, 90–91
Homestead High School	Cupertino	86–87
Horace Mann Academic Middle School	San Francisco	86–87
Hyde Junior High School	Cupertino	88–89
Irvine High School	Irvine	88–89
J. Haley Durham Elementary School	Fremont	93–94
Jacoby Creek Elementary School	Bayside	89–90
James Logan High School	Union City	82–83, 86–87
Jerabek Elementary School	San Diego	87–88
Joaquin Miller Intermediate School	San Jose	86–87
John F. Kennedy Junior High School	Cupertino	92–93
John Marshall Elementary School	Glendale	87–88
Julian Elementary School	Julian	89–90
K. R. Smith Elementary School	San Jose	87–88
Kastner Intermediate School	Fresno	92–93
La Cañada High School	La Cañada	92–93
La Mesa Middle School	La Mesa	90–91
La Paz Intermediate School	Mission Viejo	92–93
Laguna Hills High School	Laguna Hills	92–93

SCHOOL	CITY	YEAR(S) RECOGNIZED
CALIFORNIA (*continued*)		
Lakeside Middle School	Irvine	90–91
Lakewood Elementary School	Modesto	93–94
Leroy Anderson Elementary School	San Jose	87–88
Levi Bemis Elementary School	Rialto	87–88
Lincoln Elementary School	Fresno	89–90
Lindero Canyon Middle School	Agoura Hills	84–85
Los Alamitos High School	Los Alamitos	88–89, 92–93
Los Altos Intermediate School	Camarillo	86–87
Los Angeles Center for Enriched Studies	Los Angeles	92–93
Los Gatos High School	Los Gatos	86–87, 90–91
Los Primeros Structured School	Camarillo	87–88
Los Ranchos Elementary School	San Luis Obispo	89–90
Lowell High School	San Francisco	82–83
Lupin Hill Elementary School	Calabasas	85–86
Manhattan Beach Intermediate School	Manhattan Beach	90–91
Marina High School	Huntington Beach	84–85
Mayfield Junior School of the Holy Child	Pasadena	91–92
McFadden Intermediate School	Santa Ana	88–89
Meadowbrook Middle School	Poway	84–85
Meadows Elementary School	Valencia	93–94
Melvin Avenue School	Reseda	85–86
Mendocino High School	Mendocino	88–89
Mendocino Middle School	Mendocino	85–86
Menlo-Atherton High School	Atherton	86–87
Mesa Union School	Somis	86–87
Miramonte High School	Orinda	86–87, 90–91
Mission Avenue Open School	Carmichael	87–88
Mission Junior High School	Riverside	83–84
Mission San Jose High School	Fremont	86–87
Mission Viejo High School	Mission Viejo	88–89
Monte Gardens Elementary School	Concord	91–92
Montebello Intermediate School	Montebello	83–84
Montgomery High School	Santa Rosa	90–91
Moreau High School	Hayward	83–84, 88–89
Morning Creek Elementary School	San Diego	93–94
Mount Carmel High School	San Diego	88–89
Mountain View Elementary School	Fresno	93–94
Mountain View High School	Mountain View	88–89
Nathaniel Bowditch Middle School	Foster City	92–93
Neil Armstrong Elementary School	Diamond Bar	89–90
Nelson Elementary School	Pinedale	91–92
Newhall Elementary School	Newhall	93–94
Nick G. Parras Middle School	Redondo Beach	92–93
North Monterey County High School	Castroville	84–85
Norwood Creek Elementary School	San Jose	93–94

SCHOOL	CITY	YEAR(S) RECOGNIZED
CALIFORNIA (*continued*)		
Notre Dame Academy	Los Angeles	90–91
Nueva Learning Center	Hillsborough	87–88
O'Neill Elementary School	Mission Viejo	85–86
O. B. Whaley School	San Jose	89–90
Oak Grove Middle School	Jamul	88–89
Oak Hills Elementary School	Agoura	91–92
Oak Park High School	Agoura	92–93
Oakbrook Elementary School	Fairfield	91–92
Olive Peirce Middle School	Ramona	92–93
Orange Glen High School	Escondido	86–87
Pacific Union College Elementary School	Angwin	85–86
Pacific Union Elementary School	Arcata	93–94
Palms Junior High School	Los Angeles	86–87
Palo Alto High School	Palo Alto	86–87
Park Dale Lane Elementary School	Encinitas	87–88
Pepper Drive School	El Cajon	87–88
Piedmont High School	Piedmont	84–85
Pioneer Elementary School	Union City	85–86
Pioneer High School	Whittier	82–83
Pliocene Ridge Elementary School	North San Juan	93–94
Polytechnic School	Pasadena	84–85
Pomerado Elementary School	Poway	89–90
Poway High School	Poway	90–91
Presentation High School	Berkeley	84–85
Quailwood Elementary School	Bakersfield	91–92
R. J. Neutra Elementary School	NAS Lemoore	87–88, 91–92
Ralph Waldo Emerson Junior High School	Davis	88–89
Ramona Convent Secondary School	Alhambra	92–93
Rancho Buena Vista High School	Vista	90–91
Raymond J. Fisher School	Los Gatos	88–89
Red Bank Elementary School	Clovis	93–94
Redondo Union High School	Redondo Beach	88–89
Regnart Elementary School	Cupertino	87–88
Rio Vista Elementary School	Canyon County	91–92
Rolling Hills Middle School	Los Gatos	88–89, 92–93
Rosedale North Elementary School	Bakersfield	93–94
Rosemont Middle School	La Crescenta	84–85, 92–93
Ruth Paulding Middle School	Arroyo Grande	92–93
Saint Anthony's School	Fresno	85–86
Saint Francis High School	Mountain View	90–91
Saint John the Baptist School	El Cerrito	87–88
Saint Joseph High School	Santa Maria	92–93
Saint Simon Catholic School	Los Altos	91–92
St. David's Elementary School	Richmond	85–86
St. Elizabeth High School	Oakland	83–84

SCHOOL	CITY	YEAR(S) RECOGNIZED
CALIFORNIA *(continued)*		
St. Ignatius College Preparatory School	San Francisco	83–84
St. Isadore School	Danville	93–94
St. James Episcopal School	Los Angeles	93–94
St. Joseph Elementary School	Alameda	93–94
St. Mary's College High School	Berkeley	84–85
St. Thomas the Apostle School	Los Angeles	91–92
Samuel Curtis Rogers Middle School	San Jose	92–93
San Diego Hebrew Day School	San Diego	91–92
San Lorenzo High School	San Lorenzo	90–91
San Mateo High School	San Mateo	90–91
Santa Rita Elementary School	Los Altos	91–92
Santana High School	Santee	83–84
Santee Elementary School (grades 6–8)	Santee	92–93
Saratoga High School	Saratoga	88–89
Sequoia Elementary School	Santa Rosa	89–90, 93–94
Sierra Canyon School	Chatsworth	89–90
Silver Spur School	Rancho Palos Verdes	87–88
Skyline School	Solana Beach	87–88
Solana Vista School	Solana Beach	89–90
Sonoma Elementary School	Modesto	89–90
Southwest High School	San Diego	86–87
Stevens Creek School	Cupertino	87–88
Strawberry Elementary School	Santa Rosa	87–88
Sundance Elementary School	San Diego	87–88
Taper Avenue Elementary School	San Pedro	87–88
Terrace Hills Junior High School	Grand Terrace	82–83
The Bishop's School	La Jolla	90–91
The Crossroads School	Santa Monica	83–84
The Thacher School	Ojai	90–91
The York School	Monterey	90–91
Torrey Pines High School	San Diego	86–87, 92–93
Twin Peaks Middle School	Poway	83–84, 90–91
University High School	Irvine	86–87
Vacaville High School	Vacaville	86–87
Valley Center Middle School	Valley Center	88–89
Valley Christian High School	Cerritos	83–84
Valley High School	Sacramento	86–87
Valley Oak Elementary School	Fresno	93–94
Van Buren Elementary School	Riverside	93–94
Venado Middle School	Irvine	82–83
Village Elementary School	Santa Rosa	91–92
Vista High School	Vista	88–89
Walnut High School	Walnut	92–93
Walter White School	Ceres	85–86
Walters Junior High School	Fremont	88–89

SCHOOL	CITY	YEAR(S) RECOGNIZED
CALIFORNIA (*continued*)		
West High School	Torrance	83–84
West Hillsborough School	Hillsborough	93–94
West Orange Elementary School	Orange	87–88
West Valley Elementary School	Sunnyvale	85–86
Westlake School for Girls	Los Angeles	84–85
Westminster High School	Westminster	92–93
Westwood Elementary School	Santa Clara	93–94
White Oak Elementary School	Westlake Village	85–86, 93–94
Whitmore Union Elementary School	Whitmore	86–87
William H. Crocker School	Hillsborough	82–83, 88–89
Willow Elementary School	Agoura Hills	91–92
Woodbridge High School	Irvine	86–87
Woodside School	Woodside	93–94

COLORADO

SCHOOL	CITY	YEAR(S) RECOGNIZED
Alameda Junior High School	Lakewood	84–85
Arapahoe High School	Littleton	92–93
Beth Jacob High School of Denver	Denver	83–84
Carmody Junior High School	Lakewood	82–83
Cherry Creek High School	Englewood	92–93
Cheyenne Mountain High School	Colorado Springs	82–83
Douglass Valley School	Colorado Springs	85–86
Eagle Valley Middle School	Eagle	92–93
Evergreen Junior High School	Evergreen	86–87
Heritage High School	Littleton	90–91
Holmes Junior High School	Colorado Springs	83–84
Indian Ridge Elementary School	Aurora	89–90
Lutheran High School	Denver	90–91
Mrachek Middle School	Aurora	82–83
Pioneer Elementary School	Colorado Springs	91–92
Rampart High School	Colorado Springs	90–91
Regis Jesuit High School	Denver	84–85
St. Mary's Academy	Englewood	91–92
Smoky Hill High School	Aurora	90–91
South Elementary School	Castle Rock	93–94
Thomson Elementary School	Arvada	87–88
Westridge Elementary School	Littleton	93–94
Wheat Ridge High School	Wheatridge	83–84
Woodland Park Middle School	Woodland Park	88–89

CONNECTICUT

SCHOOL	CITY	YEAR(S) RECOGNIZED
Alcott Middle School	Wolcott	90–91
Amity Regional High School	Woodbridge	82–83

SCHOOL	CITY	YEAR(S) RECOGNIZED
CONNECTICUT (*continued*)		
Amity Regional Junior High School	Bethany	83–84
Amity Regional Junior High School	Orange	82–83
Anna M. Reynolds School	Newington	93–94
Avon Middle School	Avon	84–85
Benjamin Franklin School	Meriden	87–88
Bess and Paul Sigel Hebrew Academy	Bloomfield	89–90
Bi-Cultural Day School	Stamford	87–88
Cider Mill School	Wilton	85–86
Columbus Magnet School	South Norwalk	89–90
Conard High School	West Hartford	84–85
Conte Arts Magnet School	New Haven	83–84
Darien High School	Darien	86–87
East Catholic High School	Manchester	88–89
East Ridge Junior High School	Ridgefield	83–84
Eastern Middle School	Riverside	91–92
Edward Morley School	West Hartford	87–88
Edwin O. Smith High School	Storrs	92–93
Eric G. Norfeldt Elementary School	West Hartford	91–92
Fairfield College Preparatory School	Fairfield	86–87
Flanders Elementary School	East Lyme	93–94
Flood Intermediate School	Stratford	83–84
Gideon Welles Junior High School	Glastonbury	84–85
Granby Memorial Middle School	Granby	86–87, 90–91
Greenwich High School	Greenwich	88–89
Haddam-Killingworth Middle School	Higganum	88–89
Illing Junior High School	Manchester	82–83
Irving A. Robbins Junior High School	Farmington	86–87
Joel Barlow High School	West Redding	88–89, 92–93
John Wallace Middle School	Newington	92–93
King Philip Middle School	West Hartford	86–87
Mansfield Middle School	Storrs	91–92
Martin Kellogg Middle School	Newington	86–87
Memorial Middle School	Middlebury	88–89
Middlebrook School	Wilton	82–83
Middlesex Middle School	Darien	84–85
Mitchell Elementary School	Woodbury	93–94
Naubuc School	Glastonbury	89–90
New Canaan Country School	New Canaan	93–94
New Fairfield High School	New Fairfield	84–85
Newington High School	Newington	88–89
Noah Wallace School	Farmington	93–94
Northeast Elementary School	Vernon	91–92
Northwest Catholic High School	West Hartford	88–89
Notre Dame Catholic High School	Fairfield	84–85
Plainfield Central School	Plainfield	92–93

SCHOOL	CITY	YEAR(S) RECOGNIZED
CONNECTICUT (*continued*)		
Roger Sherman School	Meriden	93–94
Sacred Heart Academy	Hamden	92–93
Saint Brendan School	New Haven	89–90
Saint Francis School	New Haven	85–86
Shelton Intermediate School	Shelton	88–89
Silas Deane Middle School	Wethersfield	90–91
Southington High School	Southington	92–93
Stratfield School	Fairfield	87–88, 93–94
Tashua School	Trumbull	89–90
The Peck Place School	Orange	87–88
The Rectory School	Pomfret	93–94
Tilford W. Miller School	Wilton	87–88
Torringford School	Torrington	87–88
Union School	Unionville	91–92
Watkinson School	Hartford	83–84
West Hill School	Rock Hill	89–90
Weston Middle School	Weston	87–88
William H. Hall High School	West Hartford	84–85
Wilton High School	Wilton	82–83
Wooster Intermediate School	Stratford	82–83
DELAWARE		
Brandywine High School	Wilmington	82–83
Caesar Rodney Senior High School	Camden	83–84
Christiana High School	Newark	83–84
Corpus Christi School	Wilmington	89–90
Dover High School	Dover	86–87
St. Matthew School	Wilmington	91–92
Shue Middle School	Newark	82–83
Skyline Middle School	Wilmington	84–85
DEPARTMENT OF DEFENSE DEPENDENTS SCHOOLS		
Aschaffenburg American School	Aschaffenburg, Germany	87–88
Bahrain Elementary School-High School	Manama, Bahrain	84–85
Bonn American High School	Bonn, Germany	86–87
Coevorden American School	Coevorden, Netherlands	91–92
Curundu Junior High School	Curundu, Panama	88–89
Ft. Kobbe Elementary School	DODDS–Panama Region	89–90
Frankfurt American High School	Frankfurt, Germany	83–84
Hahn American High School	Hahn Air Base, Germany	90–91
Heidelberg High School	Heidelberg, Germany	83–84, 92–93
Heidelberg Middle School	Heidelberg, Germany	84–85
Nile C. Kinnick High School	Yokosuka, Japan	88–89

SCHOOL	CITY	YEAR(S) RECOGNIZED
DEPARTMENT OF DEFENSE DEPENDENTS SCHOOLS (*continued*)		
Rhein Main Junior High School	Rhein Main, Germany	83–84
Seoul American High School	Seoul, Korea	84–85
Sollars Elementary School	APO AP Honshu, Japan	93–94
Wuerzburg American Middle School	Wuerzburg, Germany	92–93

DISTRICT OF COLUMBIA

SCHOOL	CITY	YEAR(S) RECOGNIZED
Alice Deal Junior High School	Washington	83–84
Benjamin Banneker Academic High School	Washington	90–91
Brookland Junior High School	Washington	82–83
Browne Junior High School	Washington	84–85, 88–89
Bunker Hill Elementary School	Washington	85–86, 91–92
Duke Ellington School of the Arts	Washington	92–93
Georgetown Visitation Preparatory School	Washington	86–87
Horace Mann Elementary School	Washington	89–90, 93–94
Jefferson Junior High School	Washington	82–83, 86–87
Julius W. Hobson Senior Middle School	Washington	83–84
Lemon G. Hine Junior High School	Washington	90–91
Paul Laurence Dunbar Senior High School	Washington	92–93
Robert Brent Elementary School	Washington	87–88
Sidwell Friends Lower School	Washington	85–86
Smothers Elementary School	Washington	85–86

FLORIDA

SCHOOL	CITY	YEAR(S) RECOGNIZED
Academy of the Holy Names	Tampa	93–94
Alimacani Elementary School	Jacksonville	93–94
American Senior High School	Hialeah	83–84
Apopka High School	Apopka	92–93
Ascension Catholic School	Melbourne	85–86
Azalea Middle School	St. Petersburg	88–89
Bay Haven School of Basics Plus	Sarasota	89–90
Bayview Elementary School	Fort Lauderdale	85–86
Boca Raton Christian School	Boca Raton	89–90
Bonita Springs Middle School	Bonita Springs	90–91
Brandon High School	Brandon	82–83
C. H. Price Middle School	Interlachen	90–91
Caloosa Elementary School	Cape Coral	85–86
Caloosa Middle School	Cape Coral	90–91
Cape Coral High School	Cape Coral	88–89
Cardinal Gibbons High School	Fort Lauderdale	86–87
Chaminade-Madonna College Preparatory	Hollywood	92–93
Clearwater Central Catholic High School	Clearwater	88–89
Conway Middle School	Orlando	88–89
Coral Gables Elementary School	Coral Gables	93–94

SCHOOL	CITY	YEAR(S) RECOGNIZED
FLORIDA (*continued*)		
Coral Springs Middle School	Coral Springs	90–91
Dade Christian Schools	Hialeah	84–85
Dixie Hollins High School	St. Petersburg	83–84
Dr. W. J. Creel Elementary School	Melbourne	85–86
Eccleston Elementary School	Orlando	87–88
Eisenhower Elementary School	Clearwater	89–90
Fairway Elementary School	Miramar	89–90
Finegan Elementary School	Atlantic Beach	85–86
Floranada Elementary School	Fort Lauderdale	87–88
Forest Glen Middle School	Coral Springs	92–93
Fort Myers High School	Fort Myers	84–85
Fort Myers Middle School	Fort Myers	90–91
Gemini Elementary School	Melbourne Beach	87–88
Greenwood Lakes Middle School	Lake Mary	88–89
Griffin Elementary School	Cooper City	91–92
Gulf Elementary School	Cape Coral	87–88
Gulliver Academy	Coral Gables	91–92
Gulliver Preparatory School	Miami	90–91
H. B. Plant High School	Tampa	90–91
Hawkes Bluff Elementary School	Davie	93–94
Heights Elementary School	Fort Myers	91–92
Hendricks Avenue Elementary School	Jacksonville	85–86
Highland Oaks Junior High School	North Miami Beach	83–84
Horace O'Bryant Middle School	Key West	84–85
Hyde Grove Elementary School	Jacksonville	93–94
Interlachen Elementary School	Interlachen	93–94
J. P. Taravella High School	Coral Springs	88–89
Jackson Heights Middle School	Oviedo	85–86
Jefferson Davis Junior High School	Jacksonville	82–83
Jesuit High School	Tampa	86–87
John Gorrie Junior High School	Jacksonville	83–84
John N. C. Stockton School	Jacksonville	85–86
Kate Sullivan Elementary School	Tallahassee	85–86
Kirby-Smith Junior High School	Jacksonville	86–87
Largo Middle School	Largo	83–84
Loggers' Run Community Middle School	Boca Raton	90–91
Lyman High School	Longwood	84–85
Mainland High School	Daytona Beach	83–84, 90–91
Melbourne Central Catholic High School	Melbourne	90–91
Miami Country Day School (Elementary)	Miami	87–88
Miami Country Day School, Inc.	Miami	88–89
Miami Palmetto Senior High School	Miami	88–89
Miami Shores Elementary School	Miami Shores	87–88
Murdock Middle School	Port Charlotte	92–93
N. B. Broward Elementary School	Tampa	91–92
Neptune Middle School	Kissimmee	92–93

SCHOOL	CITY	YEAR(S) RECOGNIZED
FLORIDA (*continued*)		
New World School of the Arts	Miami	92–93
Nob Hill Elementary School	Sunrise	91–92
Norland Middle School	Miami	86–87
North Dade Center for Modern Languages	Miami	91–92
North Miami Beach Senior High School	North Miami Beach	84–85
Nova Blanche Forman Elementary School	Fort Lauderdale	93–94
Nova High School	Davie	88–89
Oak Hill Elementary School	Jacksonville	91–92
Ormond Beach Elementary School	Ormond Beach	93–94
Our Lady of Lourdes Academy	Miami	86–87
Pensacola Catholic High School	Pensacola	92–93
Pine Crest Preparatory School	Fort Lauderdale	84–85
Pine Crest Preparatory School (Elementary)	Fort Lauderdale	87–88
Pine Trail Elementary School	Ormond Beach	85–86
Pinecrest Elementary School	Miami	85–86
Rabbi Alexander S. Gross Greater Miami Hebrew Academy	Miami Beach	85–86
Ramblewood Middle School	Coral Springs	92–93
Ribault High School	Jacksonville	82–83
Rodney B. Cox Elementary School	Dade City	93–94
Rogers Middle School	Fort Lauderdale	92–93
Saint Patrick School	Miami Beach	87–88
St. David Catholic School	Davie	93–94
St. Gregory School	Plantation	87–88
St. Joseph Catholic School	Palm Bay	93–94
St. Petersburg High School	St. Petersburg	83–84
St. Rose of Lima School	Miami Shores	85–86, 93–94
St. Thomas Aquinas High School	Fort Lauderdale	84–85
Sandalwood Junior-Senior High School	Jacksonville	84–85
Sanibel Elementary School	Sanibel	91–92
Seabreeze High School	Daytona Beach	88–89
Sealey Elementary School	Tallahassee	89–90
South Plantation High School	Plantation	82–83
Southside Junior High School #211	Jacksonville	86–87
Southwood Junior High School	Miami	84–85
Spessard Holland Elementary School	Satellite Beach	89–90
Spruce Creek High School	Port Orange	92–93
Stanton College Preparatory School	Jacksonville	86–87
Terry Parker High School	Jacksonville	83–84
The Cushman School	Miami	91–92
The King's Academy	West Palm Beach	85–86
Thomas Jefferson Junior High School	Merritt Island	83–84
Thomas Jefferson Middle School	Miami	91–92
Westchester Elementary School	Coral Springs	91–92
Windy Ridge Elementary School	Orlando	93–94

SCHOOL	CITY	YEAR(S) RECOGNIZED
GEORGIA		
A. L. Burruss Elementary School	Marietta	91–92
Benjamin E. Banneker High School	College Park	92–93
Benjamin Elijah Mays High School	Atlanta	86–87
Benteen Elementary School	Atlanta	89–90
Boynton Elementary School	Ringgold	89–90
Brandon Hall School	Dunwoody	84–85
Brookwood High School	Snellville	86–87
Burroughs-Molette Elementary School	Brunswick	85–86
Christ the King School	Atlanta	85–86
Conyers Middle School	Conyers	84–85
Cook Middle School	Adel	91–92
County Line Elementary School	Winder	93–94
Crabapple Middle School	Roswell	87–88
Dalton High School	Dalton	83–84
Dalton Junior High School	Dalton	86–87
Dolvin Elementary School	Alpharetta	89–90
Duluth High School	Duluth	90–91
Duluth Middle School	Duluth	85–86
East Cobb Middle School	Marietta	89–90
Eastvalley Elementary School	Marietta	93–94
Edwards Middle School	Conyers	87–88
Elm Street School	Newnan	93–94
Five Forks Middle School	Lawrenceville	87–88
Frederick Douglass High School	Atlanta	83–84
Garden Hills School	Atlanta	85–86
George L. Edwards Middle School	Conyers	93–94
Glynn Middle School	Brunswick	83–84
Graysville Elementary School	Graysville	91–92
Greater Atlanta Christian Schools, Inc.	Norcross	88–89
Hardaway High School	Columbus	84–85
Harlem Comprehensive High School	Harlem	88–89
Hebrew Academy of Atlanta, Inc.	Atlanta	85–86
Heritage High School	Conyers	88–89
Jonesboro Junior High School	Jonesboro	88–89
Knight Elementary School	Lilburn	87–88
Lakeside High School	Atlanta	84–85
Lee County Primary School	Leesburg	89–90
Lincoln County High School	Lincolnton	86–87
Luke Garrett Middle School	Austell	83–84
Marist School	Atlanta	86–87
McCleskey Middle School	Marietta	91–92
Mount de Sales Academy	Macon	90–91
Mt. Bethel Elementary School	Marietta	85–86
Mundy's Mill Middle School	Jonesboro	92–93
Murdock Elementary School	Marietta	87–88

SCHOOL	CITY	YEAR(S) RECOGNIZED
GEORGIA (*continued*)		
Myers Middle School	Savannah	92–93
Newton County High School	Covington	86–87
North Fulton High School	Atlanta	84–85
North Whitfield Middle School	Dalton	84–85
Otwell Middle School	Cumming	90–91
Parkview High School	Lilburn	84–85
Pinckneyville Middle School	Norcross	91–92
R. D. Head Elementary School	Lilburn	91–92
St. John Neumann Regional Catholic School	Lilburn	93–94
St. John the Evangelist Catholic School	Hapeville	93–94
St. Marys Elementary School	St. Marys	91–92
St. Simons Elementary School	St. Simons Island	89–90
St. Thomas More Catholic School	Decatur	87–88
Shiloh Middle School	Lithonia	86–87
Sope Creek Elementary School	Marietta	87–88
South Cobb High School	Austell	92–93
Southeast Bulloch High School	Brooklet	92–93
Southside Elementary School	Milledgeville	85–86
Staley Middle School	Americus	89–90
Stephens County High School	Toccoa	86–87
Swainsboro High School	Swainsboro	92–93
Tapp Middle School	Powder Springs	84–85
The Howard School	Atlanta	85–86
The Savannah Country Day School	Savannah	91–92
Thomson High School	Thomson	90–91
Trickum Middle School	Lilburn	90–91
Walton Comprehensive High School	Marietta	83–84
Warner Robins High School	Warner Robins	90–91
William Milton Davis Elementary School	Marietta	93–94
Yeshiva High School	Atlanta	84–85
HAWAII		
Aikahi Elementary School	Kailua	89–90
ASSETS School	Honolulu	91–92
Hanahauoli School	Honolulu	85–86
Iolani School	Honolulu	84–85
James B. Castle High School	Kaneohe	92–93
Kaala Elementary School	Wahiawa	87–88
Kahuku High and Intermediate Schools	Kahuku	88–89
Kailua High School	Kailua	88–89
Kalaheo High School	Kailua	90–91
Kapunahala Elementary School	Kaneohe	91–92
Leilehua High School	Wahiawa	92–93

SCHOOL	CITY	YEAR(S) RECOGNIZED
HAWAII (*continued*)		
Linapuni School	Honolulu	93–94
Manoa Elementary School	Honolulu	85–86
Mililani-uka Elementary School	Mililani	91–92
Moanalua High School	Honolulu	86–87
Nuuanu Elementary School	Honolulu	85–86
Pearl Ridge Elementary School	Aiea	93–94
Princess Miriam K. Likelike Elementary School	Honolulu	91–92
Punahou School	Honolulu	84–85
Seabury Hall School	Makawao	92–93
Waiahole Elementary School	Kaneohe	89–90
Waiakea High School	Hilo	88–89
Walhe's School	Wailuku	93–94

IDAHO

SCHOOL	CITY	YEAR(S) RECOGNIZED
Frontier School	Boise	89–90
Jefferson Junior High School	Caldwell	84–85
Lincoln Elementary School	Caldwell	85–86
Lowell Elementary School	Boise	93–94
Morningside Elementary School	Twin Falls	93–94
Mullan Junior-Senior High School	Mullan	83–84
Pierce School	Pierce	85–86
Pocatello High School	Pocatello	88–89
Silver Hills Junior High School	Osburn	84–85
Weiser High School	Weiser	86–87
Westside Elementary School	Idaho Falls	87–88

ILLINOIS

SCHOOL	CITY	YEAR(S) RECOGNIZED
Academy of Our Lady	Chicago	84–85
Adlai E. Stevenson High School	Prairie View	86–87, 90–91
Adler Park School	Libertyville	91–92
Alan B. Shepard Junior High School	Deerfield	84–85
Amos Alonzo Stagg High School	Palos Hills	90–91
Arnett C. Lines School	Barrington	93–94
Arnold J. Tyler School	New Lenox	91–92
Avoco West Elementary School	Glenview	89–90
Barrington High School	Barrington	92–93
Bernard Zell Anshe Emet Day School	Chicago	87–88
Booth Tarkington School	Wheeling	93–94
Boylan Central Catholic High School	Rockford	86–87, 90–91
Brehm Preparatory School	Carbondale	92–93
Brother Rice High School	Chicago	84–85
Butterfield School	Libertyville	93–94
Carl Sandburg High School	Orland Park	84–85

SCHOOL	CITY	YEAR(S) RECOGNIZED
ILLINOIS (*continued*)		
Carmel High School for Girls	Mundelein	84–85
Caroline Bentley School	New Lenox	91–92
Carrie Busey School	Champaign	89–90
Champaign Central High School	Champaign	88–89
Champaign Middle School at Columbia	Champaign	86–87
Cherokee School	Lake Forest	87–88
Community High School	West Chicago	92–93
Community High School North	Downers Grove	83–84
Crete-Monee Junior High School	Crete	88–89
Crete-Monee Middle School	Crete	93–94
Daniel Wright Middle School	Lake Forest	86–87
De La Salle Institute	Chicago	84–85
Deer Path Junior High School	Lake Forest	86–87, 90–91
Deer Path Middle School	Lake Forest	87–88
Deerfield High School	Deerfield	92–93
Dr. Howard Elementary School	Champaign	89–90
Edgewood Middle School	Highland Park	88–89
Elm Place Middle School	Highland Park	82–83
Everett School	Lake Forest	85–86
Fairview South School	Skokie	85–86
Fenwick High School	Oak Park	83–84
Frankfort Junior High School	Frankfort	93–94
Franklin Middle School	Wheaton	87–88
Garden Hills Elementary School	Champaign	85–86
Glenbrook North High School	Northbrook	83–84
Glenbrook South High School	Glenview	83–84
Grove Avenue School	Barrington	91–92
Hadley Junior High School	Glen Ellyn	85–86
Haines School	New Lenox	93–94
Hales Franciscan High School	Chicago	84–85
Hawthorn Intermediate School	Vernon Hills	87–88
Hawthorn Junior High School	Vernon Hills	87–88
Highland Upper Grade Center	Libertyville	90–91
Hoffman Estates High School	Hoffman Estates	84–85
Holy Angels School	Aurora	87–88
Holy Cross School	Deerfield	85–86
Homewood-Flossmoor High School	Flossmoor	82–83
Immanuel Lutheran School	Palatine	87–88
Indian Trail School	Highland Park	87–88
John Hersey High School	Arlington Heights	88–89
John W. Gates Elementary School	Aurora	85–86
Kenneth E. Neubert Elementary School	Algonquin	85–86
La Grange Highlands Elementary School	La Grange	85–86
Lake Bluff Junior High School	Lake Bluff	91–92
Lake Forest Country Day School	Lake Forest	93–94

SCHOOL	CITY	YEAR(S) RECOGNIZED
ILLINOIS (*continued*)		
Laura B. Sprague School	Lincolnshire	85–86, 91–92
Leyden East Campus	Franklin	84–85
Leyden West Campus	North Lake	84–85
Libertyville Community High School	Libertyville	90–91
Lincoln Elementary School	Highland Park	87–88
Luther High School South	Chicago	83–84
Madonna High School	Chicago	90–91
Mahomet-Seymour High School	Mahomet	86–87
Maine Township High School East	Park Ridge	84–85
Maine Township High School South	Park Ridge	88–89
Maine Township High School West	Des Plaines	90–91
Marian Catholic High School	Chicago Heights	84–85
Marist High School	Chicago	86–87
Medinah Elementary School	Roselle	83–84
Mother McAuley Liberal Arts High School	Chicago	86–87, 90–91
Mt. Carmel High School	Chicago	83–84
Mundelein High School	Mundelein	92–93
New Trier Township High School	Winnetka	90–91
Niles North High School	Skokie	90–91
Niles West High School	Skokie	90–91
Nob Hill School	Country Club Hills	85–86
Northbrook Junior High School	Northbrook	91–92
Notre Dame High School	Chicago	84–85
O'Fallon Township High School	O'Fallon	86–87
Oak Terrace School	Highwood	87–88
Old Orchard Junior High School	Skokie	83–84
Oliver Wendell Holmes Junior High School	Wheeling	86–87
Palatine High School	Palatine	92–93
Prospect High School	Mount Prospect	92–93
Ravinia School	Highland Park	85–86
Regina Dominican High School	Wilmette	92–93
Rich South High School	Richton Park	83–84
Riverton Middle School	Riverton	87–88
Rockland School	Libertyville	89–90
Roosevelt School	River Forest	88–89
Saint Louise de Marillac High School	Northfield	86–87
Saint Matthias School	Chicago	85–86
Saint Stanislaus Bishop and Martyr School	Chicago	87–88
St. Damian School	Oak Forest	91–92
St. Isaac Jogues School	Hinsdale	89–90
St. Joan of Arc School	Lisle	85–86
St. Luke School	River Forest	91–92
St. Rita High School	Chicago	86–87
Schaumburg High School	Schaumburg	92–93

SCHOOL	CITY	YEAR(S) RECOGNIZED
ILLINOIS *(continued)*		
Sheridan School	Lake Forest	85–86, 91–92
Sparta Primary Attendance Center	Sparta	89–90
Springman Junior High School	Glenview	84–85
The Avery Coonley School	Downers Grove	87–88
The School of Saint Mary	Lake Forest	89–90
Thomas Junior High School	Arlington Heights	83–84
Trinity Lutheran School	Roselle	91–92
University of Chicago Laboratory High School	Chicago	86–87
Washington School	Mundelein	91–92
Weber High School	Chicago	88–89
Westbrook School	Glenview	87–88
Wheeling High School	Wheeling	86–87
William Fremd High School	Palatine	86–87
Wilmette Junior High School	Wilmette	90–91
Wilmot Elementary School	Deerfield	87–88
Wilmot Junior High School	Deerfield	83–84
Winston Churchill School	Homewood	85–86
Wood View Elementary School	Bolingbrook	87–88
York Community High School	Elmhurst	82–83
INDIANA		
Amy Beverland Elementary School	Indianapolis	93–94
Ben Davis High School	Indianapolis	83–84
Ben Davis Junior High School	Indianapolis	86–87
Boston Middle School	LaPorte	90–91
Brumfield Elementary School	Princeton	87–88, 91–92
Carmel High School	Carmel	82–83
Carmel Junior High School	Carmel	84–85
Cathedral High School	Indianapolis	88–89
Chesterton High School	Chesterton	84–85
Clay Junior High School	Clay	82–83
College Wood Elementary School	Carmel	85–86
Concordia Lutheran High School	Fort Wayne	84–85, 88–89
Culver Academy	Culver	83–84
East Elementary School	Pendleton	89–90
Eastbrook Elementary School	Indianapolis	89–90
Eastern Elementary School	Greentown	89–90
Eastwood Middle School	Indianapolis	84–85
Edward Eggleston Elementary School	South Bend	91–92
Fegely Middle School	Portage	84–85
Harold Handley Elementary School	LaPorte	91–92
Hebrew Academy of Indianapolis	Indianapolis	89–90, 93–94
Henry W. Eggers Middle School	Hammond	88–89

SCHOOL	CITY	YEAR(S) RECOGNIZED
INDIANA (*continued*)		
Holy Cross Lutheran School	Fort Wayne	85–86
Indian Creek Elementary School	Indianapolis	89–90
Indian Meadows Elementary School	Fort Wayne	87–88
Jefferson High School	Lafayette	84–85, 92–93
John F. Kennedy School	South Bend	85–86
John J. Young Middle School	Mishawaka	90–91
John Marshall High School	Indianapolis	84–85
Kesling Middle School	LaPorte	86–87, 92–93
Klondike Elementary School	W. Lafayette	91–92
LaSalle High School	South Bend	88–89
Lawrence Central High School	Indianapolis	84–85
Lawrence North High School	Indianapolis	83–84
Longfellow Elementary School	Muncie	85–86
Marian Heights Academy	Ferdinand	86–87
Mary Evelyn Castle Elementary School	Indianapolis	87–88
Muessel School	South Bend	87–88
North Central High School	Indianapolis	82–83
Perley Elementary School	South Bend	93–94
Roncalli High School	Indianapolis	92–93
St. Joseph's High School	South Bend	84–85
St. Lawrence School	Indianapolis	93–94
St. Mark Catholic School	Indianapolis	85–86
St. Paul Lutheran School	Fort Wayne	85–86
Skiles Test Elementary School	Indianapolis	85–86
Southport Elementary School	Southport	85–86
Southport Middle School	Indianapolis	88–89
Tecumseh-Harrison Elementary School	Vincennes	87–88
The Stanley Clark School	South Bend	85–86
The Summit Elementary Program	Fort Wayne	89–90
Thompkins Middle School	Evansville	86–87
Trinity School at Greenlawn	South Bend	88–89, 92–93
Valparaiso High School	Valparaiso	82–83
Warren Central High School	Indianapolis	82–83
Westchester Middle School	Chesterton	82–83
Westlane Middle School	Indianapolis	83–84
Winchester Village Elementary School	Indianapolis	87–88
IOWA		
Alden Community Elementary School	Alden	93–94
Ames Junior High School Central-Welch Campuses	Ames	82–83
Ames Senior High School	Ames	82–83
CAL Elementary School	Latimer	91–92
CAL High School	Latimer	86–87

SCHOOL	CITY	YEAR(S) RECOGNIZED
IOWA (*continued*)		
Central Catholic Elementary School	Mason City	87–88
Clive Elementary School	Des Moines	87–88
Cody Elementary School	Pleasant Valley	85–86
Erskine Elementary School	Cedar Rapids	89–90
Franklin Junior High School	Cedar Rapids	83–84
Franklin Pierce Elementary School	Cedar Rapids	87–88
Fredericksburg Community School	Fredericksburg	88–89
Garfield Elementary School	Davenport	93–94
George Washington High School	Cedar Rapids	83–84, 90–91
Grant Wood Elementary School	Cedar Rapids	91–92
Greenwood Elementary School	Des Moines	85–86
Grinnell Community Middle School	Grinnell	90–91
Harding Middle School	Cedar Rapids	90–91
Indian Hills Junior High School	Des Moines	82–83
Keokuk Middle School	Keokuk	82–83
Kirn Junior High School	Council Bluffs	83–84
Linn-Mar High School	Marion	84–85
Linn-Mar Junior High School	Marion	83–84
Metro High School	Cedar Rapids	84–85, 92–93
Northwest Junior High School	Coralville	84–85
Pella Christian Grade School	Pella	93–94
Pella Christian High School	Pella	84–85
Pleasant Valley Community High School	Pleasant Valley	83–84
Pleasant View Elementary School	Pleasant Valley	87–88
Regina Elementary School	Iowa City	91–92
St. Katherine's-St. Mark's School	Bettendorf	85–86
South East Junior High School	Iowa City	82–83
South Winnishiek Senior High School	Calmar	86–87
Thomas Jefferson Senior High School	Cedar Rapids	84–85
Trinity Lutheran School	Davenport	89–90
Valley High School	West Des Moines	83–84
Woodrow Wilson Junior High School	Council Bluffs	88–89
KANSAS		
Belinder Elementary School	Shawnee Mission	93–94
Blue Valley High School	Stilwell	88–89
Blue Valley Middle School	Overland Park	86–87
Blue Valley North High School	Overland Park	90–91
Brookridge Elementary School	Shawnee Mission	89–90
Cherokee Elementary School	Shawnee Mission	93–94
Christa McAuliffe Elementary School	Lenexa	93–94
Countryside Elementary School	Olathe	91–92
Earhart Environmental Magnet Elementary School	Wichita	89–90

SCHOOL	CITY	YEAR(S) RECOGNIZED
KANSAS (*continued*)		
Hocker Grove Middle School	Shawnee Mission	89–90
Horace Mann Alternative Middle School	Wichita	83–84
Indian Creek Elementary School	Olathe	91–92
Leawood Elementary School	Leawood	91–92
Leawood Middle School	Leawood	88–89
Meadowbrook Junior High School	Shawnee Mission	84–85
Morse Elementary School	Olathe	87–88
Northview Elementary School	Manhattan	87–88
Oak Hill Elementary School	Overland Park	91–92
Olathe South High School	Olathe	90–91
Oregon Trail Junior High School	Olathe	83–84, 92–93
Overland Trail Elementary School	Overland Park	93–94
Oxford Middle School	Overland Park	91–92
Ridgeview Elementary School	Olathe	93–94
Robinson Middle School	Topeka	84–85
Roosevelt-Lincoln Junior High School	Salina	83–84
Roseland Elementary School	Shawnee Mission	93–94
St. Mary Queen of the Universe School	Salina	85–86
Salina High School	Salina	84–85
Santa Fe Trail Junior High School	Olathe	84–85
Seaman High School	Topeka	84–85
Shawnee Mission South High School	Shawnee Mission	83–84
Shawnee Mission West High School	Shawnee Mission	83–84
Sumner Academy of Arts and Science	Kansas City	84–85
Tomahawk Elementary School	Olathe	85–86, 93–94
Topeka High School	Topeka	88–89
Topeka West High School	Topeka	83–84
Valley Park Elementary School	Overland Park	89–90
Village Elementary School	Emporia	85–86
KENTUCKY		
Arnett Elementary School	Erlanger	85–86
Assumption High School	Louisville	88–89, 92–93
Ballard High School	Louisville	86–87
Belfry High School	Belfry	92–93
Blessed Sacrament School	Fort Mitchell	93–94
Centerfield Elementary School	Crestwood	89–90
Clark Elementary School	Paducah	85–86
Crestwood Elementary School	Crestwood	93–94
Crittenden County Elementary School	Marion	85–86
Danville High School	Danville	90–91
duPont Manual-Magnet High School	Louisville	90–91
Elizabethtown High School	Elizabethtown	92–93
Fort Campbell High School	Fort Campbell	92–93
Goshen Elementary School	Goshen	85–86

SCHOOL	CITY	YEAR(S) RECOGNIZED
KENTUCKY *(continued)*		
Helmwood Heights Elementary School	Elizabethtown	85–86
Highlands High School	Fort Thomas	84–85
Holmes High School	Covington	84–85
Jackson Elementary School	Fort Campbell	87–88
Liberty Elementary School	Goshen	87–88
Louisville Male High School	Louisville	88–89
Mahaffey Middle School	Fort Campbell	90–91
Marshall Elementary School	Fort Campbell	91–92
Maryhurst School	Louisville	86–87
Murray High School	Murray	83–84
Oldham County High School	Buckner	86–87
Oldham County Middle School	Buckner	84–85
Robert D. Johnson Elementary School	Fort Thomas	91–92
Saint Xavier High School	Louisville	83–84, 88–89, 92–93
Southern Elementary School	Lexington	89–90
Stanton Elementary School	Stanton	93–94
Thomas Jefferson Middle School	Louisville	84–85
Trinity High School	Louisville	90–91
Virginia Wheeler Elementary School	Louisville	91–92
Wassom Middle School	Fort Campbell	88–89
Williamsburg High School	Williamsburg	92–93
Woodlawn Elementary School	Danville	89–90
LOUISIANA		
Alfred Bonnabel High School	Metairie	86–87
Alice M. Harte Elementary School	New Orleans	87–88
Archbishop Chapelle High School	Metairie	86–87, 90–91
Archbishop Rummel High School	Metairie	88–89
Baton Rouge High School	Baton Rouge	82–83
Benjamin Franklin Senior High School	New Orleans	88–89
Bissonet Plaza Elementary School	Metairie	85–86
Broadmoor Elementary School	Lafayette	89–90
Broadmoor Middle Laboratory School	Shreveport	86–87
Brother Martin High School	New Orleans	86–87
Caddo Middle Magnet School	Shreveport	84–85
Captain Shreve High School	Shreveport	82–83
Catholic High School	Baton Rouge	88–89, 92–93
Christ the King School	Bossier	93–94
Cope Middle School	Bossier	93–94
Edgar Martin Middle School	Lafayette	86–87
Edward Haynes School	New Orleans	87–88
Episcopal High School	Baton Rouge	86–87, 90–91
Episcopal School of Acadiana	Cade	86–87
Gentilly Terrace Creative Arts Magnet School	New Orleans	91–92
Grace King High School	Metairie	82–83

SCHOOL	CITY	YEAR(S) RECOGNIZED
LOUISIANA (*continued*)		
Isidore Newman Lower School	New Orleans	87–88
Isidore Newman School	New Orleans	84–85
Jean Gordon Elementary School	New Orleans	89–90
Jesuit High School-New Orleans	New Orleans	86–87
Lafayette Elementary School	Lafayette	83–84
Lakewood Junior High School	Luling	82–83
Leesville High School	Leesville	82–83
Little Oak Elementary School	Slidell	89–90
Lockport Junior High School	Lockport	84–85
Lusher Alternative Elementary School	New Orleans	87–88
M. R. Weaver Elementary School	Natchitoches	85–86
Mandeville Middle School	Mandeville	89–90
Marie B. Riviere Elementary School	Metairie	87–88
McDonogh 35 Senior High School	New Orleans	92–93
McKinley Middle Magnet School	Baton Rouge	83–84
McMain Magnet Secondary School	New Orleans	90–91
Metairie Park Country Day School	Metairie	86–87
Mount Carmel Academy	New Orleans	92–93
New Iberia Senior High School	New Iberia	88–89
Norbert Rillieux Elementary School	Waggaman	85–86
Northeast Elementary School	Pride	93–94
Our Lady of Divine Providence School	Metairie	93–94
Our Lady of Fatima School	Lafayette	85–86, 89–90
Parkway High School	Bossier City	84–85
Raceland Junior High School	Raceland	82–83
Romeville Elementary School	Convent	86–87
Ruston High School	Ruston	83–84
Saint Joseph's Academy	Baton Rouge	90–91
Saint Michael Catholic School	Crowley	85–86
Saint Rosalie School	Harvey	91–92
St. Anthony of Padua School	New Orleans	87–88
St. Bernard Elementary School	Breaux Bridge	87–88
St. Christopher School	Metairie	93–94
St. Francis Xavier Cabrini School	New Orleans	93–94
St. Leo the Great Elementary School	New Orleans	89–90
St. Martin's Episcopal School	Metairie	85–86
St. Mary's Dominican High School	New Orleans	88–89
St. Thomas More Catholic High School	Lafayette	86–87, 92–93
Scott Middle School	Scott	84–85
Trinity Episcopal School	New Orleans	87–88
Upper Little Caillou School	Chauvin	85–86
Ursuline Academy	New Orleans	90–91
Woodlake Elementary School	Mandeville	93–94
Woodvale Elementary School	Lafayette	87–88
Xavier University Preparatory School	New Orleans	86–87, 90–91
Youree Drive Middle School	Shreveport	83–84

SCHOOL	CITY	YEAR(S) RECOGNIZED
MAINE		
Action Elementary School	East Lebanon	93–94
Auburn Middle School	Auburn	83–84
Biddeford Middle School	Biddeford	91–92
Bowdoin Central School	Bowdoin	91–92
Camden-Rockport High School	Camden	84–85
Deering High School	Portland	82–83
Gray-New Gloucester Junior High School	Gray	84–85
Greely High School	Cumberland	86–87
Greely Junior High School	Cumberland Center	84–85
Howard C. Reiche Community School	Portland	91–92
Jordan Small School	Raymond	87–88
Junior High School of the Kennebunks	Kennebunk	83–84
Katahdin High School	Sherman Station	82–83
Kennebunk High School	Kennebunk	82–83, 90–91
King Middle School	Portland	82–83
Lake Region Junior High School	Bridgton	89–90
Miller School	Waldoboro	93–94
Mount Desert Island High School	Northeast Harbor	83–84
Mt. Ararat School	Topsham	82–83
Old Orchard Beach High School	Old Orchard Beach	90–91
Park Street School	Kennebunk	85–86
Portland High School	Portland	83–84
Presque Isle High School	Presque Isle	90–91
Skowhegan Area High School	Skowhegan	86–87
Yarmouth Junior-Senior High School	Yarmouth	86–87
MARYLAND		
Archbishop Keough High School	Baltimore	86–87
Archbishop Spalding High School	Severn	92–93
Arlington Baptist High School	Baltimore	84–85
Atholton High School	Columbia	92–93
Baltimore School for the Arts	Baltimore	90–91
Bells Mill Elementary School	Potomac	87–88
Burtonville Elementary School	Burtonville	93–94
Calvert Hall College High School	Towson	84–85, 88–89
Candlewood Elementary School	Rockville	91–92
Centennial High School	Ellicott City	84–85
Chevy Chase Elementary School	Chevy Chase	93–94
Clarksville Elementary School	Clarksville	87–88
College Gardens Elementary School	Rockville	85–86
Columbia Park Elementary School	Landover	87–88
Connelly School of the Holy Child	Potomac	88–89
DeMatha Catholic High School	Hyattsville	83–84, 90–91
Diamond Elementary School	Gaithersburg	89–90

SCHOOL	CITY	YEAR(S) RECOGNIZED
MARYLAND (*continued*)		
Eleanor Roosevelt High School	Greenbelt	90–91
Elizabeth Seton High School	Bladensburg	84–85
Frances R. Fuchs Special Center	Beltsville	91–92
Frederick High School	Frederick	92–93
Gaithersburg Elementary School	Gaithersburg	89–90
Glenelg High School	Glenelg	84 85
Good Counsel High School	Wheaton	92–93
Governor Thomas Johnson High School	Frederick	90–91
Greenbelt Center Elementary School	Greenbelt	91–92
Havre de Grace High School	Havre de Grace	90–91
Heather Hills Elementary School	Bowie	89–90
Hebrew Academy of Greater Washington	Silver Spring	87–88, 92–93
Ivymount School	Rockville	89–90, 93–94
Kenmoor Middle School TAG Magnet Center	Landover	88–89
Kettering Middle School	Upper Marlboro	92–93
La Reine High School	Suitland	84–85
Lake Seneca Elementary School	Germantown	91–92
Linganore High School	Frederick	92–93
Loyola High School of Baltimore, Inc.	Towson	86–87
Martin Luther King, Jr. Middle School	Beltsville	92–93
Mercy High School	Baltimore	84–85
Middletown Elementary School	Middletown	89–90
Middletown High School	Middletown	86–87
Milton M. Somers Middle School	La Plata	84–85
Mount Saint Joseph High School	Baltimore	88–89
Mt. Harmony Elementary School	Owings	85–86
North Chevy Chase Elementary School	Chevy Chase	89–90
Northfield Elementary School	Ellicott City	85–86
Notre Dame Preparatory School	Towson	84–85
Parkland Junior High School	Rockville	84–85
Perryville Middle School	Perryville	90–91
Poolesville Junior-Senior High School	Poolesville	86–87
Redland Middle School	Rockville	84–85, 88–89, 92–93
Richard Montgomery High School	Rockville	90–91
Riderwood Elementary School	Towson	93–94
Saint Jane de Chantal School	Bethesda	87–88
Saint Rita School	Baltimore	85–86
St. Andrew Apostle School	Silver Spring	89–90
St. Catherine Laboure	Wheaton	93–94
St. Elizabeth School	Rockville	85–86
Stone Ridge-School of the Sacred Heart	Bethesda	86–87, 92–93
Suitland High School	Forestville	88–89
The Bryn Mawr School	Baltimore	83–84
The Gilman School	Baltimore	83–84
The Park School of Baltimore	Brooklandville	83–84
Thomas S. Wootton High School	Rockville	84–85

SCHOOL	CITY	YEAR(S) RECOGNIZED
MARYLAND *(continued)*		
TRI-Services Center School	Chevy Chase	87–88
Trinity School	Ellicott City	89–90
Washington Episcopal School	Bethesda	93–94
Westland Intermediate School	Bethesda	90–91
Whetstone Elementary School	Gaithersburg	87–88
White Oak Intermediate School	Silver Spring	88–89
Wilde Lake Middle School	Columbia	84–85
William H. Farquhar Middle School	Olney	86–87
Winston Churchill High School	Potomac	90–91
Yellow Springs Elementary School	Frederick	93–94

MASSACHUSETTS

SCHOOL	CITY	YEAR(S) RECOGNIZED
Abraham Edwards Elementary School	Beverly	89–90
Acton-Boxborough Regional High School	Acton	83–84
Alice M. Barrows School	Reading	87–88
Broad Meadows Middle School	Quincy	90–91
Cathedral High School	Springfield	83–84
Charles Sumner Pierce Middle School	Milton	84–85
Claypit Hill School	Wayland	85–86
Coyle and Cassidy High School	Taunton	90–91
Dartmouth High School	North Dartmouth	84–85
Deerfield Academy	Deerfield	83–84
Fay School	Southborough	91–92
Glenbrook Middle School	Longmeadow	84–85
Groton School	Groton	83–84
Hawlemont Regional School	Charlemont	85–86
Henry C. Sanborn Elementary School	Andover	91–92
Holliston High School	Holliston	88–89
Holyoke Street School	Holyoke	83–84
James P. Timilty Middle School	Roxbury	88–89
John Glenn Middle School	Bedford	89–90
Jonas Clarke Middle School	Lexington	92–93
Josiah Quincy School	Boston	85–86
Lighthouse School	Chelmsford	84–85, 91–92
Mansfield High School	Mansfield	90–91
Marshall Simonds Middle School	Burlington	90–91
Martha's Vineyard Regional High School	Oak Bluffs	88–89
Milton High School	Milton	86–87
Monument Mountain Regional High School	Great Barrington	92–93
Nessacus Middle School	Dalton	84–85
New Bedford High School	New Bedford	83–84
Northfield Mount Hermon School	Northfield	86–87
Oliver Ames High School	North Easton	84–85
Pine Grove School	Rowley	87–88
Raymond J. Grey Junior High School	Acton	88–89

SCHOOL	CITY	YEAR(S) RECOGNIZED
MASSACHUSETTS (*continued*)		
Rockland Junior High School	Rockland	83–84
Snug Harbor Community School	Quincy	93–94
South Elementary School	Plymouth	87–88
Steward School	Topsfield	87–88
Summer Street School	Lynnfield	85–86
Sutton Elementary School	Sutton	87–88
Thayer Academy	Braintree	84–85
The Advent School	Boston	91–92
The May Institute, Inc.	Chatham	87–88
The Meadowbrook School	Weston	87–88
The Williston Northampton School	Easthampton	90–91
Tower School	Marblehead	89–90
Tucker School	Milton	85–86
W. S. Parker Middle School	Reading	84–85
Wayland High School	Wayland	86–87
Wilson Junior High School	Natick	84–85
MICHIGAN		
Abbott Middle School	Orchard Lake	84–85
Andrews Academy	Berrien Springs	84–85
Ann Arbor Huron High School	Ann Arbor	83–84
Ann J. Kellogg School	Battle Creek	85–86
Berkshire Middle School	Birmingham	84–85
Bingham Farms School	Birmingham	87–88
Bishop Foley High School	Madison Heights	83–84
Bloomfield Hills Andover High School	Bloomfield Hills	83–84
Bloomfield Hills Lahser High School	Bloomfield Hills	82–83
Bloomfield Hills Middle School	Bloomfield Hills	88–89
Bridgman High School	Bridgman	83–84
Brighton High School	Brighton	86–87
Brooks Middle School	Detroit	84–85
Caledonia Elementary School	Caledonia	87–88
Carl H. Lindbom Elementary School	Brighton	91–92
Cass Technical High School	Detroit	83–84, 90–91
Chesterfield Elementary School	Mt. Clemens	89–90
Covington Middle School	Birmingham	92–93
Cranbrook Kingswood School	Bloomfield Hills	86–87
Creative Arts Academy	Benton Harbor	87–88
De La Salle Collegiate High School	Warren	92–93
Dickinson Area Catholic School	Iron Mountain	85–86
Doherty Elementary School	West Bloomfield	85–86
East Grand Rapids High School	Grand Rapids	84–85
East Grand Rapids Middle School	East Grand Rapids	92–93
East Hills Middle School	Bloomfield Hills	90–91

SCHOOL	CITY	YEAR(S) RECOGNIZED
MICHIGAN (*continued*)		
Eastover Elementary School	Bloomfield Hills	91–92
Edwardsburg High School	Edwardsburg	92–93
Four Towns Elementary School	Waterford	93–94
Fox Elementary School	Macomb	93–94
Garber High School	Essexville	86–87
Gaylord High School	Gaylord	83–84
Gaylord Middle School	Gaylord	84–85
George P. Way Elementary School	Bloomfield Hills	89–90
Golightly Educational Center of Liberal Arts and Sciences	Detroit	93–94
Grand Rapids Christian School	Grand Rapids	83–84
Green Elementary School	West Bloomfield	87–88
Grosse Pointe North High School	Grosse Pointe Woods	84–85
Grosse Pointe South High School	Grosse Pointe	82–83
Harlan Elementary School	Bloomfield Hills	91–92
Hartland High School	Hartland	92–93
Hawkins Elementary School	Brighton	89–90
Hickory Grove Elementary School	Bloomfield Hills	87–88
Highmeadow Common Campus	Farmington Hills	93–94
Holland Christian Middle School	Holland	85–86
Holt High School	Holt	92–93
Hornung Elementary School	Brighton	87–88
Interlochen Arts Academy	Interlochen	83–84
John Page Middle School	Madison Heights	83–84
Kalamazoo Christian High School	Kalamazoo	84–85
L'Anse Creuse Middle School Central	Harrison Township	93–94
Lakewood Elementary School	Milford	87–88
Lamphere High School	Madison Heights	86–87
Lansing Catholic Central High School	Lansing	86–87
Larson Middle School	Troy	86–87
Lawton Community High School	Lawton	86–87
Longstreet Elementary School	Saginaw	85–86
Lutheran High School North	Mount Clemens	86–87
Lutheran High School West	Detroit	86–87
Maltby Middle School	Brighton	88–89
McCord Renaissance Center	Benton Harbor	92–93
Meadow Lake Elementary School	Birmingham	89–90
Mercy High School	Farmington Hills	83–84
Monteith Elementary School	Grosse Pointe Woods	89–90
Newaygo High School	Newaygo	90–91
North Christian School	Kalamazoo	87–88
North Farmington High School	Farmington Hills	92–93
Northview High School	Grand Rapids	83–84
Novi High School	Novi	86–87
Oak Ridge Elementary School	Royal Oak	89–90

SCHOOL	CITY	YEAR(S) RECOGNIZED
MICHIGAN (*continued*)		
Oakley Park Elementary School	Walled Lake	87–88
Okemos High School	Okemos	83–84
Orchard Hills Elementary School	Novi	85–86
Orchard Lake Middle School	West Bloomfield	90–91
Parcells Middle School	Grosse Pointe Woods	86–87
Parkwood-Upjohn School	Kalamazoo	85–86
Petoskey Middle School	Petoskey	86–87
Pinckney Middle School	Pinckney	90–91
Quarton Elementary School	Birmingham	85–86
Rochester Adams High School	Rochester Hills	88–89, 92–93
Rockford Middle School	Rockford	92–93
Roscommon High School	Roscommon	82–83
St. Clare of Montefalco Catholic School	Grosse Pointe Park	93–94
St. Francis Elementary School	Traverse City	87–88
St. Joan of Arc School	St. Clair Shores	93–94
St. John Lutheran School	Rochester	85–86
St. Lorenz Lutheran School	Frankenmuth	85–86
St. Mary Cathedral School	Gaylord	85–86
Sashabaw Junior High School	Clarkston	88–89
Scotch Elementary School	West Bloomfield	89–90
Seaholm High School	Birmingham	84–85
Shay Elementary School	Harbor Springs	85–86
Slauson Intermediate School	Ann Arbor	83–84
Southfield Christian School	Southfield	90–91
Southfield Senior High School	Southfield	83–84, 88–89
Southfield-Lathrup Senior High School	Lathrup Village	90–91
Southwest Elementary School	Howell	91–92
Sturgis Public High School	Sturgis	82–83
Sunset Lake Elementary School	Vicksburg	87–88
Sylvester Elementary School	Berrien Springs	85–86
The Grosse Pointe Academy	Grosse Pointe Farms	87–88, 91–92
Traverse City Area Junior High School	Traverse City	83–84, 90–91
Troy Athens High School	Troy	92–93
Walter R. Bemis Elementary School	Troy	87–88
Waukazoo Elementary School	Holland	93–94
West Bloomfield High School	West Bloomfield	86–87, 92–93
West Hills Middle School	West Bloomfield	86–87
West Ottawa Middle School	Holland	82–83
MINNESOTA		
Apple Valley High School	Apple Valley	90–91
Aquila Primary Center	St. Louis Park	89–90
Blake Lower School	Wayzata	93–94
Breck School	Minneapolis	87–88, 92–93

SCHOOL	CITY	YEAR(S) RECOGNIZED
MINNESOTA (*continued*)		
Cambridge Middle School	Cambridge	84–85
Cedar Island Elementary School	Maple Grove	89–90
Cedar Manor Intermediate Center	St. Louis	93–94
Centennial Senior High School	Circle Pines	86–87
Clara Barton Open School	Minneapolis	87–88
Clear Springs Elementary School	Minnetonka	91–92
Creek Valley Elementary School	Edina	93–94
Dassel Elementary School	Dassel	89–90
Dassel-Cokato Senior High School	Cokato	90–91
Deephaven Elementary School	Wayzata	91–92
Edina High School	Edina	83–84
Fridley Middle School	Fridley	88–89
Greenvale Park Elementary School	Northfield	93–94
Groves Learning Center	St. Louis Park	83–84, 91–92
H. O. Sonnesyn Elementary School	New Hope	89–90, 93–94
Hastings Middle School	Hastings	84–85, 88–89, 92–93
Hayes Elementary School	Fridley	89–90
Highland Elementary School	Apple Valley	91–92
Holy Family School	St. Louis Park	85–86
Hopkins High School	Minnetonka	82–83
Hopkins North Junior High School	Minnetonka	83–84
Hopkins West Junior High School	Minnetonka	83–84
Hosterman Middle School	New Hope	91–92
Hutchinson High School	Hutchinson	92–93
Irondale High School	New Brighton	92–93
John Adams Junior High School	Rochester	82–83
John F. Kennedy Senior High School	Bloomington	84–85
Mankato West High School	Mankato	92–93
Minnetonka High School	Minnetonka	88–89
Mounds Park Academy-Lower School	St. Paul	91–92
New Hope Elementary School	New Hope	87–88
Oak Grove Intermediate School	Bloomington	93–94
Oak Grove Junior High School	Bloomington	86–87
Oak Park Elementary School	Stillwater	89–90
Oak-Land Junior High School	Lake Elmo	83–84
Peter Hobart Primary Center	St. Louis Park	87–88
Pike Lake Elementary School	New Brighton	85–86
Poplar Bridge Elementary School	Bloomington	85–86
Regina High School	Minneapolis	84–85
Richfield Senior High School	Richfield	83–84
Rosemount High School	Rosemount	84–85
Saint Louis Park High School	St. Louis Park	86–87
St. Louis Park Junior High School	St. Louis Park	88–89
South St. Paul High School	South St. Paul	84–85
South View Junior High School	Edina	86–87

SCHOOL	CITY	YEAR(S) RECOGNIZED
MINNESOTA (*continued*)		
Stillwater Junior High School	Stillwater	83–84
Stillwater Senior High School	Stillwater	84–85
Stonebridge Elementary School	Stillwater	87–88
Susan Lindgren Intermediate Center	St. Louis Park	91–92
Technology Learning Campus	Robbinsdale	87–88
The Blake Lower School	Hopkins	89–90
The Blake School	Minneapolis	92–93
Valley Middle School	Apple Valley	84–85, 90–91
Valley View Junior High School	Edina	86–87
Wadena Elementary School	Wadena	87–88
Wayzata East Junior High School	Plymouth	88–89
Wayzata Senior High School	Plymouth	90–91
Wayzata West Junior High School	Wayzata	88–89
MISSISSIPPI		
Brookhaven High School	Brookhaven	83–84
Carver Middle School	Meridian	88–89
Clinton High School	Clinton	82–83
D. T. Cox Elementary School	Pontotoc	89–90
Hall's Ferry Road Elementary School	Vicksburg	85–86
Kate Griffin Junior High School	Meridian	86–87
Marion Park Elementary School	Meridian	85–86
McComb High School	McComb	82–83
Meridian Senior High School	Meridian	84–85
Northside Elementary School	Pearl	85–86
Oak Grove School	Hattiesburg	86–87, 92–93
Pearl High School	Pearl	90–91
Pontotoc Junior High School	Pontotoc	92–93
Sudduth Elementary School	Starkville	93–94
Thomas Street Elementary School	Tupelo	89–90
Tupelo High School	Tupelo	83–84
Van Winkle Elementary School	Jackson	87–88
Vicksburg High School	Vicksburg	88–89
MISSOURI		
Ballwin Elementary School	Ballwin	93–94
Barretts School	Manchester	89–90
Bellerive Elementary School	Creve Coeur	91–92
Blue Springs High School	Blue Springs	82–83
Blue Springs Junior High School	Blue Springs	86–87
Brentwood Middle School	Brentwood	83–84, 88–89
Bryan Elementary School	Nevada	93–94
Camdenton Junior High School	Camdenton	88–89

SCHOOL	CITY	YEAR(S) RECOGNIZED
MISSOURI (*continued*)		
Cardinal Ritter College Prep High School	St. Louis	83–84
Central Institute for the Deaf	St. Louis	85–86
Clayton High School	Clayton	84–85
Cler-Mont Community School	Independence	93–94
Cor Jesu Academy	St. Louis	90–91
Cross Keys Middle School	Florissant	88–89
David H. Hickman High School	Columbia	84–85
De Smet Jesuit High School	St. Louis	84–85
E. F. Swinney Elementary School	Kansas City	89–90
Fairview Elementary School	Columbia	85–86
Farmington High School	Farmington	92–93
Flynn Park School	University City	87–88
Genesis School	Kansas City	90–91
Green Trails Elementary School	Chesterfield	87–88
H. F. Epstein Hebrew Academy	St. Louis	85–86
Hanna Woods Elementary School	Ballwin	87–88
Highcroft Ridge School	Chesterfield	85–86
Holman Middle School	St. Ann	84–85
Horton Watkins High School	St. Louis	82–83
Immanuel Lutheran School	St. Charles	89–90
J. A. Rogers Academy of Liberal Arts and Sciences	Kansas City	92–93
Jackson Park Elementary School	University City	85–86
James Lewis Elementary School	Blue Springs	91–92
Jefferson Junior High School	Columbia	92–93
Jennings Junior High School	Jennings	84–85
John Ridgeway Elementary School	Columbia	85–86
Kikapoo High School	Springfield	82–83
Knob Noster Elementary School	Knob Noster	91–92
Ladue Junior High School	St. Louis	83–84
Lewis Middle School	Excelsior Springs	83–84
Lutheran High School North	St. Louis	83–84
Lutheran High School South	St. Louis	92–93
Mason Ridge School	Creve Coeur	85–86
McCluer North High School	Florissant	83–84
Meramec Elementary School	Clayton	85–86
Midway Heights Elementary School	Columbia	91–92
Missouri Military Academy	Mexico	84–85
Monett Elementary School	Monett	85–86
Nerinx Hall High School	Webster Groves	90–91
New Franklin Elementary School	New Franklin	89–90
Notre Dame de Sion	Kansas City	84–85
Oakland Junior High School	Columbia	88–89
Old Bonhomme Elementary School	Olivette	91–92
Palmer Junior High School	Independence	86–87

SCHOOL	CITY	YEAR(S) RECOGNIZED
MISSOURI (*continued*)		
Parkway Central High School	Chesterfield	86–87
Parkway Central Junior High School	Chesterfield	88–89
Parkway East Junior High School	Creve Coeur	86–87
Parkway North High School	Creve Coeur	84–85
Parkway South High School	Manchester	86–87
Parkway West Senior High School	Ballwin	82–83
Pattonville Heights Middle School	Maryland Heights	83–84
Pattonville High School	Maryland Heights	92–93
Pershing School	University City	93–94
Pond Elementary School	Grover	93–94
Ralph M. Captain Elementary School	Clayton	89–90
River Bend Elementary School	Chesterfield	91–92
Robinwood Elementary School	Florissant	89–90
Rock Bridge Senior High School	Columbia	86–87
Rockwood Eureka Senior High School	Eureka	92–93
Rolla Middle School	Rolla	92–93
Rolla Senior High School	Rolla	92–93
Russell Elementary School	Hazelwood	93–94
St. Joseph's Academy	St. Louis	92–93
St. Monica School	Creve Coeur	85–86
St. Theresa's Academy	Kansas City	83–84
Spoede School	St. Louis	87–88
The Churchill School	St. Louis	89–90
Thomas B. Chinn School	Kansas City	85–86
Thorpe J. Gordon Elementary School	Jefferson City	93–94
Ursuline Academy	St. Louis	88–89
Villa Duchesne School	St. Louis	90–91
Washington Middle School	Maryville	90–91
Westminster Christian Academy	St. Louis	90–91
Wilkinson Early Childhood Center	St. Louis	93–94
William Volker Applied Learning	Kansas	93–94
Williams Southern Elementary School	Independence	93–94
Wydown Junior High School	Warson Woods	84–85
Wydown Middle School	Clayton	90–91
MONTANA		
Bozeman High School	Bozeman	88–89, 92–93
C. M. Russell Elementary School	Missoula	85–86
Chief Joseph Middle School	Bozeman	93–94
Garfield Elementary School	Billings	87–88
Geyser Public School	Geyser	86–87
Havre Middle School	Havre	91–92
Ponderosa Elementary School	Billings	89–90

SCHOOL	CITY	YEAR(S) RECOGNIZED
MONTANA (*continued*)		
Sussex School	Missoula	87–88
Washington Middle School	Glendive	86–87
Will James Junior High School	Billings	84–85

NEBRASKA

SCHOOL	CITY	YEAR(S) RECOGNIZED
Arbor Heights Junior High School	Omaha	83–84
Beatrice Senior High School	Beatrice	82–83
Bellevue East High School	Bellevue	84–85
Blair Junior-Senior High School	Blair	88–89
Boys Town High School	Boys Town	88–89
Christ the King Catholic School	Omaha	89–90
Creighton Preparatory School	Omaha	86–87
Father Flanagan High School	Omaha	83–84
Fremont Senior High School	Fremont	86–87
Grace Abbott Elementary School	Omaha	89–90
Gretna Junior-Senior High School	Gretna	90–91
Harry A. Burke High School	Omaha	83–84
Hastings Junior High School	Hastings	84–85
Holling Heights Elementary School	Omaha	89–90
Kearney Junior High School	Kearney	82–83
Kearney Senior High School	Kearney	83–84
Lincoln East Junior-Senior High School	Lincoln	83–84
Lincoln High School	Lincoln	83–84
Lincoln Southeast High School	Lincoln	88–89
Longfellow Elementary School	Scottsbluff	91–92
Marian High School	Omaha	92–93
McMillan Junior High School	Omaha	84–85
Millard Central Middle School	Omaha	90–91
Millard North High School	Omaha	83–84
Millard North Junior High School	Omaha	86–87
Millard South High School	Omaha	82–83
Montclair Elementary School	Omaha	87–88
Norfolk Public Senior High School	Norfolk	84–85
Norris Middle School	Firth	84–85
Ralston High School	Ralston	92–93
Raymond Central Elementary School	Valparaiso	89–90
Saint Cecilia's Cathedral Elementary School	Omaha	85–86
St. John Lutheran School	Seward	85–86
St. Mary's High School	O'Neill	88–89
St. Pius X-St. Leo School	Omaha	85–86
Tri County Senior High School	DeWitt	84–85
Valley Middle/High School	Valley	92–93
Valley View Junior High School	Omaha	84–85

SCHOOL	CITY	YEAR(S) RECOGNIZED
NEBRASKA (*continued*)		
Westbrook Junior High School	Omaha	84–85
Westside High School	Omaha	83–84

NEVADA

SCHOOL	CITY	YEAR(S) RECOGNIZED
Brown Elementary School	Reno	91–92
Cannon Junior High School	Las Vegas	83–84, 88–89
Darrel C. Swope Middle School	Reno	82–83
Edward C. Reed High School	Sparks	84–85
Elko High School	Elko	82–83
Gardnerville Elementary School	Gardnerville	85–86
Grass Valley Elementary School	Winnemucca	87–88
Kenny C. Guinn Junior High School	Las Vegas	82–83
Las Vegas High School	Las Vegas	84–85
McGill Elementary School	McGill	93–94
Procter Hug High School	Reno	86–87
Reno High School	Reno	83–84
St. Viator School	Las Vegas	85–86
Stead Elementary School	Reno	85–86
Vegas Verdes Elementary School	Las Vegas	91–92
Walter Bracken Elementary School	Las Vegas	89–90

NEW HAMPSHIRE

SCHOOL	CITY	YEAR(S) RECOGNIZED
Amherst Middle School	Amherst	86–87, 90–91
Exeter Area Junior High School	Exeter	83–84
Fairgrounds Junior High School	Nashua	88–89
Frances C. Richmond School	Hanover	87–88
Hanover High School	Hanover	82–83
Hollis Elementary School	Hollis	87–88
Kearsarge Regional High School	North Sutton	83–84
Lebanon Junior High School	Lebanon	82–83
Londonderry High School	Londonderry	86–87
Londonderry Junior High School	Londonderry	84–85
Moultonborough Central School	Moultonborough	85–86
Phillips Exeter Academy	Exeter	83–84
St. Paul's School	Concord	83–84
Stratham Memorial School	Stratham	85–86
Timberlane Regional Junior High School	Plaistow	88–89
Woodbury School	Salem	89–90
Woodman Park School	Dover	85–86

NEW JERSEY

SCHOOL	CITY	YEAR(S) RECOGNIZED
Canfield Avenue School	Mine Hill	91–92

SCHOOL	CITY	YEAR(S) RECOGNIZED
NEW JERSEY (*continued*)		
Christian Brothers Academy	Lincroft	83–84
Columbia High School	Maplewood	92–93
CPC Behavorial Healthcare, High Point Elementary School	Morganville	93–94
Crossroads School	Monmouth Junction	92–93
Delbarton School	Morristown	83–84
Dwight-Englewood School	Englewood	86–87
East Brunswick High School	East Brunswick	90–91
Eden Institute	Princeton	91–92
Fair Lawn High School	Fair Lawn	90–91
George C. Baker Elementary School	Moorestown	91–92
Greenbrook School	Kendall Park	91–92
Hebrew Academy of Atlantic County	Margate	89–90
Hillside School	Montclair	87–88
Ho-Ho-Kus Public School	Ho-Ho-Kus	89–90
Irwin School	East Brunswick	89–90
Jefferson School	Summit	89–90
Lawrence Brook School	East Brunswick	91–92
Leesburg School	Port Elizabeth	91–92
Mary E. Roberts School	Moorestown	89–90
Maurice Hawk	Princeton Junction	93–94
Mill Lake School	Monroe Township	91–92
Montgomery High School	Skillman	92–93
Moorestown Friends Lower School	Moorestown	91–92
Morris Catholic High School	Denville	84–85
Mount St. Mary Academy	Plainfield-Watchung	84–85
Mustard Seed School	Hoboken	87–88
Nishuane School	Montclair	89–90
Northern Highlands Regional High School	Allendale	86–87
Our Lady Star of the Sea School	Cape May	93–94
Paramus High School	Paramus	88–89
Parkway School	Paramus	87–88
Pompton Lakes High School	Pompton Lakes	86–87
Princeton Child Development Institute	Princeton	83–84
Queen of Peace High School	North Arlington	92–93
Richard M. Teitelman School	Cape May	90–91
Ridge High School	Basking Ridge	86–87
Ridgewood High School	Ridgewood	86–87
Rutgers Preparatory School	Somerset	92–93
Sacred Heart School	Trenton	87–88
St. Paul's School	Jersey City	87–88
St. Peter Elementary School	New Brunswick	85–86
South Brunswick High School	Monmouth Junction	90–91
South Valley School	Moorestown	87–88
Spotswood High School	Spotswood	92–93

SCHOOL	CITY	YEAR(S) RECOGNIZED
NEW JERSEY (*continued*)		
The Midland School	North Branch	89–90
Upper Freehold Regional Elementary School	Allentown	93–94
Watchung School	Montclair	89–90, 93–94
West Windsor-Plainsboro High School	Princeton Junction	92–93
NEW MEXICO		
Albuquerque Academy	Albuquerque	83–84
Albuquerque High School	Albuquerque	82–83
Barcelona Elementary School	Albuquerque	93–94
Carrizozo High School	Carrizozo	83–84
Cibola High School	Albuquerque	86–87
Corrales Elementary School	Albuquerque	85–86
Eisenhower Middle School	Albuquerque	84–85
Governor Bent Elementary School	Albuquerque	93–94
Highland High School	Albuquerque	84–85
Hillrise Elementary School	Las Cruces	89–90
Hoover Middle School	Albuquerque	82–83
Jefferson Middle School	Albuquerque	83–84
John Adams Middle School	Albuquerque	86–87
John Baker Elementary School	Albuquerque	87–88
Las Cruces High School	Las Cruces	84–85
Loma Heights Elementary School	Las Cruces	91–92
Longfellow Elementary School	Albuquerque	85–86
Manzano High School	Albuquerque	82–83
McCormick Elementary School	Farmington	87–88
McKinley Middle School	Albuquerque	88–89, 92–93
Polk Middle School	Albuquerque	86–87
Rehoboth Christian High School	Rehoboth	83–84
Roosevelt Middle School	Tijeras	92–93
Taft Middle School	Albuquerque	82–83
Van Buren Middle School	Albuquerque	84–85, 92–93
Washington Middle School	Albuquerque	86–87
West Mesa High School	Albuquerque	83–84
NEW YORK		
A. Phillip Randolph Campus High School	New York	86–87
Academy of Mount Saint Ursula	Bronx	86–87
Academy of Our Lady of Good Counsel	White Plains	86–87
Alexander Hamilton High School	Elmsford	92–93
Anne M. Dorner Middle School	Ossining	88–89
Aquinas High School	New York	84–85
Archbishop Molloy High School	Briarwood	86–87
Astor Home for Children	Rhinebeck	93–94

SCHOOL	CITY	YEAR(S) RECOGNIZED
NEW YORK (*continued*)		
Baldwin Senior High School	Baldwin	90–91
Bedford Road School	Pleasantville	89–90
Benjamin Franklin Elementary School	Binghamton	93–94
Benjamin Franklin Middle School	Kenmore	93–94
Benjamin N. Cardozo High School	Bayside	83–84
Berkshire Junior/Senior High School	Canaan	92–93
Bishop Loughlin Memorial High School	Brooklyn	83–84
Blind Brook High School	Rye Brook	86–87
Blue Mountain Middle School	Peekskill	82–83
Bronxville High School	Bronxville	90–91
Brooklyn Technical High School	Brooklyn	82–83
Burnt Hills-Ballston Lake Senior High School	Burnt Hills	88–89
Byram Hills High School	Armonk	88–89
Campus East School	Buffalo	87–88
Canandaigua Primary School	Canandaigua	85–86
Carrie E. Tomkins Elementary School	Croton-on-Hudson	85–86
Catherine McAuley High School	Brooklyn	90–91
Cazenovia Junior-Senior High School	Cazenovia	88–89
Central School	Larchmont	85–86
Clayton A. Bouton Junior/Senior High School	Voorheesville	90–91
Clinton Middle School	Clinton	89–90
Clinton Senior High School	Clinton	88–89
Como Park Elementary School	Lancaster	91–92
Concord Road Elementary School	Ardsley	91–92
Convent of the Sacred Heart School	New York	90–91
Daniel Webster Magnet School	New Rochelle	93–94
Davison Avenue School	Lynbrook	91–92
Dr. Roland N. Patterson Intermediate School #229	Bronx	86–87
Eastchester High School	Eastchester	92–93
Edgemont Junior-Senior High School	Scarsdale	83–84
Edward R. Murrow High School	Brooklyn	88–89
Elmer Avenue School	Schnectady	87–88
Elmont Memorial High School	Elmont	90–91
F. E. Bellows School	Mamaroneck	87–88
Fordham Preparatory School	Bronx	83–84
Friends Academy	Locust Valley	87–88
Fulmar Road Elementary School	Mahopac	89–90
Futures Academy #37	Buffalo	85–86
Garden City Junior High School	Garden City	84–85
Garden City Senior High School	Garden City	86–87
Gardnertown Fundamental Magnet School	Newburgh	87–88
George W. Miller Elementary School	Nanuet	89–90
Glenmont Elementary School	Glenmont	89–90
Gowana Junior High School	Clifton Park	88–89

SCHOOL	CITY	YEAR(S) RECOGNIZED
NEW YORK (*continued*)		
Greece Athena Senior High School	Rochester	83–84
H. J. Kalfas Early Childhood Magnet School	Niagara	93–94
Haldane Elementary School	Cold Spring	87–88
Harbor Hill School	Greenvale	85–86
Harrison Avenue School	Harrison	85–86
Harry Hoag School	Fort Plain	87–88
Hebrew Academy of the Five Towns and Rockaway	Lawrence	87–88
Herbert Hoover Elementary School	Kenmore	91–92
Hillel Academy of Broome County	Binghamton	87–88
Holmes Elementary School	Tonawanda	89–90
Holy Family School	Hicksville	89–90
Holy Trinity Diocesan High School	Hicksville	86–87
Horace Mann School	New York	84–85
Horizons-on-the-Hudson Magnet School	Newburgh	89–90, 93–94
Houghton Academy P. S. #69	Buffalo	85–86
Hutchinson Central Technical High School	Buffalo	88–89
Irvington High School	Irvington	92–93
Irvington Middle School	Irvington	86–87
Jamaica High School	Jamaica	84–85
James P. B. Duffy School No. 12	Rochester	89–90
Jericho High School	Jericho	90–91
John Bowne High School	Flushing	92–93
John F. Kennedy High School	Somers	83–84
Kenmore East High School	Tonawanda	92–93
Koda Junior High School	Clifton Park	86–87
L. P. Quinn Elementary School	Tupper Lake	87–88
La Salle Institute	Troy	86–87, 90–91
Lake George Elementary School	Lake George	85–86, 91–92
Lincoln Elementary School	Scotia	85–86
Liverpool High School	Liverpool	84–85
Livonia Primary School	Livonia	89–90
Long Island Lutheran High School	Brookville	88–89
Longwood Middle School	Middle Island	90–91
Louis Armstrong Middle School	East Elmhurst	82–83
Louis M. Klein Middle School	Harrison	93–94
Loyola School	New York	88–89
Lynbrook High School	Lynbrook	90–91
Maine-Endwell Middle School	Endwell	88–89
Malverne High School	Malverne	88–89
Mandalay School	Wantagh	93–94
Manhasset Junior-Senior High School	Manhasset	88–89
Marion Street Elementary School	Lynbrook	85–86
McQuaid Jesuit High School	Rochester	86–87
Mercy High School	Riverhead	88–89

SCHOOL	CITY	YEAR(S) RECOGNIZED
NEW YORK *(continued)*		
Midwood High School at Brooklyn College	Brooklyn	86–87
Miller Place High School	Miller Place	83–84
Milton School	Rye	93–94
Moriches Elementary School	Moriches	89–90, 93–94
Mother Cabrini High School	New York	86–87
Mount Markham Middle School	West Winfield	90–91
Mount Saint Michael Academy	Bronx	90–91
Mount Vernon High School	Mount Vernon	86–87
Nazareth Academy	Rochester	83–84
New Hyde Park Memorial Junior/Senior High School	New Hyde Park	92–93
New Rochelle High School	New Rochelle	83–84
Newburgh Free Academy	Newburgh	86–87
Niskayuna High School	Schenectady	82–83
North Salem High School	North Salem	88–89
North Salem Middle School	North Salem	86–87
North Shore High School	Glen Head	90–91
Northport High School	Northport	83–84
Oneida Middle School	Schenectady	86–87
Orchard School	Yonkers	89–90, 93–94
Orenda Elementary School	Clifton Park	89–90
Osborn School/ Julia Dyckman Andrews Memorial	Rye	91–92
Our Lady of Lourdes School	West Islip	85–86
Our Lady of Mercy School	Hicksville	87–88
Our Lady of Peace School	Lynbrook	89–90
Our Lady of the Hamptons Regional Catholic School	Southhampton	93–94
Our Saviour Lutheran School	Bronx	87–88
Oyster Bay High School	Oyster Bay	88–89
P. S. 183, General Daniel "Chappie" James, Jr.	Brooklyn	87–88
P. S. 189, Bilingual School	Brooklyn	85–86
P. S. 206, M.-Jose C. Barbosa School	New York	87–88
Park Early Elementary School	Westbury	85–86
Paul D. Schreiber High School	Port Washington	84–85
Paul J. Gelinas Junior High School	Setauket	86–87
PEARLS Elementary School #32	Yonkers	91–92
Pelham Memorial High School	Pelham	92–93
Pequenakonck Elementary School	North Salem	87–88
Pierre Van Cortlandt Middle School	Croton-on-Hudson	84–85
Pittsford Middle School	Pittsford	86–87
Pleasantville High School	Pleasantville	90–91
Poestenkill Elementary School	Poestenkill	93–94
Port Jefferson Junior High School	Port Jefferson	86–87
Purchase School	Purchase	87–88

SCHOOL	CITY	YEAR(S) RECOGNIZED
NEW YORK (*continued*)		
Regis High School	New York	84–85
Ridge Street School	Rye Brook	85–86
Robert Cushman Murphy Junior High School	Stony Brook	83–84
Sacandaga Elementary School	Scotia	85–86, 93–94
Sacred Heart/Mt. Carmel School of the Arts	Mount Vernon	93–94
Saddle Rock Elementary School	Great Neck	93–94
Saint Catharine Academy	Bronx	92–93
St. Agnes Cathedral School	Rockville Centre	89–90
St. Francis Prep School	Fresh Meadows	83–84
St. Ignatius Loyola School	New York	85–86
St. Isidore School	Riverhead	87–88
St. Joseph's School	Long Island City	89–90, 93–94
St. Thomas of Canterbury School	Cornwall-on-Hudson	87–88
Sts. Peter and Paul School	Bronx	85–86
Salanter Akiba Riverdale Academy	Riverdale	91–92
Scarsdale High School	Scarsdale	82–83
School #54-ECC	Buffalo	85–86
School #59-Science Magnet	Buffalo	84–85
Scotia-Glenville High School	Scotia	86–87
Scotia-Glenville Junior High School	Scotia	88–89
Seth Low Intermediate School #96	Brooklyn	86–87
Sewanhaka High School	Floral Park	92–93
Shaker High School	Latham	84–85
Shaker Junior High School	Latham	92–93
Shelter Rock Elementary School	Manhasset	91–92
Shenendehowa High School	Clifton Park	90–91
Shoreham-Wading River High School	Shoreham	86–87
Shoreham-Wading River Middle School	Shoreham	82–83
Shulamith High School for Girls	Brooklyn	86–87, 92–93
Skaneateles High School	Skaneateles	90–91
South Park High School	Buffalo	88–89
Springhurst Elementary School	Dobbs Ferry	87–88
Stewart School	Garden City	87–88
Stratford Avenue School	Garden City	87–88
Stuyvesant High School	New York	82–83
Susan E. Wagner High School	Staten Island	88–89
Syosset High School	Syosset	92–93
The Academy of the Holy Names	Albany	92–93
The Astor Learning Center	Rhinebeck	87–88
The Brearley School	New York	83–84
The Bronx High School of Science	Bronx	82–83, 88–89
The Calhoun School	New York	85–86
The Douglaston School	Douglaston	85–86
The Fieldston School	Riverdale	83–84
The Fox Lane Middle School	Bedford	83–84

SCHOOL	CITY	YEAR(S) RECOGNIZED
NEW YORK (*continued*)		
The Herman Schreiber School	Brooklyn	87–88
The Nichols School	Buffalo	84–85
The Ursuline School	New Rochelle	84–85
Theodore Roosevelt Elementary School	Kenmore	93–94
Thomas Edison Elementary School	Tonawanda	93–94
Thomas Jefferson Elementary School	Buffalo	89–90
Thomas K. Beecher School	Elmira	85–86
Tottenville High School	Staten Island	86–87
Townsend Harris High School at Queens College	Flushing	88–89
Triangle Academy	Buffalo	89–90
Vestal Senior High School	Vestal	84–85
Voorheesville Elementary School	Voorheesville	91–92
Wantagh Elementary School	Wantagh	91–92
Wantagh Middle School	Wantagh	90–91
Ward Melville High School	Setauket	88–89
Waterford-Halfmoon Elementary School	Waterford	87–88
Weedsport Elementary School	Weedsport	85–86
West Corners Campus School	Endicott	87–88
West End School	Lynbrook	85–86
West Hertel Academy	Buffalo	85–86
Westbury Senior High School	Westbury	86–87
Westhill High School	Syracuse	92–93
White Plains High School	White Plains	86–87
White Plains Middle School	White Plains	86–87
William B. Ward Elementary School	New Rochelle	87–88
Woodmere Middle School	Hewlett	86–87
Xavier High School	New York	90–91
Yeshiva of Central Queens	Flushing	93–94

NORTH CAROLINA

SCHOOL	CITY	YEAR(S) RECOGNIZED
Blessed Sacrament School	Burlington	89–90
Brevard Elementary School	Brevard	85–86
Brewster Middle School	Camp Lejeune	88–89
C. G. Credle Elementary School	Oxford	89–90
Carmel Junior High School	Charlotte	83–84
Carolina Friends School	Durham	83–84
Charlotte Latin School	Charlotte	86–87
China Grove Elementary School	China Grove	89–90
Crest Senior High School	Shelby	86–87
Elon College Elementary School	Elon College	87–88
First Ward Elementary School	Charlotte	87–88
Gatesville Elementary School	Gatesville	86–87
Ira B. Jones Elementary School	Asheville	85–86
John A. Holmes High School	Edenton	84–85

SCHOOL	CITY	YEAR(S) RECOGNIZED
NORTH CAROLINA (*continued*)		
John T. Hoggard High School	Wilmington	90–91
Kinston High School	Kinston	86–87
Lee County Senior High School	Sanford	82–83
Lewis H. Powell Gifted and Talented Magnet Elementary School	Raleigh	91–92
Manteo High School	Manteo	83–84
McDowell High School	Marion	84–85
Mooresville Junior High School	Mooresville	86–87
Myers Park High School	Charlotte	86–87
Needham Broughton High School	Raleigh	83–84
North Davie Junior High School	Mocksville	84–85
Park View Elementary School	Morresville	85–86
Piedmont Middle School	Monroe	90–91
Piedmont Open Middle School	Charlotte	90–91
Providence Day School	Charlotte	86–87
Richmond Senior High School	Rockingham	90–91
Rowland Hill Latham Elementary School	Winston-Salem	93–94
Stone Street Elementary School	Camp Lejeune	87–88
W. G. Pearson Elementary School	Durham	85–86
Walter M. Williams High School	Burlington	92–93
West Rowan High School	Mount Ulla	90–91
William G. Enloe High School	Raleigh	82–83
NORTH DAKOTA		
Belmont Elementary School	Grand Forks	91–92
Benjamin Franklin Junior High School	Fargo	82–83
Beulah High School	Beulah	90–91
Century High School	Bismarck	92–93
Clara Barton Elementary School	Fargo	91–92
Crosby Elementary School	Crosby	85–86
Divide County High School	Crosby	83–84
Hazen Public High School	Hazen	82–83
Hughes Junior High School	Bismarck	84–85
Northridge Elementary School	Bismarck	89–90
Shanley High School	Fargo	83–84
Washington School	Fargo	87–88
OHIO		
Arbor Hills Junior High School	Sylvania	83–84
Aurora High School	Aurora	92–93
Barrington Elementary School	Upper Arlington	85–86
Bath Elementary School	Akron	85–86
Beachwood Middle School	Beachwood	92–93

SCHOOL	CITY	YEAR(S) RECOGNIZED
OHIO (*continued*)		
Beaumont School	Cleveland Heights	90–91
Bellflower Elementary School	Mentor	91–92
Berea High School	Berea	84–85
Berwick Science/Math/Environmental Studies Alternative Elementary School	Columbus	87–88
Bishop Watterson High School	Columbus	88–89
Brunswick Middle School	Brunswick	84–85
Canton Country Day School	Canton	91–92
Center Street Village Elementary School	Mentor	89–90
Centerville High School	Centerville	83–84, 92–93
Central Catholic High School	Toledo	90–91
Chagrin Falls High School	Chagrin Falls	88–89
Chambers Elementary School	East Cleveland	85–86, 89–90
Chaminade-Julienne High School	Dayton	88–89
Columbus Alternative High School	Columbus	84–85
Columbus School for Girls	Columbus	92–93
Columbus School for Girls, Lower School	Bexley	93–94
Cottonwood Elementary School	Cincinnati	87–88
David Smith Elementary School	Delaware	87–88
Dublin Middle School	Dublin	86–87
East Muskingum Middle School	New Concord	83–84
Eastview Middle School	Bath	82–83
Edison Primary School	Dayton	85–86
Elda Elementary School	Hamilton	87–88
Elyria Catholic High School	Elyria	92–93
Evamere Elementary School	Hudson	85–86
Evendale Elementary School	Cincinnati	87–88
Fairfax Elementary School	Mentor	87–88
Fairfield North Elementary School	Hamilton	89–90
Forest Elementary School	North Olmsted	85–86
Francis Dunlavy Elementary School	Lebanon	85–86
Freedom Elementary School	West Chester	91–92
Gesu Catholic School	University Heights	87–88
Gibbs Elementary School	Canton	85–86
Glendale Elementary School	Cincinnati	87–88
Greensview Elementary School	Upper Arlington	87–88
Harrison Elementary School	Harrison	89–90
Hastings Middle School	Upper Arlington	84–85
Heritage Elementary School	Medina	87–88
Herman K. Ankeney Junior High School	Beavercreek	83–84
Hillcrest Primary School	Richfield	87–88
Hoffman School	Cincinnati	87–88, 91–92
Hopewell Elementary School	West Chester	91–92
Hopkins Elementary School	Mentor	87–88
Hudson High School	Hudson	83–84

SCHOOL	CITY	YEAR(S) RECOGNIZED
OHIO (*continued*)		
Hudson Junior High School	Hudson	83–84
Immaculate Conception School	Columbus	93–94
Incarnation Catholic School	Centerville	89–90
Independence Primary School	Independence	93–94
Indian Hill Elementary School	Cincinnati	87–88
Indian Hill High School	Cincinnati	83–84
J. F. Burns Elementary School	Kings Mills	93–94
Jennings Middle School	Akron	84–85
John F. Dumont Elementary School	Cincinnati	87–88
Jones Middle School	Columbus	83–84
Kilgour Elementary School	Cincinnati	91–92
Kirtland Middle School	Kirtland	93–94
Lakota High School	West Chester	92–93
Lewis Sands Elementary School	Chagrin Falls	87–88
Lial Elementary School	Whitehouse	91–92
Lomond Elementary School	Shaker Heights	85–86
Louisa Wright Elementary School	Lebanon	87–88
Madeira High School	Cincinnati	84–85
Magnificat High School	Rocky River	84–85
Mariemont High School	Cincinnati	84–85, 88–89
Mentor Shore Junior High School	Mentor	86–87, 92–93
Metro Catholic Parish School	Cleveland	93–94
Morgan Elementary School	Hamilton	87–88
Mount Notre Dame High School	Cincinnati	86–87
Nativity School	Cincinnati	87–88
Normandy Elementary School	Centerville	91–92
North Olmsted High School	North Olmsted	86–87
Oakwood High School	Dayton	90–91
Olde Sawmill Elementary School	Dublin	85–86
Orange High School	Pepper Pike	90–91
Orchard Elementary School	Cleveland	93–94
Ottawa Middle School	Cincinnati	84–85
Our Lady of Perpetual Help School	Grove City	87–88, 91–92
Pepper Pike Elementary School	Pepper Pike	93–94
Perkins Junior High School	Akron	82–83
Perry Middle School	Worthington	84–85
Pine Elementary School	North Olmsted	91–92
Princeton High School	Cincinnati	83–84, 92–93
Princeton Junior High School	Cincinnati	82–83, 92–93
Regina High School	South Euclid	90–91
Revere High School	Richfield	90–91
Robert E. Lucas Intermediate School	Cincinnati	85–86
Roselawn Condon School	Cincinnati	85–86
Saint Barbara School	Massillon	85–86
Saint Bernard-Elmwood Place High School	Saint Bernard	86–87

SCHOOL	CITY	YEAR(S) RECOGNIZED
OHIO (*continued*)		
Saint Xavier High School	Cincinnati	83–84
St. Agatha School	Columbus	85–86
St. Andrew School	Columbus	91–92
St. Columban Elementary School	Loveland	89–90
St. Francis DeSales High School	Columbus	92–93
St. Gertrude School	Cincinnati	87–88
St. Ignatius Jesuit High School	Cleveland	84–85
St. James White Oak School	Cincinnati	87–88, 91–92
St. John Bosco School	Parma Heights	91–92
St. John's High School	Toledo	88–89
St. Joseph Academy	Cleveland	90–91
St. Joseph Montessori School	Columbus	93–94
St. Jude Elementary School	Elyria	93–94
St. Mary School	Cincinnati	85–86, 93–94
St. Michael School	Worthington	87–88
St. Patrick of Heatherdowns School	Toledo	93–94
St. Paul Lutheran School	Napoleon	87–88
St. Peter Catholic School	Huber Heights	89–90
St. Therese of the Little Flower School	Cincinnati	93–94
St. Thomas More School	Brooklyn	93–94
St. Timothy School	Columbus	89–90
School for Creative and Performing Arts	Cincinnati	84–85
Shaker Heights High School	Shaker Heights	82–83
Shaker Heights Middle School	Shaker Heights	86–87
Sharonville Elementary School	Cincinnati	91–92
Solon High School	Solon	90–91
Springdale Elementary School	Cincinnati	93–94
Stewart Elementary School	Cincinnati	93–94
Sycamore Junior High School	Cincinnati	86–87
Symmes Elementary School	Loveland	93–94
Theodore Roosevelt High School	Kent	84–85
Three Rivers Middle School	Cleves	87–88
Tremont Elementary School	Upper Arlington	85–86
Upper Arlington High School	Upper Arlington	84–85
Urban Community School	Cleveland	87–88
Ursuline Academy of Cincinnati	Cincinnati	88–89
Villa Angela Academy	Cleveland	86–87
W. M. Sellman Middle School	Madeira	85–86
Walnut Hills High School	Cincinnati	84–85
Walsh Jesuit High School	Stow	84–85
Western Row Elementary School	Mason	93–94
Whitewater Valley Elementary School	Harrison	93–94
William Henry Harrison High School	Harrison	90–91
William Henry Harrison Junior High School	Harrison	83–84
Willoughby South High School	Willoughby	92–93

SCHOOL	CITY	YEAR(S) RECOGNIZED
OHIO (*continued*)		
Windermere Elementary School	Upper Arlington	85–86
Woodbury Junior High School	Shaker Heights	83–84
Woodlawn Elementary School	Cincinnati	87–88
Worthington Hills School	Worthington	85–86
Worthingway Middle School	Worthington	86–87
Wyoming High School	Wyoming	82–83

OKLAHOMA

SCHOOL	CITY	YEAR(S) RECOGNIZED
Ardmore High School	Ardmore	82–83
Ardmore Middle School	Ardmore	90–91
Booker T. Washington High School	Tulsa	82–83
Byng High School	Ada	83–84
Carnegie School	Tulsa	85–86
Cimarron Middle School	Edmond	93–94
Crosby Park Elementary School	Lawton	85–86
Deer Creek Elementary School	Edmond	89–90
Douglas Learning Center	Lawton	89–90
Gans Junior-Senior High School	Muldrow	83–84
Holland Hall Middle School	Tulsa	85–86, 89–90
Hugh Bish Elementary School	Lawton	93–94
James L. Dennis Elementary School	Oklahoma City	85–86
John Marshall High School	Oklahoma City	82–83
Maryetta School	Stilwell	87–88
McKinley Elementary School	Norman	87–88
Millwood High School	Oklahoma City	83–84
Monte Cassino School	Tulsa	93–94
Norman High School	Norman	88–89
Northeast High School	Oklahoma City	83–84
Piedmont Elementary School	Piedmont	89–90
Putnam City North High School	Oklahoma City	88–89
Quail Creek Elementary School	Oklahoma City	91–92
School of Saint Mary	Tulsa	87–88
Seiling Public Schools	Seiling	84–85
Summit Middle School	Edmond	92–93
West Mid High School	Norman	88–89
Western Hills Elementary School	Lawton	89–90
Whittier Elementary School	Lawton	87–88
Wiley Post Elementary School	Oklahoma City	89–90

OREGON

SCHOOL	CITY	YEAR(S) RECOGNIZED
Alameda Elementary School	Portland	87–88
Beaumont Middle School	Portland	84–85
Beaverton High School	Beaverton	84–85

SCHOOL	CITY	YEAR(S) RECOGNIZED
OREGON (*continued*)		
Bolton Middle School	West Linn	85–86
Burns High School	Burns	86–87, 90–91
Byrom Elementary School	Tualatin	87–88
Calapooia Middle School	Albany	82–83
Cedar Park Intermediate School	Beaverton	82–83
Centennial High School	Gresham	88–89
Chapman Elementary School	Portland	89–90
Clackamas High School	Milwaukie	83–84
Corridor School	Creswell	85–86
Crater High School	Central Point	82–83
Duniway Elementary School	Portland	87–88
Floyd Light Middle School	Portland	83–84
Gilbert Park School	Portland	89–90
Gladstone High School	Gladstone	86–87
Jesuit High School	Portland	88–89
Lake Oswego High School	Lake Oswego	82–83
Lake Oswego Junior High School	Lake Oswego	84–85
Lakeridge High School	Lake Oswego	86–87
Marist High School	Eugene	84–85
McLoughlin Junior High School	Milwaukie	83–84
Monroe Middle School	Eugene	83–84
North Bend High School	North Bend	86–87
Nyssa Elementary School	Nyssa	85–86
Nyssa High School	Nyssa	84–85
Oaklea Middle School	Junction City	82–83
Obsidian Junior High School	Redmond	84–85
Ogden Junior High School	Oregon City	86–87
Oregon City High School	Oregon City	84–85
Our Lady of the Lake School	Lake Oswego	89–90
Pleasant Hill High School	Pleasant Hill	83–84
Pringle Elementary School	Salem	87–88
Renne Intermediate School	Newburg	82–83
Rex Putnam High School	Milwaukie	84–85
Riverdale School	Portland	85–86
Saint Mary's Academy	Portland	83–84, 88–89
Seven Oak Middle School	Lebanon	85–86
Slater-Filmore Grade School	Burns	91–92
South Eugene High School	Eugene	82–83
South Salem High School	Salem	86–87
Sunset High School	Beaverton	82–83
Tualatin Elementary School	Tualatin	89–90
Walker Middle School	Salem	89–90
Washington Elementary School	Medford	91–92
West Linn High School	West Linn	83–84
Westridge Elementary School	Lake Oswego	87–88
Wilbur Rowe Junior High School	Milwaukie	86–87

SCHOOL	CITY	YEAR(S) RECOGNIZED
PENNSYLVANIA		
Academy of Notre Dame de Namur	Villanova	86–87
Allentown Central Catholic High School	Allentown	83–84, 92–93
Ancillae-Assumpta Academy	Wyncote	85–86, 91–92
Arcola Intermediate School	Norristown	90–91
Bala Cynwyd Middle School	Bala Cynwyd	83–84
Baldwin School	Bryn Mawr	83–84
Benchmark School	Media	85–86
Boyce Middle School	Upper St. Clair	91–92
Buckingham Elementary School	Buckingham	85–86
Bywood Elementary School	Upper Darby	93–94
Carl Benner School	Coatesville	93–94
Carl R. Streams Elementary School	Upper St. Clair	89–90
Carson Middle School	Pittsburgh	93–94
Central Catholic High School	Pittsburgh	86–87
Central High School	Philadelphia	86–87
Chatham Park School	Havertown	85–86
Conestoga Senior High School	Berwyn	83–84
Crooked Billet Elementary School	Hatsboro	93–94
Cynwyd Elementary School	Bala Cynwyd	91–92
Delaware Valley Middle School	Milford	84–85
Dorothea H. Simmons School	Horsham	91–92
Downingtown Senior High School	Downingtown	84–85, 88–89
E. T. Richardson Middle School	Springfield	84–85
East Coventry Elementary School	Pottstown	93–94
East High School	West Chester	86–87, 92–93
East Junior High School	Waynesboro	84–85
Fort Couch Middle School	Upper St. Clair	86–87, 92–93
Fox Chapel Area High School	Pittsburgh	92–93
Franklin Elementary School	Sewickley	85–86
Franklin Learning Center	Philadelphia	92–93
Garrettford Elementary School	Drexel Hill	89–90
General Wayne Middle School	Malvern	84–85, 90–91
Glenwood Elementary School	Media	89–90
Great Valley High School	Malvern	86–87
Gwynedd Mercy Academy	Gwynedd Valley	90–91
Harriton High School	Rosemont	83–84, 92–93
Harvey C. Sabold Elementary School	Springfield	93–94
Haverford Senior High School	Havertown	86–87
Henderson High School	West Chester	86–87
Hereford Township Elementary School	Hereford	89–90
Highland Park School	Upper Darby	87–88
Hillcrest Elementary School	Drexel Hill	87–88
Holy Ghost Preparatory School	Bensalem	92–93
Independence Middle School	Bethel Park	92–93
J. R. Fugett Middle School	West Chester	90–91
John M. Grasse Elementary School	Sellersville	91–92

SCHOOL	CITY	YEAR(S) RECOGNIZED
PENNSYLVANIA *(continued)*		
Kathryn D. Markley School	Malvern	87–88
Keith Valley Middle School	Horsham	90–91
Kerr Elementary School	Pittsburgh	93–94
King's Highway Elementary School	Coatesville	93–94
La Salle College High School	Wyndmoor	84–85
Louis E. Dieruff High School	Allentown	84–85
Marlborough Elementary School	Green Lane	93–94
Mary C. Howse Elementary School	West Chester	85–86, 89–90
Mercy Vocational High School	Philadelphia	83–84
Mercyhurst Preparatory School	Erie	92–93
Merion Elementary School	Merion	85–86
Methacton High School	Fairview Village	88–89
Mount Saint Joseph Academy	Flourtown	92–93
Mt. Lebanon Junior High School	Pittsburgh	90–91
Mt. Lebanon Senior High School	Pittsburgh	83–84, 90–91
Nether Providence Middle School	Wallingford	86–87
New Eagle Elementary School	Wayne	85–86
North Allegheny Intermediate High School	Pittsburgh	88–89
North Allegheny Senior High School	Wexford	92–93
North Penn High School	Lansdale	90–91
O'Hara Elementary School	Pittsburgh	91–92
Orborne Elementary School	Sewickley	93–94
Overbrook Educational Center	Philadelphia	87–88
Penn Wynne School	Philadelphia	85–86
Pennsbury High School	Fairless Hills	84–85
Perkiomen Valley South Elementary	Collegeville	93–94
Philadelphia High School for Girls	Philadelphia	86–87
Quaker Valley High School	Leetsdale	92–93
Radnor High School	Radnor	83–84
Saint Bernadette School	Drexel Hill	85–86
St. Agnes School	West Chester	89–90
St. Gabriel's Hall School	Audubon	88–89
St. Joseph's Preparatory School	Philadelphia	84–85
Saints Philip and James School	Exton	89–90
Salford Hills Elementary School	Harleysville	93–94
Sandy Run Middle School	Dresher	83–84
Scenic Hills Elementary School	Springfield	85–86
Schenley High School Teacher Center	Pittsburgh	86–87
Scranton Preparatory School	Scranton	86–87
Sewickley Academy	Sewickley	92–93
Springfield High School	Springfield	88–89
Springside School	Philadelphia	84–85
State College Area High School	State College	92–93
Stonehurst Hills Elementary School	Upper Darby	89–90
Strath Haven High School	Wallingford	84–85
Sugartown Elementary School	Malvern	85–86

SCHOOL	CITY	YEAR(S) RECOGNIZED
PENNSYLVANIA (*continued*)		
Swarthmore Rutledge School	Swarthmore	91–92
The Harrisburg Academy	Wormleysburg	92–93
The Mercersburg Academy	Mercersburg	90–91
The Miquon School	Miquon	85–86
Tredyffrin/Easttown Junior High School	Berwyn	86–87
Trinity High School	Camp Hill	92–93
Upper Darby High School	Upper Darby	88–89
Upper Perkiomen Middle School	East Greenville	92–93
Upper St. Clair High School	Upper St. Clair	83–84, 88–89
Villa Maria Academy	Malvern	88–89
Villa Maria Academy-Lower School	Immaculata	87–88
Wallingford Elementary School	Wallingford	89–90
Welsh Valley Middle School	Narberth	83–84
West Catholic High School for Boys	Philadelphia	83–84
William T. Gordon Middle School	Coatesville	92–93
Wissahickon Middle School	Ambler	84–85
Wyomissing Area Junior-Senior High School	Wyomissing	90–91

PUERTO RICO

SCHOOL	CITY	YEAR(S) RECOGNIZED
Academia Maria Reina	Rio Piedras	88–89
Andres Grillasca Salas School	Ponce	89–90
Angela Cordero Bernard School	Ponce	87–88
Benito Cerezo Vazquez High School	Aguadilla	88–89
C. R. O. E. M. High School	Mayaguez	92–93
Colegio Ponceño	Coto Laurel	90–91
Colegio Ponceño	Ponce	91–92
Colegio Radians	Cayey	92–93
Colegio San Ignacio de Loyola	Rio Piedras	84–85
Francisco Matias Lugo School	Carolina	91–92
José Emilio Lugo Ponce De León High School	Adjuntas	90–91
Patria Latorre Ramirez High School	San Sebastían	92–93
Saint John's School	Santurce	86–87

RHODE ISLAND

SCHOOL	CITY	YEAR(S) RECOGNIZED
Archie R. Cole Junior High School	East Greenwich	88–89
Bishop Hendricken High School	Warwick	92–93
Davisville Middle School	North Kingstown	90–91
Dr. James H. Eldredge Elementary School	East Greenwich	91–92
East Greenwich High School	East Greenwich	83–84
Hugh Bain Junior High School	Cranston	82–83
La Salle Academy	Providence	90–91
Lincoln Junior-Senior High School	Lincoln	82–83, 88–89
Mount Saint Charles Academy	Woonsocket	92–93

SCHOOL	CITY	YEAR(S) RECOGNIZED
RHODE ISLAND (*continued*)		
Narragansett Elementary School	Narragansett	85–86
Narragansett High School	Narragansett	86–87
Norwood Avenue School	Cranston	87–88
St. Luke School	Barrington	93–94
St. Mary Academy-Bay View	Riverside	90–91
St. Rocco School	Johnston	93–94
South Kingstown High School	Wakefield	86–87
South Kingstown Junior High School	Peace Dale	84–85
Western Hills Junior High School	Cranston	83–84

SOUTH CAROLINA

SCHOOL	CITY	YEAR(S) RECOGNIZED
Aiken Elementary School	Aiken	89–90
Ashley River Creative Arts Elementary School	Charleston	91–92
Augusta Circle Elementary School	Greenville	93–94
Baker's Chapel Elementary School	Greenville	91–92
Buena Vista Elementary School	Greer	89–90
C. E. Williams Middle School	Charleston	92–93
Camden High School	Camden	82–83
Clifdale Elementary School	Spartanburg	89–90
Conder Elementary School	Columbia	85–86
Conway High School	Conway	84–85
Conway Middle School	Conway	92–93
Cowpens Elementary School	Cowpens	85–86
Dent Middle School	Columbia	84–85
Dreher High School	Columbia	88–89
Dutch Fork Elementary School	Irmo	93–94
E. L. Wright Middle School	Columbia	83–84
Edwards Junior High School	Central	88–89
Greeleyville Elementary School	Greeleyville	93–94
Harbor View Elementary School	Charleston	93–94
Heathwood Hall Episcopal School	Columbia	83–84
Hillcrest Middle School	Simpsonville	84–85
Irmo High School	Columbia	82–83
Joseph Keels Elementary School	Columbia	85–86, 93–94
L. W. Conder Elementary School	Columbia	93–94
Lake City Primary School	Lake City	93–94
League Middle School	Greenville	82–83
Lemira Elementary School	Sumter	89–90
Lexington Middle School	Lexington	90–91
Lonnie B. Nelson Elementary School	Columbia	87–88
Mauldin High School	Mauldin	84–85
Mitchell Elementary School	Charleston	93–94
North Springs Elementary School	Elgin	87–88
Oakbrook Elementary School	Ladson	93–94

SCHOOL	CITY	YEAR(S) RECOGNIZED
SOUTH CAROLINA (*continued*)		
Orange Grove Elementary School	Charleston	93–94
Richland Northeast High School	Columbia	84–85, 92–93
Rock Hill High School	Rock Hill	83–84
Satchel Ford Elementary School	Columbia	87–88
Shaw Heights Elementary School	Shaw Air Force Base	87–88
Socastee High School	Myrtle Beach	90–91
Spartanburg High School	Spartanburg	82–83, 88–89, 92–93
Spring Valley High School	Columbia	82–83
Summerville Elementary School	Summerville	93–94
SOUTH DAKOTA		
Central High School	Aberdeen	86–87
Dell Rapids Elementary School	Dell Rapids	93–94
O'Gorman High School	Sioux Falls	84–85
Yankton Senior High School	Yankton	86–87
TENNESSEE		
Alvin C. York Institute	Jamestown	88–89
Andrew Jackson Elementary School	Old Hickory	89–90
Big Ridge Elementary School	Chattanooga	93–94
Bradley Central High School	Cleveland	86–87
Brookmeade Elementary School	Nashville	91–92
Brown Middle School	Harrison	86–87
Central High School	Harrison	86–87
Cleveland High School	Cleveland	82–83
Collierville Middle School	Collierville	82–83
Craigmont Junior/Senior High School	Memphis	92–93
Dodson Elementary School	Hermitage	85–86
Dyersburg High School	Dyersburg	90–91
Eagleville School	Eagleville	92–93
Eakin Elementary School	Nashville	85–86
Farmington School	Germantown	87–88
Farragut Intermediate School	Knoxville	87–88
Farragut Middle School	Knoxville	86–87
Girls Preparatory School	Chattanooga	90–91
Glencliff High School	Nashville	88–89
Glendale Middle School	Nashville	91–92
Grahamwood School	Memphis	85–86
Haywood High School	Brownsville	86–87
Head Middle School	Nashville	89–90
Hillsboro High School	Nashville	84–85
Hixson High School	Hixson	84–85
Ingleside School	Athens	85–86, 89–90
Lakeview Elementary School	Nashville	87–88

SCHOOL	CITY	YEAR(S) RECOGNIZED
TENNESSEE (*continued*)		
McCallie School	Chattanooga	88–89
Meigs Magnet School	Nashville	89–90
Memphis Catholic High School	Memphis	84–85
Miller Perry Elementary School	Kingsport	87–88
Millington South Elementary School	Millington	87–88
Oak Elementary School	Bartlett	93–94
Red Bank High School	Chattanooga	92–93
Richland Elementary School	Memphis	93–94
Sacred Heart Cathedral School	Knoxville	91–92
Saint Cecilia Academy	Nashville	90–91
St. Jude School	Chattanooga	87–88
St. Mary's Episcopal School	Memphis	90–91
Science Hill High School	Johnson City	90–91
Snow Hill Elementary School	Ooltewah	85–86
Snowden School	Memphis	82–83
Thrasher Elementary School	Signal Mountain	85–86
Vanleer Elementary School	Vanleer	89–90
Westminster School	Nashville	89–90
Whiteville Elementary School	Whiteville	91–92
TEXAS		
Akiba Academy of Dallas	Dallas	85–86
All Saints Episcopal School	Lubbock	91–92
Anderson Elementary School	Spring	89–90
Anna Middle School	Anna	92–93
Arch H. McCulloch Middle School	Dallas	90–91
Armstrong Middle School	Plano	92–93
Arnold Junior High School	Houston	90–91
Austin Academy for Excellence	Garland	92–93
Bear Creek Elementary School	Houston	87–88
Bellaire Senior High School	Bellaire	83–84
Ben Milam Elementary School	McAllen	89–90
Big Springs Elementary School	Garland	87–88
Bishop Lynch High School	Dallas	90–91
Bleyl Junior High School	Houston	83–84, 90–91
Booker T. Washington Elementary School	Port Arthur	87–88
Booker T. Washington Junior High School	Conroe	92–93
Bradley Middle School	San Antonio	86–87
Brentfield Elementary School	Dallas	93–94
Bunker Hill Elementary School	Houston	91–92
Canyon Vista Middle School	Austin	90–91
Carroll Elementary School	Southlake	93–94
Castle Hills Elementary School	San Antonio	87–88
Charles M. Blalack Junior High School	Carrollton	92–93
Charlie Richard Lyles Middle School	Garland	92–93

SCHOOL	CITY	YEAR(S) RECOGNIZED
TEXAS (*continued*)		
Chisholm Trail Middle School	Round Rock	92–93
Christ the King Catholic School	Dallas	93–94
Christa McAuliffe Elementary School	Lewisville	91–92
Clark High School	Plano	92–93
Clear Lake High School	Houston	86–87
Clear Lake Intermediate School	Houston	86–87
Coke R. Stevenson Middle School	San Antonio	90–91
Corpus Christi Catholic School	Houston	89–90
Crockett Elementary-Intermediate School	El Paso	85–86
Daniel F. Ortega Elementary School	Austin	93–94
Dartmouth Elementary School	Richardson	89–90
Davis Elementary School	Plano	93–94
Desert View Middle School	El Paso	83–84
Dooley Elementary School	Plano	89–90
Douglas MacArthur High School	San Antonio	88–89
Duchesne Academy of the Sacred Heart	Houston	92–93
Dwight D. Eisenhower Middle School	San Antonio	88–89
E. B. Reyna Elementary School	La Joya	93–94
E. L. Kent Elementary School	Carrollton	93–94
East Side Elementary School	Palacios	89–90
Eisenhower High School	Houston	88–89
Fiest Elementary School	Houston	93–94
Florence Elementary School	Southlake	93–94
Flower Mound Elementary School	Flower Mound	93–94
Forest Trail Elementary School	Austin	89–90
Forman Elementary School	Plano	93–94
Fort Sam Houston Elementary School	San Antonio	93–94
Francone Elementary School	Houston	91–92
Frostwood Elementary School	Houston	89–90
Good Shepherd Episcopal School	Dallas	91–92
Greenhill School	Dallas	84–85
H. B. Carlisle Elementary School	Plano	87–88
Hamilton Park Pacesetter School	Dallas	85–86
Harwood Junior High School	Bedford	86–87
Hazel S. Pattison Elementary School	Katy	93–94
Hedgecoxe Elementary School	Plano	93–94
Highland Park Elementary School	Austin	91–92
Highland Park High School	Dallas	84–85
Highland Village Elementary School	Lewisville	93–94
Hill Country Middle School	Austin	90–91
Hill Elementary School	Austin	93–94
Holy Cross High School	San Antonio	83–84
Holy Family of Nazareth School	Irving	89–90
Huffman Elementary School	Plano	91–92
Hunters Creek Elementary School	Houston	93–94

SCHOOL	CITY	YEAR(S) RECOGNIZED
TEXAS (*continued*)		
Immaculate Conception School	Grand Prairie	85–86
Incarnate Word Academy	Corpus Christi	84–85
J. J. Pearce High School	Richardson	88–89
Jack D. Johnson Elementary School	Southlake	93–94
James Bowie High School	Austin	92–93
Jesuit College Preparatory School	Dallas	90–91
John Foster Dulles High School	Sugar Land	84–85
John Marshall High School	San Antonio	92–93
John S. Armstrong Elementary School	Dallas	85–86
John S. Bradfield Elementary School	Dallas	89–90
Juan N. Seguin Elementary School	McAllen	85–86
Kimberlin Academy for Excellence	Garland	91–92
Kingwood High School	Kingwood	84–85
L. P. Montgomery Elementary School	Farmers Branch	91–92
L. V. Berkner High School	Richardson	88–89
Labay Junior High School	Houston	88–89, 92–93
Langham Creek High School	Houston	90–91
Las Colinas Elementary School	Irving	93–94
Laurel Mountain Elementary School	Austin	91–92
Lina Milliken Middle School	Lewisville	92–93
Live Oak Elementary School	Austin	91–92
Los Encinos Special Emphasis School	Corpus Christi	87–88
Lowery Elementary School	Houston	91–92
Lozano Special Emphasis School	Corpus Christi	85–86
Mayde Creek Elementary School	Houston	89–90
Memorial High School	Houston	88–89
Memorial Junior High School	Houston	88–89
Meridith Magnet School	Temple	87–88
Merriman Park Elementary School	Dallas	89–90
Mirabeau B. Lamar Elementary School	Corpus Christi	91–92
Monsignor Kelly High School	Beaumont	84–85, 90–91
Moss Haven Elementary School	Dallas	93–94
North Loop Elementary School	El Paso	87–88
North Oaks Elementary School	Austin	93–94
Northbrook Senior High School	Houston	88–89
Northside Health Careers High School	San Antonio	90–91
Nottingham Elementary School	Houston	91–92
Olle Middle School	Houston	90–91
Parkhill Junior High School	Dallas	92–93
Pine Tree High School	Longview	88–89, 92–93
Pine Tree Junior High School	Longview	90–91
Pine Tree Middle 6/7 School	Longview	92–93
Pines Montessori School	Kingwood	85–86
Plano East Senior High School	Plano	92–93
Plano Senior High School	Plano	84–85

SCHOOL	CITY	YEAR(S) RECOGNIZED
TEXAS (*continued*)		
Pope Elementary School	Arlington	85–86
R. L. Turner High School	Carrollton	90–91
R. W. Carpenter Middle School	Plano	92–93
Raul Longoria Elementary School	Pharr	87–88
Richardson High School	Richardson	83–84
Richardson Junior High School	Richardson	90–91
River Oaks Baptist School	Houston	91–92
Robert E. Lee Elementary School	Austin	91–92
Robert G. Cole Junior/Senior High School	San Antonio	86–87, 90–91
Robert S. Hyer Elementary School	Dallas	91–92
Rockdale High School	Rockdale	84–85
Rose Shaw Special Emphasis School	Corpus Christi	85–86
Rummel Creek Elementary School	Houston	85–86
Sacred Heart School	Muenster	93–94
Saigling Elementary School	Plano	91–92
Saint Agnes Academy	Houston	83–84, 88–89
St. Elizabeth Catholic School	Dallas	87–88
St. James Episcopal School	Corpus Christi	91–92
St. Mark the Evangelist Catholic School	Plano	91–92
St. Mark's School of Texas	Dallas	86–87
St. Patrick School	Corpus Christi	85–86
St. Peter Prince of Apostles School	San Antonio	85–86
St. Thomas More Parish School	Houston	93–94
Scarborough Senior High School	Houston	86–87
Schimelpfenig Middle School	Plano	88–89
Schuster Elementary School	El Paso	87–88
Shepard Elementary School	Plano	91–92
Sidney Lanier Vanguard Expressive Arts School	Dallas	87–88
Spring High School	Spring	92–93
Stephen F. Austin High School	Austin	82–83
Strack Intermediate School	Klein	90–91
Stratford High School	Houston	83–84
T. F. Birmingham Elementary School	Wylie	91–92
T. H. Johnson Elementary School	Taylor	85–86
T. H. Rogers School	Houston	91–92
Tanglewood Elementary School	Fort Worth	91–92
The Lamplighter School	Dallas	93–94
The Parish Day School	Dallas	93–94
Thomas J. Stovall Junior High School	Houston	90–91
Travis Elementary School	Greenville	87–88
Travis Middle School	Port Lavaca	83–84
University Park Elementary School	Dallas	87–88
Ursuline Academy of Dallas	Dallas	92–93
V. W. Miller Intermediate School	Houston	88–89

SCHOOL	CITY	YEAR(S) RECOGNIZED
TEXAS (*continued*)		
Vivian Field Junior High School	Farmers Branch	92–93
W. H. L. Wells Elementary School	Plano	91–92
Wake Village School	Wake Village	85–86
West Ridge Middle School	Austin	92–93
Westlake High School	Austin	88–89
Wilchester Elementary School	Houston	89–90
William H. Atwell Fundamental Academy	Dallas	86–87
Wilson Middle School	Plano	88–89
Winston Churchill High School	San Antonio	82–83
Woodway Elementary School	Waco	85–86

UTAH

SCHOOL	CITY	YEAR(S) RECOGNIZED
Altara Elementary School	Sandy	85–86
Bonneville Elementary School	Salt Lake City	87–88
Bountiful High School	Bountiful	82–83
Brighton High School	Salt Lake City	82–83
Butler Middle School	Salt Lake City	82–83
Eastmont Middle School	Sandy	83–84
George Q. Knowlton Elementary School	Farmington	91–92
Granger High School	West Valley	92–93
Highland High School	Salt Lake City	82–83
Hillcrest Elementary School	Logan	85–86
J. A. Taylor Elementary School	Centerville	87–88
Judge Memorial Catholic High School	Salt Lake City	83–84, 88–89
Logan Junior High School	Logan	83–84
Logan Senior High School	Logan	82–83
Mound Fort Middle School	Ogden	84–85
Northwest Intermediate School	Salt Lake City	88–89
Northwest Middle School	Salt Lake City	93–94
Olympus High School	Salt Lake City	84–85
Olympus Junior High School	Salt Lake City	86–87
Rowland Hall-St. Mark's School	Salt Lake City	85–86
South High School	Salt Lake City	83–84
Timpview High School	Provo	83–84
Wasatch Elementary School	Salt Lake City	89–90
Wasatch Middle School	Heber City	82–83
West High School	Salt Lake City	88–89

VERMONT

SCHOOL	CITY	YEAR(S) RECOGNIZED
Camels Hump Middle School	Richmond	88–89
Chamberlin School	South Burlington	91–92
Craftsbury Academy	Craftsbury Common	90–91

SCHOOL	CITY	YEAR(S) RECOGNIZED
VERMONT (*continued*)		
Essex Elementary School	Essex Junction	89–90
Hardwick Elementary School	Hardwick	87–88
Hazen Union School	Hardwick	83–84
Mater Christi School	Burlington	89–90
Proctor Junior/Senior High School	Proctor	92–93
Richmond Elementary School	Richmond	91–92
St. Johnsbury Academy	St. Johnsbury	90–91
Shelburne Middle School	Shelburne	88–89
South Burlington High School	South Burlington	84–85
South Burlington Middle School	South Burlington	86–87
Waitsfield Elementary School	Waitsfield	93–94
Waterbury Elementary School	Waterbury	85–86
Woodstock Union High School	Woodstock	86–87

VIRGIN ISLANDS

Antilles School	St. Thomas	91–92

VIRGINIA

Ashlawn Elementary School	Arlington	89–90
Bishop Denis J. O'Connell High School	Arlington	92–93
Breckinridge Junior High School	Roanoke	83–84
Brookland Middle School	Richmond	84–85
Cape Henry Collegiate School	Virginia Beach	92–93
Cave Spring High School	Roanoke	82–83
David A. Dutrow Elementary School	Newport News	85–86
Denbigh High School	Newport News	86–87
Dooley School	Richmond	86–87
Douglas Southall Freeman High School	Henrico County	92–93
Dunbar-Erwin Middle School	Newport News	83–84
E. C. Glass High School	Lynchburg	82–83, 92–93
Falls Church Elementary School	Falls Church	85–86
George Mason Junior-Senior High School	Falls Church	82–83
Glenvar High School	Salem	88–89
Hampton High School	Hampton	84–85
Heritage Elementary School	Lynchburg	85–86
Heritage High School	Lynchburg	92–93
Hermitage High School	Richmond	83–84
Hidden Valley Junior High School	Roanoke	83–84
Highland Park Learning Center Magnet School	Roanoke	91–92
Homer L. Hines Middle School	Newport News	86–87, 92–93
Huntington Middle School	Newport News	84–85
James Madison Junior High School	Roanoke	86–87
Kingston Elementary School	Virginia Beach	89–90

SCHOOL	CITY	YEAR(S) RECOGNIZED
VIRGINIA *(continued)*		
Linkhorne Elementary School	Lynchburg	93–94
Lynnhaven Junior High School	Virginia Beach	86–87
Menchville High School	Newport News	83–84
Mills E. Godwin High School	Richmond	88–89
Mountain View Elementary School	Roanoke	87–88
Norfolk Academy	Norfolk	84–85, 93–94
Northside Middle School	Norfolk	92–93
Norview High School	Norfolk	88–89
Oak Grove Elementary School	Roanoke	85–86
Oakridge Elementary School	Arlington	85–86
Poquoson Elementary School	Poquoson	87–88
Poquoson Primary School	Poquoson	93–94
Prospect Heights Middle School	Orange	82–83
R. C. Longan Elementary School	Richmond	85–86
Rawls Byrd Elementary School	Williamsburg	91–92
School for Contemporary Education	Annandale	92–93
Syms Middle School	Hampton	90–91
T. C. Williams High School	Alexandria	82–83
The Madeira School	Greenway	86–87
Washington-Lee High School	Arlington	84–85
William Fleming High School	Roanoke	88–89
WASHINGTON		
Anacortes High School	Anacortes	88–89
Battle Ground High School	Battle Ground	83–84
Bellarmine Preparatory School	Tacoma	83–84, 88–89
Blaine High School	Blaine	84–85
Blaine Middle School	Blaine	85–86
Capital High School	Olympia	86–87
Cashmere Middle School	Cashmere	82–83
Charles A. Lindbergh High School	Renton	83–84
Charles Wright Academy	Tacoma	88–89
Cherry Crest Elementary School	Bellevue	87–88
Colville High School	Colville	83–84, 88–89
Curtis High School	Tacoma	82–83
Curtis Junior High School	Tacoma	83–84
Custer Elementary School	Custer	93–94
Dick Scobee Elementary School	Auburn	89–90
Eastmont High School	East Wenatchee	88–89
Emily Dickinson School	Redmond	85–86
Enumclaw Junior High School	Enumclaw	88–89
Eton School	Bellevue	91–92
Ferndale High School	Ferndale	86–87
Garrison Junior High School	Walla Walla	86–87

SCHOOL	CITY	YEAR(S) RECOGNIZED
WASHINGTON (*continued*)		
Gonzaga Preparatory School	Spokane	92–93
Hanford Secondary School	Richland	82–83
Hazelwood Elementary School	Renton	91–92
Holy Names Academy	Seattle	84–85, 90–91
Holy Rosary School	Seattle	89–90
Jefferson Middle School	Olympia	83–84
Jemtegaard Middle School	Washougal	90–91
John Campbell Elementary School	Selah	85–86
John H. McKnight Middle School	Renton	84–85
John Muir Elementary School	Kirkland	89–90
Kent Junior High School	Kent	88–89
Kent-Meridian High School	Kent	92–93
Kentridge High School	Kent	84–85
Lacamas Heights Elementary School	Camas	85–86
Lake Washington High School	Kirkland	84–85
Lake Youngs Elementary School	Kent	85–86
McAlder Elementary School	Puyallup	93–94
Mead Junior High School	Mead	82–83
Meany Middle School	Seattle	86–87
Meridian Junior High School	Kent	84–85
Mount Rainier High School	Des Moines	84–85
New Century High School	Lacey	92–93
Omak Middle School	Omak	83–84
Pasco Senior High School	Pasco	82–83
Pine Tree Elementary School	Kent	89–90
Pleasant Valley Intermediate School	Vancouver	84–85
Redmond Elementary School	Redmond	87–88
Redmond High School	Redmond	83–84
Renton Park Elementary School	Renton	89–90
Ringdall Middle School	Bellevue	84–85
Sacajawea Junior High School	Spokane	82–83
Saint Edward School	Seattle	87–88
St. Paul School	Seattle	87–88
St. Philomena Catholic School	Des Moines	91–92
Shorewood High School	Seattle	82–83
Skyline Elementary School	Ferndale	91–92
Spring Glen Elementary School	Renton	91–92
Stevens Middle School	Port Angeles	84–85
Vista Middle School	Ferndale	88–89
Washington Elementary School	Auburn	93–94
Washington Elementary School	Mount Vernon	93–94
Wenatchee High School	Wenatchee	86–87
West Valley Junior High School	Yakima	84–85
Whitworth Elementary School	Seattle	85–86
Wilbur High School	Wilbur	83–84

SCHOOL	CITY	YEAR(S) RECOGNIZED
WEST VIRGINIA		
Bridge Street Junior High School	Wheeling	82–83
Buckhannon-Upshur Middle School	Buckhannon	93–94
Capital High School	Charleston	92–93
Clay County High School	Clay	88–89
Clay County Junior High School	Clay	90–91
Clay Elementary School	Clay	93–94
DuPont Junior High School	Belle	92–93
East Dale Elementary School	Fairmont	87–88
Elm Grove Elementary School	Wheeling	91–92
George Washington High School	Charleston	83–84
High Lawn Elementary School	St. Albans	91–92
Jennings Randolph Elementary School	Elkins	85–86
Johnson Elementary School	Bridgeport	85–86
Lewisburg Elementary School	Lewisburg	93–94
Lory-Julian Elementary School	Julian	93–94
Our Lady of Fatima School	Huntington	91–92
Pleasants County Middle School	Belmont	92–93
St. Francis Central Catholic School	Morgantown	93–94
St. Marys High School	St. Marys	84–85
Tiskelwah Elementary School	Charleston	91–92
Triadelphia Junior High School	Wheeling	82–83
Troy Elementary School	Troy	93–94
Weberwood Elementary School	Charleston	87–88
West Milford Elementary School	West Milford	93–94
Wheeling Junior High School	Wheeling	82–83
Wheeling Park High School	Wheeling	83–84
Wyatt Elementary School	Wyatt	87–88
WISCONSIN		
Alexander Hamilton High School	Milwaukee	86–87
Bay View Middle School	Green Bay	93–94
Brown Deer High School	Brown Deer	83–84
Butte des Morts Junior High School	Menasha	86–87
Columbus High School	Columbus	84–85
Crestwood Elementary School	Madison	91–92
Custer High School	Milwaukee	92–93
Divine Savior Holy Angels High School	Milwaukee	84–85
East High School	Madison	88–89
Edgewood High School of the Sacred Heart	Madison	86–87
Elm Grove Lutheran School	Elm Grove	85–86
Franklin High School	Franklin	86–87
Garfield Math/Science Elementary School	Milwaukee	87–88
Hales Corners Elementary School	Hales Corners	87–88
Harold S. Vincent High School	Milwaukee	86–87

SCHOOL	CITY	YEAR(S) RECOGNIZED
WISCONSIN (*continued*)		
Horace Mann Middle School	Sheboygan	90–91
Immanuel Lutheran School	Wisconsin Rapids	87–88
James Madison Memorial High School	Madison	90–91
Jefferson Elementary School	Menasha	91–92
John Burroughs Middle School	Milwaukee	83–84
John Muir Elementary School	Madison	91–92
Kohler High School	Kohler	88–89
LaFollette High School	Madison	83–84
Lincoln High School	Manitowoc	88–89
Lincoln High School	Wisconsin Rapids	86–87
M. J. Gegan Elementary School	Menasha	87–88
Magee Elementary School	Genesee Depot	93–94
Marquette University High School	Milwaukee	83–84
Martin Luther High School	Greendale	83–84
McFarland Elementary School	McFarland	85–86
Memorial High School	Eau Clair	82–83
Merrill Senior High School	Merrill	84–85
Milwaukee German Immersion School	Milwaukee	93–94
Milwaukee Lutheran High School	Milwaukee	84–85, 92–93
Milwaukee Trade and Technical High School	Milwaukee	92–93
Morse Middle School	Milwaukee	84–85
Neenah High School	Neenah	84–85
Nicolet High School	Glendale	90–91
Northwest Lutheran School	Milwaukee	85–86
Oconomowoc High School	Oconomowoc	90–91
Owen-Withee High School	Owen	83–84
Parkview Middle School	Green Bay	87–88
Phoenix Middle School	Delavan	84–85
Pius XI High School	Milwaukee	83–84
Rufus King High School	Milwaukee	82–83
St. Alphonsus School	Greendale	93–94
St. Joseph Academy	Green Bay	88–89
St. Margaret Mary School	Neenah	87–88
St. Paul's Lutheran School	Janesville	91–92
Seymour Middle School	Seymour	93–94
Sheboygan South High School	Sheboygan	86–87
South Milwaukee Senior High School	South Milwaukee	88–89
Spring Road School	Neenah	85–86
Stevens Point Area Senior High School	Stevens Point	84–85
Stoughton Middle School	Stoughton	84–85
Valley View Elementary School	Green Bay	89–90
Van Hise Middle School	Madison	86–87
Webster Transitional School	Cedarburg	82–83
West Senior High School	Madison	84–85
Whitman Middle School	Wauwatosa	84–85

SCHOOL	CITY	YEAR(S) RECOGNIZED
WISCONSIN *(continued)*		
Williams Bay High School	Williams Bay	86–87
Wilson Elementary School	Sheboygan	89–90

WYOMING

SCHOOL	CITY	YEAR(S) RECOGNIZED
Big Piney Middle School	Big Piney	92–93
Crest Hill Elementary School	Casper	87–88, 91–92
Douglas Middle School	Douglas	82–83
Jackson Hole High School	Jackson	86–87, 92–93
Kelly Walsh High School	Casper	83–84
Pine Bluffs High School	Pine Bluffs	82–83
Pinedale Elementary School	Pinedale	89–90
Pinedale Middle School	Pinedale	90–91
Sage Valley Junior High School	Gillette	86–87
Wilson Elementary School	Wilson	93–94

Blue Ribbon Schools Program
Office of Educational Research and Improvement
U.S. Department of Education

STATE LIAISONS 1994–95

Dr. Frank Heatherly
Mathematics Specialist
Alabama Department of Education
50 North Ripley Street
Montgomery, AL 36130-3901
(205) 242-8082

Ms. Rosemary Hagevig
Education Specialist
Alaska Department of Education
801 West 10th Street, Suite 200
Juneau, AK 99801-1894
(907) 465-8715

Mr. Thomas L. Cox
Coordinator, Recognition Programs
Arizona Department of Education
1535 West Jefferson
Phoenix, AZ 85007
(602) 542-3740

Mr. James A. Hester
Program Support Manager for Evaluation
Arkansas Department of Education
4 Capitol Mall
Little Rock, AR 72201
(501) 682-4371

Ms. Norma Carolan
Research Analyst
California Department of Education
Program Evaluation and Research Division
721 Capitol Mall, P.O. Box 944272
Sacramento, CA 94244-2720
(916) 657-3799

Ms. Erlinda Archuleta
Director
Regional Educational Services Unit
Colorado Department of Education
201 East Colfax Avenue
Denver, CO 80203
(303) 866-6638

Dr. Marie Della Bella
School Approval Consultant
State Department of Education
Box 2219
Hartford, CT 06145
(203) 566-3593

Dr. Horacio D. Lewis
State Supervisor, Human Relations
Delaware Department of Education
The Towsend Building
P.O. Box 1402
Dover, DE 19901
(302) 739-2770

Dr. Phyllis D. Hines
Executive Assistant
Office of Educational Programs and Operations
District of Columbia Public Schools
215 G Street, NE, Room 108
Washington, D.C. 20002
(202) 724-4980

Ms. Beth Boltz
Program Specialist
Office of Business Citizen Partnerships
126 Florida Education Center
325 West Gaines Street
Tallahassee, FL 32399
(904) 488-8385

Ms. Gale E. Samuels
Special Projects Coordinator
Georgia Department of Education
2052 Twin Towers East
Atlanta, GA 30334-5010
(404) 656-2476

Dr. Elaine M. Takenaka
Special Programs Management Section
Hawaii Department of Education
3430 Leahi Avenue
Honolulu, HI 96815
(808) 735-9024

Ms. Judy Adamson
Elementary Supervisor
Idaho Department of Education
LBJ Office Building
Boise, ID 83720
(208) 334-2281

Mr. Fred Nunn
Illinois State Board of Education
Grants and Applications Section
100 North First Street
Springfield, IL 62777
(217) 782-9374

Ms. Betty Johnson
Chief, Office of School Assistance
Indiana Department of Education
229 State House
Indianapolis, IN 46204
(317) 232-9141

Ms. Sharon Slezak
Administrative Coordinator
Communication Services
Iowa Department of Education
Des Moines, IA 50319-3294
(515) 281-3750

Mr. Robert L. Gast
Team Leader, Information and Marketing
Kansas State Board of Education
120 S.E. 10th Street
Topeka, KS 66612-1182
(913) 296-4961

Ms. Kay Anne Wilborn
Office of Communication Services
Kentucky Department of Education
Capitol Plaza Tower, 19th Floor
Frankfort, KY 40601
(502) 564-3421

Mrs. Kay Nelson
Program Manager
Bureau of Elementary Education
Louisiana Department of Education
P.O. Box 94064
Baton Rouge, LA 70804-9064
(504) 342-3366

Dr. Horace P. Maxcy, Jr.
Coordinator
Maine Education Assessment
Maine Department of Education
State House Station 23
Augusta, ME 04333
(207) 287-5996

Mrs. Darla Strouse
Specialist
School Volunteer and Partnership Program
Maryland Department of Education
200 West Baltimore Street
Baltimore, MD 21201
(410) 333-2211

Ms. Jacqueline Peterson
Program Coordinator
Blue Ribbon Schools Programs
Division of School Programs
Massachusetts Department of Education
350 Main Street
Malden, MA 02148-5023
(617) 388-3300, Ext. 235

Ms. Ellen Carter Cooper
Education Consultant
School Development Unit
Michigan Department of Education
P.O. Box 30008
608 West Allegan
Lansing, MI 48909
(517) 373-3608

Ms. Marlys Peters
Education Specialist
Minnesota Department of Education
550 Cedar Street
St. Paul, MN 55101
(612) 297-2685

Dr. Johnny Franklin
Director of Instructional Development
P.O. Box 771, Suite 806
Walter Sillers Building
Jackson, MS 39205-0771
(601) 359-5532

Ms. Joan Solomon
Director of Urban Education
Missouri Department of Elementary and Secondary Education
P.O. Box 480
205 Jefferson
Jefferson City, MO 65102
(314) 751-2931

Mr. Duane Jackson
Foreign Language Specialist
Office of Public Instruction
Capitol Station
Helena, MT 59620
(406) 444-3129

Dr. Dean Bergman
Administrative Assistant
Nebraska Department of Education
Centennial Mall South
Lincoln, NE 68509-4987
(402) 471-2437

Ms. Vicki M. Bulter
Education Consultant
Nevada Department of Education
Capitol Complex
Carson City, NV 89710
(702) 687-3136

Dr. Robert Fournier
Consultant, Foreign Language Education
New Hampshire Department of Education
101 Pleasant Street
Concord, NH 03301
(603) 271-2717

Dr. John M. Dougherty
Program Evaluation Specialist
New Jersey Department of Education
Division of General Academic Education
225 West State Street
Trenton, NJ 08625
(609) 984-6304

Mr. Luis Delgado
Assistant Director
School Programs and Professional Development
New Mexico Department of Education
Education Building
Santa Fe, NM 87501-2786
(505) 827-6443

Ms. Susan Shipe
Associate, Capital Region II
New York Department of Education
Room 1066 EBA
Washington Avenue
Albany, NY 12234
(518) 486-5339

Mr. Dennis Stacey
North Carolina Department of Education
301 North Wilmington Street, ED BLDG
Raleigh, NC 27601-2825
(919) 715-1632

Ms. Joan Estes
Assistant Director, Elementary Education
North Dakota Department of Education
600 Boulevard Avenue, East
Bismarck, ND 58505
(701) 224-2488

Ms. Hazel Flowers
Director, Division of Equal Educational Opportunities
Ohio Department of Education
106 North High Street, Second Floor
Columbus, OH 43266-0106
(614) 466-3318

Ms. Martha Michael
Director of Effective Schools
Oklahoma Department of Education
2500 North Lincoln Boulevard
Oklahoma City, OK 73105-4599
(405) 521-4513

Ms. Patricia L. Stewart
Regional Director, Division of School Based Improvement
Pennsylvania Department of Education
333 Market Street
Harrisburg, PA 17126-0333
(717) 783-2862

Ms. Nancy Lebron Iriarte
Blue Ribbon Schools Program Coordinator
Department of Education
Office 800, Floor 8, Box 759
Hato Rey, Puerto Rico 00919
(809) 754-1315

Mr. Steve Nardelli
School Improvement Center
Rhode Island Department of Education
22 Hayes Street
Providence, RI 02908
(401) 277-2638

Dr. Bart Teal
Accreditation Supervisor
South Carolina Department of Education
707 Rutledge Building
Columbia, SC 29201
(803) 734-8333

Ms. Shirlie Moag
Gifted Education Director
South Dakota Department of Education
700 Governors Drive
Pierre, SD 57501
(605) 773-4662

Mrs. Mary Ann Lewis
Middle Grades Director
Tennessee Department of Education
8th Floor Gateway Plaza
710 James Robertson Parkway
Nashville, TN 37243-0379
(615) 532-6267

Dr. Marianne Vaughan
Assistant to the Deputy Commissioner
Texas Education Agency
1701 North Congress Avenue
Austin, TX 78701-1494
(512) 463-8998

Ms. Eileen Rencher
Director of Public Information
Utah State Board of Education
250 East 500 South
Salt Lake City, UT 84111
(801) 538-7519

Mr. Edward Haggett
School Improvement Coordinator
Vermont Department of Education
120 State Street
Montpelier, VT 65602
(802) 828-2756

Mr. Vernon Wildy
Principal/Specialist Student Needs Assessment
Virginia Department of Education
P.O. Box 6Q
Richmond, VA 23216
(804) 371-6881

Ms. Henrita Barber
Office of Testing, Planning, Research, and Evaluation
44-46 Kongens Gade, Charlotte Amalic
St. Thomas, U.S. Virgin Islands 00802
(809) 774-0100, Ext. 3082

Ms. Chris McElroy
Supervisor, School Improvement and Accreditation Program
Washington Department of Education
Old Capitol Building
Olympia, WA 98504
(206) 753-1895

Mr. David Perrine
Coordinator of Early Childhood Education
Office of Professional Development
West Virginia Department of Education

Capitol Complex, Room B-330
1900 Kanawha Boulevard, East
Charleston, WV 25305
(304) 558-7805

Ms. Ann Conzemius
Executive Assistant to the State Superintendent of Instruction
Wisconsin Department of Public Instruction
P.O. Box 7841
Madison, WI 53707
(608) 266-1771

Mr. D. Leeds Pickering
Consultant, School Improvment Unit
Wyoming Department of Education
Hathaway Building
Cheyenne, WY 82002-0050
(307) 777-6265

Ms. Lana Shaughnessy
Education Specialist
Elementary and Secondary Branch
Bureau of Indian Affairs
U.S. Department of the Interior
Code 521, MS3525, MIB
1849 C Street, NW
Washington, D.C. 20245
(202) 219-1129

Ms. Joyce G. McCray
Executive Director
Council for American Private Education
1726 M Street, NW, Suite 1102
Washington, D.C. 20036
(202) 659-0016

Dr. Mary Johnson
Project Officer, Recognition Program
Department of Defense Dependents Schools
4040 North Fairfax Drive
Room 916, Education Division
Alexandria, VA 22203
(703) 696-4490, Ext. 152

U.S. DEPARTMENT OF EDUCATION

Lois Weinberg
Director
(202) 219-2134

Kathryn E. Crossely
(202) 219-2154

Patricia A. Hobbs
(202) 219-2063

J. Stephen O'Brien
Acting Director
(202) 219-2141

Blue Ribbon Schools Program
555 New Jersey Avenue NW
Washington, D.C. 20208-5645
Telephone: (202) 219-2149
Fax: (202) 219-2106

APPENDIX C

Educational Program References

SOME of the programs used in many of the Best Schools are available through the National Diffusion Network. These programs include the following list. Note: the following programs have been nationally validated as effective by the U.S. Department of Education. Inservice training and materials are made available to schools throughout the country through the National Diffusion Network (NDN). There are state facilitators available in every state to assist schools with adoption (see Appendix D for a list of state facilitators). For more complete references concerning NDN programs, see *Educational Programs That Work: The Catalogue of the National Diffusion Network (NDN)*, 20th Edition, 1994, Sopis West, Longmont, CO 80501 or contact your state facilitator.

- *Applied Mathematics: Attainment of Algebra I Skills* is an integrated algebra, geometry, and trigonometry course, developed by the Center for Occupational Development. This is a two- to three-year course, which is a component of many TechPrep programs. Schools other than those with TechPrep programs also use the program to ensure a high level of mathematical achievement for all students in place of traditional algebra and general mathematics courses. Candace H. Todd, Center for Occupational Research and Development, P.O. Box 21689, 601 Lake Air Drive, Waco, TX 76702-1689.
- *Capacitor-Aided System for Teaching and Learning Electricity (CASTLE)* aims to improve the preparation of high school students for college or university courses in science and engineering and improves the comprehension of electricity concepts by students who will enter the work force directly from school. Melvin S. Steinberg, Physics Department, Smith College, Northampton, MA 01063.
- *Comprehensive School Mathematics Program (CSMP)* has as an underlying assumption that students can learn and enjoy mathematics more than is usually the case. The content is presented as an extension of experiences children have encountered in their development, both in real life and at the fantasy level. Children are led through problem solving situations. It is CSMP's conviction that mathematics is a unified whole and should be learned as such. CSMP is a complete K–6 curriculum. CSMP, Clare Heidema, Director, 2550 South Parker Road, Aurora, CO 80014.
- *Physics Resources and Instructional Strategies for Motivating Students (PRISMS)* is a comprehensive program that stimulates students to develop reasoning and problem-solving skills while providing learning activities about practical applications of physics for grades 10–12. Roy D. Unruh, PRISMS, Physics Department, University of Northern Iowa, Cedar Falls, IA 50614.
- *Foundation Approaches in Science Teaching (FAST)* is a multidisciplinary, inquiry science program designed to meet the special needs of middle school students in three one-year courses: FAST 1, The Local Environments; FAST 2, The Flow of Matter

and Energy through the Biosphere; and FAST, Change over Time. The program uses carefully sequenced tasks and inquiries involving both students and teachers in defining concepts, generating and testing hypotheses, correcting misconceptions, and ultimately coming to consensus on the adequacy of explanations. Between 60% and 80% of class time is spent in laboratory or field studies. The remaining time is devoted to analysis of data, small-group and class discussion, literature research, and report writing. There are separate teacher institutes for each course. Director, FAST Dissemination Project, University of Hawaii–CRDG, 1776 University Ave., Honolulu, HI 96822.

- *Growing Healthy* is a comprehensive health education program designed to foster student competencies to make decisions enhancing their health and lives, for grades K–7. Growing Healthy includes a planned sequential curriculum, a variety of teaching methods, a teacher training program, and strategies for eliciting community support for health education. Contact: Michelle Reich, School-Based Programs, National Council for Health Education, 72 Spring Street, Suite 208, New York, NY 10012, (212) 334-9470.
- *Higher Order Thinking (H.O.T.S.)* is an alternative approach to reading remediation, which consists solely of higher order thinking activities. The program has also been used for gifted children. The goal is to provide students with conceptual skills to learn content of the upper elementary school grades the first time it is taught in the classroom. The program was developed by Dr. Stanley Pogrow, University of Arizona. Chapter I H.O.T.S.: Higher Order Thinking Skills Project, University of Arizona, College of Education, Tucson, AZ 85721.
- *Institute for Political and Legal Education/Model Congress (IPLE)* introduces students in grades 6–12 to the American political, legislative, and legal processes. The curriculum, originally developed by the IPLE staff and New Jersey teachers, stresses active participation by the students through a variety of activities, including role play, simulations, case studies, and practical experiences. The core of the program is a simulation of the federal Congressional process. The research, writing, and debating skills and the self-awareness that the process generates gives students tools they can use long after the simulation ends. Rebecca McDonnel, Director, Institute for Political and Legal Education, Educational Informational and Research Center, 606 Delsea Drive, Sewell, NJ 08080.
- *Junior Great Books* is a student-centered program of interpreting reading, writing, and discussion based on the shared inquiry method of learning developed by the Great Books Foundation. The curriculum provides intensive work in constructing meaning from literature. The Great Books Foundation, 35 East Wacher Drive, Suite 2300, Chicago, IL 60601-2298.
- *Philosophy for Children* is a program that offers conceptual and cultural enrichment while providing skill improvement in comprehension, analysis, and problem solving. Teachers are trained to become expert facilitators of substantive philosophical discussion about matters of concern to children. Uses novels as texts. Matthew Lipman, Director, Institute for the Advancement of Philosophy for Children, Montclair State College, Upper Montclair, NJ 07043.
- *Systematic Teaching and Measuring Mathematics (STAMM)* is an elementary mathematics program that provides the curriculum and the means to assist in delivering the NCTM Standards. Teachers select from a variety of learning activities using concrete manipulatives, problem solving, and enrichment strategies. The program was developed to complement existing textbooks, manipulatives, and

teacher-made resources. STAMM Project Director, Jefferson County Schools, 1005 Wadsworth Blvd., Lakewood, CO 80215.

- *Systemic Technology Planning to Support Educational Reform (STPSER)* is a planning process that involves critical administrative, instructional, and support personnel from school districts in an integrated strategic planning process for technology implementation. The process features a consensus-building technique of instructional goal setting that relies on curriculum and content specialists, teachers, and administrators from the local district to provide the impetus for technology implementation that supports dramatic changes in the manner in which instruction is delivered and received. John R. Phillipo, Executive Director, Center for Educational Leadership and Technology, 165 Forest Street, Marlborough, MA 01752.
- *Talents Unlimited* is a teaching/learning model that integrates creative and critical thinking skills into any area in the regular curriculum. The program applies, at the classroom level, Dr. Calvin Taylor's research-based multiple talent approach to teaching. Talents Unlimited, 1107 Arlington Street, Mobile, AL 36605.
- *TechPrep Program* is a secondary school and two-year college program designed to prepare students to enter and complete a postsecondary technical associate degree program without need for remediation. The program is a course of study for the "middle majority" of secondary students who previously were allowed to "flow through the system" without a sense of direction and without academically challenging courses. Myrtle D. Stogner, Director, National TechPrep Demonstration Site Project, Richmond Community College, P.O. Box 1189, Hamlet, NC 28345.

Some of the other programs frequently used in the Best Schools are as follows:

- *Activities that Integrate Math and Science (AIMS)* is a program that establishes an intrinsic relationship between math and science. A whole series of math skills and science processes are interwoven in a single activity, creating a continuum of experiences, practice, and application. Students actively investigate questions that relate to the world of the student. Investigations are available in a series of books for grades K–9. Teacher training and other support materials are available. AIMS Education Foundation, P.O. Box 7766, Fresno, CA 93747.
- *Drug Abuse Resistance Education (D.A.R.E.)* was developed by the Los Angeles Police Department and the Los Angeles Unified School District to prevent drug abuse in children. The K–12 curriculum is designed to help students recognize and resist the many subtle pressures that influence them to experiment with alcohol and marijuana. In addition, program strategies are planned to focus on feelings related to self-esteem, interpersonal and communication skills, and decision making. Lessons are conducted by police officers trained in program implementation. Contact: D.A.R.E., Los Angeles Unified School District, Los Angeles, CA.
- *Here's Looking at You 2000* is a sequenced K–12 program that includes all the activities and materials, needed for implementing the program. The program teaches life skills, as well as providing drug prevention education. Contact: Robert, Fitsmahan and Associates. Educational Services District #121, Seattle, WA.
- *KidsNet–National Geographic Kids Network* is program that uses easy-to-use computer software, hands-on materials, and telecommunications to allow children to work together around the world to conduct original scientific research on real-world issues. Students share findings (via modem) with "research teammates" in the United States and other countries. Help and advice is provided by participating professional

scientists. Materials and software are purchased and owned by the school. Tuition and telecommunications are paid by subscription for each eight-week session. Units include: Weather in Action; What's in Our Water?; Hello!; Too Much Trash; Solar Energy; Acid Rain; and What are We Eating? National Geographic Society, Educational Services, Washington, D.C. 20036.

- *Project Jason* uses the Jason Classroom Network, offered through cable companies by Turner Educational Services, to carry live broadcasts from research sites. Scientists at multiple sites lead experiments and live discussions via satellite with students at interactive stations. The National Science Teachers Association has developed curriculum support materials. Lessons feature hands-on activities dealing with one or more topics that the Jason expedition explores: technology, geology, physics, biology, geography, history, and social studies. The Jason Foundation for Education, 391 Totten Pond Rd., Waltham, MA 02154.
- *Science Curriculum Improvement Study (SCIS 3)* is the third generation of a program originally developed in the post-Sputnik era of the 1960s, with funding from the National Science Foundation. SCIS 3 uses a thematic conceptual hands-on approach to actively engage students in physical, life, earth, and environmental science. Emphasis is placed on the concept of evidence as a foundation of modern science and on relationships between classroom science and everyday lives of students. Delta Education, Hudson, NH.
- *Voyage of the Mimi* is an interdisciplinary program that combines videos or videodiscs, computer software, and print material to present an integrated set of concepts in math, science, social studies, and language arts. The Voyage of the Mimi is based on the story of the ketch Mimi and her crew, who set out on the sea to locate and study whales. The Second Voyage of Mimi leads students on an adventure in Mexico to study the ancient Maya civilization. The programs were created by Bank Street College of Education, with funds from the U.S. Department of Education and the National Science Foundation, for students in grades 4–6. WINGS for Learning/Sunburst Communications, 1600 Green Hills Road, Scotts Valley, CA 95067-0002.

National Diffusion Network State Facilitators

FOR information concerning nationally validated programs disseminated by the National Diffusion Network, contact:

ALABAMA
Ms. Maureen C. Cassidy
Alabama Facilitator Project
Div. of Professional Services
Gordon Persons Building Rm 5069
50 North Ripley
Montgomery, AL 36130-3901
(205) 242-9834
Fax (205) 242-9708

ALASKA
Ms. Sandra Berry
Alaska State Facilitator
AK State Department of Education
Mail to: 801 West 10th Street
Suite 200
Ship to: P.O. Box F
Juneau, AK 99801-1894
(907) 464-2824
Fax (907) 464-3396

ARIZONA
Dr. L. Leon Webb
Arizona State Facilitator
Ed. Diffusion Systems, Inc.
161 East First Street
Mesa, AZ 85201
(602) 969-4880
Fax (602) 898-8527

ARKANSAS
Ms. Jo Cheek
State Facilitator
Arkansas Department of Ed.
Office of the Director
#4 Capitol Mall/Room 204B
Little Rock, AR
(501) 682-4568
Fax (501) 682-1146

CALIFORNIA
Ms. Susan Boiko, SF
Association of California
School Administrators
1575 Old Bayshore Highway
Burlingame, CA 94010
(415) 692-4300
Fax (415) 692-1508

COLORADO
Mr. Charles D. Beck, Jr.
The Education Diffusion Group
3607 Martin Luther King Blvd.
Denver, CO 80295
(303) 322-9323
Fax (303) 322-9475

CONNECTICUT
Mr. Jonathan P. Costa
Connecticut Facilitator
RESCUE Education Service Center
P.O. Box 909
355 Goshen Road
Litchfield, CT 06759-0909
(203) 567-0863
Fax (203) 567-3381

DELAWARE
Mrs. Linda Y. Welsh
State Facilitator Project
Dept. of Public Instruction
John G. Townsend Building
Management Information Division
P.O. Box 1402

Dover, DE 19903
(302) 739-4583
Fax (302) 739-3092

DISTRICT OF COLUMBIA
Ms. Susan C. Williams
District Facilitator Project
Eaton School
34th and Lowell Streets, NW
Washington, D.C. 20008
(202) 282-0056
Fax (202) 282-1127

FLORIDA
Ms. Judy Bishop
Florida State Facilitator
Florida Department of Education
424 FEC
325 West Gaines Street
Tallahassee, FL 32399-0400
(904) 487-1078
Fax (904) 487-0716

GEORGIA
Dr. Frances Hensley
Georgia Facilitator Center
607 Aderhold Hall, UGA
Carlton Street
Athens, GA 30602-7145
(706) 542-332 or 542-3810
Fax (706) 542-4032

HAWAII
Dr. Mona Vierra
State Facilitator
Department of Education
Office of Information and
Telecommunication Services
P.O. Box 2360
Honolulu, HI 96808
(808) 735-3107
Fax (808) 735-5217

IDAHO
Ms. Lianne Yamamoto
State Facilitator
Idaho State Department of Ed.
Len B. Jordan Office Building
Boise, ID 83720-3650
(208) 334-3561
Fax (208) 334-2228 or 2636

ILLINOIS
Dr. Shirley Menendex
Project Director
Statewide Facilitator Project
1105 East Fifth Street
Metropolis, IL 62960
(618) 524-2664
Fax (618) 524-3535

INDIANA
Dr. C. Lynwood Erb
Project Director
Indiana Facilitator Center
Education Resource Brokers, Inc.
2635 Yeager Road
Suite D
West Lafayette, IN 47906
(317) 497-3269
Fax (317) 497-3461

IOWA
Ms. June Harris
State Facilitator
Iowa Department of Education
Bureau of Planning, Research,
and Evaluation
Grimes Building
East 14th Street & Grand Ave.
Des Moines, IA 50310-0146
(515) 281-5288
Fax (515) 242-5988

KANSAS
Mr. James H. Connett
Kansas State Facilitator Project
Director, KEDDS/Link
Administrative Center, S Bldg.
217 North Water
Wichita, KS 67202
(316) 833-4711
Fax (316) 833-4712

KENTUCKY
Ms. Jannet Stevens
Kentucky State Facilitator
Kentucky Department of Education

Capitol Plaza Tower Office Bldg.
500 Mero Street
Frankfort, KY 40601
(502) 564-2672
Fax (502) 564-6711

LOUISIANA
Ms. Brenda Argo
Facilitator Project Director
State Department of Education
ESEA Title II Bureau Office
Mail to: P.O. Box 94064
Baton Rouge, LA 70804-9064
Ship to: 654 Main St., 3rd Floor
Baton Rouge, LA 70802-9064
(504) 342-3375
Fax (504) 342-7367

MAINE
Ms. Sue Doughty
Ms. Elaine Roberts
Center for Educational Services
Mail to: P.O. Box 620
Auburn, ME 04212-0620
Ship to: 223 Main Street
Auburn, ME 04210
(207) 783-0833
Fax (207) 783-9701

MARYLAND
Dr. Raymond H. Hartjen
Educational Alternatives, Inc.
P.O. Box 265
Harwood Lane
Port Tobacco, MD 20677
(301) 934-2992
(D.C. Line) (301) 870-3399
Fax (301) 034-2999 (Please call first)

MASSACHUSETTS
Ms. Nancy Love
THE NETWORK
300 Brickstone Square
Suite 900
Andover, MA 01810
(508) 470-1080 or 1 (800) 877-5400
Fax (508) 475-9220

MICHIGAN
Ms. Elaine Gordon
Michigan State Facilitator
MI Department of Education
Mail to: Box 30008
Lansing, MI 38909
Ship to: 608 W. Allegan St.
Lansing, MI 48933
(517) 373-1807
Fax (517) 373-2537

MINNESOTA
Ms. Diane Lassman and
Ms. Barbara Knapp
State Facilitator Office
The EXCHANGE AT CAREI
116 U Press Building
2037 University Avenue, S.E.
University of Minnesota
Minneapolis, MN 55414-3097
(612) 624-0584
Fax (612) 625-4880

MISSISSIPPI
Dr. Bobby Stacy
MS Facilitator Project
State Department of Education
P.O. Box 771, Suite 704
550 High
Jackson, MS 39205-0771
(601) 359-3498
Fax (601) 359-2198

MISSOURI
Ms. Jolene Schulz
Project Director
Missouri Facilitator Project
Suite A
555 Vandiver
Columbia, MO 65202
(314) 886-2165
Fax (314) 886-2160

MONTANA
Ms. Patricia B. Johnson
State Facilitator Project
MT Office of Public Instruction
State Capitol, Room 106
1300 11th Avenue
Helena, MT 59620
(406) 444-2736
Fax (406) 444-3924

NEBRASKA
Dr. Elizabeth Alfred
Facilitator Project Director
Nebraska Department of Education
301 Centennial Mall
P.O. Box 94987
Lincoln, NE 68509
(402) 471-3440 or 471-2452
Fax (402) 471-2113

NEVADA
Ms. Doris B. Betts
State Facilitator
Nevada Department of Education
Capitol Complex
400 W. King Street
Carson City, NV 89710
(702) 687-3187
Fax (702) 786-4499

NEW HAMPSHIRE
Mr. Jared Shady
NH Facilitator Center
36 Coe Drive
Durham, NH 03824
(603) 224-9461
Fax (603) 224-8925

NEW JERSEY
Ms. Katherine Wallin or
Ms. Elizabeth Ann Pagen
Education Information and
Resource Center
NJ State Facilitator Project
606 Delsea Drive
Sewell, NJ 08080-9199
(609) 582-7000
Fax (609) 582-4206

NEW MEXICO
Dr. Amy L. Atkins
New Mexico State Facilitator
Department of Educational
Foundations
University of NM
College of Education
Onate Hall, Room 223
Albuquerque, NM 87131
(505) 277-5204
Fax (505) 277-7991

NEW YORK
Ms. Laurie Rowe
State Facilitator
New York Education Department
Room 469 EBA
Washington Avenue
Albany, NY 12234
(518) 473-1388
Fax (518) 473-2860

NORTH CAROLINA
Ms. Linda Love
Project Director
Division of Development Services
North Carolina Department of
Public Instruction
301 North Wilmington Street
Raleigh, NC 27601-2825
(919) 715-1363
Fax (919) 733-3791

NORTH DAKOTA
Ms. Jolene Richardson
Division of Independent Study
North Dakota State University
State University Station
P.O. Box 5036
Fargo, ND 58105-5036
(701) 239-7287

OHIO
Ms. Mary Ellen Murray
Ohio Facilitation Center
Ohio Department of Education
Div. of Curriculum/Instruction
and Professional Development
65 South Front Street
Columbus, OH 43266-0308
(614) 466-2761
Fax (614) 752-8148

OKLAHOMA
Ms. Deborah Murphy
Oklahoma Facilitator Center
123 East Broadway
Cushing, OK 74023
(918) 225-1882
Fax (918) 225-4711

OREGON
Dr. Ralph Nelsen

Columbia Education Center
11325 S.E. Lexington
Portland, OR 97266
(503) 760-2346
Fax (503) 760-5592

PENNSYLVANIA
Mr. Richard Brickley
Project Director
Facilitator Project, R. I. S. E.
200 Anderson Road
King of Prussia, PA 19406
(215) 265-6056
Fax (215) 265-6562

RHODE ISLAND
RI State Facilitator Center
RI Department of Education
Roger Williams Building
22 Hays Street
Providence, RI 02908
(401) 277-2638
Fax (401) 277-2734

SOUTH CAROLINA
Mrs. Catherine Thomas
NDN Facilitator Project
Department of Education
1429 Senate Street, Room 1114
Columbia, SC 29201
(803) 734-8446
Fax (803) 734-8624

SOUTH DAKOTA
Dr. Wendy Bonaiuto
State Facilitator
South Dakota Curriculum
Center
435 South Chapelle
Pierre, SD 57501
(605) 224-6287
Fax (605) 224-8320

TENNESSEE
Dr. Peggy F. Harris
Tennessee State Facilitator
Tennessee Association for School
Supervision and Administration
330 10th Avenue, North
Nashville, TN 37203-3436
(615) 251-1173
Fax (615) 259-8492

TEXAS
Dr. Judy Bramlett
Texas Facilitator Project-NDN
Education Service Center
Region 6
3332 Montgomery Road
Huntsville, TX 77340-6499
(409) 295-9161
Fax (409) 295-1447

UTAH
Ms. Kathy Mannos
State Facilitator Project
Utah State Office of Education
250 East 500 South
Salt Lake City, UT 84111
(801) 538-7823
Fax (801) 538-7882

VERMONT
Mr. Howard Verman
Trinity College
McAuley Hall
208 Colchester Avenue
Burlington, VT 05401
(802) 658-7429
Fax (802) 658-7435

VIRGINIA
Ms. Judy McKnight
The Education Network of Virginia
3421 Surrey Lane
Falls Church, VA 22042
(703) 698-0487
Fax (703) 698-5106

WASHINGTON
Ms. Nancy McKay
Project Manager
Washington State Facilitator
Educational Service District 101
1025 West Indiana Avenue
Spokane, WA 99205-4400
(509) 456-7086
Fax (509) 456-2999

WEST VIRGINIA
Ms. Cornelia Toon
WV State Facilitator
Mail to: State Department of Education
Building #6, Room B-252
Ship to: 1900 Kanawha Boulevard, East
Charleston, WV 25305
(304) 558-2193
Fax (304) 558-0048

WISCONSIN
Mr. William Ashmore
State Facilitator
Department of Public Instruction
125 South Webster
P.O. Box 7841
Madison, WI 53703
(608) 267-9179
Fax (608) 267-1052

WYOMING
Ms. Nancy Leinius
State Facilitator
WY Innovation Network System
State Department of Education
Hathaway Building-Room 269
2300 Capitol Avenue
Cheyenne, WY 82002-0050
(307) 777-6226
Fax (307) 777-6234

PUERTO RICO
Ms. Maria del Pilar Charneco
Puerto Rico State Facilitator
General Council on Education
P.O. Box 5429
Hato Rey, PR 00919
(809) 764-0101
Fax (809) 704-0820

VIRGIN ISLANDS
Dr. Fiolina B. Mills
State Facilitator
Department of Education
Office of the Commissioner
44-46 Kongens Gade
Charlotte Amalie
St. Thomas, VI 00802
(809) 774-0100, Ext. 225
Fax (809) 776-5687

AMERICAN SAMOA
Ms. Sharon Stevenson
NDN Facilitator
P.O. Box 1132
Pago Pago, AS 96799
(011) (684) 633-5654 or 2401
D.C. Office (202) 225-8577
Fax (011) (684) 633-5184

GUAM
Ms. Margaret Camacho
NDN Facilitator
Federal Program Office
Guam Department of Education
P.O. Box DE
Agana, Guam 96910
(011) (671) 472-8524 or 5004 or 8901, Ext. 321
D.C. Office (202) 225-1188
Fax (011) (671) 477-4587

NORTHERN MARIANA ISLANDS
Ms. Paz Younis
NDN Facilitator
CNMI Public School System
P.O. Box 1370
Saipan, MP 96950
(011) (670) 322-9311
D.C. Office (202) 673-5869
Fax (011) (670) 322-4056

PALAU
Mr. Masa-Aki Emesiochl
State Facilitator
Department of Education
P.O. Box 189
Koror, Republic of Palau 96940
(011) (680) 488-2570 or 1003
Fax (011) (680) 488-2830

PRIVATE SCHOOL FACILITATOR
Dr. Charles Nunley
Private School Facilitator
Council for American Private Ed.
1726 M Street, NW
Suite 1102
Washington, D.C. 20036
(202) 659-0177
Fax (202) 659-0018

Parent Involvement Resources

Consumer Information Center
P.O. Box 100
Pueblo, CO 81002

National Committee for Citizens in Education
10840 Little Patuxent Parkway
Suite 301
Columbia, MD 21044
(301) 997-9300

The National PTA
700 North Rush Street
Chicago, IL 60611
(312) 787-0977

National Association of Partners in Education, Inc.
1501 Lee Highway, Suite 201
Arlington, VA 22209
(800) 48-NSPRA
Fax (703) 528-7017

The Parent Institute
P.O. Box 7474
Fairfax Station, VA 22039-7474
Fax (703) 569-9244

The National Education Goals

School Readiness: By the year 2000, every child will start school ready to learn.

School Completion: By the year 2000, the high school graduation rate will increase to at least 90%.

School Achievement and Citizenship: By the year 2000, American students will leave grades 4, 8, and 12 having demonstrated competency in challenging subject matter including English, mathematics, science, foreign language, civics and government, economics, arts, history, and geography; every school in America will ensure that all students learn to use their minds well, so they may be prepared for responsible citizenship, further learning, and productive employment in our nation's modern economy.

Mathematics and Science: By the year 2000, United States students will be first in the world in science and mathematics achievement.

Adult Literacy and Lifelong Learning: By the year 2000, every adult American will be literate and will possess the knowledge and skills necessary to compete in a global economy and exercise the rights and responsibilities of citizenship.

Safe, Disciplined, and Alcohol- and Drug-Free Schools: By the year 2000, every school in the United States will be free of drugs, violence, and the unauthorized presence of firearms and alcohol, and will offer a disciplined environment conducive to learning.

Teacher Education and Professional Development: By the year 2000, the nation's teaching force will have access to programs for the continued improvement of their professional skills and the opportunity to acquire the knowledge and skills needed to instruct and prepare all American students for the next century.

Parental Participation: By the year 2000, every school will promote partnerships that will increase parental involvement and participation in promoting the social, emotional, and academic growth of children.

Joint Statement by the President and the Governors of the United States of America, February 26, 1990. Amended by Congress, March 21, 1994.

EVELYN HUNT OGDEN – Dr. Ogden received her Ed.D. from Rutgers University in Educational Evaluation, Psychological Measurement, and Statistics. She is the author of five books, major studies, and reports on effective and ineffective schools, programs that work, strategies to increase student achievement, programs for at-risk students, reduction of school violence, and dissemination of successful practices. Dr. Ogden has served for many years on the U.S. Department of Education, Blue Ribbon Schools Selection Panel. She also serves on the U.S. Department of Education Program Evaluation Panel, which reviews and accepts or rejects research related to claims of program effectiveness. Her twenty-five years of administrative experience have included roles as Deputy Assistant Commissioner for Research, Planning, and Evaluation, New Jersey Department of Education; Director of the National Diffusion Network (NDN) Support Project; Director of Curriculum, Moorestown Public Schools, Moorestown, New Jersey; and her current position as Deputy Superintendent, East Brunswick, New Jersey. As a central office administrator, Dr. Ogden has worked directly with six schools that have been recognized as Blue Ribbon Schools of Excellence.

VITO GERMINARIO – Dr. Germinario received his Ed.D. from Rutgers University in Educational Administration and Supervision. He has teaching experience at the junior high, high school, and college level. He also taught at the Bordentown Youth Correctional Center for Men. Dr. Germinario has been an elementary and middle school principal and currently serves as superintendent for the Moorestown Township Public Schools in New Jersey. Dr. Germinario has lectured and conducted workshops for numerous school districts and private organizations nationwide on such topics as the supervision of instruction, essentials of instruction, and at-risk students. He is superintendent in a district with three Blue Ribbon Schools.